A DICTIONARY

of

MODERN BALLET

General Editors

FRANCIS GADAN

and

ROBERT MAILLARD

with the assistance of

RONALD CRICHTON

and

MARY CLARKE

METHUEN AND CO. LTD

36 ESSEX STREET · STRAND · LONDON WC2

Translated from the French
Dictionnaire du Ballet Moderne

by JOHN MONTAGUE and PEGGIE COCHRANE

First published in 1959

I.I

CATALOGUE N° 6043/U

PRINTED IN FRANCE

LIST OF CONTRIBUTORS

GEORGES AROUT

HÉLÈNE BELLEW

MARIE BRILLANT

MARIE-FRANÇOISE CHRISTOUT

MARY CLARKE

RAYMOND COGNIAT

RONALD CRICHTON

JEAN GANDREY-RÉTY

SVEND KRAGH-JACOBSEN

IRÈNE LIDOVA

MARCEL LOBET

DINAH MAGGIE

FERDINANDO REYNA

CLAUDE SARRAUTE

ANDRÉ SCHAÏKEVITCH

MAURICE TASSART

FOREWORD

.

This is a Dictionary only in the sense that the entries are in alphabetical order. A reader seeking definitions of technical ballet terms will be disappointed. It is more precisely a collection of about 650 articles describing the achievements of dancing on the stage in the course of the last fifty years. There are accounts of the artists, performers, ballets and institutions which have made their mark since Diaghilev and his Russian Ballet reached Western Europe.

The editors do not, however, confine themselves pedantically to this century. Ballets such as Giselle *and* Le Lac des Cygnes *have established themselves so firmly in the contemporary repertoire that accounts of their early history are welcome in a book of this sort. Artists like Petipa and Tchaikovsky are part of twentieth century ballet, even though they belong in time to the nineteenth ; so they are described at some length.*

The French edition of this Dictionary was published in Paris in 1957. The English version, prepared by Ronald Crichton and Mary Clarke, contains a number of important changes and additions, reflecting the change of perspective.

For production reasons it was necessary in the English edition for the coloured illustrations to appear in the same position as in the French edition. As these illustrations relate closely to their surrounding text, certain entries appear under their French titles, e.g. Théâtre Bolchoï *for* Bolshoi Theatre. *Where necessary, cross-references are given.*

THE PUBLISHER.

THE ILLUSTRATIONS
HAVE BEEN ASSEMBLED BY
FRANCIS GADAN
WHO OFFERS
HIS GRATEFUL THANKS
TO THE ARTISTS
THE OWNERS
THE LIBRARY OF THE PARIS OPERA
AND THE BRITISH COUNCIL
FOR THEIR ASSISTANCE
AND FOR THE MATERIAL
MUCH OF IT HITHERTO UNPUBLISHED
WHICH THEY HAVE KINDLY
MADE AVAILABLE.

A

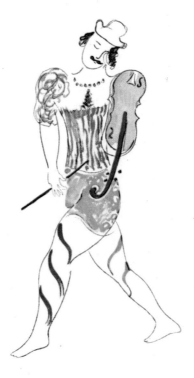

ABRAXAS. Ballet in five acts. Scenario and music: Werner Egk. Scenery and costumes: Josef Fenneker. Choreography: Janine Charrat. First performance: Berlin Municipal Opera, 21 October 1949.

The word "Abraxas" is an occult symbol for the number 365, representing power. The somewhat hectic scenario, based on various versions of the Faust legend, is nearer Heine than Gœthe. Faust, tempted by evil spirits with a vision of Archisposa, the devil's favourite concubine, signs a pact with Hell. Accompanied by Bellastriga, a feminine Mephistopheles, he ranges through time and space in pursuit of beautiful women. With the exception of the innocent Margarethe they are demons (Archisposa) or phantoms (Helen of Troy). There is no redemption; Faust is damned, and Margarethe with him. The original version of *Abraxas,* with choreography by Marcel Luipart, presented in Munich in 1948, was banned by the clergy.

ADABACHE Olga. Parisian dancer of Slavonic origin. A sharply defined stage personality, with her slender, boyish body and sensuous features. Although discovered by Lifar before the last war, her reputation was not established until 1946 when she danced Lifar's *Salomé* — a long solo on points in which she displayed an almost acrobatic agility. In *Nuit sur le Mont Chauve* by the same choreographer she proved her dramatic talent by dancing the role of a wild sorceress.

ADAMS Diana. A classical dancer, tall and dark, with a proud bearing, Diana Adams is a pure product of the American school. Born in Stanton, she later studied at the Ballet Arts School, New York, under Caton and Agnes de Mille. It was de Mille who arranged her stage début in musical comedies. At Antony Tudor's request, she joined Ballet Theatre (1944-1950), dancing in *Romeo and Juliet, Undertow, Les Sylphides, Pillar of Fire* and *Helen of Troy.* She is now one of the ballerinas of the New York City Ballet. Appeared with Danny Kaye in the film *Knock on Wood.*

ADRET Françoise. A pupil of Rouzane, Gsovsky and Nora Kiss, this Parisian dancer, who gave her first recital in 1943, never belonged to any company but followed an independent career. A disciple of Lifar, she started choreography with *Conjuration* (1948). After having been ballet mistress in Roland Petit's company, she has directed since 1954 the ballet of the Amsterdam Opera. Beside reviving the classical repertoire, she has produced many of her own works there : *Terrain vague, La Porte ouverte, Le Photographe,* and above all *Le Rêve de Véronique.*

ALEKO. Ballet in three scenes by Massine and Chagall. Music: Tchaikovsky. Choreography: Massine. Scenery and costumes: Chagall. First performance: Ballet Theatre, Mexico City, 8 September 1942. Principal interpreters: Alicia Markova, George Skibine, Hugh Laing, Lucia Chase, Antony Tudor, Rosella Hightower.

Based on Pushkin's poem *Gipsies.* Aleko, a typical romantic hero, is the mysterious stranger, jealous and sombre, who brings death into a peaceful gipsy camp in Bessarabia. Chagall's settings, with their dramatic power, reflected the violence of the plot, especially in the last scene, where a white horse suspended in a menacing sky dominates the burning village. Massine, the master of *ballets d'action,* here borrowed from Russian folklore as well as from the fiery style of gipsy dance. The surprise of the first night was Alicia Markova, the romantic ballerina, dressed on this occasion in red, and with a tanned skin, who brought to the role of Zemphira all the wild and sensual ardour required by the action.

ALEXANDRE LE GRAND. Choreographic epic in five scenes including prologue and epilogue. Scenario and choreography: Serge Lifar. Music: Philippe Gaubert. Scenery and costumes: Paul Larthe. First performance: Paris Opera Ballet, 21 June 1937. Principal dancers: Lifar, Suzanne Lorcia, Solange Schwarz, Yvette Chauviré. After hearing Gaubert's *Les Inscriptions pour les Portes de la Ville* at a concert, Lifar decided to use it for a heroic ballet on the legend of the Greek hero Alexander. The action moves from Solomon's temple in Jerusalem, to an oasis in Egypt and finally to a Babylonian palace where the hero meets his death, poisoned by the Queen. The epilogue shows Alexander climbing the slopes of Mount Olympus. Three ballerinas, among them Yvette Chauviré as the Young Jewess, represented the lands conquered by Alexander. Not for the first time, however, the main interest of the ballet lay in Lifar's own personality; his virile impetuosity and strange Asiatic features

helped to conceal some weaknesses in the general conception.

ALGAROFF Youly. A pupil of Egorova, he made his Parisian début just before the war in the Ballets de la Jeunesse. But it was in 1945, with the Ballets des Champs-Élysées and again with the Nouveau Ballet de Monte-Carlo where he created the role of Tariel in *Chota Roustaveli,* that he revealed his personality. His romantic figure makes him the ideal interpreter of poets and love-lorn princes. His subtle and restrained acting and elegant technique opened the doors of the Paris Opera to him, where he has had a successful career as *danseur noble.*

ALGUES Les. Ballet in four scenes. Scenario, scenery and costumes: L.-B. Castelli. Music: Guy Bernard. Choreography: Janine Charrat. First performance: Ballets J. Charrat, Théâtre des Champs-Élysées, Paris, 20 April 1953. Principal dancers: J. Charrat, Peter Van Dijk, Maria Fris, Pieral.

A young man simulates madness to rejoin his beloved in the asylum where she has been interned. His subterfuge is discovered and he is forced to return to compulsory liberty. The author of the scenario himself stayed voluntarily in an asylum in order to study his subject at first hand. To give a convincing picture of the climate of lunacy, the characters should have been sharply individualised and shown in depth; above all, the impression of confusion should have been conveyed by properly organised choreography. Janine Charrat submerges the real drama in long scenes of distracting gesticulation by pseudo-Giselles and inessential subsidiary characters. Nevertheless, the moments which directly illuminate the central theme without mere gibbering achieve great emotional power. Here the choreographer's talent is clearly recognisable. Guy Bernard's score, on the other hand, with its mixture of music and sound-effects, successfully recreates the extraordinary atmosphere of the world of the damned.

ALONSO Alicia. A Cuban dancer (her real name is Martínez) who has never broken the ties with her native Havana, Alicia Alonso has won international fame as ballerina of the American Ballet Theatre and the Ballet Russe de Monte-

Carlo. After early training in Havana, she went to New York and made her professional début in musicals. In 1943 she joined Ballet Theatre and except for occasional seasons in Cuba remained with that company until 1955. Then, with Igor Youskevitch, she joined the Ballet Russe de Monte-Carlo. It is hard to believe that this dazzling virtuoso dancer some years ago lost her eyesight and lived in darkness for nearly eighteen months. Small and vivacious, with a warm Southern beauty, Alonso is at her most brilliant in the *Black Swan* pas de deux, which she invests with much coquetry, but she can also be wraith-like in *Giselle,* intensely dramatic in *Fall River Legend* (she created the leading rôle), poetic in *Les Sylphides,* and witty as the Italian ballerina in *Gala Performance.* Married to the dancer Fernando Alonso, she organized the Ballet Alicia Alonso (now the Ballet de Cuba) in Havana in 1948. Much honoured by the Cuban Government, she danced in Russia in 1957-58.

AMATI Olga. A pretty brunette with romantic, elongated and delicate features, Olga Amati studied at the Scala ballet school in Milan. Prima ballerina in 1940, she danced all the leading roles in the classical ballets. Her career suffered from the understudy system which is the practice there, and she accordingly left the Scala in 1956. She has since danced at the San Carlo in Naples.

AMAYA Carmen. When this gipsy dancer first appeared in London and Paris in 1948, she had already behind her an important career in the Argentine and the United States. A gipsy dancer she most certainly is; with her vibrant rhythm, her barbaric wildness, the contortions of her face and androgynous body, she is a living embodiment of her racial instincts. But her dancing lacks that glimpse of the soul which, combined with the purely animal instinct, would raise it to the dignity of true flamenco art. She is a real "natural".

AMBOISE Jacques d'. Though his name paradoxically evokes the proud architecture of a French château on the banks of a great river, he is physically the embodiment of an unsophisticated American. Jacques d'Amboise, who was born in Massachusetts in 1934, is a leading soloist in the New York City Ballet. He dances with joyful abandon, especially in the *Western Symphony* of Balanchine, which conveys the virile movements of cowboys in the orderly terms of the classical dance. His greatest success in Europe was in Robbins' version of *L'Après-midi d'un faune,* which he danced with Tanaquil Le Clercq. A stronger technician than interpreter, he has danced many extrovert roles in ballet and in films.

CARMEN AMAYA.

AMERICAN BALLET. Founded in 1934 by Lincoln Kirstein and Edward M. M. Warburg, in collaboration with George Balanchine, the American Ballet was the earliest of the American companies. Its foundation was preceded by the creation, at the beginning of that year, of the School of American Ballet, to direct which Balanchine left Europe and settled in New York. The company of the American Ballet was therefore entirely composed of dancers recruited on the spot and trained by Balanchine. After a few performances in Hartford (Conn.) in December 1934, the company appeared in New

LOUIS BOUCHÉ.
PROGRAMME FOR THE AMERICAN BALLET. 1935.

York in the following March with a programme of seven ballets, all by Balanchine: three revivals *(Songes, L'Errante, Mozartiana)*, and four new creations of which one was *Serenade*. While attached to the Metropolitan Opera House in New York from 1935 to 1938, the company appeared in *Orpheus* (designed by Tchelitchev) and gave a memorable Stravinsky evening with *Apollon Musagète, Le Baiser de la Fée* and *The Card Party,* the score of which had been specially commissioned from the composer. After a break, the American Ballet, in association with Ballet Caravan, resumed its activities in 1941 to make a tour of South America. Two masterworks of Balanchine date from that time, *Ballet Imperial* and *Concerto Barocco*. In its short life the American Ballet played a decisive part in the history of classical dancing in the United States. Under Balanchine's guidance, and as the starting point of an admirable school of dancing, it contributed to the formation and development of a whole constellation of new choreographers and dancers: William Dollar, Todd Bolender, John Taras, Eugene Loring, Lew Christensen, John Kriza, Michael Kidd, and Nicholas Magallanes. (See above names, Balanchine and New York City Ballet.)

AMERICAN BALLET THEATRE. See *Ballet Theatre.*

AMOR BRUJO El. Ballet in one act. Scenario: G. Martinez Sierra. Music: Manuel de Falla. First performance: Teatro Lara, Madrid, 15 April 1915. The work was inspired by the great gipsy dancer Pastora Imperio, its ideal interpreter. The story is a pure product of Spanish folklore. The action takes place in one of the grottoes or *cuevas* which serve the gipsies of Granada as dwelling places. In spite of the love of her fiancé Carmelo, the young and beautiful Candelas can find neither peace nor happiness; between them falls the memory of the gipsy she formerly loved. Only magic charms can break the spell. In the flickering light of a brazier she abandons herself with all the fervour of her passion to the ritual fire dance. The charm works; the ghost of her former lover appears. A second gipsy girl successfully diverts his attention, while the two lovers are at last able to exchange the kiss of perfect love. A fiery work, full of haunting rhythms, it needs an interpretation which goes beyond mere local colour and concentrates on the dramatic situation. Its appeal, however, is so strong that there have been many new versions (Bolm; Romanoff, Ballets de Monte-Carlo, 1932; Woizikowski; Lifar, Paris Opera, 1943; Mariemma; Espanita Cortez; Antonio). But the only artist since Pastora Imperio able to meet the demands of this strange ballet with success was Argentina (Opéra-Comique, Paris, 1928).

AMOUR ET SON AMOUR L'. Ballet in two scenes. Music: César Franck *(Psyché)*. Scenery and costumes: Jean Cocteau. Choreography: Jean Babilée. First performance: Ballets des Champs-Élysées, Paris, 13 December 1948. Principal dancers: Nathalie Philippart, Jean Babilée. Taken from the *Cupid and Psyche* episode in Apuleius's *Golden Ass,* it was a choreographic poem expressing in a dreamlike atmosphere the omnipotence and fatality of love.

AMOURS DE JUPITER Les. Ballet in five scenes. Scenario: Boris Kochno. Music: Jacques Ibert. Scenery and costumes: Jean Hugo. Choreography: Roland Petit. First performance: Ballets des Champs-Élysées, Paris, 9 March 1946. The story showed some of the many disguises adopted by Jupiter in his amorous escapades among mortals. Europa (Solange Schwarz) was carried away by a monstrous bull; Leda (Irène Skorik) abandoned herself to the caresses of the swan; Danae (Nathalie Philippart) yielded to the sinful pleasure of a shower of gold; Ganymede (Ethéry Pagava) soared aloft in the talons of the divine eagle. The final scene showed the reconciliation of Jupiter (R. Petit) and Juno (Ana Nevada). The costumes, flesh-coloured tights set off by many-coloured scarves, gave the work an atmosphere of remarkable sensuality.

ANDRÉANI Jean-Paul. Leading soloist at the Paris Opéra since 1954. Pupil of Serge Peretti. He was a sensation in Lifar's ballet *Grand Pas* and created the role of the Prince in *Blanche-Neige*. He has a fine elevation, and his *grand jeté en écarté* is inimitable.

ANIMAUX MODÈLES Les. Ballet in one act, after La Fontaine. Music: Francis Poulenc. Scenery and costumes: Maurice Brianchon. Choreography: Serge Lifar. First produced: Paris Opera, 8 August 1942. Principal dancers: Solange Schwarz, Suzanne Lorcia, Yvette Chauviré, Serge Lifar, Serge Peretti.

ANNABEL LEE. Ballet in one act. Scenario and choreography: George Skibine. Music: B. Schiffmann. Scenery and costumes: A. Delfau. First performance: Grand Ballet du Marquis de Cuevas, Deauville, 26 August 1951. Principal dancers: Marjorie Tallchief, George Skibine.

Skibine has made here a most poetic transposition of Edgar Allan Poe's evocation of a couple's happiness turned to sorrow by the death of the girl and of the final reunion of the lovers in a grave by the sea. His choreography abounds in plastic invention. The music is in keeping with the romantic mood of the poem, which is recited during the ballet.

ANTONIO Ruiz Soler. Born in Seville, Antonio is an outstanding virtuoso of Spanish dancing in all its aspects. Ever since his first appearance in Paris in 1949 with Rosario—his inseparable partner for 15 years—he has captivated his audience by his extraordinary agility and lightness, his intelligent use of the castanets, his *renversés,* his acrobatic leaps, and the unmatched brilliance of his zapateado. In 1953, after parting from Rosario, he formed his own company with Rosita Segovia and Carmen Rojas among its leading dancers. He has developed this to a highly professional ensemble, whatever one may think of his somewhat complacent acceptance of public adulation.

ANTONIO BY CAPULETTI.

APOLLON MUSAGÈTE. Ballet in two scenes. Scenario and music: Igor Stravinsky. The first version was produced in Washington with choreography by Adolph Bolm (27 April 1928), but Balanchine's version for the Diaghilev company is the famous one. First performance: 12 June 1928, Théâtre Sarah Bernhardt, Paris. Scenery: André Bauchant. Costumes: Chanel. Principal dancers: Lifar, Nikitina (alternating with Danilova), Tchernicheva, Doubrovska.

In the first scene (prologue) we witness the birth and upbringing of the god Apollo. Three muses, Calliope, Polyhymnia and Terpsichore appear. Apollo confers on them the gifts of Poetry, Mime and Dancing. In an apotheosis they lead him to the heights of Parnassus. This ballet, in which for the first time the names of Stravinsky and Balanchine were linked, was a revelation. Indeed, just as Stravinsky's music marked a return to classicism, the choreography, closely allied to it, showed strict academic steps alongside arabesques with bent or turned-in knees, the first examples of the "neo-classic" style. Choreography and music combined to make this work, with its pure, clear line, a masterpiece of serene and graceful restraint. Although little to the taste of the public, Bauchant's settings brought a note of ingenuous freshness to the conventional world of classical legend. There have been notable revivals of *Apollon* under Balanchine's own direction: American Ballet, Metropolitan Opera House, New York (1937), Ballet Theatre, Metropolitan Opera, New York (1943), Paris Opéra (1947), New York City Ballet (1956), Royal Danish Ballet, Copenhagen (1957).

APPARITIONS. Ballet in five scenes (including prologue and epilogue). Scenario: Constant Lambert. Music: Liszt, selected Lambert, orch. Gordon Jacob. Scenery and costumes: Cecil Beaton. Choreography: Frederick Ashton. First performance: 11 February 1936, Sadler's Wells Theatre, London. Principal dancers: Margot Fonteyn, Robert Helpmann. Scorning the world, a poet takes refuge in dreams. Haunted by spectres of his own creation, exhausted by vain endeavours to attain the unattainable, he dies in despair. On this very romantic theme adapted from Berlioz's *Symphonie Fantastique,* Ashton composed sober, elegant and sensitive choreography; in the ball scene music, décor and choreography alike combined to create an atmosphere of fevered, tragic gaiety.

APRÈS-MIDI D'UN FAUNE L'. Ballet in one act. Scenario and choreography: Nijinsky. Music: Debussy. Scenery and costumes: Bakst. First performance: Diaghilev Ballets Russes, 29 May 1912, Théâtre du Châtelet, Paris. Principal dancer : Vaslav Nijinsky.

Who first had the idea of this ballet ? Romola Nijinsky affirms that it was her husband. According to her, in 1911, Vaslav Nijinsky (who was then 20) underwent a physical and mental evolution, which made possible a reorientation of his former tendencies; he yearned to express in dancing the sexual and emotional awakening of a youth who concentrates his frustrated passion on an object discarded by a young girl, and thus satisfies his longing: the eternal theme of juvenile aspirations and erotic fetishism.

On the other hand, if one is to believe Stravinsky, Grigoriev (stage-director of the Ballets Russes) and other witnesses, the idea of the story (a young faun is chasing nymphs; one of them drops her veil which the creature avidly seizes) and of the general form of the ballet belong to Diaghilev, influenced by his recent discovery of Dalcroze. As a matter of fact, on the way to Vienna during the winter of 1911-12, Diaghilev's company gave a number of performances in Dresden; while they were there he took Nijinsky to see the inventor of Eurhythmics at his school at Hellerau, so that he could absorb the doctrines of the master and apply them to his first ballet, which was already sketched out. In her biography of Nijinsky, Romola ignores this episode. However, the ideas of Dalcroze appealed strongly to Nijinsky; the young man was feeling his way towards a style of choreography quite different from classical dancing. Like all the innovators who preceded him, he wanted to react against academic constraints — the sacrosanct "five positions", the extended and graceful gestures — and to prove that movements hitherto regarded as heavy and ugly could be supremely beautiful if only they expressed an idea or an emotion. Indeed nothing could be further from classicism than the rhythmical movements punctuated by rigid poses which Nijinsky invented for the faun and his nymphs. In order to give the ballet the aspect of an animated bas-relief, the dancers were made to move on flat feet, heel before toe, against all established rules, to ignore the famous *en dehors* and place their bodies squarely facing the public, but with head and limbs in profile, and arms in strange angular positions. Though simple in appearance, this new technique seemed all the more difficult to the dancers because Debussy's fluid music (he had readily given Diaghilev permission to use his *Prélude à l'Après-midi d'un faune*), although it certainly produced the appropriately suggestive atmosphere, gave them little support for their novel movements. And so 120 rehearsals were needed before the ballet was ready; however, it was completed in time for the company's Paris season of 1912.

As soon as he arrived, Diaghilev invited a number of friends to the rehearsals; even before the première, the extraordinary spectacle promised by *Prélude à l'Après-midi d'un faune* (the title of the first production, later abridged) was the talk of Paris. During rehearsals, Nijinsky only "marked" his dancing. Not until the dress rehearsal did he give a complete performance of his role, to the consternation of Diaghilev's guests, who found the final movement, with the faun stretched in ecstasy across the discarded veil, indecent. Diaghilev and Nijinsky disregarded all advice and on 29 May, the curtain rose before an audience already hungry for sensation, revealing Bakst's décor, a lake bordered by trees and a hill, in front of which Nijinsky, in his mottled tights immortalized in so many photographs, and the nymphs in their pleated tunics, golden wigs and bare feet, were to perform their evolutions. The twelve minutes of the ballet crept by in a silence pregnant with astonishment at this choreographic revolution. The curtain had barely fallen when frantic applause and catcalls broke out in equal proportions; whistles blended with cheers and the audience came to blows among themselves. In the end, the cheers prevailed and, contrary to the tradition of the Ballets Russes, the *Faun* was given again. By the next morning all Paris, press and public alike, was divided into "faunists" and "anti-faunists", one side as heated as the other. A few days later Gaston Calmette, who had suppressed the notice of the première in "Le Figaro", published an incendiary editorial entitled "Un faux pas", castigating the "exhibition trop spéciale" and the "faune inconvenant avec de vils mouvements de bestialité érotique et des gestes de lourde impudeur". The attack had unexpected repercussions. The Russian Embassy saw it as an attempt to break the Franco-Russian alliance. On the streets, in the salons, even in the corridors of the Chambre des Députés, voices were raised for or against the *Faun*. The prefect of police was called upon

to stop the performances of this "obscene" ballet. Other newspapers echoed "Le Figaro" to the point of demanding that Diaghilev should apologize to the public.

But an answer was soon flung back, in "Le Matin", from the pen of Auguste Rodin. The great artist rushed ardently to the defence of Nijinsky and described in enthusiatic terms what he considered "a perfect personification of the ancient Greek ideal of beauty". It was then

NIJINSKY IN L'APRÈS-MIDI D'UN FAUNE.

Rodin's turn to be attacked by Calmette, and people fought for or against Rodin as much as the *Faun*. Petitions circulated in favour of the sculptor, signed by illustrious names: Émile Loubet, Raymond Poincaré, Clemenceau, Aristide Briand, Anatole France, Maurice Barrès, Paul Doumer, and many others. Thanks to this campaign, the *Faun* received world-wide publicity. Seats at the Châtelet became precious as gold: the Faunists had won.

* Nine years after Nijinsky's disappearance from the stage, Serge Lifar took up the challenge. His version of the *Faun* concentrated exclusively on the title-rôle. The nymphs were suppressed altogether and the plastic aspect of the work was emphasised more than the emotional character. (Paris Opera, 1932.)

L'APRÈS-MIDI D'UN FAUNE. COSTUME BY BAKST.

* It was Mallarmé's poem rather than Debussy's music which prompted Clotilde Sakharoff to create a *Faun* in her turn. In May 1938, a feminine faun appeared on the stage of the Salle Pleyel, drunk with air, sun and *joie de vivre,* and generating an astonishing amount of sensual tension.

* Unusual sensual excitement was also generated by Jerome Robbins' version of *L'Après-midi d'un faune,* (New York City Ballet 14 May 1953). The Mallarmean experts, those for whom the word is more than the meaning, and those for whom Debussy's music evokes pri-

marily an undergrowth peopled with fantastic creatures, hoofed and horned, were considerably shaken when this time the curtain rose not on a landscape, but a sunny dance studio with wide openings; instead of faun and nymphs, two young dancers in practice tights. Yet nothing could be more moving, more sensual or more enthralling than this new interpretation. The American choreographer succeeded in giving an almost incantatory power to the bare movements with which he suggested youth, the lust for life, the awakening of love, and more than anything, the admiring discovery of their real selves by the dancers fascinatedly contemplating their own image in the studio mirror, downstage. For the audience plays the part of the mirror. And it is perhaps the rôle of reflector which gives the spectator the illusion of identity with the dancers and creates an unusually strong link across the footlights.

ARGENTINA. Argentina just missed introducing into the history of dancing about 1925 a trend as original and lively as that of the Russian Ballet 15 years earlier. She brought a personal dynamism to the Spanish dance which transfigured it, or at least transfigured the idea of it still prevalent in France and elsewhere as a seductive music-hall entertainment. This artist, however, was far from being an immediate success; her merits were not recognized until 1928, the date of her version of *El Amor Brujo.* She was born in Buenos Aires in 1890, where her parents, both professional dancers of Spanish birth, were touring. Thus Antonia Mercé took the stage name of Argentina. She studied with her father, and at the age of 11 became principal dancer of the Madrid Opera. She appeared in Paris in 1923, first at the Olympia, then at the Théâtre Fémina, in the "matinées espagnoles": her talent did not escape notice, but did not yet suggest a new chapter, probably because no-one yet foresaw that Spanish dancing could transcend its local character and become a branch of the classical style. For that, no less, was Argentina's achievement. To understand the effort involved, André Levinson's definition of Spanish dancing should be recalled. He sees it as the meeting ground of the East and West: oriental dancing being concentric, "the curved arms envelop the torso, everything converges

BAKST. DESIGN FOR NIJINSKY AS THE FAUN.

1945. The choice of a name so similar to that of the great Argentina was for a Spanish dancer a risky business, for it was bound to provoke comparison. But Argentinita's choice was governed less by a wish to profit from her predecessor's reputation than by a desire to pay homage to a great artist and, as it were, to place herself under Argentina's patronage. Very quickly Argentinita dispelled the doubts that had been aroused by the news of her first appearances in France. From her first recitals in 1935, it was apparent that she was no mere copy of Argentina. She brought to the Spanish dance her own true style which, even if it did not possess the whole purity of classicism, never descended to the easy vulgarities of the music hall. Her lively wit prompted her frequently to express her personality in ironic byplay. Her parodies and pastiches were among the finest creations of the time and were achieved as much by her powers of observation and characterisa-

inwards", while classical dancing is eccentric, "the whole being, body and soul, opens out, fills the surrounding space, thrusts itself forward". In offering a synthesis of these contradictory trends, Spanish dancing found in Argentina its noblest incarnation, with its classicism, and the flawless beauty of vertical lines.

Argentina formed a company to provide a wider canvas for her style. The wisdom of her enterprise became clear when she appeared as Candelas in *El Amor Brujo (L'Amour Sorcier)* at the Paris Opera (1928): a most poignant performance and her greatest triumph. For eight years, up to the time of her death, she lived in the heady and dangerous fever of success which exhausts as much as it stimulates. But when, on the 18th July 1936, returning from a festival in San Sebastian, she collapsed on the threshold of her villa, her mission was complete.

ARGENTINITA. Spanish dancer, whose real name was Encarnación Lopez (sister of Pilar), born Buenos Aires 1898, died New York

ARGENTINA.

9

tion as by her actual dance technique. With her company she toured widely in the United States and appeared as guest artist with Ballet Theatre, her last appearance being with that company in New York in April 1945.

ARGYLE Pearl. English dancer of great personal beauty, with a quality of restrained but radiant lyricism. A Rambert pupil, who created leading roles in several Ballet Club productions, including *Mermaid* and *Bar aux Folies-Bergère* (both 1934). Leading dancer with Sadler's Wells from 1935 to 1938. For them she created the Fairy in *Le Baiser de la Fée* (Ashton, 1935) and the Serving Maid in *The Gods Go a'Begging* (de Valois, 1936). Later went to U.S.A. and died there in 1947.

ARNOLD Malcolm. English composer, born 1921. Formerly a trumpet player in the London Philharmonic Orchestra. His two ballets for Ashton at Covent Garden, *Homage to the Queen* (written for the Coronation, 1953) and *Rinaldo and Armida* (1955) are typical examples of his unproblematic, professional style and effective orchestral writing. His English Dances for orchestra, with two new numbers added, were used for MacMillan's ballet *Solitaire* (Sadler's Wells Theatre Ballet, 1956).

AROVA Sonia. Dancer of Bulgarian origin, infant prodigy from the Preobrajenska studio in Paris in the years before the last war; leading classical soloist of International Ballet (1941), then Metropolitan Ballet (1947). A fine technician, with a violent, dramatic temperament, remembered particularly for her created role in *Revanche* with the Ballets des Champs-Élysées (1951).

ASAFIEV Boris (1884-1949). An eminent musicologist and member of the Soviet Academy of Sciences, Asafiev's place in the annals of Soviet ballet is not merely that of a theoretician. Indeed, if we owe him *Letters on Russian opera and ballet* and *Studies of Tchaikovsky,* his work as a composer, from about 1930 until his death, is also considerable. He wrote about 30 ballet scores, among them *The Fountain of Bakhchisarai*

SYMPHONIC VARIATIONS. BALLET BY ASHTON.

(1934), *Prisoner of the Caucasus* (1938), and *The Flames of Paris* (1932), his most remarkable work.

ASHTON Frederick. Britain's master choreographer was born in 1906 in the Republic of Ecuador. At the age of fourteen he saw Anna Pavlova dance in Lima and his love of the dance dates from that day. After completing his education at Dover College, in England, he took lessons from Massine and Marie Rambert. It was at the latter's suggestion that his first ballet, *A Tragedy of Fashion,* was produced in 1926 as part of a London revue. It was decorated by Sophie Fedorovitch who, until her death in 1953, remained his close friend and colleague. At that time ballet in England was still almost non-existent, and in order to increase his knowledge Ashton spent a year in the company of Ida Rubinstein and worked under two great choreographers, Massine and Nijinska. The experience strengthened his ambition to be a choreographer himself, and when he returned to London, he seized every opportunity to work with the Ballet Club, the Camargo Society and the Vic-Wells Ballet. His early works *(Pomona,*

Façade (*), *Les Masques, Capriol Suite, The Lord of Burleigh, Les Rendez-vous*) were light, witty, sophisticated and charming. They reflected the excitement of the years when the young English ballet was beginning to find its feet.

In 1935, Ashton joined the Vic-Wells Ballet on a permanent basis as principal choreographer, and there followed a dazzling succession of ballets including *Le Baiser de la Fée* (*), *Nocturne, Apparitions* (*), *Les Patineurs* (*), *A Wedding Bouquet* (*) and *Horoscope*. Deeper in feeling and wider in range than their predecessors, they confirmed Ashton's remarkable gifts and also displayed the rapid flowering of Margot Fonteyn, his ideal interpreter. Together with the more dramatic and literary ballets of Ninette de Valois, to which they formed an effective contrast, Ashton's contributions transformed the Vic-Wells Ballet into an important artistic unit. From the beginning, Ashton's work had possessed a snob appeal; he brought a fashionable audience to Sadler's Wells and such cosmopolitan figures as Cecil Beaton, Lord Berners and Gertrude Stein were attracted into the orbit of English ballet. But his most important collaborators were his friends, Constant Lambert, the company's musical director, and the designer Sophie Fedorovitch, who understood him so well. *Dante Sonata* (1940), his first wartime ballet, showed a more serious side of his nature and marked the beginning of his maturity as a choreographer.

After service in the Royal Air Force, Ashton returned to his post with the Sadler's Wells Ballet and the third phase of his career began, in 1946, in the spacious surroundings of Covent Garden. His work here falls into three categories: the abstract, storyless ballets in which all emotion comes through the classic dance (*Symphonic Variations* (*), *Scènes de Ballet, Homage to the Queen, Birthday Offering*) ; the one-act dramatic ballets in which he can develop character and incident (*Daphnis and Chloe* (*), *Tiresias* (*), *Madame Chrysanthème* (*)); the spectacular three-act ballets in the tradition of Petipa (*Cinderella* (*), *Sylvia* (*)). Unlike many choreographers, he shows at the age of fifty (with about sixty ballets to his credit) no sign of declining invention; rather does his work grow in stature. His genius for arranging lyrical pas de deux, first evident in *Le Baiser de la Fée,* continues to develop. His reverence for the classic dance is perfectly expressed in his masterpiece, *Symphonic Variations*. His weakness is a tendency to rely too much on charm and prettiness. With the exception of *Dante Sonata* he has spared no more than a glance for the darker side of life, and has preferred to take refuge in the past rather than to interpret the present. Unlike the younger school of English choreographers, who have nevertheless been greatly influenced by his work, he understands the value of simplicity and quietness; his ballets are never acrobatic, fussy or pretentious.

Though his services are much in demand, Ashton rarely accepts work abroad. His most important ballets for foreign companies are: *Le Rêve de Léonor* for Les Ballets de Roland Petit (1949), *Les Illuminations* (*), based on Britten's settings of the prose-poems by Rimbaud, for the New York City Ballet (1950) and *Romeo and Juliet* (*) (three acts, music by Prokofiev) for the Royal Danish Ballet (1955).

Ashton's dancing has always been subsidiary to his work as a choreographer, though his sense of style enabled him to perform classical rôles successfully at the outset of his career and throughout it he has danced comedy, character

FRED ASTAIRE IN THE BELLE OF NEW YORK.

and mimed parts with delightful subtlety (the Dago in *Façade* ; the Spectator in *Nocturne*). He has also played two *travesti* roles with success : the Fairy Carabosse in *The Sleeping Beauty* and one of the two Ugly Sisters in *Cinderella*.

Sophisticated, amusing (like Robert Helpmann, he is a brilliant mimic), diffident and emotional, Ashton is highly sensitive to criticism, easily depressed and hurt by it, yet quietly obstinate when he knows he is right. His distinguished talents have formed the ideal counterpart to the more vigorous mind and the administrative genius of Ninette de Valois; in May 1952, he was fittingly made Associate Director with her of the Sadler's Wells Ballet, now the Royal Ballet of Great Britain.

ASTAIRE Fred. Born in Omaha (Nebraska), Fred Astaire is American in more than one way. He is the heir of the "nigger minstrels" and also of the "clog-dancers", immigrants from Ireland and Lancashire who brought their popular dances to America with their native brogues. The syncopated rhythms of the minstrels combine with the clattering footwork of the cloggers to emerge, transformed, as the tap-dance. They owe their letters patent to "the man with sophisticated feet"; to the elegance, and distinction of a style where fantasy, precision, spontaneity and the off-beat contrive a precarious, enchanting equilibrium. To all this, in the choreographic gags with which he spiced his dance numbers, Astaire added a typically Yankee humour. Hollywood lured him from Broadway, where he had remained on his own after the marriage of his sister Adele, the ideal partner of his early years, and Hollywood gave him the chance to invent a new cinema technique. The cinema, for a perfectionist like Astaire, had one particular advantage: it was possible to film each of his dances up to 30 times and to keep only the best shots of each sequence in the final editing. To this process—then a novelty—we owe *Roberta, Top-Hat* and *Shall we Dance ?* Their memory has survived the long series of films which Astaire has made since he separated from his second ideal partner—Ginger Rogers.

AUBADE. Choreographic concerto by Francis Poulenc. Scenery and costumes: J.-M. Frank. Choreography: Nijinska. First produced 29 June 1929 at a private party at the Vicomte de Noailles' house in Paris; Poulenc himself was at the piano and W. Goldschmann conducted the orchestra. Poulenc, who also wrote the scenario, wanted the ballet to be arranged in the quasi-mystical, sensual style of the painters of the School of Fontainebleau. The subject was suitable enough: the goddess Diana, devoured by an impure passion which she has so far conquered, finally, abandons herself in an ecstatic dance to the fate which will destroy her. The ballet ended with a slow, pathetic solo for Diana, a last farewell to her innocent companions. In Nijinska's choreography the compact, block movements of the ensemble were contrasted with solos composed of leaps, turns and arabesques demanding great virtuosity.

The Nemchinova-Dolin company's version (Paris, Théâtre des Champs-Élysées, 22 January 1930) was quite different. Balanchine, who did the choreography, modified Poulenc's idea by reverting to Ovid's version of the story and introducing the character of Actaeon, suppressed in Nijinska's ballet. In a revival by the Ballets de Monte-Carlo (Monte Carlo, 11 April 1936), under the direction of René Blum, the Balanchine version was danced by Vera Nemchinova and Michel Panaïeff in a restrained and distinguished setting by Cassandre. In Monte Carlo again, Lifar produced a new version of the ballet (1946): the same scenario as Balanchine's, but the action now took place in a salon with the musicians, in dinner-jackets, on the stage; the décors were by Nepo. Another version, called *Diana,* was produced by Harald Lander at the Royal Theatre in Copenhagen in 1933.

AUBERT Louis. French composer, born 1877. One of Aubert's first works was a ballet, *Chrysothemis* (Vichy, 1903). His skill as an orchestrator brought him two important commissions for the Paris Opera ballet : *La Nuit ensorcelée* (1923) and *La Belle Hélène* (1955). His main work for dancing is the musical score of *Cinéma,* a ballet by Lifar staged at the Opéra in 1954. This humorous evocation of the heroi-comic age of the silent film provided him with two of his most successful subjects: the legendary figures of Charlie Chaplin and Max Linder.

LES FÂCHEUX. AURIC'S MS. SCORE. — COSTUME BY BRAQUE. 1924.

AURIC Georges. French composer, born 1899. With five of his young friends and contemporaries, Auric's name became known overnight in 1921, when the now famous *Groupe des Six* was mentioned for the first time in an article by the critic Henri Collet, *Les cinq Russes, les six Français et Erik Satie*. Of this group, of which Jean Cocteau was ringmaster and spokesman, four were to become composers much sought after by choreographers: Honegger, Milhaud, Poulenc, and Auric himself. Cocteau started them off as ballet composers in 1921 with *Les Mariés de la Tour Eiffel*, that aggressive manifesto to which they all contributed part of the score. In *Les Fâcheux*, commissioned three years later by Diaghilev, Auric succeeded in restraining his natural fantasy without losing his exuberance. *Les Matelots*, which Diaghilev produced in the following year (1925) was quite different. Here Stravinsky's influence produced a dry, cutting, sinewy style, purposely devoid of modulation. On the contrary, in *La Pastorale* (Diaghilev Ballet, 1926), in *Les Enchantements d'Alcine* (Ida Rubinstein's company, 1929) and in *Concurrence* (Monte-Carlo, 1932), the style was deliberately gayer and livelier, heightened by the use of popular tunes. For *Les Imaginaires*, Lichine's first attempt at choreography (1934), Auric used particularly sturdy and percussive rhythms — noisy, some people called them — which made an effective contrast with the geometrical abstractions of the story.

By the time Auric started to work for the ballet again after a break of 20 years, his style had matured and had become gentle and flowing: the cerebral quality of *Les Mariés de la Tour Eiffel* was now no more than a memory. Whether for *Quadrille* (Ballets des Champs-Élysées, 1946), *Le Peintre et son Modèle* (same company, 1949) or *Phèdre* (Paris Opera, 1950), Auric's scores are now in complete accord with their subject. Expressive, frankly emotional, they have gained in depth and density without losing colour and freshness.

AURORA'S WEDDING. See *La Belle au Bois Dormant*.

AVELINE Albert. Behind this short, smiling, affable man, rather shy and retiring, one discovers a dancer and choreographer authentically French in style. Aveline was born in Paris, 1883, and entered the Opéra School of Dancing in 1894. He remained at the Opéra throughout his career. Leading dancer and maître de ballet in 1917, he later became director of the school. One cannot think of Aveline without evoking the name of Carlotta Zambelli. No better matched couple ever graced the stage. With her, he danced *Roussalka* (1911), *Cydalise et le chèvre-pied* (*) and *Les Deux pigeons* (*). He directed successful revivals of ballets by Mérante, Clustine and Staats, while his original works include : *La Grisi* (1935), *Jeux d'enfants, Elvire* (1937), and in 1950 the entertaining *La Grande Jatte* (*).

B

BABILÉE Jean. One can deduce from the intelligence and clarity, the sensibility and taste which mark both his dancing and his choreography that he comes from a family of artists and intellectuals (his father, a distinguished doctor, is also a painter). That he is a product of the Paris Opera School is also clear. Nevertheless Babilée has turned deliberately to a contemporary style of dancing, a language of the body so widely based that he can express everything. His virile grace and feline precision endow the most romantic roles, from the phantom of *Le Spectre de la Rose* to the Prince in *Giselle,* with an unequivocal charm. With his frank approach he can make characters as complex as the Joker in *Jeu de Cartes* or as tortured as the youth in *Le Jeune Homme et la Mort* seem wholesome. And always, through the simplest or the most elaborate step, through acrobatics or stylised gesture, bounding leaps or delicate *batteries,* through the slightest movement of head or fingers, he has the power of communication. All these qualities are to be found in his choreography, alike in his first ballet, *L'Amour et son amour* (*), in works full of youthful high spirits such as *Divertimento, Balance à trois* (*), and *Sables,* in the many-faceted *Til Eulenspiegel* (*) or in the experimental *Le Caméléopard* (*). In Babilée's dancing there are no empty, meaningless gestures. At his best, he transcends technique and enhances the spectator's experience: such is true dancing.

BACCHANALE. Ballet in one act. Scenario, scenery and costumes: Salvador Dali. Music: Wagner (Venusberg scene from *Tannhäuser*). Choreography: Massine. First performance: Ballets Russes de Monte-Carlo, Metropolitan Opera, New York, 9 November 1939.

The central character of Dali's "paranoiac ballet" is the mad king Ludwig II of Bavaria. In dream or hallucination Ludwig identifies himself with the heroes of legend, transforms himself into Lohengrin and finally dies while contemplating the loves of Leda and the Swan. A mixture of old legends and erotic symbols borrowed from psycho-analysis, this ballet assembled in strange confusion the Prince of Death (Chris Volkov), Venus (Nini Theilade), a Faun (André Eglevsky) side by side with Lola Montès (Milada Mladova) and Sacher Masoch (Marc Platoff).

BABILÉE BY TOM KEOGH. 1950.

BABILÉE AS THE JOKER IN JEU DE CARTES.

BACCHUS ET ARIANE. Ballet in two scenes. Scenario: Abel Hermant. Music: Albert Roussel. Scenery and costumes: G. de Chirico. Choreography: Lifar. First performance: Paris Opera, 22 May 1931, with Lifar, Spessivtseva and Peretti.

BAISER DE LA FÉE Le. Ballet in four scenes. Scenario and music: Igor Stravinsky. Scenery and costumes: Alexandre Benois. Choreography: Nijinska. First performance: Paris Opera, 27 November 1928 (Ida Rubinstein season). Principal dancers: Ida Rubinstein, Ludmilla Schollar, Anatole Vilzak.

Stravinsky, being his own scenarist, took the

precaution while writing this score of not tying the hands of future choreographers too firmly. "The strict and precise indications of the appearance and actions of the characters to be found in my score" he wrote "will form the permanent basis of the producer's work. On the other hand, the vague and imprecise indications I have given as to the place and period of the action will give the designer and the producer the necessary freedom to build up a choreographic spectacle emanating directly from the character and style of the music". Balanchine and Alice Halicka made use of this freedom in the version they staged with the American Ballet at the Metropolitan Opera, New York (27 April 1937). The action is supposed to take place in settings and costumes recalling the picturesque Switzerland of the 1830s, but a

Switzerland conceived by an artist of Slavonic origin. The story comes from Hans Andersen's *The Ice Maiden*. A fairy who had kissed a new-born child on the forehead and thus saved him from a snowstorm, returns to claim the grown man on the day of his engagement to a young village girl. The fairy carries him off to the depths of an icy lake, where for the second time she gives him a kiss in which life and death are mingled. This is the version which Balanchine produced at the Paris Opera (2 July 1947) with Tamara Toumanova, Alexandre Kalioujny and Maria Tallchief. *Baiser de la Fée* was also produced at Sadler's Wells Theatre in 1935, with choreography by Ashton and scenery and costumes by Sophie Fedorovitch. The dancers were Pearl Argyle, Harold Turner and Margot Fonteyn.

LES ORIENTALES. DÉCOR BY LÉON BAKST. 1910.

BAKER Joséphine. Her first appearance in Paris, in the *Revue Nègre* at the Théâtre des Champs-Élysées (1925), was a revelation. Indeed, in presenting this revue, Rolf de Maré was following a recent fashion, but one which already had a firm grip on public taste. In painting, the appeal of negro art dated from the beginnings of fauvism and cubism about 1910, but the general public was only affected by it considerably later; and then it was chiefly through dancing and music that the fascination of negro art manifestations, the uninhibited frenzy and the throbbing rhythms, began to gain ground. The *Revue Nègre,* therefore, while it seemed to be a startling novelty, was really the outcome of a powerful movement. Joséphine Baker created a furore in it because she embodied aspirations which so far had found no rallying point. The growing interest in primitive emotions, appealing naively and cynically by means of the frankest eroticism, had hitherto found only fragmentary expression, in certain cabaret shows, for instance; thanks to Joséphine Baker, this movement suddenly discovered a style which, far from diluting the violence and passion, magnified and exalted them, and transformed them into an art. André Levinson gave a very apt definition of this artist as "a prodigious creature with the suppleness of a monkey—a wanton idol with the appeal of a *gamin*". There were certainly moments in her dancing which reached a real and moving grandeur.

After this brilliant début, Joséphine Baker remained firmly attached to the life of the music-hall, to which she had given a new impulse. Later she sang and danced in less exotic productions of a more conventional type. In these she never failed to show taste and skill; but it was in her instinctive exoticism, a reaction against banal prettiness and salon eroticism, that her real contribution lay. She left the stage in 1947 after a long career of world-wide success.

BAKST Léon. Born St Petersburg, 1866; died Paris, 1924. By the time the Parisian public discovered Bakst through his décors for the Diaghilev Ballets Russes, his reputation was in fact already firmly established, even beyond the borders of his native Russia. As a co-founder with Diaghilev of the group *Mir Isskoustva* (The World of Art), Bakst had, before

JOSÉPHINE BAKER BY PAUL COLIN.

the beginning of the century, declared his desire to ally himself with those Russian artists who were attempting to escape from academism and to find a place for their native temperament in the renaissance of modern art. The portraits he had exhibited in Munich as early as 1899 were evidence of his talent; but it was for the Ballets Russes that he showed his real measure. His décors started a movement in European art: a movement, moreover, which remained independent of the predominant French trends of the period, for it belongs neither to cubism nor fauvism (then in the front of the battle), nor to German expressionism, with its tendency to caricature. Although using the brightest colours, and demanding from painting a luminosity and intensity which the academic formulas could no longer provide, Bakst's style nevertheless differed from the modernism of the time in its precise drawing and its refusal to dislocate form, especially the human figure, a practice so dear to the Cubists, Fauves and Expressionists. Above all Bakst represents the introduction to modern art and to the theatre of picturesque orientalism. His best ballets are like animated Persian miniatures with all their refined colours, touches of precious gold and minutely detailed drawing. This eminently seductive art had an immediate

2

BAKST BY MODIGLIANI.

midi d'un faune and *Narcisse*. In all its aspects, Bakst's art was fundamentally opposed to the austerity which the growing movement of cubism was then trying to establish. However, this modern version of baroque, unlike that of the 18th century or even the "Modern Style" of 1900, did not go so far as to obliterate the essential structures.

As well as enchanting the public with pomp and sumptuousness *(Cléopâtre, Sheherazade, Le Martyre de Saint-Sébastien)*, Bakst proved that he could work on less extravagant lines. For *Le Spectre de la Rose* (1911), he designed an almost conventional setting, and in *L'Après-midi d'un faune* (1912), went to the extreme limits of austerity with a simple décor, and an almost bare stage, concentrating all emphasis upon the Faun himself, standing out clearly against the plain background of a blue sky. With *Les Femmes de Bonne Humeur* (1917), Bakst made a curious experiment; composing a décor slightly distorted, as if seen through a curved glass. Was this a desire to escape from the conventional 18th century or an essay in distortion in the manner of the *avant-garde ?* Anyway, the experiment was not followed up, and the final version of the décor was quite normal. At least it showed that Bakst was not willing to work to a formula. Valuable as these experiments were, it is *Sheherazade,* his most important work, which remains most clearly in the memory.

success, and its fresh and vivid exoticism completely won the hearts of the elegant and worldly public of the Ballets Russes. Bakst's influence on fashion, and particularly on Paul Poiret, the leading dress-designer of the period, is well known.

Bakst brought to the theatre a feeling for the monumental, for oriental magnificence, but also for charming detail. Like Bibiena in the 18th century, he loved vast palaces and sumptuous perspectives. His fantastic architecture rejects the rigidity of classical structures and delights in curves, fluted columns, and all-enveloping decoration which gives it, immobile though it be, the appearance of movement. All the sensuality of the Orient found expression there; but as well as the "orgy of colours" which he let loose on the stage, Bakst caused some head-shaking by the unaccustomed prominence he gave to the nude in *Sheherazade, L'Après-*

NARCISSE. COSTUME BY BAKST. 1911.

LES PAPILLONS. COSTUME BY BAKST. 1914.

But Bakst's work had such grandeur, such exceptional quality, that it remains, in spite of familiarity and changing tastes, one of the most illustrious examples of theatrical art in the first quarter of the century. — Beside the ballets already mentioned Bakst designed the following works for the Diaghilev company: *Carnaval* (1910), *Narcisse* (1911), *Le Dieu Bleu* (1912), *Thamar* (1912), *Daphnis et Chloé* (1912), *Jeux* (1913), *La Légende de Joseph* (costumes only, 1914), and finally, in his most magnificent style, *La Belle au Bois dormant* (1921).

BAL Le. Ballet in two scenes. Scenario: Boris Kochno. Music: Vittorio Rieti. Scenery and costumes: Chirico. Choreography: Balanchine. First performance: Diaghilev's Ballets Russes, Monte Carlo, 9 May 1929. Principal dancers: Alexandra Danilova, Anton Dolin.

LES PAPILLONS. COSTUME BY BAKST. 1914.

It left a deep mark on the pre-1920 theatre.

Having so largely contributed to Diaghilev's triumph, Bakst was never completely dropped, even when Diaghilev felt the need for new ideas and called in such painters of the *École de Paris* as Picasso, Braque, Derain and Matisse. The love of magnificence which marked the Ballets Russes for a time was very much to the taste of that strange and compelling *animateur,* Ida Rubinstein, whose collaborator Bakst became. To him she owed much of the success of *Hélène de Sparte, La Pisanelle, Phèdre, Istar,* and especially *Le Martyre de Saint-Sébastien,* where the names of d'Annunzio and Debussy were linked with his. The collaboration with Ida Rubinstein led to a break with Diaghilev. Bakst's death, shortly before the great exhibition of Decorative Arts in Paris (1925) which summed up the new aesthetic trends and marked their acceptance by the public, was the full close of a theatrical epoch the like of which has not been seen again.

A masked ball in costumes inspired by architecture. Chirico's contribution was the most important. The ballroom, for example, was composed of architectural fragments, classical ruins, rocks and trees; at the back a great door opened to reveal a white, prancing horse. The dancers, seated along the walls, looked like plaster statues; their costumes were made of fragments of walls, columns and capitals. In a cold, pale light, a young and handsome officer pursued a masked lady. The preponderance of the decorative elements was a hindrance to the choreographer; indeed, everything in this ballet indicated a desperate search for originality.

BALACHOVA Alexandra. Pupil of the Imperial School of Moscow, she attracted notice in 1906 as the Russian Princess in *The little humpbacked Horse*. A lovely face, a sculptural figure and a brilliant technique secured her the rank of leading dancer in 1915. After leaving Russia she gave recitals at the Théâtre Fémina, Paris, and had a great success at the Opéra in 1922 as Lise in *La Fille mal gardée*. Since 1931 has devoted herself to teaching. In 1946-47 she staged a new version of *La Fille mal gardée* for the Marquis de Cuevas, revived 1957 at the Strasbourg Festival.

BALANCE À TROIS. Ballet in one scene. Scenario: Constantin Nepo. Music: Jean-Michel Damase. Scenery and costumes: Tom Keogh. Choreography: Jean Babilée. First performance: Monte Carlo (Babilée's company), 25 April 1955. Principal dancers: Yvette Chauviré, Jean Babilée, Alexandre Kalioujny.

A girl and two youths are practising in a gymnasium. The two male athletes, one lithe and supple, the other strong and muscular, show off in front of the girl. Finally she wins a competition of skill and strength which narrowly avoids disaster but ends in an atmosphere of frank, open-hearted camaraderie. Everything in this ballet is fresh, youthful and witty: a little masterpiece.

BALANCHINE George. One of the greatest living choreographers. Youthful, slightly built and, apart from a weakness for shoe-string

ties, soberly dressed; affable and smiling (whatever the official photographs may suggest), though no great talker; for a man of the theatre, extremely diffident. Such is Balanchine in these middle years of the century, which was four years old when he was born in St. Petersburg. To know that he is a constant smoker of English cigarettes or that he has a slight nervous tic which occasionally creases his features may not be very relevant. But the portrait would not be complete without some reference to the kind of Pygmalion complex which has driven him to marry, one after the other, the stars of his ballets: Tamara Gevergeva, Alexandra Danilova, Vera Zorina and Maria Tallchief all bore the name Balanchine before his present wife, Tanaquil LeClercq.

It is not, in fact, his real name. The son of a Georgian composer, he was called George Melitonovitch Balanchivadze until Diaghilev abridged and Russianised his name at one stroke. Balanchine was then only 21 but already had an eventful career behind him. Brought up in a

BALANCHINE BY LUCIEN FREUD.

CONCERTO BAROCCO. BALLET BY BALANCHINE.

family of artists, he showed at first little desire to follow in their footsteps. He refused his first piano lessons until he was threatened with early bed and no supper. When he was 9, his parents entered him for the Imperial School of Ballet, with the idea that there would be time enough afterwards to think of the army. He passed the entrance examination with six or seven other boys out of 150 candidates, but he hated the school so much that he ran away. The aunt to whom he fled had the good sense to send him back. Soon, just as he had taken to the piano when he discovered on his own the beauties of a Beethoven sonata, so he became reconciled to dancing when for the first time he trod the boards of the Maryinsky. The events of 1917 led to the closing of all the Imperial Schools, and the boy was suddenly faced with severe financial worries. He had to earn his living, as a porter in a bank, a saddler's apprentice, a cinema pianist. The ex-Maryinsky and his old school re-opened the following year, in a pitiful condition. Cold, half-starving students cut up the curtains to make themselves trousers; their old imperial uniforms had to last till 1920. Having completed his studies brilliantly in 1921, George Melitonovitch was engaged for the company. In his spare time he took classes in

piano and composition at the Conservatoire, then directed by Glazounov.

As early as 1920, he had arranged for his friends a short ballet based on Rubinstein's *Night*. Since he was unable to obtain the approval of the State theatres for his work as choreographer, he and the painter Volodia Dimitriev founded (1923) an experimental ballet-group. For lack of a proper stage, they performed in the old parliamentary amphitheatre of the Duma. The entire programme was planned by Balanchine and performed by him and his companions from the State Theatre, whose directors, however, soon banned these auxiliary activities. The young choreographer had the compensation of mounting some new ballets at the Mikhailovsky Theatre, the Comic Opera of Petrograd. These included *Le Bœuf sur le Toit* by Jean Cocteau and Darius Milhaud and a dance scene for Shaw's *Caesar and Cleopatra*. Balanchine, however, hoped to reach a larger audience. He obtained permission from the Soviet authorities to organise a tour abroad during the summer of 1924. These "Soviet State Dancers" were only four in number: Alexandra Danilova, Tamara Gevergeva, Nicolas Efimov and Balanchine himself who, at the age of 20, was the oldest of the group. They

LE BAL. COSTUMES BY CHIRICO. 1929.

appeared in Berlin, at a few German spas, at Mannheim, in London and finally in Paris, where Diaghilev engaged them for the Ballets Russes. Nijinska had just left the company and Balanchine at once took her place as maître de ballet and choreographer. There now opened for Balanchine a period of intense creative activity of which, more than thirty years later, the end is not yet in sight.

He did ten ballets in all for Diaghilev, from *Barabau* (*) to *Le Bal* (*), including *The Triumph of Neptune* (*), *La Chatte* (*), and above all *Apollon Musagète* (*) and *Le Fils Prodigue* (The Prodigal Son) (*). After Diaghilev's death and the dispersion of his company, Jacques Rouché invited Balanchine to stage *Les Créatures de Prométhée* at the Paris Opera. He fell ill, and Serge Lifar did the choreography. Later he went to Copenhagen as maître de ballet of the Royal Danish Ballet, then to London, where he worked on a musical comedy. In 1932, René Blum and Colonel de Basil summoned him to Monte Carlo to produce *La Concurrence* (*),

Cotillon (*), and *Le Bourgeois Gentilhomme*. With him he took the "baby ballerinas" Toumanova and Baronova whom he had discovered in Paris. After leaving Monte Carlo he directed six productions, among them *Les Sept péchés capitaux, L'Errante* and *Mozartiana* (*) for the "Ballets 1933". The life of this Company was as ephemeral as its name (one season at the Théâtre des Champs-Élysées followed by one in London) but it enabled Balanchine to meet Lincoln Kirstein who, with Edward M. M. Warburg, invited him to found the School of American Ballet in New York. From this school, opened in 1934, four companies and a number of masterpieces were to come. But this is another story, to be found in the article on the New York City Ballet (*). In 1947, Balanchine returned to Paris to enrich the repertoire of the Opéra with *Serenade* (*), *Le Baiser de la Fée* (*), *Apollon Musagète* (Apollo) (*) and *Le Palais de Cristal* (Symphony in C) (*).

George Balanchine's output includes about 80 ballets, not counting work for musicals and films. The one feature common to all this huge output is its musicality. Fortunately, Balanchine is not the only choreographer who appreciates and understands music, but he is probably the only one whose musical knowledge is sufficiently developed to produce a subtle "visualisation" based not only on the rhythm and melody but also on the formal structure of a score. Hence such marvels as *The Four Temperaments* (*), *Symphonie Concertante* (*), *Serenade* (*) and *Concerto Barocco* (*); hence, too, his frequent and happy collaboration, of which *Apollo, Orpheus* and *Agon* are perhaps the finest fruit, with the greatest of modern composers for ballet, Igor Stravinsky. Balanchine is rightly considered as the master of abstract, plotless ballet, but this special gift, developed since he settled in the United States, must not be allowed to steal all the limelight from his narrative ballets (*La Chatte, The Prodigal Son, Night Shadow* (*), etc.), nor from his recent versions of the classics *(Swan Lake, Nutcracker)*. Although he knows and values more than anyone the purity of the classical dance vocabulary, he has allowed it to absorb American idioms *(Western Symphony)* (*) and has profited from the example of Martha Graham. He is a choreographer without prejudice either in his aesthetic outlook or in his method of work

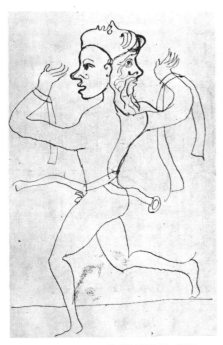

FASTES. COSTUME BY DERAIN. 1933.

the winter of 1956-57, he cancelled all his engagements in order to spend months at the bedside of Tanaquil LeClercq, stricken down by poliomyelitis. The most authentic artists are not always "sacred monsters".

BAL DES BLANCHISSEUSES Le. A young and handsome apprentice, forgetting his business, follows a street musician playing a clarinet. Pretty young laundresses flock round him. He responds to one of them and takes her by the hand; around them an improvised ball springs up. On this simple and romantic idea by Boris Kochno, assisted by the music of Vernon Duke, Roland Petit built an ingenious choreography with scenery and costumes by Stanislas Lepri. First performance: by the Ballets des Champs-Élysées, Paris, 19 December 1946. This ballet revealed the talents of the acrobatic dancer Danielle Darmance.

BAL DES CADETS. See *Graduation Ball*.

which consists, indeed, in an almost complete absence of system. This master of abstract ballet admits that he is incapable of working out new choreography on paper, without the raw material of stage and dancers. Although he wrote a preface for a study of "Labanotation" and authorized the publication of a number of his ballets according to this system, he takes no notes himself and does not believe it necessary or even desirable that a ballet should be handed down intact to posterity.

George Balanchine never wanted to be a star performer and gave up dancing quite early in his career. Even in the Diaghilev days, he usually limited his appearances to character roles, preferably the humorous ones in which he excelled. But he likes conducting, and one evening at the Théâtre des Champs-Élysées in 1952 he was even seen playing *incognito* as the clarinettist in *The Pied Piper,* that remarkable ballet by his colleague, Jerome Robbins. He is one of those rare great artists who give the impression of being as unusual in character as in talent. Fame has not turned his head; during

LEPRI. BALLETS DES CHAMPS-ÉLYSÉES.

PROGRAMME, 1946.

THE BALLAD OF READING GAOL. GENEVIÈVE KERGRIST.

BALL IN OLD VIENNA A. Ballet in one act. Scenario and choreography: Kurt Jooss. Music: Joseph Lanner, arr. Cohen. Scenery and costumes: A. Siimola. First performance: Ballet Jooss, Cologne, 21 November 1932.

BALLAD OF READING GAOL The. Choreographic poem in three scenes. Music: Jacques Ibert. Scenery and costumes: Jean-Claude May. Choreography: Jean-Jacques Etchevery. First performance: Opéra-Comique, Paris, 19 December 1947. Principal dancers: Geneviève Kergrist, Michel Rayne.

Inspired by Oscar Wilde's famous ballad, this ballet evokes the tragic story of one of the poet's fellow-prisoners in Reading Gaol: a horse-guard due to be hanged for the murder of his mistress. In three scenes (the room, the gaol and the prison yard) Etchevery's choreography and Ibert's music illustrate with sombre power some of the more poignant passages in the poem: the savage love scene followed by the crime, the grotesque visions which haunt the prisoners (rather long drawn-out and over-realistic), the despairing routine of men waiting in the condemned cell.

BALLET CARAVAN. A ballet company founded in 1936 by Lincoln Kirstein to serve as a testing ground for young American choreo-graphers: William Dollar, Lew Christensen, Erick Hawkins, Eugene Loring. The latter created *Billy the Kid* for the company, a very successful ballet in a completely new style. In the spring of 1941, the Ballet Caravan (since 1938 the American Ballet Caravan) joined the American Ballet for a South American tour. These were the company's last performances; on its return to the United States in October of the same year it was dissolved. Subsequent efforts to form American ballet companies have, however, succeeded partly because of the groundwork laid by Ballet Caravan.

BALLET CLUB. See *Ballet Rambert*.

BALLET IMPERIAL. Ballet in one act. Choreography: Balanchine. Music: Tchaikovsky. Scenery and costumes: Doboujinsky: First performance: American Ballet, Hunter College, N.Y., 29 May 1941. Principal dancers: Marie-Jeanne, Gisella Caccialanza, William Dollar.

Based on the three movements of Tchaikovsky's Second Piano Concerto. A tribute to Marius Petipa, the greatest choreographer of Imperial Russia—hence the title. The original décor suggested a hall in a palace opening on to a view of St. Petersburg under snow. The ballet is a succession of entrances, variations and pas de deux, the passages of brilliant virtuosity set off by the romantic central *andante*. This demonstration of classical grammar, enriched with Balanchine's own discoveries, was a splendid opportunity of presenting the first American ballerinas trained in his school. *Ballet Imperial* was revived for the Ballet Russe de Monte-Carlo (1945) with Mary Ellen Moylan, Maria Tallchief and Nicolas Magallanes, and for the Sadler's Wells Ballet (1950) with Fonteyn, Grey and Somes, setting and costumes by Eugene Berman.

BALLET INTERNATIONAL. A ballet company founded in New York (1944) by the Marquis George de Cuevas. Its brief existence (one season from 30 October to 23 December) at least gave the Marquis the necessary experience to take over the direction of the Nouveau Ballet de Monte-Carlo three years later (see *Grand Ballet du Marquis de Cuevas*).

BALLET RAMBERT. This English company grew out of the Ballet Club (first performance February 1931, London) which was itself an extension of ten years of pioneer work by the Polish-born dancer and teacher, Marie Rambert, a former member of the Diaghilev Ballet, who enabled her young pupils to work with such artists as Karsavina and Woizikowski. Her husband, the dramatist Ashley Dukes, opened a small theatre in Notting Hill Gate, later to be known as the Mercury, where the Club gave Sunday performances on the tiny stage with a small company of dancers using the simplest costumes and décors and usually only a piano for music. The result was distinguished out of all proportion to the resources. Markova was the principal dancer. An astonishingly high proportion of the beginners were to make their mark as dancers and were encouraged to develop latent talent for choreography or designing: Ashton, Tudor, Andrée Howard, Walter Gore and Frank Staff among the choreographer-dancers, William Chappell as dancer-designer, Pearl Argyle, Diana Gould, Maude Lloyd, Prudence Hyman, Peggy van Praagh, Hugh Laing and Harold Turner as dancers, Sophie Fedorovitch and Hugh Stevenson as designers. Markova left in 1935, and a number of the others moved on to Sadler's Wells, but new talent soon emerged from the ranks of Rambert's pupils. From the earliest days there had been occasional seasons at larger theatres (at one of which, in 1931, Karsavina appeared as a guest). When the war came, the Sunday performances at the Mercury Theatre were abandoned and the Ballet Club became the Ballet Rambert, but for practical reasons was temporarily amalgamated with two other small companies, the London Ballet and the Arts Theatre Ballet. During the most difficult period of the war, between September 1941 and March 1943, performances

were suspended, but the Ballet Rambert re-emerged on its own to dance for factory and service audiences, and soon for the general public as well. Sally Gilmour and Walter Gore were the principal dancers now and for the years immediately after the war; Paula Hinton, Belinda Wright and John Gilpin were developing rapidly. Gore was the principal choreographer, but Andrée Howard made a distinctive contribution with *The Sailor's Return* (1947). Up to now the company had concentrated on the production of new ballets by young choreographers, and the classics had not played a large part in the repertory. An exception, made possible by the increase in the size of the company, was Rambert's revival of *Giselle* (1945 and 1946), which was widely praised for the authenticity of its style; Sally Gilmour danced the title-rôle. The climax of this period was a triumphant eighteen-months tour of Australia and New Zealand, from 1947 to 1949.

Since their return to England, the pattern has remained the same. Seasons have been given in various London theatres, including Sadler's Wells; there have been provincial tours and

MARIE RAMBERT.

25

appearances at Festivals at home and abroad; the leading dancers have inevitably left, sooner or later, to join larger companies where the financial reward was less modest; new young dancers have taken their place. New choreographers and designers have been given opportunities: David Paltenghi, Michael Charnley, Cranko and Kenneth MacMillan among the former, Kenneth Rowell among the latter. In 1951, Rambert's daughter Angela Dukes and her son-in-law David Ellis formed a small experimental project called Ballet Workshop, whose Sunday performances at the Mercury Theatre, in the chances given to young choreographers, designers and composers to try out new ideas for subject-matter and treatment, did for the nineteen-fifties something of what the Ballet Club had done for the 'thirties. There was some interchange of repertory with the parent company. The Mercury was closed as a theatre in 1955; it remains as a rehearsal studio.

In the thirty-seven years of her activity in England, Marie Rambert's contribution, as teacher and as *animateur,* has been incessant and invaluable. In her teaching, while guarding the strictest technical standards, she has sought to develop the dancer's individuality to a degree not always encouraged by other English schools.

Whereas the splendidly-trained products of Sadler's Wells have a certain family resemblance in their typically English reserve, the hall-mark of a Rambert dancer is a completely developed individual artistry. Her best dancers have a gift for identifying themselves with their roles that is quite independent of technical ability; Pearl Argyle and Sally Gilmour, to take two outstanding examples who were never virtuoso dancers, have left indelible memories. Rambert's flair for detecting potential gifts for theatrical work other than dancing has been remarkable; only in the sphere of music, hampered perhaps by the lack of financial resources to maintain a first-rate orchestra, has her contribution been unimportant, though her taste in the use and selection of existing music has been both perceptive and enterprising. Her career has been compounded of indomitable courage, ruthless energy and warm-hearted devotion to the Dance.

BALLET (ROYAL DANISH). Three names illustrate the history of the Royal Danish Ballet since its origin: Vincenzo Galeotti, Auguste Bournonville and Harald Lander. Between them they symbolise a two hundred

NAPOLI. ACT III. ROYAL DANISH BALLET.

THE SLEEPING BEAUTY. DÉCOR FOR ACT II BY DELFAU. COPENHAGEN, 1957.

year old tradition, the longest of any company except that of the Paris Opera. The permanent ballet company was founded in 1748 (at the same time as the Royal Theatre of Copenhagen), on the initiative of the Frenchman Des Larches, who assumed the direction. The Italian, Vincenzo Galeotti, succeeded him. A disciple of Noverre, the master of the *ballet d'action*, Galeotti produced some fifty works, including *Les Caprices de Cupidon* (*), which has remained in the repertoire to this day and was revised by Harald Lander for the Paris Opera in 1952. The great period of the Danish Ballet, however, began in 1829, with the nomination of Auguste Bournonville, first as leading dancer and director of the School of Dancing, then as maître de ballet. Born in Copenhagen in 1805 of a French father and a Swedish mother, Bournonville studied in Paris under Gardel and Vestris. An admirable dancer, he kept alive the great tradition of male dancing in his country and transmitted it to Russia through his pupil, the famous Christian Johansson. Another pupil of Bournonville was the romantic

ballerina Lucile Grahn, who appeared with Marie Taglioni, Fanny Cerrito and Carlotta Grisi in London in the famous *Pas de Quatre* of 1845. An indefatigable worker and a man of genius, Bournonville was one of the greatest choreographers of the nineteenth century. He was the author of about fifty ballets, the most famous of which — *Napoli, La Sylphide, Far from Denmark, Kermesse in Bruges,* and *Et Folkesagn* (A Folk Tale) still constitute the basis of the repertoire of the Royal Theatre. The main task of Bournonville's successors, Hans Beck and Valborg Borchsenius, was to keep alive in all its purity the tradition he had created.

Not until 1931 was there an equally flourishing epoch in the Danish ballet. The revival was due to Harald Lander's talent as maître de ballet. A sensitive and cultured man, Lander made a careful study of Bournonville's repertoire, condensing and revising it to suit the public of today. He himself created a number of ballets, including *Qarrtsiluni* and, above all, *Études,* which has become a classic in the repertoire of several international companies.

Harald Lander's great achievements, however, must not be allowed to overshadow the works of Birger Bartholin or Børge Ralov, one of the great Danish dancers of his time, and the ideal partner of Margot Lander. Beside the Danish repertoire, the Royal Theatre includes in its programmes works by the great foreign choreographers: from Fokine, Balanchine and Massine to Ashton, Lichine, Dolin and Taras. In 1955, Ashton made his version of the three-act Prokofiev *Romeo and Juliet* for Copenhagen. Harald Lander's departure in 1951 left an opening for choreographers of the younger school: Niels Bjørn Larsen (who succeeded him as ballet master), Frank Schaufuss, and Erik Bruhn.

TWO DANCERS BY DERAIN.

One of the special characteristics of the Danish Ballet is the survival of an admirable tradition of mime. Few artists elsewhere have the technique and knowledge of Gerda Karstens, Niels Bjørn Larsen or Svend Erik Jensen. Male dancing in the Danish Ballet tends to be better than female; excellent technicians, the Danish male dancers are supremely elegant. Erik Bruhn, Poul Gnatt, Henning Kronstam, Fredbjørn Bjørnsson and Flemming Flindt are among the most distinguished. The women dancers are remarkable for their swiftness, freedom and incomparable lightness, the latter a quality rarely found to-day in the European schools. Inge Sand in *Coppélia*, Margrethe Schanne in *La Sylphide*, Mona Vangsaa in *Romeo and Juliet*, Kirsten Ralov or Toni Lander in *Études* are living examples of this tradition. The technique of the corps de ballet has undergone considerable change and improvement since Vera Volkova, one of the best teachers of to-day, came to direct the School. The production of the complete *Sleeping Beauty* in 1957 revealed great progress. There is much enthusiasm for the ballet in Denmark, as the success of the annual spring festivals in Copenhagen abundantly testifies.

FASTES. COSTUMES BY DERAIN. 1933.

BALLETS 1933 Les. As a result of serious disagreement within the Ballets de Monte-Carlo, George Balanchine left the company less than a year after its foundation to direct Les Ballets 1933. Founded (as its name indicates) in 1933 thanks to an extremely wealthy patron, Edward James, the new company, apart from Balanchine, included Boris Kochno, Vladimir collaboration of first class writers, designers and musicians; to have assembled for such a short season such distinguished names as Derain and Sauguet for *Fastes,* Milhaud and Derain for *Songes,* Koechlin and Tchelitchev for *L'Errante,* Weill and Brecht for *The Seven Deadly Sins,* and Christian Bérard for *Mozartiana* was no mean feat.

LES PRÉSAGES. BALLET BY MASSINE. LAST MOVEMENT.

Dimitriev, the young Toumanova, Roman Jasinsky and Lubov Rostova (all three "deserters" from the Ballets de Monte-Carlo), Tilly Losch (the wife of Edward James) and Nathalie Leslie (the future Krassovska). It was to have an ephemeral existence: a single season at the Théâtre des Champs-Élysées in Paris during the month of June, and a few performances in London. When Balanchine was asked to direct the School of American Ballet in the United States, it was dissolved.

The repertoire comprised five straight ballets: *Fastes, Songes, L'Errante, Mozartiana* and *Les Valses* (Beethoven), all of them by Balanchine, and two composite works: *Job,* and *The Seven Deadly Sins.* If lack of unity and consistency in such a repertoire was unsatisfactory, one must admit that Les Ballets 1933 only employed the

BALLETS DE MONTE-CARLO. After Diaghilev's death in 1929, his company, the fruit of twenty years of ceaseless activity, was dissolved. Several attempts to reassemble it led to the formation in 1932 of a new company, the Ballets Russes de Monte-Carlo. The initiative came from Colonel de Basil and René Blum, who had been running the theatrical seasons at Monte Carlo since 1925. Several members of the former Ballets Russes immediately joined the new company: Serge Grigoriev, Diaghilev's faithful regisseur first of all, his close collaborator Boris Kochno, dancers such as Alexandra Danilova, Felia Doubrovska and Leon Woizikowski and finally the two principal choreographers of Diaghilev's last seasons, George Balanchine and Leonide Massine. The new and surprising elements were the "baby ballerinas"

LES COMÉDIENS JALOUX. DÉCOR BY ANNENKOV. 1932.

whom Balanchine had discovered in the dance-studios opened in Paris in the early 'twenties by the great Russian ballerinas of the old régime. For these amazingly precocious children, Tamara Toumanova, Irina Baronova, Tatiana Riabouchinska, a new repertoire was fittingly prepared: *Jeux d'enfants, Cotillon, Concurrence, Scuola di ballo.* The company made its début in Monte Carlo and, after a tour in Belgium and Holland, opened its first Paris season at the Théâtre des Champs-Élysées (9 June 1932). Although they could hardly hope to make as deep an impression as Diaghilev's company twenty years earlier, their youthful, springlike freshness and vitality won general approval. Toumanova, pale and mysterious, with her long, dark hair down to her shoulders, in *Cotillon ;* the blonde and fairy-like Riabouchinska discovering the magic world of toys in a sur-realist nursery by Joan Miró in *Jeux d'enfants ;* the tiny Baronova with her smooth and fluent style; David Lichine, a faun-like and mascu-line athlete; the inimitable Woizikowski in his dazzling variation in *Concurrence ;* finally the noble and beautiful Rostova, remote and dreamy in her diamond-studded dress... these

are a few of the memories of that first season.

After Paris and London (where the reception was enthusiastic) the company left for America, thanks to the celebrated impresario, Solomon Hurok, who presented them at the St. James' Theatre, New York, in 1933. The arrival of the baby ballerinas (with their mamas) dressed in cheap coats, cotton stockings and berets, delighted the American press. Their success was enormous and Hurok engaged the company on many other occasions. Meanwhile, serious disagreements within the company had brought changes. Balanchine left to organise Les Ballets 1933. The preponderant role then fell to Massine, and all the company's work during this period bore the mark of his style. Besides such light-hearted works as *Le Beau Danube, Beach* and *Union Pacific,* where he could exploit his natural humour and fantasy, Massine embarked on the great series of symphonic ballets: *Les Présages* and *Choreartium* (1933). At that time, especially in its male dancers, Eglevsky, Lichine, Woizikowski, Petrov, not forgetting Massine himself, the company was unrivalled. In following the trail blazed by Diaghilev, the Ballets Russes de Monte-Carlo could pride themselves on having brought to the theatre, besides Dufy, Miró and André Masson, a stage designer of the calibre of Christian Bérard. Goncharova, Larionov and Léon Zack still made valuable contributions, but it was the School of Paris which set the tone. On the musical side, two young composers were discovered: Jean Françaix and Vladimir Dukelsky. Unfortunately, there was a grave crisis in 1935: René Blum gave up his active directorship of the company and resigned completely in 1936. This marked the end of the first period of the Ballets Russes de Monte-Carlo, perhaps its most brilliant, and certainly its most balanced and homogeneous.

Ballets Russes du Colonel de Basil. — After René Blum's departure, the company was renamed Ballets Russes du Colonel de Basil. Then began a succession of tours, first Spain, then London; in 1936 the Metropolitan Opera in New York and, the same year, Australia and New Zealand. However, the main body of the company's work up to 1940 was done in the United States and England. Two famous dancers, Alexandra Danilova and Lubov Tchernicheva, led the company which included, beside Toumanova, Baronova and Riabouchinska, some promising youngsters like Vera Zorina and George Zoritch. Massine, the resident choreographer of the company, staged his famous *Symphonie Fantastique* at Covent Garden in July 1936. But, finding himself in constant disagreement with de Basil, Massine decided to break his contract. He left the company in January 1938 in order to join the rival group which René Blum had started in Monte Carlo in 1936 after his own break with de Basil. The Colonel's company withstood the crisis caused by Massine's departure, toured even more widely and then, bidding farewell to Europe, embarked in 1938 for Australia. There they took the name *Educational Ballet*, soon changed to *Original Ballet Russe* (see below).

Ballets de Monte-Carlo. — But to return to 1936, when René Blum, backed by "Universal Art", a group of American financiers presided over by

L'ÉPREUVE D'AMOUR. DÉCOR BY ANDRÉ DERAIN. 1936.

SEVENTH SYMPHONY.
MARKOVA AND YOUSKEVITCH.

and *Les Éléments*. Massine became the artistic director when he rejoined Blum in 1938. Danilova, Toumanova, Guerard, Platoff, Zoritch and some others went with Massine to the Blum company and Hurok announced that during the 1938-39 season he would manage this new company and not de Basil's.

Then Hurok had the daring and brilliant idea of combining the two rival companies and presenting them as a single troupe at Covent Garden in the summer of 1938. Agreement in principle was reached but when Hurok arrived in London he found that Universal Art Inc. (sponsors of the Blum-Massine company) had instituted proceedings to restrain de Basil from "producing, performing, or authorizing the production of certain ballets". De Basil, ignoring this suit, started a season at Covent Garden but described his company as the Royal Covent Garden Ballet Russe. Blum's company at the Theatre Royal, Drury Lane, in the next street, launched a season which was to run concurrently. Balletomanes spent their evenings scuttling from one theatre to the other and the ensuing lawsuit aroused passionate interest in London.

Nonetheless in October 1938, Hurok signed up René Blum's company for an important tour across America. The company was a starry one, headed by Massine, Danilova, Markova, Toumanova, Slavenska, Youskevitch, Eglevsky, Lifar and Franklin, and the tour a triumph. On its return to Europe in the following year,

Sergei Denham and Julius Fleischmann, had just created a new company. Favoured with the patronage of the Principality of Monaco, it was authorised to take the name of *Ballets de Monte-Carlo*. The two stars were Vera Nemchinova and Anatole Vilzak, joined, in 1937 by Nana Gollner, an American ballerina of Russian training. There were some new names, too: Maria Ruanova, Nathalie Leslie (the future Krassovska), Hélène Kirsova. Blum's first important step was to obtain the collaboration of Fokine, who thus returned to Europe after twenty-two years absence. Blum asked him not only to revive some of his finest ballets, *Le Spectre de la Rose, Petrouchka, Carnaval, Prince Igor*, which were thus restored to life and freshness, but also to do the choreography for three new works: *L'Épreuve d'Amour, Don Juan*

HIGHTOWER, TOUMANOVA AND TALLCHIEF BY LARIONOV.

they gave an unforgettable season at the Palais de Chaillot in Paris (June 1939). Three great works by Massine were in the repertory: *Seventh Symphony, Nobilissima Visione,* and *Rouge et Noir (L'Étrange Farandole).* It was the Ballets de Monte-Carlo's last season in Europe. In September war was declared and the principal artists returned to New York to make their début at the Metropolitan Opera in November 1939.

Original Ballet Russe. — The company directed by de Basil, whom we left in Australia, where they went after the "ballet war", only returned to New York at the end of 1940. Then the long American epic of the two rival companies began. Hurok presented both in 1940, with great success, but the Original Ballet Russe tour of South America in 1940-41 soon ended in disaster with a dancers' strike in Cuba. After an attempt to play in the United States, the company returned to South America and remained there from 1942 to 1946, bringing classical ballet to Brazil, Argentina and Mexico. In 1946 de Basil, with the help of the Marquis de Cuevas and once again under the management of Hurok, gave a big season at the Metropolitan Opera New York. Alicia Markova and

Rosella Hightower headed the bill. In the summer of 1947, the company returned to Europe, revisiting London and Paris. The dancing seemed a little uneven and the décors rather worn, but the repertoire was still interesting enough to hold the attention. Riabouchinska, Morosova, Moulin, Stroganova, Jasinsky, Lichine, Dokoudovsky, and Orloff now led the company. Lichine's *Graduation Ball* had its European première and Massine's *Symphonie Fantastique* was danced in France for the first time. The season at the Palais de Chaillot was the last appearance of the Original Ballet Russe in Paris, but until his death in 1951 de Basil remained active and gave seasons in Spain. After his death George Kirsta attempted, without success, to revive the company in London.

Ballet Russe de Monte-Carlo. — Once in the United States, René Blum's company was taken over by Sergei Denham and its name altered to *Ballet Russe de Monte-Carlo.* It would be difficult to follow its wanderings through the New World during the war years. In spite of

MOZARTIANA. DANILOVA AND FRANKLIN.

CLAVÉ. BALLETS DE PARIS.
PROGRAMME, 1953 SEASON.

Diaghilev. But never having the fortune to possess a leader of the same stature, or a permanent base from which to work, they were unable to keep up with changing ideas and tastes, let alone influence them. The various companies quarrelled over the spoils of the deceased, each hoping to be the sole heir, each struggling to imitate the one great company which from 1909 to 1929 revolutionised western sensibilities. There was too much imitation; in order to be really faithful to the example of Diaghilev, they should have innovated ceaselessly, taken constant risks, discovered and backed new talents with audacity. There was certainly no lack of dancers, choreographers, composers, designers, writers, or public enthusiasm. Perhaps they lived too much on Diaghilev's impulse to develop one of their own. At least they upheld, usually with honour, a precious tradition.

N.B. — During the war and later, the theatre at Monte Carlo gave its name to two other companies; their history is sufficiently distinct from the others to demand a separate article: see *Nouveaux Ballets de Monte-Carlo*.

numerous difficulties, the company has always included artists of the calibre of Alexandra Danilova, its *prima ballerina,* Natalie Krassovska, Frederic Franklin, Igor Youskevitch. Soon, with the gradual accession of American choreographers and young dancers, it was sufficiently acclimatised to produce as typically American a work as Agnes de Mille's *Rodeo* (1942). Massine, too, added to the company's American repertoire with *The New Yorker* and *Saratoga,* but has seldom worked for them since 1945. Balanchine's *Night Shadow* (1946) was another landmark. Since 1943-44 the Ballet Russe de Monte-Carlo has toured the United States with occasional New York seasons. The company is now a non-profit making organisation under the direction of Sergei Denham. David Libidins directs all bookings. They have not returned to Europe since 1939 and many of their dancers are virtually unknown outside America.

When we examine the 25 years of their history, it becomes clear that the essential importance of the Ballets de Monte-Carlo lay in their attempt to continue the work of

CLAVÉ. BALLETS DE PARIS.
PROGRAMME, 1953 SEASON.

LES DEMOISELLES DE LA NUIT. DÉCOR BY LÉONOR FINI. 1948

BALLETS DE PARIS. After his break with the Ballets des Champs-Élysées, of which he had been both founder and maître de ballet, Roland Petit undertook the formation of a company which he could run in his own way. He had the luck to find a young patron, the twenty-three year old Prince Alessandro Ruspoli, who made it possible for the Ballets de Paris to come into being. The company made its début at the Théâtre Marigny on 21 June 1948. The leading dancers were Janine Charrat, Colette Marchand, Renée Jeanmaire, Wladimir Skouratoff, Serge Perrault and Gordon Hamilton. For the opening of this first season, Margot Fonteyn agreed to create the leading rôle in Les Demoiselles de la Nuit. In addition, Petit called on the services of some famous painters and composers: André Derain, Léonor Fini, Jean Françaix and Darius Milhaud. Massine came for the occasion to revive his Beau Danube and Janine Charrat undertook several new ballets such as La Femme et Son Ombre and 'Adame Miroir. The new company was a great success with "le Tout-Paris": this

was the first of some brilliant summer seasons at the Théâtre Marigny during which Roland Petit produced: L'Œuf à la Coque, Les Demoiselles de la Nuit, and Carmen. Carmen, first produced in London (21 February 1949) brought fame overnight to Zizi Jeanmaire, just as L'Œuf à la Coque started Colette Marchand on her brilliant career. At the end of the London season came Roland Petit's Pas d'action to music by Wagner, and William Dollar's The Duel (Le Combat).

In October 1949 the new company made a smash hit in New York. Back in Europe, Roland Petit provided a new success for Zizi Jeanmaire, La Croqueuse de Diamants, in which she danced and sang. The company disbanded after a second American tour and was not re-formed until 1953, when it presented an entirely new repertoire at the Théâtre de l'Empire in Paris. Jeanmaire had broken with her choreographer; Colette Marchand headed the bill. She appeared in two gay, sexy new ballets: Ciné-bijou and Deuil en 24 heures. Roland Petit's team included several brilliant names:

LES AMOURS DE JUPITER. NATHALIE PHILIPPART.

the designers Carzou, Beaurepaire, Clavé, the composers Thiriet and Dutilleux and the dramatist Anouilh. The great success of the season was *Le Loup,* which revealed the talent of the young Violette Verdy. There was another New York season in 1954, then once more activities had to be suspended.

But the indefatigable Roland Petit, nothing discouraged, and reunited with Jeanmaire, launched his company once again in 1955, this time at the Théâtre des Champs-Élysées. As well as his earlier successes, there was a new work by Simenon and Auric, *La Chambre,* with décor by Buffet, which introduced two new dancers, Veronika Mlakar and Buzz Miller. After another London season, the Ballets de Paris had to close down once again. Since then Roland Petit seems to have turned from straight ballet to a mixed kind of American-style "show". But his *Revue des Ballets de Paris,* presented at the Théâtre de Paris in 1956 and starring Jeanmaire, now his wife, was indifferently received.

BALLETS DES CHAMPS-ÉLYSÉES.
In its brief career this company left a brilliant mark on the history of French Ballet. The leading spirits were Roland Petit and Boris Kochno: the former a twenty year old choreographer, the latter a close collaborator of Diaghilev — thus combining the enthusiasm of youth with the wisdom of maturity. Youth was the most distinctive attribute of the dancers and ballerinas of this company; youth, with its vitality, enthusiasm, daring and its physical beauty, was the great strength of their dancing. They were the representatives of a brave new generation which had grown up silently during the war years in the studios of émigrée Russian dancers or at the Opéra School, where Lifar had been preparing the way for such a revival. Behind the young dancers could be discerned the attentive shadows of their elders, Kochno, Bérard, Cocteau, with their vast theatrical experience and memories of their own youth in the days of Diaghilev.

The origin of the Ballets des Champs-Élysées, however, goes back to 1941 and 1944, when Roland Petit gave his first performances with Janine Charrat. Their example spread slowly but surely to other young dancers until Irène Lidova, to whom the credit is due for the first attempt to organise this latent talent, arranged some performances at the Théâtre Sarah-Bernhardt just after the liberation of Paris, and introduced to a surprised and delighted public Jean Babilée, Nina Vyroubova, Irène Skorik, Nathalie Philippart, Ethéry Pagava, Colette Marchand, Serge Perrault, and Renée Jeanmaire, not to mention Janine Charrat and Roland Petit. The success of these "Soirées de la danse", staged under difficult but exciting conditions, inspired Kochno and Bérard to mould this promising material into a permanent company. It was they who suggested *Les Forains* to Roland Petit, duly produced at the Théâtre des Champs-Élysées, 5 March 1945. In June of the same year there was a short season of ballet at the Théâtre Sarah-Bernhardt sponsored by Petit's father, the proprietor of a Paris restaurant, which included *Le Rendez-vous,* with scenario by Jacques Prévert.

LE JEUNE HOMME ET LA MORT.
BALLET BY COCTEAU.

THÉATRE SARAH-BERNHARDT
DIRECTION CHARLES DULLIN

LES SOIRÉES DE LA DANSE

PROGRAMME FOR LES SOIRÉES DE LA DANSE. 1944.

Roger Eudes, the then director of the Théâtre des Champs-Élysées, also encouraged Petit to form a company and to present it at his theatre for the opening of the autumn season. Boris Kochno became artistic director, Roland Petit maître de ballet, Irène Lidova general secretary. It was to be called the Ballets des Champs-Élysées; dancers included Babilée, Skorik, Youly Algaroff, Pagava, Christian Foye, Marina de Berg and Ludmilla Tcherina (replacing Renée Jeanmaire). The programme announced for the opening night, 12 October 1945, was: *La Forêt,* an act of *La Belle au Bois dormant* rehearsed by Preobrajenska; Charrat's version of *Jeu de Cartes,* and *Les Forains.*

All Paris was there. It is difficult now to imagine the success of this memorable evening — the excited audience, the electric atmosphere and finally the innumerable recalls which greeted the creation of this first specifically French company and the courage of its young leader. The triumph owed something to the circum-

LES FORAINS. SKETCH BY CHRISTIAN BÉRARD. 1945.

stances (the war was barely over) and to the significance for a Parisian audience of a ballet like *Les Forains* which seemed to symbolise not only the period, but the very moment.

After its first tours, the company returned to Paris in 1946 with some remarkable new ballets: *Les Amours de Jupiter, Los Caprichos, Concert de danses, La Fiancée du diable;* three exciting designers, Antoni Clavé, Jean-Denis Malclès, André Beaurepaire, and a Franco-Spanish dancer, Ana Nevada. In April of the same year, the new ballet company left for London and brought with it a breath of fresh, Parisian spring air. In June, the third season at the Théâtre des Champs-Élysées was distinguished by the first production of Cocteau's *Jeune homme et la mort,* which gave Babilée an international reputation. Another success of 1946 was *La Sylphide,* revived by Victor Gsovsky for Nina Vyroubova. 1947 saw Petit's *Le Bal des Blanchisseuses* (for Danielle Darmance), and *Treize Danses,* with extravagant costumes by Christian

Dior. Jean Babilée made his first attempt at choreography with *L'Amour et son amour.* In November, *Le Portrait de Don Quichotte* by Aurel Milloss was added to the repertory. Unfortunately with the end of the year came the end also of Roland Petit's adventure owing to a disagreement with the management. The company's luck went with him.

The direction of the Ballets des Champs-Élysées now passed to Jean Robin (administrator), Victor Gsovsky (maître de ballet) and Boris Kochno, who went in search of a choreographer. His choice fell on David Lichine, who returned from the States in the summer of 1948 to produce two new works for the company—*La Création,* a ballet without music, and *La Rencontre,* which introduced the young Leslie Caron, and was the company's last success. 1949 was far from brilliant; enthusiasm had given way to lassitude and decline seemed imminent. Christian Bérard, the guardian angel, died prematurely. Boris Kochno turned to John Taras, but his views were incompatible with the temperament of his new choreographer and the season of November 1949 marked the end of the Ballets des Champs-Élysées' glorious career. Not even Massine and Auric's collaboration in *Le Peintre et son modèle* could prevent the disintegration of the company. Moreover, Roland Petit was proving a formidable rival to his old company with the Ballets de Paris, which had just made a brilliant début.

In October 1951, Kochno and Jean Robin made a fresh attempt to reorganise the company with a season at the Théâtre de l'Empire. Beside the old repertoire, there were two new productions: *Revanche* by Ruth Page and *La Damnée (The Crucifix)* by Walter Gore. The company included Jacqueline Moreau, Wladimir Skouratoff, Sonia Arova, Violette Verdy, Danielle Darmance, Hélène Traïline, Gérard Ohn and Leon Danielian. It was a brief season, however, and the company disbanded during the ensuing tour. The Ballets des Champs-Élysées left behind it many regrets and many shining memories.

BALLETS JOOSS. See article on *Jooss*.

BALLET SOCIETY. The founding, in July 1946, of the Ballet Society was the culmination of the post-war efforts of Lincoln Kirstein, George Balanchine and Leon Barzin to give the United States a ballet company of the highest quality. Successor to the American Ballet and the Ballet Caravan, the new company had more extensive aims: to present new ballets, opera-ballets, and other lyric forms with the co-operation of progressive choreographers, painters and musicians. It also aimed at improving the intellectual level of ballet through books and a scholarly review, *Dance Index*. Balanchine, the artistic director, created for it some of his most noteworthy ballets: *The Four Temperaments, Symphonie Concertante, Orpheus, Divertimento*. The Ballet Society also established the reputations of the choreographers John Taras, William Dollar, Todd Bolender, Lew Christensen, and Merce Cunningham. All in all, it can be regarded as a distinguished forerunner of the great orga-

REVANCHE. DÉCOR BY CLAVÉ. 1951.

PETROUCHKA. DRAWING BY GEORGE BARBIER.

nisation which grew out of it: the New York City Ballet.

BALLETS RUSSES DE DIAGHILEV.

The 19th May, 1909, is a red letter day in the history of ballet, a day which saw the birth of a new form of theatrical art to which we still pay tribute. On that day, the first public performance of the Ballets Russes de Diaghilev took place in Paris. The enthusiasm was indescribable. The cream of social and artistic Paris hailed the event as a miracle. Public curiosity had been sedulously fanned during the preceding weeks. Since their arrival in April, the dancers had been rehearsing feverishly under Fokine's direction. Advance publicity poured from the press. Robert Brussel of "Le Figaro" had declared himself a fervent partisan. Jean Cocteau, Jean-Louis Vaudoyer and Reynaldo Hahn, who had watched rehearsals, talked enthusiastically in the smartest circles of the marvels they had seen.

Diaghilev left nothing undone to ensure success. The Théâtre du Châtelet, shabby and inconvenient, was completely renovated. The stage was enlarged and the floor relaid with pine-wood. The front five rows of the stalls were removed to allow more room for the orchestra; boxes were lavishly upholstered in red velvet. Everything was repainted. As a final touch, on the evening of the "première" Gabriel Astruc placed fifty-two of the loveliest actresses in Paris in the first row of the dress-circle, alternating blondes with brunettes. In the balcony above them were the little ballerinas from the Opéra.

The programme consisted of *Le Pavillon d'Armide, Le Festin* and the *Danses polovtsiennes* from "Prince Igor". After this last work, the apotheosis of rhythm and colour, the enthusiasm became delirious. This public, accustomed to the tepid and lacklustre performances at the Opéra, was suddenly confronted with enchantment, and with an undreamed of perfection in

CLÉOPATRE. TCHERNICHEVA AND WOIZIKOWSKI.

40

L'OISEAU DE FEU. BULGAKOV AND FOKINE.

mirages were! The arrival of the Russian Ballet was more than an event. It was a shock, a surprise, a whirlwind, a completely new experience. *Sheherazade, Prince Igor, L'Oiseau de Feu, Le Spectre de la Rose!* Without exaggeration I can say that my life can be divided in two periods: before and after the Russian Ballet. It transformed all our ideas".

The origin of the Russian Ballet is to be found at the meeting point of two movements of artistic reform: one started at the end of the century by the small band of avant-garde painters grouped round Diaghilev and the review *The World of Art,* the other, represented principally by Fokine, concerned with theatrical dancing. Both represented a reaction against convention and the stale traditions of the preceding century. It needed someone with Diaghilev's vision, energy and genius for organisation; someone, too, who was at home in social and artistic circles in Paris, to combine those two forces and weld them into a new form of theatrical art. He succeeded, and the Russian Ballet was born.

With a powerful team, headed by the principal collaborators in *The World of Art,* Benois, Bakst and Walter Nouvel; backed in Russia

the smallest details of presentation. On 2 June, *Les Sylphides* and *Cléopâtre* renewed the miracle. In a flash, the names of Nijinsky, Pavlova, Fokine, Karsavina, Bolm and Ida Rubinstein were on everyone's lips. The whole of Paris was talking of Benois and Bakst. Two performances had sufficed to make these names, unknown the day before, famous for ever.

Diaghilev, the conjuror of these visions, was no stranger to Paris. Thanks to him, art lovers had already had a glimpse of more than one aspect of Russian art. At the Salon d'Automne of 1906, he had organised an exhibition of Russian painting and in 1907, he had arranged a series of concerts at the Opéra. Then, the following year, he staged *Boris Godounov* there and revealed the genius of Chaliapin. But the success of the ballet eclipsed all his previous efforts. Thirty years later the Academician Louis Gillet could still write:

"The Russian Ballet marked one of the turning-points of my life. I am thinking of those first, unforgettable and unsurpassed productions of 1909-1912. Those Russians! Impossible to explain how convincing their

NIJINSKY AFTER "LE SPECTRE".
DRAWING BY COCTEAU.

who brought unity and splendour to the art of the ballet.

This first period, from 1909 to 1914, was of exceptional brilliance, a long succession of triumphs diversified by a few resounding scandals which raised the company's prestige even higher. *Firebird,* Stravinsky's first ballet and a landmark in the history of music, and *Sheherazade* were the two great events of 1910. In Paris, though not in London, *Carnaval* and the revival of *Giselle* were less successful, the public preferring the exotic orientalism and barbaric colours of *Sheherazade*. For many balletomanes 1911 represents the culminating point of the company's history, with Fokine's *Petrouchka* and *Le Spectre de la Rose,* two masterpieces which, nearly half a century after their creation, remain unsurpassed.

There were three important events in the 1912 season: the scandal of Nijinsky's *L'Après-*

and Paris by official and private subsidies; supported by his incomparable dancers and a choreographer of genius, Michel Fokine, Diaghilev set out to conquer the West. His formula, a living synthesis of the three arts of music, dancing and spectacle, was so far removed from the conventions of the time that it could not fail to arouse intense interest. As far as dancing was concerned, it tended to play down the element of virtuosity so dear to exponents of the Italian school in favour of a far wider range of expression. The female dancer, all-powerful since the middle of the 19th century, still held the limelight. But the Russian Ballet rehabilitated the despised male dancer; the leaps of Nijinsky and Bolm were as warmly applauded as Pavlova and Karsavina's arabesques. Moreover, the corps de ballet, up to now kept discreetly in the background, assumed an entirely new importance; Fokine's admirably arranged ensembles in *Prince Igor* and elsewhere attracted as much attention as the virtuosity of the soloists. But the dominant feature of these productions was the close collaboration between composer, choreographer and designer. It was they, linked inseparably from now onwards,

PETROUCHKA. COSTUME FOR THE MOOR BY BENOIS.
1911.

midi d'un faune; the quarrel between Diaghilev and Fokine, who left the company in the following year, furious at Nijinsky's promotion to the rank of choreographer; Jean Cocteau's début in the world of ballet with the scenario of *Le Dieu Bleu*. People were too preoccupied with the scandal of the *Faun* to pay much attention to Fokine's *Daphnis et Chloé*, a distinguished and subtle work nevertheless. In the following year, an even greater scandal greeted the Paris première of *Le Sacre du Printemps* and quite overshadowed two less sensational novelties: Debussy's *Jeux* (the first appearance of sport in ballet) and Boris Romanov's *La Tragédie de Salomé*. The *Sacre* caused a terrific hubbub; shouts and whistles came from every side of the house, members of the audience came to blows and two of them fought a duel next morning.

The last season before the war was less exciting, although Fokine had returned and Léonide

LA BOUTIQUE FANTASQUE.
COSTUME BY BAKST (NOT USED). 1919.

Massine, whom Diaghilev had discovered the year before in Moscow, made his début as the young shepherd in *La Légende de Joseph*. *Le Coq d'or* was the first of Diaghilev's many notable experiments in the combination of singing and dancing.

Since 1912 the company had made its headquarters in Monte Carlo. Here they spent the winter, between summer visits to Paris, London and other European capitals. The outbreak of war dispersed the dancers, though Diaghilev managed to arrange American tours in 1916 and 1917. Both he and his dancers suffered real hardship for a time in Spain and Portugal, but these years were not wasted, for there and in Italy Diaghilev worked out fresh ideas coloured by the Mediterranean sunshine. At last he returned to London (1918) and Paris (1919) with some new lieutenants: Cecchetti as maître de ballet, Massine, Larionov, Goncharova, Picasso and Cocteau. Now that the ballet was cut off from Russia, the centre of gravity moved to Paris, to the painters of the École de Paris (Derain, Picasso, Braque, Matisse, Rouault) and to composers from the group *Les Six* (Milhaud, Poulenc, Auric).

SHEHERAZADE. COSTUME FOR THE CHIEF EUNUCH
BY BAKST. 1910.

LES NOCES. DÉCOR BY GONCHAROVA. 1922.

During this second period, from the end of the war up to his death in 1929, Diaghilev was constantly in search of new styles, trying to keep up with (or better still ahead of) the *avant-garde*. A slight lessening of public interest due to external circumstances and constant financial difficulties compelled him to undertake more extensive tours, with programmes designed to attract wider audiences. Nevertheless, the results were not so meagre as some critics have made out: a few extravagant failures were balanced by positive achievements of great value. And though he was always willing to revive his earlier successes, he was too discriminating (and too capricious) to allow his new works to become sterile repetitions of the old.

The new trends were already evident in *Parade* (1917), a foretaste of the shock tactics of the 'twenties which caused a fresh scandal. Massine found his real form as a choreographer

LES NOCES. SKETCH BY GONCHAROVA. 1922.

44

with a series of masterpieces which included *Les Femmes de bonne humeur* (1917), *La Boutique Fantasque* and *Le Tricorne* (1919), *Pulcinella* (1920). When Massine left, Diaghilev chose Bronislava Nijinska to succeed him. At this point, any consistent line seems to have been abandoned. Topicality was represented by *Les Biches* and *Le Train Bleu* (both 1924); *Chout* (1921) and *Renard* (1922) were a return, and a happy one, to Russian folk-legend; *Les Tentations de la Bergère* and *Les Fâcheux* (both 1924) evoked the airs and graces of the *Grand Siècle*. One masterpiece, Stravinsky's *Les Noces* (1923), dominates these years. This apparent uncertainty of direction can be partly excused by the dire necessity in which Diaghilev found himself of recapturing public favour after the financial disaster of the London revival of *La Belle au Bois dormant* (1921).

Meanwhile, a new generation of dancers and choreographers was at hand to lend lustre to the last five years of the company's existence: Serge Lifar, Anton Dolin, Alexandra Danilova, George Balanchine, Alicia Markova, and the poet Boris Kochno, who became Diaghilev's secretary. Balanchine was put straight on to choreography and together with Massine, who had returned in 1924, he was responsible for the last creations of the Russian Ballet. *La Chatte* and *Le Pas d'Acier* (both 1927) were the final tributes to modernism, but the two great achievements (only moderately successful at the time) were *Apollon Musagète* (1928) and *Le Fils Prodigue* (1929). After the London season of 1929, Diaghilev went to Germany and then on to Venice, where he died on 19th August. In spite of the efforts of Serge Grigoriev, his stage director, and of Nijinska to keep the company together, it soon disintegrated, and it became clear that without Diaghilev there could be no Russian Ballet

The balance-sheet of those twenty years is pretty impressive. Out of the sixty-odd works created by the Russian Ballet, a good third still figure in the repertory of the world's great companies. The early triumphs owed a great deal to the novelty, exoticism and atmosphere of luxury which pervaded every performance, but even without these extraneous attractions such ballets as *Prince Igor, Sheherazade, Petrouchka, L'Oiseau de Feu, Le Spectre de la Rose, Les Sylphides,* the *Faun,* the *Sacre* and *La Boutique Fantasque* remain as monuments of modern choreography.

LARIONOV. DESIGN FOR LE COQ D'OR.

45

BALLETS RUSSES

PICASSO. PROGRAMME FOR THE BALLETS RUSSES.
SEASON 1924.

the time. The music is no longer regarded as a secondary consideration, totally subservient to the dancing. With the rehabilitation of stage design and ballet music, the spectacle has become an artistic unity. The vocabulary of the dance, though it went up some blind alleys, has been developed and enriched. The male dancer, once merely the obedient partner of the ballerina, has reached fully independent status. As for the corps de ballet, Fokine, and after him Massine, immensely enhanced the rôle they had to play.

Ultimately, Diaghilev changed our entire attitude to ballet. From an entertainment designed to titillate the jaded sensations of a fashionable audience, it has become an art capable of expressing the whole range of emotions from the noblest to the basest. Antiquated forms have been swept away and new ones substituted, more fertile, more in keeping with the spirit of the age, and far worthier of the huge public for dancing which, thanks to the Russian Ballet, exists to-day.

Daphnis et Chloé, Le Coq d'or, Les Femmes de bonne humeur, Le Tricorne, Les Noces, Les Biches, Apollon Musagète are some of the most perfect theatrical spectacles of the last half-century. Countless modern works are descended from *Parade, Le Pas d'Acier, La Chatte* and *Le Fils Prodigue,* with which Diaghilev blazed the trail for the avant-garde ballet. Consult the list of painters and composers: with few exceptions, and those mainly from Central Europe, all the great names of our time are there. Our debt is not yet paid; later companies have inherited not only the enthusiastic public which the Russian Ballet created but a constellation of artists discovered and trained by Diaghilev. Twenty-five years after his death, Massine, Balanchine, Lifar, Nijinska, Dolin, de Valois and many others are still at the head of their profession.

In order to realise fully what the Russian Ballet achieved, consider the difference between a ballet performance at the turn of the century and one to-day. Instead of the old scenery laboriously painted by conscientious but mediocre professional scene-painters, brilliant and inventive settings by the finest painters of

THE SLEEPING BEAUTY. COSTUME FOR
COLUMBINE BY BAKST. 1921.

46

Cris des trois managers ensemble

(rire nègre)	(il crache)	(il siffle dans un doigt)
ENTREZ	ENTREZ	ENTREZ
mesdames et messieurs!	mesdames et messieurs!	mesdames et messieurs!
SI vous êtes dignes de vivre	SI vous voulez vivre vieux!	SI vous voulez être riches!
SI vous voulez ne plus jamais être malades!	SI vous voulez voyager pour rien!	Exigez les K!
SI vous voulez avoir la toute puissance!	SI vous voulez qu'on vous aime!	Exigez le K!
SI vous voulez plaire!	Madame! SI vous voulez une belle poitrine!	Exigez le K!
SI Exigez le K! vous voulez gagner au jeu!	Monsieur! SI vous voulez obtenir une situation prépondérante!	Exigez le K!
SI si on vous voulez faire un beau mariage!	SI Exigez le K vous êtes honnête!	SI Exigez le K!
SI!		
SI!	SI!	SI!
	SI!	
SI!	SI!	SI! SI! SI!

(les trois managers s'écroulent de fatigue)

PARADE. THE THREE MANAGERS. UNPUBLISHED MANUSCRIPT BY JEAN COCTEAU.
Collection Henry Bernard, Paris.

IGOR STRAVINSKY.

CARNAVAL. FOKINE AND FOKINA.

LARIONOV. LIFAR AND DIAGHILEV AT A REHEARSAL. 1927.

Diaghilev's Ballets Russes presented the following ballets between
the first season in 1909 (Théâtre
du Châtelet, Paris) and the last in
1929 (Théâtre du Casino, Vichy) :
1909. *Le Pavillon d'Armide, Dances
from Prince Igor, le Festin, les Sylphides, Cléopâtre*. — 1910. *Le Carnaval, Sheherazade, Giselle, l'Oiseau
de feu, les Orientales*. — 1911. *Le
Spectre de la Rose, Narcisse, Sadko,
Petrouchka, le Lac des Cygnes*. — 1912.
*Le Dieu bleu, Thamar, l'Après-midi
d'un faune, Daphnis et Chloé*. — 1913.
*Jeux, le Sacre du Printemps, la Tragédie
de Salomé*. — 1914. *Papillons, la Légende de Joseph, Midas*. — 1915. *Le
Soleil de nuit*. — 1916. *Till Eulenspiegel,
las Meninas*. — 1917. *Les Femmes de
bonne humeur, les Contes Russes, Parade*.
— 1919. *La Boutique fantasque, le Tricorne*. — 1920. *Le Chant du Rossignol,
Pulcinella*. — 1921. *Chout, Cuadro Flamenco, la Belle au bois dormant (The
Sleeping Princess)*. — 1922. *Renard*. —
1923. *Les Noces*. — 1924. *Les Tentations de la bergère, les Biches, Cimarosiana, les Fâcheux, la Nuit sur le Mont
Chauve, le Train bleu*. — 1925. *Zéphire
et Flore, les Matelots, Barabau*. —
1926. *Roméo et Juliette, la Pastorale,
Jack-in-the-box, The Triumph of
Neptune*. — 1927. *La Chatte, Mercure, le Pas d'acier*. — 1928. *Ode,
Apollon Musagète, The Gods go
a-begging*. — 1929. *Le Bal, le Fils
prodigue*.

Diaghilev also presented the
following operas and other musical
works with or without dancing (single
acts only were given of some of the
Russian operas) : 1908. *Boris Godounov*. — 1909. *Prince Igor, Ivan the
Terrible, Russlan and Ludmilla*. —
1913. *Khovanshchina*. — 1914. *Le Coq
d'or, le Rossignol, A Night in May*. —
1916. *Histoires naturelles*. — 1917. *Feu
d'artifice*. — 1920. *Le Astuzie femminili*. — 1922. *Mavra*. — 1924. *La Colombe, le Médecin malgré lui, Philémon
et Baucis, Une Éducation manquée*. —
1927. *Oedipus Rex*.

LE TRICORNE. LEONIDE MASSINE.

LE CHANT DU ROSSIGNOL. DRAWING BY MATISSE. 1920.

LE CHANT DU ROSSIGNOL. COSTUMES BY MATISSE. 1920.

49

LE RENARD. DÉCOR BY LARIONOV. 1929 VERSION.

BALLETS SUÉDOIS. Ballet company founded in Paris by the Swedish *animateur,* Rolf de Maré. When they were seen for the first time (Théâtre des Champs-Élysées, 25 October 1920) they had the advantage and the disadvantage of appearing twelve years after the Russian Ballet. While they profited from Diaghilev's success, they ran the risk of being classed as imitators. The enterprise was all the more risky because its Scandinavian origin did not endow it with a choreographic tradition comparable to Diaghilev's Russian heritage. Besides, however much they wanted to dazzle and astonish the public (and that was certainly one of their aims) the means of doing so were becoming distinctly limited. The Russian Ballet, having revealed the charm of their national folklore, and unveiled the glamour of the East, were now relying on the most advanced painters and composers of the time to astonish sophisticated Paris. And although some of Rolf de Maré's productions had a recognisably Scandinavian character and ballets like *Dansgille, La Nuit de la Saint-Jean* or *Les Vierges folles* were based on Swedish legends, they were not in essentials very different from the style of the Russian Ballet. And if one can

reproach the latter for giving too much scope to the designer, how much more so the Swedish Ballet ! With the agreement of Rolf de Maré, F. Divoire wrote: "the Swedish Ballet is primarily a combination of intelligence and painting... neither dancing, music, nor décor are individually sacrificed, but they remain subordinate to an essentially pictorial conception". There lies the essence of the achievements and the limitations of the Ballets Suédois.

This pictorial conception explains their remarkable eclecticism: artists as orthodox as Steinlen *(Iberia)* and André Hellé *(La Boîte à Joujoux)* jostle avant-garde painters like Léger, Chirico and Picabia. They were not consistently attached to any aesthetic movement, though, as their experiments became more daring, their preference for advanced modern art became clearer. Bonnard designed their first ballet, a new version by Jean Borlin of Debussy's *Jeux* (1920). Irène Lagut and Jean Hugo did *Les Mariés de la Tour Eiffel* (1921). Fernand Léger designed two ballets: *Skating Rink* (1922) and *La Création du Monde* (1923). In 1924, Chirico designed *La Jarre* and Picabia *Relâche,* an extremely original work by Erik Satie and the company's last creation. Other new works presented included *Le Tombeau de Couperin* and *L'Homme et son Désir* (designer, Audrey Parr).

On the choreographic side, the Swedish Ballet's contribution was less interesting, while the dancers (mainly Scandinavian) were no match for the Russians. The leading dancer and choreographer was the Swede, Jean Borlin (a one-time pupil of Fokine), whose appealing but rather elementary spontaneity, youthfulness and directness was bound to appear a little crude beside the complex and highly professional skill of the Russian Ballet.

Three works indisputably deserve to be remembered: *L'Homme et son Désir* and *La Création du Monde* for the contribution of their designers and of their composer, Darius Milhaud, and the extraordinary *Relâche*, for Picabia's décor and for the interpolated film by René Clair, *Entr'acte,* as well as for Satie's music. After the company's demise in 1925, Rolf de Maré continued to serve the cause of dancing by presenting music-hall revues of a superior type such as the famous *Revue Nègre* in which Josephine Baker was discovered. Perhaps it was in the music-

LÉGER. PROGRAMME FOR THE BALLETS SUÉDOIS.

JEAN BORLIN BY PER KROGH. 1920.

hall that the enterprise and taste for originality which the Ballets Suédois had always shown could best be exploited. De Maré also founded *Les Archives Internationales de la Danse* in Paris in 1931 in memory of Borlin. This valuable collection was divided in 1950 between the Musée de l'Opéra, Paris, and the Stockholm Royal Opera.

BALLET THEATRE. The American Ballet Theatre ranks among the great international companies of the 20th century. It was the first essentially American company, founded (and entirely supported) by America, to win international renown. The corner stone of this brave enterprise was laid by Mikhaïl Mordkin, a great name in the history of ballet, leading dancer with Diaghilev, partner to Pavlova, who settled in the United States in 1923. In 1937 he founded the Mordkin Ballet, in order to present the pupils of his own school. Among them was a young American dancer, Lucia Chase, who backed her master's company financially and thus enabled him to present, among other works, *Giselle* and *La Fille mal gardée*. The occasional performances of the Mordkin Ballet led, towards the end of 1939, to the formation of a more important company, for which the initiative must be credited to Mordkin's young associate, Richard Pleasant. The Ballet Theater, as it was called, made its début at the Center Theatre, New York, on the 11th January 1940. No expense was spared for this first season; the public had to be impressed, and a gigantic publicity campaign was launched. As to the company, it comprised fifteen soloists and a corps de ballet of fifty-six dancers as well as two separate groups of fourteen Negro and nineteen Spanish dancers. Eleven choreographers, eighteen composers, as many designers and three conductors all contributed to the success of this auspicious opening.

Only two of the choreographers, Eugene Loring and Agnes de Mille, were American-born. The Russian choreographers represented included Fokine, Nijinska, Bolm and Mordkin himself; the English, Antony Tudor, Anton Dolin, Andrée Howard. From the very first performance, the most popular work was Fokine's *Les Sylphides,* while Loring's *The Great American Goof* and Mordkin's *Voices of*

PILLAR OF FIRE. NORA KAYE AND HUGH LAING.

Spring were dropped during the year; so was Agnes de Mille's *Black Ritual.* Tudor's works, however, *Lilac Garden, Dark Elegies* and *Judgement of Paris,* were retained and appreciated because of their link with the traditional classical ballet. The stars of the company at that time were: Patricia Bowman, Lucia Chase, Karen Conrad, Annabel Lyon, Nina Stroganova, Viola Essen, Adolph Bolm, Antony Tudor, Edward Caton, Anton Dolin, William Dollar, Eugene Loring, Dimitri Romanoff, Leon Danielian, Leon Varkas, Hugh Laing, Vladimir Dokoudovsky and Yurek Shabelevsky. Among the corps de ballet, Nora Kaye, Alicia Alonso, Jerome Robbins, John Kriza and other future glories of the young American Ballet were beginning to show their talent. Richard Pleasant resigned as director of the company in 1941, and Gerry Sevastianov took over. Four new stars were engaged: Irina Baronova, Alicia Markova, Rosella Hightower and George Skibine. The brilliant success of Fokine's *Bluebeard,* first produced in October 1941, was largely due to these admirable newcomers.

All through the history of the Ballet Theatre,

CAPRICHOS. J. KRIZA AND R. A. KOESUN.

Russians, English, Americans, each in turn, have dominated the company and imposed their own styles and ideas. The creation of *Pillar of Fire* in 1942 inaugurated a phase of the influence of Tudor and his favourite interpreters, Hugh Laing and Nora Kaye. Kaye was a dancer of a completely new style, a pure product of the American school, whose intense personality inspired the dramatic and "Freudian" side of the Ballet Theatre's repertoire. For the more classical ballets there was the fragile and poetic Alicia Markova. Massine appears in the history of the company with the production of *Aleko* (1942). Fokine died in August of that year while he was working on *Helen of Troy,* which Lichine completed. Tudor set the tone once again with two important works for the 1943 season: *Romeo and Juliet* and *Dim Lustre*.

From 1944, the young American choreographers came suddenly into the limelight, with their dynamism, fresh ideas and new rhythms: Jerome Robbins with *Fancy Free, Interplay, Facsimile ;* Michael Kidd with *On Stage ;* the more classical John Taras with *Graziana*. London saw the Ballet Theatre for the first time in 1946 and discovered the strength and vitality of the American style, whose influence was soon to be felt in Europe. A new stage of development was marked by Agnes de Mille's *Fall River Legend* (1948) and by the revivals of such folk ballets as *Billy the Kid* and *Rodeo*. In 1950, when the company, headed by Lucia Chase and her new partner the designer Oliver Smith, celebrated its tenth anniversary, the organisers could pride themselves on a repertoire representing all the modern choreographic trends. A European tour in that year, with London and Paris seasons, revealed an unsuspected wealth of talent in the field of music as well as choreography; only décor and costumes left something to be desired. American ballet surprised Europeans by its peculiar choreographic style, a composite of modern dancing and negro rhythms, influenced both by daily life and by indigenous folklore. Dancers of the new type, John Kriza, Paul Godkin and Kelly Brown, revealed a new technique, supple, elastic and staccato, but the mixture of races, schools and temperaments allowed plenty of variety. Alicia Alonso, incomparable virtuoso of Balanchine's *Theme and Variations* and of *The Black Swan,* contrasted vividly with the impetuous Jenny Workman and Allyn MacLeerie, who seemed to have walked straight out of a Broadway musical. The company has always been headed by a great *danseur noble* — Dolin, Eglevsky, Youskevitch, Erik Bruhn.

Between 1951 and 1957 Ballet Theatre made

FANCY FREE. BALLET BY ROBBINS.

extensive tours of Europe and the Middle East, acquiring in various countries new ballets and guest artists, such as Jean Babilée, Natalie Philippart and Colette Marchand. A nomad existence of touring militates against the creation of new ballets, however, and by the mid-1950s Ballet Theatre was existing on past successes and star dancers rather than on important new creations. Valerie Bettis's ballet, *A Streetcar Named Desire,* revived for Ballet Theatre in 1954 enjoyed some success (although not in London), largely on account of Nora Kaye's poignant and distraught performance as Blanche du Bois. More successful was the creation by a young Englishman, Kenneth MacMillan, of *Winter's*

bassador of the United States. In 1958 the company danced at the Brussels World Fair and in many other European cities under the auspices of the American National Theatre and Academy (ANTA). The leading dancers were Kaye, Kriza, Bruhn, Lupe Serrano, Violette Verdy, Scott Douglas, Ruth Ann Koesun, and Michael Lland.

BALLET WORKSHOP. See *Ballet Rambert.*

BARABAU. Choral ballet in one act. Scenario and music: Vittorio Rieti. Scenery and costumes: Maurice Utrillo. Choreography: Ba-

LEMUEL AYRES. COSTUMES FOR THE HARVEST ACCORDING. 1953.

Eve for Kaye and Kriza (first produced Lisbon, 17 January 1957). To develop new choreographic talent, Ballet Theatre instituted in the spring of 1957 an exciting new venture known as Ballet Previews. Seven entirely new ballets, together with eight productions by the Ballet Theatre Workshop (founded in 1954), were presented in a Festival of Ballet at the Phoenix Theatre, New York, to sold out houses. Workshop classes are now part of the curriculum at the Ballet Theatre School in New York, which boasts a distinguished faculty. Associate schools are being established throughout the United States, in Denver, Oklahoma City and Woodstock.

After the 1956-57 tour of Europe and the Middle East, the name of the company was officially changed to *American Ballet Theatre,* a proud and deserved distinction for such an am-

lanchine. First performance: Diaghilev's Ballets Russe, Coliseum Theatre, London, 11 December 1925. Principal dancers: Léon Woizikowski, Serge Lifar, Lydia Sokolova. Based on an Italian nursery rhyme. Barabau, a sly, rich peasant, feigns death in order to trick some pillaging soldiers. Utrillo's charming backcloth looked typically French; the balance was adjusted by the Italian folk songs used in Rieti's score. Balanchine's burlesque choreography was a great success. * Sadler's Wells produced a new version of *Barabau* in 1936. Choreography: de Valois. Scenery and costumes: Edward Burra.

BARDIN Micheline. An infant prodigy in the Paris Opera's *Vie de Polichinelle ;* promoted to leading dancer in 1948. A brilliant, piquante dancer with an excellent elevation. Her main

CHAGALL. BALLET THEATRE SOUVENIR PROGRAMME. 1945-1946.

successes were: *Le Palais de Cristal* (third movement) and *Études*. Left the Opéra in 1956.

BARONOVA Irina. "The sensation of the evening... the tiny Mdlle Baronova, who danced through the final galop like a whirlwind". André Levinson was describing the début of a girl of thirteen in a divertissement by Balanchine at the Théâtre Mogador in Paris (1932). A few months later, Baronova became one of the three baby ballerinas of the Ballets de Monte-Carlo. An invaluable artist in both classical and demi-caractère roles, in the successive Monte Carlo companies from 1932 to 1940, she was later engaged as ballerina by Ballet Theatre (1941-42). A great favourite in London, New York and Paris. But the years of strenuous touring during her youth took their toll, and Baronova left the ballet at the early age of twenty-seven. After a short period as an actress, she left the stage altogether, settled in England, and devoted herself to her husband and children, until persuaded by Fonteyn to serve on the Royal Academy of Dancing in 1957. Blonde, with grey eyes, her lively temperament and warm femininity made her a fascinating Queen of Shemakhan in *Le Coq d'Or* and a tender and poetic interpreter of the slow movement of *Les Présages*.

BARTHOLIN Birger. Danish maître de ballet and choreographer. Trained in the severely classical school of Copenhagen, his career as a dancer began in 1928 with Ida Rubinstein in Paris. Danced in the Boris Kniaseff company in 1930, with Vera Nemchinova and Oboukhoff in 1931 and in a Cochran revue in London in 1932. After a period with the Ballets de Monte-Carlo (1935-36), he confined his dancing to solo recitals. Meanwhile, Bartholin had found his real vocation, choreography, with four very successful works for the Ballets de la Jeunesse (Paris, 1938-39), followed by others for the Royal Theatre, Copenhagen *(Classical Symphony, Romeo and Juliet, Parisiana)*, for de Cuevas

BARABAU. NINETTE DE VALOIS AND ASHTON.

JEUX D'ENFANTS. IRINA BARONOVA.

(L'Aigrette), and for the opera houses of Oslo and Helsinki. A firm supporter of the academic style, and a successful teacher.

BASIL Colonel Vassili de. Born Kovno 1888, died Paris 1951. His real name was Vassili Grigorievitch Voskressensky. A Russian émigré and ex-Cossack officer, known in the history of ballet as Colonel de Basil. Became an impresario in Paris; Prince Zeretelli's partner in the "Opéra Russe de Paris" (1925-30), then formed the first Ballets de Monte-Carlo company (1932) with René Blum. A clever, tenacious, energetic man, courageous to the point of folly, with an infallible flair but no real knowledge of art. Something of a genius for organisation, and an irresistible charmer, he controlled his company with a mixture of paternal affection and diplomacy. He had great powers of persuasion; if he could not inspire the artists around him, he at least knew how to make them give their best. For twenty years, he ran a ballet company under various names: Monte-Carlo, de Basil, Original Ballet Russe. For their history, see the article *Ballets de Monte-Carlo*.

BAYLIS Lilian. See *Royal Ballet*.

BEACH. Ballet in three scenes. Scenario: R. Kerdyk. Music: Jean Françaix. Scenery and costumes: Raoul Dufy. Choreography: Massine. First performance: Ballets de Monte-Carlo, 18 April 1933. Principal dancers: David Lichine, Tatiana Riabouchinska, Irina Baronova.

BEATON Cecil. English photographer, also designer and author, born 1904. His books of photographs provide an illuminating commentary on the fashionable world of the 'twenties and 'thirties, also, in a rather different vein, on wartime London. As a designer for ballet, Beaton's concern with "amusing" details of period styles is not wholly free from lapses into sentimental vulgarity, but his décor and costumes for Ashton's *Apparitions* (Sadler's Wells, 1936) included some enchanting evocations of the Romantic period. Beaton also designed *Les Sirènes* for Sadler's Wells (1946) as well as several ballets for leading American companies, notably *Les Patineurs* for Ballet Theatre, the Balanchine version of *Swan Lake* and *Les Illuminations* for the New York City Ballet, *Devoirs de vacances* for the Ballets des Champs-Élysées.

DRAWINGS BY BEATON
FOR DEVOIRS DE VACANCES.

BEACH. DÉCOR BY DUFY. BALLETS DE MONTE-CARLO. 1933.

BEAU DANUBE Le. Perhaps it was because it contained too little of the famous waltz
that *Le Beau Danube bleu* (ballet in two scenes, first
performed Count E. de Beaumont's "Soirées de
Paris", 17 May 1924) was abridged both in title
and length to *Le Beau Danube,* in one scene, for
the revival by the Ballets de Monte-Carlo, in
Monte Carlo, 15 April 1933. (Music: Johann
Strauss, orch. Désormière. Scenery: V. Polunin, after Guys. Costumes: E. de Beaumont.
Choreography: Massine.) Whatever the reason,
the ballet is a real masterpiece, still fresh despite
its years.

Nothing could be simpler than this story of
the encounter and rivalry, in the Prater of the
1860's, between an innocent young girl and the
ex-mistress, a not-so-innocent Street Dancer,
her fiancé the dashing Hussar. And nothing
could be simpler than the means used. But the
skilful interweaving of episodes, romantic,
happy, serious or comic; the portrayal of character through pure dancing; all these, and
above all the vitality of the whole ballet are
characteristic of Massine at his best. In Monte
Carlo, the main roles were danced by Massine

(the Hussar), Alexandra Danilova (the Street
Dancer), Tatiana Riabouchinska (the Young
Girl), David Lichine (the King of the Dandies),
and Irina Baronova (the First Hand).

The ballet was included in the repertoire of
many companies. Usually the spirit, if not the
actual details, of Polunin's Constantin Guys
backcloth depicting an elegant hansom bowling
through a park, and of de Beaumont's costumes,
in half-tones from beige to dark brown, broken
only by the red velvet gown of the Street
Dancer, has been retained.

* Under the title *Straussiana,* the Ballet of
the Stanislavsky and Nemirovitch-Dantchenko
Theatre presents a work by Bourmeister and
Markow on the same theme, equally lively and
well arranged, but emphasising comedy and
burlesque rather than the finesse and poetry of
Massine's *Beau Danube.*

BEAUMONT Cyril W. English writer, publisher and bookseller, born 1891. An authority on dancing whose interest, aroused by
seeing Pavlova in 1910, continues undimmed to

this day. His bookshop in central London is known to lovers of ballet the world over. Of his numerous publications, which include monographs on dancers past and present, technical primers and translations of historical works, the monumental *Complete Book of Ballets* is a noteworthy example of his encyclopaedic knowledge, patient research and precise, factual style.

BEAUMONT Count Étienne de. A passionate amateur of modern art in general and ballet in particular; one of those wealthy and discriminating patrons whose activities in the twenties were of notable value to the sophisticated theatre in Paris. De Beaumont's enthusiasm was of the practical kind. He organised a series of performances at the Théâtre de la Cigale in May and June 1924, called *Les Soirées de Paris*. Massine was the choreographer, and the dancers were former Diaghilev stars. The programmes included Cocteau's *Roméo et Juliette, Salade, Mercure* (with masterly décors by Picasso), *Le Beau Danube, Scuola di Ballo, Gaieté Parisienne*. For the last three, later revived by the Ballets de Monte-Carlo, de Beaumont himself did the scenery and costumes. A highly successful venture and one, moreover, applauded by the fashionable world of Paris. Though he sponsored no further seasons, de Beaumont remained until his death in 1956 a member of that part of the avant-garde that willingly accepts provocation provided that it is sufficiently elegant (see also *Soirées de Paris, Les.*)

BEAUREPAIRE André. Beaurepaire brings to the theatre the personality of an engraver and draughtsman. His striking décor for *Concert de Danses* (Ballets des Champs-Élysées, 1946) was a neo-Baroque fantasy. By the time he designed *Scènes de Ballet* for Ashton (Sadler's Wells Ballet, 1948) his style, though still predominantly linear, had become much starker. He also designed *La Belle au bois dormant, Ciné-Bijou* and *La Nuit* for the Ballets de Paris.

BEECHAM Sir Thomas. An English conductor and impresario, who for the greater part of this century has played a predominant role in the musical life of his country. Mainly asso-

ciated with opera and with orchestral music, his connections with the ballet have been fitful but notable. With his father, Sir Joseph Beecham, he was associated in the first London seasons of the Diaghilev Ballet (1911 and 1913) and conducted for them on various occasions. During the London season of 1928, he conducted his own arrangement of music by Handel for Balanchine's *The Gods go a'begging*. A second Handel ballet, *The Origin of Design,* followed in 1932, this time for Ninette de Valois and the Camargo Society. A celebrated wit, and a man of striking personality, regal appearance and very definite opinions as to how things, musical and otherwise, should be done. Dancers still speak with bated breath of the speed at which Beecham took certain passages in the one-act version of *Le Lac des Cygnes* at a Camargo Society performance.

BEDELLS Phyllis. English dancer and teacher, born in Bristol 1893. Phyllis Bedells, by succeeding Lydia Kyasht as prima ballerina at the old Empire Theatre in London in 1914, established the prestige of the English dancer,

APPARITIONS. COSTUME BY BEATON. 1949.

proving that ballerinas need not necessarily be Russian-born. After a long and popular stage career, including appearances with the Camargo Society and young Vic-Wells Ballet, she retired to devote herself to teaching and her work as Vice President of the Royal Academy of Dancing. In 1954 she published her reminiscences, *My Dancing Days*.

BÉJART Maurice. French dancer and choreographer of classical training. The modern dance has now claimed his attention; the style fits him like a glove. His *La Mégère apprivoisée (The Taming of the Shrew)*. showed a gift for humorous characterisation of people and situations, but his most remarkable work, far more typical of his contemporary, anxiety-laden outlook, is the celebrated *Symphonie pour un homme seul* (*) (1955). The effect created by this ballet was partly due to the use of *musique concrète*, a form of accompaniment which evidently works as a stimulus to Béjart, who used it again in *Haut-Voltage*. Since 1954 Maurice Béjart has directed with Jean Laurent the "Ballet des Étoiles" company, previously entitled "Ballet de l'Étoile".

SYMPHONIE POUR UN HOMME SEUL.
MAURICE BÉJART AND MICHÈLE SEIGNEURET.

BELLE AU BOIS DORMANT La (The Sleeping Beauty). Ballet in three acts with a prologue. Scenario: Ivan Vsevolojsky and Marius Petipa after Perrault. Scenery and costumes: Vsevolojsky. Music: Tchaikovsky. Choreography: Petipa. First performance: Maryinsky Theatre, St. Petersburg, 3 January 1890. Principal dancers: Carlotta Brianza, Paul Gerdt, Enrico Cecchetti, Marie Petipa, Varvara Nikitina.

Tchaikovsky wrote this ballet, the most brilliant in the whole classical repertoire, at the request of Vsevolojsky, the director of the Imperial Theatres. Its innumerable solos, its famous pas de deux, and its fairy-tale atmosphere helped to revive the prestige of the ballet in Russia at a particularly critical moment. There is hardly a classical matinée of any standing which does not offer an extract from *The Sleeping Beauty*, such as the Blue Bird pas de deux (see below).

The Prologue shows the christening of the Princess Aurora. The fairies come to lay at her feet all the gifts of the earth. In turn they dance before her cradle: the Fairy of the Crystal Fountain, the Fairy of the Enchanted Garden, the Fairy of the Woodland Glades, the Fairy of the Songbirds, the Fairy of the Golden Vine, and the Fairy of the Lilac. Each one is neatly characterised in music and choreography. But suddenly, with a flash of lightning, riding in a chariot drawn by rats and mice, the wicked Fairy Carabosse makes her entrance. The Master of Ceremonies had forgotten to invite her—the seventh fairy. She curses the baby princess, foretelling that at the age of sixteen years she will prick her finger and die. But the Lilac Fairy has not yet presented her gift. Now she comes forward to change the spell; the princess will indeed prick her finger but she will not die. She will sleep for a hundred years and will then be awakened by the kiss of Prince Charming. The rest of the story follows Perrault's tale. The spell is cast, the palace sleeps for a hundred years under brambles and cobwebs. Then Prince Charming is shown a vision of the Princess Aurora by the Lilac Fairy and is brought to the palace. He awakens her and their wedding is celebrated with a display of brilliant dancing.

The staging at the Maryinsky Theatre surpassed all previous efforts in grandeur and extravagance. The décor of Act III (The Wedding), with an immense staircase bordered by sparkling fountains, like the *grandes eaux* of Versailles, required the most complex stage machinery. The dress rehearsal took place on 2 January 1890 before the assembled court. The Czar showed little enthusiasm; "very nice" was all he said to poor Tchaikovsky, and the press was scornful. But the success with the public was immediate and total; tickets were resold for more than double the real price; the publishers of the music made a fortune. Out of 45 ballet performances that season, 21 were of *The Sleeping Beauty*. It was no flash in the pan; in 26 years there were 163 performances.

For Petipa, working in close collaboration with the composer, this ballet was a kind of artistic testament. At the peak of his genius, the old master poured into it all the resources of half a century's experience of classical choreography. The work is so rich that examples from every scene might be quoted: the fairy variations, the superb Rose Adagio, the lyricism of the Vision Scene, the Blue Bird pas de deux, the great adagio for Aurora and her Prince, to say nothing of the farandole and the mazurka. In 1890 Petipa attempted to stage a performance of the ballet in Paris at the Théâtre Eden but it had to be abandoned because of the cost. On 17 July 1899 it was presented at the Bolshoi Theatre in Moscow. The staging was by Gorsky and Aurora was danced by Roslavleva, one of the greatest Russian ballerinas of the time.

* The most brilliant of all revivals was Diaghilev's at the Alhambra Theatre, London (2 November 1921). Production and choreography were entrusted to Nicholas Sergueev, who reproduced the original version from notes he had taken when régisseur at the Maryinsky. Choreography for a few additional variations was provided by Nijinska, and Stravinsky partly reorchestrated the music. The scenery and costumes, of incredible magnificence, were designed by Bakst. In reviving this great classic, to celebrate the 100th anniversary of Petipa's birth, Diaghilev showed considerable courage, for the public had come by now to think of him as a revolutionary who had broken with tradition. They did not understand his fundamental belief in classicism. The dancers included the greatest names of the day: Olga Spessivtseva, Vera Trefilova, Lubov Egorova and Lydia Lopokova alternating as the Princess

Aurora; Pierre Vladimirov and Anatole Vilzak as Prince Florimund; Idzikowski and Lopokova in the Blue Bird pas de deux; Lopokova also as the Lilac Fairy. One moving detail: Carlotta Brianza who, thirty years earlier, had danced the role of Aurora now appeared as Carabosse. This part was also taken by Enrico Cecchetti, the first Carabosse, who chose it for his fiftieth anniversary performance on the stage. Other roles were danced by Felia Doubrovska, Vera Nemchinova, B. Nijinska, Ludmilla Schollar, Lydia Sokolova, Lubov Tchernicheva, Tadeo Slavinsky, Leon Woizikowski, Nicolas Zverev, Maria d'Albaicin, Nicholas Kremnev, Errol Addison, Ursula Moreton, Hilda Bewicke and, under the name of Patrikeeff in a very minor part, Anton Dolin. The season ended with a financial disaster in which the company almost foundered. Diaghilev had to leave London, abandoning scenery and costumes, but he retained in his repertoire until the end a suite of dances, mostly from the last act, which was presented as *Aurora's Wedding*. This was also a great popular success when danced by de Basil's company and has been revived on many occasions.

* Not until 2 February 1939 was there a revival of *The Sleeping Beauty* in its complete form in London, this time by the Sadler's Wells Ballet. Once again, Sergueev reproduced the choreography but ignored Diaghilev's emendations and reverted to the Petipa version. The — rather simple — scenery and costumes were by Nadia Benois. Margot Fonteyn danced Princess Aurora; Robert Helpmann was Prince Florimund, June Brae the Lilac Fairy, Mary Honer and Harold Turner danced the Blue Bird pas de deux. The ballet was an immediate and enduring popular success. At the reopening of Covent Garden on 20 February 1946, the Sadler's Wells Ballet presented a handsome revival with some choreographic alterations by Frederick Ashton and Ninette de Valois; scenery and costumes were by Oliver Messel. Once again, Fonteyn and Helpmann had the leading roles; Beryl Grey was the Lilac Fairy, Pamela May and Turner danced the Blue Bird pas de deux. This production became the company's greatest success in England and in America where it was first shown at the Metropolitan Opera House, New York, on 9 October 1949. In Paris, where it was danced at the Opéra

on 27 September 1954 with Fonteyn, Michael Somes and Beriosova, it was less universally admired. Among the company's most notable Auroras, in addition to Fonteyn, have been Pamela May, Moira Shearer, Beryl Grey, Violetta Elvin, Svetlana Beriosova, Elaine Fifield, and, as guest artists, Markova and Chauviré.

* In the Soviet Union the ballet underwent profound modifications during the years 1930 to 1938 but is now given again in the complete version by the Bolshoi company as well as at the Kirov Theatre in Leningrad. Semenova, Ulanova, Lepeshinskaya, and Struchkova are among the great Auroras.

* In 1957 Ninette de Valois staged a version similar to that of the Sadler's Wells Ballet for the Royal Danish Ballet in Copenhagen. Scenery and costumes were by André Delfau. The principal dancers were: Margrethe Schanne, Kirsten Simone, Henning Kronstam, Niels Bjørn Larsen and Lizzie Rode.

LE COQ D'OR. COSTUME BY BENOIS.
PARIS OPERA VERSION, 1948. *Musée de l'Opéra.*

* Full length productions have been essayed in the United States by Mordkin (1936) and Catherine Littlefield (1937). Nicholas Beriosoff staged the complete ballet in Stuttgart, 27 December 1957.

* *Blue Bird (L'Oiseau Bleu)* is often presented separately as a divertissement. It is a pas de deux cast in the classical formula of adagio, variation for the man, variation for the woman, coda. The fairy tale which inspires the dance is that of the beautiful captive, Princess Florisse, who is cheered in her prison by the visits of the Blue Bird, hence the man's dance is full of steps of elevation and brilliant batterie while the woman's is delicate and feminine. It is a superb vehicle for the male virtuoso and among the greatest exponents have been Cecchetti (the creator), Nijinsky, Idzikowski, Lifar, Dolin, Eglevsky, Turner, Babilée, Bruhn and Shaw.

BELLE HÉLÈNE La. See *Helen of Troy.*

BENOIS Alexandre. Born 1870 in St. Petersburg. Alexandre Benois is, together with Leon Bakst, the artist who played the greatest part in the foundation and aesthetic orientation of Diaghilev's Ballets Russes. More than anyone else, he was responsible for the capital importance given to painting, and his role went far beyond that of a mere stage designer. To Benois especially much of the credit is due for the greater cohesion and unity between the various elements in a performance, after a long decadence had reduced ballet to a mere complement of opera, and décor to an impersonal background. Through the idea of close collaboration between composer, dancer and painter, Benois achieved a unique result; the role of the dancer was enhanced, though his movements were controlled and subjected to pictorial and plastic considerations previously regarded as mere accessories. In fact, one could almost say that during the first period of the Russian Ballet, the years of the great revelation, painting was the dominant art. Benois has himself said as much: "The role of the painters was very important; not only were we responsible for the backgrounds against which Fokine, Nijinsky, Pavlova, Karsavina, Fedorova and so many others appeared; but the general idea of the productions was ours. We, the *painters* (not

PETROUCHKA. DÉCOR BY BENOIS FOR FIRST AND LAST SCENES. 1911.

professional stage designers, but "real" painters who came to stage design through our love of theatre) helped also to plan the main lines of the choreography and all the details of the production. It was this control, neither official nor professional, which lent such a particular character to our work and — I do not think I am claiming too much — contributed largely to its success".

Today, when theatrical experiment tends to extremes, the art of Alexandre Benois may seem sedate and conventional. In reality, it was revolutionary without renouncing any of the valid and permanent aspects of tradition. In the history of stage design, Alexandre Benois played a similar role to Cicèri in abolishing the unoriginal, mediocre, mass-produced work which had succeeded that of the romantic innovators. He proved that mediocrity was not inevitable and that painters were capable of evolving and renovating old theatrical formulas without impoverishing or rejecting them. If there is a chasm between contemporary art and that of the past, there is none between Benois and the great designers of the 19th century; he

achieved the same grandeur of conception and perfect unity of style with means appropriate to our time.

By the time his work for Diaghilev was seen in Paris, Alexandre Benois had behind him a career rich in knowledge and experience. Of all the painters from Russia, he was the best qualified to create a synthesis, an authentically European style. He came from a family of French origin and was closely involved with artistic life in Russia, indeed in daily contact with it. His father was Court Architect; his brother, who had also studied architecture, became a well known water-colourist and was elected to the Russian Academy in 1884. He himself studied law before becoming a painter: he spent nearly two years as an art student in Paris about 1904, before Diaghilev's arrival. Benois' influence on Diaghilev was decisive; it may well be that without Benois, Diaghilev's plans would not have materialised — certainly his technical, theoretic and historical knowledge proved indispensable. Benois was already a knowledgeable balletomane when he first met Diaghilev, and became a co-founder with him of the review *The World of Art*. He had also worked for the theatre and had been commended for his décors for *Sylvia* at the Maryinsky Theatre in 1901. It was with the Ballets Russes, however, that Benois came to play a decisive role. His décors for *Le Pavillon d'Armide* (1909) and *Giselle* (1910) prepared the way for *Petrouchka* in 1911. This, due to his gift for blending the real with the supernatural and for setting poetically conceived individual characters against a background of everyday life coloured by popular tradition, was his greatest success. His power of recapturing the essence of the most diverse periods and places gave him exceptional versatility. He could interpret with equal felicity the French classics *(Le Malade Imaginaire, Le Médecin malgré lui)*, Italian comedy *(La Locandiera, The Servant of Two Masters)*, Shakespeare *(The Merchant of Venice, Julius Caesar)*, the romantic period *(La Dame aux Camélias, Ruy Blas, La Bohème)*, or the most typical Russians *(Le Coq d'Or, Pique Dame, The Idiot)*. He adapted himself equally well to the grand scale of the Paris Opera and the more limited demands of spoken drama. His output for the ballet alone has been immense. For Diaghilev he designed *Le Pavillon d'Armide* (previously produced in St. Petersburg in 1906) and *Les Sylphides, Giselle* (1910), *Petrouchka* (1911), *Le Rossignol* (1914). He was the principal designer for Ida Rubinstein's 1928 season *(Les Noces de l'Amour et de Psyché, Le Baiser de la Fée, La Bien-Aimée, La Princesse Cygne, Boléro)*. He also designed for her *Amphion* in 1931, *Semiramis, Diane de Poitiers* and *La Valse* in 1934. For the Ballets de Monte-Carlo, he designed *Le Bourgeois Gentilhomme* (1932), *Graduation Ball* (1940), *Raymonda*

BENOIS AND STRAVINSKY.

(1946); for the Marquis de Cuevas *The Enchanted Mill* (1948); for London's Festival Ballet the complete *Nutcracker* (1957).

BÉRARD Christian (1902-1949). Born and died in Paris. As a painter, Christian Bérard belonged to the short-lived movement called neohumanism, whose aim was to restore something of the spirituality and humanity which the primarily intellectual and abstract experiments since the beginning of the century had neglected. The group came into being about 1930. The

BENOIS. SKETCH FOR SYLVIA. 1901.

64

leader was the critic, Waldemar George; the painters concerned were Eugène and Léonide Berman, Léon Zack, Hosiasson. It was not perhaps a very well-defined movement but, in its reaction from formalism towards subjective sentiment it represented a definite trend in the thought of the time and one of some value. Although they soon ceased to function as a group, the painters retained their common interests. Perhaps it was their preoccupation with the human personality which led all of them, with the exception of Hosiasson, to stage design. To the theatre they brought a new conception of space, in which mystery and suggestion played an important part. In this respect, Christian Bérard's role was considerable. Out of the simplest-seeming materials he could create a magic world. As an example of his strange powers of invention which, far from being extravagant, conjured mystery and beauty out of the most familiar scenes and objects, one has only to think of one of his first ballet décors, *Cotillon* (Ballets de Monte-Carlo, 1933). The set consisted of a single row of theatre boxes set low in a plain white wall, lined with red and lit from within, simple, refined and yet sumptuously elegant. The girls' costumes were traditional and yet subtly original: tight bodices with tulle skirts slightly longer than the conventional *tutu,* suggesting rather than revealing the lines of the body, mistily reflecting and diffusing the real colour of the dress, that was concentrated in the bodice, tightly moulded to the figure. Already in 1930, when he made his début in the theatre with *La Nuit,* he had shown what ravishing effects he could obtain with transparent materials. It was clear then that the art of Christian Bérard was a transfiguration of the familiar world, accomplished by means of the utmost simplicity.

Close and intelligent co-operation from the dressmaker was of course essential for Bérard. He suggested shapes, colours, harmonies, folds; he showed how the material should drape the body, the forms it should assume in movement. But is was up to the dressmaker to see that Bérard's ideas worked. Because of this co-operation, one could say that he was himself a *grand couturier* as much as stage designer; conversely, many *couturiers* found precious suggestions in his work for the theatre, which had considerable influence on fashion between the wars. Bérard's taste for great folds of supple, enveloping material, and the delicate harmony of his lines were not confined to his costumes; the décors showed the same sure hand at work. In his architectural sets he made dream palaces, the shape of whose unsubstantial stones was suggested less by outline than by the shadows cast by the light falling across their surface. This apparent lack of precision, however, did not exclude a romantic affection for classical forms, triangular pediments and arcades, occasionally superimposed, as in Molière's *Don Juan.* (for Jouvet) and *Symphonie Fantastique* (for Colonel de Basil's Ballet Russe, 1936). Often his décors were extremely low in tone, almost monochrome, in order to set off the dancers. Bérard's

BÉRARD. SKETCH FOR LES FORAINS. 1945.

LA RENCONTRE. STUDY FOR THE DÉCOR BY BÉRARD. 1948.

favourite colour seemed to be white, or pale grey, against which the more vivid shades of the costumes would glow in luminous relief. Even in his most simple and bare settings—and it would be hard to go further, in this respect, than *Les Forains* (Ballets des Champs-Élysées, 1945)—Bérard succeeded in creating an impression of richness by the sudden brilliance of a red, the intensity of his contrasts, the elegance of his shapes. He could endow the picturesque with the magic of dreams and suspend a halo of enchantment over a squalid scene: the melancholy and poverty-stricken jugglers and acrobats of *Les Forains* have a look of fallen lords and fairies disguised as beggar-women. After ensuring by their approval the success of Diaghilev's Ballets Russes, the arbiters of taste in Paris society found in Christian Bérard, only a short while after Diaghilev's death, a new *enfant terrible* whose fantasies—not to say caprices—they feared, adored and encouraged. But Bérard knew by instinct, better than anyone else, how to live up to his legend, to renew himself without inconsistency, to surprise

without offending. Beside *La Nuit* (1930) and *Mozartiana* (Les Ballets 1933), his work for ballet included *Cotillon* (1933), *La Symphonie Fantastique* (1936), *Seventh Symphony* (1938), for the Ballets de Monte-Carlo; *Les Forains* (1945), *La Sylphide* (1947, costumes only), *La Rencontre ou Œdipe et le Sphinx* (1948) for the Ballets des Champs-Élysées; finally *Clock Symphony* (1948) for Sadler's Wells, a revival of *La Nuit* for the Ballets des Champs-Élysées (1949), and *Caracole* (1952) for the New York City Ballet.

BERIOSOVA Svetlana. One of the younger ballerinas of Britain's Royal Ballet, Svetlana Beriosova is a dancer of rare romantic quality. Gracious in manner and aristocratic in bearing with wide and beautiful movements, she has the natural style of a ballerina. Born of a dancing family in Lithuania in 1932, she trained with Vilzak and Schollar in New York and played children's roles with the Ballet Russe de Monte-Carlo. After experience with the Cuevas ballet and Metropolitan Ballet (where Taras made for

CHRISTIAN BÉRARD. IMPRESSION OF LES FORAINS. BALLETS DES CHAMPS-ÉLYSÉES. 1945.

her his *Designs with Strings*), she joined Sadler's Wells in 1950, moving to Covent Garden in 1952. She dances the principal ballerina roles in the classics and has created those in Cranko's *The Shadow* and *Prince of the Pagodas* and Ashton's short ballet *Rinaldo and Armida*.

BERMAN Eugene. (Born St. Petersburg, 1899). Together with Christian Bérard, Berman was one of the pillars of the neo-humanist movement which, about 1930, attempted the reintegration of feeling and the human element into painting. Berman comes very close to surrealism with this desire for the expression of vaguely disturbing emotions; his work is full of mystery and troubled dreams, where apparently inert objects take on a strange power of suggestion. After settling in the United States in 1937, he workéd almost exclusively for American ballet companies, though he designed *The Devil's Holiday* (choreography Ashton, 1939), for the Ballet Russe de Monte-Carlo. Romantic themes suit him better than classical, although he loves linear perspectives and Italian architecture. With the aid of *trompe-l'œil* and other time-honoured devices, he composes a strange, lunar world, romantic yet abstract, of obsessive fixity, where man becomes an anguished puppet. The calculated effect of his powerful imagination, so realistically conveyed, has sometimes been a disadvantage, notably in his décors for *Giselle* (Ballet Theatre, 1946) where the obsessive immobility gave a bizarre emphasis to every detail and proved stronger than the personality of the dancers. Berman worked with Balanchine on two of his ballets: *Concerto Barocco* (1941), *Danses Concertantes* (1944) and with Tudor on *Romeo and Juliet* (1943). He also designed *Ballet Imperial* in 1950 for the Sadler's Wells Ballet revival at Covent Garden.

BERNERS Lord. Born 1883, died 1950; an English diplomat who became a composer after studying with Stravinsky and Casella. Berners was also a painter and a writer, an aristocratic dilettante, but well aware of the limitations of his talents. He wrote a ballet for Diaghilev (*The Triumph of Neptune,* 1926) and three for Sadler's Wells: *A Wedding Bouquet* (1937, text by Gertrude Stein, décor and costumes by Berners himself), *Cupid and Psyche* (1939) and *Les Sirènes* (1946). His music is witty, ironical and yet nostalgic for the styles he parodied: one might say, an English Poulenc.

BERNSTEIN Leonard. Born 1918 in Lawrence, Massachusetts. One of the most brilliant young American composers and conductors he is also unusually versatile, having successfully practised light as well as serious music, classical as well as popular. This versatility has been underlined by two recent events in his career: the success of the musical *West Side Story* which he wrote with Arthur Laurents and Jerome Robbins, and his appointment to the conductorship of the New York Philharmonic-Symphony Orchestra. Robbins is no new collaborator; Bernstein's ballets *Fancy Free* (1944), *Facsimile* (1946) and *Age of Anxiety* (1950) were written for him. The first of these, an immediate popular success, has become an American classic.

BESSY Claude. Promoted *danseuse étoile* at the Opéra in 1956. The creator of the Océanide in *Les Noces Fantastiques* and of Venus in *La Belle Hélène,* where her blonde and statuesque beauty was seen to advantage. Made her film début in Gene Kelly's *Invitation to the Dance* (1956).

BICHES Les. Ballet in one act. Music: Francis Poulenc. Scenery and costumes: Marie Laurencin. Choreography: Nijinska. First performance: Ballets Russes de Diaghilev, Monte Carlo, 6 January 1924. Principal dancers: Bronislava Nijinska, Vera Nemchinova, Léon Woizikowski, Anatole Vilzak.

A series of witty and mordant sketches satirising certain rather conspicuous aspects of smart life in the early twenties. There is no real plot; comings and goings, fox-trots and flirtations at a sort of party in the elegant world where sport and clothes (Chanel's influence was evident in the costumes) are competing attractions. Nijinska's distorted classicism was exhilarating, elegant, suggestive and often fiendishly difficult. The "Adagietto" made Nemchinova famous: with sleek hair, white-gloved hands, her tight blue velvet tunic lending an ambiguous quality to her figure, she strode across the stage on her points, the image of "la garçonne". Nijinska herself was the hostess, with a long, thin cigarette-holder and a long pearl necklace, assiduously trying to pair off her young friends and flirting with the *gigolo* athletes to the rhythm of a rag-mazurka: it was one of her best roles. Poulenc's irresistible music hinted at French

folk-songs and (in the original version) had singers in the orchestra pit. Marie Laurencin was the perfect collaborator. Highly original, half way between parody and comedy of manners, *Les Biches* was a minor masterpiece, often imitated but never equalled. Revived in London under the title *The House Party* by the Markova-Dolin Company (1937). First produced in the United States by the Marquis de Cuevas, with Marjorie Tallchief and George Skibine, in 1947. Has also been presented under the title *Les Gazelles*.

BILLY THE KID. Ballet in one act. Scenario: Lincoln Kirstein. Music: Aaron Copland. Scenery and costumes: Jared French. Choreography: Eugene Loring. First performance: Ballet Caravan, Chicago, 16 October 1938. Principal dancers: Loring, Lew Christensen, Todd Bolender, Marie-Jeanne.

One of the first American ballets of specifically national inspiration, *Billy the Kid* is also one of the most successful and has strongly influenced subsequent choreographers. In ele-

ven episodes, the ballet tells the sad history of Billy the Kid, a notorious outlaw who was born William Bonney in New York City towards the end of the Civil War. His tragedy is set against the relentless push westwards of the pioneers; they are seen in the first and last episodes, sometimes faltering or turned back, but inevitably moving forward across the prairie. The three leading characters are Billy, Pat Garrett his best friend who turns Sheriff, and a strange figure, Alias, Billy's nemesis. Billy kills his first man accidentally in a street brawl to defend his mother. By the time he is twenty-one, he has twenty-one crimes on his conscience. At last he is ambushed and shot in Mexico. The role of Billy was created by Loring who also danced it for Ballet Theatre when that company revived the ballet in 1948. Since then it has been danced by Charles Dickson, Ian Gibson, Michael Kidd and, notably, John Kriza.

BLAIR David. A leading young *danseur noble* of the Royal Ballet, David Blair was born in Halifax in 1932 and won a scholarship to Sadler's Wells in 1946. After six years good work with the junior company he moved to Covent Garden in 1953 and rapidly asserted his right to the principal male roles. A brilliant technician and a lively, extrovert personality, he is a good partner and sympathetic mime. His creations in *Harlequin in April* and *Pineapple Poll* were distinctive and subtle, for he can play poetic and satirical roles with equal assurance.

BLISS Sir Arthur. English composer, born 1891. He began as a member of the avant-garde but has settled into official respectability without, howevever, sacrificing his musical energy. He now holds the traditional post of Master of the Queen's Musick. Of his three ballets for Sadler's Wells, *Checkmate* (1937) has immense dramatic force, but *Miracle in the Gorbals* (1944) and *Adam Zero* (1946) are more expertly contrived for dancing and theatrical effect.

BLISS Herbert. American dancer, born in Kansas City, formed at Balanchine's School of American Ballet. Blond and elegant, with a delicate and refined style, he was a leading soloist of the New York City Ballet until he resigned in 1958 to open his own school.

BLUEBEARD. Ballet in two prologues, four scenes and three interludes, after Meilhac and Halévy's comic opera *Barbe-Bleue*. Scenario and choreography: Fokine. Music: Offenbach. Scenery and costumes: Vertès. First performance: Ballet Theatre, Mexico City, 27 October 1941. Principal dancers: Alicia Markova, Irina Baronova, Lucia Chase, Anton Dolin, Vania Psota.

Fokine's last important ballet before his death in 1942; a spectacular comedy-burlesque. The action takes place in the 16th century and concerns the comic King Bobiche and the sinister Baron Bluebeard who lives surrounded by the graves of his wives, in dread of their vengeance. Vertès's décors, in his favourite grey and pastel shades, were ravishing. Fokine's lively and witty choreography combined scenes of pure buffoonery with passages in the grand classical manner.

BLUM René. Born 1884, died 1944. Refined, courteous, as intelligent as he was sensitive, this Proustian character commanded the respect of all who met him. A brother of the socialist leader Léon Blum, he devoted his life to the theatre and to the arts. He was a man of wide artistic culture, possessing infallible literary taste, and a flair for discovering talent. He helped to make Marcel Proust known, and many others famous today, including Marcel Pagnol and Jean Anouilh. He served the theatre as director of the Théâtre de Monte-Carlo and of the Casino at Le Touquet, then he gave his best to the ballet. He and Colonel de Basil, two men completely dissimilar in character, founded the first company of Ballets Russes de Monte-Carlo. To this enterprise René Blum brought his thorough knowledge of literature, painting and dramatic art. In his relations with the company, he showed an honesty, courtesy and kindness which won all hearts. He was an expert at dealing with intrigues, jealousies and scandals. His collaboration with de Basil, however, had its ups and downs; in 1936 he broke with his partner and founded a new

enterprise, first with the assistance of Fokine, later of Massine. The final season of the Ballet de Monte-Carlo at the Palais de Chaillot in Paris, shortly before the war, was the culminating point of his career. During the German occupation, René Blum was persuaded by his sense of duty to stay in France, and, in spite of many warnings, remained cool in the face of imminent and threatening danger. Behind his nonchalant and detached appearance, which so often led people to regard him as a mere dilettante, René Blum concealed inflexible courage. He was interned in the concentration camp of Royallieu in 1941, and later deported to Germany, where he died three years later.

BOITE A JOUJOUX La. Ballet in four scenes. Music: Debussy. Scenery and costumes: André Hellé. Choreography: Jean Borlin. First performance: Ballets Suédois, Théâtre des Champs-Élysées, Paris, 15 February 1921.

BOLENDER Todd. American dancer and choreographer, member of the New York City Ballet since 1948. Remarkable for his exceptional agility in the leading roles of *Pied Piper, Four Temperaments, Western Symphony* and other modern ballets. An artist who could only have been produced by contemporary America, Bolender has worked with a number of companies since his début as a soloist with Ballet Caravan (1937), and has also danced in films. His choreography includes *Mother Goose* (1943), *Comedia Balletica* (1945), *Zodiac* (1947), *The Miraculous Mandarin* and, for television, *Peter and the Wolf* and *An American in Paris*. In January 1957, the New York City Ballet produced his ballet *The Masquers,* to Poulenc's Sextet. His ballet *Still Point* (1956), his best work to date, has also been staged at Munich.

BOLÉRO. Ballet in one act; music: Ravel. Scenery and costumes: Alexandre Benois. Choreography: Nijinska. First performance: Paris Opera, Ida Rubinstein season, 22 November 1928. Principal dancers: I. Rubinstein, Anatole Vilzak. (New version by Fokine 1934).

It is often forgotten that Ravel's famous *Boléro* was written at the request of Ida Rubinstein for this season. Ravel himself conducted the first performance. It was a great success, and the music went round the world. Nijinska revived it with her own company in 1932, dancing the lead herself, in a new décor by Goncharova. In 1954, she restaged it for the Marquis de Cuevas at the Théâtre Sarah-Bernhardt with Marjorie Tallchief and Wladimir Skouratoff. The impression was disappointing; *Boléro* had lost the charm of novelty.

* Ravel's *Boléro* inspired many other choreographers, notably Dolin, Catherine Littlefield and Serge Lifar. The latter turned it into a drama with three characters, quite foreign to the spirit of the music (Paris Opera, 1941, scenery and costumes by Leyritz). Dolin performs it as a highly mannered solo.

BOLM Adolph. Born St. Petersburg 1884, died Hollywood 1951. Bolm's fame after the first performances in Paris of Diaghilev's Ballets Russes eclipsed even Nijinsky's. A fiery dancer, of splendid physical presence, he communicated his zeal and great energy to the audience. The passionate virility of his dancing in *Prince Igor* was primarily responsible for restoring the male dancer to his rightful place in ballet as the equal of the ballerina, not just a *porteur*. Trained in the Imperial School at St. Petersburg, he graduated in 1904 and became a soloist at the Maryinsky. In 1908-09 he toured Scandinavia with Pavlova and a small troupe and in 1909 danced with Pavlova in Berlin and with Kyasht at the Empire Theatre, London. He was a member of Diaghilev's Ballets Russes intermittently from 1909 until he settled in America after the company's second tour of the United States (1917). His most famous roles were the Chief of the Polovtsian Warriors in *Prince Igor,* Amoùn in *Cléopâtre,* Pierrot in *Carnaval* and the Tsarevitch in *Firebird,* but he was equally good as Hilarion in *Giselle* and the Shah in *Sheherazade.*

In America in 1917 he organized his Ballet Intime, a troupe which Lifar considered the starting point of American ballet. It was also the starting point for Bolm of a long and fruitful career as dancer and choreographer. After having staged *Le Coq d'Or* (1918) and *Petrouchka* (1919) for the New York Metropolitan Opera, he was engaged by the Chicago Opera and subsequently worked at the Colon, Buenos Aires,

BONNAT. PROGRAMME FOR FIRST INTERNATIONAL DANCE FESTIVAL AT AIX-LES-BAINS. 1954.

and the San Francisco Opera. He was a pioneer of choreography for the films and his ballet *Krazy Kat* is said to have forecast Mickey Mouse. For Ballet Theatre he produced *Peter and the Wolf* (1940) and *Firebird* (1945) while during the 1942-43 season he was régisseur and ballet master to the company. He finally settled in Hollywood, to teach and arrange choreography for films.

BOLSHOI THEATRE BALLET. See *Théâtre Bolchoï.*

BON René. From the corps de ballet of the Paris Opera, he went to the Ballets de Monte-Carlo in 1945 and then to de Cuevas as soloist. A leading dancer in the Ballets J. Charrat, he danced the role of the White Horse in *Le Massacre des Amazones* (1951). Small in stature, lively and expressive, with exceptional elevation and brilliant batterie, he is a mercurial dancer destined for character rather than purely classical roles.

BONNAT Yves. French painter, born 1920. Bonnat belongs to no particular group, but his work, with its decorative, schematic simplicity and its architectural quality is contemporary and typically French. His most important ballet décors were for *Jeux* (Opéra-Comique, 1948) and *Septuor* (Opéra, 1950). President of the *Syndicat des Artistes Décorateurs de Théâtre* after the war. President of the *Amis de la Danse* since 1948. Technical manager of the International Dance Festival at Aix-les-Bains.

BORLIN Jean. Born Sweden 1893, died New York 1930. The choreographer and leading dancer of the Ballets Suédois. He made his début at the Stockholm Opera. Studied with Fokine in Copenhagen (1918) and came later to Paris, where he gave a solo recital at the Théâtre des Champs-Élysées in March 1920. In October of the same year, the newly constituted Ballets Suédois opened at the same theatre. Borlin was a lover of modern painting, and tried to express what he felt about it in terms of dancing. This confusion of aims may explain critical reservations made at the time about the results. Certainly his passion for art seems to have hindered his development as a choreographer. In any case, his choreographic style was radically different from that of the Russian Ballet. There was no attempt at romantic grace and fire, lightness and elevation; Borlin kept his dancers firmly on the ground, in a succession of turned-in "plastic" poses, emphasising rather than overcoming the density of the human body. But it would be unjust to imply that Borlin never achieved grace and beauty in his own style: *Le Marchand d'oiseaux* and *Les Mariés de la Tour Eiffel* were proof to the contrary.

BOS Camille. French dancer who entered the Paris Opéra at the age of eight, and was promoted to rank of *étoile* in 1928. Light and graceful, she danced practically the whole classical repertoire and appeared in the first production of *Maïmouna* (1921), *Siang-Sin* (1924), *L'Écran des Jeunes Filles* (1929), and *Divertissement*. She was for twelve years in charge of the second *quadrille* at the Opéra.

BOUCHÊNE Dimitri. French stage designer, born Saint-Tropez, 1898. Bouchêne is one of those designers who, like Christian Bérard, possess the gift of theatrical magic.

His designs are light, free, almost sketchy; architecture is suggested rather than defined. Light, clear colours; wide skies brushed in behind airy columns. His costumes are simple, with a small range of colours, material generously draped. Bouchêne's theatrical world resembles an insubstantial, hovering fairyland, ready to vanish at the least breath of wind. He designed the costumes and décors for *Les Éléments* (Ballets de Monte-Carlo, London, 1937), for *Chronica* and *The Prodigal Son* (Ballets Jooss, 1939), for *Divertissement* (1948) and *Blanche-Neige* (1951) at the Paris Opera.

BOURGEOIS Denise. Formerly at the Paris Opera where she had almost reached the top of the tree, being promoted to *première danseuse* in 1948. A notable success in two ballets by Balanchine, *Serenade* and *Le Palais de Cristal*. A very feminine dancer with an irresistible charm on the stage and off it, Denise Bourgeois is now leading dancer with the Grand Ballet du Marquis de Cuevas, but with the exception of Effie in *La Sylphide,* which she created in Lander's revival (1953), she has not yet been shown to great advantage.

BOURMEISTER Vladimir. Russian choreographer, born 1904. Director and maître de ballet of the ballet company of the Stanislavsky and Nemirovitch-Dantchenko Theatre in Moscow. Founded in Moscow (1930) by Victorina Krieger, this company, thanks to Bourmeister's efforts, has developed considerably since the war, both in the number and quality of its dancers and in the richness and variety of its repertoire. During the company's season in Paris (Théâtre du Châtelet, June-July 1956) several of Bourmeister's most important works were given: *The Merry Wives of Windsor, Les Rives du Bonheur* and *Straussiana*. Part of his new version of *Esmeralda* was also shown and, above all, his exquisitely romantic production of the full-length *Swan Lake,* dramatically far in advance of any other version of today.

BOUTIQUE FANTASQUE La. Ballet in one act. Music: Rossini, arr. and orch. Respighi. Scenery and costumes: Derain. Choreography: Massine. First performance:

Diaghilev's Ballets Russes, Alhambra Theatre, London, 5 June 1919. Principal dancers: Lydia Lopokova, Lydia Sokolova, Lubov Tchernicheva, Vera Nemchinova, Massine, Leon Woizikowski, Stanislas Idzikowski, Enrico Cecchetti. In Paris, Karsavina danced instead of Lopokova.

La Boutique Fantasque, as we know it, was suggested by a German ballet of the second half of the 19th century, with music by Bayer. In 1906, Nicolas Legat had made a new version of this in St. Petersburg, under the title of *The Fairy Doll.* Pavlova revived it in New York (about 1914), with choreography by Clustine and décors by Doboujinsky. It was a success and remained in her repertoire; later there was a new décor by Soudeikine. The new work, of course, differed considerably from the above. Massine and Derain placed the action in 1865, and though they had in mind drawings and lithographs by Toulouse-Lautrec, Derain's dark-toned set, deliberately old-fashioned, full of charm and atmosphere, was very much his own. Originally, the décor was to have been designed by Bakst; Diaghilev's change of mind led to a break between them.

The story takes place in a toy-shop: there are Tarantella dancers, strolling pedlars, kings and queens from a pack of cards, dogs, cossacks, and, as *pièces de résistance,* two Can-Can dancers. The customers, English ladies, an American family, some wealthy Russians, all admire the little dancers and quarrel over them. Finally, the Russian family buys the girl dancer; the American family, the man. They pay and leave. The shop closes for the night. Once alone, the dolls come to life. They bemoan the fate of the couple about to be separated. The two dancers decide to escape. Next day, when the customers come to collect their purchases, the shopkeeper shows them the parcels all prepared: they are opened and found empty. Furious, the customers begin to sack the shop. But the dolls come to life again and chase them out. The absurd and touching story was treated as a pastiche; the gentle episode of the toy-couple framed between burlesque character dances and passages of remarkable virtuosity. The Tarantella, for instance (Sokolova and Woizikowski); the Mazurka of the Kings and Queens; the Snob (Idzikowski); the five Cossacks and above all the Can-Can danced by Lopokova and Massine to the sound of muted trumpets. Massine's

gift for characterisation and humour, Derain's taste and invention, Rossini's lively tunes and the brilliance of the dancing made *La Boutique Fantasque* one of the greatest of Diaghilev's successes. Since then, Massine has revived the ballet many times. In the 1930's Danilova as the Can-Can dancer and Shabelevsky as the Snob gave these characters new life. Ballet Theatre mounted *La Boutique Fantasque* in 1943 and Massine danced it with the Sadler's Wells Ballet in 1947 when Moira Shearer was the Can-Can dancer, Rassine the Snob. The Opéra-Comique in Paris revived the ballet in 1950 for Solange Schwarz, Michel Rayne and Paul Goubé.

BOVT Violetta. A pupil of the Bolshoi Theatre School who has spent most of her career in the company of the Stanislavsky Nemirovitch-Dantchenko Theatre. Among the roles she has danced are Natasha in *Les Rives du Bonheur* and Odette-Odile in *Lac des Cygnes.* Of medium height and well proportioned, she has a very sound technique but sometimes sacrifices lyricism to virtuosity. She appeared in Paris during the summer of 1956 at the Théâtre du Châtelet, with the troupe of the Stanislavsky Theatre.

BOZZONI Max. *Danseur-étoile* at the Paris Opéra (1948), he specialises in demi-caractère parts. An excellent actor, notably as Hilarion in *Giselle* and as the truculent Agamemnon in *La Belle Hélène.*

BRAE June. This lovely girl, who glowed on stage as with an inner fire, brought a touch of exoticism to the early years of British ballet. First seen at the Ballet Club, she was a leading dancer with the Sadler's Wells Ballet from 1936 to 1942, creating the Rich Beauty in *Nocturne,* the seductive Black Queen in *Checkmate* and the tipsy Josephine in *A Wedding Bouquet.* She retired from the stage after marriage but returned briefly in 1946 to create the principal female role in Helpmann's *Adam Zero* and to dance with the newly formed Sadler's Wells Theatre Ballet.

BRAQUE Georges. Born 1882 at Argenteuil. When, in 1924, Diaghilev commissioned Braque to design the décors for *Les Fâcheux,* he was only confirming the widespread feeling that, despite the revolutionary nature of his cubism, Braque was really a classic painter in the great French tradition. The idea of commissioning him to do a modern transposition of the 17th century and of rediscovering the elegance of the period of Louis XIV through his eyes was so successful that Braque's name has become inseparably linked with the production. There was no attempt, in costumes or setting, at authenticity. Out of memories and half-forgotten impressions, Braque invented new harmonies. His costumes were not only beautiful designs in themselves, but were also an essential element in the total effect. There were the servants, dressed like characters of the Italian comedy, to contrast with their more richly-clad masters. But best of all were the women's costumes. Certain of these, with skirts of varying lengths, short and yellow in front, long and brown behind, formed a sort of moving décor, for, according to whether they faced the public or turned away from it, the effect was completely different in colour and feeling. But there was nothing aggressive; Braque's work harmonised perfectly with the general rhythm of the production, submitting to it even when setting the tone. The same merits were found in *Salade* for the "Soirées de Paris" (1924), and in *Zéphyre et Flore* for Diaghilev (1925).

BRAYER Yves. French painter, born 1907. Brayer is one of those painters who have brought to stage design the gift of spontaneity and elimination, and the ability to make a strong general impression without an accumulation of detail. In *Joán de Zarissa* (Paris Opera, 1942), Brayer revealed his individual technique of introducing out-of-scale elements to produce a sense of the grandiose, notably in the chapel scene, where two gigantic candlesticks towered over an almost empty stage. His monumentalising tendency, however, is happily tempered by the sobriety of his colour schemes. Others décors: *L'Amour Sorcier* (1943), *Lucifer* (1948), *La Tragédie de Salomé* and *Nautéos* (1955) all for the Paris Opera.

BRIANSKY Oleg. Born in Brussels of Russian parents, made his début with the Ballets des Champs-Élysées in 1946. Dolin engaged

him for London's Festival Ballet, where he won a place for himself as soloist, notably in the pas-de-deux from *Don Quixote*. A tall dancer, with a fine presence, dark and flashing eyes, he has a sound classical technique. He was a brilliant partner to Toumanova. Toured Latin America with Beryl Grey, 1957.

BRIEUX Yves. French dancer, trained at the Paris Opera, appeared before the war with Geneviève Ione. Now devotes himself to teaching; started the male classes at the Conservatoire National in Paris. He was the choreographer for *Incantation* (Ballets J. Charrat) and *Pas des déesses* (Ballet de l'Étoile).

BRITTEN Benjamin. Born 1913. One of the most versatile, accomplished and prolific musicians of his generation. World fame has come to him principally through such operas as *Peter Grimes, The Rape of Lucretia* and *The Turn of the Screw*, which have, in no uncertain fashion, put English opera on the map. Only recently has he written a ballet, *The Prince of the Pagodas* (1957). The first three-act ballet by an English composer, it is composed mainly in a modern extension of the tradition of Delibes and Tchaikovsky, but the second act contains a remarkable evocation of oriental dance music. The score exploits to the full Britten's gift for instrumental colour and atmospheric description. Earlier orchestral works, notably the sets of variations on themes by Frank Bridge and Purcell, and the song-cycle *Les Illuminations,* had already been used for ballets by Ashton, Alan Carter, Cranko, MacMillan, Robbins, Gore and others.

BRONZE HORSEMAN The. Ballet in four acts and nine scenes. Scenario: P. Abolimov, after Pushkin's poem. Music: Glière. Scenery and costumes: Bobychev. Choreography: Zakharov. First performance: Kirov Theatre, Leningrad, June 1949 (100th anniversary of Pushkin's birth). Principal dancers: Dudinskaya, Sergueev.

A prologue describes the construction of St. Petersburg by Peter the Great. The action then moves to 1824, a century later: over the happy and flourishing city towers a statue of

LA BOUTIQUE FANTASQUE. BACKCLOTH AND COSTUMES BY DERAIN. OPÉRA-COMIQUE, PARIS, 1950.
Bibliothèque-Musée de l'Opéra, Paris.

Peter the Great, the Bronze Horseman. Two young people, Eugene and Paracha, fall in love. But 1824 is the year of the terrible flood: Paracha is swept avay by the torrent. The grief-stricken Eugene tries to escape but falls, exhausted. As he dies, he curses the Bronze Horseman, which to him seems a symbol of the State, indifferent to the people it condemns to suffering and destruction. *The Bronze Horseman* was the first Soviet ballet in which the principal role was given to a male dancer. Ensemble dances, mainly "demi-caractère", alternate with lyrical pas de deux. The realistic décors and ingenious stage-machinery were impressive, particularly in the flood scene, where the swirling waters of the Neva swept away a sentry box, planks and a drowning man.

BRUHN Erik. Danish dancer, trained in the ballet school of the Copenhagen Royal Theatre, he joined the Royal Danish Ballet in 1947, advancing rapidly to soloist rank. He was soon sought after by foreign companies, especially the American Ballet Theatre, which he joined in 1956.

THE CAGE. NORA KAYE.

Blond, virile, and exceptionally handsome, with a precise and subtle style, Erik Bruhn is the embodiment of all that is meant by the title *danseur noble*. His great roles are James in *La Sylphide*, Albrecht in *Giselle* and Siegfried in *Le Lac des Cygnes*, but he can be dazzling in the Bournonville tarantellas of *Napoli*, sadly romantic in *A Folk Tale*. He made his début as choreographer with *Concertette*, a ballet created in Copenhagen in 1953, to music by Morton Gould. In 1958 returned to Copenhagen.

C

CAGE The. Ballet in one act. Music: Stravinsky (Concerto in D for strings). Costumes: Ruth Sobotka. Scenario and choreography: Jerome Robbins. First performance: New York City Ballet, New York, 14 June 1951. Principal dancers: Nora Kaye, Yvonne Mounsey, Nicholas Magallanes.

A highly controversial ballet. Some saw it as a drama of unnatural love, others as a demonstration of the habits of the praying mantis, while the programme implied that it was based on the initiation rites of a mythical cult. However, a full explanation of the meaning is not necessary. The deliberate ugliness of this dark, sombre ballet, writhing with animal cruelty and human passion, attains a kind of ferocious, pagan grandeur, half realistic, half symbolic. The lighting constitued the main décor. Ruth Sobotka's costumes were far from attractive but the realistic way in which their sequins moulded the bodies of the female cohort and the two male victims was fully in keeping with the choreographer's intentions. Nora Kaye, predatory and passionate, was an incomparable ringleader.

CAMARGO SOCIETY The. Founded in London 1930 by P. J. S. Richardson, Editor of

The Dancing Times, and Arnold Haskell, with a group of men and women distinguished in the arts, to give subcription performances three or four times a year with dancers drawn mainly from the emergent companies of de Valois and Rambert. De Valois's *Job* and Ashton's *Façade* were among the ballets thus produced. In 1932, the economist J. M. Keynes became the Society's treasurer and organised a public season at the Savoy Theatre with Olga Spessiva (Spessivtseva) and Lydia Lopokova. Sir Thomas Beecham and Constant Lambert conducted. In 1933, two gala performances were given at Covent Garden. The object was by now achieved; the Vic-Wells Ballet and Ballet Club had been enabled to show their work in central London, and public opinion had been stirred by the revelation of native talent. The new ballets and the outstanding funds were made over to the Vic-Wells, and after helping to finance the production of Ashton's *Apparitions* (1936), the Camargo Society ceased to function.

CAMÉLÉOPARD Le. Ballet in four scenes by Alain Vigot and Jean Babilée. Music: Henri Sauguet. Scenery and costumes: Jacques Noël. Choreography: Babilée. First performance: Ballets Jean Babilée, Théâtre des Champs-Élysées, Paris, 18 June 1956. Principal dancers: Babilée, Dick Sanders.

The action takes place during "the last days of a declining civilization"; the curtain bears the name of Antioch, but the décor shows a decadent metropolis where men and beasts adore the Cameleopard. One day, the king assumes the god's place. The people are deceived, but the animals kill the impostor. Babilée designed the king's role to suit his own particular talent: with great bounding leaps he paraded almost naked through the dream city, wearing a great maned helmet.

CAPRICCIO ESPAGNOL Ballet in one act. Music: Rimsky-Korsakov. Choreography: Massine and Argentinita. Scenery and costumes: Mariano Andreu. First performance: Ballets de Monte-Carlo, Monte Carlo, 4 May 1939. Principal dancers: Argentinita (later Mia Slavenska), Alexandra Danilova, Massine, Michel Panaieff.

CAPRICES DE CUPIDON Les. The Florentine Vincenzo Galeotti, maître de ballet in Copenhagen, composed this one-act ballet in 1786: gay and fresh, it has lost nothing of its period style, thanks to the care with which the Danes have preserved it. Harald Lander revised Galeotti's choreography with a fastidious, delicate, and slightly quaint fantasy for the Paris Opera (27 February 1952) with scenery and costumes by Chapelain-Midy. The scene is the Temple of Love—an arbour hung with grapes. Couples of various nationalities and ages perform appropriate dances. But playful Cupid blindfolds them all and pairs them off according to his whim. So the Quaker finds himself with the Negress, the Old Man with the Young French Girl, and so on, in hilarious confusion.

CAPRICHOS Los. Ballet in one act. Music: Padre Soler, Raphael Angles and Mateo Albeniz, arr. and orch. Tony Aubin. Scenery and costumes: Antoni Clavé. Choreography: Ana Nevada and Juanito Garcia. First performance: Ballets des Champs-Élysées, Paris, 11 March 1946.

The theme is drawn from Goya. A young

LOS CAPRICHOS. BALLET BY HERBERT ROSS.

maja (A. Nevada), indifferent to her various legitimate suitors, falls passionately in love with a torero (R. Petit). He soon abandons her to lonely regrets and nightmares. Clavé's red and black décor gave the work its distinction.

(*) The ballet in four scenes by the young American choreographer Herbert Ross (Choreographers' Workshop, New York, 1949) was very different in spirit and style. The music was Bartok's *Contrasts ;* scenery and costumes were by Hélène Pons. Ross illustrated some of the most dramatic and hallucinatory of Goya's engravings: the dance of the mad women, the macabre dance of a man with the dead body of a woman, the *autodafé*. In the repertory of Ballet Theatre since 1950.

C A R A C O L E. Ballet by George Balanchine. Music: Mozart's Divertimento No. 15 in B flat. Costumes: Christian Bérard. First performance: New York City Ballet, New York, 19 February 1952. Principal dancers: Adams, Hayden, LeClercq, Tallchief, Wilde, Eglevsky, Magallanes, Robbins.

A plotless ballet for 16 dancers (including 3 men). The equestrian title refers to the style of the choreography as well as the red and white costumes with plumes and harnesses. Balanchine has since abandoned both the title and Bérard's costumes. The New York City Ballet now gives the work under the name of the score, *Divertimento No. 15,* in ornate but conventional costumes by Mme Karinska.

C A R M E N. Ballet in five scenes by Roland Petit, based on the opera. Music: Bizet. Scenery and costumes: Antoni Clavé. Choreography: Roland Petit. First performance: Ballets de Paris de Roland Petit, Princes Theatre, London, 21 February 1949. Principal dancers: Renée Jeanmaire, Roland Petit.

When the curtain rose on the décor of the first act, the audience of the première broke into enthusiastic applause. Clavé's five sets, the costumes of the cigarette-girls, Carmen's brief tunic and the gold dust on her body, the blaze of the Toreador's finery, all contributed to the great success of the ballet which ran for 4 months in London, 8 weeks in Paris and 3 months in the United States. The critics reacted with equal violence, reproaching Roland Petit with what François Mauriac, in *La Table Ronde,* called: "a crime against *Carmen*". In fact, Roland Petit had cut Mérimée's story very judiciously, omitting the picturesque digressions and the folklore background. His choreography blended realism and classicism with a great deal of humour and frank eroticism without descending to vulgarity or obscenity. The love scene in Carmen's room — with its ravishing blue window — was extremely sensual but always dramatically relevant. The same could be said of the final scene of Carmen's death, outside the bullring, with the drum-beat underlining the struggle between the lovers. Although the main emphasis was on the two protagonists, Petit devised some colourful incidental episodes: the fight in the first scene, the tavern of Lillas Pastia, the murder of the traveller and the pursuit of the fatuous Toreador by a crowd of hysterical women. Clavé's décors and accessories were in perfect harmony with the choreography, the burning colours enhancing the dramatic atmosphere. Above all, there was the masterly interpretation of the title-role by Renée Jeanmaire. Dazzling, mocking, seductive, passionate and vindictive, she blazed upon the stage. Beaumont called it a performance worthy to stand beside Elssler's Esmeralda and Karsavina's Thamar.

C A R N A V A L. Ballet-pantomime in one act. Scenario and choreography: Fokine. Music: Schumann, orch. Rimsky-Korsakov, Liadov, Tcherepnine and Glazounov. Scenery and costumes: Bakst. First performance: Diaghilev's Ballets Russes, Theater des Westens, Berlin, 20 May 1910. Principal dancers: Thamar Karsavina, Vera Fokina, Bronislava Nijinska, Ludmilla Schollar, Vaslav Nijinsky, Adolph Bolm.

An adaptation of a ballet produced by Fokine at St. Petersburg earlier in the same year. Columbine, Harlequin and Pantalon from the *Commedia dell'arte* and the wistful Pierrot intrigue, frolic and suffer with the characters of the youthful Schumann's romantic imagination, against Bakst's simple setting, designed deliberately to dwarf their Biedermeyer figures. *Carnaval* was no great success with the Parisian public, drunk with the splendour and colour of *Sheherazade* and *Prince Igor,* but was beloved

CARMEN. THE INN OF LILLAS PASTIA. DÉCOR BY CLAVÉ. 1949.

elsewhere. Revived by Diaghilev in 1918 (London, Coliseum), in a slightly modified version, with Lydia Lopokova and Stanislas Idzikowski, it has since been included in the repertoire of numberless companies, but has rarely achieved the elusive combination of gaiety, sadness and hair-trigger precision required for a good performance.

CARTER Alan. Now Ballet Master at the Bayerische Staatsoper in Munich (since 1954), Alan Carter was born in London in 1920. He studied with Astafieva and Legat and was a soloist with the Sadler's Wells Ballet from 1938-40, creating among other roles that of Harlequin in *Harlequin in the Street*. He served in the R.A.F. from 1940-46, afterwards organised his own ballet company and did important work on several dance films, including *The Red Shoes* and *Invitation to the Dance*. In Munich his prin-

cipal ballets have been: *The Miraculous Mandarin, House of Shadows, Vier mal vier* and *The Prince of the Pagodas* (1958). He is married to the dancer and ballet mistress Joan Harris.

CARZOU Jean (b. 1907). One of the most brilliant stage designers of recent years. He was well known as a painter when, in 1952, Maurice Lehmann, then Director of the Paris Opera, commissioned him to do the décor of the Inca scene in *Les Indes Galantes*. The result, a barren, sun-parched landscape in striking contrast to the exotic costumes, encouraged Roland Petit to invite Carzou to design *Le Loup* in 1953. The closely woven lines of the new décor, with their mysterious shadows and perspectives, made a strange, poetic, almost surrealist effect. But Carzou is really closer to romantic nostalgia than to metaphysical anguish. In the theatre, he is less of a painter than an illustrator, reviving an

LES INDES GALANTES. DRAWING BY CARZOU.

18th-century tradition half forgotten in France. Although he would seem the obvious person to re-design the old ballets, his new décors for *Giselle* (Paris Opéra, 1954) were neither understood nor accepted by the public, still less by the balletomanes, always suspicious of innovations in the sacrosanct "classics".

CASSANDRE (b. 1901 in Kharkov, of French parents). One of the creators of the modern poster. Cassandre imposes a kind of rejuvenated classicism on the discoveries of modern painting. His first work for the theatre, Giraudoux's *Amphitryon 38* (1934) showed the same rigorous, formal style. His blend of sensitive understanding of tradition with lively invention can be found in all his décors, especially those for Lifar's *Le Chevalier et la Damoiselle,* where his stylised forests and architectural compositions have, for all their modernity, much of the purity and geometrical structure of Renaissance painting. His power of drawing the maximum effect from architectural perspectives was shown in *Aubade* and *Mirages*. Pursuing his geometrical style to its logical extreme, Cassandre produced in *Dramma*

per Musica a kind of glorified architect's diagram: an idea transfigured into a composition of dreamlike beauty.

His most important décors: *Aubade* (Ballet de Monte-Carlo, 1936), *Le Chevalier et la Damoiselle* (Paris Opera, 1941), *Dramma per Musica* (Nouveau Ballet de Monte-Carlo, 1946), *Les Mirages* (Paris Opera, 1947), *Cordélia* and *Coup de Feu* (both for de Cuevas, 1951), *Chemin de Lumière* (Munich State Opera 1951).

CASSE-NOISETTE. Ballet in two acts and three scenes. Scenario: Marius Petipa, after Alexandre Dumas's version of Hoffmann's story. Music: Tchaikovsky. Scenery: M. Botcharov and K.-M. Ivanov. Costumes: Vsevolojsky and Ponomarev. Choreography: Lev Ivanov. First performance: Maryinsky Theatre, St. Petersburg, 18 December 1892. Principal dancers: Antonietta Dell'Era, Paul Gerdt, Legat.

The success of *The Sleeping Beauty* encouraged Vsevolojsky, the director of the Imperial Theatres, to commission another ballet from Tchaikovsky. The subject of *Casse-Noisette* aroused the composer's interest and he set to work with enthusiasm, later cooled by disagreements with the administration. In spite of his difficulties, he produced a brilliant score whose beauties are by no means confined to the familiar suite of dances drawn from it. These excerpts, which were played in public some months before the ballet, had more success than the complete ballet. Petipa's scenario, with its somewhat unhappy combination of human and supernatural elements, was partly to blame. In time, however, *Casse-Noisette* became popular with the public, especially with children, and it is now everywhere accepted as one of the great classical ballets. It contains long passages of mime and much mediocre choreography, but the snowflake scene and the superb pas de deux and variations for the Sugar Plum Fairy and her Prince in the last act — together with the enchanting music — have given it immortality.

The ballet opens with a children's Christmas party, originally set in early 19th century Germany (Hoffmann's own period), now usually shown as 19th century St. Petersburg. The President and his wife receive their guests, grown-ups and also the young friends of their children Clara and Fritz. There is general dancing and merrymaking until one of the guests, Drosselmeyer the magician, arrives. He brings strange Christmas presents; the clockwork toys, a vivandière and a soldier, Harlequin and Columbine, dance for the children, to their intense delight. Clara is presented with a toy Nutcracker which Fritz covets. There is a quarrel and the toy is thrown aside. Soon bedtime approaches; the guests leave and the drawing room is dark and deserted. But Clara, thinking of her Nutcracker, cannot sleep. She creeps downstairs to look for the toy and witnesses a battle between the toy soldiers and an invading army of mice. Her Nutcracker is leading the toy soldiers and rushing to his aid she hits the King of the Mice with her slipper. This ensures a victory for the toy soldiers, and the Nutcracker is transformed into a handsome prince. In gratitude, he takes Clara on a visit to the Kingdom of Sweets. To reach this delectable place, they have to cross snowy wastes where they see the snowflakes dancing together. In the Kingdom of Sweets they are welcomed by the Sugar Plum Fairy who commands a feast of dancing for Clara's entertainment. Spanish, Arab, Chinese and Russian dancers appear. Then the Sugar Plum Fairy herself dances for

LE CHEVALIER ET LA DAMOISELLE. DÉCOR BY CASSANDRE. 1941.

MARIA TALLCHIEF AND NICHOLAS MAGALLANES
IN CASSE-NOISETTE.

her guest and the ballet concludes with the Waltz of the Flowers.

The ballet requires very skilful staging by a company rich in character dancers and mimes if it is to make its full effect. Ivanov's choreography was somewhat hampered by the lack of continuity in the action, but his snowflake scene remains one of the great passages in classical dance. A multitude of ballerinas, all dressed in white and bearing wands clustered with sparkling snowflakes, perform very simple steps which, however, create figures of rich invention as they swirl through the falling snowflakes. The Waltz of the Flowers is also simple but harmonious while the pas de deux and variations for the Sugar Plum Fairy and the Prince are the epitome of the formal, classical *danse d'école*. The Sugar Plum Fairy's variation, all crispness and brilliance, is a testing piece for a ballerina.

 * The most remarkable revivals of *Casse-Noisette* in Russia have been those of Gorsky in 1919, Lopoukhov in 1929 and Vainonen in 1934. The ballet is frequently given in Russia not only by the professional companies but also in student performances by scholars of the Bolshoi School. In the West, the most noteworthy versions have been the full-length production by

Sergueev (based on his notes of Ivanov's choreography) for the Sadler's Wells Ballet (January 1934), with Alicia Markova and Stanley Judson (later Harold Turner); by Boris Romanov, in two acts, for the Ballets de Monte-Carlo (April 1936) with décors and costumes by Alexeieff, and Vera Nemchinova and Anatole Oboukov in the leading roles; by J. J. Etchevery for the Opéra-Comique, Paris (February 1947), décors by Paul Colin, and Kergrist and Paul Goubé as principal dancers. In the United States, the Ballets Russes de Monte-Carlo first presented the ballet (October 1940) in décors by Alexandre Benois, with Alicia Markova and André Eglevsky. Balanchine created a new version (February 1954) for the New York City Ballet, with Maria Tallchief and Nicholas Magallanes and using children from the School of American Ballet. Festival Ballet, in London, staged a version by Nicholas Beriosoff (1950) in décors by George Kirsta and danced by Alicia Markova and Anton Dolin. A new production, with choreography by David Lichine, after Ivanov, designed by Alexandre Benois, was first produced by Festival Ballet in December 1957 with Natalie Krassovska and John Gilpin and children of the Arts Educational Schools. The second act (third scene), The Kingdom of Sweets, is frequently danced in the form of a divertissement.

CECCHETTI Enrico (1850-1928). His whole life might be summed up in the one word "theatre". Both his parents were dancers; he was born in the dressing-room of an old theatre in Rome; he died while giving a lesson at La Scala in Milan, where he had been teaching since 1925. While still very young he left Italy and went to Russia, where he spent more than half his life at the Imperial Theatre of St. Petersburg, first as dancer then as professor. With Diaghilev's company he danced in various character-roles, creating Pantalon in *Le Carnaval* when nearly 60, the Chief Eunuch in *Sheherazade,* and the Showman in *Petrouchka.* To celebrate his fiftieth anniversary on the stage, in 1922, he appeared as Carabosse in *The Sleeping Princess.* But his tremendous reputation was based on his work as teacher and maître de ballet, which exercised a decisive influence on modern dancing.

After the death of Carlo Blasis, the famous

Italian master of the romantic period, teaching reverted to haphazard methods, passive and mechanical. Cecchetti thoroughly revised the curriculum, incorporating all the known techniques in his method. Thus he borrowed from the Italians their brilliant and acrobatic technique. He balanced the *adagio* and *allegro* (i.e. the slow and strong tempos) so as to form all-round dancers and ballerinas. Taking the basic lesson, he elaborated a logical progression of the various exercises, execution of which ensured the absolute independence of all the movements of the body: each exercise answered a definite purpose and was a necessary preparation for the following. Cecchetti re-established the notion of "legato", i.e. the harmonious linking up of two or more steps. He strengthened the arabesque, emphasised the plastic and aesthetic effects of the *épaulement ;* finally he developed the exercise of the *pliés* which slowly transform the tendons of the foot into a lever for the soft silent leap called *ballon.* Through his teaching, he gave dance a unity which it greatly lacked before: he established, so to speak, its modern grammar and syntax.

Cecchetti taught Olga Preobrajenska while she was a leading dancer at the Maryinsky theatre in St. Petersburg. He formed Nijinsky and Pavlova, Karsavina and successive generations of Russian or European dancers such as Lifar, Dolin and Ninette de Valois. He even taught Alicia Markova, when he was very old and she was still a child. Diaghilev and Pavlova alike held him in the highest esteem as a teacher. Cecchetti wrote a treatise of the academic dance which has never been published; but through his pupils, the masters of to-day, he has had a powerful effect on contemporary ballet.

Although charming in everyday life, he was strict and punctilious in the class-room. He rejected purely mechanical execution, demanding from his pupils a real understanding of each exercise. Idleness and stupidity would make him lose all control. Pupils and friends alike held him in great esteem for his directness and his acute judgment. He was the first to acknowledge that one cannot create genius where it does not exist. "In school," he would say to his pupils, "you learn what I want; on the stage, you will dance as you want, or rather... as you can."

The basic principles of his method, which prescribes certain exercises for each day of the week, were recorded by a brilliant pupil, Stanislas Idzikowski, and Cyril Beaumont, and published in London in 1922 under the title *A Manual of the Theory and Practice of Classical Theatrical Dancing,* with a preface by Cecchetti. Further volumes, dealing with the theory and practice of allegro and primary work for children have been issued subsequently, culminating in a textbook on Advanced Allegro by Margaret Craske and Derra de Moroda. There are Cecchetti teachers and Cecchetti societies throughout the world. In England, the Cecchetti Society, founded in 1922 at the instigation of Cyril Beaumont, was the first to seek to perpetuate the teaching of the master. Now incorporated in the Imperial Society of Teachers of Dancing it has done invaluable work throughout the British Commonwealth.

CENDRILLON. Marius Petipa, with Cecchetti and Ivanov, produced a three-act ballet on the theme of Perrault's fairy story at the Maryin-

CECCHETTI BY PICASSO.

sky Theatre, St. Petersburg, in 1893. A sumptuous production, with incredibly luxurious costumes, it is now remembered as the first success of Pierina Legnani in Russia. Fokine also turned to Perrault for his one-act ballet (in three scenes) for the Original Ballet Russe. Music: Frédéric d'Erlanger. Scenery and costumes: Goncharova. First performance, Covent Garden, London, 19 July 1938. Principal dancers: Tatiana Riabouchinska, Paul Petrov. An over-decorated ballet of thin choreographic invention, this was once described as "les deux cents baisers", a mocking reference to another unsatisfactory work.

* Infinitely more successful was the ballet in three acts on the same theme with music by Prokofiev which was staged at the Bolshoi Theatre in Moscow in November 1945. Scenario: Nicholas Volkov. Choreography: Rostislav Zakharov. Scenery and costumes: P. V. Williams. Principal dancers: Lepeshinskaya or Ulanova, and Gabovitch. This version was planned by the Kirov Theatre of Leningrad while Ulanova was a member of that company and it was created during the war when the Kirov was evacuated to Molotov. At the Bolshoi, the role of Cinderella was danced by Olga Lepeshinskaya and Ulanova. It was not produced in Leningrad until 1946, under Sergeev, with Dudinskaya and Balabina sharing the title role.

* Frederick Ashton used the Prokofiev score, but a slightly different scenario, when he staged *Cinderella* for the Sadler's Wells Ballet in 1948 with scenery and costumes by Jean-Denis Malclès. Envisaged for Fonteyn, the role of Cinderella was actually created by Moira Shearer owing to Fonteyn's indisposition. The Prince was Michael Somes. Ashton's version has its bleak passages, but a hauntingly tender role for Fonteyn (which she soon made very much her own) and much wild comedy for himself and Robert Helpmann as the Ugly Sisters. Alfred Rodrigues produced a three-act ballet, also to the Prokofiev music, at La Scala, Milan in 1955, with scenery and costumes by André Beaurepaire and Violette Verdy and Perugini in the principal roles.

CHABOUKIANI Vakhtang. A Georgian dancer and choreographer who is a hero in the Soviet Union and also — thanks to his films and one visit to America — outside. He graduated from the Leningrad school in 1929 but, despite a troublesome knee, his virtuosity seems unimpaired today. His technique is extraordinary even by Russian standards and his elevation, in his prime, was unequalled. His

COMPOSITION FOR LA CHAMBRE BY BERNARD BUFFET. 1955.

CENDRILLON. DÉCOR BY GONCHAROVA. 1938.

neat black moustache accentuates his Caucasian appearance; it is difficult to imagine a dancer better qualified to dance the role in *Taras Bulba* which he created. Now ballet master at Tiflis, he is the choreographer of many ballets, mostly character works: *Heart of the Hills* (1938), *Laurencia* (1939), *Sinatle* (1948), *For Peace* (1953), *Othello* (1957).

CHAGALL Marc (b. Vitebsk, 1887). Chagall made a surprisingly late theatrical début considering that the fairy-tale quality of his painting seems so well-suited to Russian ballet. It was not until 1942 that he designed a ballet, *Aleko,* for Ballet Theatre. *Firebird* followed in 1945 for the New York City Ballet. In the event, Chagall brought nothing new to the technique of stage-designing. He simply adapted his style as a painter to the conventional type of ballet décor. Indeed, his backcloths are merely Chagall paintings greatly enlarged: on this scale they illuminate the whole stage, radiating poetry and magic.

CHAMBRE La. Ballet in one act by Georges Simenon. Music: Georges Auric. Scenery and costumes: Bernard Buffet. Choreography: Roland Petit. First performance: Ballets de Paris, Théâtre des Champs-Élysées, 20 December 1955. Principal dancers: Veronika Mlakar, Buzz Miller.

"A rectangular orange glow of light in the nocturnal darkness—it is a window—a window in a room—a room, a den where men are born, love, hate, die—sometimes even are killed."

Bernard Buffet's set, at once realistic and fantastic, created an appropriate atmosphere for Simenon's theme. In a sordid hovel bedroom, barely visible, a man is murdered. Neighbours appear, then the police, and an inspector who reconstructs a mysterious, dreamlike *crime passionel*. It is Kafka's rather than Simenon's world.

CHANT DU ROSSIGNOL Le. Ballet in one act. Music: Stravinsky. Scenery and costumes: Matisse. Choreography: Massine.

First performance: Diaghilev's Ballets Russes, Paris Opera, 2 February 1920. Principal dancers: Karsavina, Sokolova, Idzikowski. Adapted from the Stravinsky opera which Diaghilev had produced at the same theatre in May 1914, with scenery and costumes by Benois and dances by Boris Romanov.

Based on Andersen's fairy-tale of the rivalry between the marvellous nightingale, favourite of the Emperor of China, and the mechanical nightingale, a gift from the Emperor of Japan. The real nightingale, jealous of the enormous artificial bird, glittering with precious stones, is banished by the angry Emperor. But when he falls ill and Death comes to claim him, the real nightingale returns. By its beautiful singing, it revives the Emperor and charms even Death into giving up her victim. Promising to return every night to sing to its master, the nightingale flies away. Matisse's white and turquoise-blue décors and his costumes, especially Death's heavy red cloak lined with black, were exceptionally striking. Karsavina was the real, Idzikowski the mechanical, nightingale. Sokolova was Death, a part she repeated when Diaghilev revived the ballet in 1925 with new choreography by Balanchine, and Markova as the real nightingale.

CHAPELAIN-MIDY Roger. French painter and stage designer, born 1904. With his traditional affiliations, Chapelain-Midy was well qualified to take his place among those artists engaged in reviving and refreshing the classical repertoire of the Paris Opera. This movement started about 1920, when Jacques Rouché, the then director, engaged such painters as Dresa, Dethomas and Piot, and has continued, with varying fortunes, up to the present day. Chapelain-Midy has successfully recreated the spirit of 18th century stage spectacles and has brought a new freshness to the old formula of symmetry and axial perspective, softening the rigours of classicism with clear colours and charming, romantic allusions. His work for the Opéra includes *Les Caprices de Cupidon* and part of *Les Indes Galantes* (1952), as well as numerous opera décors.

CHAPPELL William. English dancer and designer, born 1908. A pupil of Marie Ram-

bert, he joined Ida Rubinstein's company in 1929-30, when he had the experience of working under Nijinska and Massine. Appeared in the early seasons of the Ballet Club, notably in *L'Après-midi d'un faune,* joined Sadler's Wells as soloist in 1934 and remained with them until the war, dancing among other rôles the Strange Player in de Valois' *The Haunted Ballroom,* a sailor in *Rio Grande, Façade* (Popular Song), the Friend in *The Rake's Progress* and the Shepherd in *The Gods go a'Begging.* At the Ballet Club, Rambert had soon discovered his talent for designing (*Lysistrata, Bar aux Folies-Bergère,* etc.) and he subsequently provided many bright and charming décors for Sadler's Wells including several versions of Ashton's *Les Rendez-vous, The Jar, Les Patineurs* and *Coppélia* (two versions, 1940 and 1946). Chappell has also designed for other ballet companies, including International Ballet, and is now a successful producer and designer of plays and revues.

JANINE CHARRAT. LE MASSACRE DES AMAZONES.

CHARRAT Janine. She holds a very special place in contemporary French ballet: she is one of the few dancers who have not been connected with the Paris Opera and have yet acquired an international reputation both as dancer and choreographer. Her first teacher was Jeanne Ronsay, a specialist in oriental dance, from whom Janine Charrat acquired an expressive suppleness of movement. Her facility and her vigorous imagination prevented her from submitting entirely to the strict discipline of the classical ballet. In the film *La Mort du Cygne* (1936) she played the part of a "petit rat" and showed herself already a remarkable actress. In 1941 she met Roland Petit, and produced some short ballets with him. This was her apprenticeship as a choreographer. But her real master was Serge Lifar; *Jeu de Cartes* (*) of which she made a version in 1945 for the Ballets des Champs-Élysées, *Concerto* (Opéra-Comique), *Cressida* (Nouveau Ballet de Monte-Carlo) all show his influence.

In 1948, she rejoined Roland Petit, in the Ballets de Paris, for which her works include *La Femme et son Ombre* and, notably, *'Adame Miroir* in collaboration with Jean Genêt and Darius Milhaud. This unusual ballet, danced by an all-male cast against a strange décor of mirrors, showed exceptional mastery. *Abraxas* for the Berlin-Municipal Opera followed in 1949. In 1951, Charrat founded her own company and made for it *Le Massacre des Amazones* (*), *Herakles, Le Colleur d'affiches* and *Les Algues* (*). Finding that the cares of administration left her little time for choreography she abandoned it in 1956 to produce *Les Sept péchés capitaux* for La Scala, Milan and *Le Joueur de flûte* for the Colon Theatre, Buenos Aires. But she reformed the Company in 1957 and toured successfully in America.

Janine Charrat has already an impressive career behind her. As a dancer she is both sensitive and forceful. As a choreographer, she is full of ideas, though her reliance on instinct leads to occasional lack of clarity and theatrical effect. But her work shows touches of real originality which yet fit perfectly into her neo-classical style.

CHASE Lucia. The good angel of the American Ballet Theatre, Lucia Chase is a Connecticut Yankee by birth. She went to New York to attend the Theatre Guild School and there started ballet lessons with Mikhail Mordkin.

She joined the Mordkin Ballet on its formation in 1937 and danced ballerina roles in *Giselle,* and *La Fille mal gardée*. When this group was incorporated in the newly formed Ballet Theatre in 1940, Miss Chase remained as a dancer and

LUCIA CHASE.

from 1945, with Oliver Smith, has been Director of the company. Although never a strong classical dancer, Miss Chase has created several unforgettable character roles, notably the Elder Sister in *Pillar of Fire* and the Stepmother in *Fall River Legend*. A brilliant comedienne, she also dances in *Three Virgins and a Devil* and *The Judgement of Paris* (Tudor). The money she inherited from a rich industrialist family has enabled Miss Chase to maintain Ballet Theatre through its lean years as well as its good ones. Ballet in America owes much to her for she has constantly placed the well-being of the company before her own ambitions as an artist.

CHATFIELD Philip. "A small, fair boy with unbelievably long legs comes up twice every week on the milk train from Bournemouth, so as to be at the nine o'clock class. He is twelve years of age, and one day apologizes, solemnly, for being stupid; he then explains that he has been up all night in an air raid shelter, and that he had to stand on the milk train. He is very tired, he adds gravely." That is how Ninette de Valois records a wartime memory of Philip Chatfield. His seriousness, hard work and devotion to ballet have brought him now to the position of principal soloist with the Royal Ballet. A tall, strong and virile dancer, with exceptionally good ports de bras (well displayed in the role of Aminta in *Sylvia*), he is a dependable partner and a popular artist. Married to the ballerina Rowena Jackson.

CHATTE La. Ballet in one act. Scenario: Sobeka, alias Boris Kochno. Music: Henri Sauguet. Scenery and costumes: Gabo and Pevsner. Choreography: Balanchine. First performance: Diaghilev's Ballets Russes, Monte-Carlo, 30 April 1927. Principal dancers: Olga Spessivtseva, Serge Lifar.

From one of Aesop's fables: a young man in love with a cat prays Venus to transform her into a woman. His prayer is granted but Venus, rather maliciously, causes a mouse to appear. The woman chases it and is changed back into a cat; the young man dies of despair. The décor was made of constructions of transparent talc against a background of black American cloth; talc was also used for the costumes. Balanchine's choreography, with its stress on male dancing, was an excellent vehicle for the radiant beauty of the young Lifar. Nikitina succeeded Spessivtseva in the title-role. One of the most popular of Diaghilev's later ballets.

CHAUVIRÉ Yvette. The pride of the Paris Opera, and known as La Chauviré Nationale, Yvette Chauviré represents classical tradition in all its purity. Her romantic appearance and nobility of bearing are the result of ceaseless work. She has modelled her body into a work of art, studying every detail, refining every movement. Her dancing has the delicacy of precious lace, or rare tapestry. She is a "terre-à-terre" dancer, more flower than bird, with superlative arabesques *piqués,* precise *déboulés,* slow and voluptuous *dégagés.* Boris Kniaseff stabilised and purified her technique, Serge Lifar made her conscious of her personality. Yvette Chauviré's career at the Opéra was stormy and irregular: she escaped more than once, gave recitals, tried her hand at choreography, danced in America, in London. In 1957 the Opéra terminated her contract, then begged her to return for guest performances. She remains the most valuable intepreter of the Opéra's great classical repertoire, while she created the principal roles in a number of important new ballets, e.g. *Le Roi Nu* (1936) and *David Triomphant* (1937). She was promoted to *danseuse étoile* in 1941, after her remarkable creation in *Istar,* an 18-minute ballet which is virtually a solo. *Les Mirages* (1947) was an even greater success: she danced Man's Shadow, his cold, spectral and poignant alter ego. Away from the Opéra, Yvette Chauviré appeared in two important ballets, *Dramma per Musica* for Lifar's Nouveau Ballet de Monte-Carlo (1946), and *L'Écuyère,* which was especially composed for her. More than any other ballerina, Yvette Chauviré is the admiration of the younger generation of French dancers; she is one of the great

CHAUVIRÉ IN (1) MIRAGES, (2 AND 3) THE DYING SWAN, (4) GISELLE. DRAWINGS BY GENEVIÈVE LABORDE.

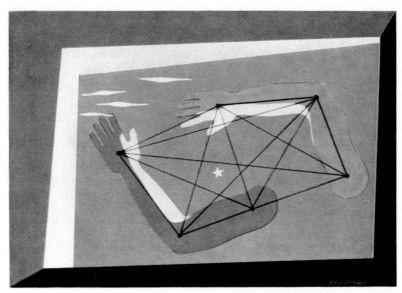

CHECKMATE. CURTAIN BY MCKNIGHT KAUFFER. 1937.

classical dancers of the present day. Her guest appearances with the Royal Ballet in 1958 brought her great popularity in London.

CHECKMATE. Ballet in one scene with a prologue. Scenario and music: Arthur Bliss. Choreography: Ninette de Valois. Scenery and costumes: E. McKnight Kauffer. First performance: Vic-Wells Ballet, Théâtre des Champs-Élysées, Paris, 15 June 1937. Principal dancers: June Brae, Harold Turner, Pamela May, Robert Helpmann. Revived, Royal Opera House, Covent Garden, November 1947.

A dramatic ballet played out in terms of the game of chess. *Checkmate,* with the aid of powerful choreography and bright yet menacing backcloth and costumes, holds the audience in spite of the tendency of Bliss's vigorous music to extend crucial scenes beyond the limits of the dancers' physical endurance and thus weaken their effect. The prologue shows a game of chess in progress between Love and Death: Love has a premonition of defeat. In the ensuing action the Red Knight, fighting to protect his King and Queen from the onslaught of the masterful Black Queen (the best female role in any de Valois ballet) falls a victim to her beauty and is slain by her. She is free to subjugate the senile and terrified Red King—Checkmate !

CHEVALIER ERRANT Le. "Choreodrama" in two acts and four tableaux. Scenario: Elisabeth de Gramont, with poems by Alexandre Arnoux. Music: Jacques Ibert. Scenery and costumes: Pedro Flores. Choreography: Serge Lifar. First performance: Paris Opera, 26 April 1950. Principal dancers: Lycette Darsonval, Christiane Vaussard, Micheline Bardin, Espanita Cortez, Serge Lifar. A chorus, ranged in tiers at one side of the stage, comment on the action. An unusual picture of Don Quixote, the "wandering knight", half Adonis, half archangel.

CHEVALIER ET LA DAMOISELLE Le. Ballet in two acts. Music: Philippe Gaubert. Scenery and costumes: A. M. Cassandre. Choreography: Lifar. First performance: Paris Opera, 2 July 1941. Principal dancers: Solange Schwarz, Yvette Chauviré, Serge Lifar, Serge Peretti, Paul Goubé, Renée Jeanmaire.

A fair Damoiselle is fated to be changed every evening into a doe. One night in the forest she is surprised by a wandering knight. Enchanted with the pretty animal, he tries to play with her, but is wounded by one of her horns. In self-defence he strikes back and unwittingly breaks the spell: the doe resumes human shape. The couple dance a passionate pas de deux. Her three esquires appear and challenge the knight. The second scene is a tournament. The three esquires oppose the knight with lance, sword and dagger. He is victorious, and is united to the Damoiselle in a triumphant and joyful finale.

Le Chevalier et la Damoiselle is one of the most considerable of modern French ballets. Lifar's neo-classic choreography is at once lyrical and stylised. Cassandre's scenery and costumes resemble medieval illuminated books. Solange Schwarz danced the complex role of the heroine beautifully; Lifar gave the knight the grave and romantic allure of a Tristan.

CHICAGO BALLET COMPANY. See *Ruth Page.*

LE CHEVALIER ET LA DAMOISELLE.
LIANE DAYDÉ AND MICHEL RENAULT.

CHIRICO Giorgio di. Italian painter, born in Greece in 1888. Came to Paris in 1911, and had won a considerable reputation in avant-garde circles by the time Rolf de Maré invited him to design *La Jarre* (from a Sicilian story by Pirandello) for the Ballets Suédois. Five years later came *Le Bal* for Diaghilev. It was the fantastic aspect of Chirico's painting that appealed to Diaghilev as it did to the surrealists, who claimed him for one of their own. The dancers in Kochno's ballet, disguised as columns, capitals and pieces of walls, pale patches of clear colour moving in a pale, cold light, have a family resemblance to the large seated figures in Chirico's early paintings, with fragments of buildings in their laps.

Chirico's remaining work for the theatre reflects his increasing reaction from modernism: *Pulcinella* (1930), for the ballet of the Russian Opera in Paris; *Les Bacchantes* (1937): *Bacchus et Ariane* (Paris Opera, 1938); *Protée* (de Basil, 1938). His final return to academic tradition and the cult of the Italian masters was shown in his designs for *The Legend of Joseph* (La Scala, 1951) and *Don Quixote* (Florence May Festival, 1953). Little remained, however, in these works of the strange poetry of the early Chirico.

CHISTOVA Nina. A young dancer surely destined for fame in the Bolshoi Theatre Ballet, Chistova has a beautiful line and a most expressive body that illuminates, in particular, the roles of romantic heroines. Like all other soloists of the Bolshoi she has a strong yet supple technique. When she dances Paracha in *The Bronze Horseman* she turns soli and pas de deux into pure poetry by the grace of her movements. In London, she was especially admired as Juliet's young friend in *Romeo and Juliet,* warm and vivacious, adorable in her pas de deux with the troubadour.

CHOREARTIUM. Choreographic symphony in four movements. Music: Brahms, 4th symphony. Drop curtain: G. Annenkov. Scenery and costumes: C. Terechkovitch and E. Lourié. First performance: De Basil's Ballets Russes, Alhambra Theatre, London, 24 October 1933. Choreography: Massine. Principal dancers: Irina Baronova, Alexandra Danilova, Tatiana Riabouchinska, Nina Verchinina, David Lichine, Paul Petrov.

CHOREARTIUM. IRINA BARONOVA AND D. LICHINE.

Massine's first symphonic ballet, *Les Présages,* ensured the success of the first London season of de Basil's Ballets Russes, and *Choreartium,* his second symphonic ballet, was the note of challenge on which de Basil ended the historic season. Although, like *Les Présages,* the ballet required a huge cast of dancers, there was no vestige of plot. Every movement stemmed directly from the music, each solo or ensemble corresponding strictly to the musical development. The first movement was perhaps the most striking; in front of a curtain depicting a dim horizon crossed by a rainbow, dancers appeared in steadily increasing groups, creating a living lansdcape that dissolved into new groupings, equally harmonious. The solos, conceived as peaks of intense lyricism and often extremely difficult technically, sprang naturally from the ensembles and thus did not impede the progress of the ballet. In the second movement, Nina Verchinina's barefoot dance in the manner of the Wigman school was remarkably impressive. The four movements were very different in style; the first being joyous, the second sombre, the third light-hearted and the fourth, again, full of foreboding. *Choreartium* has not been seen for a great many

years in Europe, but it ranks as one of the great creations of Massine and heralded the complete success of his *Symphonie Fantastique* in 1936.

CHOUT (The Buffoon). Russian legend in six scenes. Music: Serge Prokofiev. Scenery and costumes: Michel Larionov. Choreography: Larionov and T. Slavinsky. First performance: Ballets Russes de Diaghilev, Gaîté-lyrique, Paris, 17 May 1921.

Diaghilev had a particular affection for this old folk-tale about a buffoon who fools seven of his colleagues. He decided to use it for a ballet and asked Prokofiev (whom he called his "second spiritual son", the first being Stravinsky) to write the music in 1915, many years before its eventual production. *Chout* was largely Larionov's work. Massine was absent, so, in addition to designing the décors and the costumes, Larionov had to guide the steps of the dancer Slavinsky in his début as choreographer. The ballet was not a great success. Prokofiev's aggressive and brightly-coloured music attracted more attention than the décors and costumes (also brightly coloured; a sophisticated, cubist version of traditional Russian folk-art) and the choreography.

CHRISTENSEN Lew. Brother of Harald and Willam, and with them an architect of the San Francisco Ballet. Of Danish origin, the brothers were born in Utah. Lew studied with his uncle and then at the School of American Ballet. Danced title roles in *Orpheus* and *Apollo* with the American Ballet (1934) and worked with Ballet Caravan, Dance Players and the San Francisco Opera Ballet. After war service, he became ballet master and dancer with Ballet Society (1946-48). Choreographer of *Filling Station* and *Pocahontas* (for Ballet Caravan), *Jinx* (*) (for Dance Players), and *Con Amore* for New York City Ballet. Married to Gisella Caccialanza.

CINÉ-BIJOU. Ballet in one act. Scenario: J.-P. Grédy. Music: Pierre Petit. Scenery: André Beaurepaire. Costumes: René Gruau. Choreography: Roland Petit. First performance: Théâtre de l'Empire, Paris, 17 March 1953.

Principal dancers: Colette Marchand, Roland Petit, Georges Reich, Serge Perrault.

CINÉMA. Ballet in three scenes by Ręné Jeanne. Music: Louis Aubert. Scenery and costumes: Touchagues. Choreography: Lifar. First performance: Paris Opéra, 11 March 1953. Principal dancers: Lifar (Chaplin), Youly Algaroff (Max Linder), Paulette Dynalix (Musidora),

should the effect of his décors be judged from the gouaches sometimes described as designs but usually done afterwards. In fact he uses small working models which he constructs himself out of pieces of cardboard, matches and bits of string.

Clavé has an extraordinary gift for utilising space on the stage; he is more producer than painter. He thinks in terms of the total effect,

LA PEUR. CURTAIN BY CLAVÉ. REVUE DES BALLETS DE PARIS. 1957.

Liane Daydé (Mary Pickford), Michel Renault (Rudolf Valentino), Lycette Darsonval (Marlene Dietrich).

CLAVÉ Antoni. Born at Barcelona, 1913; settled in Paris, 1939. Clavé is one of the two or three great revelations of contemporary stage-design. His décors have been largely responsible for the success of several recent French ballets. He infused new life into ballet design at a time when it seemed that everything had been said and that new discoveries were unthinkable. Oddly enough, his work as a painter did not suggest any particular talent for the theatre, nor

not from the point of view of decoration alone. Under these conditions, the décor becomes an infinitely richer and more complex element in the ballet. In his paintings, with their thick lines and heavy textures, the predominant blues, reds and blacks are kept on one plane. In his décors, dark frameworks stretched like a net in space stand out against a luminous background, accentuating the bright colours and emphasising the depth of the stage. This delineation of space is further enhanced by the use Clavé makes of the screens, movable objects and accessories which play such a vital role in his designs: the chairs, the wheels and the bed in *Carmen,* the revolving door in *Deuil en 24 heures,* which really does revolve; the bicycles and bric-à-brac in *Ballabile*. His style is so flexible and his invention so abundant that he is equally at home in the dramatic intensity of *Carmen* and the irony of *Deuil en 24 heures*. His range alone puts him among the leading stage designers of the day. He has designed: *Los Caprichos* (1946), *Carmen* (1949) and *Revanche* (1951), for the Ballets des Champs-Élysées; *Deuil en 24 heures* (1953) and *La Peur*

CLÉOPATRE. Ballet in one act. Choreography: Fokine. Music: Arensky, with additions by Taneev, Rimsky-Korsakov, Glinka, Moussorsky and Glazounov. Scenery and costumes : Bakst. First performance: Diaghilev's Ballets Russes, Théâtre du Châtelet, Paris, 2 June 1909. Principal dancers: Anna Pavlova, Ida Rubinstein, Tamara Karsavina, Vaslav Nijinsky, Michel Fokine.

CLAVÉ. LE MARCHÉ AUX PUCES. PROJECT FOR DÉCOR. 1949.

(1957) for the Ballets de Paris; *Ballabile* (1950) for the Sadler's Wells Ballet at Covent Garden; *Susanna and the Barber* for Ruth Page's Chicago Opera Ballet (1956).

CLAVIER Josette. A sparkling Parisian dancer who made her début at the Opéra at the age of fourteen in *Les Malheurs de Sophie*. Première danseuse in 1951. Left the Opéra in 1955 to become principal dancer of the short-lived "Ballets de la Tour Eiffel" founded by Pierre Lacotte. Has since danced in Janine Charrat's company and appeared as guest artist with London's Festival Ballet in 1956.

An adaptation of an earlier Fokine ballet *Une Nuit d'Égypte* (Maryinsky Theatre, St. Petersburg, 21 March 1908) with complete score by Arensky. Bakst's imposing and sumptuous setting showed the façade of a temple flanked by massive, rock-hewn figures. The Nile could be seen in the distance. It was destroyed by fire during a South American tour and replaced for the London revival of 1918 by a new décor by Robert Delaunay, and costumes by his wife, Sonia. Amoûn, the young betrothed of the priestess Ta-hor, falls a victim to the charms of the Queen, Cleopatra. He is arrested and condemned to death. The Queen intercedes to save him and grants him one blissful night of love, but at dawn she has him poisoned. Ta-hor tries vainly to bring him back to life, then falls grief-stricken over his dead body. One of the many attractions of the ballet was the entrance of Ida Rubinstein as Cleopatra, swathed like a mummy and unwound in a prolonged, intricate and spectacular sequence. This was her début in the theatre; her talent for mime, her great beauty and wonderful figure compensated for her restricted technique.

CLOCK SYMPHONY The. Ballet in four movements. Music: Haydn. Scenery and costumes: Christian Bérard. Choreography: Massine. First performance: Sadler's Wells Ballet, Covent Garden, 25 June 1948. Principal dancers: Moira Shearer, Alexander Grant.

CLUSTINE Yvan. Born Moscow, 1860, died Nice, 1941. After a long career at the Maryinsky Theatre in St. Petersburg, became premier danseur and maître de ballet at Monte-Carlo (1905) where his partners were Carlotta Zambelli and Natacha Trouhanova. Later engaged as choreographer at the Paris Opera and created *La Roussalka* (1911), *Suite de Danses* (1913—still in the repertoire) and *Hansli le Bossu*. In 1914, Clustine became Pavlova's regular choreographer and spent 18 years touring with her. Some of the most popular ballets in her reper-

CLÉOPÀTRE. LUBOV TCHERNICHEVA.

toire were his work, including *The Fairy Doll*, *La Péri* (*), *Amarilla,* and *Pavlova Gavotte.* Clustine's work for the Paris Opera forms part of the new movement started by the immense success of the first Diaghilev seasons.

COCTEAU Jean. Born 1889, Maisons-Laffitte, near Paris. It is a commonplace to say that Jean Cocteau, as a creative artist and as an instigator, has played a capital role in the growth and ultimate success of modern art. That role has been Protean; Cocteau has appeared as a glorified cheapjack, entertaining the crowd with amusing patter to entice them down difficult and dangerous paths; a prophet, pointing the way to artists uncertain of their direction; as an artisan jack-of-all-trades, constantly trying out new techniques and materials for the pleasure of proving anew the instinctive skill of his own hands. But also, as an artist genuine enough to create his own brand of magic and to present his contemporaries with a theatre of illusions, in which each could see beyond himself. He has left a trail of snobbery in his wake, and his many followers have often mistaken his wit, talent and fantasy for their own

CLAVÉ. SKETCH FOR BALLABILE.

The theatre, by its artifice and its serious potentialities, was bound to attract him, and within the theatre the ballet offered him unique opportunities. Cocteau's role in the history of ballet during the last forty years has been considerable, extending beyond the works for which he was nominally responsible. In the earliest days, he designed two posters for Diaghilev, and wrote the scenario for *Le Dieu Bleu* (1912). Towards the end of the war, he became and remained one of the Russian Ballet's spiritual leaders. It was through Cocteau that Picasso began to work for the ballet; he made the *Groupe des Six* known and introduced them to the theatre. The production of *Parade* (*) in 1917 — in which Picasso and Satie collaborated with him — was a theatrical event of considerable importance and the beginning of a new period in the evolution of the Russian Ballet. *Parade,* of which he was the chief instigator, was a clear example of a tendency to which he has remained faithful: the use of traditional forms to clothe topical allusions barely disguised and at first sight quite out of place. There was always an element of affectation about Cocteau's determined up-to-dateness, but by sticking to his guns he finally succeeded in creating a valid, contemporary equivalent of the faded allegories of the past. *Les Mariés de la Tour Eiffel* (*) and *Le Train Bleu* (*) were further stages in the creation of this familiar yet whimsical mythology, transforming banalities into symbols, poeticizing everyday life without robbing it of its brutal immediacy, and without prettifying it in the 18th century manner. The age of rococo saw the growth of a mythology full of charming conventions in which the ladies of the Court assumed the attributes of the divinities of Olympus; of Circe, or of Venus. Cocteau rejected this elegant masquerading and filled his Olympus with typists, telegraphists, photographers and acrobats, complete with their banal paraphernalia, and yet contrived, by some touch of personal magic, to endow them with the power of legendary figures.

When he subsequently transferred his attention to the great dramas of antiquity, *Oedipus Rex* or *Phèdre* (*), he appeared to have changed his subject-matter. But in reality he was only reversing his previous procedure: having deified the commonplace, he was now familiarising the divine. One of his more recent ballets, *Le Jeune Homme et la Mort* (*) was the logical and perhaps

JEAN COCTEAU BY HIMSELF.

final outcome of this two-directional movement, which only a poet could have conceived and carried out. Cocteau's contribution to the ballet has not been confined to the role of scenarist. He has always taken an active and usually a predominant part, imposing his visions by all available means. On occasion he has designed the décors as well, apparently simple, but really the result of complex and subtle elaboration. All his work proves that poetry is not made with words alone but springs from a certain way of looking at things, of bringing the dead to life and transfixing the living, of showing the most ordinary people in a new and unfamiliar light. Cocteau, who has contrived to remain in the avant-garde with a success that eluded Diaghilev himself, has also remained a poet, annoying, stimulating and enchanting the successive decades. — Ballets and related works: *Le Dieu Bleu* (1912); *Parade* (1917); *Le Train bleu* (1924), *Oedipus Rex* (1927) for Diaghilev's Ballets Russes; *le Bœuf sur le toit* (Fratellini brothers, Comédie des Champs-Élysées, Paris, 1920); *Les Mariés de la Tour Eiffel* (Ballets Suédois, 1921); *Roméo et Juliette* (Soirées de Paris, 1924); *Le Jeune Homme et la Mort* (Ballets des Champs-Élysées, 1946);

DÉCOR BY JEAN COCTEAU FOR PHÈDRE. *Bibliothèque-Musée de l'Opéra, Paris.*

Phèdre (Paris Opera, 1950); *La Dame à la Licorne* (Munich State Opera, 1953). Ballet décors: *L'Amour et son Amour* (Ballets des Champs-Élysées, 1947), and the above-mentioned *Phèdre* and *La Dame à la Licorne.*

COLIN Paul. Born Nancy, 1892. Colin and Cassandre, during the period 1925-1930, were among the creators of the modern French poster. Most of the new poster designers favoured a purely graphic style, but Colin, faithful to the painter's point of view, insisted on using colour to define shape and volume. One of his first posters was for the Ballets Suédois at the Théâtre des Champs-Élysées; it immediately attracted favourable comment and the interest of theatre and music-hall directors. In 1925 Rolf de Maré commissioned him to design all the décors for the famous *Revue Nègre* in which Joséphine Baker made her triumphant début. Paul Colin has been busy ever since designing posters for ballet seasons from Joséphine Baker to Katherine Dunham (1948 and 1953). Mention should also be made of the numerous décors he designed for

the Paris Opera: *Prélude Dominical* and *L'Orchestre en liberté* (1931), *Le Cantique des Cantiques* (1938); for the Opéra-Comique: *Comme ils s'aiment* (1941), *Casse-Noisette* (1947), *Guignol* (1949). He also provided very original decorations for various revues at the Casino de Paris and for Jean Borlin's ballet *Sculpture nègre* (1929).

COMBAT Le. Scenario and choreography: William Dollar. Music: Raffaello de Banfield. Scenery and costumes: Marie-Laure. First performance: Ballets de Paris, Prince's Theatre, London. Principal dancers: Janine Charrat, Wladimir Skouratoff.
   This ballet, really a long pas de deux, tells the story of Clorinda, the pagan Princess, killed in a duel with her lover, Tancred, who does not realise her identity. It was Banfield's début as a composer. The costumes, black tights with hoods trimmed with tassels, were designed by the Vicomtesse de Noailles. Dollar's ingenious choreography, long perambulations and swift gallops on points, culminated in an astonishing, lyrical pas de deux where the ballerina, almost

inert, allowed herself to be guided entirely by her partner. Colette Marchand and Milorad Miskovitch made their names in this ballet in New York in 1949, during the first American season of the Ballets de Paris. Two American companies, Ballet Theatre and the New York City Ballet, have revived *Le Combat* under the title of *The Duel,* with a modified, but not superior, décor. *Walter Gore composed a different version, to music by Monteverdi, for himself and Paula Hinton in 1952, called *Tancredi and Clorinda.*

CONCERTO BAROCCO. Ballet in three movements. Choreography: Balanchine. Music: J. S. Bach (Concerto for two violins and orchestra in D minor). Scenery and costumes: Eugene Berman. First performance: American Ballet, New York, 28 May 1941. Principal dancers: Marie-Jeanne, Mary Jane Shea, William Dollar.

This much revived work was arranged for ten girls (including two soloists) and a man who appears in the adagio only. The two soloists correspond more or less to the two solo violins

but Balanchine does not attempt a "note for note" equivalence. His treatment of the famous score is thoroughly sensitive and the strictly academic style of the choreography perfectly matches Bach's pure classicism. In recent revivals (by the Grand Ballet du Marquis de Cuevas and the Royal Danish Ballet, for example) Berman's designs have been replaced by practice tunics and a plain backcloth.

CONCURRENCE. Ballet in one act. Scenario, scenery and costumes: André Derain. Music: Georges Auric. Choreography: Balanchine. First performance: Ballets Russes de Monte-Carlo, 12 April 1932. Principal dancers: Irina Baronova, Tamara Toumanova, Leon Woizikowski.

This lively and amusing ballet was a memorial to the jovial and colourful personality of André Derain. The drop curtain set the tone: Harlequin and Pierrot, guitars strapped to their backs, leading a circus girl balancing on a piebald horse towards the gaily-painted town on which the curtain rises. The story concerns two rival tailors, and the décor showed their shops facing

LE COMBAT. MELISSA HAYDEN AND WILLIAM DOLLAR.

97

one another in the little square surrounded by toy-town houses. The tailors go to shameless lengths to entice one another's customers, but everyone gets new clothes, and the rivals are finally reconciled over their handsome profits. There was a memorable burlesque variation for Woizikowski as a ragged tramp. A contrast to the comic scenes was provided by a group of young girls who remained totally indifferent to the general agitation. An element of virtuosity was introduced by their competing fouettés, in which the young ballerinas, headed by Touma-nova, particularly excelled. Altogether, the work revealed an unexpectedly gay and witty side of Balanchine's talent. George Auric's music, with its reminiscences of popular songs, barrel organs and squeaky musical boxes, was just what was required.

CONSERVATOIRE The *(Konservatoriet eller et avisfrieri)*. Ballet in two acts. Music: H. Paulli. Choreography: August Bournon-ville. Composed by Bournonville in 1849 in memory of his years of study at the Paris Opéra under Vestris, in the 1820's. A charming, old-fashioned ballet based on an intrigue at the Paris Conservatoire between the young dancers, their professor and his old housekeeper. *Konser-vatoriet* remained in the repertoire of the Royal Danish Ballet until 1941, when Harald Lander and Valborg Borchsenius made a new version of the first act under the title *Le Conservatoire*. In this new form, the ballet is a simple but charm-ing classroom demonstration of French classical dancing in the style of Vestris, a tradition which the Danish school has preserved intact.

CONSTANTIA. Ballet in three movements. Scenario and choreography: William Dollar. Music: Chopin. Scenery: Horace Armistead. Costumes: Grace Houston. First performance: International Ballet New York, 31 October 1944. Principal dancers: Marie-Jeanne, Yvonne Patter-son, Dollar.

Based on an earlier work (1936) by Dollar called *Ballet Classique,* in which his master, Ba-lanchine, collaborated in the "larghetto". The final version, *Constantia,* completely remodelled, is by Dollar alone. The music used is Chopin's Second Piano Concerto dedicated to the Polish singer Constantia Gladowska—hence the title. The choreography follows the score closely. Three soloists and a corps de ballet, in simple costumes, translate the subtlest nuances into terms of dancing. Revived for the Grand Ballet du Marquis de Cuevas (1947), Original Ballet Russe (1946), and the American Ballet Theatre (1951), it has proved an ideal vehicle for the talents of Rosella Hightower.

CONTES RUSSES. Choreographic mi-niatures. Music: Liadov. Scenery and cos-tumes: Michel Larionov. Choreography: Mas-sine. First performance: Diaghilev's Ballets Russes, Théâtre du Châtelet, Paris, 11 May 1917. Principal dancers: Sokolova, Tchernicheva, Idzikowksi, Woizikowski. A suite of scenes and dances based on Russian folklore. One of them, *Kikimora,* had already been produced at San Sebastian the previous year. Massine, with much assistance from Diaghilev and Larionov, worked at the ballet in Rome, adding two more episodes, *Baba Yaga* and *La Princesse Cygne,* and a finale. A new version, considerably longer, was given in London in 1918. Tchernicheva, in a beautiful Russian costume, scored a great

AUGUST BOURNONVILLE.

LA CONCURRENCE. DÉCOR BY ANDRÉ DERAIN. BALLETS DE MONTE-CARLO, 1932.

success as the Swan Queen. Larionov's gay designs and Liadov's beautifully finished miniatures fitted perfectly. One of Diaghilev's happiest incursions into Russian folklore.

COPLAND Aaron. Born Brooklyn, New York, 1900. Copland studied in Paris, where he was a distinguished pupil of Nadia Boulanger. Stravinsky was another important influence. From these two he learned, and has never forgotten, the virtues of precision, economy and rhythmic vitality. His work is often strongly coloured by Jazz and American folklore, particularly in the highly distinguished contributions he has made to American ballet: *Billy the Kid* (1938) for Loring, *Rodeo* (1942) for Agnes de Mille, and *Appalachian Spring* (1944) for Martha Graham. His Clarinet Concerto, written for Benny Goodman, was used for Jerome Robbins' *Pied Piper* (New York City Ballet, 1951).

COPPELIA. Ballet-pantomime in two acts and three tableaux. Scenario: Ch. Nuitter and Saint-Léon. Music: Léo Delibes. Scenery:

Chambon, Despléchin and Lavastre. Costumes: Paul Lormier. Choreography: Arthur Saint-Léon. First performance: Théâtre Impérial de l'Opéra, Paris, 25 May 1870. Principal dancers: Giuseppina Bozzacchi, Louise Fiocre, the mime Dauty.

From Hoffmann's famous tale *The Sand Merchant* concerning Coppelia, "the girl with enamel eyes", a lovely automaton built by the learned scientist Dr. Coppelius. Coppelia is so lifelike that Franz, Swanilda's young fiancé, falls in love with her. One night, accompanied by friends, Swanilda manages to enter the magician's house and finds out the secret of her lovely rival. But the girls dally, amusing themselves by winding up the numerous automatons in this fantastic workshop. Suddenly Coppelius arrives and they all flee, except Swanilda who hides behind a curtain. She watches as young Franz climbs through the window and is seized by the magician who forces him to drink a narcotic. Coppelius now hopes to realize his long-cherished dream of giving life to his loveliest doll by transferring to her the life-blood of a young human. We watch the moving and pathetic transformation of 'Coppelia" into the most appealing of young girls but, unlike Dr. Coppelius, we realise that it is not the doll who has come to life, but Swanilda, who has taken her place. When Franz at last wakes up, Swanilda tells the old toymaker he has been tricked and drags her young lover away. The third and last act of the ballet celebrates their reconciliation and closes on a grand divertissement. An excellent example of the ballet-pantomime, *Coppelia* is the masterpiece of Arthur Saint-Léon, a dancer and maître de ballet at the Paris Opera. It maintains a perfect balance between pantomime and dance, introducing soli, pas de deux and character dances without in any way disrupting development of the story. It is a light-hearted and continuously popular work. The quaint charm of some of the mimed sequences adds to the enjoyment of the modern spectator while Léo Delibes' honeyed music is a constant enchantment.

Coppelia has a permanent place in the reper-

ÉLIANE BONABEL. DANCER AT THE BARRE.

SOLANGE SCHWARZ IN COPPÉLIA.

toire of the Paris Opera where it is still staged in its original choreography, even the role of Franz being generally danced by a ballerina *en travesti*. However, at the Paris Opera it is now customary to suppress the third act and to end the ballet with the awakening of Franz and the disillusionment of Dr. Coppelius. There have been many célebrated interpreters of Swanilda at the Paris Opera. The little Giuseppina Bozzacchi, who created the role at the age of 16, died soon afterward during the seige of Paris. Carlotta Zambelli and later Solange Schwarz were famous successors.

* In England the ballet was staged at the Empire Theatre as early as 1884 in a one-act version. The full ballet was first danced by Adeline Genée in London in 1906. It was produced by the Sadler's Wells Ballet, in a two act version by Sergueev, based on the Russian production of Ivanov and Cecchetti, in 1933 with Lydia Lopokova. Later, Mary Honer danced the three-act version (1940), with Helpmann as Franz, and in 1946 the ballet was revived at Covent Garden with Fonteyn and Shearer dancing Swanilda; Rassine, Turner and John Hart dancing Franz, and Helpmann clowning his way superbly through the part of Dr. Coppelius.

In 1951, the production was completely overhauled and redesigned by Osbert Lancaster. Nadia Nerina and David Blair danced the principal roles.

* Harald Lander's version for the Royal Danish Ballet, which stresses character dancing rather than classical, is one of the best integrated contemporary productions. Margot Lander was one of Denmark's great Swanildas; she has now been succeeded by Inge Sand. Niels Bjorn Larsen is still a magnificent Dr. Coppelius. This version has also been reproduced for London's Festival Ballet and danced by Toni Lander and Belinda Wright, with Flemming Flindt and John Gilpin.

* The René Blum Company presented a version by Zverev which starred Vera Nemchinova and the ballet remains in the repertory of the present Ballets Russes de Monte-Carlo where it was danced with special brilliance by Alexandra Danilova. For Ballet Theatre, in 1942, Irina Baronova danced Swanilda and indeed there are few ballerinas who have not essayed this delightful and rewarding part.

COQ D'OR. Le. Opera-ballet in three acts. Scenario: V. Bielsky, adapted by Alexandre Benois. Music: Rimsky - Korskov. Scenery and costumes: Goncharova. Choreography: Fokine. First performance: Diaghilev's Ballets Russes, Paris Opera, 21 May 1914. Principal dancers: Tamara Karsavina, Alexis Boulgakov, Enrico Cecchetti.

Alexandre Benois was responsible for both the idea and its scenic realisation. The story comes from Pushkin's famous satirical poem. The feeble old King Dodon, threatened by powerful enemies, consults a mysterious astrologer who gives him a golden cockerel which can warn him by its crowing of approaching dangers; in exchange, Dodon promises to grant the astrologer his dearest wish. During a battle, in the course of which his sons are slain, the King is confronted with the beautiful Queen of Shemakhan and carries her home to make her his wife. But the astrologer claims her for himself. Dodon breaks his promise and kills him. The cockerel avenges his master by, in his turn, killing the King. All the action was mimed or danced, the singers being concealed in the orchestra pit. This was one of Diaghilev's many experiments in the combination of singing and dancing, of which other examples were *Les Noces, Les Biches, Barabau, Ode* and *Renard.* Goncharova's décors and costumes, blazing with reds, yellows and gold, were among the

GONCHAROVA. STUDIES FOR LE COQ D'OR. CENTRE: KARSAVINA.

LE COQ D'OR. CURTAIN BY NATHALIE GONCHAROVA. 1914.

most brilliant ever designed even for this company. *Le Coq d'Or* was the last ballet Fokine arranged for Diaghilev.

* In September 1937, Fokine made a new, shortened and purely choreographic version of the ballet for the de Basil company. Irina Baronova danced, superbly, the Queen of Shemakhan.

COTILLON. Ballet in one act. Scenario: Boris Kochno. Music: Emmanuel Chabrier. Scenery and costumes: Christian Bérard. Choreography: Balanchine. First performance: Ballets Russes de Monte-Carlo, 12 April 1932. Principal dancers: Tamara Toumanova, Lubov Rostova, Leon Woizikowski, David Lichine.

A ball in a white room surrounded by a row of theatre boxes, hung with red. A succession of episodes, some gay and turbulent, some tinged with a mysterious, half-sensuous melancholy, as varied as the lights and shadows of Chabrier's music. Bérard dressed the ballet with exquisite Parisian simplicity and elegance. The girls wore tulle skirts, studded with stars, diamonds and musical symbols, over coloured petticoats; the men, gaily coloured tail-coats. The "baby ballerinas", brought a note of curiously moving freshness to this delightful work.

CRANKO John. John Cranko is the first South African choreographer to win an international reputation. Born in Rustenburg, South Africa, in 1927, of wealthy parents, he made his first ballets in Johannesburg and at the University of Cape Town (where there is a department of ballet directed by Dulcie Howes). He joined the Sadler's Wells Theatre Ballet in England in 1946 and after staging some experimental works for a ballet production club convinced Ninette de Valois that although he would never be a good dancer he might become a good choreographer. With the Sadler's Wells Theatre Ballet he was allowed to create a number of ballets over a period of years on the same group of dancers, a policy that rewarded the company with *Sea Change, Pastorale, Pineapple Poll, Harlequin in April* (*) (which he considers to be his best work) and *The Lady and the Fool.* In 1952 his *Bonne Bouche* was staged at Covent Garden, followed in 1953 by *The Shadow* and in 1957 by *The Prince of the Pagodas* (*), a three-act ballet with a score commissioned from Benjamin Britten.

Cranko has also worked for the Ballet Rambert, the New York City Ballet, the Scala and the Paris Opera. He was sole author of the eccentric and highly successful revue *Cranks* and the completely unsuccessful musical *Keep Your Hair On.* His youth and boundless enthusiasm drive him forward at a tremendous pace. His ballets range from high comedy to tormented psychological probings, and his lively and inquiring

LE COQ D'OR.
COSTUME BY ALEXANDRE BENOIS.
PARIS OPERA VERSION, 1948. *Musée de l'Opéra.*

mind seizes ideas, magpie fashion, from all quarters. His talents are abundant and obvious although as yet his powers of concentration and selection are not fully matured. His gifts and his weaknesses were well displayed in *The Angels* which he made for the smaller company of the Royal Ballet in 1957. To a commissioned score by Richard Arnell, Cranko tried to explore in movement the rewards and penalties of genius. Passages of beautiful plastic invention were cancelled out by other passages of tortuous, meaningless dancing.

CRÉATION La. Ballet by David Lichine. First performance: Ballets des Champs-Élysées, Paris, 12 November 1948.

An experimental ballet without music danced in practice costume in front of black curtains: an attempt to dramatise the creative processes of the choreographer, feeling his way towards the expression, through movement, of new ideas. Attempts had been made many years previously by Rudolf van Laban and various Dalcroze

COTILLON. COSTUMES BY BÉRARD. 1932.

disciples to compose ballets without music. Lichine's essay, although not entirely convincing, was a useful reaction against the opposite tendency: the absolute subjection of dancing to music. During the first season, the role of the Choreographer was danced alternately by Lichine and Jean Babilée, with Leslie Caron as his Ideal, Nathalie Philippart as his Uncertainty, Hélène Sadovska as his Temptation and Hélène Constantine as his Idea.

CRÉATION DU MONDE La. Ballet in one act. Scenario: Blaise Cendrars. Music: Darius Milhaud. Scenery and costumes: Fernand Léger. Choreography: Jean Borlin. First performance: Ballets Suédois, Théâtre des Champs-Élysées, Paris, 25 October 1923.

This work marked an important date both in the annals of the Ballets Suédois and in the history of the contemporary theatre. The cult of Negro Art, started by the Cubists about 1910, had by now spread far beyond the circles of the avant-garde. A wide public was familiar with the obsessive rhythms of negro music and dancing, yet the theatre had not so far assimilated them into a serious art-form. With *La Création du Monde,* Léger and Milhaud at one stroke achieved the synthesis in a work which was clearly of more than ephemeral value. Cendrars imagined totemistic deities creating a negro world out of primitive matter: trees, monstrous birds, insects, animals, gradually detach themselves; finally, man and woman emerge. The savage grandeur of the subject was matched by Léger's bold designs and by the barbaric rhythms of Milhaud's evocative score.

* Ninette de Valois made a new version of the ballet for the Camargo Society (London, 26 April 1931) with scenery and costumes by Edward Wolfe. Two years later, it was taken into the repertory of the Vic-Wells Ballet.

CRÉATURES DE PROMÉTHÉE Les. To honour the centenary of Beethoven's death, Jacques Rouché, director of the Paris Opera, decided to mount a new version of the ballet *Die Geschöpfe des Prometheus* which Beethoven wrote for the famous Italian choreographer Salvatore Viganò, and which was first performed in Vienna in 1801. Balanchine was invited to do the choreography but had to abandon the work through illness, and Lifar took over. The first performance took place two years later (Paris Opera, 30 December 1929). Scenery and costumes: Quelvée. Principal dancers: Olga Spessivtseva, Suzanne Lorcia, Serge Lifar, Serge Peretti.

The authors of the scenario, MM. Chantavoine and Lena, proposed an exact re-creation of Viganò's ballet and when Lifar objected asked for their names to be withdrawn. In Lifar's new version, Prometheus is no longer a minor figure but the central character, around whom revolve the "creatures" he has brought to life. His first act, treated as narrative ballet in the style made familiar by the Ballets Russes, conformed to the choreographer's known opinion: in Lifar's eagerness to "rehabilitate male dancing", he transformed it into a virtual solo for Prometheus. The second act, on the whole, was more traditional in form. It took place, in the presence of Apollo, on the peristyle of a Doric temple;

LÉGER. COSTUME FOR CRÉATION DU MONDE. 1923.

a succession of ensembles and classical variations introduced Muses, Shepherds and Bacchantes, followed by Pan and Eros. The new ballet was a mixture of styles, but with it Lifar, 24 years of age and with only one previous ballet (*Renard*) to his credit, brought new life to the Opera. Such audacity naturally provoked hostile criticism, but the ballet, in spite of reservations, was a great success with those who saw it as a work capable of reviving the active role which the Paris Opera seemed to have renounced.

CROQUEUSE DE DIAMANTS La. Ballet by Roland Petit and Alfred Adam. Lyrics: Raymond Queneau. Music: Jean-Michel Damase. Scenery and costumes: Wakhevitch. Choreography: Roland Petit. First performance: Ballets de Paris, New York, 31 October 1950. Principal dancers: Zizi Jeanmaire, Roland Petit, Gordon Hamilton.

The authors of this ballet, which is strictly speaking not a ballet at all but a miniature "musical" with songs as well as dancing, were in two minds how to describe it. Anyway, the mixed genre became a favourite of Roland Petit's. A girl gangster, operating with her gang in the Halles quarter of Paris, seduces the boy from the local bistro and fortifies herself with diamonds, which are to her what spinach was to Popeye. A sketchy theme, but the good humour was contagious. The big success was Jean-Michel Damase's music; two of his songs, "la Croqueuse de diamants" and "la Rue Montorgueil", became famous.

CUADRO FLAMENCO. Suite of Andalusian dances. Scenery and costumes: Picasso. First performance: Gaieté-Lyrique, Paris, 17 May 1921 (during season of Diaghilev's Ballets Russes).

Diaghilev became fascinated by Spanish dancing during his wartime visits to the peninsula, when Massine was preparing *Le Tricorne*. Back in Madrid in 1921, he decided to transport some genuine gipsy dancers to dance during the Russian Ballet's seasons in Paris and London. Twelve dancers were invited, including a girl, Maria Dalbaicin, of outstanding beauty, a dwarf, and a legless cripple who danced on his stumps. Picasso designed a special set with a false proscenium, so that the dancers should not

PICASSO. TWO DANCERS. 1925.

look lost on the huge stage, but Stravinsky wisely insisted that the flamenco singing and the guitar music should not undergo any "improvement". The present craze for flamenco music had not started, and the novelty of the proceedings caused a furore in both capitals.

CUEVAS Marquis George de. A fantastic and rather superb character, one of the most popular figures of contemporary ballet. For his own pleasure he runs a company of 45 dancers and takes infinite delight in their performances. Born in Chile of Spanish extraction with a Danish mother, he bears the title of Marquis de Piedra Blanca de Guana de Cuevas. In 1927, he married the granddaughter of John D. Rockefeller. Deeply sensitive and generous, he has the real knack of making people like him: the kisses he dispenses so liberally earned him the nickname of "The kissing Marquis". In 1953, he gave a huge party on Lake Chiberta and was severely reprimanded by *L'Osservatore Romano*, the official organ of the Vatican. Much offended, the Marquis sued for libel. George de Cuevas lives for his ballet company, following it across the world or directing operations by telephone from his apartment in Paris. He also owns a villa in Cannes, a chalet in Austria and an apartment in New York. Astonishingly youthful and dynamic, his finely-drawn features look as though they were engraved on a medal, and he wears the numerous decorations won in the service of art with irreproachable elegance. He has a habit of writing things down as they occur to him in a little school notebook. One of these observations is worth quoting: "The only way to endure the boredom of living is to give one's life to somebody or something." The Marquis de Cuevas has given his to the ballet .

CYDALISE ET LE CHÈVRE-PIED. Ballet in two acts and three scenes. Scenario: G. A. de Caillavet and R. de Flers. Music: Gabriel Pierné. Scenery: Maxime Dethomas. Choreography: Léo Staats.· First performance: Paris Opera, 12 January 1923. Principal dancers: Carlotta Zambelli, Albert Aveline.

The young faun Styrax falls in love with the King's favourite dancer, Cydalise, but the call of the forest proves too strong and lures him back. The theme provided a contrast between sylvan elements — nymphs, dryads, fauns — and the elegant gallantries of the courtiers of Versailles. The dance of the malicious little faun was reminiscent of Fokine's *Daphnis et Chloé*. The court scenes were treated in the manner of Molière's divertissements.

D

DALCROZE Émile-Jacques (1865-1950). He was the inventor of a system of musical education, based on movement and known as "Eurhythmics". He was born in Vienna of Swiss parents and studied music first at the Geneva Conservatoire, then in Paris under Delibes, finally in Vienna under Bruckner. In 1910 he founded an Institute at Hellerau, near Dresden,

which attracted students of all ages and callings: philosophers, singers, men of the theatre and amateurs. Diaghilev and Nijinsky paid some visits there early in 1912 and the influence of Dalcroze was clearly seen in Nijinsky's subsequent works for the Russian Ballet, *L'Après-midi d'un faune, Le Sacre du Printemps* and *Jeux*. Marie Rambert, a Dalcroze pupil, gave lessons to the Diaghilev company and worked with Nijinsky on the *Sacre*. Mary Wigman, Hanya Holm, Fokine, Kurt Jooss, Uday Shan-kar, and Balanchine (at least in the early part of his career) were also, in their various ways, influenced by Dalcroze's teachings.

The system is based on gymnastics, musical theory and the study of rhythm. Dalcroze believed, with reason, that the ear could more easily assimilate the pattern of a phrase of music, and eventually of a whole piece, if the body reproduced it — time, intervals, and even harmonic modulations — in movement. The simultaneous employment of mind and senses led to a rare degree of self-control.

Although the name of Dalcroze is closely linked with the history of the dance during the first half of this century, he never considered the dance as an end in itself, he did not teach technique, and theatrical dancing played no part in his method. Eurhythmics teach dancers more about music than about dancing and indeed are of even greater value to musicians than to dancers. His theories gave rise to bitter controversies and to often mediocre displays by would-be adepts (of whom he himself for the most part disapproved) which did much to discredit him, but the importance of his teaching is now universally recognised.

The Hellerau school was transferred in 1920 to Austria where Dr. Ernst Ferand and Mrs. Christine Baer-Frissell conducted the Hellerau-Laxenburg School until it was closed on the Nazi invasion of Austria in 1938. The thousands of pupils who graduated from this school are now teaching all over the world. Dr. Ferand himself went to the United States. Dalcroze taught at the central school in Geneva until his death but his work has been continued there and Geneva is still the headquarters of the Dalcroze method.

Many ballet schools, including the Royal Ballet School in England, find Dalcroze eurhythmics valuable for developing a dancer's response to music. The method may be studied in his books

SALVADOR DALI. DÉCOR FOR LABYRINTH. BALLET RUSSE DE MONTE-CARLO, 1941.

Rythmique, art et éducation and *Musique, éducation et eurythmie,* written in French but now translated into many languages.

DALE Margaret. One of the first dancers to specialise in the production of ballet for television; formerly a soloist with the Sadler's Wells Ballet. For BBC Television she has directed studio performances by many of the famous companies and dancers of the world, including Ulanova and the Bolshoi Ballet, Fonteyn and the Royal Ballet, the Moiseyev Ensemble, the Chinese Classical Theatre.

DALI Salvador. Born 1904 at Figueras, Catalonia. There is something essentially theatrical about surrealist painting, with its carefully contrived effects and dramatic spacing of objects. But in spite of obvious affinities, the use of surrealist art in the theatre is a risky business. No paint-ings exhibit the advantages and disadvantages of the process more clearly than those of Salvador Dali. They represent a moment petrified, to which the passage of time can add nothing, because any movement robs their oppressive stillness of its mysterious power. Similarly, the substitution of three dimensions for two produces a tangible reality on the stage far less potent than the painted illusion on the canvas. Nevertheless, the temptation to invite Dali to design for the theatre was understandably strong. The result was what one might expect: his décors are at once intriguing, disconcerting, and disappointing. Their effect is instantaneous, but it does not last beyond the first shock.

Dali designed the décors and costumes of two of Massine's ballets for the Ballet Russe de Monte-Carlo, *Bacchanale* (1939) and *Labyrinth* (1941), both produced in New York. He designed *Sentimental Colloquy* and *Mad Tristan* for Ballet International (New York, 1944), and *Café de Chinitás* for Ballet Theatre (Detroit, 1944).

LA DAME A LA LICORNE. REINHOLM, DEEGE AND MLAKAR.

DAMASE Jean-Michel. Born 1928, Paris. During the cold and anxious winter of 1944, Roland Petit was only able to use a piano for his "Soirées de la Danse" in the vast Théâtre Sarah-Bernhardt: his pianist was the sixteen year old Jean-Michel Damase, Premier Prix du Conservatoire and later Grand Prix de Rome (1947). The story goes that hearing the young virtuoso's playing of some Schumann gave Roland Petit the idea of using the music for his Oscar Wilde ballet *Le Rossignol et la Rose*. This early contact with the ballet was successfully followed up: Damase has written the scores for the celebrated *Croqueuse de Diamants* (Ballets de Paris, 1950), *Piège de Lumière* (de Cuevas, 1952) and *Balance à trois* (Babilée, 1955).

DAME A LA LICORNE La. Ballet by Jean Cocteau. Music: Jacques Chailley. Scenery and costumes: Cocteau. Choreography: Heinz Rosen. First performance: Theater am Gärtenplatz, Munich, 9 May 1953. Principal dancers: Geneviève Lespagnol, Veronika Mlakar, Boris Trailine.

Based on the famous tapestries in the Musée Cluny in Paris. The principal characters are the Lady, the Knight and the Unicorn, with a corps de ballet of white unicorns. Cocteau's treatment and staging were, as usual, unconventional. The orchestra played on rostrums at one side of the stage, in full view of the public. His costumes were equally original: the Lady wore an immensely long velvet train of bright scarlet; the Knight rode a lion which formed part of his costume; the Unicorn, by contrast, was dressed in simple white tights with a white mask surmounted by a horn. The whole had something of the controlled, formal violence of the Japanese theatre. The young Veronika Mlakar was a touching Unicorn. The ballet has been restaged for the Ballet Russe de Monte Carlo in America and for the Paris Opera Ballet.

DANILOVA Alexandra. The last link between ballet in the Western world and the tradition of the Russian Imperial Schools, Danilova worked in the Maryinsky Theatre in Leningrad until 1924. At that time she left the Soviet Union with Balanchine and Efimov and was soon engaged by Diaghilev. She became the most noted ballerina of the last years of the Ballets Russes (1925-1929). Her very individual style, her long, agile limbs, her strange Madonna-like face, allowed her to dance any type of role. Not only did she excel in the classical repertoire but she created important roles in ballets as different as *The Triumph of Neptune, Le Pas d'Acier, Apollon Musagète, The Gods go a'Begging* and *Le Bal* From 1932 she danced with de Basil's Ballets de Monte-Carlo until, in 1938, she joined Massine's Ballet Russe de Monte-Carlo where she remained, with few interruptions, until 1952.

The acknowledged queen, the unrivalled interpreter of Massine's ballets, *Le Beau Danube, Gaieté Parisienne, Capriccio Espagnol, La Boutique Fantasque,* throughout this period, she created, in America since the second world war, some important Balanchine ballets, *Danses Concertantes* (1944), and *Night Shadow* (1946). Her fame and popularity in the United States are already legendary. Her dancing in *Swan Lake* and *Coppelia* has been applauded from coast to coast and

BOLM AS THE POLOVTSIAN WARRIOR.

the dazzling characterisation of her Street Dancer in *Le Beau Danube* enchants the public as much today as when she first danced it. More than thirty triumphal years have elapsed since her first *Firebird,* in 1924, on the stage of the old Maryinsky. Alexandra Danilova (Choura to all her friends) is beloved not only by her public but by her colleagues, her pupils (she is a born teacher), and by all stage folk. Her wit and gaiety and her elegance are proverbial. Diaghilev, in the last speech he ever made to his company, complimented them all and said: "It is not possible to kiss you all, and so I will not try. But you, Choura, I still must kiss." He kissed her and departed. Neither Danilova nor the company ever saw him again.

DANCES FROM PRINCE IGOR (Polovtsian Dances). Ballet in one act. Music: Borodin. Scenery and costumes: Nicholas Roerich. Choreography: Michel Fokine. First performance: Diaghilev's Ballets Russes, Théâtre du Châtelet, Paris, 19 May 1909. Principal

ALEXANDRA DANILOVA. LA BOUTIQUE FANTASQUE.

DANCES FROM PRINCE IGOR. DÉCOR BY ROERICH. 1909.

dancers: Sophie Fedorova, Hélène Smirnova, Adolph Bolm.

In the original production of Borodin's opera, *Prince Igor,* at the Maryinsky Theatre, St. Petersburg (4 November 1890) the dances were arranged by Lev Ivanov. But this version was completely eclipsed by Fokine's, which was included in the opening programme of Diaghilev's Ballets Russes in Paris. *The Polovtsian Dances* met with triumphant success, and contributed largely to the sudden fame of Diaghilev's company. When the dancers surged downstage to the footlights, the whole audience sprang to their feet and shouted their enthusiasm. After years of domination by the ballerina, a legacy from the Romantic era, the male dancer was at last superbly restored to his rightful place in ballet.

Productions since 1909 have all been based on Fokine's choreography or have been influenced by it, for neither he nor the designer, Nicholas Roerich, left much scope for their successors. The beauty of the dances, with their roots in the folk-lore of Russia, is derived as much from their expressive qualities as from their animation.

The role of the Chief Warrior is vitally important, yet how few dancers after Bolm, its peerless creator, have been able to dominate the ballet ! Perhaps only Leon Woizikowski, Yurek Shabelevsky and Alexandre Kalioujny have succeeded. The ballet subtly contrasts the savage joy of the victorious warriors with the langour of their captives and the carefree gaiety of the young Polovtsians. Staged or danced indifferently, it becomes a slightly ridiculous illustration of the colourful and evocative score. Although included in the repertoire of many international companies, the *Dances from Prince Igor* are rarely performed within their proper operatic context with chorus and soloist.

DAPHNIS ET CHLOÉ. Dramatic ballet in one act, three scenes. Scenario (after Longus) and choreography: Fokine. Music: Ravel. Scenery and costumes: Bakst. First performance: Diaghilev's Ballets Russes, Théâtre du Châtelet, Paris, 8 June 1912. Principal dancers: Tamara Karsavina, Vaslav Nijinsky, Adolph Bolm.

This ballet seems to have been pursued by bad luck. The scenario was turned down by the Imperial Theatres of St. Petersburg in 1904. Diaghilev liked it and commissioned the music from Ravel for the first season of the Ballets Russes. But the score was not ready until 1912, the year of L'Après-midi d'un faune, and Diaghilev, absorbed by the arrangements for Nijinsky's ballet, lost interest in Daphnis, which was not given until the end of the season, when it failed to make the effect that it deserved. Diaghilev and Fokine were by now on bad terms, and the latter left the company when the season was over. In fact, Daphnis was one of Fokine's finest works. He had treated Longus's story of the pastoral loves of a boy and girl in the groves of Mitylene in a manner reminiscent of Isadora Duncan's "Greek" dances, like them inspired by antique vase paintings. There were also some admirably devised ensembles. It can have been no easy task, for though Ravel's score is one of the finest ever written for ballet, some sections are overlong for dancing.

Ill-luck pursued subsequent Diaghilev revivals as well. Fokine's version was revived at the Paris Opera in 1921, and there have been numerous new versions by other choreographers, notably Lifar (Paris Opera) and by Ashton for Sadler's Wells (Covent Garden, 5 April 1951) with Fonteyn and Somes. John Craxton set the ballet boldly and successfully (except for the anachronistic pirates) in modern Greece. This Daphnis has gradually revealed itself as one of Ashton's finest works, too.

DARK ELEGIES. Ballet in two scenes. Music: Gustav Mahler. Choreography: Antony Tudor. Scenery and costumes: Nadia Benois. First performance: Ballet Club, Duchess Theatre, London, 19 February 1937. Principal dancers: Peggy van Praagh, Maude Lloyd, Agnes de Mille, Antony Tudor, Walter Gore, Hugh Laing. Singer: Harold Child.

There is no story, but an abstract yet intensely human portrayal of grief and bereavement in a

DAPHNIS ET CHLOÉ. DÉCOR FOR ACT II BY BAKST. 1912.

LYCETTE DARSONVAL IN LA TRAGÉDIE
DE SALOMÉ.

simple village community mourning the loss of
its children. Movements and groupings wonderfully convey an agony hardly to be borne and
yet stoically endured until the resignation suggested by the last pages of Mahler's *Kindertoten-
lieder.* Nadia Benois' sombre, stormy backcloths and severe costumes gave the tragedy a
maritime setting.

DARSONVAL Lycette. A devoted pupil of
Zambelli, Lycette Darsonval personifies the
style and *esprit* of the Paris Opera ballet. A
brilliant, lively ballerina, she makes great use of
her feminine seductiveness and smiling coquetry.
Her body is slim, delicate and nervous, her feet
strong, her back muscular. Vivacious and
light, she is always ready to risk the most dangerous feats of skill. To the French public she
typifies "la danseuse", but to English and
American audiences her style seems somewhat
mannered. She was a delicate Oriana in *Oriane
et le Prince d'Amour* with Lifar, then a vibrant
Sylvia and a sincere and feminine Giselle. Pro-

moted to the rank of *étoile* in 1940, she created
the principal role in *Salomé* (1954). Darsonval
has worked outside the Opéra on many occasions. In 1933, she danced in the Doucha
Lesprilova Company; later, she formed her own
troupe with which she toured Europe, North
Africa, and, in 1956, the United States. In 1957
she was appointed Director of the Paris Opera
School of Dance but continues to appear as a
ballerina.

DAVID TRIOMPHANT. Ballet in two
acts and three scenes. Scenario from the *Book
of Kings.* Scenery and costumes: Fernand Léger.
Choreography: Lifar. First performance: Cité
Universitaire, Paris, 15 December 1936, with
music by Debussy and Moussorgsky. Principal
dancer, Mia Slávenska. Revived at the Opéra,
26 May 1937, music by Rieti with rhythms by
Serge Lifar.

A ballet dominated by the principal character,
like Lifar's *Icare, Aeneas,* and *Alexandre le Grand.*
The story of the shepherd David, who slays
Goliath, succeeds Saul as King and marries his
daughter, Melchola. Some of the rhythms in
the composite score were dictated by Lifar to
Rieti who then orchestrated them, a method used
by Lifar on other occasions also. Léger's
décor, in hard and bold colours, gave an
unexpected violence to the work.

DAYDÉ Liane. Étoile at the Paris Opera
since 1950. A Parisian of Moorish descent, she
is small and frail, her doll-like face lit by enormous dark eyes with long eyelashes. Engaged
in the corps de ballet at the age of fourteen, she
was trained by Léo Staats, Carlotta Zambelli and
Blanche d'Alessandri. She created the title role
in *Blanche-Neige (Snow White)* which perfectly
suited her child-like charm, and also Juliet in
Lifar's *Roméo et Juliette* (1955). Although
magnificently trained, Daydé has a tendency to
rather fussy and affected movements; when she
forgets these mannerisms she is capable of fine
performances for she is an accomplished actress
As guest artist with Festival Ballet she danced
Giselle in London (1957) and later appeared in
the same ballet, partnered by Michel Renault, at
the Bolshoi Theatre, Moscow, where she had a
great success.

DEBUSSY Claude (1862-1918). There are few composers whose names occur so frequently in the programmes of dance recitals and yet, in all his varied output, only three works were written expressly for dancing: *Jeux, La Boîte à Joujoux* and *Khamma*. Apart from the piano pieces, whose picturesque titles are fatally attractive to recitalists, some of his larger works have been used many times by choreographers. To take three very dissimilar examples: the *Petite Suite* (in Büsser's orchestration) was one of the "Ballets rythmiques" which Jacques Rouché mounted at the Paris Opera in 1922; the *Three Nocturnes* were interpreted by Loie Fuller with the aid of veils and changing lights; David Lichine used the *Danse Sacrée et Danse Profane* for his *Protée* (de Basil, 1938). Most remarkable of all is the success as ballet music of the short, atmospheric masterpiece *L'Après-midi d'un faune* (see article). Of the works Debussy specifically wrote for ballet, *Jeux* is by far the most distinguished. Whether it is good ballet music is another matter. Nijinsky's original version for Diaghilev (1913) and Borlin's for the Ballets Suédois (1920) have both disappeared. The Ballets Suédois also presented a version of *La Boîte à Joujoux,* a children's ballet written for Debussy's daughter "Chouchou" and orchestrated by Caplet. *Khamma,* commissioned by Maud Allan in 1912, was left unfinished at the composer's death. It was completed and orchestrated by Koechlin, but not performed until 1947. There is far finer music in the mystery play *Le Martyre de Saint-Sébastien,* which d'Annunzio and Debussy wrote for Ida Rubinstein, who performed it at the Paris Opera in 1911.

DÉJEUNER SUR L'HERBE Le. Ballet in one act. Scenario: Irène Lidova. Music: Joseph Lanner, orch. Tcherepnin. Scenery and costumes: Marie Laurencin. Choreography: Roland Petit. First performance: Ballets des Champs-Élysées, 14 October 1945. Principal dancers: Marina de Berg, Nathalie Philippart, Irène Skorik, Jean Babilée, Ethery Pagava, Roland Petit. A slight ballet, remembered now for the youth and freshness of the dancers and the delicacy of the costumes.

DELANNOY Marcel. French composer, born 1908. *Le Fou de la Dame,* an early work (1929), was a mixture of dance and song, in the style of the medieval "chansons de gestes". Delannoy's first real ballet was *Le Pantoufle de vair,* a modern version of the Cinderella story, first produced at Chicago, then in Paris (Opéra-Comique, 1935). The lively score includes a blues and a rumba. Twenty years later came another, and more considerable, fairy-tale ballet. *Les Noces Fantastiques* (Paris Opera, 1955) takes place partly in a harbour, partly under the sea. The contrast is ably reflected in the dramatic and richly orchestrated music.

DELFAU André. A designer with the typically French gift of being simple without being dry. His ballet décors are usually reduced to essentials, with the details standing out clearly against a plain background. The costumes, with their carefully co-ordinated colours, are designed to help the dancers. In fact, Delfau is more concerned to find the correct style for a given ballet than to impose a style of his own.

DELFAU. COSTUME FOR TRAGEDY AT VERONA.

Hence the considerable variety in his décors: *L'Ombre de la nuit* (de Cuevas, 1945); *Sérénade* and *Apollon Musagète* (both Paris Opera, 1947); *Tragedy at Verona* (1950) and *Annabel Lee* (1951) both for de Cuevas, and *Night Shadow* (1954) for the Royal Danish Ballet. His recent designs for *The Sleeping Beauty* (Royal Danish Ballet, Copenhagen, 1957) are among his most interesting. The décors are minutely detailed in the 18th century tradition, but the costumes have a characteristic simplicity.

DELL'ARA Ugo. After studying at the Opera in Rome, he became a leading dancer there in 1939. Since 1946 he has been principal dancer at La Scala, Milan, appearing in *La Follia di Orlando* (Milloss) and *Les Sept Péchés Capitaux* (Charrat). Appointed maître de ballet at La Scala, he created there *Conte d'hiver* (1955), *Lumawig et la flèche* (1956), etc.

DE MILLE Agnes. "This is the story of an American dancer, a spoiled egocentric wealthy girl, who learned with difficulty to become a worker . . ." So begins Agnes de Mille's autobiography *Dance to the Piper,* which she wrote in 1951 after she had worked her way to the top of her profession. With Eugene Loring, Ruth

LES DEMOISELLES DE LA NUIT.
COSTUMES BY LÉONOR FINI. 1948.

Page, and Catharine Littlefield she occupies an important place in the history of American ballet. Like them, she searched for an original style which would blend classical dancing with the rhythms and expressionism of the New World. Through her works, Agnes de Mille helped the American ballet to liberate itself from the traditions that had been imposed in the United States for the preceding twenty years by former collaborators of Diaghilev. She recognised the significance of Martha Graham's work and incorporated many of Graham's discoveries into her choreography. Her ballets often draw their inspiration from American history, folklore or the stuff of everyday American life. In this connection, *Rodeo* (*), *The Harvest According* (*), and *Fall River Legend* (*) are particularly successful.

Born in New York, a niece of the film producer Cecil B. de Mille, she really began her career in London with the Ballet Rambert. There she created roles in Tudor's ballets *Gallant Assembly* (1937), *Dark Elegies* (1937), and *Judgement of Paris* (1938). She also gave concerts of her own dance compositions. Her first ballet was *Black Ritual* for Ballet Theatre (1940), which was danced by a Negro troupe. For Ballet Theatre she also choreographed *Three Virgins and* a *Devil* (1941), *Tally-Ho* (1944), *Fall River Legend* (1948), which is probably her masterpiece, and *The Harvest According*. *Rodeo or The Courting at Burnt Ranch* (first performed in 1942 by the Ballet Russe de Monte-Carlo, after it had emigrated to the United States) made her name. She followed up this success with her ballets in the musical *Oklahoma !,* which helped to change the pattern of musical comedy production in the United States. Among many films and musicals

A white cat, transformed into a woman by the love of a young man, cannot withstand the pull of her natural instincts. She returns to her cat world and in seeking to regain her the young man falls to his death. Léonor Fini's scenery showed an attic hung with newspapers, then a bare bedroom with the window opening to tempting tiles and rooftops, finally *les toits de Paris,* where the young man dies. The costumes and the famous, delicious cat masks,

CURTAIN BY ANDRÉ DERAIN FOR LA CONCURRENCE. 1932.

for which she has staged the dances are *Carousel, Bloomer Girl, Brigadoon*. Agnes de Mille's style is harshly realistic without ever lacking humour and poetry; she is generally more at ease in popular or dramatic scenes than in classical passages and has a tendency sometimes to get out of her depth, for instance in *The Rib of Eve* (Ballet Theatre, 1956).

DEMOISELLES DE LA NUIT Les. Ballet in one act, three scenes. Scenario: Jean Anouilh. Music: Jean Françaix. Scenery and costumes: Léonor Fini. Choreography: Roland Petit. First performance: Ballets de Paris, Théâtre Marigny, Paris, 21 May 1948. Principal dancers: Margot Fonteyn, Roland Petit, Gordon Hamilton.

the sensitive and strange choreography and the evocative music, together with Fonteyn's uncanny realisation of the cat, Agathe, endowed this ballet with an intense atmosphere of feline sensuality.

DENISHAWN. First a school, opened in Los Angeles in 1915 by the newly married Ruth St. Denis and Ted Shawn, then a widespread educational and artistic influence on dancing in the United States, with a company that toured widely at home and visited the Orient in 1925-26. St. Denis and Shawn believed that dance students should be able to learn all forms of movement expression, including ballet, the dances of primitive peoples and the highly developed dance techniques of countries such as Spain, India and Japan. Later, they investigated the German modern dance and from the teaching at Denishawn and the performances of the company grew the first shoots of the American modern dance. These were nurtured and strengthened by the next generation of dancers—all students of Denishawn—Martha Graham, Doris Humphrey, Charles Weidman, Jack Cole, and the composer and conductor, Louis Horst. St. Denis and Shawn separated in 1931 to follow separate paths, but both retained their interest in the cultural and educational aspects of dancing. Shawn now, at Jacob's Pillow in Massachusetts, organises an annual summer festival of dance and dance instruction which he calls the University of the Dance.

DERAIN André. Born Chatou 1880, died Chambourcy 1954. The distinguished painter made his début as stage-designer with *La Boutique Fantasque* (Ballets Russes, 1919). The engagement of Picasso for *Parade* (1917), and of Derain for the above-mentioned ballet marks Diaghilev's desire to enlarge the hitherto almost exclusively Russian basis of the Ballets Russes by the addition of modern French painting. Derain was an apt choice for the transition, for this first contribution was, in spirit at least, closer than it appeared in the style of the Russian designers. Benois in *Petrouchka* and Larionov in *Contes Russes* had adapted the imagery of popular folklore to the stage as Bakst had adapted the style of oriental miniature painting. In *La Boutique Fantasque,* Derain used another form of popular imagery, naive, cheerful, rudimentary, typically French; but he used it with a refinement and a self-consciousness that were also typical of the artistic experiments of the period, when many artists were sugaring the pill of cubism and other recent developments with a deliberate recourse to a style based on popular art. The prestige of the Douanier Rousseau, of primitive art in general and Negro art in particular, are all reflected in *La Boutique Fantasque* which, from the artistic point of view, is a much more original, complex and significant work than it appears today. The story of the toys which come to life for one night was admirably suited to Derain's approach, apparently child-like but in reality very sophisticated. The furniture

painted on the scenery, the "flat" landscape without perspective, the composition on two planes which showed the dancers in such sharp relief, were cunning transcriptions of the traditional style of old-fashioned toy-boxes.

The gentle irony and the entirely personal re-interpretation of a past style, owing nothing to pastiche, was typical of Derain's work for the theatre. So was his ability to make the fashions of the preceding generation look charming rather than ridiculous; in this case Derain prepared the way for the re-habilitation of the 1900's, soon to be completed by Jean Hugo. Derain was to perform similar miracles of inventive re-interpretation in *La Concurrence,* one of the most perfect works of its kind that the modern theatre has produced, and for which he also wrote the scenario; in *Salade,* an evocation of the 18th century commedia dell' arte, and in *L'Épreuve d'amour* with its delicious chinoiserie. It is interesting to observe that Derain's sympathy with the styles of the past never, in his stage designs, betrayed him into the abuse of technical skill which makes some of his easel paintings look like deliberate essays in academicism.

A technical point worth mentioning is his extraordinary gift for designing costumes for

COSTUME BY DERAIN FOR SONGES. 1933.

DESIGNS WITH STRINGS. SIX DANCERS OF THE ROYAL DANISH BALLET.

dancing; each one adding a new and yet harmonious element to the total effect; each one equally satisfying in repose and (far more unusual) in movement. Décors for Diaghilev: *La Boutique Fantasque* (1919), *Jack in the Box* (1926); for the "Soirées de Paris": *Gigues* (1924); for "Les Ballets 1933": *Les Songes, Fastes*; for the Ballets de Monte-Carlo: *La Concurrence* (1932), *L'Épreuve d'amour* (1936). For other companies: *Salade* (Paris Opera, 1935), *Harlequin in the Street* (Sadler's Wells, 1938); *Les Femmes de bonne humeur* (de Cuevas, London, 1949); *Mamz'elle Angot* (Sadler's Wells Ballet, Covent Garden, 1947); *Que le diable l'emporte* (Ballets de Paris, 1948); *Valses* (Opéra-Comique, 1951).

DESIGNS WITH STRINGS. Ballet in one act by John Taras. First performance: Metropolitan Ballet, Edinburgh, 6 February 1948. Principal dancers: Sonia Arova, Svetlana Beriosova, Celia Franca, Erik Bruhn.

Taras's ballet to Tchaikovsky's Trio in A minor, his most successful work up to now, was composed in a style very much influenced by his master, Balanchine. Six dancers, four girls and two boys, group and separate according to the choreographer's inspiration. The combinations of strictly academic steps with the curves imposed by the choreography on the dancers' bodies, the weaving of their arms, created an ebb and flow of movement that was heightened, here and there, with a simple, human gesture. The

ballet originally had an adolescent flavour and a hint of unrequited love, echoed in the music, but the broken circle of friendship soon closed again. Revived subsequently for the Grand Ballet du Marquis de Cuevas, the Royal Danish Ballet and the American Ballet Theatre, *Designs with Strings* reached a wider audience but lost the charm of its first youthful interpreters.

DETHOMAS Maxime. Born 1867, died 1924. A designer who made an important contribution to the French theatre in the first two decades of this century. The work of Dethomas, Piot and Dresa for Jacques Rouché, first at the Théâtre des Arts in Paris in 1910 and later at the Opéra, had an influence comparable to that of the Russians Bilibine and Golovine. Dethomas, with his sober, powerful but essentially traditional designs, accomplished a discreet but far-reaching renovation at a time when the artistic standards of the Opéra had become lax on both sides of the footlights. His output was enormous, and much of his work was anonymous. His most notable décors for the Opéra included: *Goyescas,* and *Sylvia* (1920), *Taglioni chez Musette* (1921), *Impressions de music-hall, Maimouna* (1922), *Cydalise et le Chèvre-pied* (1923).

DEUIL EN 24 HEURES. Ballet in five scenes by Roland Petit. Music: Maurice Thiriet. Scenery and costumes: Clavé. Choreography:

Roland Petit. First performance: Ballets de Paris, Théâtre de l'Empire, Paris, 17 March 1953. Principal dancers: Colette Marchand, Serge Perrault, Hélène Constantine, George Reich.

Clavé's happy décors make even a funeral seem joyful. A young coquette of the "belle époque" loses her husband in a comic duel. Abandoning her room decorated with the portraits of her dead husbands, she drives gaily in a cab to Maxim's to console herself with matchiches and can-can. The dances have irresistible zest and wit and Thiriet's music is a gay, mocking parody. The very "French" style of this ballet has earned it great success abroad as well as in Paris.

DEUX PIGEONS Les. Ballet in three acts. Scenario: Régnier. Music: André Messager. Choreography: Louis Mérante. First performance: Paris Opéra, 18 October 1886.

DETHOMAS. COSTUME FOR IMPRESSIONS DE MUSIC-HALL. *Musée de l'Opéra, Paris.*

In 1919, Aveline produced a new version for Carlotta Zambelli, which was virtually a new work.

Pepio is bored by village life, in spite of his fiancée, Gourouli. A gipsy caravan arrives, and the young man leaves everything to follow one of the girls, Djali. The faithful Gourouli follows him, and finding him disillusioned by life on the road, wins him back. The strength of the ballet lay in the contrasting styles of the two feminine roles, discreet classicism for Gourouli, and rapid, nervous character dances for Djali. A magnificent pas de deux for Gourouli and the gipsy chief was a triumph for Carlotta Zambelli and Albert Aveline. Today, *Les Deux Pigeons* is mainly remembered for Messager's music.

DE VALOIS Dame Ninette. The Director and principal architect of Britain's Royal Ballet, Ninette de Valois, whose real name is Edris Stannus, was born in Ireland in 1898. A shy and introspective child, she once electrified her mother by demanding to dance an Irish jig in the middle of a children's party. This sudden, passionate conviction of her own ability may have been the first pointer towards her future life. Encouraged by her mother, she attended dancing classes, became a child prodigy and claims to have danced *The Dying Swan* on the end of every pier in England. Her training, however, under Lila Field, Espinosa and Cecchetti, was sound and when, in 1923, after a period in pantomimes, revues and opera ballets, she decided to try for the Diaghilev ballet she was at once accepted and soon attained the rank of soloist.

Her interest was aroused not only by the ballets in which she danced, but by the whole organisation and administration of that great company. In those precious years she was equipping herself for the work ahead and when she left Diaghilev in 1925, to open her own school under the ambitious title of Academy of Choreographic Art, it was her professed object to train dancers and choreographers for a British repertory ballet. Such an ambition then seemed absurd, but she maintained a link between her school and the avant-garde theatres of the time by producing ballets and dance dramas (performed by her pupils) at the Abbey

DEUIL EN 24 HEURES. THE DUEL SCENE. DÉCOR BY CLAVÉ. 1953.

Theatre, Dublin, and the Festival Theatre, Cambridge, and also staged opera ballets and dances in Shakespeare's plays at the Old Vic in London. In 1928 she arranged a ballet to Mozart's *Les Petits Riens* which was presented by Lilian Baylis at the Old Vic as a curtain-raiser. In 1931 came a great step forward. Lilian Baylis that year reopened Sadler's Wells Theatre in North London and invited de Valois to transfer her school to within the walls of the theatre and to undertake responsibility for the opera ballets. She envisaged a possibility of presenting occasional full evenings of ballet.

The young company, originally consisting of six girls with de Valois as ballerina, was named the Vic-Wells Ballet. It subsequently became the Sadler's Wells Ballet and ultimately was honoured with the title of Royal Ballet. Thus, by steadfast determination and faith in the potentialities of British ballet, the dynamic young choreographer guided her company to fame.

In the beginning de Valois was obliged to compose nearly all the new ballets herself. Later, the demands of teaching and direction absorbed more and more of her time, for throughout her career she has been intensely concerned with the training of dancers and the

perfecting of an English school. Her first great success was *Job*, a Masque for Dancing (1931), and since then her principal works have been *Création du Monde* (1931), *The Haunted Ballroom* (1934), *The Rake's Progress* (1935), *The Gods go a' Begging* (1936), *Barabau* (1936), *Checkmate* (1937), *The Prospect Before Us* (1940) and *Don Quixote* (1950). Her style reflects her personality: instead of improvising in front of the dancers as is the habit of many choreographers, Ninette de Valois works out every detail in advance and arrives at the rehearsal with a precise plan, notes and drawings. Among her most celebrated works, many have been inspired by paintings or literature and most of the scenarios have been written for her — *Job* (*) (based on Blake's Vision of the Book of Job) by Geoffrey Keynes, *The Rake's Progress* (*) by Gavin Gordon, and *Checkmate* (*) by Arthur Bliss. A born organiser, she has a miraculous gift for making use of ideas which have been submitted to her. Because of their literary content, her ballets tend to contain many character dances. The choreography is often complex, made up of many tiny movements, neat and expressive. Curiously, she seems to have a predilection for composing masculine roles; she has created many of these, but only one feminine role, the Black Queen in *Checkmate*, has been endowed with real life.

A woman of remarkable intelligence and practical common sense, de Valois is a persuasive talker and has great personal charm. She can achieve her objects by logical argument or Irish blarney. She can be alternately exasperating or inspiring, will change her mind three times in five minutes, yet never loses sight of her long-term objective and never forgets loyal service from a colleague.

The recipient of many honours, she is the first to disclaim personal merit and to express gratitude to those who helped her build a national ballet. Her attitude is best expressed in the famous rebuke delivered to the Covent Garden audience one evening when forced, against her will, to take a curtain call. "Ladies and gentlemen", she snapped, "it takes more than one to make a ballet company." Nevertheless, it is doubtful whether, without that one

NINETTE DE VALOIS.

person at its head, the Sadler's Wells Ballet would have prospered so remarkably and so consistently.

In *Invitation to the Ballet* and *Come Dance With Me* de Valois has written, firstly, of her work, secondly of her life. It is significant that she originally planned to call the autobiography *The Tale of a Jig*.

DIAGHILEV Serge de. Pride of place in the marvellous story of modern ballet belongs, not to a dancer or designer, not even to a choreographer, though there has been no lack of exceptional talent in any of these directions, but to the director of a ballet company, a courageous and far-sighted *animateur*, a dilettante of genius, Sergei Pavlovitch Diaghilev. He was born on the 19th March 1872 in the province of Novgorod where his father, an officer in the Imperial cavalry, was garrisoned. Childhood and schooldays were spent in the town of Perm. As a pupil, Diaghilev was already a budding member of the intelligentzia, preferring music to normal studies, and when he came to St. Petersburg as a law-student in 1890, the temptations became correspondingly greater. The city of Peter had a vigorous artistic life and through his cousin, Dima Filosofov, he met a number of young men passionately interested in new, and predominantly Western, ideas. Their leaders were Alexandre Benois and Walter Nouvel, two names which recur again and again in Diaghilev's later life and which were to be intimately associated with the Russian Ballet. Music and the theatre were Diaghilev's main interests now, but after a few unsuccessful attempts at composition he gave up all hope of an active musical career and decided to devote his life to discovering and backing the artistic talents of others. For a young man of twenty-three, this was a bold decision. He explained his point of view in a letter, ironical but revealing, written in 1895 to his stepmother, Mme Panaëv-Diaghilev: "I am, firstly, a charlatan, though rather a brilliant one; secondly, a great charmer; thirdly, frightened of nobody; fourthly, a man with plenty of logic and very few scruples; fifthly, I seem to have no real talent. None the less, I believe that I have found my true vocation—to be a Maecenas. I have everything necessary except money—but that will come !"

With his energy and his self-confidence Diaghilev soon began to assert himself in his new circle. His friends introduced him to fresh spheres of interest and gave him (a provincial among metropolitans) his bearings. They had much to put up with; he was overbearing and a bit of a bully, but they owed it to him and his extraordinary capacity for fighting and overcoming difficulties, and for securing generous financial backing, that some of their dreams came true. Art, though it never altogether superseded music, now became his devouring passion, and 1897 saw the first of a series of admirably arranged exhibitions, in this case watercolours by modern English and German painters. But the task of educating the public, which was to occupy Diaghilev for the whole of his working life, could not be accomplished by exhibitions alone. In association with Filosofov, Nouvel and others, he founded the illustrated review *Mir Isskoustva* (*The World of Art*) which to some extent was a Russian equivalent of the *Yellow Book,* though the scope was wider and the work to be done, especially in the setting of new standards of typography and presentation, far greater. Contributors included the writers Rozanov, Merejkovsky and Soloviov and the painters Serov, Levitan, Korovine, Benois, Somov, Bakst and Golovine, many of them future collaborators in the ballet. The review lasted for six eventful years. Further exhibitions not only brought new developments in Scandinavia and Paris to St. Petersburg and revealed Russian painters of the past and present to their own people (notably in the exhibition of Historic Russian Portraits from 1705 to 1905), but began to attract the attention of Western eyes.

Meanwhile, in 1899, a turning point had been reached in Diaghilev's career with his appointment as special assistant to the new Director of the Imperial Theatres, Prince Serge Volkonsky. Diaghilev's job was to edit the theatre year-book and he did it, typically enough, brilliantly and extravagantly. His downright opinions, fearless originality and sophisticated tastes made him so many enemies that, two years later, he was dismissed. But this contact with the life of the great theatres had shown him where his true path lay and had revealed to him (here the influence of Benois was decisive) the possibilities of ballet as an art-form. Far from discour-

DIAGHILEV BY STRAVINSKY. 1921.

DIAGHILEV BY CHALIAPINE. 1910.

aging him, his dismissal only confirmed his belief in himself. He knew now what he was worth, and his will and energy were equal to his ambition. Of this period Robert Brussel wrote: "To the visitor in Russia, the most striking thing about Diaghilev was the authority he wielded in the most varied circles . . . a *grand seigneur* with the power to charm and persuade. Even his enemies, and God knows they were numerous, were inclined to give way when they felt the force of his personality". Such was Diaghilev on the threshold of his main career: large, handsome, dandified, with a monocle and a white lock in his dark hair which earned him the nickname "Chinchilla"; faithful but demanding to his friends, sure of himself and of his new mission which, since his activities at home were to be limited by official conservatism, was to take the best from Russia and show it to the West.

An opening was at hand, for the success of the portrait exhibition of 1905 was remarked in Paris and the organisers of the new Salon d'Automne offered him generous space in the Grand Palais for a Russian exhibition in 1906. Bakst designed the setting, Benois wrote a historical essay for the catalogue. The success of the exhibition and the support of such influential Parisians as the Comtesse Greffulhe and Missia Edwards (later Mme J.-M. Sert), encouraged Diaghilev to return to Paris each year to show different aspects of Russian culture. In 1907 he organised a series of concerts of Russian music at the Opéra; and in 1908, again at the Opéra, a production of Mussorgsky's *Boris Godounov* with Chaliapine in the title role. But the climax came with the triumphant season of the Ballets Russes at the Châtelet in May and June 1909. The vitality, the novelty and the sheer magnificence of the performances won the Russian Ballet an immediate place among the major achievements of contemporary art. The second season, a year later, was a new triumph.

Such a miracle owed nothing to luck—it was the result of close collaboration between the artists involved, musicians, painters, dancers and

SOLEIL DE NUIT. DÉCOR BY LARIONOV. BALLETS RUSSES, 1915.

LE TRICORNE. DÉCOR BY PICASSO. BALLETS RUSSES, 1919.

choreographers, and the man responsible for this collaboration was Diaghilev himself. The painters were Benois, Roerich, Bakst, Golovine, close friends of his for more than ten years; the musicians, Tcherepnine, Borodin, Glazounov, whose works he had performed at concerts in St. Petersburg and Paris, and Stravinsky, who was his own recent discovery. The dancers came from the Imperial Theatres and were already famous in Russia; Paris and London brought them world renown. Michel Fokine, a young and original choreographer of the new school, as ardent an innovator and reformer as Diaghilev himself, completed the most exceptional company ever seen in the European theatre.

From then on, Diaghilev's life was the Russian Ballet, the twenty years of whose momentous history are retraced in the article *Ballets Russes de Diaghilev*. Restless, curious, always on the alert for new talent and the sudden shifts of the avant-garde, the one thing which Diaghilev abhorred was repetition; he was bound to move away from the predominantly Russian inspiration of his first seasons. "He exchanged his national costumes for something more European, and became a polyglot, an arbiter dominating the artistic destinies of two continents" (R. Brussel). The perilous nature of the task made it all the more attractive to a man of Diaghilev's temperament. In time the influence of Cocteau, whom he met in 1912, his admiration of the painters of the École de Paris, and his determination to be in the vanguard of new artistic movements gradually estranged him from most of his early collaborators, Benois, Bakst and Fokine among them. His violent and imperious character tended to inflate petty squabbles into serious disagreements. But he pressed onwards, refusing to be disconcerted by defections. Nijinsky, for instance, was his great favourite; for more than five years he had watched jealously over his career. But when he heard of his marriage, Diaghilev was so furious that he expelled him forthwith from the company. Similarly, when he learned that Stravinsky, whom he regarded as his "spiritual son", was working for Ida Rubinstein, herself a deserter from the company and now a would-be rival, he was heard to express publicly the hope that "someone would blow up

THAMAR BY P. COLMAN
SMITH. — POSTER BY
MARTY FOR THE BAL-
LETS RUSSES. 1910. —
BENOIS. DIAGHILEV
AT A REHEARSAL OF
PETROUCHKA, 1911.
— PICASSO AND STRA-
VINSKY BY COCTEAU.
— MASSINE, BAKST
AND DIAGHILEV BY
PICASSO. ROME, 1917.

BOURDELLE. NIJINSKY AS HARLEQUIN. 1912. — DIAGHILEV,
STRAVINSKY, PROKOFIEV AT THE PIANO, MASSINE AND
GONCHAROVA BY LARIONOV. — THE HORSE IN PARADE
BY PICASSO. — APOLLINAIRE AND DIAGHILEV BY LARIONOV.
1917.

artists who are still the leaders of modern ballet. After his death, people began to wonder what was the secret of his power, how he had been able to control his various forces so long and so well. Some ascribed to him real creative talent, but they were at a loss to say in what it had consisted. And indeed, though he was neither painter, choreographer nor composer, the sum total of his achievements surely amounted to an act of creation. Others described him as an impresario of genius, but Diaghilev was not concerned with box-office returns and formulas for success; his sole criterion, to which all other considerations were sacrificed, was his sense of what was artistically right. Yet that in itself would not have been enough to sustain him through those momentous twenty years, had he not, as Alexandre Benois has said, also possessed "his speciality — *will-power*". It was only when this dilettante of genius "began to *will,* that things began to happen, to shape themselves and to exist".

those old barracks with their public and their performers who fancy themselves as artists just because they have masses of money to throw about and can afford to buy themselves composers".

After this period of hectic glory came the war with its attendant difficulties and the Russian revolution, which cut him off for ever from his native country. Regular seasons were resumed in London in 1918 and in Paris the following year. Perhaps post-war audiences were a little less enthusiastic, but they never lacked curiosity. There were too many tours, too many quarrels with old friends, too many near-failures. All these, together with the constant strain of devising new ballets to satisfy a fickle public whose snobbishness sometimes recoiled on itself, gradually wore out even this most dynamic and generous of men who, though he loved luxurious surroundings, asked so little luxury for himself. In his last years, absorbed in his new passion for collecting books, Diaghilev even began to lose interest in the ballet. At the end of the London season of 1929 he retired by stages to his beloved Venice, a sick man. He died there, of diabetes, on the 19th August, and was buried in the cemetery of San Michele.

The importance of the part he had played in the running of the company now became brutally apparent; he was irreplaceable. And yet, he left behind him a unique repertoire, and a company containing the best dancers and choreographers of the day — a whole galaxy of

The man and his achievement have never ceased to fascinate. In 1954 Richard Buckle, former editor of the magazine "Ballet" and critic of "The Observer", arranged a comprehensive, imaginative and nostalgic exhibition at the Edinburgh Festival to mark the twenty-fifth anniversary of Diaghilev's death. Later, it was brought to London. Perhaps the last word should be with Jean Cocteau, his associate for nearly twenty years, who wrote for an earlier exhibition (Paris, 1939) "do not forget that this prince of the theatre, this man of splendours, was himself poor. Behind the palace doors, the duns were waiting to pounce on his old, furlined coat. And however much this sublime pauper depended on Maecenases, Diaghilev himself was the real Maecenas . . . those who helped him owe him fortunes still".

DIEU BLEU Le. Ballet in one act. Scenario: Jean Cocteau and Federico de Madrazo. Music: Reynaldo Hahn. Scenery and costumes: Bakst. Choreography: Fokine. First performance: Diaghilev's Ballets Russes, Théâtre du

Châtelet, Paris, 13 May 1912. Principal dancers: Karsavina, Nijinsky.

A ballet in the style of Hindu dancing, made by Fokine after close study of Indian art. Bakst's magnificent décor showed the court of a temple in a tropical forest, surrounded by orange-coloured rocks. In the foreground, garlands of intertwined serpents; at the back, a sky of violent, glowing blue. Giant lotus petals opened to reveal Nijinsky as Krishna, his body painted blue and silver, his costume heavy with pearls and embroidery. In spite of these attractions, the ballet was not a success. The weak link was probably the music: Hahn's delicate talent was not suited to oriental evocations on the grand scale.

DIEUX MENDIANTS Les. See *Gods go a'Begging, The.*

DIGNIMONT André. Born Paris, 1891. A French painter of pretty women, with a sentimental tenderness for the charm of the "grisettes" and for the feminine fashions of the second half of the 19th century so prettily displayed in the coloured plates of the "Magasin des Modes", in the comedies of Labiche, and echoed in the music of Chabrier. He gives us the elegance and luxury of stuffed satin furniture, crinolines, silk fringes and pompons, without the tedious pomposity of the period. His affectionate approach is similar to Derain's, but his designs are less precise and his colours softer. He payed the way for the rehabilitation of the fashions of the 1900's. Décors for the Paris Opera: *Namouna* (1934), *La Grisi* (1935), *Suite en blanc* (1943), *Guignol et Pandore* (1944), *La Grande Jatte* (1950).

DIVERTIMENTO No. 15. See *Caracole.*

DOBOUJINSKY (or Dobuzhinsky) Mstislav. Born Novgorod, 1875, died New York, 1957. To the end of his working life, Doboujinsky remained a link with the early days of the Russian Ballet. In the early years of the century he had been a contributor to Diaghilev's review *The World of Art* in St. Petersburg, and had worked for the Moscow Art Theatre. For the Ballets Russes he designed *Papillons* (1912) and *Midas* (1914). Unlike other Russian designers in exile, such as Benois, Goncharova and

LE DIEU BLEU. COSTUME BY BAKST. 1912.

Larionov, who have been influenced by international styles, traditional or contemporary, Doboujinsky in his subsequent career remained obstinately faithful to Russian folklore and to the sumptuous style of Diaghilev's first ballets. Less refined than Benois and less spectacular than Bakst, Doboujinsky compelled respect for his knowledge, skill and solid achievement. Besides the two ballets for Diaghilev mentioned above he designed: *The Fairy Doll* for Pavlova (1915); *The Sleeping Beauty, Harlequinade* and *Raymonda* (1934) for the Lithuanian Ballet; *Coppélia* for the Ballets de Monte-Carlo (1935); *Casse-Noisette* for Sadler's Wells (1937); *Ballet Imperial* for the American Ballet (1941); *Danses Polovtsiennes* for the Paris Opera (1949); *Le Prisonnier du Caucase* for de Cuevas (1951); *Coppelia* for Ballet Rambert (1957).

DOLIN Anton. His real name is Patrick Healey-Kay; he was born in Sussex, but he is of Irish descent and unmistakeably Irish temperament.   He had intended to be an actor but, under the guidance of Seraphine Astafieva, became a dancer instead.   He danced in the corps de ballet in Diaghilev's ill-fated revival of *The Sleeping Princess* (London, 1921).   Two years later he was re-engaged by Diaghilev as a soloist. Watching him perform acrobatic exercises in the rehearsal room at Monte Carlo, Cocteau conceived the idea of a ballet about the modern craze for sport; the result was Nijinska's *Le Train Bleu,* with Dolin in the rôle of Beau Gosse.   In *Les Fâcheux,* he had a spectacular solo on his points. But the "beau gosse" soon showed that, though he has never underrated these qualities, there was more to him than brilliance and showmanship.   With his clean, virile attack, his faultless precision and his admirable partnering, he became a very fine dancer indeed, excelling particularly in the older classics and in modern works.

He left the Ballets Russes in 1925, rejoining before the end; in the interval, he formed a small company with Vera Nemchinova.   After Diaghilev's death Dolin, together with Alicia Markova, appeared in London with the Camargo Society (for which he created the rôle of Satan in *Job,* 1931) and danced leading roles with the Vic-Wells Ballet.   From 1935 to 1937 'hese two young but already famous and experienced dan-

DOLIN WITH NATHALIE KRASSOVSKA IN GISELLE.

cers led their own company, the Markova-Dolin Ballet.   Subsequently he crossed the Atlantic to play a leading part in the foundation of the American Ballet Theatre, for which he created the title-rôle in Fokine's *Bluebeard.*   Since 1950, his abundant energies have been chiefly devoted to the successful foundation of yet another company, London's Festival Ballet, of which he is artistic director as well as leading dancer.

As a choreographer, his solo version of Ravel's *Bolero* and his popular reconstruction of the famous *Pas de quatre* of 1845 have overshadowed more ambitious creations.   One of the most articulate of dancers, Dolin has written two books of memoirs, *Divertissement* and *Ballet-go-round,* and a biography of Markova.   He is an excellent teacher and has generously coached younger dancers, among them Kriza, Gilpin and Blair.

DOLLAR William.   Born in St. Louis, Missouri, Dollar is one of that first generation of American classical dancers, trained entirely in America, who took their places in the world ballet scene in the period 1939-42.   A disciple of Balanchine, from whom he learned style and principles of choreography, without surrender-

ANTON DOLIN BY MAURICE TASSART.

ing his own personality, he has been at the heart of ballet development in America during the last twenty years. As a dancer, he created roles as diverse as the Joker in Balanchine's *Card Game* and the cavalier in *Ballet Imperial*. As a choreographer he is the author of *Five Gifts* (Ballet International 1943), *Constantia* (*) (1944) and *Le Combat* (*) (1948) which was commissioned by Roland Petit. Maître de ballet of Ballet Society in 1946 and the Grand Ballet du Marquis de Cuevas in 1948, Dollar now devotes most of his time to teaching.

DOUBROVSKA Felia. Trained in the Imperial School at St. Petersburg and a fellow graduate, in 1913, of Olga Spessivtseva, Doubrovska typified the classical dancer of adagio and elevation. Her développés, her running steps and leaps were all of great beauty. Despite these gifts, however, her career was not spectacular and when she left Russia in 1920 she was only a second soloist. Engaged forthwith by Diaghilev, she became one of the most devoted servants of his company and remained until its dissolution in 1929. She appeared in a great variety of ballets, for example *Les Noces* and *Les Biches,* but it was not until the arrival of Balanchine and the trumphs of his early ballets that her special qualities were appreciated—her slender body, her long but supremely delicate legs, supple torso and proud head, with its fine but strong features. If it was Massine's *Ode* which brought her first to the attention of the general public, it was *Apollon Musagète* and, above all, *Le Fils Prodigue* (1929) which displayed her cat-like grace and the incomparable beauty of her line. A worthy partner to Lifar, she yielded nothing to him in her dramatic dances and was an unforgettable Temptress in *Le Fils Prodigue*. This success was the summit of a career which she continued, after the death of Diaghilev, in Anna Pavlova's company. She appeared as ballerina in *Orpheus in the Underworld* which Balanchine staged at the Théâtre Mogador in 1933 and in 1938-49 she was principal dancer at the Metropolitan Opera House, New York. Now teaching at the School of American Ballet, she is loved and revered by the young generation of American dancers.

DRAMMA PER MUSICA. Ballet by François-Michel. Music: J. S. Bach. Scenery and costumes: Cassandre. Choreography: Lifar. First performance: Nouveau Ballet de Monte-Carlo, 2 May 1946. Principal dancers: Yvette Chauviré, Alexandre Kalioujny, Edmond Audran, Boris Trailine.

Lifar's first important ballet outside the Paris Opera. Based on a secular Cantata by Bach, written in honour of the Queen of Saxony. Lifar's austere choreography was in perfect harmony with the music; a little mannered, with subtle parodies of 18th century court dances. Cassandre's décor, derived from 17th century treatises on mathematical perspective, set pure line against a sepia background; the costumes, in beige and brown, were equally severe. The theme of the ballet was explained in a spoken prologue: a noble Lady persuades her lover to return from hunting and rejoin her. Yvette Chauviré as the Lady had one of her great triumphs: her noble, measured style and the precision of her arabesques were perfectly suited both to the choreography and the décor. *Dramma per Musica* was subsequently revived at the Paris Opera (28 June 1950) but immediately withdrawn following a disagreement between Cassandre and the management.

DOUBROVSKA IN LE FILS PRODIGUE.

LA PÉRI. MARGOT FONTEYN AND MICHAEL SOMES.

DRESA Jacques. Born 1869, died 1929. Drésa, Piot and Dethomas were the faithful collaborators of Jacques Rouché, first at the Théâtre des Arts (1910), later at the Paris Opera, when Rouché was engaged in a complete renovation of the artistic side of the productions. Dethomas contributed a powerful sense of form and design; Drésa's gifts were of a lighter nature, with greater fantasy; he was ideally suited to recreate the elegant artificiality of 18th century court spectacles, hoop skirts and powdered wigs, formal gardens and beauties disguised as goddesses, all done without the slightest suggestion of pastiche. His tasteful and pleasing designs brought fresh life to the Opéra and helped to prepare the public for later, and more drastic, innovations. His large output included the following ballets: *Le Sicilien* (1910), *Les Aveux Indiscrets* (1912) for the Théâtre des Arts; *Castor et Pollux* (1919) and *L'Écran des jeunes filles* (1929) for the Paris Opera.

DUDINSKAYA Nathalie. A pupil of Vaganova, trained in the Leningrad school, Doudinskaya was first noticed in 1931 and became in a very short time one of the great Soviet ballerinas. Of medium height and rather thin, nothing at first distinguishes her; but she has all the fine qualities of Russian dancers, beautiful ports de bras, remarkable speed and ballon. No matter how dizzy the speed of her dance, nor how complicated the steps, she remains precise, light and undismayed. She has an expressive body and her gifts as an actress have enabled her to excel as much in ballets of strong sentiment *(Laurencia)* as in those of simple lyricism *(The Bronze Horseman, Cinderella)*.

DUEL The. See *Le Combat*.

DUFY Raoul (1877-1953). Dufy's contribution to the theatre is by no means so outstanding as one might expect from the exceptional charm, skill and wit of his painting. It is true that he was never asked to design a work really worthy of his talent, but it is also true that his style of painting, in which the effect of improvisation is deliberately calculated, is very difficult to transfer to the stage. The very essence of stage design lies in the constant modifications caused by the movement of the actors and the changes in the lighting. Under these conditions, Dufy's exquisitely balanced washes of colour and calligraphic suggestions appear little more than charming, superficial decoration. Moreover, the predominant blues in his palette are a disadvantage: blue on the stage tends to look grey unless it is very strongly lit. Nevertheless the charm of his décors was certainly considerable; coming from anyone less distinguished, they would have seemed remarkable. Beside the décor for *Le Bœuf sur le toit* (Comédie des Champs-Élysées, 1920), Dufy designed scenery and costumes for three ballets: *Frivolant* (Paris Opera, 1922), *Beach* (Ballets de Monte-Carlo, 1933), *Epsom* (de Basil, 1938).

DUKAS Paul. Born 1865, died 1935. Two major works in the slender output of this distinguished French composer have served as ballet music, with unequal success. They are: *L'Apprenti Sorcier* (1897), one of his first compositions, and *La Péri* (1912), one of his last. *L'Apprenti Sorcier* is universally known as a symphonic poem. In spite of the colour and rhythmic vitality of the score, it has never won as a ballet (the first version was given at St. Petersburg in 1916) the success of *La Péri*. This work, described by Dukas himself as a "poème dansé", was contemporary with Florent Schmitt's *Tragédie de Salomé*, Vincent d'Indy's *Istar* and Ravel's *Daphnis et Chloé*; it is a typical product of that opulent period, and of the first years of the Russian Ballet. *La Péri* would have been danced by them if Dukas and Diaghilev had been able to agree about the principal dancer; the composer wanted Trouhanova, to whom he had dedicated the work. Nevertheless, the luscious score has taken its place in various choreographic versions in the repertory of more than one distinguished company, including the Paris Opera and the Royal Ballet of Great Britain.

DUKELSKY Vladimir (Vernon Duke). A remarkable case of a composer, Russian by birth (1903) and training, who found his musical salvation in the American idiom. His first ballet, *Zéphire et Flore* (Diaghilev's Ballet Russe, 1925) was neo-classical in style, half waybe tween Rachmaninov and Stravinsky. At that time, Dukelsky was only 22 and had just arrived from Russia. Shortly afterwards, he decided to settle in the States, where he changed his name to Vernon

Duke and became a well known composer of light music for films and revues. Two later ballets, *Jardin public* (de Basil, 1935) and *Le Bal des Blanchisseuses* (Ballets des Champs-Élysées,

ISADORA DUNCAN BY JOSÉ CLARA. 1927.

1946) both of which were largely based on jazz, showed that the transformation had been successfully accomplished.

DUNCAN Isadora. As a small child, Isadora would dance while her mother played the piano or recited poems. At six, she conducted her first school of dance, gathering together the neighbours' children, even infants, and teaching them arm movement. By the time she was ten

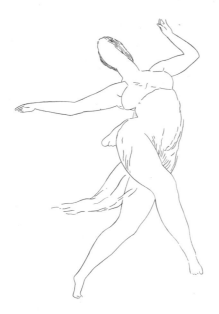

ISADORA DUNCAN BY DUNOYER DE SEGONZAC.

but I cannot explain it". It is not surprising that the schools she founded in Russia, France and America, did not survive after her death. She conveyed her ideal through example, stimulating poets, painters and musicians, dancers and choreographers, among them Fokine. "I didn't invent dance", she said. "It existed before me, but it was sleeping and I woke it up". She also said that all the crucial events of her life had taken place by the sea, and it was by the sea (at Nice), that she died, strangled by a scarf which had caught in the wheel of the car in which she was driving.

DUNHAM Katherine. The Afro-American dancing of Josephine Baker and the revue "Blackbirds" startled Europe after the First World War; Katherine Dunham, with an entertainment based on the living traditions of the Carribean Negroes had something of the same effect after the Second. Dunham, who directed her own company, is not only a dancer but a trained anthropologist, with a degree from the University of Chicago. Theory backed by experience

she had so many pupils that she gave up gradeschool and with her sister Elizabeth gave dance lessons in the wealthiest families of San Francisco. She herself took classes in classical dance — an early photograph shows her on points and in tights. But she did not suffer academic constraint very long; she became interested in the theories of Delsarte as taught by Genevieve Stebbins (who danced in a Greek tunic before a curtain and copied her poses from classical statuary), and put her ideas into practice at some recital performances. Finding, however, that she could not express herself freely even in her own recitals without causing a scandal, Isadora boldly left for Europe where she gave free rein to her whims and to her instinctive talent.

For Isadora Duncan, Nature was the great teacher. She believed that the human body should pattern itself on the undulations of the wind, the sea, and the clouds, guided by the movement of breathing and the rhythms of the heart. All this was rather vague; Irma Duncan, one of her disciples and spiritual daughters, describes Isadora's failure to analyse one of her dances in front of a class: "It is strange", she exclaimed, "I created it and can dance it any time,

KATHERINE DUNHAM.

enabled her to bring Voodoo rites and Haitian dances to the stage without losing any of their frenzied, sensuous spontaneity. *Shango* (first performed at the Théâtre de Paris, 1948), the sacrifice of the White Cock to the God Yoruba, is based on ceremonies still current in the West Indies; *Bahiana,* one of her greatest successes, is a dance of seduction from Bahia, in which a fisherman brings back a wife at the end of a rope. *L'Ag'ya* and *Rites du Passage* are dance dramas based on authentic material gathered in primitive communities, but *Nostalgia, Blues, Flaming Youth* and *Ragtime* are concerned with the pursuits of Negroes living in the industrialised cities of the twentieth century. Katherine Dunham, aided by the brilliant décors of her husband John Pratt, and by some marvellously expressive dancers—Vanoye Aikens, Lenwood Morris, Eartha Kitt, Tommy Gomez, Lucille Ellis, Richardena Jackson—recreated the ritual atmosphere of the dances of possession, war and love from Cuba, Mexico or the Martinique, and contrasted them with the enchantments of Harlem. In recent years she seems to have lost the secret of this subtle blending of knowledge and theatrical instinct which made her immediate post-war seasons so irresistible, but their impact still exerts an influence as do her films, notably *Cabin in the Sky* (1940), *Carnaval of Rhythm* (1942) and *Stormy Weather.*

DUTILLEUX Henri. French composer, born 1916. Dutilleux studied at the Paris Conservatoire and was awarded the Premier Grand Prix de Rome shortly before the war, in 1938. His career as a composer, therefore, did not really begin until 1945. In spite of a comparatively small output, he has won a place among the most important young modern French composers. His music for Roland Petit's ballet *Le Loup* (Ballets de Paris, 1953), severe but expressive, was one of the chief factors in the work's success.

DYNALIX Paulette. A lively brunette with twinkling eyes and a merry wit, Paulette Dynalix, a pupil of Carlotta Zambelli and a première danseuse at the Paris Opera since 1942, sparkles with intelligence and gaiety. She has danced a large number of roles (including Giselle at the age

of 19) but there is one, above all, which she has made her own, although it is played *en travesti* and entirely in mime. This is Franz in the ballet *Coppelia,* the booby who prefers a doll to his pretty fiancée. In recent years she has given more time to teaching and is understandably popular with her young pupils.

E

ÉCUYÈRE L'. Ballet by Constantin Nepo. Music: Joseph Kosma. Scenery and costumes: C. Nepo. Choreography: Lifar. First performance: during an Yvette Chauviré recital, Paris, Salle Pleyel, 21 February 1948. Principal dancers: Chauviré, Michel Renault, Guylaîné, Max Bozzoni.

CHAUVIRÉ AND RENAULT IN L'ÉCUYÈRE.

EGK Werner. One of the leading German composers of the middle generation, born 1901. From 1936-41 conductor at the Berlin State Opera. Director of the Hochschule für Musik, 1950-53. Now lives in his native Bavaria. Egk's most important works have been written for the theatre (opera and ballet), for which his style, vigorous, direct, clear-cut and unproblematic, is eminently suited. Of his four ballets, the most considerable are the large-scale works *Joán de Zarissa* (Paris Opera, 1942), which has an important part for the chorus, and *Abraxas* (Munich State Opera, 1948; new version Berlin Municipal Opera, 1949). Two short ballets followed: *Ein Sommertag* (Berlin Municipal Opera, 1950) and *Die Chinesische Nachtigall* (Munich State Opera, 1953).

EGLEVSKY André. Trained in Paris by Volinine and in London by Nicholas Legat, Eglevsky made his début at the age of 14 and with the rank of premier danseur in the company of Colonel de Basil. At 19, in René Blum's Ballets de Monte-Carlo, he won an immense success with his interpretation of the fiancé in *L'Épreuve d'Amour* (1936). After appearing as principal classical cavalier with all the big companies in America for some ten years, he returned triumphantly to Europe in 1946 with Ballet Theatre, dancing in *Helen of Troy,* and in 1947 with the Grand Ballet du Marquis de Cuevas, dancing not only in *Giselle* and *Le Lac des Cygnes* but also in *Tristan Fou* by Massine and Dali. Towards the end of 1950 he danced with the New York City Ballet in the great classical pas de deux (with Maria Tallchief) and created a leading role in *Scotch Symphony.* He has remained with that company with few interruptions ever since. Eglevsky is tall and heavily built, but possesses a remarkably soft and supple technique, a catlike grace and an exceptional jump. His slow, controlled pirouettes are inimitable. He is a strong and reliable partner and has an endearing, easy charm on the stage. Inheriting the Russian schooling of the Imperial Ballet, he is one of the great classical dancers of today. He is also a fine teacher.

EGOROVA Lubov. Trained in the Imperial Ballet School of St. Petersburg, and a contemporary of Fokine (they both graduated in 1898), Egorova was immediately engaged at the Mary-

JOAN DE ZARISSA. COSTUME BY YVES BRAYER. 1942.

insky as a coryphée, a most unusual honour. Her progress was rapid and her triumphs in *Giselle, Raymonda, La Belle au Bois Dormant* and above all as Odette-Odile in *Le Lac des Cygnes* were such that she received the title of ballerina in 1914. The grave, almost severe beauty of her face, her technique which stressed lyricism and expression rather than with virtuosity, her perfect arabesque and her eloquent adagio earned her much success. She left Russia after the Revolution and joined Diaghilev in London in October 1921 to dance the role of the Princess Aurora in *The Sleeping Princess.* In 1923 she opened her school of dance in Paris to which she has devoted herself ever since. In 1937-38 she undertook the artistic direction of the Ballets de la Jeunesse, a company of twenty young dancers led by Jean Weidt. Most of the troupe came from Egorova's studio, among them Geneviève Moulin, Tatiana Leskova, George Skibine and Youly Algaroff.

ÉLÉMENTS Les. Ballet in one act. Music: J. S. Bach (Suite in B Minor). Scenery and costumes: Dimitri Bouchêne. Choreography: Fokine. First performance: Ballets de Monte-Carlo, direction R. Blum, London, 24 June 1937. Principal dancers: Nini Theilade, Igor Youskevitch.

A romantic allegory based on the recurring patterns of nature, culminating in the apotheosis of Zephyr and Flora. Both the scenery of Bouchêne, suggesting an open-air theatre, and the choreography of Fokine helped to create a formal and dignified atmosphere reminiscent of the elaborate productions in favour at the beginning of the 18th century.

ELFES Les. Ballet in one act. Music: Mendelssohn (Overture to *A Midsummer Night's Dream,* second and third movements of Violin Concerto). Scenery: Visconti. Costumes: Mme Vialet. Choreography: Fokine. First performance: Ballet Fokine, Metropolitan Opera, New York, 26 February 1924.

Les Elfes may be considered as a pendant to Fokine's earlier and more famous essay in pure dancing, *Les Sylphides.* Chopin's music had inspired diaphonous visions of a romantic dreamworld. Mendelssohn's, the best fairy music ever written, suggested a different kind of romanticism, earthier and tinged with humour, for the elves and sprites of Shakespeare's "wood near Athens". Fokine had already produced a ballet based on the *Dream* in St. Petersburg in 1906: Nijinsky was one of the elves. Unlike *Les Sylphides, Les Elfes* never became a classic, but it was twice revived by the Ballets de Monte-Carlo: in 1937, under Fokine's direction, at Monte Carlo itself, and again in the United States during the 1942-43 season, with Mia Slavenska and Igor Youskevitch. (A rather unconvincing version, with new scenery and costumes by Goncharova, was presented by the "Théâtre d'Art du Ballet" at Monte Carlo, 2 February 1957.)

ELVIN Violetta. Born in Moscow as Violetta Prokhorova and trained at the Bolshoi school, she came to England in 1945 with her first husband, the writer Harold Elvin, whose name she has kept. She danced with the Sadler's Wells Ballet from 1946 to 1956, much loved for her charm and warm, Slav personality. Her pale expressive face, framed in rich black hair, her aristocratic technique, most moving in adagio, and above all her eloquent ports de bras made her a fine interpreter of the great classical roles: Odette-Odile, Princess Aurora and Giselle.

ENTRE DEUX RONDES. Scenario and music: Marcel Samuel-Rousseau. Scenery and costumes: Nadine Landowski. Choreography: Lifar. First performance: Paris Opera, 24 April 1941. Principal dancers: Solange Schwarz, Serge Lifar.

In one of the rooms in the Louvre devoted to sculpture, a Degas dancer comes to life and flirts with the marble Apollo. When the museum attendant comes back on his round, everything returns to normal. A charming divertissement for two principals and a group of young coryphées who surround the ballerina. The ballerina role is technically demanding as it involves a mixture of classical style, near-acrobatics and the exaggerated positions caught in the paintings of Degas.

ÉPREUVE D'AMOUR L'. Ballet in one act. Scenario: André Derain and Michel Fokine. Music: Mozart. Scenery and costumes: Derain. Choreography: Fokine. First performance: Ballets de Monte-Carlo, 4 April 1936. Principal dancers: Vera Nemchinova, André Eglevsky, Helen Kirsova.

The score upon which this ballet is based has a curious history; although written by Mozart for a Carnival in 1791, it was only rediscovered in 1928. The ballet roughly follows the theme suggested by the composer. An avaricious and bitter Chinese Mandarin wishes to marry off his daughter to a rich ambassador; but she is in love with a penniless young man. The latter, with the help of his friends, temporarily steals the wealth of his rival. When the ambassador recovers his riches, it is already too late; the mandarin has resigned himself to the marriage. As the nuptial procession moves away, butterflies and monkeys dance around the mandarin; he understands at last that only greed separates men and animals. Derain's décor was a witty modern adaptation of those paintings *à la chinoise* which were so popular in the 18th century, while

Fokine's choreography was full of felicitous touches.

"There are very few ballets which have the subtle wit and refinement of this production", wrote Cyril Beaumont after the London première. "It has the fragrance of a blend of rare Pekoe, in which every ingredient is rightly proportioned and combined." To the personal triumphs of the leading dancers, must be added the remarkable performance of Anatole Oboukhov as one of the three Strangers.

ESCUDERO Vincente (b. circa 1889, Valladolid). Considered the greatest flamenco dancer ever to appear on the stage, Escudero is a true Castillan, haughty and austere, violent both in his loves and hatreds. He has been dancing since the age of ten, when he used to stow away on the Spanish railways so as to dance from village to village. Later, he danced on all the stages of the world, alone or with Carmita Garcia. He partnered Argentina in *El Amor Brujo.* Exceptionally articulate among dancers, he is able to explain his own theory and practice clearly, both in words and diagrams. His exacting *Decalogue,* for instance, lists the true principles of flamenco. He abhors "the effeminate, the mechanical, the academic", and protests violently against "ridiculous, spineless little dances": the true flamenco is a dance of "fire and bronze", overflowing with natural force. Unlike many dancers, Escudero never exploits folklore for cheap personal success, but devotes all his genius to presenting the dances his of country in their purest form. His haughty, graceful gestures are almost liturgical in their solemnity. His poised and responsive body, his infinitely varied *zapateados,* the snapping of his fingers, the brief crack of his knuckles on wall or table, all these recreate on the stage the rhythms of his native Spain, while the sinuous movements of his hands and arms, recalling the *mudras* of India, transport the spectator to the heart of gipsy dancing and to the deep nostalgia of all wandering tribes.

ESMERALDA La. Ballet in three acts, five scenes. Scenario and choreography: Jules Perrot. Music: Cesare Pugni. Scenery: W. Grieve. Costumes: Mme Copère. First perform-

ESCUDERO BY CAPULETTI.

ance: London, Her Majesty's Theatre, 9 March 1844. Principal dancers: Carlotta Grisi, Jules Perrot. Revived St. Petersburg, 21 December 1848, with Fanny Elssler.

Although not as popular as *Giselle* and *La Sylphide, La Esmeralda* is one of the few ballets of the romantic period to remain in the repertory. It is a large scale *ballet d'action* inspired by Victor Hugo's *Notre-Dame de Paris,* in which dancing is relegated to occasional divertissements: in the first act, the "Cour des Miracles"; in the second, a fête at the castle; in the third, the rescue of Esmeralda from execution. Perrot's formula for the choreography fits the melodramatic immensity of the subject: a large number of first-rank dancers, an impressive corps de ballet, and a lion's share for the ballerina. Carlotta Grisi, the first to dance the role, made Esmeralda a delicate and pathetic figure. Fanny Elssler, on the other hand, showed her as seductive and sensual. Indeed, this was Elssler's greatest role and she chose it for her sensational farewell performance at the Bolshoi Theatre in Moscow (14 March 1851) when more than 300 bouquets were thrown on to the stage. But Perrot came up against censorship difficulties in Russia. The subject was regarded as suspect and the ending was altered on the instruction of Czar Nicholas I.

The completely revised version by Marius Petipa, produced in St. Petersburg in 1886, was a triumph for Mathilde Kschessinska, its first interpreter. Another great Russian ballerina,

Spessivtseva, established her reputation in the role of Esmeralda; when she first danced the part (1918), both the audience and her partner were moved to tears. Petipa's version remains, in general outline, the one still played in Russia, Soviet audiences being partial to these grandiose and rather old-fashioned spectacles. It is interesting to note that Perrot's version was never included in the repertoire of the Paris Opera; the only performance ever given in France took place at the Théâtre de la Porte Saint-Martin (1856) with Maria Scotti in the title role. In 1956 the Parisian public saw an astounding and dazzling Esmeralda, the Soviet dancer Eleanora Vlassova, who appeared in a production by V. Bourmeister, after Petipa, presented by the Moscow Stanislavsky Ballet. (Only the second act was given; the music was by Drigo.)

London's Festival Ballet is the only company outside Russia to include *Esmeralda* in its repertoire. Presented originally as a full-length ballet, it has now been condensed to a one-act divertissement. (Choreography: Beriosoff. Décor: Nicholas Benois. First performance: Festival Hall, London, 15 July 1954. Principal dancers: Krassovska, Gilpin, Briansky, Wright, Dolin, Beckett.)

ETCHEVERY Jean-Jacques. Born in Paris, he studied with Lydia Karpova, Nicholas Zverev and Gustave Ricaux. From 1940 to 1944, danced with the Nouveaux Ballets de Monte-Carlo and composed the choreography of several ballets, among them *La Péri* by Dukas. Shortly after the Liberation, he directed the "Compagnie de l'Oiseau Bleu" for which he produced a number of ballets, including *La Bourrée Fantasque* (Chabrier). Appointed maître de ballet at the Paris Opéra-Comique, he choreographed *La Chanson du Mal aimé, Ballade de la Geôle de Reading* (*), and other works. In several ballet films made for American Television, Etchevery showed a great interest in production and stagecraft, a taste which he later indulged on becoming maître de ballet at the Théâtre Royal de la Monnaie, Brussels (December 1953). After some charmingly stylised works based on nineteenth-century paintings and engravings *(Les Bals de Paris, Manet, Opéras-ballets)* he was, in 1956, given the title of producer as well as choreographer. In *The Miraculous Mandarin*

(Bartok) and *Le Masque de la mort rouge* he invented a distinctive neo-expressionist style. His masterpiece remains *Pelléas et Mélisande* (*), first produced at the Enghien Festival in 1953.

ÉTRANGE FARANDOLE L'. Ballet in four movements. Music: Shostakovitch (first symphony). Scenery and costumes: Matisse. First performance: Ballets de Monte-Carlo, Monte' Carlo, 11 May 1939. Principal dancers: Alicia Markova, Igor Youskevitch, Nathalie Krassovska, Frederic Franklin. Originally called *Rouge et Noir*, later *L'Étrange Farandole*. In America, the first title was resumed.

A symbolic ballet about the fate of Man and Woman, caught between spiritual and material forces, ultimately condemned to solitude. The action was obscure but also unimportant; the real and considerable interest lay in Massine's remarkable transposition of music into movement by means of bewilderingly rich and varied choreography. He was greatly assisted by Matisse's simple but extremely telling costumes: tights of various contrasting colours: red, yellow, blue and black. The Man and the Woman, by contrast, were dressed entirely in white. The pattern of their movements, weaving through the constantly changing groups of the large corps de ballet over forty strong, formed a visual equivalent to the development of the music. The total effect was solemn and powerful, like a moving fresco. It was one of Massine's most important ballets, a worthy successor to *Seventh Symphony* and *La Symphonie Fantastique*. *L'Étrange Farandole* has never been danced in England, but was much admired in the United States.

ÉTUDE. Choreographic composition by Bronislava Nijinska. Music: J. S. Bach. Scenery and costumes: Boris Bilinsky. First performance: "Opéra Russe à Paris", Théâtre des Champs-Élysées, 27 January 1931.

One of the first "abstract" ballets. Bilinsky designed a back-drop of a night sky of stars with the signs of the Zodiac. The dancers, in pale blue tunics with great wing-like capes, moved in majestic architectural patterns, interrupted by a pas de quatre and two brief solos, a Bourrée and a Minuet. Nijinska planned this

LES FÂCHEUX. DÉCOR BY GEORGES BRAQUE. BALLETS RUSSES, 1924.

remarkably forward-looking work in 1920, when she was still at Kiev. It remains a model of its kind and has had many revivals: Teatro Colon, Buenos Aires, 1926-27 (under the choreographer's direction); Opéra-Comique, Paris, 3 June 1932; Ballets de Monte-Carlo, 10 April 1934.

ÉTUDES. Ballet in one act. Choreography: Harald Lander. Music: Czerny's Études, arranged by Knudage Riisager. First performance: Royal Theatre, Copenhagen, 15 January 1948. Principal dancers: Margot Lander, Brenaa, Jensen. First performance at the Paris Opera: 19 November 1952. Scenery: Moulène. Principal dancers: Micheline Bardin, Renault, Kalioujny. First performance by London's Festival Ballet, Royal Festival Hall, 8 August 1955. Principal dancers: Toni Lander, Gilpin, Polajenko, Dolin.

To set the atmosphere, we are provided with a glimpse, through a gap in the curtains, of a class of "petits rats" being instructed by their teacher, who is armed with the traditional baton. Then the curtains part and the lights pick out successive groups of dancers who are working at horizontal barres erected on the stage. As the lights grow stronger, we see ensembles practising various movements based on simple, double or triple rhythms. The movements follow each other as in a canon or a fugue, blossoming out finally into the unity of a coda, with all the legs aligned in a triumphant *grand battement*. The exercises become progressively more difficult, passing from the barre to centre practice. Male dancers join the girls. Finally, the ballerina appears with her two partners and adds the indispensable romantic note to this parade of academic dance. Variations and adages alternate with dazzling series of *déboulés, grands jetés, pirouettes* and *fouettés*, the rhythm of movement accelerating into an astonishing crescendo of virtuosity. In this masterly exhibition of classical technique, exercises become dance, just as certain instrumental studies are in themselves music. *Études* marvellously and revealingly displays the style and schooling of a ballet company.

EVDOKIMOV Gleb. Magnificently virile, of superb bearing and blessed with an almost faultless technique, this artist of the Bolshoi Ballet is as successful in classical roles as in the character of the fiery and untamed Nur Ali in *The Fountain of Bakhchisarai*. His powers of mime and expression are such that he pours into this role as much colour and animation as would be produced by an entire corps de ballet of western origin. Yet in London, in 1956, his performance in the peasant pas de deux of *Giselle* (Act I) received just as much acclaim.

F

FAÇADE. Ballet in one act. Music: William Walton. Choreography: Frederick Ashton. Scenery and costumes: John Armstrong. First performance: Camargo Society, Cambridge Theatre, London, 26 April 1931. Principal dancers: Lydia Lopokova, Alicia Markova, Frederick Ashton.

Ashton's celebrated *divertissement* has no story: it is a series of satirical character dances suggested by Walton's brilliant music which, originally written to accompany the recitation of poems by Edith Sitwell, affectionately parodies traditional music of other countries and popular dances of the nineteen-twenties. The wit, freshness and vitality of the result have kept *Façade* uninterruptedly in the repertory of the Rambert and Sadler's Wells companies. John Armstrong re-designed décor and costumes in 1940 without however improving on his delightful original version.

FACHEUX Les. Ballet in one act. Scenario: Boris Kochno, after Molière's comedy-ballet. Music: Georges Auric. Curtain, scenery and costumes: Georges Braque. Choreography: Bronislava Nijinska. First performance: Diaghilev's Ballets Russes, Monte Carlo, 19 January 1924. Principal dancers: Lubov Tchernicheva, Anatole Vilzak, Anton Dolin.

The subject comes straight from Molière: Éraste, a lover on his way to a rendez-vous, is delayed by all sorts of tiresome people: gossips (Schollar and Nikitina), a card-player (Woizikowski) who spreads his enormous cards on the pavement, an enthusiast for dancing (Nijinska), players of battledore and shuttlecock (the best episode) and of bowls. Éraste is forced by these "fâcheux" to take part in their various pursuits; the succession of episodes serves as a pretext for variations with more mime than dancing. Auric's deft score gave the work its unity. Braque's scenery—a little square surrounded by 17th century houses—was in characteristic ochres and greens; his costumes were original and tasteful. All the elements of

FAÇADE.
HAROLD TURNER AND WILLIAM CHAPPELL.

success were present; but the ballet proved disappointing. A lack of spontaneity in the development of the action, too much straining after effect and some rather indifferent choreography prevented it from being more than a " succès d'estime ". Diaghilev, however, had a partiality for *Les Fâcheux* ; a second version was produced three years later with new choreography by Massine (Théâtre Sarah-Bernhardt, Paris, 28 May 1927).

FACSIMILE. Ballet by Jerome Robbins. Music: Leonard Bernstein. Scenery: Oliver Smith. Costumes: Irene Sharaff. First performance: Ballet Theatre, Broadway Theatre, New York, 24 October 1946. Principal dancers: Nora Kaye, Jerome Robbins, John Kriza.

Contemporary loneliness and restlessness is the subject of this psychological ballet for "three insecure people", set against an anonymous, timeless, desolate background: "Small inward treasure does he possess who, to feel alive, needs every hour the tumult of the street, the emotion of the theatre, and the small talk of society" (Ramon y Cajal).

MANUEL DE FALLA BY PICASSO. 1920.

FALLA Manuel de. Born 1876, died 1946. Before the first war, he spent seven years in Paris in friendly contact with such musicians as Paul Dukas, Debussy and Ravel before returning to his native Spain, where he composed the highly distinguished ballets, *El Amor Brujo* and *Le Tricorne*. Although superficially similar, these two works are really quite unalike both in inspiration and form. Both were originally intended by the composer for Diaghilev's company. But when Falla began writing *El Amor Brujo,* only one interpreter seemed desirable: the famous Pastora Imperio, who finally created the main role in Madrid (April 1915), thirteen years before Argentina's triumphant revival in Paris. The obsessive rhythms of the "Dance of Fear" and the "Ritual Fire Dance" are typical of the powerfully dramatic and evocative score. *Le Tricorne* (Ballets Russes, 1920) is more aggressive and masculine; in contrast with the tragic intensity of *El Amor Brujo,* Falla gives free rein to a strong sense of farcical humour. In both ballets he made use of the melodic and rhythmic resources of Spanish (particularly Andalusian) folk music. But he approached the music of his native land with real love and understanding; it was far more to him (and consequently to us) than mere local colour.

FALL RIVER LEGEND. Ballet in one act. Scenario and choreography: Agnes de Mille. Music: Morton Gould. Scenery: Oliver Smith. Costumes: Miles White. First performance: Ballet Theatre, Metropolitan Opera House, New York, 22 April 1948. Principal dancers: Alicia Alonso (alternating with Nora Kaye), Diana Adams, Muriel Bentley, John Kriza, Ruth Ann Koesun.

The ballet is based on a famous murder case of the 1890's, which inspired the popular jingle

> *Lizzie Borden took an axe*
> *And gave her mother forty whacks.*
> *When she saw what she had done*
> *She gave her father forty-one.*

The young woman of Fall River in the state of Massachusetts was accused of killing her father and step-mother with an axe. In real life she was acquitted; in the ballet she is hanged.

Agnes de Mille tells the story as a flashback in the mind of the condemned Lizzie. We see her happy childhood, the death of her mother, the arrival of the jealous stepmother. There is a brief hope of happiness when she grows up and a young clergyman falls in love with her, but the stepmother opposes the marriage. Lizzie believes that her only chance of escape has been snatched from her; she takes a hatchet and kills her father and stepmother. There is a tragic dream sequence in which she meets her own mother again and is upbraided for getting blood on her clothes. Then the scene returns to the foot of the gallows.

FANCY FREE. SKETCH FOR THE DÉCOR BY OLIVER SMITH.

De Mille shows great skill in transposing the psychologically relevant aspects of the story into dance and in conveying a nightmare atmosphere by the different rhythms, gestures and general pattern of the dances. The style is classical with modern overtones, resembling in places the ballet in *Oklahoma!* The music of Morton Gould and the ingenious, mobile décors of Oliver Smith, together with the trim costumes of Miles White, contribute to the provincial atmosphere, the conflicting moods of puritanism and revolt. A well-constructed ballet, *Fall River Legend* can survive changes in cast but will be remembered as one of the great successes of Nora Kaye.

FANCY FREE. Ballet in one act. Scenario and choreography: Jerome Robbins. Music: Leonard Bernstein. Scenery: Oliver Smith. Costumes: Kermit Love. First performance: Ballet Theatre, Metropolitan Opera House, New York, 18 April 1944. Principal dancers: Janet Reed, Muriel Bentley, Shirley Eckl, Harold Lang, John Kriza, Jerome Robbins.

A hot summer night in New York. A bar, a street light, a backcloth of twinkling lights in the skyscrapers. Three sailors on shore leave —and only two girls. Each sailor shows off his paces in a dance, which reveals much of his character. The first is a cheerful extrovert, the second a sentimental charmer, the third a sophisticate. But the contest proves nothing; the girls are unable to choose and the sailors come to blows. The girls slip away and presently three bruised and battered sailors find themselves alone in the bar. They swear off women and chew a stick of gum. Then, under the street light, they see a blonde. "No women" says the first sailor. "No women" the others agree. And then one of them slicks off in pursuit, the others follow and as they career offstage the curtain falls.

A smash hit from its first performance, *Fancy Free* has proved itself to be indestructible. It is a cornerstone of Ballet Theatre's repertory, inspired a musical and a film *(On the Town)*, and has been cheered all over the world. Sailors and girls come and go, but the ballet does not seem to suffer. John Kriza alone of the original cast remains, irreplaceable, inimitable.

FARRON Julia. An invaluable artist of the Royal Ballet, she trained first at the Cone School and joined Sadler's Wells in 1936. A dancer of rare intelligence and strong personality, she has enlivened many mime roles but also excels in purely classical work. Her sparkling Neapolitan Dance in the third act of *Le Lac des Cygnes* is as memorable as the embittered Puritan woman she created in *A Mirror for Witches*. Married to Alfred Rodrigues.

FASTES. Ballet in one act. Scenario, scenery and costumes: André Derain. Music: Henri Sauguet. Choreography: Balanchine. First performance: Ballets 1933, Théâtre des Champs-Élysées, Paris, 7 June 1933. Principal dancers: Tilly Losch, Tamara Toumanova, Roman Jasinsky.

A square in ancient Italy: rose-coloured houses baking in the fierce sun. An antique land of heat and heavy shadows, a fit setting for the rites and dances of a pagan festival; hideous masks, grotesque heads balanced on bodiless legs, triple-masked priests of Lupercal. The

FEDOROVITCH. COSTUME FOR NOCTURNE.
Collection G. B. L. Wilson, London.

choreography made less impression than Derain's powerful décor and costumes.

FEDOROVA Sophie. A graduate of the Moscow School (1899), and one of its best character dancers, Fedorova, with her speed and vivacity, became famous in *La Fille mal gardée, Don Quixote,* and *Esmeralda.* In 1909, she shared the triumphs of the first Paris season by Diaghilev's Ballets Russes with Karsavina, Karalli and Smirnova. She appeared in *Le Pavillon d'Armide* and *Le Festin* but was noticed in particular for her performance as the Young Polovtsian Girl in the Dances from *Prince Igor.* Afterwards, she joined Pavlova's company.

FEDOROVITCH Sophie. Painter and designer, born 1893 in Minsk (Russia) came to England in 1920. She designed over twenty ballets, mainly for the Ballet Club and Sadler's Wells. Eleven of these were for Ashton, for whom she was the ideal collaborator. Fedorovitch was a modest and unassuming person, and an artist of great integrity, with considerable influence on the artistic policy of Sadler's Wells. Her stage designs, while never obtruding themselves, had an unmistakeable simplicity, elegance and poetry. Decoration was pared to essentials; colour she used sparingly but often boldly. Her sketches were mere indications, but her supervision of their execution was meticulous and her judgement unerring. Among her most notable décors were *Les Masques* (1933), *Nocturne* (1936), *Horoscope* (1938), *Dante Sonata* (1940), *La Fête étrange* (1940) and, the finest of all, *Symphonic Variations* (1946). She died in 1953.

FEMMES DE BONNE HUMEUR Les. Ballet in one act. Music: Domenico Scarlatti, arr. Tommasini. Scenery and costumes: Bakst. Choreography: Massine. First performance: Diaghilev's Ballets Russes, Teatro Costanzi, Rome, 12 April 1917. Principal dancers: Lydia Lopokova, Lubov Tchernicheva, Enrico Cecchetti, Stanislas Idzikowski, Leon Woizikowski, Leonide Massine.

Although it was produced during a difficult period in the career of the Ballets Russes, this ballet had an enormous and well deserved success. Name and theme come from a comedy

LES FEMMES DE BONNE HUMEUR. DÉCOR BY BAKST. BALLETS RUSSES, 1917.

by Goldoni. Carnival time in Venice: the "good-humoured ladies" and their accomplice, the wily *trattore* Niccolo, amuse themselves with practical jokes. They tease and mystify the handsome Rinaldo, the betrothed of Costanza, the old Marchese de Luca, and his sister, the Marchesa Silvestra. The comedy unravels itself in mistaken identities and misunderstandings; each fresh intrigue dissolves into laughter and the whole thing has an enchanting swiftness and assurance. To find suitable music, Diaghilev ransacked more than a hundred scores: the choice of Scarlatti was a happy one. Massine followed the music closely, taking hints from the dances and theatrical styles of the past, and particularly from the commedia dell'arte. The result was some really dynamic choreography, witty without vulgarity, blending classical dancing with stylised movements from every-

day life. Bakst's décor showed a little Venetian square dominated by the inevitable campanile. Everything—not forgetting the exceptionally brilliant cast—combined to make a ballet of the highest quality; no mere pastiche or reconstruction, but "a new and vital work where the past is only a faint background suggestion, an echo subdued by the centuries" (André Levinson).

Revivals: Marquis de Cuevas, London 1949, (décors: Derain); Opéra-Comique, Paris, 1952 (décors: André Masson) and 1957.

FESTIN DE L'ARAIGNÉE Le. Ballet-pantomime by Gilbert de Voisins. Music: Albert Roussel. Scenery and costumes: Maxime Dethomas. Choreography: Léo Staats. First performance: Théâtre des Arts, Paris, 3 April

1913. Revival: Opéra-Comique, Paris, 5 December 1922. New version: Paris Opera, 1 May 1940. Choreography: Albert Aveline. Scenery and costumes: Leyritz.

This divertissement by Léo Staats, based on an enchanting score by Roussel, portrays the world of insects. The principal characters are a spider, waiting at the centre of her web for her prey; ants, a pair of praying mantis, a mayfly. The oriental ballerina Sara-Djeli created the title-role. At the Opéra-Comique it was danced by an acrobat, Mado Minty. The version currently performed was choreographed by Aveline for the classical ballerina Suzanne Lorcia. Her magnificent dégagés, strong renversés and abrupt équilibres were most effective.

* Andrée Howard made a new version for the Sadler's Wells Ballet with scenery and costumes by Michael Ayrton (New Theatre, London, 20 June 1944).

FÊTE ÉTRANGE La. Ballet in two scenes. Music: Gabriel Fauré. Scenario: Ronald Crichton, based on an episode in *Le Grand Meaulnes*. Choreography: Andrée Howard. Scenery and costumes: Sophie Fedorovitch. First performance: London Ballet (with Ballet Rambert), Arts Theatre, London, 23 May 1940. Principal dancers: Maude Lloyd, Frank Staff, David Paltenghi.

Children in carnival costume are celebrating a betrothal, dancing and playing in the wintry sunlight on the terrace of the young bride's castle. A country boy, wandering in the woods, stumbles on the scene; his happiness mounts to ecstasy when the bride allows him to dance with her. But the mood changes as the bridegroom arrives, and gazes uncomprehendingly at them. He leaves in proud disillusion; the young guests melt away; as evening falls, the bewildered boy retraces his steps to the woods. Andrée Howard's tenderly flowing choreography, the crisp, clear colours of Sophie Fedorovitch's costumes against the pearly grey background, combined with the haunting chromaticism of Fauré's piano pieces and songs to evoke the strange mood of adolescent wonder suggested by a chapter in Alain-Fournier's novel *Le Grand Meaulnes*.

FIELD John. Born in Doncaster (1921) and trained by Shelagh Elliott-Clarke in Liverpool, John Field joined the Sadler's Wells Ballet in 1939. A good mime and fine dancer, he soon

LE FESTIN DE L'ARAIGNÉE. SUZANNE LORCIA.

became a soloist and on his return from war service achieved the rank of premier danseur. He appeared in all the great classical ballets (usually partnering Beryl Grey or Beriosova). In 1956 he was appointed Resident Director of the Sadler's Wells Theatre Ballet, which is now incorporated in the Royal Ballet. Married to the dancer Anne Heaton.

FIFIELD Elaine. A perfectly placed dancer of elegant build, with exceptionally beautiful feet, Fifield is an ideal exponent of classical choreography. She came to England from Australia in 1945, aged 15, and soon became a leading dancer with the Sadler's Wells Theatre Ballet. By 1956 she was a ballerina of the Royal Ballet, but in 1957 returned to Australia to lead the Borovansky Ballet. She created the principal roles in *Pineapple Poll*, *Madame Chrysanthème* and *The Miraculous Mandarin*. Her Odette-Odile in *Le Lac des Cygnes* is particularly poignant and memorable.

FILLE MAL GARDÉE La. Ballet-pantomime in two acts and three scenes. Music: attributed to J. W. Hertel. Scenario and choreography: Jean Dauberval. First performance: Bordeaux, 1786.

The oldest ballet still in the modern repertory. The story resembles the pseudo-rustic comedies fashionable shortly before the French revolution. Despite its wealth of episodes, it can be reduced to one simple idea: Lise is deeply in love with young Colin, but her mother Simone, a rich farmer's wife, wishes her to marry the son of a wealthy vine grower. Lise is stubborn and wily, and after a thousand schemes and devices she gets her own way. In Russia, during the 19th century, *Vain Precautions* (a version by Didelot, after Dauberval, for the Imperial Theatres) was a favourite with the public and a popular vehicle for leading dancers. The ballet was revived at the Paris Opera (19 September 1827) with music arranged by Hérold.

* Revived in London at the beginning of the century by Anna Pavlova, with herself as Lise, Novikoff as Colin, and Cecchetti as Mother Simone, a role traditionally danced by a man.
* New York, 1938, by Mordkin. Scenery

ELAINE FIFIELD AND ALEXANDER GRANT IN MADAME CHRYSANTHÈME.

and costumes: Serge Soudeikine. Principal dancers: Lucia Chase (Lise), Mordkin (Simone).

* Ballet Theatre staged a revised version (two acts, four scenes) by Nijinska, 1940, with Baronova, and later Alicia Alonso, as Lise.
* In Europe, a condensed version was produced for Renée Jeanmaire by the Ballets du Marquis de Cuevas with choreography by Alexandra Balachova, herself a famous Lise in Russia at the beginning of the century. Scenery: Coletti. First performance: 27 November 1947:

FILS PRODIGUE Le (The Prodigal Son). Ballet in three scenes. Scenario: Boris Kochno. Music: Sergei Prokofiev. Scenery and costumes: Georges Rouault. Choreography: Balanchine. First performance: Diaghilev's Ballets Russes, Théâtre Sarah-Bernhardt, Paris, 21 May 1929. Principal dancers: Serge Lifar, Felia Doubrovska, Anton Dolin, Leon Woizikowski.

The last ballet produced by Diaghilev before

LA FILLE MAL GARDÉE. COSTUMES BY SERGE SOUDEIKINE FOR THE MORDKIN BALLET.

his death. The theme is from the familiar biblical parable. Rouault's designs were only ready at the last moment; Diaghilev, to make sure, had him locked in his hotel bedroom, where his meals were served to him. The first set, luminous and highly coloured, evoked the bright blue sky and burning sun of the Near East. The second scene (the orgy) took place in front of an open tent with a single huge table of which striking use was made in the choreography. In this otherwise exclusively masculine scene there was one woman, the temptress, who made a sensational, lascivious entrance and danced a solo with a large, purple cape. In this ballet Diaghilev laid particular emphasis on the dancers' acting. Lifar's performance in the title role was astonishingly virile and expressive. The last scene when, covered in rags, he crawled towards his father's threshold, has become part of ballet history. "I shall never dance like that again", he said later. Balanchine's choreography, influenced by Byzantine ikons, was a combination of classical steps, acrobatics and mime; all the resources of the human body were brought into play. Le Fils Prodigue was one of the starting points of modern choreography.

* Lichine made a new version for the de Basil company in 1939 which he danced with Sono Osato. This was revived after the war (1947) with Roman Jasinsky and Renée Jeanmaire.

* The Prodigal Son. Ballet in two acts, six scenes, by Kurt Jooss. Music: Fritz Cohen. Choreography: Jooss. Scenery and costumes: Hein Heckroth. First performance: Ballets Jooss, Amsterdam, 6 October 1933.

* The Prodigal Son. Ballet in five scenes, based on Biblical paintings from Dalarna. Choreography: Ivo Cramer. Music: Hugo Alfven. Painter: Rune Lindström. First performance: Royal Swedish Ballet, Stockholm, 1957. Principal dancers: Bjørn Holmgren, Elsa Marianne von Rosen.

FINI Leonor. As a stage designer Leonor Fini is in no sense an innovator, but her décors are marked, like her paintings, by an acute sense of the fantastic, the surrealist gift of transfiguring reality. Even before the action of the ballet has begun the nervous, feline poetry of her designs creates an atmosphere full of sinister suggestions, so adroitly presented that the spectator does not realise their significance until it is too late to escape. She can even endow 18th century themes with disturbing, dramatic overtones.

Her décors include: Le Rêve de Léonor (Ballets des Champs-Élysées, 1945); Le Palais de Cristal (Paris Opera, 1947); Les Demoiselles de la Nuit (Ballets de Paris, 1948); Le Spectre de la Rose (La Scala, Milan).

FLAMES OF PARIS The. Ballet in four acts and seven scenes. Scenario: Nicholas Volkov and V. Dimitriev. Music: Boris Asafiev. Scenery and costumes: V. Dimitriev. Choreography: V. Vainonen. First performance: Kirov Theatre, Leningrad, 20 November 1932.

A great historical fresco depicting the class struggle in the Paris of 1792. We pass from a ball at the Palais de Versailles, majestic and stately, to a popular fête celebrating the capture of the Tuileries. The only character common to both scenes and styles is the actress Mireille, who plays the role of a galante in an interlude ("Les ruses de l'Amour") during the ball at Versailles and then, after the triumph of the revolution, leads the sans-culottes in a frenzied carmagnole. Ensemble dances and mime scenes play an essential part in this romantic-heroic melodrama. Understandably enough, it had a great influence on the realist movement in the U.S.S.R., although some Russian critics objected to its excessive reliance on crowd movements at the expense of individual characterization. The ballet was revived at the Bolshoi Theatre, Moscow (6 June 1933) in a slightly revised version with more scope for dancing. The version currently produced on the Soviet stages dates from 1950 and consists of four acts and five scenes.

FOKINE Michel (1880-1942). One of the founders of modern ballet and its first great choreographer, Fokine's name is primarily associated with the dazzling early years of Diaghilev's Ballets Russes. Both company and choreographer were the product of the same artistic movement but, while it is true that Diaghilev gave him his great opportunity, it must not be forgotten that Fokine's reforms had been planned and in part tested in St. Petersburg before the Diaghilev Ballet was formed. At the beginning of his career, at least, he was the right man in the right place.

Fokine was born at St. Petersburg on the 22nd April, 1880. He joined the Imperial Ballet School of the Maryinsky Theatre as a boy

LE FILS PRODIGUE. SKETCH FOR DÉCOR BY ROUAULT. 1929. *Collection Serge Lifar, Paris.*

of eight and was a pupil successively of Platon Karsavin, Pavel Gerdt and Nicholas Legat. He had a passion for art, and spent his free time in the museums. He impressed his teachers by his precocity (top of the class not only in dancing but in drawing as well) as much as he worried them by signs of temperamental instability. When he was barely 13, he attracted attention by his performance of the role of Luke in Ivanov's *The Magic Flute*. He left the School in 1898 and, exceptionally, was engaged as soloist at the Maryinsky without passing through the corps de ballet. On 26th April of that year he made his début in the pas de quatre from *Paquita,* with Egorova, Sedova and Oboukhov. The ballets he appeared in were of the old, elaborate, spectacular type. More often than not, the story was merely a peg on which to hang a succession of brilliant dances for the soloists; the male dancer was there to lift the ballerina; the corps de ballet simpered in the background; almost anything, music, costumes, etc., could be and often was changed at the ballerina's whim.

Though he became one of the finest dancers in the company, his real vocation lay elsewhere and he began to study with Johansson for a diploma in choreography. He also revealed himself, from 1902 onwards, as a most original teacher whose working methods forecast his later reforms. He did not neglect the daily "barre" but he attached less importance to it than to individual expression and to the development of the pupil's creative ability. Ordinary movements such as walking or running would be subjected to a minute analysis, and free improvisation was encouraged. Technique was taught as a means, not an end. The dancer Gorchovka once said that it was difficult for anyone accustomed to his methods to work for anyone else. He was above all a stickler for correct style — "he would commit murder for that".

In 1904 he wrote a scenario based on Longus's *Daphnis and Chloe* and submitted it to the management of the Imperial Theatres. Its main interest today lies in the explanatory notes in which Fokine revealed his plans for the reform of ballet: "Dancing should be expressive. It should not degenerate into mere gymnastics. It should reflect the feelings of the character portrayed. Above all, it should be right for the place and period indicated by the subject ...

MICHEL FOKINE.
ETCHING BY SEGUIN-BERTAULT.

Expressive dancing needs suitably expressive music; not the old waltzes, polkas, pizzicatos and galops, but something that conveys the same emotions as the movements of the dancer ... Ballets should no longer consist entirely of isolated numbers, entries, and so on. There should be unity of conception. The action of a ballet should never be suspended to allow a *danseuse* to acknowledge applause ... Instead of the traditional dualism music-dancing, complete and harmonious artistic unity of the three elements, music, painting and movement ...". Needless to say, the scenario was rejected and the management viewed his ideas with some suspicion. Nevertheless Fokine was consumed with enthusiasm and dreamed of the day when he might succeed Petipa as maître de ballet. In a wider sense he did indeed become the old man's successor and carried the torch of the great tradition of innovators inherited from Noverre far beyond the confines of the Imperial stages.

Sensitive as he was to the influence of the artistic movements of the time, Fokine was very much in sympathy with the ideas propagated by

Diaghilev's review *Mir Isskoustva* and found support there for his constant concern with questions of style. At this time, also, there were two important events for him in the world of dancing: the appearance of a company of Siamese dancers, who aroused his interest in arm movements, usually neglected in academic teaching, and (1905) the arrival of Isadora Duncan. Her dancing showed him many new possibilities, but Diaghilev exaggerated when he said that "Isadora's influence on Fokine was the very foundation of his creative activity". He shared to the full her desire to liberate the dance from outworn conventions, but he never approved of her ignorance of academic rules and, for his part, refused to renounce them. In any case, Fokine's profound originality was evident at the very outset of his career as a choreographer. His first ballets (1905) were *Acis and Galatea* and *The Dying Swan* (*), the latter arranged for Pavlova who, with Karsavina, was his most fervent disciple. There followed *A Midsummer Night's Dream* and *La Vigne*, which was warmly praised by Petipa (both 1906). *Eunice* (1907) was evidently inspired by Duncan, but it was followed by a ballet in the old, spectacular tradition, *La Tapisserie Enchantée*, performed at the Maryinsky as *Le Pavillon*

d'Armide. With this work he made his début as choreographer on the great stage which Petipa had at last vacated, but he still met with discouraging opposition from conservative circles.

In 1908 came *Une Nuit d'Égypte* and *Chopiniana*, later to become famous as *Cléopâtre* and *Les Sylphides*. But there was a still more important event. Through Benois, a keen supporter of new tendencies in the ballet, he had made the acquaintance of Diaghilev and of his circle of painters and musicians, who offered him precisely the opportunity he needed. The coming together of Fokine and Diaghilev, and the invitation to the young choreographer to join the new Russian Ballet for the Paris season of 1909 was decisive for both of them. Fokine assumed responsibility for the entire repertory given in Paris: *Le Pavillon d'Armide* (*), *Les Sylphides* (*), *Cléopâtre* (*), and one new ballet, the *Dances from Prince Igor* (*), in which he achieved new and overwhelming effects by the simplest means. As for Diaghilev's dancers, the majority of them, headed by Pavlova, Karsavina and Ida Rubinstein, shared Fokine's ideas and were willing collaborators.

As premier danseur noble and sole choreographer, Fokine's position in the Russian Ballet was unique, but it was not unchallenged for

LES SYLPHIDES. BALLET BY FOKINE. 1909.

CLÉOPÂTRE. COSTUME BY BAKST. 1909.

Fokine and Diaghilev, matters went from bad to worse. Diaghilev seemed to be tiring of Fokine's style and to find it already old-fashioned; he was becoming more and more occupied with Nijinsky, whose first ballet *L'Après-midi d'un faune* was being rehearsed in secret. Then Fokine's *Daphnis and Chloe* (*), that long-cherished project and a favourite work, partly misfired through no fault of his own, and he left the company. He returned to Russia to mount *Papillons, Islamey* and *Judith*. Two years later, after Nijinsky had been expelled, Fokine was persuaded by Diaghilev (in the course of a telephone conversation of five hours' duration) to return, as dancer and choreographer. He mounted *Papillons* (*) for the company and three new works, *La Légende de Joseph* (*), *Le Coq d'or* (*) and *Midas*. It was his last season with the Russian Ballet. When the war came he returned to Russia, but neither there nor elsewhere could he ever find another company to which he could attach himself permanently. Though he was by no means played out, the greatest innovator of 20th century ballet seemed to have got out of step.

In Russia, he produced several new works: *Eros, Francesca da Rimini, Stenka Razine, Orpheus and Eurydice* (all 1915) and *L'Apprenti sorcier* (1916). He left for good in 1918, worked in Stockholm, Copenhagen and in London, and then settled in the U.S.A. The only product of these years of wandering to have survived is

long. For the 1910 season he produced *Carnaval* (*), *Sheherazade* (*) and *L'Oiseau de Feu* (*), in which he danced himself with Karsavina. The last two, immensely successful with the public, were splendid examples of the still novel genre of the dramatic one-act ballet. The one was brutally, the other tenderly, exotic; both were full of characterisation as well as of spectacle.

For the 1911 season, because Diaghilev wanted Nijinsky to be without rival as leading male dancer, Fokine was engaged as choreographer only. He was deeply hurt, but put his heart and soul into four new ballets: the charming *Le Spectre de la Rose* (*), *Narcisse* (*), *Sadko* and the masterly *Petrouchka* (*). 1912 saw *Le Dieu Bleu* (*), which reflected his interest in oriental dancing and *Thamar* (*), another exotic. Between

DRAWING BY PICASSO.

Les Elfes (*) (1924). Some years later, Ida Rubinstein commissioned him to do a number of ballets for her: *La Valse* (*) (1931), *Sémiramis* and *Diane de Poitiers* (1934). Then, with René Blum and the Ballets de Monte-Carlo, he found his old form with the mellow yet youthful *L'Épreuve d'Amour* (*) (1936). *Don Juan* (1936) and *Les Éléments* (*) (1937) also had distinction. Two ballets for de Basil followed, *Cendrillon* (*) (1938) and *Paganini* (*) (1939). Back in America, he produced *Bluebeard* (*) for Ballet Theatre in 1941 and *Russian Soldier,* for the same company in 1942. Danced to Prokofiev's symphonic suite "Lieutenant Kije", and dedicated to the Russian soldiers of the second world war, this was Fokine's last ballet. He died suddenly in New York on 22 August 1942.

Fokine's works are the best possible illustrations of his theories. The range of style and subject matter was immense. He rehabilitated the male dancer and gave the corps de ballet an entirely new function. He welded mime and pure dancing into an indissoluble whole. He was not concerned with sensationalism but, like a true follower of Noverre, with the expression of truth. A number of his finest ballets are still danced by the world's leading companies but all too often they are performed without regard to Fokine's simplest maxim: "If there is to be truth in the dance, the performer must have heart and brain so that there will be feeling and style."

FOLKESAGN Et (A Folk Tale). Ballet in three acts by August Bournonville. Music: Niels W. Gade and I. E. P. Hartmann. First performance: 20 March 1854, Royal Theatre, Copenhagen. Inspired by a Danish folk story about a changeling. A young girl, Hilda, has been carried off when a baby by trolls who jealously guard her and try to prevent the young man Junker Ove from approaching her. However, truth triumphs in the end when it is revealed that the disagreeable Birthe, supposed heiress to a rich estate, is the real daughter of the trolls. The ballet is a perennial favourite with the Danish public. Erik Bruhn is the finest Junker Ove of our day; Ulla Poulsen was the most celebrated Hilda. Margot Lander used to dance the rôle of Birthe with success; Kirsten Ralov was her successor.

COSTUME BY BAKST FOR THE FIREBIRD. 1910.

FONTEYN Dame Margot. "Who is the little Chinese-looking girl?" said Ninette de Valois, watching the junior class at the Sadler's Wells School. "She's not Chinese—her name is Hookham", replied the teacher. Miss Hookham, whose father came from Yorkshire and whose mother is part-Irish, part-Brazilian, soon changed her name to Fonteyn. Today she is prima ballerina assoluta of the Royal Ballet of Great Britain; a product of the organization to which she has given so much distinction in return.

Margot Fonteyn joined the Sadler's Wells School in 1934 after a childhood spent in England (where she was born) and in China (where her father worked). Among her early teachers were Goncharov and Astafieva, who first aroused in her a passionate love of the dance. Subsequent influences were Preobrajenska in Paris and Vera Volkova with whom she worked after the war in London. But her everyday training throughout her career has been at Sadler's Wells.

Her pre-eminence has been achieved with humility and unselfishness, and with a quiet, unspectacular determination to give of her best. Her natural gifts were considerable; she is beautifully built and is blessed with a genuine response to music; she has developed an unrivalled talent for minutely studied characterisation. Karsavina, who taught her the role of the Firebird, has praised her quality of "artistic logic"; John Martin of the *New York Times* wrote that "she is able to see the choreographer's intentions better than he has seen them himself." In Fonteyn's dancing there is an innate sense of proportion; the details are related to the whole, and technique is never used as an end in itself. There are strong undercurrents of feeling kept in check, at times rather too firmly, by a natural reserve which has something in it of English schooling but is also a personal quality. This quality, because it is both unspectacular and un-obvious, is particularly hard to define. Invariably elegant, she can be witty, and she can flash fire, but perhaps most typical of her is a tenderness, at once wistful and radiant, perfectly suited to the roles made for her in such ballets as *Nocturne, The Wise Virgins, Symphonic Variations, Cinderella* and *Daphnis and Chloe* by Frederick Ashton, of whose choreography she is the ideal interpreter.

She inherited the roles of Giselle and Odette-Odile at a very early age after Markova left the Sadler's Wells Ballet. In 1939 she danced Aurora in *The Sleeping Beauty* for the first time, and it was in the new production of this ballet at Covent Garden in 1946 that she set the seal on her reputation. Other milestones have been her appearance in Paris in Roland Petit's *Les Demoiselles de la Nuit,* her triumphant tours with the Sadler's Wells Ballet in North America, her visit to Australia in 1957. In the spring of 1958, returning to London from her fifth American tour, she was dancing with a new-found joy and sureness. Her Giselle, in particular, after study with Karsavina, achieved a new poignancy and beauty.

Married to Dr. Roberto de Arias of Panama. President of the Royal Academy of Dancing since 1954.

MARGOT FONTEYN.

FORAINS Les. Ballet by Boris Kochno. Music: Henri Sauguet. Scenery and costumes: Christian Bérard. Choreography: Roland Petit. First performance: Théâtre des Champs-Élysées, 2 March 1945. Principal dancers: Nina Vyroubova, Roland Petit, Ethery Pagava, Christian Foye, Marina de Berg, Hélène Sadovska.

A travelling circus sets up its booth in the outskirts of a town. A little practice, then the performance in front of a few apathetic onlookers, and the troupe moves on again . . . Petit's first important ballet, and the real beginning of his career as a choreographer. It was presented during a recital of his works, soon after he had left the Opéra, and was composed in feverish haste. "We never thought about the work's future", said the composer Sauguet, "we wrote it for that one evening". Petit set each section as Sauguet brought him the music; Bérard

THE FOUNTAIN OF BAKHCHISARAI. MAYA PLISSETSKAYA.

ransacked the street markets for scraps of material and bits of tinsel; the ballet was just ready on the day of the première. The artists' friends were pressed into service as supers, to represent the spectators on the stage. Not all the choreographic "numbers" were of equal merit, but Petit wonderfully caught the moment when the performers began to believe in themselves and their subsequent tired, hopeless resignation. This, with the inspired simplicity of Bérard's set, Sauguet's melancholy, steam-organ tunes and the youth and charm of the dancers made Les Forains into a success which encouraged the formation of the Ballets des Champs-Élysées, whose repertory it subsequently adorned.

FOUNTAIN OF BAKHCHISARAI
The. Ballet in four acts, with prologue. Scenario: N. Volkov, after Pushkin. Music: Boris Asafiev. Scenery and costumes: V. Khodassevitch. Choreography: R. Zakharov. First performance: Leningrad, Kirov Theatre, 22 September 1934, with Galina Ulanova.

The grounds of a large country house in Poland in 1783. The nobles dance mazurkas and cracoviennes in the moonlight; Maria falls in love with Vaslav. Then a Tartar invasion, the slaughter of the Polish fighters, the mansion set on fire, Vaslav killed and Maria abducted by the Khan Girei. He takes her to his harem in Bakhchisarai but grants her plea for solitude. His respectful love for Maria arouses the jealousy

of his former favourite, Zarema, who stabs her. The Khan orders the immediate death of Zarema and spends the rest of his days mourning the chaste Maria beside the fountain he has built to her memory. She appears in his imagination as she was in life, always evading him and eluding his grasp. He is left alone beside his "fountain of love, fountain of sorrow".

One of the most beautiful ballets in the Soviet repertoire, *The Fountain of Bakhchisarai* has retained its popularity for over twenty years despite its uninteresting score. The highlights of the choreography are the national dances of the first act, the jealous dance of Zarema, Maria's lonely musings in captivity, and the superb Tartar dance in the last act. Nevertheless, the ballet depends for its success on the interpretation of the three principal characters. Girei, a mime role, must dominate the action throughout and has been played by the great character dancers Gusev and Lapauri. The two feminine roles are directly opposed: Maria is gentle and lyrical and must convey an innate innocence. Zarema is sensual, full of force and fury. The great Soviet ballerinas have chosen one or other of the roles to suit their own temperament: thus Tcherkassova and Plissetskaya have danced the jealous favourite; Vassilieva, Struchkova and Lepeshinskaya have appeared as Maria. But the most sensitive and moving Maria is unquestionably Ulanova; when she dances, the character becomes, as it was to Pushkin, a symbol of inward, spiritual beauty.

FOURBERIES Les. Choreographic comedy in two acts by Robert Manuel and Serge Lifar, after Molière's *Fourberies de Scapin*. Music: Tony Aubin, after Rossini. Scenery and costumes: Roland Oudot. Choreography: Lifar. First performance: Paris Opera, 27 February 1952. Principal dancers: Nina Vyroubova, Liane Daydé, Madeleine Lafon, Serge Lifar, Michel Renault, Max Bozzoni. Unfortunately the ballet retained very little of the zest and verve of Molière's original.

FOUR TEMPERAMENTS. Ballet by George Balanchine, to the music of Hindemith's Theme and four variations for piano and strings. Scenery and costumes: Kurt Seligmann. First performance: Ballet Society, New York, 20 November 1946. Principal dancers: Gisella Caccialanza, Tanaquil LeClercq, Mary Ellen Moylan, Elise Reiman, Todd Bolender, Lew Christensen, William Dollar, Francisco Moncion.

Probably Balanchine's masterpiece and certainly one of the finest abstract ballets. The choreographer's visual counterpoint to the music does not "illustrate" the composer's intentions; it "illuminates" them, which is more difficult and much more rewarding. Balanchine himself has said that it forms "a negative to Hindemith's positive plate". Three couples dance the theme. Other groups, with soloists, represent the four medieval temperaments: melancholy, sanguine, phlegmatic and choleric. The complete cast of 24 dancers (including six men) comes together in the "choleric" variation, which forms the finale. Balanchine's choreography derives its exceptional richness of expression partly from the combination of classical with modern elements, including (notably in the man's solo in the "phlegmatic" movement) Martha Graham's technique of contraction, relaxation and falls. The ballet was originally projected by Kirstein and Balanchine for the American Ballet in 1941 as *The Cave of Sleep* with décor and costumes by Tchelitchev. It did not materialise. *The Four Temperaments* has become one of the cornerstones of the repertory of the New York City Ballet.

FRANCA Celia. Director of the National Ballet of Canada since its foundation in 1950, Celia Franca was a dancer with Ballet Rambert and International Ballet in England before joining the Sadler's Wells Ballet in 1941. Raven-haired and of striking appearance, she excelled in dramatic roles such as the Queen in Helpmann's *Hamlet*. With *Khadra* (first produced by the Sadler's Wells Theatre Ballet 1946) she established a reputation as a choreographer. Undaunted by hardships and difficulties, she has done remarkable pioneer work in Canada not only in the direction of the company but in the guidance of its school.

FRANÇAIX Jean. French composer, born 1912. A brilliant pupil of Nadia Boulanger, who gave him a sound technical foundation which ensures that his music, witty, charming, facile, rarely touching the deeper emotions, is always beautifully turned. He has written several ballets: *Beach* (1933), *Scuola di Ballo*, an adaptation of pieces by Boccherini (1933), *Le Roi nu* (1936), *Verreries de Venise, Le Jugement du fou, Les Malheurs de Sophie* (1948), *Les Demoiselles de la nuit* (1948), *Le Jeu sentimental, La Lutherie enchantée, La Dame dans la Lune* (1958).

LES FOURBERIES. COSTUME BY ROLAND OUDOT. 1952. *Bibliothèque-Musée de l'Opéra, Paris.*

FRANKIE AND JOHNNY. Ballet in one act. Scenario: Michael Blandford and Jerome Moross after the ballad of that name. Music: Jerome Moross. Scenery: Clive Rickabaugh. Costumes: Paul DuPont. Choreography: Ruth Page and Bentley Stone. First performance: Page-Stone Ballet, Chicago, 19 June 1938. Principal dancers: Ruth Page and Bentley Stone.

There are several versions of the semi-blues ballad upon which the ballet is based. In the old Chicago of the 90's, Frankie is a prostitute, Johnny her faithless pimp. When Frankie learns from a barman that her lover is double-crossing her, she goes and shoots him. Three women in the uniform of the Salvation Army act as a sort of chorus, introducing and commenting on the action. The ballet is now in the repertory of the Ballets Russes de Monte-Carlo.

FRANKLIN Frederic. English dancer, born in London, trained in Liverpool, he made his name with the Markova-Dolin Ballet, in 1935 but the greater part of his career has been with the Ballets Russes de Monte-Carlo, which he joined in 1938. A good actor, handsome and easy in manner, Franklin created many roles in the ballets of Massine, notably the Baron in *Gaieté Parisienne* and the spirit of creation in *Seventh Symphony*. In 1939 he went with the company to America, where he created the Champion Roper in *Rodeo*, Stanley in *A Streetcar Named Desire* and the principal male role in *Danses Concertantes*. Maître de ballet to the Ballets Russes de Monte-Carlo from 1944-56, he now devotes much time to teaching.

FULLER Loie. (1862-1928). This American dancer might have been born to illustrate Mallarmé's paradox that "la danseuse n'est pas une femme qui danse" because she is not a woman but a metaphor returning aspects of human form, sword, chalice or flower, and because she does not dance, but suggests through the language of movement what paragraphs of prose would hardly suffice to express. When she danced, Loie Fuller was neither a woman nor a dancer but a flower, a butterfly, a flame or a storm. Though she was early attracted to the theatre, she studied acting and singing before

JULES CHÉRET. POSTER FOR LOIE FULLER.

she became a dancer. Her vocation was suggested, not by academic dancing, but by Tanagra statuettes, Greek vases and Pompeian frescoes, from which she derived a new and very different plastic language. From the time of her first appearances, about 1890, she declared herself as a resolute innovator, discarding the conventional tutu for a long, pleated tunic based on the traditional Greek costume. Walking, rhythmical running, flexions of the torso, movements of the hips and the shoulders replaced the classical *jetés battus* and the use of points. More important were her scenic innovation, or rather her exploitation of lighting effects, which were virtually the raison d'être of her greatest successes, the *Snake Dance* for instance and the *Fire Dance,* in which she moved about, draped in transparent veils, on a glass floor lit from below by a red light. In another dance she used mirrors to create, by herself alone, the illusion of several dancers. She showed equal skill in obtaining bizarre effects by the use of shadows. These tricks, for years now commonplaces of the music-hall, seemed at the time genuinely original and exciting.

For more than a quarter of a century, Loie Fuller toured America and Europe, at first alone, then with a small company. She was particularly appreciated in France, where she was one of the great attractions of the Exposition Universelle (Paris, 1900) and returned again and again. Though she may have influenced Isadora Duncan, her methods of staging were of far greater importance than her actual dancing.

G

GAIETÉ PARISIENNE. Ballet in one act. Scenario, scenery and costumes: Étienne de Beaumont. Music: Offenbach, arr. and orch. Manuel Rosenthal. Choreography: Massine. First performance: Ballets de Monte-Carlo, Monte Carlo, 5 April 1938. Principal

dancers: Leonide Massine, Nina Tarakanova, Frederic Franklin, Igor Youskevitch.

A gay and rowdy evocation of the Paris of the Second Empire, based largely on Offenbach's operetta *La Vie Parisienne*. Massine, as the little Peruvian visitor who, though his pockets are stuffed with gold, never quite gets beyond the fringe of the fun, made himself a role to measure. The first half, full of movement and intrigue, is excellent, but from the can-can onwards the comic invention begins to flag and the noise and the "period" vulgarity become tedious. Nevertheless, assisted by Rosenthal's effective arrangement of Offenbach's exhilarating tunes, the ballet has become one of Massine's most popular works and has remained in the repertoire of several companies.

GALA PERFORMANCE. Ballet in two scenes. Music: Serge Prokofiev. Scenario and choreography: Antony Tudor. Scenery and costumes: Hugh Stevenson. First produced: London Ballet, Toynbee Hall Theatre, London, 5 December 1938. Principal dancers: Peggy van Praagh, La Reine de la Danse (from Moscow); Maude Lloyd, La Déesse de la Danse (from Milan); Gerd Larsen, La Fille de Terpsichore (from Paris).

GALA PERFORMANCE. BALLET RAMBERT.

Three famous ballerinas, each supreme in her own country, consent to appear at the same gala performance. At the beginning, the audience sees the coryphées limbering up on the stage before curtain rise. The three great ladies appear. The viewpoint changes, and the succeeding displays are seen from the front. Dignity and decorum are maintained until the fall of the curtain when, tempted by applause and bouquets, the submerged rivalries come boiling to the surface. The choreography, while gently mocking the conventions of 19th century ballet, contrasts the schools of France, Italy and Russia. The satire is most effective when least exaggerated; unfortunately few companies today resist the temptation to overplay it. Tudor wrote *Gala Performance* for the opening night of his own company, the London Ballet. It has passed into the repertory of several others, including the Ballet Rambert, the Royal Swedish Ballet, American Ballet Theatre and the National Ballet of Canada.

GAIETÉ PARISIENNE. HIGHTOWER AND MASSINE.

GAUBERT Philippe. (1879-1941). French composer and conductor (Paris Opera and Conservatoire) who died shortly after the successful première at the Opéra of his two-act ballet, *Le Chevalier et la Damoiselle,* a neo-classic work of considerable accomplishment. Other ballets by Gaubert were: *Philotis* (1914), *Fresques* (1922) and above all *Alexandre le Grand* (Opéra, 1937), based on his symphonic suite *Inscriptions pour les portes de la ville.*

GELTZER Catherine. Trained in the Imperial School at Moscow, she devoted the whole of her career, which stretched over forty-four years, to the Bolshoi Theatre. Of medium height, dark and brilliant, she possessed remarkable lightness and a strong stage personality. She was not altogether successful as the dream heroines of the romantic ballets, but in roles requiring attack and brio she was incomparable. Diaghilev invited her to Paris in 1910 but decided that her style was foreign to that of his company. In Moscow, however, she was considered the first ballerina in all Russia. At the time of the coronation of King George V in 1911 she danced at the Alhambra Theatre in London, partnered by Vassili Tikhomirov,

whom she married. It was for Geltzer that the title "people's artist" was created in the Soviet Union in 1921.

GENÉE Dame Adeline. Danish ballerina and idol of London in the Edwardian era, trained by her uncle Alexander Genée. Tiny, blonde, feather-light, and fragile as porcelain, she was nevertheless an excellent technician and a fine example of good schooling. Prima ballerina at the Empire Theatre in London from 1897-1909, she made several triumphant tours of America and visited Australasia before Pavlova. She retired officially in 1914 but continued to appear until 1917 and subsequently returned for occasional charity performances. She was the first President of the Royal Academy of Dancing.

GEORGIADIS Nicholas. Greek painter and designer, born 1925, studied in Athens, New York and London. Has been closely associated with the rise to fame of the young English choreographer Kenneth Mac Millan, for whom he has designed *Danses Concertantes, The House of Birds* (both Sadler's Wells Theatre Ballet, 1955), *Noctambules* (Sadler's Wells Ballet,

1956) and *Winter's Eve* (American Ballet Theatre, 1957). In his décors and costumes, Georgiadis uses broad masses of brilliant colour with elegant and sometimes weird calligraphic suggestions of architectural structure and ornament. *The Burrow* (Mac Millan, Royal Ballet, 1958) showed that he could work equally happily with a deliberately restrained colour scheme.

GERSHWIN George. (1898-1937). His attempts to marry Jazz with serious music, though they brought him immense popularity, may not (with the possible exception of the opera *Porgy and Bess*) prove to be of permanent value. But some of his music will live, because he had a rare and individual gift of melody. His *Rhapsody in Blue* and *An American in Paris* have been danced many times. A notable version of the former was Dolin's for the Nemchinova-Dolin Ballet (Paris, 1928); of the latter, Ruth Page's for the Ruth Page-Bentley Stone Ballet (Cincinnati, 1936). Massine used Gershwin music for his *New Yorker* (Ballet Russe de Monte-Carlo, New York, 1940).

CARLOTTA GRISI.

GILMOUR Sally. Rambert's first Giselle and a dancer of exceptional poignancy and intelligence, Sally Gilmour was born in Malaya in 1921. Her creation of the woman changed into a fox in *Lady into Fox* first brought her fame. She danced most of the Rambert repertory, being able to play zany, childlike comedy as well as tragic parts. Now married with several children, she is living in Australia.

GILPIN John. One of the finest male dancers of the day, he has been since 1950 a star of London's Festival Ballet. Of medium height, blond and with an open, childlike face which might have come from a portrait by Gainsborough, he possesses a remarkable technique. A child actor, he also studied dance at the Cone-Ripman school until, deciding his first love was the ballet, he joined Ballet Rambert. Rambert established him as a classical dancer and with her company he toured Australia. In 1949 he partnered Jeanmaire in Paris in *Arlequinade* then, after some months of indecision, he joined the newly-formed Festival Ballet. Now he carries on his young shoulders the entire classical and romantic repertory. A light and poetic Spectre de la rose (with beautiful *épaulement*), a lively Franz in *Coppelia*, a brilliant virtuoso in *Études,* Gilpin has partnered nearly all the great ballerinas of today. In 1957, in the title role in *Witch Boy* (choreography by Jack Carter), he tackled with success his first strongly dramatic part.

GISELLE or **THE WILIS.** Fantastic ballet in two acts. Scenario: Vernoy de Saint-Georges, Théophile Gautier and Jean Coralli. Music: Adolphe Adam. Scenery: Ciceri. Choreography: Jean Coralli (and Jules Perrot). First performance: Paris, Académie Royale de Musique, 28 June 1841. Principal dancers: Carlotta Grisi, Lucien Petipa.

This moving choreographic elegy, the masterpiece of its period, was the product of collaboration. Théophile Gautier conceived the idea of a ballet based on the legend of the Wilis in Heine's *De l'Allemagne ;* Vernoy de Saint-Georges, the skilled librettist, helped to adapt it. The first programme ascribed the choreography to Jean Coralli but the critics even then declared

BAKST

BAKST. COSTUME FOR PAVLOVA IN GISELLE.

that Jules Perrot, maître de ballet at the Opera, had composed some of the best sequences for his wife Carlotta Grisi, who played Giselle. Collaboration was in those days quite usual. In any case, *Giselle* was an immediate success. Carlotta Grisi, then only 22, became the idol of the public and the equal of the two great romantic ballerinas, Marie Taglioni and Fanny Elssler.

The opening scene shows vintage time in the Rhineland, with hunting horns sounding through the forest. Giselle, a village maiden, is in love with Loys, who is really the nobleman Albrecht philandering in peasant disguise. The forester Hilarion, who has been rejected by Giselle, discovers Albrecht's secret and exposes his duplicity. The shock is too great for Giselle. Her delirious happiness is turned to despair and her mind gives way. Pathetically she repeats the little dance she performed with Albrecht when she trusted him, then she collapses and dies.

The second act takes place in the haunted world of the Wilis, maidens like Giselle who in life loved dancing too well. Dead before their wedding day, they are now condemned to dance all night long and woe to any traveller caught in their accursed round. Hilarion is their first

LUCIEN PETIPA AS LOYS.

SPESSIVTSEVA IN THE MAD SCENE
FROM GISELLE.

victim; he is driven towards the lake and drowned. Albrecht, coming to pray by the tomb of Giselle, sees her in her ghostly shape as a Wili. She is compelled by Myrtha, the Queen of the Wilis, to draw her lover into the dance, but she succeeds in saving his life by urging him to stay near to the protecting cross that surmounts her tomb. With the coming of dawn, the Wilis return to their graves. Giselle bids Albrecht a last farewell before she too disappears. Distraught and crazed with grief, he collapses on her grave.

The success of *Giselle* is mainly due to the delicate balance maintained between dance and drama, and by the contrast achieved between the simple, human tragedy of the first act and the supernatural happenings of the second. The choreography has survived almost without change, except for some amendments in the first act probably made by Petipa in Russia towards the end of the 19th century. The second act is the very apotheosis of the "ballet blanc". The world of the Wilis is created by the use of a most expressive choreographic language; steps of elevation, arabesques and grands jetés, release these creatures from the earth. Each step, each movement is relevant; choreography and plot are indissolubly blended. The spirit of romanticism is so perfectly captured that the ballet today may be admired as a period piece as well as a living drama. The music of Adam, simple and tuneful, is theatrically right even though it could not withstand transference to the concert hall.

In addition to its other qualities, *Giselle* provides a superb role for the ballerina, intensely difficult in interpretation, infinitely rewarding if well done. It calls for perfection of technique, great acting ability, and a appreciation of period style, so that the real world of the first act and the dream world of the second may be realised and united in the role of Giselle. Elssler, excelling in the drama of the first act, soon challenged Grisi. Taglioni, Grahn and Cerrito all danced Giselle. In Russia, Andreyanova, Muravieva and Grantzow were eventually succeeded by Pavlova and Karsavina, then by Galina Ulanova. Although constantly preserved in the repertory in Russia, *Giselle* disappeared from the Paris Opera stage for many years. Thus, Carlotta Zambelli learned the original choreography from Adelina Théodore in Paris, but danced Giselle for the first time in St. Petersburg in 1901. Diaghilev showed *Giselle* in Paris in 1910 (Opéra, 18 June), with

Karsavina and Nijinsky. In 1924 there was a famous revival with Olga Spessivtseva and Aveline. Spessivtseva was succeeded by Chauviré, later by Daydé. Alicia Markova danced Giselle for the first time with the Vic-Wells Ballet (1 January 1934) and has since become one of its greatest exponents, appearing with many different companies. Margot Fonteyn and, recently, Beriosova have been the great Giselles of the Sadler's Wells Ballet. With the Ballets Russes de Monte-Carlo, Toumanova; with Ballet Theatre, Alicia Alonso; with the Royal Danish Ballet, Margot Lander; with Ballet Rambert, Sally Gilmour.

The role of Albrecht, although less difficult, requires great stage presence, good acting and a fine technique, for in 1841 the male dancer still held an honoured position in ballet. Jules Perrot (named *Perrot l'aérien*) danced it himself, after Petipa. Among his great successors may be mentioned Nijinsky, Anton Dolin, Igor Youskevitch, Serge Lifar, George Skibine, Borge Ralov, Robert Helpmann, Michael Somes, and Erik Bruhn.

The most famous settings for the ballet are those designed by Alexandre Benois, which were used at the Paris Opera until 1954 when a Carzou décor was substituted. Carzou, like Berman (who designed *Giselle* for Ballet Theatre) proved too individual a designer and soon the Opéra restored the Benois settings. In Enggland, the ballet has been well designed by Hugh

ULANOVA IN THE MAD SCENE FROM GISELLE.

Stevenson (for Rambert and Festival Ballet) and by James Bailey for Sadler's Wells.

Giselle is now in the repertory of nearly all the world's ballet companies. Among the finest contemporary productions are Leonid Lavrovsky's for the Bolshoi Theatre Ballet, Marie Rambert's for her own company, Anton Dolin's for Ballet Theatre and Festival Ballet, Mary Skeaping's for the Royal Swedish Ballet, and Sergueev's for the Sadler's Wells Ballet.

GLIÈRE Reinhold. Born Kiev, 1875. Died 1955. Studied at the Moscow Conservatoire, where he later became professor of composition. Wrote symphonies, chamber music, operas and several ballets, including *Chrysis* (1912), *Egyptian Nights* (1925) and *The Comedians* (1930). His best known work was *The Red Poppy* (1926-27), the first Soviet ballet on a revolutionary subject. A second version (1949) was even more successful. Another big ballet *The Bronze Horseman* came in 1949. Glière's music is romantic in the Russian academic tradition, and quite unproblematic.

GODS GO A'BEGGING The (Les Dieux Mendiants). Ballet in one act. Scenario: Sobeka (Kochno). Music: Handel, arr. and orch. Beecham. Choreography: Balanchine. First performance: Diaghilev's Ballets Russes, His Majesty's Theatre, London, 16 July 1928. Principal dancers: Danilova, Woizikowski.

The ballet was hastily put together by Kochno and Balanchine at the end of a London season, using one of Bakst's décors for *Daphnis and Chloe* and the 18th century costumes designed by Juan Gris for *Les Tentations de la Bergère*. The only characters to be dressed simply were a serving-maid and a shepherd; they were revealed at the end as two gods in disguise, amusing themselves among the mortals at a pastoral picnic à la Watteau. The ballet was a great, and rather unexpected, success.

* New version by de Valois for the Vic-Wells Ballet, 21 February 1936, with scenery and costumes by Hugh Stevenson. Principal dancers: Pearl Argyle, William Chappell.

* Another version by David Lichine for the de Basil company, with décor by Juan Gris after Bakst, was produced in 1937.

GISELLE. DÉCOR FOR ACT I BY BENOIS. PARIS OPERA VERSION. 1924.

Principal dancers: Alexandra Danilova, Yurek Shabelevsky.

GOLEIZOVSKY Kassian. Russian dancer and choreographer, born 1890. One of the rare modernists in Soviet ballet. He was trained at St. Petersburg, but went to Moscow in 1910 where, under the influence of Gorsky, he broke with academic tradition and a few years later founded his own dance studio in order to do experimental work of an avant-garde nature. There was a strong element of physical culture and gymnastics; he upheld the sculptural beauty of the nåked body and banished conventional ballet costume. With the Revolution his influence increased and numerous young artists were attracted by his ideas. He invented the notion of a "collective" dance company with discipline strict to the point of anonymity. His methods of staging were equally original: massed movements against cubist or "constructivist" décors. In 1925 he was invited by the government to work at the Bolshoi Theatre, where he staged *Joseph the Handsome* and *Theolinda*. The latter was a parody of classical ballet, an unheard of audacity for the period. Goleizovsky can be regarded as a forerunner of the style later known as neo-classicism. When his fame spread abroad, Diaghilev tried to get him to Paris, but he was unable to leave Russia and remained there in a climate ever more unfavourable to experiment. Later he made new versions of the dances from *Prince Igor* and *The Fountain of Bakhchisarai* (Minsk, 1939).

GOLLNER Nana. Born in Texas, she studied dancing as a remedial exercise after recovering from infantile paralysis, and eventually became the first American ballerina of the Ballet Russe de Monte-Carlo (René Blum's company 1936-37). Subsequently ballerina with Ballet Theatre (1939-41, 1943-45), Original Ballet Russe (1941-43), International Ballet (1947). A beautiful woman and a strong dancer, she appeared in character as well as classical roles, for instance Helen of Troy, and the Street Dancer in *Beau Danube* as well as *Swan Lake* and *Giselle*. Now teaching, with her husband Paul Petroff, in California.

GISELLE. SKETCH FOR DÉCOR BY CARZOU, PARIS OPERA. 1954.

GOLOVINE Alexandre; (1864-1930). One of the team of Russian artists, already famous in their own country, whom Diaghilev introduced to the West with his first productions in Paris. The Ballets Russes suddenly revealed a new decorative art, equally remarkable for its sense of composition and for the intensity of its colour. Golovine's essentially Slavonic style united barbaric violence with precious, oriental refinement. He was never so precious as Bakst, but he was more forceful. On the other hand his more exclusively national outlook prevented him from undertaking Bakst's wide range of subjects. Golovine designed part of the décor of two of the operas which Diaghilev gave at the Paris Opera, *Boris Godounov* (1908) and *Ivan the Terrible* (1909). His most notable work in Europe was the first version of *L'Oiseau de Feu* (1910). He also collaborated with Korovine in the Diaghilev revival of *Lac des Cygnes,* Act II (London, 1911).

SERGE GOLOVINE AND HARRIET TOBY.
LE MOULIN ENCHANTÉ.

GOLOVINE Serge. He is a dancer in every sense of the word. His body has been shaped by rigorous training, and his life is dedicated to the dance. Born in Monaco of a Russian father and Breton mother, he knew much hardship during his childhood. He started his career at the studio of Julie Sedova in Nice, and has ever since accepted wholeheartedly the gruelling life of a dancer. Years of hard work in the ranks of the corps de ballet at the Paris Opera brought him eventually to a glorious début in 1950 with the Grand Ballet du Marquis de Cuevas, when he electrified the audience by his dancing in *The Black Swan* pas de deux. Since then he has become one of the most brilliant classical dancers of his generation and his lightness and elevation are legendary. He is a graceful Spectre de la rose, a soaring Blue Bird, and a pathetic Petrouchka. Silent, withdrawn, a little mysterious, Serge is the eldest of a family of dancers: his sister, Solange, and his two brothers, Georges (Gavriloff) and Jean, have chosen the same profession.

GONCHAROVA Nathalie. One of the Russian artists who have made the greatest contribution to stage design. Her powerful imagination has never upset the artistic unity of her work; the demands of a given subject have always meant more to her than the mere opportunity for self-expression. Her ballet décors have shown a marked inclination towards the style of popular art, towards bold, simplified outlines and clear, joyous colours. This approach is neither naive nor patronising. It is sincere, scholarly and based on considerable experience. Before she came to Paris in 1914, Goncharova had been an active member of the Russian avant-garde; she and Larionov were the leaders of the movement called "rayonnisme", one of the ancestors of the abstract art of to-day. Her décors for the Diaghilev revival of *Le Coq d'or* demonstrated to perfection the twin sources of her inspiration: popular and modern art. They were like giant manuscript illuminations, glowing with reds and golds, and making short work of academic perspective; two-dimensional in their emphasis on flat planes of colour yet at the same time suggesting depth by the very intensity of the colours and by the avoidance of shadows. Subsequently, with subjects which were not drawn from Slavonic folklore, for instance her costumes for *Le Mariage d'Aurore* and her set for *Cinderella,* she showed that she was equally at home with a quieter palette. The full extent of her range was revealed by the extreme, almost monochromatic, economy of her set and costumes for Stravinsky's *Les Noces,* which was one of the greatest achievements of the Russian Ballet's second period. In nothing that she has done has Goncharova pandered to sensation or fashion. She is one of the finest designers of the contemporary theatre. Principal décors: for the Ballets Russes: *Le Coq d'Or* (1914), *Liturgie* (project, 1915), *Sadko* (revival, 1916), *Les Noces* (1923), *Renard* (costumes, 1922), *Le Mariage d'Aurore* (some costumes, 1922), *L'Oiseau de Feu* (revival, 1926); for the Ballets de Monte-Carlo: *Igrouchka* (1938), *Bogatyri* (1939); for de Basil: *Cinderella* (London, 1938). Other décors include *Tsar Saltan* (National Theatre of Latvia, 1932), *Boléro* (Nijinska, 1933), *La Vie Parisienne* (Chauve-Souris, New York, 1933), *La Foire de Sorochinsky* (Ballets Russes de Paris, 1940), *Cœur de diamant* (de Cuevas, 1949).

GORE Walter. English dancer and choreographer, now ballet master at the Opera House, Frankfurt, Walter Gore worked with Marie Rambert off and on for nearly twenty years. He was one of the first male dancers to make a reputation at the Ballet Club and although his fame has never perhaps been sufficiently widespread he ranks as one of the best of English character dancers. He danced with the Vic-Wells Ballet between 1931-35 and created the role of the Rake in *The Rake's Progress,* returning in 1952 to give several remarkable performances of this role.

He danced most of the Rambert repertoire and such classical roles as Albrecht in *Giselle.* For Rambert he made his first ballet, the poignant *Valse Finale* (1938) and after war service in the Navy returned to Rambert as soloist and choreographer, creating *Simple Symphony, Mr. Punch, Concerto Burlesco* and *Antonia,* and reviving *Confessional* and *Bartlemas Dances* (first produced for the Oxford Ballet Club).

Since leaving Rambert, Gore has worked with many companies in Europe and Australia. For a short time he ran his own company, the Walter Gore Ballet (1953). Among his most successful recent works have been *Carte Blanche* (1953) for the Sadler's Wells Theatre Ballet,

Crucifix (first produced in Paris) in which his wife Paula Hinton danced the leading part of a girl burned as a witch, and *Ginevra,* produced in 1956 for the Ballet der Lage Landen in Holland. His first new ballet at Frankfurt, *Die im Schatten Leben* (to Britten's Variations on a Theme of Frank Bridge), may prove to be his masterpiece, though it will be rivalled by *The Night and Silence,* created for the 1958 Edinburgh Festival Ballet. Gore's taste for eccentric and violently dramatic ballets sometimes overshadows his true gifts of gaiety, tenderness and deep pity. He has suffered from working with too many groups for short periods of time and now needs a long-term appointment and congenial atmosphere in which to consolidate his achievements.

GOOD-HUMOURED LADIES The. See *Les Femmes de bonne humeur.*

GORSKY Alexander. Born St. Petersburg 1872, died Moscow, 1924. Dancer, choreographer and teacher, a product of the Imperial School of St. Petersburg. He became premier danseur in 1900. By then, he had been teaching for four years under Gerdt, had assisted

WALTER GORE AS THE RAKE.

Vladimir Stepanov to evolve his system of dance notation, and had introduced it to Moscow by using it to produce *The Sleeping Beauty* at the Bolshoi in 1898. Towards the end of 1900 he was appointed maître de ballet at the Bolshoi and settled in Moscow, where, under the influence of Stanislavsky's Art Theatre, his ideas gradually clarified and their revolutionary nature became apparent. Gorsky's aim was to restore the dramatic and human appeal of ballet, stifled beneath a mass of meaningless conventions. He needed dancers who were accomplished mimes and actors and, instead of the usual frigid symmetrical arrangements, an expressive, pliable corps de ballet capable of sustaining continuous dramatic action. He even made intelligent use of the wooden ranks of supers—usually hired soldiers. Great importance was attached to the authenticity of national dances. His favourite designers Golovine and Korovine shared his aims. Everything was made as realistic as possible; for the shipwreck in *Le Corsaire* (1912) the machinist Waltz constructed a special machine weighing more than a ton; in *Salammbo* (1910) Gorsky

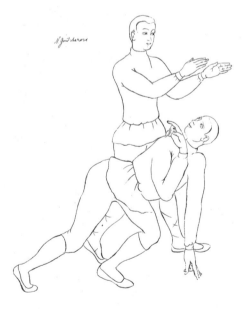

GONCHAROVA. STUDY FOR LES NOCES. 1923.

staged a scene with monstrous, writhing reptiles, which was banned. The press was inclined to be hostile and Gorsky's old master Petipa openly disapproved. But apart from these orgies of realism Gorsky accomplished much valuable work, including four different versions of *Lac des Cygnes* and many new productions of classical ballets. His reputation spread rapidly; in 1911, he was invited to London to produce *The Dance Dream* at the Alhambra for the Coronation of George V. Diaghilev wanted him to do the choreography of Tcherepnine's *The Red Masks,* but the project fell through. From the purely choreographic point of view Gorsky was not an innovator, but his general influence was invigorating and he communicated his enthusiasm to a whole group of younger artists as devoted as himself.

GRADUATION BALL or *Bal des Cadets.* Ballet in one act. Scenario and choreography: David Lichine. Music: Johann Strauss, arr. and orch. Antal Dorati. Scenery and costumes: Alexandre Benois. First performance: Original Ballet Russe, Theatre Royal, Sydney, 28 February 1940. Principal dancers: Tatiana Riabouchinska, David Lichine, Nicholas Orloff, Borislav Runanine, Igor Schwezoff, Leskova, Denisova, Moulin.

The title explains the setting. The cadets of a military school are invited to a dance at a seminary for young ladies in Vienna. The ballet is a series of divertissements and episodes, comic and sentimental. The old general flirts with the headmistress, there is a fouetté competition, a naughty pupil who performs an impromptu solo, a brilliant variation for a young drummer and a romantic pas de deux. A light-hearted ballet, sometimes grossly over-exaggerated, it can become in the hands of artists (such as the original cast or the present dancers of the Royal Danish Ballet) a charming and nostalgic work. Now in the repertory of several European and American companies.

GRAHAM Martha. Martha Graham's art is very much of her time and place. Her family were New England Presbyterians and included several clergymen. Her father was a specialist in mental diseases; from him Martha learned

GONCHAROVA. COSTUMES FOR THE FAIR AT SOROCHINSK.
BALLETS RUSSES DE PARIS. 1940.

MARTHA GRAHAM.

muscles loosen but do not grow slack. There is no conflict either between the body and space or the ground which serves as a "barre" for every day practice. Leaps are never abrupt and aggressive: the body seems to bounce lightly into space. Falls never degenerate into slumps: an easy, controlled progress allows the body to halt in impossible momentary equilibriums before taking off in another direction. In spite of appearances to the contrary, Graham was not influenced by the European techniques of Laban and Wigman; she had established the basis of her own method before she came into contact with theirs.

Martha Graham showed an early interest in specifically American themes; she derived much, for example, from the direct and simple mysticism of the Indians. She then turned to social and psychological problems, e.g. the puritanism in which she had been raised, the behaviour of women, etc. With a fully trained company at her disposal, she gradually moved towards more universal, dramatic themes. For her, the scenario of the ballet is relatively unimportant. What matters in *Night Journey,* for example, is not the myth of Oedipus and Jocasta, but the emotions which spring from the situation; a heroine at once wife and mother, a hero ravaged by inner strife, a dancing chorus stressing the universal significance of the drama. Even her most poetic and gay ballets, like *Canticle for Innocent Comedians,* show a deep attention to human psychology. The foremost American musicians, painters and sculptors have worked with her on her ballets so closely that music, décor and costumes seem an integral part of the choreography. Martha Graham has already produced more than one hundred ballets, among them *Primitive Mysteries* (1931), *Frontier* (1935), *American Document* (1938), *Every Soul is a Circus* (1939), *Letter to the World* (*), *El Penitente* (1940), *Punch and the Judy* (1941), *Deaths and Entrances, Cave of the Heart* (1947), *Errand into the Maze, Night Journey* (1947) and, "the crown of a fabulous career", *Clytemnestra,* a full evening work first produced at the Adelphi Theatre, New York 1 April 1958.

how to judge people's motives from their outward movements. He was, however, opposed to her becoming a dancer; it was only after his death, when she was already 16, that she could start her professional studies.

She entered the school of Ruth St. Denis and Ted Shawn in 1916, and this was her first contact with the theories of Delsarte. Although she danced in the Denishawn troupe, she was already moving towards another conception of ballet, something more contemporary and socially significant. The composer Louis Horst, then musical director at Denishawn and passionately interested in the dance, advised her to spread her wings and she left the school in 1923.

After appearing in various productions, Martha Graham made her independent début in New York in 1926. She was to become one of the most original of modern choreographers and the founder of a new school of movement. Delsartism had taught her the links between body and mind, the importance of elementary movement analysis in perfect muscular coordination and control of balance. It also taught her to harmonize movement and breathing, a technique which she later developed as the basis for her method, now used in many American schools in the teaching of classical dance. Her own troupe is the best possible illustration of her method; her dancers impress by their great ease and muscular coordination, the least movement entailing the participation of the whole body. Even relaxation is controlled: the

GRAND BALLET DU MARQUIS DE CUEVAS. One of the few companies whose existence is still due to private initiative. The initiative in this case was twofold: the passionate enthusiasm of the Marquis himself and the understanding generosity of his wife, a granddaughter of John D. Rockefeller. Its origins go back to 1944, when the Marquis formed his first company in New York. It was called *Ballet International* and gave an autumn season at the Park (renamed for the occasion the International) Theatre. There were classical revivals, and a number of new ballets: *Constantia* (William Dollar), *Mad Tristan* (Massine), *The Mute Wife* (Antonia Cobos), *Sebastian* (Edward Caton). There was no further season, but the experience encouraged de Cuevas to take over (in 1947) the company which Eugene Grunberg had been running for three years in Monte Carlo with Serge Lifar as maître de ballet (see *Nouveau Ballet de Monte-Carlo*).

De Cuevas accordingly arrived in Europe with an imposing general staff of choreographers, dancers and maîtres de ballet: Rosella Hightower, Marjorie Tallchief, André Eglevsky, George Skibine, Bronislava Nijinska, William Dollar, Nicolas Beriosoff, Yvonne Patterson, Anna Cheselka. There was soon friction between the newcomers and the European artists, who included Yvette Chauviré, Renée Jeanmaire, Ludmilla Tcherina, Janine Charrat, Olga Abadache, Alexandre Kalioujny, Youly Algaroff, Wladimir Skouratoff and Boris Trailine. Very few Parisian stars were still in the company when, as the *Grand Ballet de Monte-Carlo,* it gave its first Paris season at the Alhambra (7 November 1947). The American dancers were the stars of the memorable opening programme, consisting of *Variations* (Nijinska), *Roméo et Juliette* (Lifar) and *Tableaux d'une exposition* (Nijinska).

In the ensuing eleven years the de Cuevas company has become world-famous. Its present repertoire consists of more than 60 ballets,

ROSELLA HIGHTOWER AND WLADIMIR SKOURATOFF
IN COUP DE FEU. DE CUEVAS BALLET, 1952.

some of them by members of the company who were given their chance as choreographers: George Skibine, Ana Ricarda, Wladimir Skouratoff and Serge Golovine. In 1950, the company ceased its annual visits to Monte Carlo and became independent, as the *Grand Ballet du Marquis de Cuevas*. It must have visited more countries than any other modern company. Tours are usually preceded by a long season in Paris, which has become almost an annual event. In the autumn season of 1955 there were no important novelties and the company appeared tired. Very sensibly, de Cuevas waited until 1957 before appearing in Paris again. This time there were five new ballets, notably *La Corrida* (Lichine) and *La Fiesta* (Enriquez Martinez).

With strong financial backing and a substantial and varied repertoire, the Cuevas ballet owes much of its success to the brilliance of its dancers, the majority of whom have remained, with some short interruptions, faithful to the company. Another factor has been the widespread popularity of the big classics, which few of the smaller touring companies can afford to produce. The de Cuevas productions are calculated to appeal to the general public, which likes virtuoso dancing from the soloists and a large corps de ballet, rather than to the élite. Really successful new works have been rare; *Piège de lumière* (Taras), *Idylle* and *Le Prisonnier du Caucase* (Skibine), and *Le Moulin Enchanté* (Lichine) are among the exceptions. But there have been excellent revivals of works by Fokine, Massine, Balanchine and Nijinska. These form the basis of the company's repertoire with the great classics, *Giselle, Le Lac des Cygnes* (Act II) and the inevitable *Black Swan* and *Blue Bird* pas de deux.

GRANDE JATTE La. Ballet by Pierre Bertin. Music: Fred Barlow. Choreography: Albert Aveline. First performance: Opéra de Paris, 12 July 1950. Principal dancers: Lycette Darsonval, Jacqueline Moreau and Michel Renault. A Sunday outing at the end of the last century, complete with polkas and quadrilles.

GRAND PAS. "Ballet académique" by Serge Lifar. Music: Brahms, orch. Tony Aubin. First performance: Paris Opera, 17 June 1953 (see *Variations*).

BALLET DE MONTE-CARLO

PROGRAMME BY DERAIN FOR THE FIRST SEASON OF THE DE CUEVAS BALLET, 1947.

GRANT Alexander. Now principal character dancer in Britain's Royal Ballet, Alexander Grant was born in New Zealand in 1925 and came to England on a R.A.D. scholarship in 1946. Within a few months he was dancing at Covent Garden and in 1947 made his name as the comic, lovelorn barber in Massine's *Mam'-zelle Angot*. Since then he has created the Jester in *Cinderella*, Sancho Panza in *Don Quixote*, Pierre in *Madame Chrysanthème* and many other roles. He dances the Miller in *Le Tricorne*, Eros in *Sylvia*, Neapolitan Dance in *Le Lac des Cygnes*, and, most notably, Petrouchka. Unimpressive in the classroom, he comes to life on stage. A truly theatrical personality, he enlivens any part in which he appears.

GRECO José. In America he is considered one of the finest Spanish dancers of the day, and his annual tours are triumphant progresses, but in Europe he is less well known and perhaps less appreciated. He started his career with Argentinita and for a long time was her partner. Afterwards he danced in the company of Pilar Lopez before forming his own troupe. In addition to his natural gifts and brilliant personality, he has excellent style which gives his performances great homogeneity. More at ease in solos or dances for small groups than in large ensembles, his finest creations have been his *Farruca,* and, above all, *El Cortijo.* Cinemagoers will remember his dancing in the film devoted to the great matador Manolete, and also in *Around the World in Eighty Days.*

GREY Beryl. An exceptionally gifted child, Beryl Grey became a member of the Sadler's Wells ballet at the age of fourteen; in the following year (1942) she was already dancing ballerina roles, notably Odette-Odile. A tall dancer of great fluency, she has excelled by the sheer quality of her dancing rather than by gifts of interpretation. A great favourite of the English public, she ranked second only to Fonteyn in popularity when, in 1956, she resigned from the Royal Ballet in order to devote her energies to guest appearances in England and abroad. In

LA CORRIDA. COSTUMES BY CAPULETTI.
DE CUEVAS BALLET, 1957.

1957 she was the first English ballerina to dance in Russia (Moscow, Leningrad, Kiev and Tiflis) and has recorded her experiences in a book. Warm-hearted and loquacious, she is an excellent public speaker.

GRIGORIEV Serge. A former student of the Imperial School of St. Petersburg, Grigoriev was engaged by Diaghilev as *régisseur général* for the Paris season of 1909. He also made occasional appearances as a dancer in character parts in *Le Pavillon d'Armide, Sheherazade* (the Shah) and later in *La Boutique Fantasque* (the Russian merchant) and *Le Chant du Rossignol* (the Emperor), but his work as *régisseur* was far more important. He had the thankless but necessary task of maintaining absolute discipline in the company and seeing that Diaghilev's orders were scrupulously carried out. The comprehensive training he had received in St. Petersburg enabled him to combine the roles of producer, maître de ballet and coach. Imperturbable, meticulous and tactful, he was Diaghilev's most faithful collaborator, the only one to remain in the company for the whole twenty years (1909-1929) without interruption. After Diaghilev's death, he was unable, in spite of valiant efforts, to keep the troupe together. In 1932 he was engaged as *régisseur* by Colonel de Basil and worked both with the Ballets de Monte-Carlo and the Original Ballet Russe. His phenomenal memory—he can reconstruct the details of a ballet after as much as forty years—has been particularly valuable to the Royal Ballet, fort which he and his wife Lubov Tchernicheva have staged important revivals of *The Firebira* (1954) and *Petrouchka* (1957). They have also helped Festival Ballet with Fokine revivals and have mounted *The Firebird* in Milan. Grigoriev is the author of a valuable book of memoirs: *The Diaghilev Ballet, 1909-1929.*

GRIS Juan. Born Madrid 1887, died Boulogne-sur-Seine 1927. Gris, who occupies an important place in the history of cubism, was a latecomer to stage design. He worked for the Ballets Russes for the first time in 1924, the year of Braque's *Les Fâcheux* (it was some years before cubism reached the theatre; the first manifestations in painting date from 1907, Picasso's first décor, *Parade,* from 1917). By 1924 the heroic period was over, and the contributions to the theatre of both Gris and Braque were more notable for their extreme refinement and professional skill than for startling innovations of the kind cubism might have provided earlier on. Their designs revealed the strong affinities between cubism and the purest classicism. Both artists in fact were called on to re-interpret the 17th or 18th centuries in modern terms. The ballet Gris designed for Diaghilev in 1924 was *Les Tentations de la Bergère ;* in the same year he superintended the *Fête merveilleuse* given in the Galerie des Glaces at Versailles, and designed two of the operas given by the Ballets Russes at Monte-Carlo, Gounod's *La Colombe* and Chabrier's *Une Éducation manquée.*

JOSÉ GRECO WITH ARGENTINITA.

Pygmalion (Metropolitan Ballet), *La Perle* (Ballets de Paris), *L'Aigrette* (de Cuevas), and a popular showpiece pas de deux, *Grand Pas Classique.*

GSOVSKY Tatiana. A Russian dancer from St. Petersburg who came to Germany in 1925 and has had great influence there as choreographer and teacher. Ballet mistress at the (East) Berlin State Opera 1945-52. After two years at the Teatro Colon (Buenos Aires) she returned to (West) Berlin where she resumed teaching and founded her own company, the Berliner Ballett, in 1955. Her thirty-odd ballets include *Hamlet, Der Idiot, Turandot, Orpheus.* Among her many notable German pupils were Maria Fris, Natasha Trofimova, Peter van Dijk and Gert Reinholm. Formerly married to Victor Gsovsky.

GSOVSKY Victor. Choreographer and distinguished teacher. Born St. Petersburg. Has been maître de ballet to numerous companies: Berlin State Opera (1925), Paris Opera (1945), Ballet des Champs-Élysées (1946), Metropolitan Ballet (1947), Munich State Opera (1949). He now teaches in Paris. Colette Marchand, Irène Skorik, Violette Verdy and Serge Perrault were among his pupils. His ballets include *Mascarade* and *La Sylphide* (Ballets des Champs-Élysées), *Dances of Galanta* and

H

HAMILTON Gordon. Dancer of Australian origin, who studied under Egorova in Paris. After making his début with the Anglo-Polish Ballet, he joined the Sadler's Wells Ballet to play character parts. In 1946 he joined the Ballets des Champs-Élysées, and appeared in *La Sylphide, Carmen,* and *La Croqueuse de Diamants.* Small, lively and red-haired, he is a remarkable mime. He is now maître de ballet for classical productions at the Vienna State Opera, whose company is acquiring increased renown.

HAMLET. Ballet in one scene. Scenario (after Shakespeare) and choreography: Robert Helpmann. Music: Tchaikovsky. Scenery and costumes: Leslie Hurry. First performance: Sadler's Wells Ballet, New Theatre, London, 19 May, 1942. Principal dancers: Margot

Fonteyn, Celia Franca, Robert Helpmann, David Paltenghi, John Hart, Alexis Rassine.

Hamlet has been slain by Laertes. As he dies and his body is borne away, memories crowd through his disordered brain. He sees his mother the Queen; his royal father's ghost; the usurping King, his uncle; Ophelia, and her brother Laertes. But their identities tend to merge, events are twisted and strange motives revealed. Hamlet confuses his mother with Ophelia, who appears to divide her affections equivocally between Hamlet and Laertes; the personages of the Court themselves act the play scene. The drama works itself out in this distorted form; the cortège is resumed as final darkness falls. Helpmann's sensational and cunningly designed extravaganza, compressed into the bare twenty minutes of Tchaikovsky's Fantasy-Overture, was admirably served by Leslie Hurry's lurid setting, with its baroque curves melting surrealistically into sinister human forms.

HARLEQUIN IN APRIL. Ballet in two scenes. Music: Richard Arnell. Scenario and choreography: John Cranko. Scenery and costumes: John Piper. First performance: Sadler's Wells Theatre Ballet, London, 8 May 1951. Principal dancers: David Blair, Patricia Miller, Stanley Holden.

In Piper's mysterious setting of a burnt-out theatre with charred proscenium and tattered red curtain (suggested by the disaster in the Theatre Royal at Hanley in 1949, when the company was playing there on tour) Cranko staged a symbolic parable of the hopelessness of man's endeavour, and of his indestructibility. Harlequin, gay, lithe and adventurous is born, discovers Columbine, his ideal, pursues her and overcomes her guardian unicorns. But she fades from his grasp, an illusion. Harlequin dies, disconsolate. Pierrot, the other side of man's nature, absurd, cowardly and incapable of learning from experience, goes blundering on, trying incorrigibly to emulate Harlequin.

Harlequin in April was suggested by lines from T. S. Eliot's poem *The Waste Land,* beginning:

> *April is the cruellest month, breeding*
> *Lilacs out of the dead land, mixing*
> *Memory and desire, stirring*
> *Dull roots with spring rain . . .*

HARLEQUIN IN APRIL.

HART John. A pupil of Judith Espinosa, John Hart joined the Sadler's Wells Ballet in 1938, soon becoming a leading soloist. Blond, virile and of cheerful disposition, he danced nearly all the important classical solos before joining the Royal Air Force. After the war, he returned to the company and made a new reputation in character parts, notably the Corregidor in *The Three Cornered Hat,* The Shopkeeper in *La Boutique Fantasque,* Dr. Coppelius and Kostchei in *The Firebird.* Ballet Master to the Royal Ballet since 1955, he is also a skilled photographer.

HARVEST ACCORDING The. Ballet in one act. Music: Virgil Thomson. Scenery and costumes: Lemuel Ayers. Choreography: Agnes de Mille. First performance: 1 October 1952, Ballet Theatre. Principal dancers : Gemze de Lappe, Kelly Brown, Ruth Ann Koesun.

"Life, life is the tillage, and death is the harvest according." These lines from Walt Whitman were the inspiration of this work, styled by Agnes de Mille "Rondo in heroic vein." The ballet is in three parts: childhood, games, war — the whole seen through a woman's eyes. Altogether it presents the eternal cycle of events, valid for all countries and all epochs. The action of the ballet takes place in New England at the time of the War between the States. The music is based on American folksong, old hymns and modern songs. The departure of the soldiers, their return, the loneliness of the girl whose fiancé does not come back, the women at work during the men's absence — these are the most striking scenes of a work which stands halfway between folklore and dramatic ballet.

HASKELL Arnold. One of England's leading authorities on ballet, Haskell was born in 1903. He was a joint founder of the Camargo Society in 1930. His interest in the national company culminated in his appointment in 1946 as Principal of the Sadler's Wells School, now the Royal Ballet School. He is a Vice-President of the Royal Academy of Dancing. Haskell has been active as writer, journalist and lecturer; his many books include *Balletomania* and a life of Diaghilev.

HAYDEN Melissa. Canadian by birth, she was a member of Boris Volkoff's Canadian Ballet, which she left in 1945 to join Ballet Theatre. She is now a star of the New York City Ballet and one of the few dancers in that famous company who, in physique and style, may be described as in the international class and not specifically American, whether she dances in *Interplay, Le Combat,* or *Four Temperaments.* Small, well-proportioned, and very musical, she has assimilated technique to the point where she can forget it. She moves like an amazon, with head held high, proudly conquering the stages of the world.

HELEN OF TROY. Ballet in prologue and three scenes, based on Offenbach's operetta *La Belle Hélène,* by David Lichine and Antal Dorati. Music: Offenbach, orch. Dorati. Scenery and costumes: Marcel Vertès. Choreography: Lichine. First performance: 10 September 1942, Ballet Theatre, Mexico City. Principal dancers: Irina Baronova, Rosella Hightower, André Eglevsky, Jerome Robbins.

The ballet was started by Fokine shortly before his death, as a successor to the highly successful *Bluebeard.* Lichine took over the plot and turned it into a comic ballet, full of burlesque touches and "gags". The free and easy way in which the characters of this danced operetta are presented — the little lambs applauding the dancing of Paris (a Hollywood jeune premier), Hermes' tricks as he sits by the nuptial couch, munching an apple or knitting — never fails to win laughter but it cannot be claimed that the work is entirely successful. Nevertheless it has been a staple item in Ballet Theatre's repertoire for many years.

* Also inspired by Offenbach's operetta, John Cranko produced *La Belle Hélène,* a ballet-bouffe in four scenes. The new scenario was by Marcel Achard and Robert Manuel, the musical arrangement by Louis Aubert and Manuel Rosenthal. The scenery and costumes, as in *Helen of Troy,* were designed by Marcel Vertès. First performance: Paris Opera, 6 April 1955. Principal dancers: Yvette Chauviré, Claude Bessy, Michel Renault, Max Bozzoni. Despite some conventional buffoonery, Cranko made clever use of the classic language of ballet to produce music-hall effects, and there was plenty

of opportunity for dancing. The tutus with bustles, the old dandies wearing "boaters", the pleasure-steamer setting out for Cythera, and Helen's rococo room were delightful examples of the good taste with which Vertès interpreted the bad taste of the 1860's.

HELPMANN Robert. "Talented, enthusiastic, extremely intelligent, great facility and vitality, witty, cute as a monkey, quick as a squirrel; a sense of the theatre and his own possible achievements therein" — this was Ninette de Valois' verdict in 1933, after Robert Helpmann, an unknown young Australian, had been at the Sadler's Wells School for a week. From the beginning of the 1933-34 season until he resigned in 1950, Helpmann was a leading dancer and mime in the Sadler's Wells Ballet.

Born in Australia in 1909, Helpmann studied under Novikov with the Pavlova company and appeared in musicals in Australia before coming to England. While studying at the Wells School he danced in the company's corps de ballet and immediately attracted attention. In no time he became a soloist, and was soon dancing leading roles in the new ballets by de Valois and Ashton. A fine partner, he appeared with Fonteyn in all the classical ballets and shared her early triumphs. Never a strong technician, he disguised his limitations by artistry and a strong sense of the theatre. He excelled alike in romantic parts (*Apparitions, Nocturne*) and character parts, dramatic (the Red King in *Checkmate*) and comic (the Bridegroom in *A Wedding Bouquet* and Mr. O'Reilly in *The Prospect Before Us*). He was equally notable as Satan in *Job* and in the title-role of *The Rake's Progress*.

During and immediately after the war, Helpmann made an important contribution as a choreographer. In contrast to Ashton's more lyrical style, Helpmann's approach in his principal ballets *Hamlet, Miracle in the Gorbals* and *Adam Zero* (in each of which he danced the leading male role) was strongly dramatic. He has since employed his remarkable gifts as producer and actor, mainly of Shakespeare, and has recently been much associated with the Old Vic. In 1958, he returned successfully to the Royal Ballet as guest artist, reviving *Hamlet* and *Miracle in the Gorbals,* and appearing for the first time in his career as Petrouchka.

LA BELLE HÉLÈNE. DÉCOR FOR SCENE I BY VERTÈS. 1955.

HENZE Hans Werner. This young German composer (born 1926, Gütersloh, Westphalia) is an important figure in the post-war musical scene. His interest in ballet dates from 1948, when he saw a performance by the Sadler's Wells Ballet at Hamburg. His direction in 1951-52 of the small ballet company attached to the theatre at Wiesbaden, and which included the dancers Maria Fris, Denise Laumer, Wolfgang Leistner, Peter van Dijk and the choreographer Erich Walter, marked an important stage in the revival of ballet in Germany. Henze's ballets include *Jack Pudding* (Wiesbaden, 1951), *Pas d'action* (Munich Festival, 1952) and the controversial *Maratona di Danza* produced by Luchino Visconti at the Berlin Festival, 1957. His Third Symphony was performed as a ballet under the title *Anrufung Apoll's* (Wiesbaden, 1951). Other works for the stage in which dancing plays an important part are *Der Idiot,* a ballet-pantomime after Dostoievsky (Berlin Festival, 1952), and his most considerable achievements so far, the operas *Boulevard Solitude* (Hanover, 1952) and *König Hirsch* (Berlin Festival, 1956). He was recently commissioned to write a three-act ballet *Ondine* for the Royal Ballet.

Henze studied in Germany with Wolfgang Fortner and in Paris with René Leibowitz. His approach to music is undogmatic, his pen is fluent and his invention copious. His gift for dramatic expression he shares with many of his countrymen, but few of them have possessed his command of rhythmic suppleness, and his extraordinary sense of instrumental colour is very much his own.

HIGHTOWER Rosella. Born at Ardmore, Oklahoma, Rosella Hightower first became aware of ballet when she saw Colonel de Basil's company in 1933 at Kansas City, where her family had settled. Discovered by Massine in 1938, she came to Europe, and soon rose to be a soloist in the Ballets Russes de Monte-Carlo. In 1944 she was a principal dancer with Ballet Theatre, but her real dedication dates from the day when she replaced Alicia Markova, who was indisposed, in *Giselle*. In 1947 Hightower joined the Marquis de Cuevas's company in Europe and embarked on a dazzling career. Her famous roles include the pas de deux *Black Swan, Piège de Lumière, Constantia, Inès de Castro, Rondo Capriccioso,* as well as all the ballets in the classical repertoire. She tried her hand at choreography with *Henry VIII* for the Markova-Dolin company in 1946 and *Scaramouche* for the Marquis de Cuevas. Returning to Ballet Theatre in 1955, she divided her time for two years between that company and de Cuevas. She married Jean Robier, painter and scene-designer.

ROBERT HELPMANN IN DANTE SONATA.

A product of the American school of classic dancing, Rosella Hightower is one of the first American ballerinas to have achieved international fame. Taught first by an American, Dorothy Perkins, and then by Russians in New York and Paris, Hightower brings to contemporary ballet the vitality and dynamism of a youthful race, moulded by the traditional classical school. A brilliant dancer, by sheer hard work she acquired a romantic style which is contrary to her nature. Her dancing is free and spontaneous, and there exists no technical difficulty that she cannot overcome; her slender body is a perfect instrument. Her response to music is immediate; there is nothing affected or "pretty" about her vigorous, passionate dancing. She has given much thought to the question of make-up, and makes effective use of her fascinating green eyes.

HINDEMITH Paul. Born Hanau, 1895. The gradual metamorphosis of the *enfant terrible* of the musical 'twenties into the benign but still very active senior composer of the 'fifties, so clearly a pillar of the German academic tradition in its finest aspects, is no longer a matter for surprise. The indications were always there, in the traditional training at the Frankfurt Conservatoire and, even when he was shocking the public with the works of the inter-war period (the operas with their "contemporary" subject matter, divas in the bath and typewriters in the orchestra, and the short concertos laid out for small, contrasted groups of instruments, with their astringent harmony and muscular counterpoint), in his practical, utilitarian outlook on musical problems. In the 'thirties came a settling down and broadening out with large-scale works such as the opera *Mathis der Maler,* which reflected, in part from the angle of personal experience, the deeper preoccupations of the time. Hindemith is one of the great musical all-rounders of the century: composer, theorist, pedagogue and executant—he plays numerous instruments and has won distinction as violist and as conductor. Diaghilev's death in 1929 robbed the world of a Hindemith ballet from the first period: a score to be called *Number 13,* about bicycle racing, was under consideration. But *Nobilissima Visione* (Massine, Ballets de Monte-Carlo, 1938) is one of the finest works of

ROSELLA HIGHTOWER IN PIÈGE DE LUMIÈRE.

the ensuing decade, while *Herodiade* (for reciter and chamber orchestra, written for Martha Graham in 1944) and *The Four Temperaments* (Theme and Variations for piano and strings) are sterling examples from the output of the years spent in America. This last work, produced by the Ballet Society in 1946, is one of Balanchine's masterpieces.

HIRSCH Georges. As Administrator of the Réunion des Théâtres Lyriques Nationaux (the two national opera houses of France), to which post he was appointed in 1946, it was Hirsch's task to reconstruct a team which the war years had disrupted and disbanded. He also made some controversial promotions, leading to the usual scandals. At the Opéra, it was Hirsch who reinstated Serge Lifar as maître de ballet and who, at the beginning of 1947, engaged Balanchine to stage various productions including *Le Palais de Cristal,* and to direct revivals such as *Le Baiser de la fée* and *Apollon Musagète.* As for the Opéra-Comique, it was thanks to Hirsch that regular and successful evenings of ballet were instituted there. His taste was catholic. He initiated a series of experiments, without favouring any particular style or school and without alarming his conservative public. Hirsch's term of office ended in 1951. He was reappointed in 1956, in spite of violent opposition from his opponents. Since that date, there have been two important revivals: *Le Martyre de Saint-Sébastien* and *La Symphonie fantastique*.

HOMME ET SON DÉSIR L'. Ballet in one act. Scenario: Paul Claudel. Music: Darius Milhaud. Scenery and costumes: Audrey Parr. Choreography: Jean Borlin. First performance: Ballets Suédois, Théâtre des Champs-Élysées, Paris, 6 June 1921.

Claudel and Milhaud wrote this "poème plastique" in Brazil in 1917-18. It was there, also, that Audrey Parr designed the setting which Claudel had imagined: four superimposed tiers on which the allegorical action (man, imprisoned by desire, watched over by the hours and by the two faces of the moon, is released from his struggles by woman, at once love and death) could be worked out simultaneously. Milhaud's imaginative score, written for vocal quartet, twelve solo instruments and percussion, shows, like *La Création du monde,* a preoccupation with barbaric colour and rhythm. It had a double origin in the impression made on the composer by the myriad sounds of nightfall in the virgin forest, and also by Nijinsky's last performances in Rio before his mental collapse. *L'Homme et son désir* was one of the Swedish Ballet's most important productions.

HONEGGER Arthur. Born 1892, died 1955. Although he was born at Le Havre, Honegger came of German-Swiss stock and studied at the Zürich Conservatoire before completing his musical education in Paris. In spite of his years of residence in Paris and his membership of the Groupe des Six, his music retained a sober, individual sturdiness, its innate romanticism tempered with a respect for form and a fondness for contrapuntal complexity. One of his earliest works, *Les Dicts des jeux du monde* (1919), was commissioned by Jeanne Ronsay as a suite of dances. Two years later, he contributed a funeral march to the gay manifesto *Les*

Mariés de la Tour Eiffel which Les Six wrote for the Ballets Suédois. From 1921 also dates a far more important and typical work, *Horace Victorieux,* originally intended for stage performance and described by the composer as a "symphonie mimée". His first real ballet was *Skating Rink* (Ballets Suédois, 1922). The press summed it up neatly: "English title, Swedish ballet, Italian scenario, Swiss music—a typically Parisian event. Everything went as smoothly as on roller-skates". In 1928 he arranged some Bach music for Nijinska's *Les Noces de l'Amour et de Psyché* (Ida Rubinstein season). In 1931 came *Amphion,* for Ida Rubinstein again, a scenic cantata to a text by Paul Valéry. *Sémiramis* (1934, described as an "action chorégraphique") and *Cantique des Cantiques* (Lifar, 1938) made use of the Ondes Martenot in the orchestra. Further ballets included *L'Oiseau Blanc* (1937, Salle Pleyel), the last two acts of *Chota Roustaveli,* a Georgian legend in four acts, the other two being written by Tibor Harsanyi and Tcherepnin (Lifar, Nouveaux Ballets de Monte-Carlo, 1946) and, for the Paris Opera, *L'Appel de la Montagne* (1945) and *La Naissance des Couleurs* (1949). To English audiences, Honegger as a composer of ballet is best known by the piano pieces which Andrée Howard used for *Lady into Fox* (1939).

HOWARD Andrée. An English choreographer of great intelligence, taste and artistry, a dancer for the connoisseur and a dancer of no mean talent, Andrée Howard was an original member of Rambert's Ballet Club. She studied with Egorova, Preobrajenska, Kschessinska and Trefilova as well as with Rambert and in 1933 spent a few months with the Ballets Russes de Monte-Carlo.

She returned to Rambert as soloist and choreographer and worked with her until the war. Afterwards she took charge of classes in choreographic production at the Sadler's Wells School and was appointed resident choreographer to the Sadler's Wells Theatre Ballet when it was founded in 1945. She has also created ballets for the Sadler's Wells Ballet at Covent Garden, the most recent being *Veneziana* (1953).

Howard's gift for choreography was apparent in the early ballets which she made in association with Susan Salaman, namely *Our Lady's Juggler*

(1933) and *Mermaid* (1934) which was based on the Hans Andersen story. *Death and the Maiden,* in which she created the role of the Maiden, has remained a classic of the Rambert repertoire from 1937 until today. *Lady into Fox* (1939) and *The Sailor's Return* (1947), both based on stories by David Garnett, were exceptionally successful examples of ballets which derive their inspiration from literature. *La Fête Étrange* (*) was similarly based on a novel; it captured the emotions and the atmosphere rather than the mere incidents of the story and is probably her masterpiece. In *The Fugitive, Mardi Gras* and *A Mirror for Witches* she has handled strongly dramatic themes with considerable power while her wit and humour have been exploited in *The Rape of the Lock, La Muse s'amuse, Carnival of Animals* and *Selina* (1948) which burlesqued all the conventions of the ballets of the Romantic era and in which she herself gave a brilliant performance as a very inefficient witch.

Howard's sensitivity to music has been evident in all her ballets; she has worked frequently with young composers, guiding and encouraging them. She is perhaps the most English of all choreographers, with a tendency towards under-statement that sometimes means loss of contact with her audience. On the other hand, her ballets have a subtlety that ensures their enduring freshness.

HUGO Jean. Born Paris, 1894. This painter's work for the theatre appears deceptively light-hearted; more than once he has proved to be a real innovator, never trying to be sensational, but producing ideas elegant enough to be immediately acceptable and valuable enough to be retained as obvious acquisitions to stage design. As early as 1921, for instance, with his costumes for *Les Mariés de la Tour Eiffel* he reasserted the charm of the fashions of 1900, thus paving the way for the present-day vogue for "La Belle Époque" and Edwardianism. More important, though, Hugo has invented a twentieth century romanticism, without grandiloquence or affectation. In the realm of ballet his work has been characterised by a "depersonalising" of the body, achieved through original use of body tights. In *Roméo et Juliette* (Soirées de Paris, 1924) and, twenty years later, in *Les Amours de Jupiter* (Ballets des Champs-

JEAN HUGO. DÉCOR FOR ROMÉO ET JULIETTE. SOIRÉES DE PARIS, 1924.

Élysées) he has shown what can be achieved with the simplest materials. In *Roméo et Juliette* the tights were black and tended to merge the dancers with the scenery, which consisted of black curtains; only a splash of colour on the tights defined the silhouette, while the huge white collars framing the faces of the dancers gave them a strangely impersonal character. In *Les Amours de Jupiter,* on the contrary, every dancer had a clearly defined outline, moving in shadowless space and thus constituting an independent form. The flesh-coloured tights, with the minimum of drapery, achieved the maximum of simulated coldness yet, at the same time, an intensity of expression, using the nude as a means of tranquil provocation, free from vulgarity. Hugo also designed *Les Cent Baisers* (1935) for the Ballets de Monte-Carlo.

HUGO Valentine. Her art is often allied to surrealism by a certain taste for the strange, and by her power of transfiguring a world apparently composed of simple elements into a haunted place, as shown in the setting she designed in 1947 for Debussy's *Pelléas et Mélisande.* But with the ballet *Les Malheurs de Sophie,* produced at the Opéra in 1948, the feminine element becomes dominant, a femininity expressing itself in embroidered flounces and sentimental reverie. At once clear and complex, innocent and morbid, the art of Valentine Hugo can stimulate the most diverse emotions. Among her other décors may be mentioned *Vogue* (Soirées de Paris, 1924) and *Quadrille* (Ballets des Champs-Élysées, 1945).

HUMPHREY Doris. Her mother was a pianist, her father a photographer and she came of an old American family of intellectuals. Born in Chicago, she began to dance at the age of eight and composed her first ballet *Persephone and Demeter* when seventeen. She began studying at Denishawn in 1917 and Ruth St. Denis, impressed by her gifts, advised her to concentrate on dancing and choreography. In 1928 Humphrey left Denishawn to found her own school and company with Charles Weidman. She devoted much time and deep thought to the discovery of a basic dance that would depend upon the laws of motion alone. She concluded that all movement is situated in an "arc between two deaths", at one end perfect equilibrium, at the other complete submission to the pull of gravity. Her great trilogy, *Theatre Piece, With My Red Fires,* and *New Dance* (completed in 1936) strongly impressed the younger school of American modern dancers, to whom she was both an inspiration and a practical teacher. After her retirement as a dancer, she choreographed mainly for the company of José Limon *(Lament for Ignacio Sanchez Mejias, Story of Mankind, Ruins and Visions).* Frail, red-haired, with a sharp intellect and dominating personality, she imparted her ideas to students through the choreographic courses which she taught in New York. A pioneer of modern dance, she exerted a powerful influence until her death in December 1958.

I

IBERT Jacques. Born in 1890, he is one of the most brilliant composers of the modern French school. A former director of the Réunion des Théâtres Lyriques, he has divided his prolific output between orchestral music, opera and ballet. There are six ballets by Jacques Ibert: *Rencontre* (1925), which anticipates the lively score he was to write later for *Les Amours de Jupiter ;* the *Ballad of Reading Gaol,* based on Oscar Wilde's poem, a moving, soberly lyrical work; *Escales* (Opéra, 1948), a series of short tableaux danced to a symphonic suite which had earned the composer fame in the concert hall in 1924; and finally *Diane de Poitiers* (1934) and *Le Chevalier Errant* (1950), both staged at the Opéra and undoubtedly his most important works. In the first, Ibert develops his conception of "court ballet", the divertissement which provides an opportunity for entrées enclosing varied episodes in which singing is mixed with dancing. The composer has adroitly included in his score choice pages from the time of the Renaissance: popular airs, *Danceries,* Passereau's *Il est bel et bon,* Clément Jannequin's *Chant des oiseaux.* A work of equally large dimensions (by the same librettist, Mme Elizabeth de Grammont) is *Le Chevalier errant,* which makes great use of massed choruses. Here, too, Jacques Ibert has composed a score distinguished not only by the brilliance of its style but also by its danceable qualities.

ICARE. Ballet by Serge Lifar. Rhythms by Georges Szyfer. Scenery and costumes: Paul Larthe. First performance: Paris Opera, 9 July 1935. Principal dancer: Serge Lifar.

Icarus lifts himself from the earth on wings made by his father Daedalus. A group of boys and girls watch his efforts, at first fruitless, then crowned with success. Icarus flies away, and disappears in the direction of the sun. But the sun melts the wax on his wings; one of them falls to the ground and Icarus crashes tragically to earth. He dies, immobilised in an attitude resembling the silhouette of a crashed aircraft. This ballet, neo-Greek in its presentation and neo-classic in its choreography, was a culminating point in Lifar's work, even though its revolutionary importance may sometimes have been exaggerated. No matter what Lifar himself may have said, *Icare* did not emancipate ballet from music; though limited to percussion instruments, there is still a musical score. It was the choreographer who imposed his "rhythms" on the composer Georges Szyfer, at that time conductor at the Opera. But did Petipa behave any differently in regard to Tchaikovsky? The importance of *Icare* lies rather in the unusually expressive use made of classical elevation by a prodigious actor-athlete. Serge Lifar at the age of 30 could depict, in a most dramatic fashion, the struggle of man against gravity. But it was a role made to measure and practically unique; he can hardly by replaced.

IDYLLE. Ballet in one act. Scenario, scenery and costumes: Alwyn Camble. Music: François Serette. Choreography: George Skibine. First performance: Grand Ballet du Marquis de Cuevas, Theatre de l'Empire, Paris, 2 January 1954. Pincipal dancers: Marjorie

IDZIKOWSKI IN LE TRICORNE.

Tallchief, George Skibine, Wladimir Skouratoff. A white fence, two bare, twisted trees. A black horse (with a green twig in his mane to show that he comes from the country) is frolicking in the field with a white filly. Some exercises at the fence (which becomes a barre) to loosen up the muscles, a little flirting, some lovers' quarrels, some tender exchanges. But now there arrives on the scene the circus horse, grey-coated, beplumed and splendid. Captivated at once, the filly is led away into the striped circus tent where the couple are going to perform. Here the dancing changes in style and rhythm: no longer poetic and sensitive, it develops great virtuosity, but it is virtuosity with a purpose, and for once the famous 32 fouettés are made to signify something —the proud gaiety of the young, coquettish filly dancing round the circus where she has found her happiness. At the end of the performance the filly, intoxicated with pleasure and love, tears the red plume and the golden epaulettes from her partner in order to have him as he is, for herself alone. A cruel disappointment ensues: stripped of his trappings, the splendid animal is only a poor little horse who goes sadly away, while the giddy young filly returns to her rustic lover once more. This ballet is full of real dancing, the ingenuity of the steps constantly and perfectly illustrating the central idea.

IDZIKOWSKI Stanislas. This Polish-born dancer was a star pupil of Cecchetti and made his début at the Empire Theatre in London. He danced with Pavlova's company before joining Diaghilev in 1915, appearing for the first time

Boutique Fantasque — he was unrivalled. His performance as the White Cat in *Contes Russes* always reduced Diaghilev to helpless laughter. He had a personal triumph in Balanchine's *Jack-in-the-Box* (to music of Satie), although the ballet was not popular.

He is the author, with Cyril Beaumont, of "The Theory and Practice of Classical Theatrical Dancing", the standard textbook on the Cecchetti Method of teaching.

LES INDES GALANTES. DÉCOR FOR THE TABLEAU DES FLEURS BY MOULÈNE.
Théâtre de l'Opéra, Paris.

as Harlequin in *Carnaval*. He remained with Diaghilev until 1926, returning in 1928. Since that date, except for some guest performances in the early 'thirties (notably with the Vic-Wells Ballet where he created the lead in Ashton's *Les Rendez-vous*), he has been teaching in London. At the same time he pursues his hobby of carving miniature replicas of buildings and furniture.

Idzikowski was primarily a character dancer with a prodigious technique, although his interpretation of *Le Spectre de la Rose* was also celebrated. Tiny in stature, with an up-tilted nose and animated face, he had a special gift for grotesque and artificial comedy. He could perform difficult steps at great speed and jumped easily, sharing with Nijinsky an ability to seem suspended in the air. In the ballets of Massine —*Les Femmes de bonne humeur, Le Tricorne, La*

ILLUMINATIONS. Ballet by Frederick Ashton. Music: Benjamin Britten. Scenery and costumes: Cecil Beaton. Lighting: Jean Rosenthal. First performance: New York City Ballet, New York, 2 March 1950. Principal dancers: LeClercq, Hayden, Magallanes. The idea of this work, which is still in the repertoire of the New York City Ballet, was suggested to the choreographer by the life and poems of Rimbaud. Music for soprano (or tenor) and strings accompanies a series of passionate tableaux evoking episodes in the life of the poet.

IMPRESSIONS DE MUSIC-HALL. Choreographic sketches by Nijinska. Music: Gabriel Pierné. Scenery and costumes: Maxime Dethomas. First performance: Paris Opera,

8 April 1927. This work was inspired by the variety performances then at the height of their vogue. Though the general level was undistinguished, a few episodes stood out: the "Sisters" (an allusion to the Dolly Sisters), by Mlles Binois and Cérès; an eccentric variation by Aveline in imitation of the clown Fratellini; and the entrance of Carlotta Zambelli in an immense hat-box carried by two grooms—the last role to be performed at the Opéra by that great artist.

INDES GALANTES Les. Opera-ballet in a prologue and four acts by Fuzelier (1735). Spoken commentary: René Fauchois. Music: Jean-Philippe Rameau. Scenery and costumes: Arbus and J. Dupont (Le Palais d'Hébé), Chapelain-Midy (Les Sauvages), Carzou (Les Incas), Fost and Moulène (Les Fleurs), Wakhevitch (Le Turc généreux). Choreography: Albert Aveline, Harald Lander, Serge Lifar. First performance: Paris Opera, 18 June 1952.

Perhaps the most rewarding of the Opéra's controversial attempts to revive its post-war fortunes by staging huge spectacles. "A musical for rich snobs", muttered some of the faithful adherents of *Coppelia* and the ballet in *Faust*. But it was a serious and not unconvincing attempt to revive the theatrical splendour and magnificence which appealed to Rameau's contemporaries. The succession of changing and contrasting scenes, the hundreds of elaborate costumes, the raging sea complete with shipwreck, the volcano belching stones, flames and scented smoke, the earthquake, the Persian garden à la française perfumed with the scent of roses; none of this, realized though it was by the most up to date technical methods, would have been disowned by an artist at the court of Louis XV. There were occasional minor faults of style, but on the whole the conventions of a vanished epoch were recreated and respected with surprising success; the various elements, vocal, instrumental, decorative, choreographic, combined harmoniously in a powerful assault on ear and eye.

INGHELBRECHT Désiré-Émile. French conductor and composer, born Paris, 1880. Inghelbrecht was the regular conductor for the Ballets Suédois, and worked with Diaghilev for a short time in 1927, when he had some notable differences of opinion with the great man and some of his dancers about tempi. For the Ballets Suédois he wrote the score of *El Greco* (1920); for the Opéra, *Le diable dans le beffroi*, based on the tale by Edgar Allan Poe (1927), and *La belle aventure* (1927). In that year also he orchestrated Fauré's Theme and Variations for a ballet, given at the Opéra, called *Rayon de Lune*. In 1933 the Opéra-Comique presented a ballet, *Jeux de Couleurs*, based on Inghelbrecht's charming nursery-rhyme suite "La Nursery".

INGLESBY Mona. English dancer, at one time a member of the Ballet Rambert which she left in 1940 to found her own company Interna-

LES INDES GALANTES. COSTUME FOR A SAVAGE BY CHAPELAIN-MIDY.
Bibliothèque-Musée de l'Opéra, Paris.

tional Ballet. She was at the same time director, choreographer and ballerina of this company. (See below.)

INTERNATIONAL BALLET. British company founded in 1941 by Mona Inglesby, its artistic director and principal dancer. Her aim was to bring classical ballet to audiences which had rarely if ever seen it before; to this end, the company played frequently in large cinemas and in other places not normally associated with theatrical performances. Their efforts were rewarded by enormous audiences and their tours became an annual event in many British provincial towns. The mainstay of the repertory was the series of revivals directed by Nicholas Sergueev, who mounted *Giselle, Lac des Cygnes, The Sleeping Beauty, Coppelia* and a number of Fokine's masterpieces. Massine revived two of his ballets: *Gaieté Parisienne* and *Capriccio Espagnol*. New works produced included some by Mona Inglesby herself, notably *The Masque of Comus,* given at the London Coliseum in 1946 with the text of Milton's poem spoken by actors, the original songs of Henry Lawes and additional music by Handel. Dancers appearing with the company included Moira Shearer, Nina Tarakanova, Sonia Arova, Harold Turner and Algeranoff. Designers included Sophie Fedorovitch, William Chappell and Rex Whistler. The International Ballet paid visits to Italy, Spain and Switzerland. In

ISTAR. YVETTE CHAUVIRÉ.

spite of considerable success, the cost of maintaining a full-size company without an official subsidy proved too great, and activities had to be suspended in 1953. A school of ballet, formerly attached to the company, remains in operation in London.

INTERPLAY. Ballet in one act four movements. Theme and choreography: Jerome Robbins. Music: Morton Gould. First performance: Billy Rose's *Concert Varieties,* Ziegfeld Theatre, New York, 1 June 1945. Principal dancers: John Kriza, Janet Reed, Jerome Robbins. First performance by Ballet Theatre, Metropolitan Opera House, New York, 17 October 1945. Scenery: Oliver Smith. Costumes: Irene Sharaff. Principal dancers: John Kriza, Janet Reed, Harold Lang.

The four movements are called Free Play, Horse Play, Byplay, and Team Play. The first and last are competitive ensembles for the eight dancers, the second is a crazy solo for a male soloist, the third a pas de deux to a sentimental blues. Brilliant, lively, witty and expertly constructed, *Interplay* has a surface appeal of simple fun and games and underlying recognition of the rivalry, particularly keen in the United States, between classical ballet and modern dance. It has one been of the greatest successes of the Ballet Theatre repertoire. On 23 December 1952 Robbins restaged the work for the New York City Ballet, but the dancers of this company have never quite captured its gaiety, warmth and comradeship.

ISTAR. Ballet in one act on the symphonic poem by Vincent d'Indy. Revived at the Paris Opera in a new version by Serge Lifar, 31 December 1941, with Yvette Chauviré.

The original version was mounted in 1924 by Ivan Clustine for Natasha Trouhanova. The idea was the same: the Assyrian goddess Istar descends to the infernal regions to set free the Son of Life. On her way she must pass through seven gates, at each one of which a guardian relieves her of one of her veils. The seven gates are represented musically and choreographically by as many variations in both senses of the word. The musical theme is not heard in its pure form until the end of the work — symbolising Istar's virtual nudity. Chauviré's performance of the extremely difficult solo part (the other characters are of no importance) definitely established her reputation.

J

JACK IN THE BOX. Dances by Erik Satie, orch. Darius Milhaud. Scenery and costumes: André Derain. Choreography: Balanchine. First performance: Diaghilev Ballet, Théâtre Sarah-Bernhardt, Paris, 3 July 1926. Principal dancers: Stanislas Idzikowski, Alexandra Danilova. This suite of three dances was a pretext for presenting Idzikowski, with his prodigious elevation, in the role of an amusing and mischievous jumping jack. Three girls, one coal-black (danced by Danilova) played with him as if he were a rubber ball. The background of the set was made of movable cardboard clouds.

JACKSON Rowena. A New Zealand-born dancer of quiet integrity, since 1952 a ballerina of the Royal Ballet, Rowena Jackson has a special gift for fast and brilliant turns. She holds the world record for multiple *fouettés* performed *sur place*. She has danced a sensitive Odette-Odile, a good Aurora and a likeable Swanilda. Invaluable in secondary roles, her speed, ease and precision are best seen in the Blue Bird pas de deux, as one of the "Blue Girls" in *Les Patineurs,* and in the solos which Ashton composed for her in *Variations on a theme of Purcell* and *Birthday Offering.* She danced *Giselle* for the first time in 1958. Married to Philip Chatfield.

JACOB Gordon. Born London, 1895. English composer, pupil of Stanford at the Royal College of Music in London where he subsequently (until his retirement in 1954) spent many years as Professor of theory, composition and orchestration. In the early days of the Vic-Wells Ballet he wrote two scores for the company, *The Jew in the Bush* (1931) and *Uncle Remus* (1934). Jacob is the author of (among other books) a student's manual, "Orchestral Technique". An expert practitioner himself, his association with the ballet was appropriately continued with a number of orchestrations and arrangements of music written for other purposes including *The Lord of Burleigh* (Mendelssohn), *Apparitions* (Liszt, selected by Lambert), *Promenade* (Haydn) and *Mam'zelle Angot* (Lecocq), all for Sadler's Wells.

JARDIN AUX LILAS (Lilac Garden). Ballet in one act. Music: Ernest Chausson. Choreography: Antony Tudor. Scenery and costumes: Hugh Stevenson. First performance: Ballet Club, Mercury Theatre, London, 26 January 1936. Principal dancers: Maude Lloyd, Peggy van Praagh, Antony Tudor, Hugh Laing.

La Belle Époque — or its English equivalent, the Edwardian era; Chausson's ardent *Poème ;* Stevenson's summer garden heavy with the scent of lilacs in bloom; these are the ingredients of Tudor's masterly study of frustration underlying perfect manners. Caroline is about to be married to a man she does not love and is forced to give up her lover, whom she is desperately seeking among her guests. Her fiancé's former mistress is also present. Furtive meetings soon disturbed, hurried partings, imploring glances. The tension mounts inexorably; by the end of the ballet we know only that it will not easily be resolved.

* Revived by Tudor for Ballet Theatre, Center Theatre, New York, 15 January 1940. Scenery and costumes: Raymond Sovey. * New York City Ballet, 1951. * National Ballet of Canada, 1954.

JARRE La (The Jar). Ballet in one act. Scenario: Pirandello (from his short story, *La Giarra*). Music: Alfredo Casella. Costumes and scenery: Giorgio de Chirico. Choreography: Jean Borlin. First performance: Ballets Suédois, Théâtre des Champs-Élysées, Paris, 19 November 1924.

One of Pirandello's stories of Sicilian peasant life. A battle of wits between Don Lollo, whose fine new wine-jar is broken, and the hunchback, Zi'Dima, who gets inside it to mend it, and, having completed his work, can't get out until the exasperated Don Lollo breaks it again. Casella's sturdy and colourful music was chiefly responsible for the atmosphere of brutal good-humour and physical well-being.

* New version by Ninette de Valois for the Vic-Wells Ballet, with scenery and costumes by William Chappell, Sadler's Wells, London, 9 October 1934.

JEANMAIRE Renée. Darling of New York, idol of London, and spoilt child of her native Paris, "Zizi" Jeanmaire owes her fame to the role of Carmen, which she created with the Ballets de Paris in 1949. The charming, smiling little dancer that she had been till then was transformed overnight into an international star. Her pallid face and cropped hair have now become part of her personality. A former "petit rat" of the Paris Opera, Zizi received her training from Volinine and Kniaseff, and it was

RENÉE JEANMAIRE IN CARMEN.

Serge Lifar who launched her on her career in *Aubade* (Nouveau Ballet de Monte-Carlo). In 1950, *La Croqueuse de Diamants* revealed her to be the possessor of a voice at once raucous and sensual. This was the beginning of a new career as film star *(Hans Christian Andersen, Folies-Bergère)* and musical comedy star on Broadway *(The Girl in Pink Tights)*. Married in 1954 to Roland Petit, who has arranged many dance sequences for her, she demonstrated her versatility yet again in *La Revue des Ballets de Paris* (October, 1956).

JEU DE CARTES. Ballet in three hands. Music: Stravinsky. Scenery and costumes: Pierre Roy. Choreography: Janine Charrat. First performance: Ballets des Champs-Élysées, Paris, 12 October 1945. Principal dancers: Jean Babilée, Irène Skorik, Roland Petit, Youly Algaroff, Nathalie Philippart.

The subject of this ballet, which is danced by the characters of a pack of cards, is a game of poker bedevilled by the tricks of a malicious Joker who can transform himself at will into a different card in each successive hand. The first version of *Jeu de Cartes* was presented at the Metropolitan Opera, New York, 27 April 1937, by the American Ballet. Choreography: Balanchine. Scenery and costumes: Irene Sharaff. It was revived in 1940 under the title *Poker Game* by the Ballets Russes de Monte-Carlo with a brilliant cast comprising Alicia Markova, Alexandra Danilova, Frederic Franklin, Igor Youskevitch and André Eglevsky. Balanchine's version was not a success, however, and dropped out of the repertoire.

When the Ballets des Champs-Élysées was founded in October 1945, Boris Kochno suggested to the young Janine Charrat that she should arrange a ballet to Stravinsky's score. Finding the existing book unsuitable, she devised her own scenario and made the ballet a drama of the card world—flirtations and jealousies fanned by a sardonic and baleful joker. The dancers were dressed in white body tights ornamented with the symbols of their various suits and performed against a simple brick-coloured backcloth. The work was enthusiastically received, the Parisian press acclaiming the young choreographer and her Joker, Jean Babilée, whose astonishing performance

THE JAR. DÉCOR BY CHIRICO. BALLETS SUÉDOIS, 1924.

will be remembered in the history of the dance. *Jeu de Cartes* was Charrat's first full-scale ballet, and remains one of her best works. The choreography, neo-classical in style, is a perfect vehicle for the dramatic action and each role is clearly characterized; the ensembles are clear, ingenious and yet strictly logical.

JEUNE HOMME ET LA MORT Le. Dances, sets and costumes described to Roland Petit, the choreographer, by Jean Cocteau. Scenery: Wakhevitch. Music: J. S. Bach. First performance: Ballets des Champs-Élysées, Paris, 25 June 1946. Principal dancers: Nathalie Philippart, Jean Babilée. When the curtain rises one wonders how on earth the dancers are going to be able to move in this attic encumbered with tables, chairs and stools, cluttered with plaster casts, drawings, squares, frames, canvases, bits of wire—a typical artist's studio. And now the painter himself, dressed in overalls, gets up from the couch on which he has been lying, looks at his wrist watch, impatiently stubs

out his cigarette and begins to exhibit every sign of the most feverish anxiety. At last, "she" arrives—a little trollop. He adores her, but she makes fun of him. An intensely poignant drama unfolds before us. With broken jerky movements they pursue each other round the attic—she, haughty and cold; he, mad with grief, humble, suppliant and loving, and it suddenly becomes clear that not a stick of furniture in this bohemian glory-hole is superfluous; each one has its part, however humble, to play in the action. The girl leaves; the young man hangs himself. The attic walls fly away, revealing the roofs of Paris under the night sky with the Eiffel Tower ablaze with light in the distance. Death appears: placing her mask over the face of the young man, she reveals herself as the girl of the previous scene and leads him away across the rooftops.

All this is expressed in dancing at once strikingly realistic and profoundly poetic, combining the most daring acrobatics with a humanised, academic classicism. The choreography,

LE JEUNE HOMME ET LA MORT. DÉCOR BY WAKHEVITCH.

based on violently syncopated rhythms, was rehearsed to jazz music. It was not until the day of the first performance that the dancers knew that the music to which it was to be danced was in fact Bach's Passacaglia. The contrast between its calm, sonorous classicism and the impetuous movements and highly-strung emotions expressed by the dancers underlines both the clash of wills and the isolation of the tormented pair and intensifies the drama to the highest possible degree. The choice of this music is perhaps Cocteau's greatest *trouvaille* in a ballet which is surely destined to become a classic.

JEUX. Ballet in one act. Theme and choreography: Nijinsky. Music: Debussy. Scenery and costumes: Bakst. First performance: Diaghilev's Ballets Russes, Théâtre des Champs-Élysées, Paris, 15 May 1913. The first character to appear is a tennis ball, lost in a garden beside some tennis courts. A moment later a young man, armed with a racket, bounds on to the stage and begins to hunt vaguely for the lost ball, obviously bored by the game. Two young girls arrive just in time to revive his spirits. He flirts with them, cannot make up his mind between them and finally they avoid a

scene by returning to their game. This ballet, Nijinsky's second, was far from making the same impact as *L'Après-midi d'un faune*. It was dropped from the repertoire after a few performances, despite the presence of Karsavina, Schollar and Nijinsky himself in the cast and the incontestable novelty of a ballet on a contemporary theme. Neither the famous dancer nor his collaborator Diaghilev were true choreographers. But, since later versions have been no more successful, the failure may not have been due to the choreographer alone.

* At the first performance of the newly-formed Swedish Ballet of Rolf de Maré at the Théâtre des Champs-Élysées, 24 October 1920, Jean Borlin presented a ballet to Debussy's score in a setting by Pierre Bonnard.

* The American Ballet Theatre staged *Jeux* at the Center Theatre, New York, on 23 April 1950, with choreography by William Dollar, scenery and costumes by David Ffolkes, and Nora Kaye, Norma Vance and Igor Youskevitch as principal dancers.

JEUX D'ENFANTS. Ballet in one act. Book: Boris Kochno. Music: Georges Bizet. Scenery and costumes: Joan Miró. Choreography: Leonide Massine. First performance: Ballets Russes de Monte-Carlo, Monte Carlo, 14 April 1932. Principal dancers: Tatiana Riabouchinska, Tamara Toumanova, David Lichine, Leon Woizikowski.

Miró's set, brightly coloured shapes like paper cut-outs against an expanse of pale grey, was a sensation. A surrealist nursery, where toys and games come to life and wake up the child; a top, rocking-horses, two rackets and a shuttlecock, four amazons, soap bubbles, three sportsmen, and finally a mysterious Traveller for whom the child develops a passion. For each "entry" Massine devised humorous choreography of great freshness and originality. The top, clothed from top to toe in close-fitting banded tights, performed a dazzling series of *fouettés en tournant*. At daybreak everything becomes quiet once more, the toys are still and the little fair-haired girl returns to reality. The creation of this ballet is bound up with the débuts of the "baby ballerinas", Riabouchinska as the child and Toumanova as the top, who brought to the work the guarantee of their youth and whose exceptional personalities were destined to colour the whole of the first period of the Ballets Russes de Monte-Carlo.

* Albert Aveline arranged a ballet for the "petits rats" (aged from 8 to 15) of the Paris Opera to the same music by Bizet, which was performed on the stage of the Opéra itself, 16 July 1941; scenery by Dresa and costumes by Marie-Hélène Dasté. The action takes place in a school playground. Little girls in blue aprons and boys in red shirts and black ties play happily together under the watchful eye of their starchy governesses—a pretty divertissement, generally used as a curtain-raiser.

JINX. Ballet in two scenes by Lew Christensen. Music: Benjamin Britten (Variations on a Theme by Frank Bridge), arr. Colin McPhee. Scenery and costumes: George Bockman. Choreography: Lew Christensen. First performance: Eugene Loring's "Dance Players", National Theater, New York, 24 April 1942.

Jinx (bringer of ill-luck) is the story of an old clown whom the circus director keeps on out of pity, but whose evil influence brings persistent bad luck to the troupe. The other actors ostracise him and finally kill him, but he comes to life again, his sinister power in no way diminished. At the first performance, Lew Christensen himself played the part of Jinx. A revised version was presented by the New York City Ballet, City Center, New York, 24 November 1949. Principal dancers: Janet Reed, Francisco Moncion, Herbert Bliss.

JOAN DE ZARISSA. Ballet in four scenes. Scenario and music: Werner Egk. Scenery and costumes: Yves Brayer. Choreography: Serge Lifar. First performance: Paris Opera, 10 July 1942. Principal dancers: Lycette Darsonval, Solange Schwarz, Yvette Chauviré, Serge Lifar, Serge Peretti.

The story of a 15th century Don Juan who is suitably punished for his debauched and unscrupulous life by dying miserably of remorse, tormented by the ghosts of his victims: Isabelle, whose husband he killed in a duel and Florence, whom he won at a game of dice and whom he drove to suicide. Brayer's Flemish-Burgundian sets in reds, browns and black, reinforced the brutal atmosphere of the story. The ballet

JANET REED IN JINX.
DRAWING BY JUNE RYAN.

was a synthesis of German expressionism and academic dance. Certain passages in *Jcán de Zarissa,* notably the scenes of fighting and the pas de deux, recall *Le Chevalier et la Damoiselle* produced in the previous year, but the work as a whole is heavier and more tragic. The women's dances, with their mannered movements like figures from Van Eyck paintings, were the most memorable thing in the ballet. In Joan, Lifar found the last and most powerful of all the "heroic" roles of his career.

JOB. A masque for dancing in eight scenes. Scenario: Geoffrey Keynes. Music: Ralph Vaughan Williams. Choreography: Ninette de Valois. Scenery and costumes: Gwendolen Raverat. First performance: Carmago Society, Cambridge Theatre, London, 5 July 1931. Principal dancers: Anton Dolin, Stanley Judson, John McNair.

This very individual work was suggested by the famous engravings made by William Blake in 1825 to illustrate the biblical story of Job. Both Gwendolen Raverat and John Piper (who re-designed the ballet for the Covent Garden revival in 1948) captured something of Blake's mystical power, so nobly echoed in Vaughan Williams's majestic score. De Valois's deceptively simple choreography encompassed with equal success Job's spiritual anguish, Satan's evil grandeur, and the visions of the angelic host. *Job* has become one of the cornerstones of the Sadler's Wells repertory. Dolin, Helpmann and Grant have been the most notable interpreters of the great role of Satan.

* *Job:* oratorio by Nicolas Nabokov for two solo voices, male chorus and orchestra, adapted from the Book of Job by Jacques Maritain. Choreography: Balanchine. First performance: Ballets 1933, Théâtre des Champs-Élysées, Paris, June 1933. Dancing proper had very little place in this twenty-minute ballet; the production consisted mainly of the projection of lantern slides of engravings from a 16th century English bible.

JOOSS Kurt. When *The Green Table* carried off first prize at the international choreographic competition organised by Les Archives Internationales de la Danse in Paris in 1932,

the winner's name was almost unknown Yet the 31-year-old Kurt Jooss had been active in the theatre, especially in the sphere of dancing, for some time past. The son of a singer, Jooss was passionately fond of music. He entered the Stuttgart Conservatoire, where he followed courses in singing, piano and harmony, at the same time studying diction and general theatre craft. His love of the dance was increased by long months of work under Rudolf von Laban, whose acquaintance he made in 1920, and was still further intensified by the performances of Mary Wigman. He decided to found a comprehensive school of theatrical art in the country. The paternal estate in Württemberg lent itself admirably to such an enterprise, but it also required in the director a thorough knowledge of farming, so Jooss set off for Ulm to learn agriculture. But his longing to dance was so strong that he returned to Laban at the National Theatre in Mannheim. This time he worked with the master for three years, first as pupil, later as assistant and principal dancer. In the summer of 1924 he became "director of movement" at the Municipal Theatre, Münster, which at that time formed part of the German avantgarde. The dance group, known as the *Neue Tanzbühne,* gave whole evenings of ballet there and also made tours. The company included the Estonian Aïno Siimola (who some years later became Jooss's wife) his future partner, Sigurd Leeder, and the young musician Fritz Cohen, who was to become the company's regular composer. Interrupting what already amounted to an imposing series of ballets, one of which was a surrealist work, *The Ghosts,* danced without music, Jooss went to Paris and Vienna to extend his knowledge of classical dancing. Afterwards he founded the Folkwangschule at Essen in collaboration with Leeder and a year later a Dance Theatre Studio was attached to it. He was at once asked to supervise the dancers at the Essen Opera, and soon afterwards appointed maître de ballet. His own group provided the opera ballets. It was then that the famous choreographic competitions were instituted for which he composed the subsequently famous *Green Table,* with financial help from the Essen Opera. The group won its independence and thus the Ballets Jooss, soon to become world famous, came into existence. With the rise of Nazism

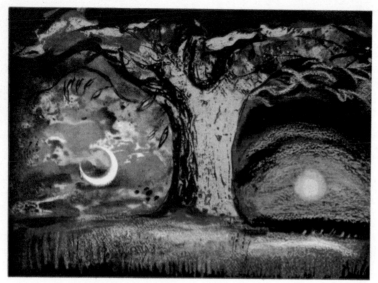

JOB. DÉCOR BY JOHN PIPER. COVENT GARDEN, 1948.

Jooss renounced the advantages offered him by his school in Essen and in 1934 left with his troupe for England, not returning to Germany till fifteen years later—as a British subject. In association with Leeder, Jooss established his school at Dartington on a estate where the American owners Mr. and Mrs. Elmhirst were trying the experiment of transplanting to the country various enterprises generally concentrated in towns: craft centres, a library, a "progressive" school, a theatre. Pupils came from all over the world to study the Jooss method of dance, scenic and costume design, musical accompaniment, choreography and Laban's famous method of dance notation. The war interrupted this peaceful, devoted existence. After an American tour the company rejoined their founder, who had remained in England; they all joined the forces, and on the conclusion of peace resumed touring. In 1949 Jooss reopened his school in Essen, while Leeder remained in England and started teaching in London. Jooss considers that all art, however abstract, possesses some human content directly related to its time. Though classical ballet has sufficed to embody human tendencies for close on two centuries, yet it no longer has the power to express our immediate problems. It is thus that the so-called "modern" techniques have arisen in response to the needs of those things that cannot find adequate expression through the classical dance vocabulary. Jooss aims at a synthesis of contemporary and classical dance techniques, in order to be able to express everything. Though deeply musical, Jooss asserts the independence of choreography, which he maintains should be accompanied by music, not subservient to it. For this reason, the accompaniment (whether music or just sound) of his ballets is generally composed afterwards or in collaboration with the choreographer. Some ballets are even danced in silence. But this does not prevent Jooss sometimes choosing existing music composed for other purposes; his main concern is to find what is right for a particular idea. It is possible that some of Jooss's ballets may appear out-of-date to-day, because they depict the preoccupations of a given period. But none the less they have played an important part in the evolution of theatrical dancing and it is conceivable that Jooss, the eternal seeker, may yet produce ballets in a new style to match our time.

K

KALIOUJNY Alexandre. One of the younger generation of Russo-Parisian dancers, trained in Paris by former ballerinas of the Imperial Ballet. At the age of 14, he won first prize in the Brussels international dancing competition, but gave up dancing shortly afterwards to devote himself entirely to sport, becoming in 1941 athletic champion of Paris. Returning to the stage after the war, he worked with the Nouveau Ballet de Monte-Carlo (1946). His height, nobility of style and powerful technique won him admittance to the Paris Opera in 1947. There he danced in notable premières (the first movement of *Le Palais de Cristal,* and *Zadig*) as well as taking the major roles in *Le Baiser de la Fée,* and the *Polovtsian Dances.* But suddenly he interrupted his career to join Renée Jeanmaire in a revue in New York. He returned to the Opéra at the end of 1956, after dancing in Jean Babilée's company. An essentially Slav artist, Kalioujny restored to French ballet the virile bravura of the Russians of the golden age.

KARALLI Vera. Trained at the Imperial ballet school in Moscow, she was the favourite pupil of Gorsky. She presents the unique example of a dancer who, immediately she was engaged at the Bolshoi Theatre, made her début in a leading role (*Lac des Cygnes,* September 1906). She was an excellent actress, whose beauty bore witness to her Greek descent — the classical lines of her face, her enormous black eyes, and slightly aquiline nose. Slim, with slender, graceful legs, she possessed ballon and an ability to "travel" quite out of the ordinary, while the public also delighted in her adage and her supple, expressive port de bras. Karalli became a ballerina of the Bolshoi in 1915. She danced twice with Diaghilev's company: in 1909 in *Le Pavillon d'Armide* and ten years later in the roles of Thamar and the Polovt-

KARSAVINA IN LE PAVILLON D'ARMIDE.

sian Girl. After that she virtually retired and made only a few further appearances.

KARSAVINA Tamara. Prima ballerina of the Imperial Russian Ballet and of the Diaghilev Ballet, Tamara Karsavina by her artistry, dramatic gifts and rare intelligence was an ideal exponent of the then revolutionary ballets of Michael Fokine and set an example for following generations. Her presence in the Diaghilev ballet ensured its initial success as surely as did the presence of Nijinsky. Diaghilev recognised her unique gifts and had a warm personal affection for her; for him she returned to the company again and again, appearing even during the last London season in 1929, when she danced in *Petrouchka*.

The daughter of a celebrated Russian dancer, Platon Karsavin, she was born in St. Petersburg in 1885 and trained in the Imperial Ballet School under Johansson, Gerdt, Sokolova and Cecchetti and in Milan under Beretta. She made her début at the Maryinsky in 1902 and appeared there in many famous ballets, including *Le Lac des Cygnes* and *Giselle*. Karsavina was an early and ardent supporter of Fokine's plans for the reform of ballet-making and was inevitably attracted to the avant-garde group of young artists who formed the nucleus of the company for Diaghilev's first Paris season (1909).

Karsavina's reputation stood high in Russia, where her sensitive and beautifully phrased dancing was in great contrast to the acrobatic virtuosity of some of her predecessors, but in Western Europe her fame was unrivalled. For Diaghilev she created principal roles in *Les Sylphides, Carnaval, L'Oiseau de feu, Petrouchka, Narcisse, Le Spectre de la Rose, Thamar, Daphnis and Chloe, Le Coq d'Or, Le Tricorne, Pulcinella,* and *Roméo et Juliette.* Of these, *Le Spectre de la Rose,* which she danced with Nijinsky, and *L'Oiseau de feu* are imperishably associated with her name. She was also one of the greatest exponents of Giselle in our time.

Karsavina had a perfectly proportioned body, dark hair, moon-pale skin and great prune-coloured eyes; even Diaghilev, walking into her bathroom by mistake one day, stopped to exclaim "Mais Tata, que vous êtes jolie !" Her beauty, although romantic in its languor, was by no means cold; she had a warm and rich personality on stage and a quality of womanliness which set her apart from Pavlova and Spessivtseva, who represented a colder and more ethereal kind of beauty. Her technique was so sure that in the theatre it never obtruded; she had a high but soft jump, beautiful ports de bras, and a body expressive from head to foot.

The most remarkable aspect of her artistry, however, was her range of style and characterisation. Chaste and classical in *Les Sylphides* and *Giselle,* she could suggest strong passions in *Thamar* —for which role Diaghilev gave her the clue to the characterisation by saying "Omission is the secret of art: draw your eyebrows in a single line." In *L'Oiseau de feu,* for ever associated with her name, she created a supernatural being of such power that one critic wrote of "ses yeux adamantins et son sourire d'une douceur cruelle." Fokine in arranging this part for Karsavina made use of her greatest gifts and on the first night in Paris (25 June 1910) her performance caused a furore. In *Le Spectre de la Rose,* which she danced with Nijinsky, Karsavina achieved a completely different characterisation; the evocation of an inno-

cent young girl returning from her first ball.

Karsavina's sympathy with a choreographer's ideas enabled her to interpret the work of many different artists. Fokine, who adored her, was the author of her greatest triumphs. For Nijinsky she created a leading role in *Jeux,* for Massine the vigorous peasant woman who is the Miller's Wife in *Le Tricorne,* and also a leading role in *Pulcinella,* while for Nijinska she created the role of Juliette in *Roméo et Juliette* (1926) dancing with the young Serge Lifar.

Karsavina's marriage in 1915 to the British diplomat Henry Bruce (who died in 1951), took her to several capitals of Europe but she ultimately settled in England. After the death of Diaghilev she proved a warm friend to the struggling British ballet, consenting to dance with Rambert's pupils and persuading Rambert herself that the girls were sufficiently accomplished to appear in *Les Sylphides.* She also danced for the Camargo Society.

Her presence in London has been an invaluable link for British dancers with the great traditions of the Russian Ballet and she has

TAMARA KARSAVINA.

passed on her knowledge most generously. Her classes in mime have the same quality of inspiration as her performances on the stage. When the Sadler's Wells Ballet revived *L'Oiseau de feu* in 1955 she personally coached Fonteyn in the role of the Firebird.

Her book *Theatre Street* (1930) paints a vivid picture of her early career and of a dancer's training in the Imperial Ballet School. Sargent, Glyn Philpot, Serov, Bakst, Cocteau, Jacques-Émile Blanche, Randolph Schwabe, Wilfrid de Glehn, and Mtislav Doboujinsky are only some of the artists who have painted her, while she has provided equal inspiration to writers and poets. The French critic R. Brussel wrote: "You are a great virtuoso, but the prestige of your technique is forgotten because of the charm of your art."

KAUFFER Edward McKnight. Poster designer and book illustrator, born in America in 1891 and died there in 1954. Most of his working life was spent in London, where he became one of the leading commercial artists of the inter-war years. Kauffer did little work for the theatre, but his striking abstract designs for de Valois's *Checkmate* (1937) were an integral part of that ballet's success. He also designed a curtain for one of the Camargo Society's performances and decorated productions of Shakespeare's *Othello* and Pirandello's *Henry IV* for the English actor Ernest Milton.

KAYE Nora. Although an impeccable performer in *Lac des Cygnes* and *Giselle* she appears to best advantage in modern dramatic roles, where her gifts of mime and her virtuosity are unrivalled. Her striking appearance, her Asiatic face with high cheekbones and deep-set eyes, and her simple bearing make her unforgettable. Born in New York of Russian parents, her real name being Nora Korev, she studied first with Fokine and Tudor at the School of American Ballet, and made her début with the Metropolitan Opera company. Joining Ballet Theatre in 1939, she became a leading dancer in 1942, after her performance as Hagar in *Pillar of Fire,* a role which she has never shared. This is, indeed, her finest role, closely followed by those in *Fall River Legend* and *The Cage.* In turn voluptuous and humorous, despairing or passionate, she has a sure sense of dramatic gesture and a personality strong enough to hold attention in even a second-rate ballet.

KELLY Gene. He is the first, the only choreographer to have seen in the cinema a mode of expression. Instead of filmed ballets Kelly has produced real ballet-films. Indeed, shaped in terms of the camera, the dances which occur throughout *An American in Paris, On the Town* or *Singing in the Rain* do not have the irritating character of interludes or "turns" but are an integral part of the action. Better still, they mark it out with heel and toe as it goes along. Backed by long experience on Broadway — where he played Pal Joey in 1940 — this prematurely bald bookworm with the muscles of an athlete, this university graduate and one-time tap-dancing teacher combines wide choreographic culture with the practical knowledge of a technician. It was not long before he was snapped up by Hollywood. From being merely a choreographer, he achieved the rank of director with *Invitation to the Dance,* in which his partner (succeeding Judy Garland, Rita Hayworth and Leslie Caron) was Claire Sombert. Famous for his good humour, his kindness, for the diversity of his gifts as dancing-partner and actor, he is himself the best of his performers, thus justifying Bob Hope's crack: "Every time Gene Kelly begins to dance, Fred Astaire begins to count his money. "

KEOGH Tom. This painter's style has been compared with Bérard's, and indeed they have some mannerisms in common, both using costumes, for instance, consisting of sumptuous, elegant rags. Keogh also possesses the older artist's ability to compose a lively, colourful ensemble in a bare and simple set. But he is less mysterious, less subtle than Bérard; by contrast with the melancholy, reticent poetry of *Les Forains,* for example, with its grace and distinction and wealth of implication, the colouring of a décor by Keogh is like a rowdy, joyful fête chiefly notable for its truculence. Keogh designed two ballets for the Ballets des Champs-Élysées, *Le Portrait de Don Quichotte* (Milloss, 1947) and *Till Eulenspiegel*

(Babilée, 1949). Other ballet décors include *Balance à trois* (Babilée's company, 1954) and *Les Belles Damnées* (Ballets de Paris, 1955).

KHACHATURIAN Aram. Born 1903, at Tiflis. An outstanding example of the survival of the type of 19th century nationalist composer drawing his inspiration from the wealth of native folksong, a procedure still officially encouraged in present day Russia. Khachaturian's native district is Armenia, and he uses the oriental colour of its songs and dances vigorously and without sophisticated inhibitions. The concert public knows him best from the piano and violin concertos and from the suite from the ballet *Gayaneh* (1942), which include the popular "Sabre dance". His output includes another considerable ballet, the four-act *Spartacus*.

KIDD Michael. American dancer and choreographer, famous for his work on numerous films *(Seven Brides for Seven Brothers, Merry Andrew)* and musical comedies *(Finian's Rainbow)*. He first became known as a choreographer with the ballet *On Stage* (1945). After dancing under Balanchine in various companies in the United States, he was with Ballet Theatre from 1942 to 1947. As a dancer, he distinguished himself in *Billy the Kid, Fancy Free* and *Interplay*.

KIRSOVA Helen. Born in Denmark, she was a member of the Ballets de Monte-Carlo from their foundation in 1932. Interpreter of many roles in the company's repertoire, she created the part of the Butterfly in *L'Épreuve d'Amour*. In 1936-37 she toured Australia with the de Basil company and settled in Sydney. There she opened a school and formed her own company in 1941. Her chief works as choreographer are *La Révolution des parapluies, Faust,* (on Heine's scenario) and *Variations symphoniques.* She retired from the theatre in 1947. Her book on Soviet ballet—*Ballet in Moscow Today*—appeared in 1956.

KIRSTEIN Lincoln. Prime mover in the establishment of classical ballet in the United States. Writer, historian, and scenarist, he founded the School of American Ballet in 1934, with Edward W. Warburg, Balanchine and

KEOGH. PROGRAMME FOR THE BALLETS DE PARIS, 1955-1956.

Dimitriev. He was also one of the founders of the American Ballet, Ballet Caravan and the Ballet Society. Today he is a director of the New York City Ballet.

KNIASEFF Boris. Dancer, choreographer and teacher. Born at St. Petersburg, he was a pupil of Goleizovsky. He emigrated in 1920 to Bulgaria, and four years later to France, where he soon made his name in Paris. From 1932 to 1934 he was maître-de-ballet at the Opéra-Comique. He opened an academy in 1937 and became a highly respected and successful teacher. Among the pupils of this "master of the stars" were Yvette Chauviré, Renée Jeanmaire and Youly Algaroff. After the war he worked as a choreographer, notably for Colonel de Basil and the Ballets de Paris. Among his ballets are *La Légende du Bouleau* (1930), and *Études symphoniques* (1948). In 1953 he settled in Switzerland, where he opened a school in Lausanne and then in Geneva. In recent years he has developed a new teaching method of his own which starts with a "barre par terre" and has unusual features in the centre practice. He claims that it substantially reduces the years of training. A brilliant and passionate personality, Kniaseff upholds an ideal of pure dancing inherited from Olga Spessivtseva, whose partner he was in 1928.

KOCHNO Boris. Diaghilev engaged him as his private secretary in 1921, a young émigré from the Ukraine, very slim and very dark, who soon attracted the attention of the followers of the Russian Ballet. He wrote poetry, and wrote it moreover in an extraordinarily ornate hand, adorned with arabesques and flourishes so elegant and so firm that they could be mistaken for engravings. But his accomplishments were not confined to verse and calligraphy; he had an ear for music and an eye for painting. Not unnaturally, he gravitated towards the ballet. In essence he was (like Diaghilev) a dilettante who knew how to make the best of his enthusiasms. Kochno appeared on the programmes of the Ballets Russes (often under the pseudonym of Sobeka) as the author of the scenario of many of the ballets of the last period. *Les Fâcheux* (*), *Zéphyre et Flore* (*), *Les Matelots* (*), *La Chatte* (*), *The Gods go a-begging* (*), *Ode* (*), *Pastorale, Le Fils prodigue* (*), and *Le Bal* (*). He also wrote the libretto of Stravinsky's opera *Mavra*. But in reality he did much more than write the scenarios. He advis-

ed on all aspects of production and, from 1925 onwards, he played a leading part in the artistic orientation of the company. When Diaghilev died in 1929 Kochno, more than anyone else, was regarded as a possible successor to the throne, and it was the regret of his life that he was not able to regroup Diaghilev's company and continue his work.

After the collapse, he collaborated in ballets for revues in London, and in 1932 wrote two scenarios for the Ballets Russes de Monte-Carlo, *Cotillon* (*) and *Jeux d'Enfants* (*). The following year he worked with Balanchine and the Ballets 1933, then rejoined the Monte Carlo company until 1937. After the war, he undertook, with notable success, the artistic direction of Roland Petit's Ballets des Champs-Élysées when that company was formed in 1945. Kochno has recently published a large and sumptuous book, *Le Ballet*.

KONDRATOV Yuri. Certainly one of the most gifted dancers of the Bolshoi Theatre ballet, although he is inclined to appear off-hand and perhaps is too well satisfied with easy effects. Sure of himself, he sometimes treats his partner a trifle carelessly, albeit with remarkable skill. He is a wonderful Don Basilio in *Don Quixote,* though the big pas de deux, the solos and finale afford him irresistible opportunities for showing off.

KOROVINE Constantine. Russian painter and stage designer, born Moscow 1861, died France 1939. One of the creators of the new Russian theatre, with more than 200 décors in St. Petersburg to his credit before his work was revealed to the West in the first Paris season of the Ballets Russes in 1909. His style is even more strongly and obsessively dramatic than that of other Russian designers of the period. The art of Korovine and Golovine forms a visual equivalent to the music of Rimsky-Korsakov, Borodin and Mussorgsky. Korovine was one of the Russian artists whose work, at once barbarous and refined, changed the taste of the European public in the years immediately before the first war. Décors for the Ballets Russes include *Le Festin* (1909), *Russlan and Ludmilla* (Opera, 1909), *Les Orientales* (1910).

BORIS KOCHNO.

In addition, for the Opéra Privé de Paris he designed *Prince Igor* (1927) and for Colonel de Basil's company *Danses Slaves et Tziganes* (1939).

KOUZNETSOV N. Trained at the Kirov Theatre school in Leningrad, he is a very expressive dancer and a sensitive and lyrical partner. As Eugene in *The Bronze Horseman* his great acting ability enables him to dominate the scene of the flood, despite the magnitude of the stage effects. In the mad scene (act IV, scene II) he can be overwhelming.

KRASSOVSKA Natalie. Her real name is Natalie Leslie, Krassovska being her mother's maiden name; she was born in Leningrad. Discovered by Balanchine, and a protégée of Lifar, she made her début in 1932 with the Ballet Nijinska. The formal beauty of her face and her assured technique made her one of the principal classical dancers of the Monte-Carlo ballet, in France (1936) and in the United States. An excellent performer in *Giselle*, *Les Sylphides*, *Le Lac des Cygnes*, she was leading dancer with London's Festival Ballet 1950-55. In 1957 she was engaged for a while by the Marquis de Cuevas, but returned to Festival Ballet to dance in their new production of *The Nutcracker*.

KREUTZBERG Harald. Born in 1902 at Reichenberg (Bohemia). He entered the Dresden ballet school at an early age, later became a pupil of Mary Wigman, and then studied expressionist dancing at Rudolf von Laban's school. The Swiss maître de ballet Max Terpis engaged him to dance at Hanover and then at the Berlin Opera. To play the part of a madman he had his head shaved, and since then has always appeared thus on the stage. At the Salzburg Festival of 1927 Max Reinhardt gave him the role of the master of ceremonies in *Turandot*, and in 1928 he played Puck in *A Midsummer Night's Dream*. With Reinhardt he went to New York. During 1929-30 he toured the United States and Canada with Yvonne Georgi, and in 1932 with Ruth Page. Since then Kreutzberg has given recitals on his own, consisting of dance and mime of his own composition, for instance: *Aufruhr, Apokalyptischer Engel, Tanz des Hofnarren*. Combining free dance with drama, Kreutzberg is one of the leading figures in contemporary German dance. His influence in the United States has been considerable and has greatly assisted the spread of expressionist dancing in the New World.

KRIZA John. Once described as "Mr. Ballet Theatre in person", John Kriza has been with that American company since 1940, starting in the corps de ballet and reaching the rank of principal male dancer by 1955. Born in Chicago of Czech-American parents, he started dancing at the age of five and also trained as an athlete so he could join a that gymnastic association. But Kriza is a born dancer. He appeared first with Ruth Page and Bentley Stone in Chicago, then tried musicals in New York before finding his true métier with Ballet Theatre. A good classical dancer, he is nevertheless at his best in character roles of either dramatic or comic nature, for instance his created roles in *Fancy Free, Interplay, Los Caprichos, Winter's Eve*, and as Hermes in *Helen of Troy*, in *The Combat* and in the name part in *Billy the Kid*. Possessing abounding good humour and much boyish charm, Kriza is a favourite with Ballet Theatre audiences all over the world. Apparently quite indefatigable, he often dances three or four ballets on one programme and "relaxes" on vacation by working on his farm.

KRONSTAM Henning. Danish dancer, pupil of Harald Lander and Vera Volkova. Engaged by the Royal Danish Ballet in 1952, he early specialised in romantic roles; his performance as the Poet in *La Somnambule* in 1955 marked a turning-point in his career. He consolidated his success with the creation of Romeo in Ashton's *Romeo and Juliet* in the same year, and was promoted solo-dancer in 1956. In 1957, when *La Belle au bois dormant* was revived, he made a perfect Prince Florimund. He appeared at the Festival of Aix-en-Provence in 1955 and 1956.

KSCHESSINSKA Mathilde. Five years after graduating in 1890 from the Imperial Ballet School in St. Petersburg, Kschessinska was dancing all the principal roles in the repertoire of the Maryinsky Theatre. Daughter of a well-known dancer of Polish origin, she was a pupil of Johansson and Cecchetti. Petite, slight and dark, with sparkling black eyes, she combined Russian expressiveness with Italian technical virtuosity. She was the first Russian to master the famous 32 fouettés. Her warm and generous temperament and exceptional dramatic ability made her the idol of the public. Delirious audiences forced her to repeat the celebrated coda from the *Talisman* five or six times. Although not a dancer of exceptional elevation, neither was she purely a terre à terre dancer; gifted with a lively imagination, she knew how to use her technique to the best advantage. Among her numberless triumphs one may mention *The Talisman, Esmeralda, Fiammetta* and *Pharaoh's Daughter.* She enjoyed the most influential connections and her caprices were to be feared. Once when a fine was imposed on her for wearing a costume of her own choice, she ignored the punishment and instead provoked the resignation of Prince Volkonsky, at that time director of the Imperial Theatres. She danced before the Parisian public for the first time in *Coppelia* at the Opéra, on the 25th June, 1909. Though Diaghilev several times invited her to take part in his performances, it was not until 1911 that he succeeded in presenting her before the London public in *Le Lac des Cygnes,* in which she danced with Nijinsky. Having left Russia at the beginning of the Revolution, she settled in Paris with her husband the Grand Duke André, and thenceforth devoted herself to teaching. From her famous school have come generations of dancers, among them Tatiana Riabouchinska.

L

LABAN Rudolf von. A Hungarian dancer and teacher, born at Bratislava in 1879, who became a sort of high priest cum philosopher, a great influence on all aspects of the modern dance. He studied painting in Munich and dancing in Paris and, at a time when theatrical dancing outside Russia had reached its lowest

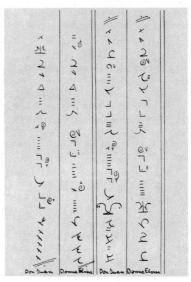

CHOREOGRAPHIC NOTATION
BY RUDOLF VON LABAN.

ebb, he attempted to find a code of movement, derived from nervous, intellectual and emotional responses of the human body, that would be all-embracing and not limited by a rigid technical system.

He travelled widely, making observations and discoveries in each place where he settled, and influencing local dancers by his teaching and by his thinking. In Germany, his most famous pupils were Mary Wigman and Kurt Jooss. These in turn have passed on the ideas and the inspiration of Laban to new generations of dancers. The teaching of Laban is at the root of the proudly American form of modern dance, and his influence on the classical ballet has been seen in the work of many choreographers.

Jooss worked with Laban for some years from 1921, and subsequently put into practice in his stage productions the theories he had evolved in the studio. In some ways the Ballets Jooss provided the finest examples of Laban's method, for although Laban had been responsible for many productions (his most famous works are *Titan, Agamemnon* and *Night*) he was more philosopher, pioneer and teacher than choreographer.

Mary Wigman has described how, when she worked with him in Ascona in 1913, Laban would stand, tambourine in hand, trying like Dr. Jekyll to change his personality at will from handsome hero to terrifying caricature. He was a genius at improvisation and a gifted mime. He could, by himself alone, give a brilliant impression of an infantry regiment parading through the streets of Vienna. He would make his pupils dance to words and phrases or to short poems of their own composition. His attitude to music was independent; early in his career he wrote ballets without any music at all, but so far relented as to admit percussion instruments and, finally, specially comissioned scores.

Laban invented a system of dance notation which has been perfected by Albrecht Knust and by the Dance Notation Bureau in New York, where it is taught as *Labanotation*. During World War II he evolved a kind of remedial gymnastics for factory workers in Manchester. In 1953 he moved to an estate in Addlestone, Surrey, and there founded the Art of Movement Studio. The "questing mind" was never still until death claimed Laban in 1958.

LABISSE Félix. Born 1905. It would be a mistake to judge Labisse's work as a stage designer from his ballet décors alone, distinguished as these have been; the whole body of his varied and inventive work in the theatre deserves to be taken into account. Probably his most remarkable décors have been for straight drama, notably those for the Barrault-Renaud company's production of Salacrou's *Les Nuits de la colère,* Kafka's *Le Procès* and Claudel's *Partage de Midi.* Though less important, his design for ballet, with their strange, tense, disturbing atmosphere achieved by precise means, are clearly from the same hand. A very successful example was *Piège de lumière* (de Cuevas, 1952), which showed the same rather dry, precise drawing and deliberate coldness which are to be found in his paintings. In the rarified atmosphere which he created on the stage the dancers stood out, appropriately enough, like insects vibrating in the light. But one of the charms of the fantastic world created by Labisse is that all its elements are borrowed from a scrupulously observed reality; the unusual effect, far from being gratuitous,

comes from the manner in which the painter organises and represents what he has observed. Décors for ballet: *Zadig* (Paris Opera, 1948); *Paris Magie* (Opéra-Comique, 1949); *Piège de lumière* (de Cuevas, 1952); *Le Martyre de Saint-Sébastien* (Paris Opera, 1957).

LAC DES CYGNES Le *(Swan Lake).* Ballet in four acts. Story: V. P. Begitchev and V. Geltzer. Music: Tchaikovsky. Scenery: Bocharov and Lavogt. Choreography: Marius Petipa and Lev Ivanov. First performed in its entirety at the Maryinsky Theatre, St. Petersburg, 27 January 1895. Principal dancers: Pierina Legnani, Pavel Gerdt, Bulgakov.

This work is one of the most beautiful in the whole classical repertory. Tchaikovsky based the music on his rejected opera *Ondine,* which was turned down by the Imperial Theatre as "unworthy to be included in the repertory". In 1875, when he was asked to compose the music for *Le Lac des Cygnes,* Tchaikovsky went back to this score and, much to his surprise, it was accepted in its new form. The first version was staged at the Bolshoi Theatre in Moscow (4 March 1877), with choreography by Julius

LABISSE. PROJECT FOR COSTUME.
LA SYMPHONIE FANTASTIQUE.

Reisinger. The ballet was a failure; the score was mutilated by the conductor and the ballerina, Karpakova, who was influentially protected, was pretty rather than accomplished. Subsequent revivals in Moscow in 1880 and 1882 were also unsuccessful. In 1893 Marius Petipa, who had already produced Tchaikovsky's *The Sleeping Beauty*, submitted a scenario for a new version of *Le Lac des Cygnes* to the management of the Imperial Theatres. The score was sent from Moscow and Petipa, working with his assistant Ivanov, sketched out the action. The second act (the lakeside) was given at a concert in memory of Tchaikovsky in February 1894 but the first performance of the complete work did not take place until the following year, having been delayed by court mourning after the death of the Emperor Alexander III. It is difficult to decide precisely which portions of the work should be ascribed to Petipa and which to Ivanov, but it is generally believed that Petipa was responsible for the overall conception and for the brilliant dances of act III, while Ivanov may have composed the lyrical passages of the second act and probably the whole of the last act.

LE LAC DES CYGNES.
VIOLETTA ELVIN AND GIULIO PERUGINI.

In the grounds of a magnificent castle, Prince Siegfried is drinking with his friends and watching the dances of the peasants. His mother comes to upbraid him for the company he keeps and tells him that the following night, at a ball in his honour, he must choose a bride. The Prince's carefree mood is broken; he sees the end of youthful irresponsibility and when a flight of swans passes overhead he suggests a shooting party, as temporary distraction. The second act takes place by the shore of a lake. The light is fading and the ruins of a castle can be dimly seen on a crag. Siegfried, who has chosen to shoot alone, watches the swans crossing the lake and takes aim at their leader. To his amazement the swan, on reaching land, is transformed into a beautiful girl, the Princess Odette. She tells him that she and her companions are victims of the magician Rothbart, whose spell can only be broken if a man who is heartwhole and faithful will swear to redeem her. Siegfried, who is falling in love for the first time, gives his oath and in dancing with him Odette forgets for a little while her fear and her sorrow. She warns Siegfried of the magician but with the coming of day she has to submit to his power and, once more a swan, flies away. The third act is the ballroom of Siegfried's castle. Still haunted by the memory of Odette, he can take little interest in the dancing or in the prospective brides his mother has assembled. Suddenly there is a fanfare and a stranger enters. It is Rothbart in disguise and with him is his daughter, Odile, whom he has caused exactly to resemble Odette. Siegfried is deceived; joyously he dances with the girl and asks for her hand. The pleading figure of the real Odette at the window is unnoticed. As he swears his love to Odile, Siegfried realises he has been tricked and, mad with grief, rushes from the ballroom to the shore of the lake. There (act IV) he finds Odette once more. She is in despair; all is lost and after a tender farewell she throws herself into the lake of tears. Siegfried follows her, for he is unable to live without her. But the double sacrifice breaks the magician's spell; Rothbart's castle crumbles to the ground and the lovers are reunited.

The story on which the ballet is built is far from being as puerile as it may appear. It is difficult to resist the disturbing atmosphere which somehow imbues the work with poetry

LE LAC DES CYGNES AT THE BOLSHOI THEATRE, MOSCOW. ACT II.

and is heightened by Tchaikovsky's sad and lovely music. The theme, certainly, might have been drawn from some German legend, but the interest centres rather in the use which has been made of it; it bears the imprint of the dying century, a period addicted to symbolism and the ambiguity between reality and dreams.

From the point of view of choreographic interest, the second act is the most perfect, and it is frequently given alone, being virtually complete in itself. The dancer does not exist who does not long to attempt the great adagio. This pas de deux between Odette and Siegfried is superbly lyrical and touching, while Odette's variation is an exquisite composition. The dance of the swans, simple but beautiful in its moving patterns, tests the quality of a *corps de ballet* while the pas de quatre for the four cygnets, technically difficult, always wins applause when well done—although only the Russians today soften the accent and preserve the artistic unity of the dance. The third act contains a rich combination of court and character dances, culminating in the brilliant pas de deux and variations for Siegfried and Odile. A dance of malevolent seduction, it is a high spot of technical virtuosity for both executants and is frequently danced as a divertissement (called *The*

Black Swan, because it is customary to dress Odile in a black tutu, in contrast to the white swan's feathers of Odette).

The choreography of the fourth act, which is musically the finest, is muted but hauntingly beautiful. A great ballerina and a good corps de ballet can make this a tragic and moving episode.

Le Lac des Cygnes is one of the great classics bequeathed to us by the 19th century and the role of Odette-Odile calls for exemplary gifts. The second and fourth acts require an intensity of emotion and a pure, lyric style, while the third act (Odile) demands dazzling technical virtuosity and an actress clever enough to suggest that she is impersonating herself in another character. The two characters are diametrically opposed and yet there must be enough resemblance to deceive Siegfried. Few dancers emerge from the ordeal with complete success. After Pierina Legnani, creator of the role, the greatest exponents have been Kschessinska, Preobrajenska, Trefilova, Karsavina, Pavlova, Semenova, Ulanova, Plissetskaya, Spessivtseva, Markova, Fonteyn, Elvin, Fifield, Vinogradova. As Odette, in the one-act version, Danilova, Nemchinova, Doubrovska, Baronova, Toumanova, Chauviré, Margot Lander,

Rosella Hightower and Vyroubova have been outstanding. The role of Siegfried is less complex, but it too makes heavy demands, for the dancer must be able to invoke a romantic mood, must be an excellent partner and must be capable of dancing the very difficult variation in act III. After Mordkin and Nijinsky, came Dolin, Helpmann, Somes and Blair; in Russia, Messerer, Vilzak, Chabukiani, Yermolaev, Sergeyev, Kondratov, Fadeyechev. In the one-act version, or in *The Black Swan,* Idzikowski, Lifar, Oboukhov, Youskevitch, Eglevsky, Skibine and Bruhn have been notable.

Le Lac des Cygnes has probably been produced, in its one-act form, in every country which has a ballet company; it is now danced even in Japan. The first full-length production outside Russia was however undertaken by the youthful Vic-Wells (now Royal) Ballet in London in 1934 with Markova as Odette-Odile and Robert Helpmann as Siegfried. This version was by Nicolai Sergueev, reconstructed from his notes of the St. Petersburg production. Since 1934 it has been revised and several times re-designed but it is undoubtedly the production which has made the full-length *Lac des Cygnes* familiar and popular in the Western world and has prompted the revivals by the Royal Swedish Ballet, the National Ballet of Canada, and other companies.

In Russia, the full version is the cornerstone of the ballet repertory in most theatres throughout the Soviet Union. The Bolshoi Ballet has used a version by Gorsky and Messerer for some years, but is constantly revising and replanning the production. Bourmeister, at the Stanislavsky and Nemirovitch-Danchenko Theatre in Moscow, in 1953, produced a new version that used the original score of Tchaikovsky, replacing some hitherto unused music and transposing the familiar "Black Swan" music to the first act. For romantic atmosphere and dramatic conviction this production is undoubtedly the finest to be seen today. All the character dances are an integral part of the ensemble, the "cardboard" swans give an illusion of complete reality, the corps de ballet of swans is closely involved in the drama and has enchaînements of great beauty and complexity, and the ballet ends with a terrific fight between Siegfried and the owl-magician Rothbart (an important character), followed by the collapse of Rothbart's castle and the flooding of the lake.

LACOTTE Pierre. Although he had risen rapidly to the rank of premier danseur at the Paris Opera, in 1953 Lacotte decided to try his fortune elsewhere. With fifteen of his companions, he produced a show at the Théâtre de Paris for which he arranged the choreography. Two years later he resigned from the Opéra and founded the *Ballets de la Tour Eiffel,* presenting his first programme at the Aix-les-Bains Festival. There, and later at the Champs-Élysées Theatre in Paris, he achieved a *succès d'estime* but did not attract a wide public. Tall and dark, Lacotte is an excellent dancer, with an elegant style, but still seeking his true métier.

LAFON Madeleine. A fine exponent of the French classical style, as taught at the Paris Opera, Lafon's apparent immunity from fatigue is proverbial. She makes light of every difficulty, has a phenomenal memory and was able to take over the name part in *Blanche-Neige* (when Daydé fell ill) simply by having watched it in rehearsal, and without further instruction. Promoted *danseuse étoile* in 1952, she danced a sparkling Swanilda in *Coppelia,* the swaying, impalpable "Chimère" in *Mirages* and the ballerina role in *Études.* In 1957 she left the Opéra and went to the Opéra-Comique.

LAING Hugh. English dancer born in the West Indies. Pupil of Craske, Rambert and Preobrajenska, he made his début at the Ballet Club in London in 1932. He created leading roles in many of Antony Tudor's ballets and became a principal soloist in Tudor's London Ballet, founded in 1938. The following year he went with Tudor to America and joined Ballet Theatre as a principal dancer on its foundation. Dark and strikingly handsome, Laing makes up in emotional intensity for what he lacks in technique. His created roles in the Tudor ballets, *Jardin aux Lilas, Pillar of Fire, Romeo and Juliet, Undertow* and *Dim Lustre,* all bear the stamp of his personality. In 1950 he joined the New York City Ballet dancing, notably, the leading role in Balanchine's *Prodigal Son.*

LAMBERT Constant. English composer, conductor and critic, born 1905, died 1951. The first Englishman to write a ballet for Diaghilev (*Roméo et Juliette,* 1926). The choreographer was Nijinska, for whom he wrote a second work, *Pomona* (1927). Lambert was associated with the flowering of English ballet from the earliest days, and for some twenty years was musical director and principal conductor for the Camargo Society and later for Sadler's Wells, in whose artistic policy he played a leading part. His work as a conductor left him all too little time for composing, but he wrote two important ballets for the Wells: *Horoscope* (1938) and *Tiresias* (1951) as well as arranging scores from the music of other composers, and one of his choral works, *The Rio Grande,* was used for a ballet by Sadler's Wells in 1935. He used to declaim, inimitably, the Gertrude Stein text for Ashton's *A Wedding Bouquet* in the later, non-choral version. Lambert's influence on English music extended well beyond the frontiers of ballet; he was a colourful and striking personality, a brilliant talker and, in his book *Music, Ho !* as in his journalism, a trenchant and controversial writer. His early death was a sad loss.

LANCASTER Osbert. A comic draughtsman in the English tradition, a brilliant newspaper cartoonist and the author of entertaining books on architecture and interior decoration, born 1908. In the theatre, Lancaster remains essentially a graphic artist, not always happy in colour combinations, but with a remarkable gift for pin-pointing the atmosphere of place and period by means of witty and significant architectural detail. His talents are well displayed in his décors for two comic ballets by John Cranko, *Pineapple Poll* and *Bonne-Bouche.* He also decorated the 1954 Covent Garden revival of *Coppelia,* the one-act version of *Napoli* for London's Festival Ballet, and operas for the Glyndebourne Festival company.

LANDER Harald. At the Royal Danish Ballet School the young Lander studied first with Hans Beck, a pupil of Bournonville, and later with Gustave Uhlendorff, receiving a sound classical training. In 1925, when Fokine was invited to Copenhagen as ballet master, Harald Lander decided on his career. He became a fervent disciple of the new reforms in ballet and went with Fokine to America, where he stayed for two years. Returning to Denmark, the

OSBERT LANCASTER. DÉCOR FOR BONNE-BOUCHE. 1952.

young choreographer remounted the works of his master — *Les Sylphides, Petrouchka, Prince Igor* — and after his appointment as ballet master (1932) inaugurated a great revival at the Royal Theatre. He was primarily responsible for cutting away dead wood, injecting new life and transforming the Royal Danish Ballet from a rather moribund organisation into the superb company that it is today. In addition to teaching and supervising the revival of the Bournonville ballets, Lander created a number of works, among them: *L'Apprenti Sorcier, Bolero, La Valse, Qarrtsiluni* and *Études*. In 1951 he was guest

ÉTUDES. BALLET BY HARALD LANDER.

choreographer at the Paris Opera, in 1953 ballet master there, and in 1956 he became a French citizen. He has revived the 18th century Galeotti ballet *Les Caprices de Cupidon* for the Paris Opera, also *Études,* his masterpiece. Subsequent productions: *Hop-Frog* (1953), *Printemps à Vienne* (1956), *Concerto aux Étoiles* (1956), *La Valse* (1958). A small man of strong passions, he is a strict disciplinarian but a lively, amusing personality and a brilliant talker. As a dancer, he was at his best in character ballets or in Spanish dances, for which he had an unusual flair.

LANDER Margot. In 1917 Margot Florentz-Gerhard entered the school of the Royal Danish Ballet. There she was trained in the pure French style which has been taught in Denmark since the time of Bournonville. In 1932 she married Harald Lander, then ballet master of the Royal Theatre, and it was under her married name that she established herself as the star of the Danish ballet. A brilliant interpreter of the great Danish classical rôles (Teresina in *Napoli*, Rosita in *Far from Denmark*), her gifts as a comédienne enabled her to triumph equally in *Coppelia* and *L'Apprenti Sorcier*. But her finest parts were Giselle and La Sylphide. On her second marriage (to Erik Nyholm) in 1950 she left the stage at the peak of her career, after experiencing at her farewell performance the greatest ovation ever known in the Danish theatre.

LANDER Toni (Toni Phil). Born in Copenhagen, and trained in the Royal Danish Ballet School, she was a pupil of Harald Lander whom she married in 1950, the year she was promoted solo-dancer. After leaving Copenhagen in 1951 she worked and danced under her husband's direction in Paris, helping him to revive *Études* at the Paris Opera. Since 1952 she has been one of the stars of London's Festival Ballet, dancing Odette in *Swan Lake,* Swanilda in *Coppelia,* and the great classical pas de deux. Her finest role is that of the ballerina in *Études,* in which her perfect mastery of technique is displayed in both allegro steps and adage. In 1958 she created the leading rôle in the Françoise Sagan ballet, *Le Rendez-vous manqué*.

LANE Maryon. Born in South Africa and now a soloist in the Royal Ballet, she is a dancer of intense individuality. Small and pert, she excels in modern character roles — the Urchin in *Café des Sports,* the waif in *Laiderette,* the Hypnotist's assistant in *Noctambules* — but her classical technique is sure and her Swanilda in *Coppelia* is enchanting. An intelligent and witty dancer, she nevertheless has a slight tendency to overplay some roles. Married to David Blair.

LAPAURI Alexander. An extremely useful member of the Bolshoi Ballet, he would prove a priceless asset to any western ballet company. No western dancer could surpass him. Big, blond and handsome, he is always at the top of his form and equally gifted both dramatically and lyrically. An ideal partner, he never cheapens his impeccable technique by meaningless spectacular display. Thanks to his great strength and art in partnering, his partner appears to be light as air and he carries her easily above him, almost carelessly on one uplifted arm. An excellent Paris in *Romeo and Juliet,* a remarkable Hilarion in *Giselle,* and a fine Don Fernando in *Laurencia,* he is noted above all for his superb portrayal of Khan Girei in *The Fountain of Bakhchisarai.*

LARIONOV Michel. Born in 1881 at Tiraspol near Odessa. The influence of Larionov on the Russian Ballet was considerable and went far beyond the designing of a few distinguished décors. What is important to stress is the character of this artist: his passion for the dance, his constant searching for new and more expressive forms and ideas, his liking for pushing matters to the furthest limit and for inventing a new vocabulary. There was no affectation in Larionov's modernism; he was never concerned with being fashionable, but the integrity and childlike directness of his work sometimes made it, quite incorrectly, appear deliberately sensational. As a young painter in Moscow he was influenced by Cézanne and later by Cubism. About 1910, he initiated the movement called "rayonnisme"; he and his friend Malevitch now appear as precursors of abstract art. His arrival in Paris in 1914 with Nathalie Goncharova brought him to the centre of the whirlpool. From this time forward, Larionov's life became more and more closely bound up with the fortunes of the Diaghilev Ballet. He did not confine himself to designing; he advised on every aspect of new productions, including the choreography, at this crucial time when Diaghilev was proving the value of his new aesthetic, based on the closest possible collaboration between designer, composer and dancers. From the earliest years, with Bakst and even more with Benois, the Russian Ballet had attached great importance to the functions of the designer. Thus, having guided Massine's first steps as choreographer in the *Midnight Sun* in 1915, Larionov was called in by Diaghilev once again to help Slavinsky with the choreo-

graphy of *Chout* in 1921. During this whole period Larionov's influence was as great as that of the new, post-Fokine choreographers; there was a shift from purely pictorial to plastic values, from rich profusion to something approaching visual austerity. The change was evident in Larionov's own work. In *Renard* he abandoned the brilliant, folk-art colours of his earlier designs for a deliberate, low-keyed simplicity devoid in his case of any sophistication. Lifar has pointed out how deeply Larionov's influence affected Massine as a choreographer, with his fondness for bizarre, broken and angular movements and groupings. But in spite of his intellectual probings, Larionov's work has never become cerebral. He has remained entirely spontaneous and sincere, an ingenuous and good-natured giant with a sense of fun.

Décors for the Ballets Russes: *Midnight Sun* (1915), *Kikimora* (1916), *Children's Tales* (1917), *Chout* (1921), *Renard* (1922, revised 1929). For other companies: *Sur le Borysthène* (Paris Opera, 1933), *Port Said* (Woizikowski Ballet, 1935).

LARSEN Niels Bjorn. Danish dancer and choreographer, born in Copenhagen and trained at the school of the Royal Danish Ballet. He

LARIONOV BY JUAN GRIS.

was appointed soloist in 1942 and served as ballet master at the Royal Theatre from 1951 to 1956. A most talented actor, imaginative and witty, he is a brilliant mime equally capable of interpreting the Charlatan in *Petrouchka,* Dr Coppelius, Angelok in *Qarrtsiluni* and the Musician in *Symphonie Fantastique.* Choreographer of several ballets, among them *Drift* (1950) and *Capricious Lucinda* (1954), he has directed the Tivoli pantomime theatre since 1957.

LAURENCIA. Ballet in three acts and six scenes. Scenario: E. Mandelberg. Music: Alexander Krein. Scenery and costumes: S. Virsaladze. Choreography: Vakhtang Chabukiani. First performance: Kirov Theatre, Leningrad, 22 March 1939. Principal dancers: Nathalie Dudinskaya, Chabukiani. Based on the play by Lope de Vega, the ballet is set in Spain at the end of the 15th century, in the tiny village of Fuente Ovejuna. The countryside is groaning under the tyranny of the lord of the manor, the cruel and debauched Don Fernando. Attracted by a young peasant girl, Laurencia, he attempts to assert his *droit du seigneur,* but is repulsed. Immediately after Laurencia's marriage to Frondozo, Don Fernando has the girl seized and taken to his castle, while her husband is thrown into prison. She returns to the village, wretched and bedraggled, and incites the people to revolt. They storm the castle, rescue Frondozo and kill the Commendador. Then they set fire to the castle and celebrate their victory by dancing in the light of the flames. With Plissetskaya and Kondratov in the main roles, *Laurencia* is one of the most successful productions at the Bolshoi Theatre in Moscow today. Chabukiani has also staged it in Tiflis and this version, with Chabukiani as Frondozo, is recorded in the film *Masters of Georgian Ballet.*

LAURENCIN Marie. Born 1885, died 1957. One of the rare painters whose work can be transferred directly to the stage without loss or alteration of quality. It is only necessary to enlarge Marie Laurencin's water-colours, preserving their simplified design and soft colours, for their tender charm to spring to life on the stage. It happened with her designs for *Les Biches,* where (with expert advice from Mme Chanel) the costumes lent a gracefulness, modest, self-effacing yet intriguing, which was extraordinarily becoming to the dancers. Unlike many ballet designers, she never relied on the naive charms of popular art. Her contribution was more personal: a discreet, feminine elegance and a secret melancholy of colour which were quite inimitable. Marie Laurencin designed the following ballets: *Les Biches* (Diaghilev's Ballets Russes, 1924), *Les Roses* (Soirées de Paris, 1924), *Un Jour d'été* (Opéra-Comique, 1940), *Le Déjeuner sur l'herbe* (Ballets des Champs-Élysées, 1946).

LECLERCQ Tanaquil. It was in 1956 in Copenhagen that this star of the New York City Ballet was struck down by poliomyelitis, in the course of a long and successful European tour. No more tragic illness could afflict a dancer. Supple and strong as steel, her slender body was admirably suited to the highly-disciplined cho-

LA LÉGENDE DE JOSEPH. COSTUME BY BAKST. 1914.

MARIE LAURENCIN. DANCERS. 1949.

reography of Balanchine, that ascetic of the dance. Captivated by the intelligence of this young American of French descent, he promoted her to his company in 1946 and less than ten years later she became his wife and the favourite interpreter of his works. Précise, cool and brilliant, she was also an enchanting comédienne, excelling in *Bourrée Fantasque* and *Western Symphony*. Jerome Robbins also made full use of the unique charm of this dryad of Fifth Avenue, in his *L'Après-midi d'un faune*. He exploited her "legginess" in *The Pied Piper* and her weaving arms in *The Cage,* in the role of the Praying Mantis which she inherited from Nora Kaye. But it is as the perfect incarnation of Balanchine's neo-classicism that Tanaquil LeClercq will be remembered, and as that she will never be forgotten.

LÉGENDE DE JOSEPH La. Ballet in one act. Scenario: Harry von Kessler and Hugo von Hofmannsthal. Music: Richard Strauss. Scenery: José-Maria Sert. Costumes: Léon Bakst. Choreography: Michel Fokine. First performance: Diaghilev's Ballets Russes, Paris Opera, 14 May 1914. Principal dancers: Maria Kouznetsova, Leonide Massine, Alexis Bulgakov. The plot contrasts the opulent splendour of Potiphar's household (treated by the designers in the style of Veronese) with the simplicity of the pastoral life led by Joseph and his family. Potiphar's wife, bored with the empty luxury of her life, is attracted by the candid innocence of the young shepherd. He repulses her, and she contrives his ruin. Joseph is condemned; he awaits torture and death with serene calm. An archangel descends from heaven, sets him free and leads him away. Potiphar's wife strangles herself with her ropes of pearls. This adaptation of the biblical episode was a failure in spite of a lavish production; there was too much mime, too little dancing and the public was beginning to feel sated with the exotic luxury of Diaghilev's productions. The ballet's only real claim to distinction was the revelation of Diaghilev's latest discovery, Leonide Massine, who danced Joseph.

LÉGER Fernand. Born 1881, died 1955. Léger's contribution to the theatre was considerable, not so much in the quantity as in the quality and originality of his décors. He instinctively grasped that the theatre presented a painter with quite different problems from easel pictures or murals. In connection with Léger, more than with anyone else, it is important to remember an essential rule of stage design: the necessity (and the difficulty) of establishing a unity between the décor and the actors, firstly because the décor is a stable element while the actors are mobile, secondly because the décor occupies the whole volume of the stage — width, depth and height — while the actor is confined to the ground level. Few painters seem to have given much thought to this problem: Léger, together with Picasso, is one of those who have foreseen or understood it and succeeded in solving it. Sometimes, as in *Skating Rink*, Léger made the dancer an element of the décor, sometimes he made the décor itself into an actor, with its own part to play in the action — a method which proved highly successful in *La Création du Monde* (1923), with its barbaric, abstract shapes, masks and costumes. Léger had a kind of natural directness and childlike emphasis, which enabled him to find clear, simple answers to complex questions. Décors by Léger for the Ballets Suédois: *Skating Rink* (1922) and *La Création du Monde* (1923); for the Paris Opera: *David Triomphant* (1937) and Milhaud's opera *Bolivar* (1950).

LEHMANN Maurice. Born 1895. Although he studied acting at the Paris Conservatoire with dictinction, he has made his name not as an actor but as a director of various Parisian theatres, including some very famous ones. He was in charge successively of the Renaissance, Empire, Ambigu, Édouard VII and Porte Saint-Martin, presenting both musical shows and straight plays. But it was at the Mogador and the Châtelet that he unmistakably showed his preference for large-scale, spectacular productions and thus prepared the way for his entry to the Opéra in 1945. Under his direction (1945-46 and again in 1951-56), the two national opera houses, and above all the Opéra, mounted a number of sumptuous spectacles and attracted bigger audiences than ever before. The effort involved in these productions of *Les Indes Galantes, Oberon* and *The Magic Flute* was repaid by a success of a kind usually associated with much more popular types of entertainment. Maurice Lehmann has been reproached with using effects more appropriate to musicals at the Châtelet than to serious works, but what his critics really seem unable to forgive is the success of his unorthodox methods. In the domain of choreography, it was Lehmann who brought Harald Lander, from the Royal Danish Ballet, to the Opéra. It was also at his instigation that the "Défilé du corps de ballet" was instituted (see *Opéra de Paris*).

LEPESHINSKAYA Olga. Apart from Ulanova — the undisputed idol of Soviet ballet — the Moscow public divides its favours between Olga Lepeshinskaya and Maya Plissetskaya. Unlike the latter, the tiny Lepeshinskaya is distinguished less by her grace and beauty than by her almost masculine vigour and force. Some critics have remarked on a certain lack of grace in her port de bras and of flowing line in her arabesques. But the Bolshoi audience always receives her enthusiastically, for her charm is irresistible. She was the first artist for 120 years to graduate from the Bolshoi

school with the title of danseuse-étoile (1933). The virtuosity of her technique, which makes her stand out at once even among the brilliant Bolshoi company, her elevation, her impressive strength, enable her to interpret any role with éclat. She excels more especially in all those in which technical virtuosity holds an important place.

LEPRI Stanislas. This painter's contribution to contemporary ballet came during that recent period when young French companies were trying, often with some success, to revive the miracles of Diaghilev's Ballets Russes. But though the attempts were interesting, they were often, probably from lack of funds, somewhat limited in scope. Thus for *Le Bal des Blanchisseuses* (Ballets des Champs-Élysées, 1946) Lepri did no more than hang lines of washing across the stage. The result was attractive and created a certain amount of atmosphere, but it did not properly speaking amount to a décor. Nor was the schematised kitchen on the backcloth of *L'Œuf à la Coque* (Ballets de Paris, 1949), although it confirmed the designer's good taste, particularly original. The costumes for

LÉGER. CURTAIN FOR LA CRÉATION DU MONDE, 1923.

LETTER TO THE WORLD. BALLET BY MARTHA GRAHAM.

these two ballets, on the other hand, were vivid and imaginative, and made up for the modesty of the décors.

LETTER TO THE WORLD. Ballet by Martha Graham. Music: Hunter Johnson. Scenic elements: Arch Lauterer. Costumes: Edythe Gilfond. Spoken text from poems by Emily Dickinson. First performance: Martha Graham's company, Bennington College, Vermont, 11 August 1940.

Martha Graham describes *Letter to the World* as "a drama about Emily Dickinson as a poet and as a woman of New England. The action takes place in the world of her imagination and of her poetry rather than in the day to day world of Amherst, Massachusetts, where she lived." Each episode is linked to a poem and each character represents some aspects of the poet's personality. Thus the character of the grandmother, while evoking the artist's Puritan ancestry, also expresses the fear and anguish of death. The wonderful world of childhood finds its ideal expression in the Fairy Queen, while the world of love and passion is expressed in the tempestuous scene beginning "Dear March, Come In" and in the dance of the young lovers. But, withdrawing from the world and its disappointments, the poet regains her solitude to dedicate herself to her work:

> *This is my letter to the world,*
> *That never wrote to me, —*
> *The simple news that Nature told,*
> *With tender majesty.*

The work may perhaps be criticised for a lack of simplicity and of continuity but for the choreographic language and the means of expression employed by Martha Graham there can be nothing but admiration. How wonderfully she captures the spirit of Emily Dickinson in the first episode, "Because I see New Englandly" !

LEVINSON André. It is doubtful whether, before André Levinson, ballet criticism in France really existed. Of course, the press published accounts of ballet performances. But these were the work of men of letters, amateurs who confined themselves to personal impressions, and often did no more than reproduce the opinions of one small section of the public. In other cases the articles were written by music, dramatic or art critics, who concentrated accordingly on the score, the action or the décor. It was only in 1922 that articles began to appear in "Comœdia" in which ballet was criticised as such, from the point of view of its principal element—dancing. The author, a Russian born in St. Petersburg in 1887, wrote excellent French. Not only did André Levinson give choreography its due, but he stressed the fundamental importance of classic French ballet, whose long and glorious tradition, apparently forgotten in Paris, had survived in Russia, thanks to Marius Petipa. André Levinson had long been opposed to the tendencies of Diaghilev's Ballets Russes and in particular to those of Fokine. For him, Diaghilev's mistake lay in subjugating the dancer "to the haughty dictatorship of the scene-designer," in giving "the musical element precedence over choreographic inspiration", in having deformed dancing in imitation of the conventions of pictorial and plastic art. For him the dance should be, in the words of Paul Valéry, "l'acte pur des métamorphoses": that is to say, it should be self-sufficient, an end in itself. Levinson died prematurely in 1933. His books include: *La Danse au théâtre* (1924), *La Danse d'aujourd'hui* (1929), a *Life of Noverre, Marie Taglioni*, an essay on *La Argentina*.

LICHINE David. Dancer and choreographer, born at Rostov-on-the-Don, 1910. Having left Russia for France with his family when still a child, he studied dancing in Paris under Mme Egorova. He was engaged by Nijinska in 1928 for Ida Rubinstein's company, and then appeared with Pavlova. But it was with the Monte Carlo Ballet (1932-40) that he made his name as one of the best dancers of his generation. Supple, elegant, graceful, as much at home in character dancing as in classical, he created many important roles: the King of the Dandies in *Beau Danube*, the Traveller in *Jeux d'Enfants*, and the Hero in *Les Présages*. Emigrating to the United States in 1940, he settled in 1952 in Los Angeles where, under the patronage of A. H. Taylor, he founded a school of dancing and the "Los Angeles" ballet company. With several of his young pupils and his wife Tatiana Riabouchinska as ballerina, this company appeared in Paris at the Théâtre de l'Empire in March 1954.

As a choreographer, Lichine began with *Nocturne* (1933), based on *A Midsummer Night's Dream*, and *Les Imaginaires* (1934). As a result, de Basil encouraged him to undertake more important works, notably *Le Lion Amoureux, Francesca da Rimini* (1937), *Protée* (1938), a "choreographic dream" to Debussy's "Danse sacrée et danse profane", with décor by Chirico, and a new version of *The Prodigal Son*. For de Basil (in Australia, in 1940) he staged his most popular ballet, *Graduation Ball* (*). In the United States he made *Helen of Troy* (*) for Ballet Theatre. For de Cuevas, *Le Moulin Enchanté* (*) and *Corrida*. For Festival Ballet, a new version of *The Nutcracker* (*). Skilful and ingenious, he has neither the technical weight nor the artistic culture of a Fokine or a Massine; nevertheless,

he excels in episodes for a few characters and especially in pas de deux. In those respects *La Création* (*) and above all *La Rencontre* (*), both staged for the Ballets des Champs-Élysées in 1948, must be accounted highly individual successes.

LIFAR Serge. Born at Kiev in 1905 into a prosperous family, Serge Lifar describes himself in his autobiography *(Du temps que j'avais faim)* as a spoilt child and unruly schoolboy, a dreamer interested most of all in the things he was not required to know, especially music. The hardships of war soon cast a shadow over this happy childhood, which was finally brought to an end by the Revolution. By the time he was 16 he had already worn several uniforms, but not as yet a pair of dancing shoes. The revelation came one day in 1921 in Bronislava Nijinska's studio in Kiev. Having nothing special to do, he looked in there with a friend. The great Nijinsky's sister would not accept him for her private classes, but she also taught at the State Central Studio where tuition was free and open to all. The young man hurried there and set himself to make up for lost time. Not for long, however, for Nijinska left a month later to rejoin Diaghilev in Paris. Lifar continued the studies which had barely begun until the end of 1922, working mostly on his own. Then a telegram arrived from Nijinska in Paris, asking for the best pupils of her old school to make up the numbers of the Russian Ballet. By pure chance, Lifar came to benefit from this opportunity. One of the boys asked for could not be found; Lifar obtained permission to go in his place. After incidents on the way and at the frontier that almost cost him his life, he succeeded in reaching Warsaw. He arrived in Paris on 13 January 1923, in company with Unger, Lapitzky and the brothers Hoyer. What happened next belongs to the history of the Russian Ballet. Lifar is the first to admit that he knew practically nothing on his arrival, 18 years old. But his passion for work and his rapid progress attracted the attention of Diaghilev. He made an inconspicuous début in *Aurora's Wedding* at Monte Carlo in the following April, but it was not long before more and more important roles were assigned to him, and in 1924 Diaghilev sent him to Turin to complete his studies with the veteran Cecchetti. By the

LES NOCES FANTASTIQUES. CURTAIN BY ROGER CHASTEL.
Bibliothèque-Musée de l'Opéra, Paris.

end of that year he had become a star and had been entrusted with the choreography of *Zéphire et Flore,* but the new task was too much for him at that stage, and he had to content himself with dancing a leading role under Massine's direction.

His rise to fame continued; he had made himself indispensable. In addition to the big classical roles, he danced in nearly all the ballets of Balanchine, Massine and Nijinska, beside Karsavina, Spessivtseva, Nemchinova and Nikitina. In 1929 he successfully realised his first completed choreography—a new version of Stravinsky's *Renard* (*). All this work did not prevent him from occasionally incurring the director's displeasure by accepting social invitations. But his quarrels with Diaghilev never reached a final breach and when the great impresario died in Venice on 19th August 1929, Lifar was at his bedside in company with Boris Kochno. Before the end of that year, his name figured on the bills of the Paris Opera as choreographer. Balanchine, who had been engaged by Jacques Rouché to mount *Les Créatures de Prométhée* (*), had fallen ill and Lifar completed

the ballet, introducing enough of himself into the work for the two librettists to insist on withdrawing their names. Then Boris Kochno invited him to London with Nikitina, Tcherkas, Efimov and Domansky, to arrange the ballets for a Cochran revue. Here he composed his third ballet, *La Nuit* (*), for which Christian Bérard designed his first décor. On his return to Paris he, with all his companions except Nikitina, was engaged at the Opéra. Balanchine, though restored to health, had resigned.

Lifar was now twenty-five. Neither too tall nor too short, broad-shouldered and exceedingly narrow-waisted, with admirably shaped legs, he was remarkable alike for his beautifully proportioned body and his strongly individual features. Two years earlier, perhaps at Diaghilev's suggestion, he had had the good sense to have his nose flattened, thereby accentuating his Asiatic appearance. "Beautiful as a rare monkey" was how Cyril Connolly, years later, described the young Lifar. As a dancer he is in a class by himself and we will try to explain why. It is not purely a question of technical ability. On this point he was handicapped in comparison with other male dancers, such as the former pupils of the Imperial School in St. Petersburg, who had started younger and had a more methodical training. Elevation, strength ? He had plenty and to spare, but others had still more. He himself supplies the explanation in his *Traité de la danse académique,* when he says in substance that it is not so important to jump very high, as to give the impression that the jump lasts for a long time. That is where a very rare quality comes in, the ability to transform even the most banal gesture; it is as hard to define as a great actor's "presence". For want of a more scientific term, we call it the "genius" of dancing, and Lifar possesses this "genius" in the highest degree. He also possesses a keen sense of drama and a lyricism, the full significance of which was only revealed much later, when his outstanding athletic qualities were less strongly in evidence. Such then was the dancer, maître de ballet and choreauthor (Lifar invented this rather uncouth term himself to underline the creative role of the choreographer), who was henceforward to rule the Paris Opera ballet, relegating Léo Staats and Albert Aveline to second rank. He took immediate, violent and revolutionary action. The institution of regular weekly evenings of ballet, which freed the dancers from their unenviable role of stopgap for operatic programmes of insufficient weight and length, was one of the results. It was to Lifar's efforts to rehabilitate the dance, also, that we owe the lowering of the auditorium lights during a performance and the abolition of many of the regular subscribers' superannuated privileges. "He thinks he's a second Wagner," the old gentlemen complained, little realising how near the mark they were. Like Wagner, Lifar placed perseverance, immense self-confidence, a sense of political expediency and irresistible personal charm at the service of his talent. Hence the innumerable controversies he has aroused, as much on the purely human plane as on the artistic. Jacques Rouché let the malcontents grumble, while according Lifar a free hand to graft the spirit of the Russian Ballet on to the venerable institution. Within the space of three months, between 16 February and 22 May 1931, Lifar mounted three ballets: *Prélude dominical, L'Orchestre en liberté* (*) and *Bacchus et Ariane* (*). He was a prodigiously dynamic maître de ballet, his enthusiasm was contagious, and the dancers worked with a will. New ballets multiplied, surrounded by noisy but efficient publicity frankly centred on Lifar, who seemed to be collecting new roles. Having obtained a degree of celebrity usually reserved for film stars, he became, and remains, the only dancer whose name is known throughout the length and breadth of his adopted country. The benefits to the Opéra were considerable. The war and the occupation, far from breaking the spell, marked the peak of this brilliant epoch. Lifar, who made the mistake of regarding the occupying forces as just so many more spectators to applaud him, was dismissed after the Liberation. He removed to Monte Carlo, where he arranged several ballets before the Marquis de Cuevas took over the resident company. But his departure from the Opéra had left a great void in Paris and in 1947 Georges Hirsch summoned him back as maître de ballet. As various unions were opposed to his appearing himself on the stage, he did not make his come-back as a dancer until February 1949, in *L'Après-midi d'un faune.*

Perhaps it is a pity that Lifar did not take

L'ORCHESTRE EN LIBERTÉ. 1931.
COSTUME BY COLIN. *Museé de l'Opéra, Paris.*

advantage of the occasion offered to leave the stage for good. Better adapted by nature to resist the oncoming of age than most dancers, he nevertheless miscalculated his physical powers. Until his farewell performance in *Giselle* on 5 December 1956, and despite his extraordinarily youthful appearance, he presented his dismayed admirers with a mere shadow of the former "dieu de la danse".

Leaving aside the revivals of such classical masterpieces as *Giselle,* all of which bore the unmistakable mark of his personality, Lifar staged more than 50 ballets at the Opéra. Among them mention must be made of *Icare* (*), *Le Chevalier et la Damoiselle* (*), *Suite en blanc* (*), *Joán de Zarissa* (*), *Phèdre* (*), *Les Mirages* (*), and *Les Noces fantastiques* (*). All these works have certain characteristics in common the study of which permits one to determine, far better than any abstract study, their creator's "neo-classical" doctrine. First of all, most of them are ballets d'action; that is to say, narrative, and tragic rather than comic. Lifar, an admirable tragedian, lacks a sense of humour and his incursions into comedy and satire—*Guignol et Pandore, Fourberies* (*), *Cinéma* (*)— have been unsuccessful. The male dancer always takes an important place, though not so preponderantly as has often been said. It is certainly true that the leading roles occupy the choreographer's attention almost exclusively, reducing the ensembles to little more than decorative accompaniment. With rare exceptions *(Cinéma, L'Inconnue)* the subjects are mythological, legendary, poetic or even abstract, never contemporary or realistic. In his horror of realism, Lifar avoids mime and treats precise situations allusively, which often leads to a certain degree of obscurity. As for his choreographic vocabulary, it is basically academic, with contributions from acrobatics and, more rarely, folk dancing. Particularly noticeable are the abundance of ornament (turns, entrechats, etc.), beaten steps, symbolic gestures and those positions of the feet which other choreographers had already employed incidentally, but Lifar has codified under the name of "sixth" and "seventh" positions. For Lifar, the instinctive artist, wants to be a theorist as well. In numerous writings and lectures he has pleaded the cause of neo-classicism with as much enthusiasm as he has used to illustrate it on the stage. In his *Manifeste du chorégraphe* (1935) he claimed for dancing priority over music and décor. His published works on the ballet, often controversial, include: *La Danse, Histoire du Ballet russe, Serge de Diaghilev, Auguste Vestris, Les Trois grâces du XXe siècle.*

Lifar can never be accused of excessive modesty. One may smile at his literary activities, his interminable harangues, his passion for being photographed or interviewed, and certain very Parisian scandals, such as the imitation, at President Lebrun's expense, of Vestris's capricious refusal to dance before Marie-Antoinette, or the recent duel with the Marquis de Cuevas. But is cannot be denied that he has done a great deal for ballet in France. He has raised the prestige of male dancing and roused the Opéra from its lethargy. Many of the finest French

SERGE LIFAR IN ICARE.

dancers—Solange Schwarz, Lycette Darsonval, Yvette Chauviré and Nina Vyroubova—owe him a great debt. Utterly egotistical and self-centred, he does not bear malice. Capable of the greatest generosity when his own laurels are not in question, he has made no fortune for himself and continues to live a bohemian existence, careless in his dress, travelling 2nd class in the "métro" and eating a sandwich lunch at the counter. Much may be forgiven an artist who carries love of his profession to such lengths.

LILAC GARDEN. See *Jardin aux lilas.*

LIMON José. Born in Mexico in 1908, José Limon studied in the U.S.A. He pursued his artistic and scholastic studies side by side and in 1930 entered the Humphrey-Weidman school. These teachers persuaded him to abandon the painting career which had been his first choice in favour of the dance, foreseeing in Limon the great modern dancer-choreographer that he was to become. He writes his ballets on a wide diversity of subjects, often creating dances of purely musical inspiration such as his *Chaconne in D Minor* (Bach). He handles dramatic subjects with great power; *The Moor's Pavane, Emperor Jones* and *The Traitor* live long in the memory. His company has grown from a tiny group to a well-integrated ensemble with a high reputation not only in the United States, but in South America and in Europe. Of magnificent appearance, with almost Aztec features, he is a commanding figure on the stage, but a gentle and persuasive teacher.

LINDEN Anya. An English beauty and a ballerina of the Royal Ballet, with a special gift for portraying childish or *gamine* characters. Born in Manchester, studied with Kosloff in Los Angeles during the war and on returning to England joined the Sadler's Wells School in 1947. She entered the Covent Garden company in 1951, was made a soloist in 1954 and ballerina in 1958. Linden's range is considerable, extending from pure classicism to a variety of modern roles. In MacMillan's *Noctambules,* for instance, she created the touching role of the Poor Girl; in his *Agon* (1958) she danced with a coolness and sharpness of attack that was near to the style of the New York City Ballet.

LITTLEFIELD Catherine. For more than fifteen years—from 1935 when she created her first ballet until 1951, the year of her untimely death—she was indisputably one of the most vital personalities in American stage dancing. Born at Philadelphia in 1908, she was taught to dance by her mother, Caroline, and her sister Dorothie was also a fine dancer. Catherine later studied with Luigi Albertieri, Léo Staats and Egorova. She first appeared on the stage at the age of 15 in the Ziegfeld Follies and became *première danseuse* at the Philadelphia Opera (1925-33). In 1935 she arranged her first ballet, the third act of *Daphnis and Chloé,* and in the same year founded her own company, the Littlefield Ballet (known also as the Philadelphia Ballet). This was the first American ballet company to tour Europe; it was warmly

SERGE LIFAR IN ICARE.

greeted in Paris, London and Brussels. There was a strong American flavour in the repertoire and among the best known works were *Barn Dance* (Philadelphia, 1937), to popular tunes of the late 19th century, *Terminal* (Paris, 1937), and *Café Society* (1938), a satire on smart night clubs in New York. Catherine Littlefield also staged several ice ballets and did the choreography for Sonja Henie's revues. The Littlefields played an important part in the development of American ballet. It was a double tragedy that both sisters should die so young.

LONDON'S FESTIVAL BALLET. This popular and highly successful company originated in a tour made in 1949 by two great English dancers, Alicia Markova and Anton Dolin, with a small group of young colleagues. The group evolved into a full company and, as the Festival Ballet, made its bow to the London public at the Stoll Theatre in the following year. It now gives annual London seasons at the

LYDIA LOPOKOVA BY PICASSO.

Royal Festival Hall, the great modern concert hall which can be converted into a theatre, and has toured the U.S.A., Canada and Europe (including several appearances at Monte Carlo) with increasing success. Markova left in 1952, but a number of young dancers have risen to star rank, notably Belinda Wright and John Gilpin. The general style, bearing the clear imprint of the artistic director, Anton Dolin, is exhilarating and brilliant rather than subtle. The company has gained much from the accession of Copenhagen dancers, notably Toni Lander, and it has provided an excellent framework for such distinguished guest artists as Charrat, Chauviré, Danilova, Fonteyn, Toumanova, Massine and the Hungarians, Kovach and Rabovsky. The repertory includes revivals of *Giselle, Lac des Cygnes* (act II), *Casse-Noisette* (in a new version by Lichine with décor by Benois, 1957), *Sheherazade, Petrouchka* and other works by Fokine. Harald Lander has reproduced *Études* and a one-act version of the Danish classic *Napoli*. Of the modern works, the most popular has been *Symphony for Fun* (1952) by the young English choreographer Michael Charnley (also responsible for *Homage to the Princess* in honour of the marriage of the Prince of Monaco) and the most original, *Les Deux Errants* (1956) by a member of the company, Wolfgang Brunner. For the European tour and London season of 1958, Markova rejoined the company as guest artist.

LOPOKOVA Lydia. Trained in the Imperial Ballet School at St. Petersburg, Lopokova went to Paris in 1910 to join Diaghilev and never returned to Russia. She was so successful in *L'Oiseau de feu* that an American impresario invited her to the United States, where she danced for five years. She rejoined Diaghilev, left and rejoined again on several occasions, but her charm and artistry made her ever welcome.

Lopokova, quite different in style from Diaghilev's other dancers, was his greatest comedienne, tiny but perfectly proportioned, with clear-cut features. She danced with a vitality and bubbling vivacity that were enchanting, and made great use of her eloquent little hands. Her blonde hair would shine under the lights, her blue-green eyes would sparkle, and her happy smile would irradiate the whole theatre.

LE LOUP. PROJECT FOR THE FIRST SCENE BY CARZOU. 1953.

Massine understood her best (just as Fokine understood Karsavina) and Lopokova was at her most lovable in the comedy roles which she created in his ballets, such as Mariuccia in *Les Femmes de bonne humeur* (1917), the Can-Can Dancer in *La Boutique fantasque* (1919) and the Street Dancer in *Le Beau Danube* (first version, 1924). She also created one of the acrobats in the cubist ballet *Parade* (1917); the designs on her white body-tights were painted by Picasso himself. Lopokova inherited from other dancers certain Russian character parts in which she was highly effective (Polovstian Girl in *Prince Igor* and Snow Maiden in *Le Soleil de nuit*). Though light and swift, she was not particularly strong technically; nevertheless, in the 1921 revival of *The Sleeping Princess* in London, she appeared in several roles (Princess Aurora, Lilac Fairy, Blue Bird pas de deux).

In 1925 she married the economist J. M. (later Lord) Keynes and settled in England. Before retiring, she created the Milkmaid in Ashton's *Façade* (Camargo Society, 1933) and danced *Coppelia* for the Vic-Wells Ballet.

LORCIA Suzanne. Entered the dancing school of the Paris Opera at 10 years of age, was engaged in the company at 14, and promoted to grand sujet at 16, when she was chosen for the part of Djali in *Les Deux pigeons*. This auspicious début proved to be the beginning of a star career that was to last for 20 years. Lorcia's dark, characteristic beauty, combined with a solid technique, marked her for roles demanding authority and distinction. She was particularly admired in *Les Créatures de Prométhée, Alexandre le Grand, Le Festin de l'araignée* and *Sylvia*. She has remained at the Paris Opera as instructor to the petits sujets.

LORING Eugene. Born in 1914 at Milwaukee, Wisconsin, he studied under Boris Glagolin before entering the School of American Ballet. Short of stature but of a strong and muscular physique, he made his mark as a character dancer when he was with the company of the Metropolitan Opera, New York. A sensitive and cultured artist and an excellent pianist, he made his début as a choreographer in 1936 with Ballet Caravan, thereafter creating in succession *Harlequin for President, Yankee Clipper* (1937), *Billy the Kid* (*) and *City Portrait* (1939). After a period with Ballet Theatre for which he mounted *The Great American Goof* (1940) he founded his own company, Dance Players, in November 1941. Although he had some excellent dancers, such as Lew Christensen, Michael Kidd and Janet Reed, the company survived for barely a year. During this brief time he presented several new works *(Prairie* and *The Invisible Wife)* inspired by the life and history of the American people. In this respect Loring, in company with Agnes de Mille and Catherine Littlefield, is one of the pioneers of American ballet. He now directs the American School of Dance in Hollywood.

LOUP Le. Ballet by Jean Anouilh and Georges Neveux. Music: Henri Dutilleux. Scenery and costumes: Carzou. Choreography: Roland Petit. First performance: Ballets de Paris, Théâtre de l'Empire, Paris, 17 March 1953. Principal dancers: Violette Verdy, Claire Sombert, Roland Petit, George Reich, Jean-Bernard Lemoine. A kind of cruel fairytale, mimed and danced, *Le Loup* reflects the pessimism of Jean Anouilh tempered by the poetry and humour of Georges Neveux. On his wedding day a young husband elopes with a gypsy girl. With the connivance of an animal tamer he makes his young wife believe he has been transformed into a wolf. The bride leaves on the arm of the being she takes to be her husband. Gradually she discovers that her companion is indeed a wolf. More remarkable still, she feels herself drawn towards this creature who, unlike the men she has known, is frank, brave and loyal. But when the inhabitants of the village discover that a wolf is living among them they set out to destroy it. The dramatic action is admirably and economically told; the tension never sags. Roland Petit's choreography has the same qualities; clear, subtle and supple it reflects the slightest nuance of feeling while remaining consistently interesting as dancing. Dutilleux's score and Carzou's beautiful sets, poetic and desolate by turn, are worthy of one of the most distinguished works presented by the Ballets de Paris.

M

MACMILLAN Kenneth. The youngest English choreographer to gain an international reputation, MacMillan's rise has been remarkably rapid. He was born in Scotland, trained at the Sadler's Wells School, and has danced for both of the companies. His first ballets were made for the Sadler's Wells Choreographic Group, an experimental organisation run by the dancers themselves. The promise revealed was so unmistakable that Ninette de Valois immediately invited him to do *Danses Concertantes* and *House of Birds* for the Sadler's Wells Theatre Ballet; in the following year (1956) he made *Noctambules* (*) for Covent Garden and, again for the company at Sadler's Wells, *Somnambulism* and *Solitaire*. An invitation from the American Ballet Theatre soon followed: the controversial *Winter's Eve* (1957) was the result. MacMillan's ballets show an unusual vein of fantasy with a streak of eccentric comedy; still more personal to his style is a compassion for lonely or unhappy people, revealed in choreography of great expressiveness. He explored the tensions and emotions of a persecuted community in *The Burrow* (1958) and returned to pure dancing in *Agon* (Royal Ballet, 1958). In *Journey* (Ballet Theatre, 1958), he created a remarkable work for Nora Kaye and a male corps de ballet about an individual's solitary journey towards death.

MADAME CHRYSANTHÈME. Ballet in five scenes. Music: Alan Rawsthorne. Scenario: Vera Bowen and Frederick Ashton, after Pierre Loti. Choreography: Frederick Ashton. Scenery and costumes: Isabel Lambert. First produced: Sadler's Wells Ballet, Covent Garden, London, 1 April 1955. Principal dancers: Elaine Fifield, Alexander Grant.

Pierre, a French sailor on shore leave in

Nagasaki, "buys" Madame Chrysanthème as his temporary wife. He grows attached to her and is persuaded that she loves him. But when he returns for a last farewell before rejoining his ship, he finds her contentedly counting her silver dollars, the fruits of her "marriage". He steals away unseen. The faded charms of Loti's story provide a surprisingly apt vehicle for Ashton's evocation, at once subtle and sharp, of Japanese dance movements, which Elaine Fifield performed with exquisite detachment. Isabel Lambert's delicate, transparent screens and Rawsthorne's bitter-sweet music have the same quality of discreetly suggestive elegance.

MAGALLANES Nicholas. Dancer of Mexican origin. Dark-haired and exotic, elegant in style, he is a product of the American school. A soloist with Ballet Caravan in 1941, he was next with the Ballet Russe de Monte-Carlo (1943-47). He joined the New York City Ballet at its foundation, and has become one of the principal interpreter's of Balanchine's ballets. As much at home in classical roles as in character dances, he created leading parts in *Les Illuminations* and *The Cage*.

MARCHAND Colette. Tall and slender, with very shapely legs, Colette Marchand, a deserter from the Paris Opera, conquered two continents in 1949 in the guise of a befeathered vamp in Roland Petit's *L'Œuf à la Coque*. This ballet decided her career, and although she was an excellent classical dancer, she turned to the music-hall and the cinema. She starred with Maurice Chevalier at the Théâtre de l'Empire in 1953, and her later greatest successes were with the Ballets de Paris, in *Ciné-Bijou* and *Deuil en 24 Heures* in which she was a sprightly and seductive "merry widow".

MARÉ Rolf de. A Swedish industrialist and patron of the arts, Rolf de Maré deserves an honourable place in the history of contemporary ballet as the founder of the Ballets Suédois and subsequently of the *Archives Internationales de la Danse*. The creation of the former was an imaginative and hazardous enterprise; he ran it with Scandinavian thoroughness, knowing what he wanted and, in spite of his gentle manner, prepared to fight for it passionately. The Ballets Suédois were his main concern, but he also played a notable part in the Parisian theatrical life of the 'twenties and, with Jacques Hébertot, was closely connected with the Théâtre des Champs-Élysées at one of its most brilliant periods. Among other distinguished productions there was the famous *Revue Nègre* which introduced Josephine Baker. De Maré assisted in the publication of important periodicals such as "La Danse". He published a commemorative volume about the Ballets Suédois and, in 1931, founded the *Archives* in their memory, with his own collection as a nucleus. The director was Pierre Tugal.

COLETTE MARCHAND

AND ROLAND PETIT IN CINÉ-BIJOU

DÉCOR BY GEORGIADIS FOR MACMILLAN'S HOUSE OF BIRDS. 1955.

There were facilities for free study, and a studio for experimental work. To the lasting regret of balletomanes, the enterprise had to be abandoned in 1950, when the collections were divided between the Paris Opera and the Royal Opera at Stockholm.

MARIÉS DE LA TOUR EIFFEL Les. Entertainment devised by Jean Cocteau. Music: Germaine Tailleferre, Georges Auric, Arthur Honegger, Darius Milhaud, Francis Poulenc. Décor: Irene Lagut. Costumes and masks: Jean Hugo. Choreography: Jean Cocteau and Jean Borlin. First performance: Ballets Suédois, Théâtre des Champs-Élysées, Paris, 18 June 1921. The argument of this strange but enjoyable ballet may be briefly recalled. It is the fourteenth of July, and we are on the first storey of the Eiffel Tower. A military band can be heard in the distance. The décor

LES MARIÉS DE LA TOUR EIFFEL. COSTUME BY
JEAN HUGO. 1921.

—ridiculous and charming, like a picture-postcard of 1900 trimmed with lace—represents an unorthodox view of the Champ de Mars, the wings showing the metal structure of the Tower. A hunchbacked photographer enters, and sets up his camera, which promptly gives birth to an ostrich. A green-clad huntsman who happens to be passing aims his gun, fires, and shoots down a telegram, an enormous blue placard which a telegraphist displays to the audience, announcing the arrival of a wedding party. And arrive it does, to the sound of a passably solemn march. Behind all this buffoonery, the piece took a decidedly satirical turn, with the *petite bourgeoisie* in their Sunday'best assembled on the stage as a sitting target for Cocteau's cruellest wit. During the ballet two phonograph horns, on each side of the stage, acted as commentators, explaining the action like a mechanical Greek chorus. The audience was deeply shocked, and the performance ended in uproar. On the day after the première, Jean Cocteau announced to the outraged public "for weeks and weeks we have been working day and night to amuse you"—but no one believed him. The work had indeed required a great deal of rehearsing. Hampered

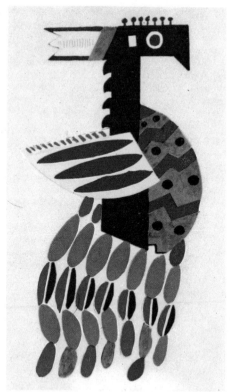

LA CRÉATION DU MONDE. COSTUME BY LÉGER
1923.

by their cardboard masks, the dancers could hear neither the music nor the voices from the loud speakers, and their movements had consequently to be timed with rigorous precision. It all sounds rather childish today, but at the time it was a kind of manifesto—less brutal perhaps than the earlier *Parade*—of the ideas of the group for which Cocteau was the spokesman. It was also a serious attempt to rehabilitate the commonplace events of daily life as material for art, to strip them of their apparent banality and to reveal their poetic truth. From the musical point of view, the work marked the incursion into the theatre of the group of composers known as "Les Six", then in the

LES MARIÉS DE LA TOUR EIFFEL. COSTUME BY
JEAN HUGO. 1921.

front line of battle. Décor and costumes were in perfect accord with the rest of the production. In attempting this return to the fashions of 1900, Jean Hugo rediscovered the charm and elegance of a period which was still regarded as old-fashioned and ridiculous, and showed us for years to come how to look at "la belle époque".

MARKOVA Alicia. She has become a legend in her own lifetime, a dancer surrounded by an aura of poetry, fragility and mystery. In 1920, as a small girl of ten years, she made her début on the London stage and was called a "miniature Pavlova". It was, in fact, the example of Pavlova which inspired the fragile and sickly little English girl Alicia Marks when she began to dance and when she grew into an artist. In 1925 she was given her stage name of Markova by Diaghilev, who discovered her in the studio of Astafieva. Her career began with the Ballets Russes, with whom she danced Stravinsky's *Le Rossignol,* in 1925, and Sauguet's *La Chatte,* in 1928. Diaghilev had

JEAN COCTEAU
IN LES MARIÉS DE LA TOUR EIFFEL. 1921.

great hopes for his "little English girl" and she has justified his faith. After his death, the second period of her career began; a period during which she helped immeasurably in the establishment of English ballet as an inspiration to the young choreographers at the Ballet Club and as the first English classical ballerina at Sadler's Wells.

From 1935 to 1938 she led the company which she founded with Dolin and which bore their names. They pioneered ballet in the English provinces and ever since Markova has been pioneering. Throughout her career as a great international ballerina, she has always been eager to dance for new audiences and to take classical ballet to new countries. As ballerina of the Ballet Russe de Monte-Carlo (1938-41) she first conquered the American public and created roles in Massine's *Rouge et Noir* and *Seventh Symphony*. Joining Ballet Theatre in 1941, she danced a surprisingly large range of parts, including creations in *Aleko* and in Tudor's *Romeo and Juliet*. After a period of recital and guest performances with Dolin, her fellow pupil at Astafieva's and her constant partner throughout her career, she founded with him in 1950 a new company, Festival Ballet, with which she danced until 1952. Then, as guest artist in New York, London, Paris, Copenhagen, and many other cities she reaffirmed her position as the foremost romantic dancer of her day. In 1958 she returned to Festival Ballet as guest artist for the European tour and London season.

Markova has attained, by ceaseless devotion to her art, an ethereal quality which makes her seem an incorporeal spirit. Her manner of dancing is inimitable: gossamer-light, she seems to float gently through the air, softly alighting on the ground. Her port de bras are of perfect grace, her batterie precise and rapid, her small, flexible feet twinkle as she performs the most complex, tiny movements. Her name will always be associated with the ballet *Giselle* (which she first danced with the Vic-Wells Ballet 1 January 1934), and her unerring sense of period has caused her to be known as "la nouvelle Taglioni". In *La Sylphide, Pas de Quatre,* and *Bolero 1830* she recreates a vanished epoch. It is ballerinas such as Markova who give to the classical dance its grandeur and also its purity.

ALICIA MARKOVA IN PAS DE QUATRE.

MARTYRE DE SAINT-SÉBASTIEN Le.

This mystery play in five acts, the product of the collaboration of two very distinguished names, the poet Gabriele d'Annunzio and the composer Claude Debussy, included only a limited amount of dancing, but it cannot be ignored by lovers of ballet. First performed in 1911 by Ida Rubinstein, with luxurious décors by Bakst, it is one of the outstanding works of its period, and if only for her courage in presenting it, Ida Rubinstein's name should be preserved in the annals of the theatre. As a truant from the Russian Ballet, she wanted to assert her independence with a new work more significant and more sumptuous than anything Diaghilev had produced. In some respects at least she achieved her aim.

* There was a notable revival at the Paris Opera in July 1957, in a new production by Lifar and Maurice Jacquemont with décor by Felix Labisse. The role of the martyr saint, formerly taken by Ida Rubinstein herself, was brilliantly performed by Ludmilla Tcherina, whose first appearance at the Opéra this was.

MARKOVA AND DOLIN IN CASSE-NOISETTE.

MASSACRE DES AMAZONES Le.

Ballet in one act by Janine Charrat and Maurice Sarrazin. Music: Ivan K. Semenoff. Scenery and costumes: Jean Bazaine. Choreography: Janine Charrat. First performance: Compagnie Janine Charrat, Théâtre Municipal, Grenoble, 24 December 1952. Principal dancers: Janine Charrat, René Bon.

Human intelligence (the Amazons) versus animal instinct (the wild horses they seek to master). The Queen of the Amazons is slain in a struggle with an untameable white horse. The animals massacre the surviving women. The end of the ballet, when the white horse carried the dead queen's body away, had a savage, mysterious poetry. Bazaine's set suggested archaic Greece with a few bold and summary strokes. René Bon was a mettlesome white horse. Charrat's clear-cut profile was seen to admirable advantage beneath a heavy, plaited wig.

MASSINE Leonide. Born Moscow, 1894.

Of all living choreographers Massine is the one whose work occupies the largest place in the international repertoire. This is due not only to the size of his contribution but to its variety

LE MARTYRE DE SAINT-SÉBASTIEN.
COSTUME FOR AN ARCHER BY BAKST.

and, above all, to the theatrical quality which is the basic denominator of all his ballets. If we allow that Balanchine is *par excellence* the choreographer-musician and Lifar the choreographer-dancer, then we may class Massine as the choreographer-actor. A Massine ballet needs to be acted as much as it needs to be danced.

It is surely significant that Massine studied acting and dancing simultaneously at the Imperial School in Moscow and that his early promise as an actor threatened to weight the scales in favour of the drama. At this point, in 1913, he was discovered by Diaghilev. This meeting altered the whole course of his career. Diaghilev had recently quarreled with Nijinsky, and was searching for a young artist with sufficient talent to replace him. The seventeen year old youth was naturally delighted with the prospects offered him by the Russian Ballet, and a long and fruitful collaboration began. At first Massine was placed in the expert hands of Maestro Cecchetti, whose job it was to give a final polish to the company's new recruits, but he did not have to wait long before making his début in an important part. On 14 May 1914, he created the title-role in Fokine's *Légende de*

Joseph at the Paris Opera. It is not difficult to imagine Massine as he was at that time: forty-three years have barely changed him. His black hair, though it has become sparse, has not turned white. The huge, dark eyes beneath thick brows and the ascetic features have lost none of their distinction. He is only of medium height, but so slim and well-proportioned that he appears tall on the stage. Thanks to rigorous and continual practice, he is still lithe and active; his agility and endurance still astound young dancers called to work with him.

His energy was always phenomenal. He was never satisfied with normal hours of rehearsal. He would call the artists together after the performance or on the train during tours to put the finishing touches to a scene or explain some modification of detail. The dancers of the Russian Ballet experienced this super-abundant energy for many years after 1915, when he arranged his first ballet, *Le Soleil de nuit* (*). This was followed by *Las Meninas, Les Femmes de bonne humeur* (*), *Parade* (*) and *Contes Russes* (*). Note the variety of subject: Russian folklore, Velasquez, Commedia dell' arte, Cubism. There is only space here to mention the most important of his subsequent ballets. *La Boutique fantasque* (*), *Le Tricorne* (*), *Pulcinella* (*) and his new version of *Le Sacre du printemps* (*) also belong to his first period with the Russian Ballet, from 1914 to 1921. In that year his contract expired, and because he had been showing signs of increasing independence, Diaghilev did not renew it. Massine spent the next four years in Paris and London, dancing and teaching. He was recalled to the fold in 1924 and remained with the company until 1928, during which time he produced *Cimarosiana, Zéphire et Flore* (*), *Les Matelots* (*), *Mercure* (*), *Le Pas d'acier* (*) and *Ode* (*). Since Diaghilev's death, two companies have had the benefit of Massine's continued collaboration: de Basil's from 1932 to 1936 with *Jeux d'enfants* (*), *Le beau Danube* (*), *Scuola di ballo* (*), *Les Présages* (*), *Choreartium* (*), *La Symphonie fantastique* (*); the Ballet Russe de Monte-Carlo thereafter with *Gaieté Parisienne* (*), *Seventh Symphony* (*), *Nobilissima visione* (*), *Capriccio espagnol* (*), *L'Étrange farandole* (*), *Bacchanale* (*), etc. Since 1940 new ballets have been fewer (they have included *Aleko* (*) for Ballet Theatre in 1924, a new version of *Mam'zelle Angot* for

Sadler's Wells in 1947 and the choreographic mystery *Laudes Evangelii* for the Perugia Festival in 1952), but he has produced and danced in revivals of his earlier ballets for more companies than can be listed here. At various times during his career he has done ballets for operas, revues and films (notably *The Tales of Hoffmann* and *Neapolitan Fantasy,* in both of which he danced himself).

This formidable list shows a remarkable homogeneity. Massine places dancing at the service of music, painting, literature, even philosophy and religion. He treats his various subjects like a dramatist; even his "symphonic ballets" are more programmatic than abstract. The *Symphonie fantastique* of course is an exceptional case, because he had only to follow and amplify Berlioz's own scenario; but *Les Présages* (Tchaikovsky), *Seventh Symphony* (Beethoven) and *L'Étrange farandole* (Shostakovitch) introduce dramatic symbols such as the Man, the Woman, the Spirit of Creation, Passion, and so forth. *Choreartium* (Brahms), with nameless protagonists and no overt narrative, is the nearest approach to an abstract ballet.

Massine's choreography is predominantly "terre à terre". He seems willing to accept the fact that human beings do not fly and, like Fokine before him, makes comparatively little use of elevation. Supernatural characters, on the other hand, such as the allegorical figures in the first movement of *La Symphonie fantastique,* are treated differently. In brief, he adapts his style to his subject, which is why he has been able to succeed in so many genres, from the comic to the religious, by way of such specialities as the Commedia dell'arte and Spanish dancing, which latter he studied during the Diaghilev company's visits to Spain during and after the first war. The only branch of dancing he seems to have neglected, both as choreographer and dancer, is the purely academic. There is little trace of virtuosity for its own sake in his ballets, just as no memory survives from his performances of classical enchaînements perfectly executed. Rather do we think of the fiery, passionate Miller, the raffish Can-Can dancer, the bemused Prince Ivan, the provincial Peruvian, the Barman of *Union Pacific,* the poet of *Symphonie fantastique,* a great Petrouchka, or the Hussar in *Beau Danube,* standing quietly at the side of the stage and riveting our attention while memory

steals over him with the first strains of the Blue Danube waltz.

Since he prizes dramatic expression above all else, Massine is unrivalled, as his symphonic ballets prove, in combining mime with dancing and in devising mass ensembles in which each component element has a part to play. Balanchine arrives at rehearsal empty-handed, with his inspiration (and his musicianship) as sole intermediary between music and dancers. Massine does not embark on a new ballet until, in the course of long and detailed study, he has dissected the score and determined the role to be played by each dancer or group of dancers. He covers reams of paper with choreographic notation (he uses the Stepanov method), plans, diadrams and sketches. When the ballet is finished, he films it for reference in future revivals.

In such a vast output, stretching over so long a period of time, there have of course been occasional failures and some works have begun to seem dated. Nevertheless, Massine con-

MASSINE IN SOLEIL DE NUIT, 1915.

225

15

quered new worlds for ballet, taking Fokine's reforms a stage further and enriching the repertoire with a considerable number of works of great value. Away from his work, Massine is sparing of words and gestures, more like a thinker than an artist concerned with movement. His second wife and faithful collaborator is a young woman who lived in the same street in Moscow. Nowadays choreography occupies him less than the upbringing of his children, both of whom are studying dancing. However, he is still very much concerned with ballet. He is preparing an important treatise (which will be his first published work) on the art of choreography, as well as making a study of the folklore of the North American Indians (he has become an American citizen). The book on choreography may well reveal him as the Noverre of the 20th century.

MATELOTS Les. Ballet in five scenes. Scenario: Kochno. Music: Auric. Scenery and costumes: Pedro Pruna. Choreography: Massine. First performance: Diaghilev's Ballets Russes, Gaîté-Lyrique, Paris, 17 June 1925.

Principal dancers: Nemchinova, Sokolova, Woizikowski, Slavinsky, Lifar.

Low life and high jinks in a Mediterranean seaport. A sailor tests his fiancée's virtue by returning in disguise with two of his companions. She refuses their advances and all ends happily. *Les Matelots* marked Massine's return to the Diaghilev company and gave Lifar his first important created role as the French sailor. The comedy was broad but inventive. The three sailors danced a card-playing variation perched on chairs; there was, by contrast, a touching solo for the girl (Nemchinova). Auric's music was based on popular tunes including some sea-shanties taught him by the English painter, Nina Hamnett. The ballet was more successful in Paris than in London, although Massine augmented the cast there with a spoon-player whom he found entertaining theatre queues in the West End.

MATISSE Henri (1869-1954). Matisse's principal contribution to the theatre is represented by two vastly different works: *Le Chant du Rossignol* (1920) for the Diaghilev Ballets

LES MATELOTS. DÉCOR BY PRUNA. 1926.

L'ÉTRANGE FARANDOLE. CURTAIN BY MATISSE. 1938.

Russes and, nineteen years later, *L'Étrange farandole* for René Blum's Ballets de Monte-Carlo. In his paintings, Matisse implies space mainly by means of colour, flat colour, without shading or modulation, a procedure totally different to the methods of the stage designer, who deals in real space, which needs no plastic conventions to make it perceptible. In *Le Chant du Rossignol* Matisse solved the problem by creating the impression of a painting, deliberately disguising the real depth of the stage. As far as possible, the dancers were disposed not in depth but vertically, in human pyramids. Even the Emperor's bed—an essential element in the décor—was made to obey this law of verticality. The public enjoyed the beauty of the white and turquoise spectacle without realising how original it was. The décor and costumes for *L'Étrange farandole* (1939) belong to a later stage in Matisse's development, and are related to the mural painted some six or seven years previously for the Barnes Foundation at Merion (Pennsylvania) of which the subject was precisely "La Danse". This décor consisted of a few, thrusting lines of the utmost simplicity, with costumes equally bare of irrelevant detail. There was an effective drop-curtain, like a huge paper cut-out. There is a curious paradox in this extreme refinement and economy of means, because it is precisely at the moment when the décor appears to efface itself and allow the maximum of expression to the dancing, that it begins to play its capital if unobtrusive part in the total effect.

MAY Pamela. Said to possess the most beautiful arabesque in English ballet, Pamela May was a contemporary of Fonteyn in the Sadler's Wells Ballet and the second ballerina in that company to dance Aurora in *The Sleeping Beauty*. Her classical purity of line could sometimes seem cold, but when she played roles such as a Child of Light of Ashton's *Dante Sonata* she conveyed an emotional frenzy rarely seen in English ballet. Now teaching at the Royal Ballet School, she plays mime roles with great distinction at Covent Garden.

MELIKOVA Genia. A ballerina of the de Cuevas company since 1954, she is a lithe and accomplished dancer, excelling in such Balanchine ballets as *Concerto Barocco*. She was born in Marseilles of Russian parents and studied with Sedowa, then with Schollar, Vilzak and Schwezoff in New York. After appearing in musicals on Broadway she danced with the American Ballet Theatre for a short time before returning to Europe. She created a leading role in Cranko's *Cat's Cradle* (Cuevas, Paris 1958).

MERCURE. "Poses plastiques" in three scenes. Scenario and choreography: Massine. Music: Erik Satie. Scenery and costumes: Picasso. First performance: Soirées de Paris, Théâtre de la Cigale, 15 June 1924. The production of *Mercure* was one of the most eagerly awaited of Étienne de Beaumont's "Soirées de Paris". Picasso's name was enough by itself to arouse intense curiosity. The surprise was complete. First of all, it could hardly be considered a ballet in the traditional sense of the word. The programme described it as "poses plastiques"; and in fact dancing only played a secondary part. It was a series of faintly erotic *tableaux* based on Greek mythology. The most

PAMELA MAY. THE PROSPECT BEFORE US.

prominent features were Picasso's weird "constructions" of cardboard and wire, which were moved about the stage, competing for attention with the dancers when they were not themselves engaged in moving them. For the tableau called "Night", Picasso had devised a metal contraption with a "construction" inside it based very freely on the female form which swung back and forth, silhouetted against a night sky in which the stars themselves were mobile. It was too much for the public, but Diaghilev was so enthusiastic that he revived it with his own company three years later (Théâtre Sarah-Bernhardt, 2 June 1927). It was no more successful on that occasion.

MESSEL Oliver. One of the most successful English theatrical designers of the last thirty years, Oliver Messel (born 1904) was a discovery of the impresario C. B. Cochran. He is perhaps not at his happiest as a ballet designer—his costumes are sometimes overladen with detail and his nostalgic evocations of baroque architectural fantasies stand up poorly to the wear and tear of constant use, but the sets for the prologue and last act of the spectacular Covent Garden revival of *The Sleeping Beauty* (1946) have a sense of grandeur and theatrical magic. Messel also designed Lichine's *Francesca da Rimini* (de Basil, 1937), Helpmann's *Comus* (Sadler's Wells Ballet, 1942) and Ashton's *Homage to the Queen* (Sadler's Wells Ballet, 1953).

METROPOLITAN BALLET The.
One of the companies which sprang up in England after the war, when the popularity of ballet was at its height, only to founder for lack of a large official subsidy. The Metropolitan Ballet was formed by Cecilia Blatch and Leon Hepner in 1947, and it was primarily the courage and devotion of Mrs. Blatch which kept it going until the end of 1949. In spite of its name, it had no permanent home, but gave London seasons in various theatres and toured at home and abroad. The first maître de ballet was Victor Gsovsky; he was succeeded by Nicholas Beriosoff and Celia Franca. Many distinguished dancers, English and foreign, appeared with the company. There was the usual backbone of classical revivals, and some interesting new creations. The Metropolitan will be remembered for Taras's *Designs with Strings* (1948) and

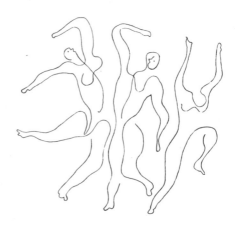

PICASSO. STUDY FOR MERCURE. 1924.

for the opportunities it offered to the young Svetlana Beriosova. Other new ballets included works by Andrée Howard, Frank Staff and Rosella Hightower (*Pleasuredrome,* 1949).

MILHAUD Darius.
Born 1892, Aix-en-Provence. He was the member of the "groupe des Six" whose music caused the most fuss at the time. In fact its most prominent features, polytonal writing, Latin American and Negro rhythms (with a fondness for percussion), gentle melanchony alternating with sunny lyricism which, in view of Milhaud's origins, one is tempted to call Jewish and Provençal respectively, were established before the group was officially formed. *L'Homme et son désir* was written (with the poet Claudel) some years before its noisy première with the Ballet Suédois, in Paris (1921). There followed: *Le Bœuf sur le toit* (1922) a hilarious Cocteau fantasy for the Fratellini clowns; *La Création du Monde* (1923), one of his finest works, for the Ballets Suédois; *Salade* for the Soirées de Paris and *Le Train Bleu* (both 1924), an "opérette dansée", for Diaghilev. Milhaud's output has continued to be enormous and there can be few people who know the whole of it. The general impression has been one of increasing relaxation, yet he remains one of the big personalities of modern music. More recent ballets include *Les Songes* (Ballets 1933), and two works for the Ballets de Paris, *'Adame Miroir* (1948) and *La Rose des vents* (1958). Milhaud orchestrated Satie's *Jack*

MELIKOVA IN CONSTANTIA.

in the Box for Diaghilev (1926) and *La Bien-aimée* (Schubert-Liszt) for Ida Rubinstein (1928). A "scenic cantata", *La Sagesse*, was commissioned by Rubinstein from Claudel and Milhaud in 1935, but the war intervened before it could be performed.

MILLOSS Aurel. A Hungarian dancer and choreographer (born 1906) who has made his reputation in Italy, the country which at first sight seemed the least likely to welcome his style. He was a pupil of Laban and Victor Gsovsky, and gave dance recitals in Germany, where he succeeded Kreutzberg as principal dancer at the Berlin Opera. In 1937 he went to Naples as maître de ballet at the San Carlo and subsequently worked for the Rome Opera (1938-45) and for la Scala, Milan (1951-52). His style, at once individual and composite (half classical and half central European), very different from what was then expected in Italian opera houses, aroused violent opposition, particularly for his use of expressionism, his minutely detailed production methods and his deliberate avoidance of virtuosity. But he stuck bravely to his guns and soon made his name outside Italy. Invitations came from the Ballets des Champs-Élysées (*Le Portrait de Don Quichotte*, 1947) and from de Cuevas (*Coup de Feu*, 1952). In 1953-54 he ran his own company in São Paulo, Brazil. It appears that his style has gained in flexibility and that he now makes greater use of classical technique. Other ballets include: *La Follia di Orlando, Marsyas, Creature di Prometeo,* and versions of *Jeu de Cartes* and *The Miraculous Mandarin*.

MIRACLE IN THE GORBALS. Ballet in one act. Music: Arthur Bliss. Scenario: Michael Benthall. Choreography: Robert Helpmann. Scenery and costumes: Edward Burra. First performance: Sadler's Wells Ballet, Princes Theatre, London, 26 October 1944. Principal dancers: Robert Helpmann, Pauline Clayden, Celia Franca, David Paltenghi.

A mysterious stranger appears in the streets of a dockside quarter of Glasgow and restores to life a young girl who has drowned herself. The crowd, at first impressed by the miracle, is later incited by an official, who recognises and fears the stranger's power and its effect on his own authority, to kill him. Benthall's modern morality was staged by Helpmann in a theatrically effective blend of realism and stylisation. The squalid *milieu*, unequivocally captured by Burra's décor and costumes, was observed in detail. The most convincing individual portrait was the official (clearly a minister of religion, his denomination tactfully obscure), whose conflicting emotions were finely shown by David Paltenghi. Helpmann's own performance was restrained and authoritative. The scene of his murder was brutally realistic. Bliss's music, written in close collaboration with the choreographer, was unashamedly direct in its impact, with some effectively simple touches, notably the suggestion of Scottish dance rhythm in the Suicide's dance of deliverance after her restoration to life, when her ecstasy gradually communicates itself to the onlookers.

MIRAGES. Ballet in one act. Scenario: A. M. Cassandre and Serge Lifar. Music: Henri Sauguet. Scenery and costumes: Cassandre. Choreography: Lifar. The ballet was rehearsed at the Paris Opera in 1944, but the performance was postponed until three years later (15 December 1947) when Lifar had been reinstated. The principal dancers were Yvette Chauviré and Michel Renault.

A dreamlike, allegorical fantasy remarkable for Sauguet's limpid and extremely danceable music and Cassandre's austere, architectural set with floating clouds, which dissolves in the final sunrise into a bare and peaceful landscape. The ballet provides Chauviré with one of her finest roles, yearningly romantic yet conveyed through purely classical movement.

MIRO Joan. Born in Catalonia, 1893. This painter's contribution to ballet has been confined to two very dissimilar works. In 1926 he and Max Ernst were invited by Diaghilev to design drop curtains, accessories and costumes for Nijinska's *Roméo et Juliette*. The most memorable thing about this was the row made at the Paris première by the painters' brother surrealists, who considered their participation in a "bourgeois manifestation" an act of treachery and turned up in force to demonstrate their disapproval. Miró's second assignment, the setting and costumes for Massine's *Jeux d'enfants* (Ballets de Monte-Carlo, 1932) was a very

JEUX D'ENFANTS. DÉCOR BY MIRÓ. 1932.

different matter, and far more successful. It was a modern version of a theme — dolls and toys brought to life — that has attracted innumerable choreographers. Miró's toys and shapes were not picturesque, traditional or "popular", but surrealist and abstract. The décor was immensely effective. With its blacks and whites, bold primary colours and clear outlines, it had much of the charm, at once compulsive and disturbing, of Miro's paintings. It is sad that he has not designed more ballets.

MISKOVITCH Milorad. Born in Yugoslavia. Came to Paris in 1946 and studied with Preobrajenska and Boris Kniaseff. After serving his apprenticeship in the companies of de Basil and de Cuevas he joined the Ballets de Paris, proving his star quality in *Le Combat* in 1949. He has partnered Yvette Chauviré, Lycette Darsonval and Janine Charrat and gained an international reputation when he partnered Alicia Markova in her recitals in Europe and America in 1954. He founded a small, eclectic company, Les Ballets 1956, and presented *Prométhée* by Maurice Béjart and Ohana, in which he gave his finest performance to date, also *L'Échelle* and *Quatuor*. Fair, athletic yet slim in build, with fine features. Miskovitch combines a strong and ardent personality with the noble elegance of the classical cavalier.

MISS JULIE. Ballet in four scenes, based on Strindberg's play. Music: Ture Rangström. Scenery and costumes: Allan Fridericia. Choreography: Birgit Cullberg. First performance: Riksteatern, Vasteros, Sweden, 1 March 1950. Principal dancers: Elsa-Marianne von Rosen, Julius Mengarelli.

It was after seeing Roland Petit's ballet *Carmen* that Birgit Cullberg and the Swedish ballerina Elsa-Marianne von Rosen had the idea of a ballet based on Strindberg's famous play, which describes the downfall of a young woman of good family who falls in love with a handsome but coarse-grained manservant. The affair leads her into deep water; she steals money from her father, and finally commits suicide. The story is told in four scenes of mounting dramatic tension. The very original choreography is a blend of classical and modern styles. The most successful of contemporary Swedish ballets.

MOISSEYEV Igor. A man whose name is now inseparably linked with a new, professional kind of Soviet folk dance. Born in Kiev in 1906, Igor Moisseyev passed his childhood in Paris and afterwards studied at the Bolshoi Ballet School in Moscow, making his début with the company in 1924. From dancing leading roles, he progressed to the position of ballet master and early in his career began to infuse new life into the classical vocabulary of steps by introducing folk dance elements. His success at a folk dance festival held in Moscow in 1937 encouraged him to devote all his energies to safeguarding and develooping the Soviet

MISS JULIE. ELSA-MARIANNE VON ROSEN
AND JULIUS MENGARELLI. STOCKHOLM, 1950.

Union's wonderful heritage of folk art. He travelled throughout the sixteen republics, across the steppes, through the forests of Central Asia, the mountains of the Caucasus, the rich cornfields of the Ukraine. He was as much fascinated by the variegated costumes and the local musical traditions as by the dances themselves, and longed to combine and balance the various elements in a theatrical spectacle. The idea of a national folk ballet gradually became of more and more importance to him. He had found his vocation. But "you can't collect Russian dances as you collect stamps", he said. It was necessary to live in the spirit in which these dances had been developed and to absorb something of local customs, climates and behaviour. So Moisseyev visited folk festivals and village dances. He recruited dancers from all over the Soviet Union and then he established a school in Moscow where general education is provided as well as daily classes in classical ballet and character dancing. The famous Ensemble which he has created performs many ancient dances, ranging from the hunting dances of the north to labour dances from Byelorussia, Lithuania, Karelia, Armenia and Uzbekistan, and the lyric love dances from Georgia. Folk dance is regarded as "an inexhaustible source of creative inspiration" and with the preservation of tradition Moisseyev seeks to combine "talented improvisation". Thus alongside the traditional hopaks and the stately dances of courtship, he shows brilliant new creations: the celebrated *Football Dance,* a marvellously comic choreographic version of a football match, *The Partisans,* which is a dramatic tribute to guerilla warfare, *Poem from Moscow,* a pas de deux of Chekovian sensibility about a shy lover who wins his girl, and the vigorous *Sailors' Dance* with its typically Soviet respect for the well-oiled machine.

The Moisseyev dancers, by their vitality, expertise and abounding delight in movement, have won all hearts, in Paris, London and New York as well as throughout the Soviet Union. They may perhaps

MOISSEYEV ENSEMBLE. THE PARTISANS.

be criticised for exaggerating too strongly the colours of national costumes, but it must be remembered that they dance frequently in giant arenas and the impact of their performance must reach thousands of spectators at a time. Moisseyev has been three times the recipient of a Stalin prize and holds the title of People's Artist of the USSR. His reputation now stands as high outside Russia as within.

MONCION Francisco. A classically trained dancer with a superb body and smouldering personality, he was born in the Dominican Republic and is a product of the School of American Ballet. Soloist with Ballet International (1944), he danced with principal ‹roles in *Sebastian* and *Mad Tristan*. Today (and since 1950) a star of the New York City Ballet, he is an excellent interpreter of *La Valse, The Prodigal Son* and *Orpheus*. He created the male role in Robbins' *L'Après-midi d'un faune* but would be as much at home in the Nijinsky version. A gentle personality and a very good painter, he choreographed his first ballet, *Pastorale,* in 1957.

MORDKIN Mikhail. Born Moscow 1881, died New Jersey 1944. One of the great male dancers of the Moscow school, magnificently virile, a strong partner, an exciting personality. Trained in the Imperial School he became pre-

mier danseur at the Bolshoi Theatre in 1900. During the first season of Diaghilev's Ballets Russes in Paris he danced in *Le Festin* and *Le Pavillon d'Armide*. Independent by nature, he left the company to tour with Anna Pavlova for two years and to partner her, most memorably, in *Autumn Bacchanale*. After a quarrel, he left Pavlova and returned to Russia. From there, he organised small companies for tours abroad and eventually became maître de ballet at the Bolshoi Theatre in Moscow. He remained in Russia until 1923 when he emigrated to the United States and in 1927 opened a school in New York. His work as a classical teacher had a considerable influence, for he trained many American dancers. In 1937, with financial help from his pupil Lucia Chase, he founded the Mordkin Ballet, which in 1939 formed the nucleus of the American Ballet Theatre.

MOREAU Jacqueline. Parisian dancer, trained at the Opéra and appointed *première danseuse* in 1948. In 1951 she joined the Ballets des Champs-Élysées and danced in the first performance of *Revanche*. Since 1952 she has been a ballerina of the de Cuevas company. Technically strong, dark and vivacious, with a brilliant and very personal style, she personifies the conventional type of Paris Opera dancer. A charming interpreter of *La Tertulia, Pastorale* and *Duo,* she dances all the classical repertoire.

MORT DU CYGNE La (The Dying Swan). Almost an improvisation, arranged for Pavlova by Fokine at short notice for a charity performance in St. Petersburg in 1905, it has become the most famous solo in all ballet. Pavlova called on the choreographer to ask him to suggest some music for a dance just when he was playing *The Swan* of Saint-Saëns. Looking at her slender body and lovely neck he thought "she is just made for the Swan". The structure of the dance is simple, built almost entirely on *pas de bourrée* and the expressive use of the arms. Fokine sketched out the steps, and then Pavlova danced it while he walked alongside, curving her arms and correcting details of poses. It lasts only a few minutes yet Pavlova by her artistry was able to suggest in that time all the poignancy of a beautiful bird in its last trembling agony before it submits to death. *La Mort du Cygne* made Pavlova's reputation and remained her greatest glory. Wearing the white feathered costume which Bakst designed, she will always be remembered as the "immortal swan".

Yet others have danced this solo which represented, in Fokine's view, the transition between the old and new worlds of ballet. He saw it not as a display of technique but as a "symbol of the everlasting struggle in this life of all that is mortal. It is a dance of the whole body and not of the limbs only; it appeals not merely to the eye but to the emotions and the imagination." Karalli and Egorova danced it during Pavlova's lifetime, and Markova now gives it a touching, elegiac quality. Chauviré, in a rather different version, is profoundly moving, but it is Ulanova who best conveys, with her proud carriage and the strong beat of her arms, the immortal soul of the swan, unconquerable by death.

MOULÈNE Maurice. Born Paris, 1901. As head of the scene workshops at the Paris Opera since 1934, responsible for making working models from artists' designs, Moulène occupies one of the key posts in the French theatre. His skill and judgment in interpreting the ideas of so many different (and often very distinguished) artists is the more praiseworthy in that he is himself a designer of distinction, as he proved in the flower episode in the famous revival of *Les Indes Galantes* (1952), and, also at the Opéra, the 1949 version of Lifar's *Roméo et Juliette* and Lander's *Études* (1952).

MOULIN ENCHANTÉ Le. Ballet in three scenes. Scenario: Léandre Vaillat and David Lichine. Music: Schubert, orch. Cloez. Scenery and costumes: Alexandre Benois. First performance: Cuevas Ballet, Théâtre des Champs-Élysées, Paris, 14 July 1949. Principal dancers: Rosella Hightower, André Eglevsky, David Lichine, Lili Ann Oka.

A "homage to the choreographers of the nineteenth century"; pastoral romanticism with a pretty set, tuneful music and a wonderful role for the male dancer — originally Eglevsky and later Serge Golovine.

MOYLAN Mary Ellen. American dancer, born at Cincinnati. A pupil of Balanchine at the School of American Ballet, she made her début at the age of 16 in the operetta *Rosalinda* and in 1944 joined the Ballet Russe de Monte-Carlo. With that company she danced many Balanchine ballets, including *Ballet Imperial* and *Danses Concertantes,* as well as classical roles and Zobeide in *Sheherazade.* Subsequently (1950) she joined Ballet Theatre and then became prima ballerina at the Metropolitan Opera, New York. She has an excellent technique and great beauty, but lacks something in fire and passion on stage.

MOZARTIANA. Ballet in five movements. Music: Tchaikovsky (Suite no. 4, "Mozartiana"). Scenery and costumes: Bérard. Choreography: Balanchine. First performance: Ballets 1933, 7 June 1933. Principal dancers: Tamara Toumanova, Roman Jasinsky.

MULYS Gérard. A pupil of Gustave Ricaux at the Paris Opera. Made his début at the age of 18 as *danseur étoile* at the Nice Opera. Maître de ballet of the de Cuevas company but was forced to give up dancing in 1948 through eye trouble. Engaged by Georges Hirsch in 1957 to restore the fortunes of the ballet at the Opéra-Comique. Mulys has championed the classical tradition in his books on Fokine and on the Monte Carlo Ballet. He has himself danced many famous roles: the Negro slave in *Sheherazade,* the Moor in *Petrouchka,* the Prince in *Swan Lake* and Albrecht in Marie Rambert's first production of *Giselle* in London, 1946.

N

NABOKOV Nicolas. Born 1903. Composer of Russian origin, trained in Germany and France, now an American citizen. His ballet-oratorio *Ode* was produced by Diaghilev's Ballets Russes in 1928. Five years later another "oratorio", *Job,* was staged by Les Ballets 1933. His next ballet, *Union Pacific* (de Basil, Philadelphia, 1934) was a very different affair, a lively American comedy about the building of the transcontinental railroad, with music based on popular songs. In the same year the Paris Opera gave *La Vie de Polichinelle,* a ballet in the style of the Commedia dell'arte. Nabokov's memoirs *Old Friends and New Music* (1951) give a valuable picture of the Diaghilev ballet in its last years and a fascinating account of Stravinsky in America. Since the war, Nabokov has occupied important administrative posts in the international musical world and has held a professorship at the Peabody Conservatoire, Baltimore.

NAPOLI or **The Fisherman and his Fiancée.** First performed 29 March 1842, Royal Theatre, Copenhagen. *Napoli* is the most celebrated of all Danish ballets and August Bournonville's masterpiece. On to a simple love story the choreographer has grafted brilliant folklore scenes embellished with numerous solos and ensembles. As the result of a temperamental "incident" in 1841, Bournonville was obliged by royal command to take a holiday away from Denmark. He went to Italy, where he gathered the material for *Napoli.* The ballet opens with lively scenes on the quayside of Santa Lucia in Naples. The beautiful Teresina returns the love

VERA NEMCHINOVA BY GONCHAROVA.

of one alone of her admirers, the handsome young fisherman, Gennaro. She scorns Giacomo the spaghetti-seller and Peppo the lemonade-seller who are, in her mother's eyes, more eligible suitors. While out sailing with Gennaro, a storm upsets the boat and Teresina is lost. Gennaro is inconsolable. A friendly monk gives him a picture of the Madonna and urges him to search for his beloved. The second act is set in the Blue Grotto, where Teresina, transformed into a naiad, is condemned to live. Gennaro finds her and, by grace of the Madonna's portrait, changes her back to human form. The third act, choreographically the best, culminates in a tarantella danced to celebrate the betrothal of Gennaro and Teresina. The music is by Paulli, Helsted, Gade (for the Blue Grotto act) and H. C. Lumbye. *Napoli* is a firm favourite in the Copenhagen repertory, chosen for many festive occasions and conducted occasionally by the King himself, who always sends champagne to the dancers. Traditionally all children from the Danish Ballet School make their first appearance on the bridge in the last act of *Napoli,* waving flags and cheering on the tarantella dancers. Bournonville himself was the first Gennaro, later Hans Beck and for the last twenty years, until his retirement in 1958, Borge Ralov. Margot Lander, Mona Vangsaa and Kirsten Ralov are the most recent interpreters of the role of Teresina.

* In 1954 Harald Lander mounted a one-act version, omitting most of the mime scenes, for London's Festival Ballet.

NEMCHINOVA Vera. One of the stars of Diaghilev's "second generation". Grigoriev engaged her in 1915 in Moscow, where she was studying privately with Nelidova. Her progress by modern standards was slow, but steady. Her first big chance came in 1919 when she took over the can-can in *La Boutique Fantasque* from Lopokova. In 1920 she created a role in *Pulcinella*. Stardom came in 1924 with *Les tentations de la bergère, Cimarosiana* and above all *Les Biches*. A year later came *Les Matelots*. With a face full of character, a tiny waist, magnificent legs and points of steel, Nemchinova combined a rare muscular strength with great capacity for expression. She was at once a classical stylist and a typically modern dancer. In 1926 she and Zverev abruptly left the company for an engagement in London where, in the following year, she founded the Nemchinova-Dolin ballet with Dolin and Oboukhov. Leading dancer at the Lithuanian State Opera, Kaunas, 1930-35. Later appeared with Blum's Ballets de Monte-Carlo (notably in *L'Épreuve d'amour,* 1936), Original Ballet Russe and as guest artist with Ballet Theatre. Now lives and teaches in New York.

NERINA Nadia. A South African who completed her training in England and quickly rose to ballerina status with the Royal Ballet at Covent Garden, Nadia Nerina is a small, strong dancer with a magnificent and exciting jump. Her speed and sharpness of attack have been exploited by Ashton in the solos he composed

for her in *Homage to the Queen* and *Birthday Offering*. Brilliant in demi-caractère roles such as Mam'zelle Angot, Swanilda in *Coppelia,* the Doll in *Petrouchka*, she also excels in abstract works like *Ballet Imperial* and *Scènes de Ballet,* and has danced all the great classical roles.

NEW YORK CITY BALLET. In a brief account of his career as a dancer and choreographer, George Balanchine wrote "It is not for me to comment on the New York City Ballet: this would be like a father telling you about his own children." The simile is apt, for it is impossible to think of the New York City Ballet

LA VALSE. BALLET BY BALANCHINE.

without thinking of Balanchine, its progenitor.

From the point of view of administration, the New York City Ballet is the dance company based on the New York City Center of Music and Drama, which also houses opera and drama companies. This privately owned organisation sponsors productions in its own theatre, the City Center. Prices are lower and the atmosphere less formal than at the Metropolitan Opera. A rough parallel might be drawn (methods of finance apart) with the two London opera houses, Sadler's Wells and Covent Garden.

The New York City Ballet in its present form came into being in 1948, but its history really

Duncan's former studio, in January 1934. Dorothie Littlefield taught the juniors, while Balanchine and Pierre Vladimiroff taught seniors and professional students.

From the school grew companies: the American Ballet, Ballet Caravan, and, after the war, Ballet Society (see articles) which Kirstein formed with Balanchine as artistic director. Ballet Society in due course was invited to make its home at the City Center as a subsidiary of the opera company. The first programme by the New York City Ballet was given on 11 October 1948 and

goes back to 1933 when a young American, Lincoln Kirstein, asked Balanchine if he would like to go to America to found a school and a ballet company. This meeting took place in London, where the season of Balanchine's company *Les Ballets 1933* was drawing to an end. Balanchine was interested. With the assistance of Edward M. M. Warburg and Vladimir Dimitriev, the Balanchine-Kirstein project was carried through. The School of American Ballet opened its doors in New York, in Isadora consisted of three Balanchine ballets: *Concerto Barocco, Orpheus* and *Symphony in C.* By the beginning of 1949 the company was an entirely independent unit: the ballet season opened on 13 January 1949 to a completely sold-out house (despite the date). The programme included *Four Temperaments, Time Table* (by Tudor), and *Symphony in C.*

New York City Ballet thus absorbed its predecessors and much of their by now distinguished repetory of new ballets by Balanchine and his young American disciples. Tudor and Robbins were also invited to make ballets. After fifteen years, Balanchine and Kirstein had a permanent theatre for their company: the ambitions of 1933 had been achieved.

Though London has seen all too little of it, the European public has had more than one opportunity to admire the discipline and brilliant, vigorous technique of the admirably integrated company, with its strict classical training but thoroughly modern outlook. In one respect, however, the foreign tours give an incom-

GLUCK'S ORPHEUS (1936).
COSTUMES BY TCHELITCHEV.

plete picture of the New York City Ballet. Because Balanchine and his assistant director, Jerome Robbins, avoid bringing ballets with which Europe is already familiar, and because transport costs have to be kept to a minimum, they do not tour their full-length production of *The Nutcracker* which is enormously popular in New York and Chicago. The company has a home, but it is not affluent and much of the repertoire is austerely mounted. This tendency to austerity, however, is not only a reflection of economic trends, but also of Balanchine's personal taste. Dancing, and its relation to music, is to him all-important. Décor is therefore the weakest facet of this American company, though these strictures do not apply to the admirable lighting of Jean Rosenthal, while certain ballets —for example *Orpheus,* designed by Isamu Noguchi, Beaton's *Illuminations,* and *The Prodigal Son* with décor and costumes by Rouault—set a remarkably high standard.

The company possesses a number of leading dancers of the first order: Maria Tallchief, Tanaquil LeClercq, Diana Adams, Patricia Wilde, Melissa Hayden, Yvonne Mounsey, Allegra Kent, Nicholas Magallanes, Francisco Moncion, Todd Bolender, Roy Tobias, Jacques d'Amboise, Robert Barnett, Jonathan Watts and André Eglevsky.

In 1958 the New York City Ballet toured Japan and Australia.

NIGHT SHADOW (See *Somnambule, La*).

NIJINSKA Bronislava. She is a real child of the theatre; from her earliest years she shared the life of dancers on tour and used to help her brother Vaslav Nijinsky paste up the bills advertising the performances of her father's company. The two children entered the Imperial School of St. Petersburg at the same time; she graduated a year later than he did, in 1908. She, as well as her brother, took part in the first two Paris seasons of the Diaghilev Ballet. In 1911, when Vaslav was forced to resign from the Maryinsky Theatre, she demanded as a protest that her own contract be annulled as well. Her request was granted, but from that moment she was forbidden to use the title "artist of the Imperial Theatres". In the ranks of Diaghilev's Russian Ballet her advance was

LES BICHES. CURTAIN BY MARIE LAURENCIN.

rapid. In 1910 she had danced Papillon in *Carnaval,* in 1911 the Street Dancer in *Petrouchka* and the Bacchante in *Narcisse ;* by 1912 she was sharing the role of the Doll in *Petrouchka* with Karsavina. Physically, she was small, supple and muscular. She resembled her brother, with her narrow eyes and high cheekbones. Nobody could call her pretty, but she danced with immense conviction and showed a remarkably intelligent grasp of her various roles. She could dance the Valse in *Les Sylphides* as well as the Polovtsian Girl in *Prince Igor,* and she sometimes replaced her brother in the title-role of *L'Après-midi d'un faune.* When war broke out she returned to Russia; the Revolution found her at Kiev, where she had opened a dancing school. She was an excellent teacher, sharing to a certain extent the theories of Laban, but in favour of completing and enriching the classical school by the discoveries of the masters of modern dance rather than rejecting it altogether for entirely new methods. This intelligent application of new discoveries to old principles is typical of Nijinska's outlook. In 1920, still at Kiev, she gave two demonstrations of her experience as a teacher: theoretically, in the publication of an essay *L'École du mouvement, théorie de chorégraphie* and practically, in the production by her pupils of her first important ballet, *Études* (*). In the following year she rejoined Diaghilev in London and was asked by him to arrange some new numbers for the great revival of *The Sleeping Beauty,* in which she also danced. She became one of the principal soloists and also maîtresse de ballet. Moreover, Diaghilev soon discovered that in her he had found a choreographer worthy to succeed Massine. She produced eight ballets for him: *Renard* (*), *Les Noces* (*), *Les Tentations de la Bergère* (*), *Les Biches* (*), *Les Fâcheux* (*), *La Nuit sur le Mont-Chauve* (1924), *Le Train Bleu* (*) and *Roméo et Juliette* (*). Though certain of her works, *Les Biches* for example, were immediately successful, others caused considerable controversy, even her masterpiece *Les Noces,* which so pleased Diaghilev that he decreed she should henceforth be billed as "La Nijinska". She left the company in 1924; her subsequent activities have been too numerous to chronicle in full. She produced various ballets at the Paris Opera, including *Rencontres, La Naissance de la lyre* and *Impressions de music-hall* (*). She was

NIJINSKA BY COCTEAU.

the sole choreographer for Ida Rubinstein's 1928 season, with *Les Noces de l'Amour et Psyché, Le Baiser de la fée* (*), *La Bien-aimée, La Princesse cygne, Boléro* (*). In 1929 she produced *Aubade* (*) for the Vicomte de Noailles. After working for the Opéra Russe de Paris she formed her own company, for which she created *Variations* (Beethoven) and *Les Comédiens jaloux* (1932). For the Ballet Russe de Monte-Carlo she made *Les Cent Baisers* (1935). In 1937 she became artistic director of the Polish Ballet. In 1938 she settled in U.S.A., where she has worked among others for Ballet Theatre and International Ballet: *Pictures from an Exhibition* and *Brahms Variations* (1944). She revisited Paris in 1947 with the de Cuevas company.

As teacher and choreographer Nijinska remains, for all her originality and occasional "modernity", pre-eminently the product of a State school in the great tradition. She understands that tradition, and her development of it has consequently left its mark on modern choreography. Some of her work has been over-complicated, neo-classical in the dryest sense. But her best work has (apart from its immediate theatrical virtues) extended the range of movement available to choreographers, notably in her typical distortion of classical steps and positions, always elegant and expressive, never merely wilful. There is some resemblance to her brother' experiments in flat, two-dimensional movement, but while his inspiration came from Greek vases, hers seems to have more in common with medieval art.

Though she has spent less time in England than in France and America, Nijinska's influence on English ballet has been more considerable than many people now realise. She spent some time with the Markova-Dolin company in 1937 and revived *Les Biches* and *La Bienaimée* for them. De Valois worked under her in the Russian Ballet and Ashton in Ida Rubinstein's company. Both are in her debt as choreographers; indeed de Valois has said that she regards Nijinska's tuition as "the most vital influence and help in her career".

NIJINSKY Vaslav. A strange and enigmatic figure, Nijinsky occupies a legendary place in the history of ballet. His name alone symbolises flight, yet this new Icarus had but a short career. His wings were soon clipped; just ten years after he made his début he left the stage for ever.

Born at Kiev on 28th February, 1890 of Polish parentage, Nijinsky was the child of travelling dancers. It was not surprising that he should be entered for the Imperial Ballet School in St. Petersburg in 1900. Silent and uncommunicative, he displayed from the first an exceptional gift for dancing and also rare powers as a mime. He was a favourite pupil of Nicholas Legat, while another teacher, Pavel Gerdt, used to say "Russia's coming great actor is a pupil of the ballet school, the little Nijinsky." He was first noticed in 1905 when he danced as a faun in a student performance of *Acis and Galatea* and the following year the teacher Oboukov proposed that he should be engaged at the Maryinsky Theatre, two years ahead of the usual time. But the young dancer refused this exceptional offer, preferring to complete his full course of training. Thus it was not until 1908 that he made his official début in the ballet in Mozart's *Don Giovanni,* after having created the part of the Slave in Fokine's *Pavillon d'Armide.* His dancing was immediately applauded, but the ballets in which he appeared made little demand on his gifts as a creative artist. Many pas de deux were allotted to him at the side of Mathilde Kschessinskaya,

who warmly encouraged him, and of Tamara Karsavina. He continued his studies under the strict discipline of Enrico Cecchetti.

In the winter of 1908 Nijinsky made the acquaintance of Diaghilev, who was to have a profound influence on his career. Diaghilev was already thinking of taking a Russian Ballet company to Paris in the spring of 1909 and the affection which he felt for the boy Nijinsky undoubtedly stimulated this desire. Nijinsky, in fact, was one of the sensations of that first Paris season. The Parisian public had for years treated male dancing with disdain, but they acclaimed Nijinsky as a second Vestris. In *Cléopâtre, Le Pavillon d'Armide, Le Festin,* and above all *Les Sylphides,* he won remarkable ovations and received extravagant tributes. His evocation of the Romantic period in *Les Sylphides* astonished Paris. The Comtesse de Noailles wrote of him, in this ballet, many years later, with nostalgia: "Désespoir de Werther, répréhensible amertume de Musset !"

NIJINSKY IN LE SPECTRE DE LA ROSE.

The following year in Paris Nijinsky danced three important new roles, all displaying his special gifts. In *Le Carnaval* he was the mischievous, lascivious Harlequin; in *Sheherazade,* the magnificent golden slave; in *Giselle,* the princely Albrecht. The following winter, back in St. Petersburg, there was a stupid incident over costume which caused Nijinsky to send in his resignation to the Imperial Theatres. Diaghilev immediately engaged him as a member of the permanent ballet company he was then establishing. In future, every programme of the Diaghilev Ballet Russe tended to be built round the personality of Nijinsky. With the exquisite Karsavina, he created *Le Spectre de la Rose* and *Petrouchka,* two utterly different ballets in both of which he was unforgettable. When she saw him in *Petrouchka,* Sarah Bernhardt called him the greatest actor in the world. He was at the height of his fame in those few years before the first World War. Fokine arranged *Le Dieu Bleu* for him, but Diaghilev was already dreaming of making him into a choreographer.

After introducing him to the theories of Dalcroze, Diaghilev encouraged him to compose a ballet to Debussy's *L'Après-midi d'un faune* (*), drawing his inspiration from antique bas-reliefs. A strange, angular work, diametrically opposed to the classical style in which Nijinsky had been trained, it won, after an initial scandal, general acceptance by its originality. But Fokine was disheartened and dissatisfied and attributed the failure of his *Daphnis and Chloe* to the inordinate amount of rehearsal time that had been given to *The Faun.* He left the company, and Diaghilev gave his place to Nijinsky. Though ably seconded by Léon Bakst and Marie Rambert, the young choreographer could not support such a position. The work was made all the harder because he composed very slowly and experienced much difficulty in communicating his wishes to the dancers. In 1913 he arranged two works: *Jeux* (*), a ballet in a contemporary setting about emotional involvements and a game of tennis, and *Le Sacre du Printemps* (*). *Le Sacre* was Nijinsky's most powerful and revolutionary ballet. He sought to depict the primitive rites of spring and the gradual emergence of human feeling. It required one hundred and twenty rehearsals and, although magnificently performed, provoked violent dissension in the

NIJINSKY AFTER SHEHERAZADE.
DRAWING BY COCTEAU.

audience. It had only six performances in London and Paris. The dancers disapproved of his penchant for "turned in" feet and legs, the stiffness and angularity of his arbitrary contortions. The public would not follow him.

In the autumn of 1913, Diaghilev's Ballets Russes sailed for South America — without Diaghilev. During the voyage, Nijinsky was seen much in company with a Hungarian dancer, Romola de Pulska, and when the company reached Buenos Aires they were married. One night in Rio de Janeiro, Nijinsky, without giving any excuse or explanation, refused to dance *Le Carnaval* and Diaghilev, considering this a breach of contract, dismissed him at the end of the tour. From this date the sun of Nijinsky began to set. A London engagement which he obtained ended in disaster. In 1914 he was interned in Budapest, but early in 1916, thanks largely to the intervention of Diaghilev, he was released and danced with the Ballets Russes again in North America. In New York, in October 1916, he produced his last ballet, *Till Eulenspiegel* (*), but the tour which followed was chaotic. Nijinsky, quite incapable of the administrative responsibilities which he had demanded, became every day more detached from life and more obsessed with a mania about persecution. Nevertheless, he danced again for Diaghilev in Spain in 1917 and then took part in a South American tour. It was apparent, however, that he was mentally very ill. The tour ended in Buenos Aires on 26th September 1917 and that night Nijinsky danced for the last time, in his two greatest roles, the spectre of the rose and Petrouchka.

The Nijinskys returned to Europe and settled in Switzerland. There the dancer's mind gradually clouded over and he was put away in an asylum. He survived for thirty years, being delivered by death on 11th April 1950.

This short and thickset young man, with his powerful limbs and strange, Mongolian features, was offstage an unimpressive and inarticulate person. Yet in the theatre he was transformed and once he began to dance his whole being was illumined with some fire of genius. The powerful limbs helped him to jump, the slanting

eyes and high cheekbones responded wonderfully to make-up, but the greatest miracle that occurred was the change in his personality. Alexandre Benois, who many times watched him prepare for a performance wrote, "the fact that Nijinsky's metamorphosis was predominantly subconscious is, in my opinion, the very proof of his genius."

NIKITINA Alice. "The most adorable cat that ever danced in a talc petticoat", wrote W. A. Propert of Nikitina's performance in the title-role of *La Chatte,* which she took over from Spessivtseva for the first Paris performance (1927), having learned it, by her own account, in under two hours. Nikitina was one of the personalities of the final Diaghilev period. She came from St. Petersburg and studied with Preobajenska, Egorova, Legat and Cecchetti. Before joining Diaghilev she had danced at the Ljubljana opera and with Boris Romanov's Ballets Romantiques. With Diaghilev, she created roles in *Zéphire et Flore* and *Ode* and appeared in *Le Pas d'acier, Apollon Musagète* and *Le Bal.* Nikitina is also a coloratura soprano — a pupil of Tetrazzini — who has appeared in opera in Italy and elsewhere. She now divides her time between singing and teaching dancing.

NOBILISSIMA VISIONE (St. Francis). Choreographic legend in one act and five scenes. Scenario: Massine. Music: Hindemith. Scenery and costumes: Tchelitchev. Choreography: Massine. First performance: Ballets de Monte-Carlo (René Blum), Drury Lane Theatre, London, 21 July 1938. Principal dancers: Nini Theilade, Massine.

The five scenes present the story of St. Francis of Assisi. Son of a cloth merchant, he leads a carefree life in his father's shop — young, handsome and rich, with nothing but contempt for the poor. He decides to become a soldier, and goes in search of a warrior's glory. But he is quickly disillusioned by the brutality of military life. In a vision he sees Poverty, his bride to be, and discovers his true vocation. He returns home, distributes his father's possessions to the poor, casts away his own fine clothes, and gives himself to a life of medita-

ALICE NIKITINA. DRAWING BY PRUNA.

NOBILISSIMA VISIONE. DÉCOR BY TCHELITCHEV. 1938.

tion. During his wanderings he tames a ferocious wolf. The ballet ends with the meeting of St. Francis and Poverty and their mystic union at a frugal wedding-feast.

Hindemith's serious, powerful music, composed in close association with the choreographer, perfectly fitted the development of the action. Tchelitchev's simple, stylised décor was chiefly remarkable for ingenious lighting. Massine danced the title-role himself. His terre à terre choreography was largely based on the hieratic, angular poses of Byzantine art. He made effective use of the hand-language known as "chironomy", which added surprising intensity to certain passages, notably the scene where the corps de ballet, in four tiers, beat out the verses of the "Song of the Creatures" with their fluttering hands.

NOCES Les. Choral ballet in four continuous scenes. Words and music: Stravinsky. Scenery and costumes: Goncharova. Choreography: Nijinska. First performance: Dia-

ghilev's Ballets Russes, Gaîté-Lyrique, Paris, 13 June 1923. Principal dancer: Felia Doubrovska.

One of the most original and (when it first appeared) disconcerting of Diaghilev's productions, by reason of Stravinsky's percussive score, violent and yet austerely impressive and moving, Goncharova's unusually severe décor and, finally, Nijinska's angular and geometric choreography. The subject—traditional wedding rites of Russian peasants—had occurred to the composer many years before, and the music was finished, apart from the orchestration, by 1917. Diaghilev was enthusiastic, but there was much discussion between the various collaborators before the final form was achieved. It had been intended to mount it as spectacular work in the manner of *Coq d'or,* but the trappings were pared down to essentials and Goncharova's final décor consisted of wings and backcloth of neutral colour and movable flats with simple windows and doors and a marriage bed to indicate changes of scene. The costumes were

LES NOCES FANTASTIQUES. BESSY, VAN DIJK AND VYROUBOVA.

uniformly black and white. Stravinsky's orchestration was equally austere: four grand pianos and percussion. The singers and the pianos were accommodated at either side of the proscenium opening. Nijinska's poses and pyramidal groups had a deliberately Byzantine stiffness; the women were on point almost continuously, to emphasise their height. The ballet reached a controlled climax of great intensity, to the sound of clanging bells.

It was not a work to which anyone could remain indifferent. In Paris (1923) its qualities were recognised (not without some dissent) but conservative London (1926) was seriously disconcerted by this ballet which was so little an "entertainment". It was hotly defended by H. G. Wells. A revival of *Les Noces,* while Nijinska and Goncharova are still here to superintend it, is much to be desired.

NOCES FANTASTIQUES Les. Ballet in two acts, four scenes by Serge Lifar. Music: Marcel Delannoy. Scenery: Roger Chastel. Costumes: André Levasseur. Choreography: Lifar. First performance: Paris Opera, 9 Fe-

bruary, 1955. Principal dancers: Nina Vyroubova, Claude Bessy, Peter van Dijk.

A youth leaves his betrothed to go to sea; the ship is wrecked and he is washed up on a magic island. He is claimed by the queen but, mindful of the girl he left behind him, spurns her and is thrown back into the sea to drown. As a spectre, he returns to port on a phantom ship and bears away his bride to a ghostly wedding in the skeleton hull in the depths of the sea. The wreck and its spectral crew disappear; the lovers are transfigured.

Both choreography and music of this adroitly constructed neo-romantic fantasy have considerable dramatic impact. The atmosphere is sustained by stylised décors and ingenious costumes. Nina Vyroubova, exquisitely tender as the fiancée, was admirably partnered by Peter van Dijk, with his strong technique and romantic presence. Claude Bessy was a seductive and authoritative queen of the *Océanides*.

NOCTAMBULES. Ballet in two scenes. Music: Humphrey Searle. Scenario and choreography: Kenneth MacMillan. Scenery and costumes: Nicholas Georgiadis. First performance: Sadler's Wells Ballet, Covent Garden, London, 1 March 1956. Principal dancers: Leslie Edwards, Maryon Lane, Nadia Nerina, Brian Shaw.

"A little variety theatre in the back streets". A hypnotist bungles his act: to quieten the angry public, he hypnotises them. Poor girl finds rich young man; the soldier lives dreams of glory; the faded beauty recaptures her youth. Duped by his own magic, the hypnotist carries her off. His little assistant, crazed with jealousy, is left alone in the empty theatre. MacMillan's bravura choreography is lit by flashes of real tenderness: the qualities unite in the role of the assistant, admirably portrayed by Maryon Lane. Searle's highly dramatic music and Georgiadis's tarnished theatre, with its tiers of deserted boxes, heighten the impression of macabre hallucination.

NOUVEAUX BALLETS DE MONTE-CARLO. Between 1942 and 1947 two companies, with the patronage of the principality of Monaco, attempted in spite of wartime restrictions to revive the great tradition of the Ballet Russe de Monte-Carlo founded several years previously by René Blum. His company left Europe on the declaration of the second World War and went to the U.S.A., where it passed under the direction of Serge Denham and gradually became an American company. Marcel Sablon, the director of the Monte Carlo theatre, took up the threads again in 1942. The "Nouveaux Ballets de Monte-Carlo", as the company was called, consisted mainly of dancers who had escaped from Paris, but there were also local recruits, notably from the studio of Julie Sedova at Nice. Geneviève Kergrist, Marie-Louise Didion and Marcelle Cassini were the principal danseuses, with Lucienne Berggren and Ludmilla Tcherina. Among the men were Gérard Mulys and Paul Goubé and some new youngsters, Edmond Audran, Boris Trailine, Jean-Jacques Etchevery and Serge Golovine, who were making their début. New Ballets included *L'Indiscret* by Tony Gregory and *Stenka Razine* by Nicolas Zverev. The latter was the company's ballet master, in charge of the revival of the Fokine classics: *Sheherazade, Carnaval, Petrouchka, Les Sylphides.*

* There was a gap from 1944 to 1945, when Prince Louis II of Monaco invited the impresario Eugène Grunberg to re-form the company, which was now called the " Nouveau Ballet de

DRAMMA PER MUSICA. DÉCOR BY CASSANDRE.

A DANCER.
DRAWING BY LÉONOR FINI.

Monte-Carlo". Serge Lifar was artistic director and produced several important works: *Dramma per Musica, Chota Roustaveli, Salomé, Noir et Blanc, Roméo et Juliette*. In addition to regular seasons at Monaco, they visited London in the summer of 1946 for a season at the Cambridge Theatre, when the above-mentioned works were shown, and also Chauviré's unforgettable Giselle. The dancers, headed by Yvette Chauviré and Janine Charrat, included Renée Jeanmaire, Ludmilla Tcherina, Wladimir Skouratoff and Alexandre Kalioujny. In the spring of 1947 the company was acquired by the Marquis de Cuevas and became, under his direction, the "Grand Ballet de Monte-Carlo". In 1950 the company severed its connection with the principality and, after important internal changes, changed its name once again to the "Grand Ballet du Marquis de Cuevas". Since then, Monte Carlo has had no permanent company attached to the theatre; Christmas and Easter seasons are given by visiting companies.

NOVARRO Luciana. A classical prima ballerina at La Scala, Milan (1946), with a supple and expressive line, who specialised in modern character roles, of which she was a sensitive and intelligent interpreter. She left La Scala in 1957 to devote herself entirely to choreography, in which field she had made an excellent beginning with *Stelle vere* (1955) and *Sebastian* (1956).

NUIT La. Ballet by Boris Kochno. Music: Henri Sauguet. Scenery and costumes: Christian Bérard. Choreography: Serge Lifar. First performance: C. B. Cochran's 1930 Revue, Palace Theatre, Manchester, 4 March 1930. Principal dancers: Alice Nikitina, Serge Lifar. Bérard's début in the theatre. The setting for Kochno's story was a dark and gloomy street. Poor boy meets rich girl; to them everything seems possible, but every time they come together, a stone wall rises between them and forces them back to their solitude. A "pièce noire" of a ballet born more than fifteen years before the time when Petit's *Le Rendez-vous* made the genre popular.

* Revived by Ballets des Champs-Élysées, Paris, 19 April 1949, as a tribute to the recently deceased Christian Bérard, with new choreography by Janine Charrat. Principal dancers: Irène Skorik, Youly Algaroff.

NUIT DE LA SAINT-JEAN La. Ballet in one act. Music: Hugo Alfvén. Scenery and costumes: Nils de Dardel. Choreography: Jean Borlin. First performance: Rolf de Maré's Ballets Suédois, Théâtre des Champs-Élysées, 25 October 1920.

St. John's (Midsummer) Eve is celebrated annually in Sweden by singing, games and dancing, interrupted only by the short Northern night and resumed with the dawn. The theme made a strong sentimental appeal to Jean Borlin and his dancers. The result was spontaneous and authentic, a breath of fresh air in a period of ceaseless aesthetic experiment and search for novelty. The designer, Nils de Dardel, reproduced the traditional costumes of his homeland with a freshness quite unlike the avant-garde sophistications of most of the Ballets Suédois productions. This was one of their most successful ballets.

NUIT EST UNE SORCIÈRE La. Ballet in one act. Story: André Coffrant. Music: Sidney Bechet. Choreography: Pierre Lacotte. Scenery and costumes: Bernard Daydé. First performed at the Aix-les-Bains Festival, 2 August 1955.

A reaction against the academicism of the Paris Opera. Pierre Lacotte had just resigned his position there as premier danseur to found the "Ballet de la Tour Eiffel", and was ripe for such an apparently revolutionary subject: a young sleepwalker who kills his entire family, under the influence of a negro servant "releasing his primitive forces". The story, in spite of its psychoanalytical pretensions, is unconvincing. So many gratuitous deaths produce nothing but repulsion or boredom. Nevertheless the ballet left some pleasant memories: Bernard Daydé's fantastic attic with its dusty bric-à-brac; the pas de deux between Pierre Lacotte and Josette Clavier; Sidney Bechet's score.

NUTCRACKER The. See *Casse-Noisette*.

O

OBOUKHOV Anatole. Trained at the Imperial Ballet School of his native St. Petersburg. Graduated at the same time as Olga Spessivstseva and Felia Doubrovska (1913), premier danseur 1917. Left Russia in 1920. Western audiences saw him for the first time with the Théâtre Romantique Russe, where he made a great success in *Giselle* (1924). Slender, light, with great natural distinction, Oboukhov was an ideal danseur noble, with impeccable batterie and soaring jetés. In 1927-28 he appeared with the Nemchinova-Dolin ballet in London, then, as his wife Nemchinova's partner, with the Kaunas Opera. Subsequently joined the Ballets Russes de Monte-Carlo (1935-37) and Original Ballet Russe (1940). Now lives and teaches in America.

ODE. Spectacle in two acts. Scenario: Boris Kochno. Music: Nabokov, to words by Lomonosov. Scenery and costumes: Tchelitchev, in collaboration with Pierre Charbonnier.

Choreography: Massine. First performance: Diaghilev's Ballets Russes, Théâtre Sarah-Bernhardt, Paris, 6 June 1928. Principal dancers: Ira Beliamina, Serge Lifar.

Massine's last ballet for Diaghilev and one of the strangest productions of the final years. Nabokov's cantata was a setting of an ode on the Aurora Borealis by the 18th century Russian poet Lomonosov. The most remarkable feature was Tchelitchev's décor, which included phosphorescent costumes, rows of dolls suspended on cords, slide and film projections on the backcloth, and ingenious lighting. Diaghilev, by now secretly tired of constant novelty, took little interest.

ŒUF A LA COQUE L'. Ballet in one act. Music: Maurice Thiriet. Scenery and costumes: Stanislas Lepri. Scenario and choreography: Roland Petit. First performance: Ballets de Paris, Princes Theatre, London, 16 February 1949. Principal dancers: Colette Marchand, Renée Jeanmaire, Nina Vyroubova, Roland Petit, Wladimir Skouratoff, Gordon Hamilton, Serge Perrault.

A light-hearted romp in a fantastic kitchen full of pots and pans and dishcloths. Cooks and scullery boys in white caps and aprons put the chickens into the oven. A gigantic egg hatches into Vyroubova, Jeanmaire and Marchand, all devastating in black silk tights and feathers. Music-hall acrobatics blended with classical dancing. Written for Colette Marchand, a witty dancer with exquisite legs.

OISEAU DE FEU L' *(The Firebird)*. Ballet in two scenes. Scenario and choreography: Fokine. Music: Stravinsky. Scenery and costumes: Golovine (Firebird's costume by Bakst). First performance: Diaghilev's Ballets Russes, Paris Opera, 25 June, 1910. Principal dancers: Tamara Karsavina, Michel Fokine, Vera Fokina, Bulgakov.

Diaghilev returned to St. Petersburg after his Paris triumph in the summer of 1909, determined on a new season the following year, with new works. One of them was to be based on the Russian fairy-tale of the Firebird, for which Fokine, aided by the *régisseur* Grigoriev, worked out a scenario collating several versions of the story. Though he knew he was a dilatory worker, Diaghilev asked his former teacher of harmony Anatole Liadov to write the music. Three months later, he asked how he was getting on. "Spendidly," replied Liadov, "I've bought the ruled paper". Diaghilev then remembered Igor Stravinsky, the talented young pupil of Rimsky-Korsakov, whose orchestral fantasy *Fireworks* had impressed him at a concert in the previous year, and who had orchestrated two pieces for *Les Sylphides*. Diaghilev's advisers were doubtful about his youth and inexperience but Fokine was agreeable, and the commission for the *Firebird* was accordingly transferred. Stravinsky, a hard worker and an expert craftsman, was ready on time. Choreographer and composer worked in perfect harmony.

A clearing in a forest at night: a tree laden with golden apples, gleaming in the darkness. A young prince, Ivan Tsarevich, is stalking the Firebird for her gorgeous plumage. The first time she eludes him, but when she returns he captures her. She pleads for her freedom and in exchange gives him one of her golden feathers, by means of which he can summon her aid. Twelve princesses appear, to play with the golden apples in the moonlight. The prince is transfixed by the beauty of one of them. She returns his feelings but implores him to flee; they are captives of the Immortal Kostchei, a wizard who imprisons anyone caught in his domain. A horde of demons appear, followed by the terrible Kostchei himself, who prepares to cast a spell over the young prince. But the Tsarevich waves the magic feather, the Firebird appears and compels the demons into a frenzied dance. They fall into an exhausted sleep. The Firebird takes the Tsarevitch to a hollow tree where there is a box containing a huge egg, the soul of Kostchei. The wizard tries in vain to prevent the prince from destroying the egg, but he hurls it to the ground. Kostchei and his court disappear for ever. The scene is transformed. The Princess comes to meet the Tsarevich as his bride, the freed captives of Kostchei join in the rejoicing at a traditional Russian wedding.

Pavlova disliked the music, and so the chief role was given to Karsavina, whose wonderful performance set the crown on the ballet's success and the atmosphere of mysterious enchantment produced by the perfect fusion of music, décor and choreography.

* For Diaghilev's 1926 revival in London (Danilova and Lifar) he commissioned a new décor from Goncharova. This production

MARJORIE TALLCHIEF AND GEORGE SKIBINE IN CONCERTO. OPÉRA-COMIQUE, 1958.

was revived for the Royal Ballet by the Grigorievs for the 25th anniversary of Diaghilev's death (Edinburgh Festival, 1954; Fonteyn, Somes, Beriosova, Ashton). This was a revival in the best sense of the word and proved that the work had lost none of its magic.

 * Adolph Bolm restaged *The Firebird* for Ballet Theatre in 1945 (Markova, Dolin, Diana Adams, John Taras), with décor and costumes by Marc Chagall.

 * The Chagall sets were acquired by Balanchine for the New York City Ballet in 1949 when he made an entirely new version to a shorter score, arranged by Stravinsky himself. This contained a spectacular pas de deux (for Maria Tallchief and Moncion) but had little fairy-tale atmosphere. Acclaimed by critics and audiences in New York, it was much disliked in London. Chagall eventually refused permission for the use of his designs.

 * Lifar produced *The Firebird* at the Paris Opera in 1954 with new décor and costumes by Wakhevitch. If not entirely successful, it was brilliantly interpreted by Vyroubova and Algaroff.

OPÉRA-COMIQUE. Although the second opera house of Paris and of France has never, as a home of ballet, acquired the importance or the fame of the Opéra, it has seen considerable activity and over a hundred different ballets have been produced there during the last fifty years. During the first quarter-century, we find names celebrated in various spheres of dancing: Cléo de Mérode, Mistinguett, Albert Aveline and, last but not least, Argentina, who danced her famous version of *El Amor brujo* there on many occasions. 1926 saw the production of Ravel's fantastic opera *L'Enfant et les Sortilèges,* to a text by Colette which requires dancers as well as singers. In 1933 Constantin Tcherkas was appointed choreographer and principal dancer; he remained for twenty years. One of his most successful works was *La Pantoufle de Verre* (1935) in which he appeared himself with Solange Schwarz. 1936 was a stormy year of quarrels and strikes culminating in the resignation of the director, Gheuzi; the fortunes of the Opéra-Comique remained somewhat uncertain until in 1939 it was formally amalgamated with the Opéra as the Réunion des Théâtres Lyriques. The years

PAVANE POUR UNE INFANTE DÉFUNTE. ESPANITA CORTEZ AND JACQUES CHAZOT.

of war and occupation produced little of interest in the second house in the realm of ballet.

Full activity was resumed in 1946 under a new director, Henri Malherbe, who instituted full programmes of ballet with a new maître de ballet, Jean-Jacques Etchevery, and with new soloists including Geneviève Kergrist (from the Opéra) and Lucienne Berggren. Etchevery's works have included *La Précaution inutile, La Ballade de la geôle de Reading, Concerto* (Tchaikovsky) and *La Chanson du mal aimé.* There was another *Concerto* (Prokofiev) from the hand of Janine Charrat. 1950 was Massine's year, with revivals of *La Boutique fantasque, Les Femmes de bonne humeur, Le Beau Danube* (in which he danced his old part) and a new work, *Le Bal du Pont du Nord.* Dancers during this period included Solange Schwarz, Christiane Vaussard, Paul Goubé, Michel Rayne. In 1951 two visitors from the Opéra, Darsonval and Kalioujny, gave a memorable performance of *Le Cygne noir.* Unfortunately one of the periodical waves of official economy led to the suppression of the ballet programmes after six years of intense and rewarding activity. The decision was rescinded early in 1957, when Gérard Mulys, the new maître de ballet, began to reassemble the company. Performances started again in June with two Massine programmes, and in 1958 Skibine produced there his very successful *Concerto* to music by André Jolivet, with décors by Delfau, and Marjorie Tallchief and Michel Rayne in the leading roles.

OPÉRA DE PARIS. With a programme of ballet every Wednesday evening and a series of performances each July which amount to a festival, the ballet at the Paris Opera has regained the position it held with such brilliance during the 18th and 19th centuries. The Opéra has had many homes, from the Jeu de Paume de la Bouteille of 1671 up to the sumptuous "Palais Garnier" opened in 1875; their stages were graced by such dancers as Mlles. Prévost, Sallé and Camargo, Louis Dupré, Noverre, Gaëtan and Auguste Vestris, Gardel, Dauberval, Duport, Marie Taglioni, Perrot and Saint-Léon, not to mention foreign celebrities. The Opéra saw the first performances of *La Sylphide* (1832), *Giselle* (1841), *Le Corsaire* (1856), *Coppélia* (1870) and *Sylvia* (1876), works which have remained in the repertory from New York to Leningrad.

But about 1900, the ballet fell into a decline. This was the period of the "vieux abonnés", rich elderly gentlemen who took season tickets in the front rows of the stalls, whence they could ogle the dancers and applaud their little protégées. The "vieux abonnés" were picturesque individuals but poor judges of art; they did not care if the ballets were no more than insipid and conventional pretexts to show off the étoiles and their surrounding coryphées to the best advantage. Nobody was interested in ballet as an art.

The rehabilitation of ballet at the Opéra and elsewhere is principally due to Diaghilev and his company, and to the intense interest and enthusiasm aroused by their first season in Paris, which spread gradually from the influential circles who flocked round Diaghilev to the general public. There was no question, at that time, of the Opéra itself producing dancers, choreographers and designers of comparable brilliance, but there was clearly a golden opportunity to learn from the Russians and to turn the newly awakened interest in ballet to good account. Yet although the Opéra had unsuspected wealth of material to

MIRAGES. DECOR BY CASSANDRE. 1944.

GUIGNOL ET PANDORE. DÉCOR BY DIGNIMONT. 1944.

hand in the teachers and dancers who, in spite of the indifference of their management and their audience, had at least maintained the fine traditions of the French school, it was some time before much improvement was shown. The worthy Léo Staats had been maître de ballet since 1907. In 1914 Ivan Clustine produced his *Suite de Danses,* which derived from Fokine's *Les Sylphides.* In that same year, Jacques Rouché, a friend and admirer of Diaghilev, who had been doing excellent work as director of the Théâtre des Arts, became director of the Opéra, a post which he held for thirty years.

Slowly but surely, Rouché brought the Opéra ballet back to life. His first important production was the 1918 revival of Rameau's opera, *Castor et Pollux,* with the abundant dances arranged by an Italian choreographer, Nicola Guerra. But this return to the past, like Diaghilev's *Sleeping Princess* of 1921, came before its time and in spite of a strong cast (Aïda Boni, who was succeeded by Carlotta Zambelli, Janine Schwarz and Albert Aveline) aroused no great enthusiasm. Rouché applied Diaghilev's formula of collaboration between the arts to local resources, which were by no means poor. His

designers included Dethomas, Drésa, Piot, and Brianchon; his composers, Pierné, Roussel, Ibert, Dukas. The great Russians also made their contribution: Bakst designed for the Opéra, Fokine revived *Daphnis et Chloé* in 1921, and Pavlova appeared in *La Péri* in the same year. Olga Spessivtseva was engaged in 1924 to dance *Giselle* and *Soir de fête,* the first step towards the rebuilding of the classical repertoire and the breaking of the tradition of the great Milanese stars. Though Rouché was no slavish imitator, and disagreed with some of Diaghilev's innovations, he started a class of eurhythmics whose teacher, Mme Pasmanik, was responsible for many productions in the Dalcroze method, which provoked considerable controversy. He was also able to provide Ida Rubinstein with an ideal setting for her spectacular productions (*Arthémis troublée* and *La Tragédie de Salomé* in 1922; and Nijinska's *Le Baiser de la Fée, La Bien-Aimée* and *Boléro* in 1928).

New ballets during this period included *La Nuit ensorcelée* (1923), a fantastic, Hoffmannesque work by Émile Vuillermoz, Bakst and Staats and, in the same year, *Cydalise et le Chèvre-pied* by Pierné, Dethomas and Staats. *Istar* and *Siang-*

ISTAR. DÉCOR BY BAKST. 1924.

Sin in 1924 inaugurated a series of ballets on oriental themes. Nijinska's *Impressions de music-hall* (1927) showed that contemporary subject-matter was not neglected. The stars of the company were Carlotta Zambelli, Camille Bos, Anna Johnson, Lucienne Lamballe, Josette de Craponne, Albert Aveline, Gustave Ricaux and Léo Staats. Suzanne Lorcia, Solange Schwarz, Marie-Louise Didion and, among the men, Serge Peretti, Roger Ritz and Paul Goubé were beginning to make their mark.

The year 1929 was a decisive one. Diaghilev died in August. His company was disbanded and his principal collaborators were in demand all over the world. Some of the rich inheritance fell to the Opéra: Rouché asked George Balanchine to do the choreography for *Les Créatures de Prométhée* and, when he fell ill, suggested that Serge Lifar should take over. This aroused violent opposition, the "vieux abonnés" demanding the instant expulsion of the "Cossack" from the "Temple of Terpsichore". But Rouché held firm and on 30th December 1929 *Prométhée* was presented with great success. Lifar was subsequently engaged as premier danseur and choreographer, positions which, apart from a short period after the liberation,

he held for more than a quarter of a century under four successive directors: MM. Rouché, Lehmann, Hirsch and Jacques Ibert.

Lifar brought with him to the Opéra something of the spirit of the Ballets Russes, though he was still at the beginning of his career as a choreographer and was as yet no rival to Fokine or Massine. His early ballets were criticised for deficiencies in ensemble work and for his tendency to concentrate almost exclusively on his own roles. But this period included—in addition to the revivals of *Giselle* and *Le Spectre de la Rose* in 1932 with Olga Spessivtseva—two fine new ballets in the style of the Commedia dell'arte: *La Vie de Polichinelle* and *Salade*. Lifar the choreographer may be a subject for debate, but Lifar the dancer undeniably aroused the enthusiasm of the public, drew large crowds to the Opéra, and brought about a revival of interest in its ballet which would have been inconceivable before he joined the company. It was at this period that the Wednesday evening ballet programmes were instituted.

On the 9th of July 1935, Lifar's *Icare* was given for the first time. This ballet (fully dealt with elsewhere, as is Lifar's work as a whole) created world-wide interest, aroused passionate controversy, and placed its choreographer and his company in the forefront of the world of ballet. Lifar had found his feet, and the succession of new ballets of high quality continued up till 1942. He enriched his choreographic vocabulary, gave greater opportunities to his feminine partners and paid more attention to the role of the corps de ballet. *David Triomphant, Le Cantique des Cantiques, Alexandre le Grand, Oriane et le Prince d'Amour, Le Chevalier et la Damoiselle, Joán de Zarissa, Suite en Blanc* (an abstract ballet in the neo-classic style), *Les Animaux Modèles* and *Entre deux Rondes*, are the major works of this period.

But Lifar's pre-eminent role must not be allowed to eclipse the work of the distinguished teachers, particularly Gustave Ricaux, Carlotta Zambelli and Albert Aveline, who were forming the coming generations of dancers in the purest classical tradition. Nor should one forget the other choreographers attached to the Opéra: Léo Staats, who retired in 1936, and Albert Aveline. The latter was responsible for several notable ballets, including *La Grisi, Un Baiser pour rien* (1936), *Elvire* (1936), *Les Santons* (1938), *Le Festin de l'Araignée, Jeux d'Enfants* and *La Grande Jatte* (1950).

With the liberation came a new epoch. Lifar had been dismissed and his works removed from the repertoire. Maurice Lehmann succeeded Jacques Rouché and tried to keep the ballet going with the few resources at his disposal. But the crisis caused by Lifar's dismissal, the financial difficulties, the loss of many of the stars and of members of the corps de ballet, threatened the company's existence. In March 1947, Georges Hirsch took the initiative by inviting Balanchine to return from America. He staged revivals of three of his old ballets, *Apollon Musagète, Le Baiser de la Fée* and *Serenade,* and gave the Opéra a new work, *Le Palais de Cristal,* of the highest quality. With him he brought two brilliant guest stars: Tamara Toumanova and Maria Tallchief. Lifar returned at the end of 1947 and took up the threads with *Mirages,* already prepared before

his dismissal in 1944. During the next ten years he produced some 20 new works, including: *Zadig, Septuor, Le Chevalier Errant, Phèdre, Dramma per Musica, Blanche-Neige, Roméo et Juliette* (two versions) and *Les Noces Fantastiques,* one of the finest ballets in the Opéra's repertoire.

One of the principal events of the last ten years was the spectacular and successful revival in 1952 of Rameau's *Les Indes Galantes,* which deployed all the resources of the magnificent theatre and atoned for the comparative failure of the earlier revival of *Castor et Pollux.* Maurice Lehmann, director at the time of this revival, was also responsible for inviting two distinguished foreigners, Harald Lander (1952) who acted as ballet master and revived the Galeotti ballet *Les Caprices de Cupidon* as well as his own *Études* (admirably suited to show off the large company), and John Cranko, who produced *La Belle Hélène* in 1955. Other guest choreographers included Nicolas Zverev, who staged accurate revivals of Fokine's *Petrouchka, Danses Polovtsiennes, Sheherazade* and *Le Spectre de la Rose.* Finally, during his second term as administrator of the National Theatres, Georges Hirsch invited Massine to revive his *Symphonie fantastique.* The Opéra

PHÈDRE. BALLET BY COCTEAU AND LIFAR.

ballet has made tours abroad, to North America, London, and Moscow, and has offered the hospitality of its stage to three great foreign companies: the Sadler's Wells Ballet, the New York City Ballet, and the Bolshoi Theatre Ballet.

The company has been equally strong in dancers promoted from its own ranks and in guest artists. After Suzanne Lorcia, Solange Schwarz, Nina Vyroubova and Micheline Bardin, the eye, but provides the balletomane with a unique opportunity of following, season by season, the gradual progression of the various artists through the imposing hierarchy, the traditional formations through which the humblest "petit rat" can climb to stardom. The rules are strict and each stage through which the young dancers must pass is rigorously defined. They join the school as children (minimum age 8 years, maximum 12) and are given suitable opportu-

SOIR DE FÊTE. DÉCOR BY JEAN-DENIS MALCLÈS. *Théâtre de l'Opéra, Paris.*

the public applauded Lycette Darsonval and Yvette Chauviré. Liane Daydé, Christiane Vaussard, Madeleine Lafon, Claude Bessy, Josette Amiel, and now Marjorie Tallchief are among their juniors. On the male side, apart from Serge Lifar and Serge Peretti (the first to be given the title danseur-étoile), Alexandre Kalioujny, Michel Renault, Jean-Paul Andréani, Youly Algaroff, Peter Van Dijk, George Skibine and Max Bozzoni have all made their mark since the war. Thirteen years ago, the *Défilé du corps de ballet* was instituted to display, at gala performances and on special occasions, the entire ballet company to the strains of Berlioz's Trojan March. The spectacle is not only a pleasure to nities to familiarise themselves with the stage by appearing in some of the productions. When they are about 15, they take the examination for entry to the Deuxième Quadrille; the members of the Premier Quadrille, who take their classes with them, are recruited from the best of these pupils. The Coryphées and Petits Sujets are dancers drawn from the ranks for small ensemble work. Next come the Grands Sujets who perform dances requiring three or four performers, sometimes a solo or pas de deux. Promotion from one category to another is decided by strict annual examinations. Thus the best of the Grands Sujets become Premiers Danseurs; then, a very small number of these are nominated for the coveted rank of Étoile. It is according to this hierarchy, corresponding to a period of training extending over ten years (sometimes less, often more) that the members of the entire company appear in the *Défilé,* as living symbols of a great tradition reborn.

Thanks to rigorous selection, strict training, and regular examinations, the level of the corps de ballet of the Opéra is very high. More than one obscure *sujet* could be a star in an inde-

than others, the more sensitive and talented being sometimes paralysed with fear, while mediocrities perform happily. This does much more real harm than the notorious and much exaggerated "favouritism" which is in any case no monopoly of the Paris Opera. Rightly or wrongly, all young dancers believe they are potential stars. French dancers, particularly, are confirmed individualists, happier as soloists than as members of a team. When they remain

BLANCHE-NEIGE. DÉCOR BY BOUCHÊNE FOR ACT I. 1950.

pendent company. Also the institution of the "petits rats" ensures that the humblest dancer has considerable stage experience and a thorough knowledge of every aspect of dancing. The company's style has remarkable homogeneity — always an asset in ballet even when the style has its defects. The *style Opéra* is characterised by a tendency to neglect the upper part of the body: its exponents are apt to forget that dancing involves not only the legs but the back, torso, head and arms as well. Moreover, the observance of a rigid hierarchy is not without its drawbacks. Until the grade of Grand Sujet is passed, a dancer's promotion depends on examinations, which always affect some children more

for years in the lower grades, in virtual anonymity, they tend to become bored and embittered. Some of them join the ephemeral, smaller companies, where there is more chance of being noticed; others resign themselves to an unspectacular but secure future at the Opéra. The latter, loyal and dependable though they may be, more employees than artists, constitute a real danger to a permanent company, for they tend to give dull, routine performances. Routine is the Opéra ballet's worst enemy. New productions and a continual enlargement and variation of the repertory is the solution for this great company, so glorious in the past and so rich in promise for the future.

BERNARD BUFFET. L'OPÉRA DE PARIS. 1956.

ORCHESTRE EN LIBERTÉ L'. Ballet in one act. Scenario: P. Franz and P. Gsill. Music: Henry Sauveplane. Scenery and costumes: Paul Colin. Choreography: Lifar. First performance, Paris Opera, 16 February 1931. Jazz versus classical music: negroes, representing jazz instruments, launch a violent attack on the musicians of the symphony orchestra. Finally the conductor succeeds in imposing his authority on the combatants and assembles them for a final, harmonious apotheosis. Suzanne Lorcia (the Flute), Lifar (the Violin), Lucienne Lamballe and Peretti (the Cymbals) danced the principal roles. Paul Colin's costumes ingeniously represented the different instruments.

ORIANE ET LE PRINCE D'AMOUR. Ballet in two acts. Scenario: Claude Seran. Music: Florent Schmitt. Scenery and costumes: Pedro Pruna. Choreography: Lifar. First performance: Paris Opéra, 7 January 1938. Principal dancers: Lycette Darsonval, Serge Lifar, Paul Goubé.

Florent Schmitt's score had been written in 1934 for Ida Rubinstein, but not used. The action takes place in 14th century Avignon where Oriane, a kind of Provençal Thamar, holds her court of love. Inquisitive and per-verse, bored by her usual distractions, she is tempted to evil deeds by gold offered her by a Mongol merchant. The Prince of Love appears, but her reputation scares him away. In desperation she holds a "fête des fous". A mysterious masked fiddler fascinates her; he unmasks and is revealed as Death.

P

PAGANINI. Ballet in one act, three scenes. Scenario: Rachmaninov and Fokine. Music: Rachmaninov (Rhapsody on a theme of Paganini). Scenery and costumes: Serge Soudeikine. Choreography: Fokine. First performance: de Basil company, Covent Garden, London, 30 June 1939. Principal dancers: Dimitri Rostov, Baronova, Riabouchinska.

Rachmaninov himself suggested the use of his rhapsody and provided a new, quiet ending.

The famous violinist (impressively mimed by Rostov) was shown beset by trials, temptations and tribulations of a mainly allegorical nature, from which he was finally rescued by his genius (Baronova). There was much demonic paraphernalia, some of it perilously near unconscious humour, and a beautiful solo, in the central episode, for Riabouchinska as a Florentine beauty.

PAGAVA Éthéry. Appeared as a child prodigy in the early recitals of Janine Charrat and Roland Petit during the war and at 13 became a star of the Ballets des Champs Élysées, making a sensation in the role of the little acrobat in *Les Forains* (1945). The following year she created Ganymede in *Les Amours de Jupiter*. Three years later she gave unforgettable interpretations of the Sleepwalker in *Night Shadow* and Juliet in *Roméo et Juliette* with the de Cuevas company. Born in France of Georgian parents, Éthéry Pagava was a pupil of Egorova. She has a lyrical technique, a pale face with a Russian cast of features, big brown eyes, and a warm, endearing personality. Now dancing as guest artist with various companies.

PAGAVA IN NIGHT SHADOW.

PAGE AND AROVA IN REVANCHE.

PAGE Ruth. American dancer and choreographer, born Indianapolis, now resident in Chicago where she directs the Chicago Opera Ballet, but often to be found in Paris or at her farm near St. Tropez. Ruth Page is an American with a cosmopolitan outlook. She went to Chicago at an early age to study with Ivan Clustine, then maître de ballet of Pavlova's company, and she was a member of that company during its last tour of South America. Returning to Chicago, she worked with Adolph Bolm and became première danseuse of his Ballet Intime. She danced at the Colon, Buenos Aires, at the Metropolitan Opera, New York, made several Oriental tours, danced in Russia in 1930, and then sealed her reputation with the recitals given during a three year partnership with Harald Kreutzberg (1932-34). With Bentley Stone she formed the Page-Stone Ballet in 1938, toured for eight seasons throughout the United States and took the first American ballet company to South America (1940). Nicholas Remisoff was principal designer for this company, later called the Chicago Ballet Company and now reborn as the Chicago Opera Ballet. Major productions, sometimes with Stone's assistance, were *Guns and Castanets* (1939), the story of *Carmen* to Bizet's music, *Americans in Paris* and *Frankie and Johnny* (1938), *The Bells* (1946) and *Billy Sunday* (1948), later restaged for the Ballet Russe de Monte-Carlo.

Ruth Page showed some of her work in Paris (1950) with a company called Ballets Américains. Her style shocked and surprised by its often daring realism and its frank humour. There was much controversy, but she was acclaimed in Paris in 1957 when she produced *Revanche* (*), her masterpiece, for the Ballets des Champs-Élysées. This was brilliantly decorated by Antoni Clavé, who has also designed *Susanna and the Barber* for her.

Her activities have been many and she is constantly in search of new ideas. A lively talker, she is happiest in the company of artists and has been able to commission interesting scores from Americans and handsome designs from Frenchmen. Her vitality is as remarkable as her youthful appearance and her generous hospitality.

LE PALAIS DE CRISTAL.
TWO COSTUMES BY LÉONOR FINI. 1947.

PALAIS DE CRISTAL Le (Symphony in C). Ballet by Balanchine. Music: Bizet (Symphony in C major). Scenery and costumes: Léonor Fini. First performance: Paris Opera, 28 July 1947. Principal dancers: Darsonval, Toumanova, Bardin, Lafon, Kalioujny, Ritz, Renault, Bozzoni.

Balanchine returned to Paris in 1947 to revive three earlier ballets for the Opéra and to mount —after only two weeks' preparation—this highly successful new work. Léonor Fini designed a baroque, architectural set, using the vast cyclorama as a backcloth. The four movements of Bizet's youthful symphony were danced by four groups of soloists and corps de ballet, each group clothed in bejewelled costumes of a predominating colour: red, blue, green, white. The whole cast of 56 dancers combined in the finale, a superb demonstration of classical dancing (and also of the choreographer's musicality). The ballet was conceived as a tribute to the Opéra ballet and the solo variations were, so to speak, made to measure.

* As *Symphony in C* the ballet was produced by Balanchine, without décor, for Ballet Society, New York City Center, 22 March 1948. Principal dancers: Maria Tallchief, LeClercq, Magallanes, Moncion. It remains in the repertory of the New York City Ballet.

* Revived by Royal Danish Ballet, 1953. Principal dancers: Inge Sand, Mona Vangsaa, Borge Ralov, Erik Bruhn.

PAPILLONS. Ballet in one act. Music: Schumann, orch. Tcherepnine. Scenery: Doboujinsky. Costumes: Bakst. Choreography: Fokine. First performance: Diaghilev's Ballets Russes, Monte Carlo, 16 April, 1914. Fokine danced the only male role, that of Pierrot; Karsavina was the Young Girl. A slight work in the vein of *Carnaval,* which broke no new ground but was an obstinate success.

PARADE. Ballet in one act. Scenario: Jean Cocteau. Music: Erik Satie. Curtain, scenery and costumes: Picasso. Choreography: Massine. First performance: Diaghilev's Ballets Russes, Théâtre du Châtelet, Paris, 18 May 1917. Principal dancers: Lopokova, Chabelska, Massine, Zverev, Woizikowski, Statkewicz.

Diaghilev had leisure enough during the war

REVANCHE. BALLET BY RUTH PAGE. COSTUME BY CLAVÉ.

years to sense that new artistic movements were crystallising and that for his return to Paris he must show them and not rely on pre-1914 Russian exoticism. With a sure instinct he chose a powerful team: Cocteau, Picasso and Satie. But *Parade* exacerbated the public even more than it would have done anyway because it came at one of the crucial phases of the war, when feelings in Paris were running the gamut from aggravated nationalism to resigned defeatism.

There was nothing in the subject itself to shock or surprise: one of the street "parades" in which the performers in a travelling circus appear one by one to do one of their numbers and attract the public inside. But if the subject was harmless, its unsentimental treatment was something new. Rival managers bawl enticements through megaphones but neither they nor the Chinese conjurer, the acrobats and the other "attractions" arouse any enthusiasm, and the self-confidence of the performers dwindles into anxiety, fatigue and disappointment. It is

LÉONOR FINI. PAS DE DEUX.

interesting to note that what shocked people most of all was not the more or less realistic conjurer and acrobats, not even the managers, fantastically clothed like cubist sculptures, but the horse, none other than our old circus friend with a loose skin and two pairs of human legs. In fact, the most familiar element caused the greatest surprise. From the point of view of theatrical technique, Picasso solved the problem of the relationship of actor to décor with the same brutal intransigeance that he brought to his painting. The managers' costumes, about nine feet tall, were virtually mobile scenery, but they nevertheless appeared far more "alive" than the dancers in their comparatively realistic costumes. The music contained its share of provocations too, incorporating some of the newer sounds of daily life, typewriters, aeroplane engines, hooters, etc. It was the radical reversal of normal values, the mixture of concession (presenting cubism, as it were, on a popular level) and provocation (the glorification of banalities) that so incensed the public. *Parade,* even if it now sounds rather tame and obvious, like so many things once considered shocking, remains a milestone, one of the works that changed the face of modern ballet.

PICASSO. THE MANAGER
FROM NEW YORK (PARADE, 1917).

PARIS OPERA BALLET. See *Opéra de Paris*.

PAS D'ACIER Le. Ballet in two scenes. Music: Prokofiev. Constructions and costumes after designs by Georges Yakoulov. Choreography: Massine. First performance: Diaghilev's Ballets Russes, Théâtre Sarah-Bernhardt, Paris, 7 June 1927. Principal dancers: Felia Doubrovska, Lubov Tchernicheva, Alice Nikitina, Massine, Serge Lifar, Leon Woizikowski.

Diaghilev's one attempt to come to terms with post-revolution Russia, where the painter Yakoulov had made his designs some years previously. Diaghilev was desperately curious about conditions there and discussed with Prokofiev the possibilities of a return visit. Prudence won the day. The two parts of *Le Pas d'acier* were of unequal value. The first showed a series of ineffective and unconvincing episodes from daily life. The second, in a double-tiered constructionist setting of the type used by Meyerhold, with mobile elements in the décor, was a glorification of the modern factory. Massine arranged the choreography (somewhat hampered by the setting) in block movements. In the finale the décor began to move as well: wheels whirred, pistons went in and out, lights flashed on and off. Movement and music increased in a breathless crescendo up to the fall of the curtain.

PATINEURS Les. Ballet in one act. Music: Meyerbeer, arr. Constant Lambert. Choreography: Frederick Ashton. Scenery and costumes: William Chappell. First performance: Sadler's Wells Theatre, London, 16 February 1937. Principal dancers: Harold Turner, Mary Honer, Elizabeth Miller, Margot Fonteyn, June Brae, Pamela May, Robert Helpmann.

A series of *divertissements* in a skating rink: snowy trees, screens of white trellis-work, hanging lanterns glowing in the dusk; fur-trimmed clothes and muffs. The music, salvaged from Meyerbeer's operas, has exactly the right tingling vivacity. Ashton devised his gay dances to exploit the growing technical capacity of the young Vic-Wells company, and in particular the brilliance of Mary Honer and Harold Turner. The display of youthful high spirits was composed with such skill and humour that *Les Patineurs* has remained in the repertory for twenty years, and its popular appeal shows no signs of fading. A larger cast and another skating rink, in the background, were introduced in 1956 when the Royal Ballet had expected to dance it in the giant Bolshoi Theatre.

* Revived by Ashton for Ballet Theatre, Broadway Theatre, New York, 2 October 1946. Scenery and costumes: Cecil Beaton. Principal dancers: John Kriza, Hugh Laing, Nora Kaye.

PAVILLON D'ARMIDE Le. Ballet in one act and three scenes. Scenario: Alexandre Benois, from Théophile Gautier's story *Omphale*. Music: Tcherepnine. Scenery and costumes: Benois. Choreography: Fokine.

Fokine produced one scene from this ballet, as *La Tapisserie Enchantée,* in April 1907 with

PARADE. DRAWING BY GEORGE BARBIER.

PARADE. CURTAIN BY PICASSO. 1917.

the pupils of the Imperial School of St. Petersburg. The full version was given at the Maryinsky Theatre under the new title on 25 November, with Pavlova, Gerdt and Nijinsky. It was included in the programme of the first performance of Diaghilev's Ballets Russes in Paris, 19 May 1909, with Karalli and Mordkin at the répétition générale and Pavlova and Fokine at the première. Nijinsky danced the part of the favourite slave. It was a transitional work, in which Fokine had not yet fully broken with the style of Petipa. Its great qualities and the magnificence of Benois's décors à la Louis XIV were eclipsed by the barbaric vigour and novelty of the dances from *Prince Igor* which followed it. One of the sets and some of the costumes were subsequently used for *Le Mariage d'Aurore.*

PAVLOVA Anna. One of the greatest, and certainly the most internationally famous, of all dancers. Anna Pavlova was a paradoxical figure, who had next to no influence on the artistic development of the ballet; yet, by her world tours, she did more than any single person to sow the seeds of the present widespread popularity of theatrical dancing.

She was born in St. Petersburg in 1882, a delicate child, brought up in poverty. A performance of *The Sleeping Beauty* at the Maryinsky Theatre, to which her mother took her as a Christmas treat, fired her with the ambition to become a dancer. When she was ten, she was admitted to the Imperial Theatre School, where her principal teachers were Johannson and Gerdt. She made her début at the Maryinsky, as première danseuse, in 1899; by 1906 she was prima ballerina, associated with the new ideas of Fokine, but still undergoing intensive study with the maestro Cecchetti. Following the example set by Taglioni, Pavlova began to make tours abroad, and in 1909 accompanied Diaghilev to Paris where, notably in *Les Sylphides,* she contributed to the company's sensational success. She appeared again with the Russian Ballet in Diaghilev's London season of 1911, but by this time she had made up her mind to go her own way at the head of her own company. She resigned from the Maryinsky Theatre after the season of 1913 and in the following year paid what was to be her last visit to Russia. During the war she toured the Americas with her company and starred in a full-length film, *The Dumb Girl of Portici*.

The war over, Pavlova returned to her London home (Ivy House, Hampstead, bought some years previously), which became her headquarters for the rest of her life. Here she would rest between tours, with her husband, Victor Dandré, her animals and her beloved and much photographed swans; ceaselessly planning, rehearsing, teaching and giving auditions. Her successive partners included Mordkin, Novikov, Volinine and Vladimirov. The Russian and Polish girls in her first company had been replaced by English dancers, who made up with their discipline and reliability for their lack of Slavonic fire. "Why do you always go about with your lips tucked in, expressing nothing?" she would complain. "Cry when you want to cry and laugh when you want to laugh". But she looked after her girls like a mother, and gave them a splendid training which some of them are still passing on to others; they rewarded her with loyal devotion. Few corners of the globe were left unvisited by Pavlova's company. They toured the whole American continent; the East, including Japan, China, India and Java; Australia and New Zealand; and, of course, Europe. Whatever the conditions, however primitive the theatre, however unsophisticated the public, Pavlova danced, and left an abiding memory.

To describe Pavlova's appearance is to describe the prototype of the Russian dancer: smooth, dark hair framing the pale, oval face, high cheek-bones, "eyes the colour of ripe, dark brown cherries", the head beautifully poised on a swan-like neck, the body straight, slim and supple, beautiful arms and superb insteps. Her features are familiar from a dozen rather indifferent paintings; the photographs, which record her range of facial expression, are more revealing. What did she dance? Some works from the old Maryinsky repertory, notably *Giselle*, but mostly ballets made for her, *The Fairy Doll, Autumn Leaves, Christmas, Oriental Impressions*. More typical, because in these she could shine alone, or with a chosen partner, were the short dances, evocations of a bygone period, of a mood of nature, a flower, or a living creature: *Gavotte*

Pavlova, Autumn Bacchanale, Californian Poppy, Dragonfly, and, most celebrated of all, *The Dying Swan*, which Fokine had arranged for her to Saint-Saëns's music as far back as 1905. The titles suggest *Kitsch*, and that is exactly what most of her repertory was, undistinguished in music and décor and often in choreography as well, but transformed and elevated by her genius to the highest degree of poetry and truth. Her dancing transcended technique, though she worked incessantly to master it. "Her body was a perfect instrument of expression; it would instantly respond to the mood of a dance, just as a tuning-fork vibrates to a blow" (C. W. Beaumont). So great was her personal magnetism that she could communicate the intensity of her feelings with equal ease to the hardened critic and the most naive spectator; like all really great performers, she could make the whole audience hang on to the slightest movement.

All this could have been at the service of Diaghilev, but Pavlova and he, the two most powerful personalities in the world of the dance, met in a headlong clash of irreconcilable opposites. Diaghilev's influence was achieved by a

LE PAVILLON D'ARMIDE. COSTUME BY BENOIS.

ANNA PAVLOVA.

calculated appeal to the intelligentsia of Paris, London, Monte Carlo and a few more European cities. Pavlova knew that her mission was to take the Dance to the whole world, and she was adored by audiences incomparably larger than Diaghilev reached or would have cared to reach. She remained uninfluenced by and even hostile to the modern trends which Diaghilev did so much to encourage. But whatever her views on Art, the Dance was her province, and no aspect of it, old or new, escaped her notice. Wherever she went, she sought out and studied genuine traditional dancing; she worked with Japanese teachers and with the great Indian dancer, Uday Shankar. She left behind her a trail of young girls, and boys as well, determined to become dancers. Even today, her name is not only a legend but an inspiration to the young; children are still learning to dance because their mothers saw Pavlova years ago.

As a woman, she was single-minded, perfectly aware of her supremacy, yet mercilessly self-critical: nothing distressed her more than an ovation for what she knew, by her standards, to have been an indifferent performance. The ceaseless travelling exhausted her and aggravated her quick temper and tyrannical ways, but it was Pavlova who worked the hardest of all and who often practised alone in darkened theatres after the others had gone home. She died in 1931, at the Hague, at the outset of yet another tour. Her powers had hardly shown any signs of failing, and she was spared the misery of decline and the long years of retirement.

PEINTRE ET SON MODÈLE Le. Ballet in one act. Music: Auric. Scenery and costumes: André Balthus. Choreography: Massine. First performance: Ballets des Champs-Élysées, Paris, 9 November 1949. Dancers: Irène Skorik, Youly Algaroff. A vehement and acrobatic pas de deux with a lively score and an original décor: an artist's studio with walls made of empty frames. The painter tries unsuccessfully to capture his elusive model and put her in a frame.

PELLÉAS ET MÉLISANDE. Ballet by Jean-Jacques Etchevery. Music: Gabriel Fauré. First performance: Enghien Festival, 13 June 1953. Principal dancers: Geneviève Kergrist, Michel Rayne.

Based on the incidental music written by Fauré for Maeterlinck's play. An austere and original conception in which Noverre's *ballet d'action* is refined and spiritualised to the point of amalgamation with the abstract ballet. The décor is formed by groups of dancers in black tights who represent in turn the castle walls, a gateway, a boat and Mélisande's bier. The love scenes and the death of Mélisande are treated allusively, but the choreography nevertheless is powerfully expressive and, in the scene where Golaud and Pelléas are reconciled over Mélisande's body, intensely pathetic.

PERETTI Serge. A pupil of the Paris Opera school who became in 1941 the first male dancer to receive the title of "étoile", hitherto reserved for the fair sex. A true danseur noble, with an impeccably clean and brilliant style, who could afford to underline his perfect mastery with a touch of irony. His *Tambourin* (Rameau) was a gem of pure classical dancing. Peretti shone in all the important new ballets produced at the Opéra in the period between the wars, from *Les Créatures de Prométhée, Salade* and *La Vie de Polichinelle* to *Le Chevalier et la Damoiselle* and *Joán de Zarissa*. In 1944 he was appointed maître de ballet and in 1945 produced his own ballet, *L'Appel de la Montagne*. Shortly afterwards he retired and is now teaching.

PÉRI La. Ballet in one act. Music: Paul Dukas. Scenery and costumes: René Piot. Choreography: Ivan Clustine. First performance: Théâtre du Châtelet, Paris, 22 April 1912 with Natasha Trouhanova.

ANNA PAVLOVA IN THE DYING SWAN.

The Péris of oriental legend are immortal beings, messengers of the spirit and of light. In this tale, one of them is robbed of the lotus of eternal youth by the Prince Iskender. However, for love of the Péri, he hands back the talisman and she is able once again to ascend into the heavens. The theme had already been used in the Romantic period, notably in a ballet by Gautier, Coralli and Burgmüller (Paris Opera, 1843; Carlotta Grisi and Lucien Petipa). Diaghilev planned to use it for a new ballet by Fokine with music by Dukas and décor by Bakst, but was unwilling to accept Trouhanova, the composer's choice, as the principal interpreter. Accordingly she presented it herself in 1912, with choreography by Clustine. Pavlova revived this version in 1921 at the Paris Opera. In the same year the Opéra's own company produced a new version by Léo Staats which remained in the repertory for some time and was danced in 1931 by Spessivtseva and Peretti.

* Lifar made a new version in 1946 for the Nouveau Ballet de Monte-Carlo. It was taken into the repertory of the Paris Opera two years later, and became one of Chauviré's most distinguished interpretations.

* In England, Ashton has made two versions of the ballet, the first for the Ballet Club (16 February 1931, Markova), the second for the Sadler's Wells Ballet (Covent Garden, 15 February 1956, Fonteyn and Somes). This version, an extended pas de deux, was subsequently modified. The original setting by Ivon Hitchens was abandoned. The present décor and costumes are by Levasseur.

PERRAULT Serge. A brother of Lycette Darsonval, and like her a pupil of the Paris Opera. His most distinguished work has been done outside that organisation. He took part in Petit and Charrat's recitals in 1944 and danced with the Ballets des Champs-Élysées in 1946. In the following year he and Colette Marchand left the Opéra to lead the Metropolitan Ballet. In 1948 he created the role of the Toreador in Petit's *Carmen* (Ballets de Paris), in 1951 the male lead in Charrat's *Grieg Concerto* and in 1953 the Dandy in Petit's *Deuil en 24 heures*. He is a sound classical dancer whose sense of comedy and unselfconscious, nonchalant charm make him an admirable interpreter of character parts.

PERUGINI Giulio. Italian classical dancer, born in Rome. A pupil of Ettore Caorsi and Gennaro Corbo he is now premier danseur at La Scala, Milan, and a backbone of the ballet company. He regularly partners guest ballerinas who appear there and has also created leading roles in many new productions.

PETIPA Marius (1822-1910). His dates proclaim him a man of the 19th century, but he has left his mark on our own time and no survey of modern ballet can ignore him. Petipa's long career forms a direct link between Vestris and Diaghilev. He saw the fusion of the French and Italian schools of dancing out of which came the Russian school and, through the influence of the Ballets Russes, the rebirth of ballet in the Western world. His own works still occupy an important place in the modern repertory. He was born at Marseilles. Both his father Jean and his elder brother Lucien were well known dancers and choreographers; his mother, Victo-

DANCERS BY DEGAS.

THE SLEEPING BEAUTY. COSTUME BY BAKST FOR PAVLOVA.

rine Grasseau, had been an actress. Marius, following in the family's footsteps, made his début as a dancer at the age of nine, at the Théâtre de la Monnaie in Brussels. At sixteen he was premier danseur and maître de ballet at Nantes, where he made his first attempts at choreography. Lucien, meanwhile, had been engaged by the Paris Opera, and the family joined him in the capital, where Marius became a pupil of Vestris. In 1840 he made a highly successful appearance at the Comédie-Française, partnering Carlotta Grisi at a gala benefit performance for the great actress, Rachel. He became premier danseur at the Bordeaux Opera and then at the Royal Theatre in Madrid, but had to leave Spain after a duel with a French diplomat. For a short time he returned to Paris, but his father had been appointed to the Imperial Theatre in St. Petersburg and Marius soon followed him there. He arrived in Russia on 20 May 1847 and remained there for the rest of his life. He married in succession two

Russian dancers, Marie Sourovtchikova and Lubov Leonidovna. The daughter of the first marriage, Marie M. Petipa, also became a dancer.

The prestige of French maîtres de ballet and choreographers had already been established in Russia by Didelot, Duport and several others. Marius Petipa soon showed that he was an excellent premier danseur and a strict but efficacious teacher, but since the great Jules Perrot was in charge at St. Petersburg and there were guest choreographers such as Saint-Léon, it was many years before he was able to produce ballets of his own at the Imperial Theatres. In 1858 he became maître de ballet. His first great success was La Fille du Pharaon (1862); thereafter he established himself more and more firmly in the saddle and from 1869 onwards his position at the Imperial School and Theatres, as sole arbiter of new ballets and revivals, engagement and promotion of dancers, was unchallenged for nearly forty years.

At this period the choreographer had despotic control not only over the music of his ballets but over every aspect of the production. The composer worked directly to his orders, following a detailed plan with requests for "lively music . . . a touch of fantastic colour . . . so many bars for a grotesque dance . . . " and so on. The music was duly composed, to the choreographer's specification, at the piano, and only rarely did the orchestration, when it was completed, serve to disguise the poverty of the initial inspiration. Scenery and costumes were "executed", without much attempt at style, by craftsmen who were specialists in trompe-l'œil. The dancing itself was suffering from academic anaemia. Male dancing was practically non-existent: a little discreet partnering, almost entirely confined to "lifts", some mime and character roles, the latter usually comic. Petipa began to vary the ensembles with solos and pas de deux in addition to the role, hitherto preponderant, of the ballerina. He gave full play to the ballerina's virtuosity, but allowed some scope to the other soloists as well; mime began to play an increasingly subservient role to pure dancing. Perhaps Petipa had less dramatic imagination than Perrot and Saint-Léon, but as an inventor of "pas" he was unsurpassed, and many of his brilliant pas de deux and solo variations remain today, in and out of their context, as

MARIUS PETIPA.

touchstones of the art of the classical dancer.

Oddly enough, the most successful period of Petipa's career was ushered in by an event which appeared at first to threaten his authority: the arrival in St. Petersburg about 1880 of the Italian stars, Zucchi, Legnani, Brianza and Cecchetti, whose dazzling, acrobatic style infused new life into theatrical dancing. Enrico Cecchetti, with his impressive pirouettes and jumps, revealed to the St. Petersburg public unsuspected possibilities in male dancing. Petipa, brought

Petipa's disposal, was providentially to hand. The result of their collaboration were the three masterpieces, *The Sleeping Beauty* (1890), *Casse-Noisette* (1892), *Le Lac des Cygnes* (1895), the last two in collaboration with Ivanov. Petipa was beginning to delegate some of his work (though his assistant, Ivanov, was not always given credit for his share) but if the lion was old, his claws were still powerful. One of his last works, *Les Millions d'Arlequin* (1900), showed remarkable rejuven-

MARYINSKY THEATRE, St. PETERSBURG.

up in the pure French classical tradition, had reservations about the new technique, but its success with the public forced him to accept it. And so, with exemplary skill and taste, the old master set himself to blend French grace and elegance with Italian fire and brilliance. From this union, aided by the physical and temperamental aptitude of the Slavonic artists, sprang the Russian style which Diaghilev was the first to reveal to western Europe.

Another new development at that time turned out to be a blessing in disguise. The post of composer of ballet music to the Imperial Theatres was suppressed, and the line of obedient musical hacks, of whom Pugni and Minkus were perhaps the least unworthy, was extinguished. But Tchaikovsky, who was prepared to put his genius for melody and orchestration faithfully at

ation, but his task was practically finished.

A new generation, Pavlova, Karsavina, Fokine, was preparing to take over from Preobrajenska, Kschessinska and Trefilova. Male dancing was to be reborn, brilliantly, with Vaslav Nijinsky. New trends in music and in all branches of theatrical art were in the air. The younger and more progressive public was won over by Isadora Duncan and by the music of Debussy and Strauss. In painting, Bakst, Benois and Golovine were beginning to assert themselves. Petipa's most gifted pupils, Fokine, Legat, Gorsky, considered their master outmoded, and were mounting experimental ballets in smaller, unofficial theatres. Prince Volkonsky, the director of the Maryinsky, supported the modern movement and had more than one clash of opinion with the ferocious old guardian of the classical tradition, but Volkonsky's replacement by Teliakovsky made things no easier for Petipa; he was retired in 1904, published his memoirs two years later and died, still in St. Petersburg, in 1910.

It was the end of a fabulous life. He had provided his adopted city with 54 new ballets, 17 revivals and the dances for 34 operas. Furthermore he had bridged the gap between romantic and modern ballet and in doing so had prepared the way for the Russian Ballet, with all its consequences.

PETIT Roland. Born at Villemomble, near Paris. As a child he used to dress up, recite and dance to the mechanical piano in his father's brasserie. At the age of nine he joined the class of Gustave Ricaux at the Paris Opera. He was an impatient, unruly, insatiably curious pupil, with a passion for jazz, the cinema and the theatre, and he suffered accordingly from the strict and monotonous discipline. At 16 he entered the corps de ballet. An elegant dancer, with a noble carriage, long slim legs and individual physique, his pale face framed by black curly hair, he was clearly designed for romantic and heroic roles. Serge Lifar had taken him under his protection and it was due to him that Petit created the role of Carmelo in *L'Amour Sorcier* (1943). He had been associated with Janine Charrat since 1941, and with her had made his début as choreographer and producer in the recitals which they gave together during the war. In 1944, when Paris was liberated, Roland Petit left the Opéra, and towards the end of the year organised the famous "Soirées de la Danse" at the Théâtre Sarah-Bernhardt, which led to the formation of the Ballets des Champs-Élysées.

His choreography for *Les Forains* (*) in March 1945 brought him fame overnight, and placed him at one bound at the head of the younger generation of French dancers. With Kochno and Irène Lidova, he founded the Ballets des Champs-Élysées (*) in October 1945, and he remained as their director, maître de ballet and leading dancer until the end of 1947. For them, he created *Le Rendez-vous* (*), *La Fiancée du Diable*, *Les Amours de Jupiter* (*), *Le Jeune Homme et la Mort* (*), *Treize Danses*, *Le Bal des Blanchisseuses* (*). He then decided to

found a new company over which he would have absolute control, and thus was born the Ballets de Paris (*). In the ensuing eight years he produced a series of brilliant new ballets, including *Les Demoiselles de la Nuit* (*), *L'Œuf à la Coque* (*), *Carmen* (*), *La Croqueuse de Diamants* (*), *Le Loup* (*), *Deuil en 24 Heures* (*), *La Chambre* (*) During this period Petit visited Hollywood to do film ballets for Renée Jeanmaire and Leslie Caron. He also began to turn his attention to the music-hall, and seemed to withdraw more and more from pure ballet.

Roland Petit differs from other choreographers in that his ballets need his own presence, his own dancers and his own particular "ambiance". Apart from *Ballabile* (Sadler's Wells Ballet, 1950), he has worked only for his own companies. He has never produced large-scale, spectacular works or handled a large corps de ballet; he prefers small, concentrated ballets and likes to build them round the personality of his dancers. He cares for the immediate impact

ROLAND PETIT BY COCTEAU.

Hommage
à Christian Bérard
et Henri Sauguet

Valentine Hugo

Entrée d'Hélery Pagava et de Roland Petit dans "Les Forains"

VALENTINE HUGO. PAGAVA AND PETIT IN LES FORAINS. 1946.

only and is not troubled by long-term policies. His ballets are not confined to dancing alone; his company are expected to mime and, on occasions, to sing. His style has been compared to champagne; it has also been called melodramatic. Certainly both the style and the man thrive on contrasts: himself he can be at once frivolous and serious, passionate and cruel. His training at the Opéra gave him a solid technical foundation, but the rest he has learned from everyday life, from newspapers, magazines and films. He knows the world from touring with his company, literature from plays, art from the décors of his ballets. Like a true child of the people, he is self-educated. Though he loves his profession, he fears and shuns the world of ballet with its sacrifices, drudgery and poverty. He wants to popularise ballet and adapt it to the needs of our time, he loves the sensational and flatters public taste. He works to please himself and hates any form of constraint; loves the unexpected, detests inactivity. He conceives his ballets himself from beginning to end; his musical feeling is impeccable. He uses dancing, never as an abstract language, but as a vehicle for portraying emotions—desire, suffering, love. He seasons classical movements with gestures drawn from life: his dancers smoke, telephone, take a shower, without disturbing the unity of the style. He constructs admirable *adages* and erotic pas de deux, frank without being offensive. His choreography is economical; nothing is wasted, every gesture tells. In spite of the sensational aspect of his work, he is a genuine choreographer working on a solid foundation of knowledge and experience, and he has had considerable influence on his younger contemporaries. He is no revolutionary, but he has skilfully used all the theatrical resources at the disposal of a modern choreographer to express a fascinating personality.

PETROUCHKA. Burlesque scenes in four tableaux by Igor Stravinsky and Alexandre Benois. Music: Stravinsky. Scenery and costumes: Benois. Choreography: Michel Fokine. First performance: Diaghilev's Ballets Russes, Théâtre du Châtelet, Paris, 13 June 1911. Principal dancers: Tamara Karsavina, Vaslav Nijinsky, Alexander Orlov, Enrico Cecchetti.

Petrouchka originated in the mind of its composer as a short piece in the manner of a *Konzertstück* for piano and orchestra, in which the solo instrument suggested an animated puppet furiously combating the orchestra with "diabolic arpeggios"; the band responding with "menacing fanfares" and finally subduing the poor puppet. According to Stravinsky himself, his search for a suitable title ended with the sudden realisation that the real subject was the puppet Petrouchka, a kind of traditional Russian equivalent of the English Punch. By other accounts, it was Diaghilev who thought of the title when Stravinsky first played him the music. In any case it is clear that Diaghilev immediately realised its possibilities for ballet and was thereby consoled for Stravinsky's failure to begin work on *Le Sacre du Printemps,* the agreed subject for the successor to the *Firebird.* The new piece became the second scene of the ballet as we now know it. Benois, who was asked to design the décor and to amplify and complete the scenario, insisted that Stravinsky's name should appear with his own as part-author. The choreography was entrusted to Fokine. Collaboration was close and, though not without incident, gloriously successful.

The scene is St. Petersburg, 1830, in the Carnival which precedes Lent. The Butter Week fair is being held in Admiralty Square. The crowd of townsfolk and peasants, in spite of the bitter cold, is enjoying the sideshows: gipsy fortune tellers, rival street dancers. The sound of a drum calls attention to a curtained booth in the middle of the stage. The old showman appears and displays to the crowd his three puppets: the pretty, doll-like Ballerina, the sad-faced, insignificant Petrouchka, and the splendid Moor, dressed in green and gold satin. They enact a little scene in which Petrouchka and the Moor are rivals for the Ballerina's love. After a blackout, we are shown Petrouchka's cell. There he bemoans his fate, his hopeless love for the Ballerina, his subservience to his master the Showman, and his sentient heart inside a puppet's body. The Ballerina visits him, but her agitated delight frightens her away. Next we are shown the cell of the Moor. He is playing idly with a coconut; when he fails to crack it with his scimitar he believes it must be sacred and accordingly worships it. When the Ballerina arrives, to execute a flirtatious dance with a toy trumpet, he makes an easy conquest, but they are interrupted by the lovelorn Petrouchka. The Moor speedily despatches him. Another blackout, and then the scene returns to Admiralty Square. The light is failing, but the merrymaking is in full swing. Coachmen and nursemaids dance together, carnival figures erupt through the crowd, a drunken merchant throws away his money, and soon it begins to snow. Suddenly the crowd becomes aware of tumult behind the curtains of the puppets' booth. Out runs Petrouchka, pursued by the Moor and the Ballerina. Struck down by the Moor's scimitar, Petrouchka dies in the snow. The crowd, horrified by the tragedy, call for the Showman, but he picks up the body and reveals it as no more than a puppet of sawdust. The merrymakers drift away from the scene. The Showman slowly makes his way homeward, dragging the puppet behind him. Suddenly he hears ghostly laughter; above the booth appears the ghost of Petrouchka, defying him for the last time. Terrified, the Showman runs from the scene. The figure of Petrouchka becomes inanimate again and swings helplessly over the edge of the booth as the curtain falls.

Fokine's choreography was a complete success, contrasting brilliantly the massed movement and dancing of the crowd with the solo

HIGHTOWER AND GOLOVINE IN PETROUCHKA.

passages for the three puppets. The dancing is not virtuoso but intensely expressive. The first and last scenes seethe with life; every kind of character is present, from aristocrats to stable boys. The main "streams of movement" are prescribed but there are limitless opportunities for the individual dancers to develop the characters they play. The roles of the three puppets are more precisely defined; while not allowing them real humanity, Fokine brings out their different natures. The Moor is indolent and stupid, the Ballerina is pert and silly, Petrouchka is awkward, inarticulate but broken-hearted. Benois's setting and his costume designs for the multitude of characters at the fair did much to give life to the ballet. In addition, the first performances had the advantage of Nijinsky's extraordinary interpretation of Petrouchka, a character he in some ways resembled (although in fact he had difficulty in remembering the steps and was prompted from the wings by Fokine at the first performance).

An undisputed masterpiece, *Petrouchka* has conquered the world. Diaghilev kept it constantly in his repertory and it has since been revived by most of the world's big companies. No other choreographic version has approached Fokine's. Among important revivals have been those by Bolm (Metropolitan Opera New York, 1919); Fokine (Royal Danish Ballet, 1925); Nijinska (Colon, Buenos Aires, 1932); Fokine (Monte-Carlo Ballet, 1936); Zverev and Lifar (Paris Opera, 1948); Beriosoff (Festival Ballet, London, 1950); Nijinska (de Cuevas company, Paris, 1953); and finally Grigoriev and Techernicheva (Royal Ballet, London, 1957).

PHÈDRE. Tragedy for dancing by Jean Cocteau. Music: Georges Auric. Scenery and costumes: Jean Cocteau. Choreography: Serge Lifar. First performance: Paris Opera, 14 June 1950. Principal dancers, Tamara Toumanova, Lifar.

Racine's tragedy retold by Cocteau in terms of dancing. His décor, at first sight childishly simple, was in reality a brilliant solution of the problem. He used a small, raised stage within a stage on which curtains parted to reveal *tableaux vivants* representing episodes, e.g. the death of Hippolyte, which in Racine are described but not seen. Phèdre trailed a great red cloak; each of the other characters wore a simple costume in one distinctive colour, with wig to match. Lifar's choreography, as usual, avoided straightforward mime yet

PETROUCHKA. COSTUME BY BENOIS FOR A STREET DANCER. PARIS OPERA. 1947.
Bibliothèque-Musée de l'Opéra, Paris.

contrived to make the story clear. Auric's music had a dramatic force very different from the light-hearted gaiety of his scores for Diaghilev. Toumanova was a superbly striking Phèdre.

PICASSO Pablo. Born at Malaga, 1881. An artist so avid for experiment with new forms and techniques as Picasso was bound sooner or later—in Paris, at least—to try his luck in the theatre. What he did there was, as usual, disconcerting to conventional minds, who were so disturbed by the fresh impact of his designs that they could not perceive the underlying respect for and understanding of what was valuable in the work of the past. Picasso accepted the convention of the picture-frame stage with the imaginary "fourth wall", but he put it to all sorts of fresh uses.

His first work for the theatre was the highly controversial *Parade* (1917), an attempt to penetrate beyond outworn conventions to the profound reality of things and objects even to the extent of deliberately emphasising the banality of common objects. *Parade* was duly hissed by the people who would neither forego the chance of being seen anywhere where the work of cubist painters was on show nor fail to jeer at it. As a matter of fact, though *Parade, Pulcinella* and *Tricorne* seemed so new, in none of them did Picasso invent radically new forms of theatrical scenery. The apparent novelty was due to his original way of defining space and depth by means of strong linear constructions, emphasising the distance between flat surfaces and colours by means (notably in *Pulcinella*) of intersecting planes and wilful distortions of traditional perspective. An example of his acceptance of theatrical artifice was his use, in *Cuadro Flamenco*, of a stage within a stage to isolate, and thus give additional importance to, a small group of dancers.

Picasso is one of the few modern designers who have seriously studied the relationship between the performer and the scenery. His costumes, even when they are mainly naturalistic, as in *Tricorne*, always play an active role in the total effect of the décor. In two ballets they have gone further. The "managers" in Parade were not so much characters in the ballet as mobile decorative elements, a kind of liaison between the scenery and the dances. In

PULCINELLA. DÉCOR BY PICASSO. 1920.

Mercure he depersonalised the dancers to the highest possible degree, disguising them by means of flat constructions made of cardboard and wire.

The strange world of his cubist paintings seemed stranger still in the theatre and its brutal intransigeance even more difficult to accept there than on canvas. But though each new stage design from his hand appeared at first to be unacceptable, the strong impression left on the spectator's mind underwent a gradual transformation. As the effects of the brutal but

PICASSO. DANCERS. 1919.

salutary shock wore off, it became clear that there was no going back and that henceforward conventional designs would look pale by comparison. And so Picasso's contribution to the theatre has been of the same quality as his work in other branches of art. In quantity, it has been limited to a handful of experiments, largely because even in Paris the theatre depends ultimately on the general public which will not accept innovations wholeheartedly until they have passed into common currency.—Décors for Diaghilev: *Parade* (1917), *Le Tricorne* (1919), *Pulcinella* (1920), *Cuadro Flamenco* (1921), drop-curtain for *Le Train bleu* (1924). For "Les Soirées de Paris": *Mercure* (1924). In 1946 he designed a drop-curtain for *Le Rendez-vous* (Ballets des Champs-Élysées).

PIED PIPER The. Ballet by Jerome Robbins. Music: Aaron Copland (Clarinet Concerto). First performance: New York City Ballet, 4 December 1951. Principal dancers: Janet Reed, Todd Bolender, Melissa Hayden, Tanaquil LeClercq, Jerome Robbins.

Copland's concerto is dedicated to Benny Goodman. In the ballet, the soloist walks on to the bare stage (there is no décor) and takes up his position to one side. As he begins to play, dancers appear in practice costume and dance to his music. The concerto is in two movements, slow and fast, joined by a cadenza for the soloist. The first is lyrical, the second full of rhythm. Both are eminently danceable, as Robbins's gay and subtle choreography shows. The animation on the stage grows as more and more dancers are involved up to the final curtain. *The Pied Piper* is a brilliantly simple idea, carried out with exhilarating skill.

PIÈGE DE LUMIÈRE. Ballet in three scenes. Scenario: Philippe Hériat. Music: Jean-Michel Damase. Scenery: Felix Labisse. Costumes: André Levasseur. Masks: Marie Molotkoff. Choreography: John Taras. First performance: Grand Ballet du Marquis de Cuevas, Théâtre de l'Empire, Paris, 23 December 1952. Principal dancers: Rosella Hightower, Wladimir Skouratoff, Serge Golovine.

The scenario of this original and fantastic ballet, about escaped convicts hiding in virgin forest and catching exotic insects for a living, was the work of the novelist, Philippe Hériat. The décor by Labisse strikingly suggests a world of shadows where tropical plant and animal life mysteriously coalesce; the undertones of savagery are dramatically conveyed by Damase's music. When the curtain rises, a new, young fugitive joins the gang. As night falls, the men erect a light trap, a pyramid-shaped structure, to attract the insects. Immediately they are drawn to it from the surrounding darkness, beautifully coloured butterflies among them, fluttering helplessly round the trap until they are caught on it and picked off by the convicts. Two of the insects, an Iphias and a Morphide, are in love, but they too are captured; the Iphias struggles with the young convict to save the Morphide; he dies, but smears the convict's bare chest with his pollen.

He is transformed into an Iphias. The most spectacular scene is the procession of convicts dragging the inert, captured butterflies. Taras cleverly contrasts the strength of the hunters with the fragility of the insects, the music rises to a barbaric grandeur, and the mood is sustained by Levasseur's butterfly costumes which contrive to be at once timeless and superbly elegant.

PIERNÉ Gabriel. French conductor and composer, born 1863, died 1937. He conducted one ballet for Diaghilev, and that a distinguished one, *L'Oiseau de feu* (1910), but his own ballet music was written for the two national companies in Paris. His most important ballet was *Cydalise et le Chèvre-pied,* tenderly and ironically pastoral (Opéra, 1923). Also for the Opéra were *Impressions de music-hall* (1927) which contained some skilful examples of musical parody and *Images* (1935) written expressly for the pupils. *Giration* (1934) was performed at a gala at the Opéra-Comique.

PILLAR OF FIRE. Ballet in one act. Music: Arnold Schönberg. Scenery and costumes: Jo Mielziner. Choreography: Antony Tudor. First performance: Metropolitan Opera, New York, 8 April 1942. Principal dancers: Nora Kaye, Annabelle Lyon, Lucia Chase, Hugh Laing, Antony Tudor.

A psychological drama danced to Schönberg's *Verklärte Nacht,* which was based on a German poem called *Woman and the World.* The period is "the turn of the century". A young woman, Hagar, fears that she will lose the man she loves to her flirtatious younger sister. She is terrified of being left an old maid, like her elder sister, and gives herself to a man she does not love. The episode brings her nothing but shame and misery; then, in the midst of her despair, the man she loves returns to her with sympathy and understanding. The ballet ends with the lovers walking away into the forest, their shoulders touching. *Pillar of Fire* is probably Tudor's masterpiece, an extension of the method first used in *Jardin aux Lilas* to express through movement the strain and stress of emotional upheaval. Superbly interpreted by Nora Kaye, it established her as a dramatic ballerina and made Tudor's name in America.

PICASSO. STUDY FOR THE CURTAIN FOR LE TRICORNE. 1919.

PIPER John. An English painter and designer (born 1903) of marked versatility and, at his best, remarkable imaginative power. He began as an abstract painter but has become a neo-romantic with strong affiliations to the English landscape painters of the early 19th century. His work for the Sadler's Wells companies includes *The Quest* (Ashton, 1943), the 1948 revival of de Valois' *Job* and a number of ballets for Cranko, of which *Harlequin in April* (1951) is perhaps the most distinguished and the sets for *The Prince of the Pagodas* (1957), embracing a rich assortment of technical devices and a partial return to his abstract manner, certainly the most ambitious. Other examples were *Sea Change* (1949) and *The Shadow* (1953). Piper has also done notable work for Britten's English Opera Group.

PLISSETSKAYA Maya. A ballerina of the Bolshoi Theatre Ballet, remarkable for her beauty, her brilliant technique and her passionate personality. She comes from a dancing family; trained at the Bolshoi and graduated in 1944. Her arms are exceptionally eloquent, her long legs beautifully proportioned, her whole body expressive. Her sensitive face reflects every nuance of emotion and her dancing is young and feminine. Her elevation is unequalled, her movements beautifully controlled and very musical. She is always in perfect accord with her partner. A romantic dancer *par excellence* she is a superb Aurora in *The Sleeping Beauty,* magnificent Zarema in *The Fountain of Bakhchisarai,* a delightful Quiteria in *Don Quixote.* But her finest role is Odette-Odile in *Le Lac des Cygnes.* She dominates the stage, performs prodigies of technique, but never sacrifices the quality of her characterisation. She is a profoundly moving Odette, and a dazzling Odile. One of her teachers remarked: "You cannot say 'she dances well' or 'she acts well'. Her performance is a complete synthesis of choreography, music and acting."

POKER GAME. See *Jeu de Cartes.*

POOLE David. South African dancer, who started with the Cape Town Ballet Club and joined the Sadler's Wells Theatre Ballet in 1947. Intelligence, sensitivity and rare ability as a mime (particularly as Pierrot in *Le Carnaval),* soon brought him to the status of principal dancer. In 1956 he joined Ballet Rambert for a time, then worked with Jooss in Germany and returned to South Africa in 1957. In 1958 returned to Europe to take part in Ballets Premières at the Edinburgh Festival.

POULENC Francis. Poulenc's ballet music shows the lighter side of his nature, affectionate, ironical and tender. As a member of Les Six, he contributed to their joint production, *Les Mariés de la Tour Eiffel,* in 1920. Diaghilev drew from him one of his best works, the score for *Les Biches* (1924), a period piece which has lost none of its charm. *Aubade* (1929), a short ballet which has been much performed, is a chamber concerto for piano and 18 instruments. His most recent ballet is *Les Animaux modèles* (Paris Opera, 1942). Poulenc's engaging music, with its rhythmic vivacity and bitter-sweet charm, has made a strong appeal to choreographers, who have made considerable use of

PLISSETSKAYA IN LAC DES CYGNES.

works written for other purposes. Examples are: Jean Borlin's solo *Sculpture Nègre* of 1929 (Rhapsodie Nègre), Ashton's *Les Masques* in 1933 (Trio for piano, oboe and bassoon), Walter Gore's *Paris-Soir* (1939) and *Hoops* in 1953 (both piano music, the latter orch. Leighton Lucas).

PREOBRAJENSKA Olga. When she applied, as a child, for admittance to the Maryinsky ballet school in St. Petersburg, she was nearly rejected on medical grounds, but she became, with Kschessinska and Trefilova, one of the great Russian stars of the early part of the century. She joined the corps de ballet in 1889, and became prima ballerina nine years later, by which time she was an established popular favourite, well able to hold her own with the visiting stars from Milan. Preobrajenska was small and infinitely graceful, with an enchanting smile and eyes sparkling with intelligence. Her technique was perfection itself, she had a rare feeling for music, her gestures were eloquent and her movements beautifully pre-

cise. Each enchaînement was a work of art.

She was loved and respected not only by the public but by her colleagues for her personal qualities and for the example she set of single-minded devotion and hard work. She danced almost the whole of the classical repertory: *Coppelia, La Fille mal gardée, Paquita, La Belle au bois dormant, Raymonda, Le Talisman*. She made numerous tours in Europe and America, including a season with Diaghilev at Monte Carlo in 1911.

Since her early years she has been a great teacher and her charm and wit on stage are evident also in the class-room. She taught at the State School in Petrograd from 1917 to 1921, and from 1924 up to the present time in Paris. Among her most famous pupils are Baronova and Toumanova, but there are few dancers, indeed few ballerinas, of today who have not worked with her in the famous Sudios Wacker.

PRÉSAGES Les. Choreographic symphony in four movements. Music: Tchaikovsky

LES PRÉSAGES. DÉCOR BY ANDRÉ MASSON. 1933.

(Fifth Symphony). Scenery and costumes: André Masson. Scenario and choreography: Massine. First performance: Ballets de Monte-Carlo, 13 April 1933. Principal dancers: Nina Verchinina, Irina Baronova, Tatiana Riabouchinska, David Lichine, Leon Woizikowski.

The first of Massine's symphonic ballets. *Les Présages* inaugurated a new chapter in the history of ballet, but one which could claim Viganò as an 18th century predecessor. The ballet has the same general, allegorical theme as the symphony: man's struggle with fate. There is no story, and no characters, only symbols —Action, Passion, Fate, Frivolity, the Hero. Massine composed a remarkable visual and plastic equivalent to the intensely dramatic music; the choreography seemed to flow out of the music, not to be imposed upon it. It was particularly notable how solo variations or pas de deux were welded into the complex ensembles without disturbing the flow of movement. Masson's highly-charged décor was in danger of overwhelming the dancers (some critics preferred the ballet in practice dress) but though emphatic, it was not out of key; in fact the work was remarkable for the close correlation of mood between dancing, décor and music. *Les Présages* proved a wonderful vehicle for the young company and revealed the astonishing precocity of its soloists. Woizikowski's experience was invaluable in the brief but incisively dramatic interventions of Fate.

PRINCE IGOR. See *Dances from Prince Igor.*

PRINCE OF THE PAGODAS The. Ballet in three acts. Music: Benjamin Britten. Scenario and choreography: John Cranko. Scenery: John Piper. Costumes: Desmond Heeley. First performance: Sadler's Wells Ballet, Covent Garden, London, 1 January 1957. Principal dancers: Svetlana Beriosova, Julia Farron, David Blair, Leslie Edwards.

Cranko's fantastic fairy-tale is spread over three acts, each with substantial divertissements, filled with endless choreographic invention but attenuating the interest. On the whole, the skill rather than the feelings of the distinguished collaborators appears to have been involved. There are moments of beguiling brilliance and a long scene in the second act (where the Prin-

cess Belle Rose arrives in the Land of the Pagodas) where music, décor and dancing combine to give an impression of enchanted exoticism. The ballet was seen to greater advantage in the 1958 season, by which time certain alterations had been made.

* New version with choreography by Alan Carter, scenery and costumes by Fabius Gugel, Munich State Opera, 17 March 1958.

PRISONNIER DU CAUCASE Le. Ballet in three scenes based on Pushkin's poem. Music: Khatchaturian (from the *Gayaneh* ballet music). Scenery and costumes: Doboujinsky. Choreography: Skibine. First performance: de Cuevas Ballet, Théâtre de l'Empire, Paris, 4 December 1951. Principal dancers: Marjorie Tallchief, George Skibine.

A Russian officer fighting the Circassians is taken prisoner; he is rescued by a Circassian girl. He escapes, and she stabs herself in despair, having lost her love and betrayed her country. An eagle hovers over her body as the curtain falls. The first scene (the battle) is full of leaps, turns and sabre thrusts. After the officers's capture there is an impressive slow march of the captives. The second scene, in the Circassian camp, has wild victory dances in the manner of *Prince Igor*. The final scene is elegiac rather than epic, a long pas de deux for the lovers. The ending, with the officer's escape and the girl's suicide, is swift and dramatic. One of the best of the de Cuevas company's new productions.

* There have been various Russian versions of the same story, including one by Lavrovsky, with music by Asafiev (Maly Theatre, Leningrad, 1938).

PRODIGAL SON The. See *Fils Prodigue, Le.*

PROKOFIEV Serge (1891-1953). The composer relates in his autobiography that his mother offered him a holiday abroad as a reward for his excellent work at the St. Petersburg Conservatoire. Fortunately for him his choice settled on London, where Diaghilev was giving his London season; the date was 1914. He was duly introduced, and Diaghilev asked him to write a ballet on a subject from Russian

PROKOFIEV BY GONCHAROVA.

country and became involved in the polemics which beset Soviet composers. During the ensuing years he wrote two more ballets, both large-scale works: *Romeo and Juliet* (1940) and *Cinderella* (1945). The aggressive vitality had died down and the bright colours were somewhat paler, but the style, with its side-slipping harmonies and straightforward rhythms, remained the same. Just how much political pressure really affected Prokofiev's development, it is too soon to say. The enfant terrible had become a middle-aged man, and, unlike Stravinsky, he was an instinctive rather than an intellectual artist (he had a more spontaneous gift of melody than the greater master has ever possessed). Though they are unequal, the two big works are big indeed by the side of most recent ballet scores. Among other works by Prokofiev which have been used for ballet are the *Classical Symphony* (Tudor's *Gala Performance,* 1938), *Peter and the Wolf* (Bolm, Ballet Theatre and Staff, Cambridge Arts Theatre, both 1940) and the suite *Lieutenant Kijé* (Fokine's *Russian Soldier,* Ballet Theatre, 1942).

legend. Prokofiev, whose mind was occupied with an opera on Dostoievsky's *The Gambler,* was not enthusiastic. "Opera is a dying artform" objected Diaghilev, " ballet is the thing now". And there the matter seemed to end. Prokofiev returned to Russia, but the idea began to germinate. He returned to Western Europe again the following year and saw Diaghilev in Rome, where they discussed new plans which culminated some years later in the ballet *Chout* (1921), after the composer's *Ala and Lolly,* later arranged as an orchestral suite, had been rejected. Prokofiev spent the years 1923-33 based on Paris, composing and touring—he was an excellent pianist. During this period he wrote two more ballets for Diaghilev, *Le Pas d'Acier* (1927) and *Le Fils Prodigue* (1929), which was the company's last new production. The time for picturesque, national legends was over; the former was an impression of a Soviet factory, the latter (one of Prokofiev's finest works) was based on the biblical parable. In 1932 he wrote *Sur le Borysthène* for Lifar and the Paris Opera. Two years later he, who had become so prominent a figure in the Western musical world, returned definitely to his native

PRUNA Pedro. Painter and stage designer, born in Barcelona. Pruna's clear colours, pure line, and taut atmosphere lose none of their uneasy tension in the theatre, and seem to acquire an additional coldness. The footlights reveal a world of controlled violence, a violence expressed in elementary contrasts that owe something to folk art. The result is a somewhat devitalised limpidity, of which *Les Matelots* (Ballets Russes, 1925) was the best example. Pruna's other décors include *La Pastorale* (Diaghilev Ballet, 1926), a revival of *Les Matelots* (Ballets de Monte-Carlo, 1933); and, at the Paris Opera, *La Vie de Polichinelle* (1934), *Le Roi Nu* (1936), *Oriane et le Prince d'amour* (1938).

PULCINELLA. Ballet in one act. Music: Stravinsky, after Pergolesi. Curtain, scenery and costumes: Picasso. Choreography: Massine. First performance: Diaghilev's Ballets Russes, Paris Opera, 15 May 1920. Principal dancers: Karsavina, Tchernicheva, Nemchinova, Massine, Idzikowski, Zverev, Cecchetti.

The subject is taken from a manuscript of

1700 found by Diaghilev in Naples, which contained various comedies relating to the traditional character of Punchinello. Stravinsky relates. in his memoirs that the working-out of the ballet was particularly difficult, necessitating long discussions between Massine, Diaghilev, Picasso and himself. It is based on a typical commedia dell'arte theme of amorous intrigue, full of disguises, beatings and duckings. Massine produced an impression of high spirits and good humour through adroit use of classical virtuosity: double tours en l'air, entrechats and fouettés, which give irresistible vitality to the title-role. Picasso's décor was a perfect example of economy and simplification. The setting —blue, white and black—represented a perspective of houses by the sea, as simple as a folding screen, yet full of light and air and space. Pulcinella wore a loose white smock with red vest and black mask; an effective contrast with the foppish elegance of the neatly tailored costumes and plumed hats of the cavaliers. The music, as well as the scenario, was the result of Diaghilev's antiquarian browsing. The tunes and fragments he had unearthed in Italy and in London (modern scholarship has thrown doubt

on their authorship, but they remain splendid tunes) were put to wonderful use by Stravinsky, who welded them into a brilliant score that is far more than pastiche.

Q

QARRTSILUNI. Ballet in one act. Story and music: Knudage Riisager. Scenery and costumes: Svend Johansen. Choreography: Harald Lander. First performance: Royal Theatre, Copenhagen, 21 February 1942. Principal dancer: Niels Bjørn Larsen.

The theme of this ballet was suggested to Knudage Riisager by reading the story of a Greenland expedition by the Danish explorer, Knud Rasmussen, which explains in a collection of folk-tales that the word Qarrtsiluni means the calm preceding a great event that is about to take place. In the ballet the event awaited is the return of the sun to the Eskimos after six months of total darkness. The principal rôle is that of the sorcerer, Angekokken, and it is under his impetus that the tribe's dancing grows more and more frenzied, to reach its peak as the sun appears above the mountains.

Qarrtsiluni shows a primitive ritual as did *Le Sacre du Printemps* but the style and character of the dance makes it a profoundly original work. It was revived under Lander's direction at Palermo in 1949 and has also been faithfully produced by Jean Weidt.

R

PULCINELLA. DRAWING BY PICASSO. 1918.

RADICE Attilia. One of Italy's greatest dancers. Born 1913, she entered the school of La Scala, Milan, at the age of ten and studied with Gini and Cecchetti. Eventually she be-

PULCINELLA. DÉCOR BY SEVERINI. VENICE, 1940.

came prima ballerina assoluta of La Scala and won a considerable reputation abroad. Svelte and immaculate, she is as much a star off-stage as on. Now prima ballerina at the Opera in Rome, she is also a sound teacher.

RAKE'S PROGRESS The. Ballet in six scenes. Scenario and music: Gavin Gordon. Choreography: Ninette de Valois. Scenery and costumes: Rex Whistler. First performance: Sadler's Wells Theatre, London, 20 May 1935. Principal dancers: Alicia Markova, Walter Gore, Harold Turner.

Several of de Valois's ballets have been inspired by pictures: this one was based on the series of engravings by Hogarth. In six scenes which blend dance and mime with economy and dramatic force, we watch the young gentleman dissipate his fortune in riotous living, whoring and gambling, until he dies miserably in the mad-house. Every stroke in the choreography tells; only the faithful, insipid betrayed girl refuses to come to life. The final scene in Bedlam can still, after more than twenty years, chill an audience to the bone. Rex Whistler's décor wonderfully caught the sober elegance of 18th century London. Gordon's music, though

it has no claim to originality, fits the action like a glove. Gore, Helpmann and Poole have been outstanding among the many interpreters of the title-role.

RALOV Borge. Danish dancer and choreographer, the first in the history of the Royal Danish Ballet to receive the title First Solo Dancer (1942). Born in Copenhagen, he entered the Royal Ballet School in 1918, and became a soloist in 1933. A great stylist, he was as good in the classics and the works of Fokine as in the Bournonville ballets. His Albrecht in *Giselle,* his Petrouchka, his Spectre of the Rose, his poet in *Les Sylphides* were all outstanding. Perhaps his most famous role was that of Gennaro in *Napoli* which he danced until his farewell performance in 1957; his interpretation ranks with those of Bournonville and Hans Beck. Choreographer of *Widow in the Mirror* (1934), *Twelve with the Mail Coach* (1942) and *The Courtesan* (1953), he is also a good teacher and now works largely for Danish television.

RAMBERT Marie. Born in Warsaw in 1888 as Myriam Ramberg, Marie Rambert has had as varied and unusual a career as any dancer of our time. Early in the present century she went to Paris to study medicine, but became interested in the theories of Jacques Dalcroze and began to study with him. In 1912, when Nijinsky was rehearsing *Le Sacre du Printemps,* Diaghilev engaged her to help his dancers disentangle Stravinsky's complex rhythms. While she worked with the Ballets Russes she, the exponent of Dalcroze eurhythmics and a passionate admirer of Isadora Duncan, developed an abiding love for the classical ballet and started to study again, but this time with Enrico Cecchetti. After the war, Marie Rambert settled in London, where she married the dramatist, Ashley Dukes, and soon opened her own school of dancing. By the mid-twenties her pupils were giving recitals, and in 1926 she danced herself in *A Tragedy of Fashion,* the first work by a young pupil of hers called Frederick Ashton, decorated by a young designer called Sophie Fedorovitch. She continued to dance certain roles after the founding of the Ballet Club a few years later, but it is as a teacher, and as a vital influence on successive generations of young dancers, choreographers and designers in her adopted country that Marie Rambert will be remembered.

As a teacher, Rambert has a real love of technique and will exclaim with joy over an intricate step perfectly executed, but her greatest contribution has been in the moulding of interpretative artists. No Rambert dancer worthy of the name has ever lacked understanding of his or her role, and Rambert's gift for production, and for instilling an appreciation of meaning and style, deserves to be employed by the world's larger companies. Her infectious enthusiasm and her gift for detecting latent talent in shy or diffident young people have been of inestimable value to the ballet in England. A woman of wide culture, Marie Rambert has an instinctive appreciation of new developments in painting, literature and the theatre and of their potential application to the dance; it is possible that her outlook was widened by her early experience outside the range of classical ballet (see also *Ballet Rambert*).

RAVEL Maurice (1875-1937). In a tribute published after Ravel's death, Serge Lifar described the composer's work as "une musique parfaitement dansante", but pointed out that, strictly speaking, Ravel had written only one ballet. This is not so paradoxical as it may seem. Ravel's music abounds in dance forms and dance rhythms, but a dance, even a dance on the scale of *La Valse* or *Boléro* does not in itself make a ballet, which has become, since the days of Diaghilev, a microcosm of which the music is only one element. Ravel's music is written with such immense care, is so polished and so self-sufficient that the most accomplished choreography is apt to seem superfluous. Nevertheless he had no objection to his works being used for ballet and himself made orchestral versions of some of them for that purpose, thus *Ma Mère l'oye* (Théâtre des Arts, Paris, 1911; later versions include Cranko's *Beauty and the Beast,* 1949), *Valses nobles et sentimentales* (as *Adélaïde, ou le langage des fleurs,* Trouhanova, Châtelet, Paris, 1912; later versions include Lifar, Paris Opera, 1938 and Ashton, Sadler's Wells Theatre Ballet, 1947, original title) and *Le Tombeau de Couperin* (Ballets Suédois, 1920). There have been innumerable versions of the *Pavane pour une Infante défunte* and other short piano pieces have similarly figured in the programmes of dance recitals. Andrée Howard used the Introduction and Allegro together with the Alborada del gracioso for *Mermaid* (Ballet Club, 1934).

Ravel's masterwork for the ballet, of course, is *Daphnis et Chloé,* conceived in the early days of the Diaghilev venture and finally produced in 1912. *Daphnis* is one of the finest scores ever commissioned by the Russian Ballet or any other company, but here again Ravel's self-sufficiency is evident; from the theatrical point of view it would have benefitted from closer cooperation between composer and choreographer. A further ballet for Diaghilev was projected but did not materialise. Ravel offered him *La Valse,* a "choreographic poem" originally entitled *Wien* and begun in 1917, but he astutely divined the same disadvantage and declined it. Ravel was mortally offended and when he met Diaghilev at Monte Carlo in 1925 during the rehearsals for the opera *L'Enfant et les sortilèges* (Balanchine was arranging the dances for artists from the Russian Ballet) refused to shake his hand. Diaghilev was furious and contemplated a duel, but at the end of his life, growing tired of the "musiquette"

284

which the younger composers were providing for him, he thought of turning to Ravel once again. *La Valse* was produced by Ida Rubinstein, with choreography by Nijinska, in 1929. She remounted it in a new version by Fokine in 1931; subsequent versions have been made by Balanchine (New York City Ballet, 1951) and Ashton (La Scala, Milan, 1958). The famous *Boléro* was also written for Rubinstein (1928). She had asked Ravel to orchestrate some pieces by Albéniz, but the rights had been given to the Spanish composer, Arbos. *Boléro* was composed instead, in an ill humour. Here again, the self-sufficiency is noticeable: one of Ravel's biographers, Hélène Jourdan-Morhange, has pointed out that he treats the solo instruments of the orchestra as if they were ballerinas themselves; the real ones have little to add. A curious point about *Boléro* is that neither in speed nor character does it resemble the classical Spanish bolero.

REED Janet. A tiny American dancer with a huge personality. Born in Oregon, she was a soloist at the San Francisco Opera before joining Eugene Loring's Dance Players. For Ballet Theatre she created roles in *Fancy Free, Undertow, On Stage !* and *Tally-Ho*—all character parts. Yet her classical technique is strong and in San Francisco she danced the first full-length production of *Swan Lake* to be given in the United States. Joining New York City Ballet in 1950 she showed her ballon in *Symphony in C* and her gifts as a comédienne in *Bourrée Fantasque* and *Pied Piper*.

REICH George. An American dancer and choreographer, who works in Paris, where he directs his own company Ballet Ho, with which he tours the music-halls. Formerly premier danseur with Roland Petit's Ballets de Paris. His work has real inventiveness and provides excellent material for the acrobatic brilliance of his small but select group of dancers. He has also appeared in the film *La Garçonne*.

RELÂCHE. Ballet in two scenes by Francis Picabia, with a film entr'acte by René Clair. Music: Erik Satie. Scenery: Picabia. Choreography: Jean Borlin. First performance: Ballets

MAURICE RAVEL BY BENOIS.

Suédois, Théâtre des Champs-Élysées, Paris, 4 December 1924.

Relâche was the swan song of the Ballets Suédois, and a rather sad one. The painter Picabia had the upper hand. He was at that time a member of the dadaist school; the ballet was intended to annoy, and annoy it did. *Relâche* was typical of the Ballets Suédois in the supremacy given to the designer and in the desire for modernity at all costs, but like many of their productions, it had its compensations. The film entr'acte, which marked the début as director of the young René Clair, was a remarkable piece of avant-garde cinema.

RENARD. Burlesque ballet with voices, in one act. Text and music: Igor Stravinsky. Scenery and costumes: Larionov. Choreography: Nijinska. First performance: Diaghilev's Ballets Russes, Paris Opera, 18 May 1922. Principal dancers: Nijinska and Idzikowski.

A fable about a cock who, after some narrow

escapes, outwits a cunning and greedy fox. Stravinsky wrote *Renard* in Switzerland during the first war when, though his music was moving rapidly away from the "Russian" style of his early works, he was still deeply engrossed in Russian folklore. There are four singers, two tenors and two basses, in the orchestra pit. The small orchestra includes a cimbalom.

RELÀCHE. FRONTISPIECE FOR SATIE'S SCORE BY PICABIA. 1924.

The work was written for the Princess Edmond de Polignac, at whose house Diaghilev first heard it. The Russian Ballet presented it in the style of a fairground entertainment in a décor by Larionov almost as simple and restrained as Goncharova's for *Les Noces*. Nijinska herself danced the title-role; it was her first complete ballet for Diaghilev. Revived in 1929 with new choreography by Lifar (his first ballet) and revised décor by Larionov. Lifar doubled the dancers with acrobats, dressed in identical costumes and masks, undistinguishable to the audience.

* New version by Fedor Lopoukov, Academy Theatre, Leningrad, 1929.

* New version by Balanchine for the Ballet Society, with scenery and costumes by Esteban Francés, New York, 1947.

RENAULT Michel. A Parisian dancer, trained by Gustave Ricaux and Serge Peretti. He has had a meteoric career at the Paris Opera since he became a danseur-étoile there at the age of 18 years, in 1947. Renault has a strong, if rather flamboyant technique, and is more at ease in the light sparkling rôles than in the romantic repertoire. His handsome Latin looks and temperament, dazzling charm and lively, spirited personality have endeared him to the French public. He has created numerous roles at the Opéra during the last six years, including *Études, Nautéos, Roméo et Juliette* and has danced in revivals of *Sylvia, Elvire, Salade, Guignol et Pandore, Le Chevalier et la Damoiselle, Mirages*. In 1957 he succeeded Serge Lifar as Albrecht in *Giselle,* and danced the role with success in Leningrad and Moscow when he visited Russia as Daydé's partner in 1958.

RENCONTRE La (Œdipe et le Sphinx). Ballet in one act. Scenario: Boris Kochno. Music: Henri Sauguet. Scenery and costumes: Christian Bérard. Choreography: David Lichine. First performance: Ballets des Champs-Élysées, Paris, 8 November 1948. Principal dancers: Leslie Caron, Jean Babilée.

Cocteau had already treated the myth of Oedipus in his play, *La Machine Infernale*. This time he and his designer, Christian Bérard, set the tragedy against the unusual background of an open-air, acrobatic circus. At the back, a monumental archway set in a low, curved wall. In front of it, the sphinx reclined on a giant trapeze of red plush, suspended and secured by ropes, and connected to the ground by rope ladders. It was one of Bérard's most striking sets. Lichine suggested the battle of wits between Oedipus and the monster by means of sober, elliptical choreography based on acrobatics. The defeated sphinx (Leslie Caron, in white, all-over tights) was left at the end hanging head downwards from her trapeze. Babilée was a formidable Œdipus.

RENDEZ-VOUS Le. Ballet in one act and three scenes by Jacques Prévert. Music: Joseph Kosma. Drop curtain: Picasso. Scenery: Brassaï. Costumes: Mayo. Choreography: Roland Petit. First performance: Théâtre

RENARD. CHOREOGRAPHIC SKETCHES BY LARIONOV.

Sarah-Bernhardt, Paris, 15 June 1945. Principal dancers: Marina de Berg, Roland Petit, Daniel Seillier.

Performed at one of Petit's Soirées de Danse which preceded the foundation of the Ballets des Champs-Élysées. *Le Rendez-vous* was taken into the repertory of the new company, and Babilée subsequently danced the role of the hunchback. It was the successor to *Les Forains,* and Petit's second important work; a sombre and rather sentimental story of the back streets of Paris, powerfully reinforced by Brassaï's photomontage décor. A young man meets the loveliest girl in the world, but destiny steals her from him and he goes to his death. It was in this ballet that Petit first showed his gift for erotic pas de deux; he also used mime and realistic gesture. Kosma's score included a song, "Les Portes de la Nuit", which was used later in Marcel Carné's film of that name.

LE RENDEZ-VOUS. DRAWING BY MAYO.

REVANCHE. Ballet in four scenes, with a prologue. Scenario: Ruth Page and Nicolas Remisov. Music: Verdi (from *Il Trovatore*). Choreography: Ruth Page. Scenery and costumes: Antoni Clavé. First performance: Ballets des Champs-Élysées, Théâtre de l'Empire, Paris, 17 October 1951. Principal dancers: Sonia Arova, Jacqueline Moreau, Wladimir Skouratoff, Gérard Ohn.

Like Petit in *Carmen,* Ruth Page took her music and her subject from a famous opera. The story of *Il Trovatore,* notoriously melodramatic and extravagant, makes a complicated but eventful ballet scenario. Ruth Page's choreography could not be said to equal Verdi's music, but it had some striking passages and the designs of Clavé ensured the ballet's success.

RIABOUCHINSKA Tatiana. Fair and delicately built, with swift, precise movements, Tatiana Riabouchinska was one of the three "baby ballerinas" engaged by René Blum and de Basil for the first season of the Ballets de Monte-Carlo in the spring of 1932. Young as she was, Riabouchinska had already danced in Paris and New York before joining the Monte Carlo company. A second generation dancer, she was a pupil of Mathilde Kschessinska to whom perhaps she owed her aristocratic style and

her stage presence. She had a special gift for evoking the wonders of childhood and for suggesting a fragile, ineffable gaiety. On 14 April 1932 she created the Child in *Jeux d'Enfants* and had her first personal triumph. She was partnered by David Lichine who later became her husband. As the Young Girl in *Le Beau Danube,* Rosina in *Scuola di Ballo,* Frivolity in *Les Présages,* the Florentine Beauty in *Paganini,* the Golden Cockerel in *Coq d'Or,* the Junior Girl in her husband's *Graduation Ball,* and also in the Prelude of *Les Sylphides* she will never be forgotten. She has danced with Ballet Theatre, the Original Ballets Russes (in London in 1947), the Ballets des Champs-Élysées and many other companies. Now living in California, she supervises the dance education of her daughter Tania.

RICARDA Ana. Born in San Francisco, she studied classical dancing with Legat, Vladimiroff, Celli and Volinine, and Spanish dancing with Argentina, Escudero and La Quica. A fragile, elegant dancer she personifies refinement rather than an ardent temperament. Composed her first ballets for the Metropolitan Opera in New York, where she was première danseuse from 1941-46, and also danced with the Markova-Dolin company in America. In 1949 she joined the de Cuevas company and mounted *Del Amor y de la Muerte*. Since then she has composed for this company *Dona Ines de Castro* (1952), *Tertulia* (1952), and *The Song of Unending Sorrow* (1957). A tireless researcher, she goes to great pains to ensure the historical accuracy of her ballets.

RICAUX Gustave. His career as a dancer was ending as Spessivtseva's sojourn at the Paris Opera began. A brilliant premier danseur he was also a first-class teacher and through his professional classes handed on the pure French style to many generations of dancers. Peretti, Brieux, Petit and Babilée were but some of his pupils. He retired in 1951 and now lives quietly in a village in the south of France.

RIETI Vittorio. Born in Alexandria (Egypt) of Italian parentage in 1898. Studied in Milan, and in Rome under Respighi. His fluent, lively, unequal music combines Parisian chic with more robust Italian qualities. His first ballet was *Noah's Ark* (1923). He wrote two for Diaghilev: the choral *Barabau* (1925) and *Le Bal* (1929). During the composition of the latter, Diaghilev asked Rieti to make so many alterations that, in delivering the manuscript, the composer ironically asked him to accept the dedication. Rieti contributed to the composite score of *David Triomphant* (Paris Opera, 1937), one of Lifar's experiments in "rhythmic ballets". In 1939 he settled in New York. Since the war he has written *Le Triomphe de Bacchus et Ariane* (1948) and *La Licorne* (1948), but the most important of his recent works for ballet has been the arrangement of the Bellini music for *Night Shadow* (New York, 1946). Balanchine also used music by Rieti (a series of waltzes) for his *Waltz Academy*, first produced by Ballet Theatre in 1944.

RIMSKY-KORSAKOV Nicholas Andreyevitch (1844-1908). If we except the dances in his many operas and the excellent schooling he gave to his pupil Stravinsky, Rimsky's contribution to the ballet was, though considerable, entirely posthumous. He reluctantly accepted to conduct some of his own works in Diaghilev's 1907 concerts in Paris, but that was before the formation of the ballet company. After his death, an excerpt from the opera *Mlada* was used in the composite score of the ballet *Cléopâtre*, and a complete opera, *Ivan the terrible*, with Chaliapin in the title-role, also figured in the Paris season of 1909. In the next year came what was to become his most celebrated contribution to the ballet repertory, the symphonic suite *Sheherazade*, shorn of its third movement and saddled with a new scenario which had next to nothing to do with the original. The result was undeniably effective, and the music intended to portray the shipwreck of Sinbad did very well for the scenes of massacre in the harem. *Sheherazade* marked a step forward in the use of concert music for ballet. For the 1911 season, Fokine used the sea-bed scene from the opera *Sadko*. In 1913, Diaghilev mounted Mussorgsky's opera *Khovanschina*, which Rimsky-Korsakov had completed. Two operas were included in the next year's programmes, *A Night in May* and *Le Coq d'or*, the latter being arranged by Fokine entirely in mime and dancing with the singers in the orchestra pit. With Gon-

RIABOUCHINSKA AND MASSINE
IN LE BEAU DANUBE.

289

charova's radiant designs, this was one of Diaghilev's most brilliant productions. In 1915, the young Massine made his début as choreographer with *Le Soleil de Nuit,* for which he used music from yet another opera, *The Snow Maiden.*

A large number of other companies and choreographers have laid Rimsky-Korsakov under contribution: Fokine for *Igrouchki* in 1921 (Fantasy on Russian themes for violin and orchestra); Nijinska for *La Princess Cygne* (1928). De Basil revived *Le Coq d'or* in 1937 in a shortened version, without singers, the music arranged by Tcherepnine. Finally, Massine used the *Capriccio Espagnol* for his ballet of that name in 1939.

ROBBINS Jerome. Now in his fortieth year (he was born in New York in 1918), Robbins is the most gifted and influential of the younger American choreographers. He spent a year at New York University before devoting himself to the theatre. He studied classical ballet with Tudor, investigated the techniques of modern, oriental and Spanish dancing, learned to play both the piano and the violin and took a course in acting with Elia Kazan. In 1940 he joined Ballet Theatre and remained with the company until 1944, rejoining for the London season of 1946. His dancing triumphs were in character roles—in *Aleko, Petrouchka, Helen of Troy, Three Virgins and a Devil*—but he made his name with his first ballet *Fancy Free* (*). This was one of the greatest successes in modern ballet and he followed it up the next year with the equally brilliant and extrovert *Interplay* (*). Afterwards came *Facsimile* (*) and when he joined the New York City Ballet he pursued this more introspective vein in *The Guests* (1949), which deals with social ostracism, and *The Age of Anxiety* (1950) based on Auden's poem.

A witty, lively and tremendously popular choreographer of musicals *(On the Town, Miss Liberty, The King and I, West Side Story)* he is also Associate Artistic Director of the New York City Ballet (since 1949) and has made for that company ballets of many different styles. He is almost alone among choreographers in being able to turn from psychological themes to erotic dramas *(The Cage)* (*) and thence to light-hearted, jazzy works such as *Pied Piper* (*) and *Jones Beach.* In *Fanfare,* danced to Britten's Young Person's Guide to the Orchestra and presented in New York as a tribute to Queen Elizabeth II on Coronation Night, 1953, he made a plotless ballet in pure classical style yet enlivened with his own bright humour. Perhaps the most emotionally mature of his ballets is *L'Après-midi d'un faune* (*), which retains the essential Debussy, rejects the mythology of Mallarmé and captures the very spirit of young America.

More visual and less abstract than Balanchine, he nevertheless resembles the master in his knowledge of music and in the importance he accords to the lines of movement. He cares about the sufferings of humanity as well as about the arrangement of classical steps, and although he can improvise brilliantly he can also express with deep sympathy the joys and woes of ordinary people.

RODEO or **The Courting at Burnt Ranch.** Ballet in three scenes. Book: Agnes de Mille. Music: Aaron Copland. Scenery;

THE IMMORTAL KOSTCHEI. COSTUME BY GONCHAROVA. 1934.

RODEO. DÉCOR BY OLIVER SMITH. 1941.

Oliver Smith. Costumes: Kermit Love. Choreography: Agnes de Mille. First performance: Ballet Russe de Monte-Carlo, Metropolitan Opera, New York, 16 October 1942. Principal dancers: Frederic Franklin, Agnes de Mille.

The ballet, set in the American South-West, deals with the problem that has confronted every woman from earliest times — how to get her man. A tomboyish Cow Girl sighs for the Head Wrangler, is persuaded by the Champion Roper to discard her breeches for a scarlet frock, becomes the belle of the local ball and is eventually carried off by the Champion Roper himself. The choreography mixes some lively evocations of riding and roping at the rodeo with a square dance interlude (complete with "caller"), some sentimental episodes and an exhilarating Saturday night social for the finale. Copland's score, vigorous yet tuneful, is abundantly theatrical with many hints of American folk songs. Oliver Smith's settings admirably capture the "Western" atmosphere of the Ballet.

* Revived for the American Ballet Theatre, 1950, with John Kriza and Allyn McLerie.

RODRIGUES Alfred. South African dancer and choreographer, trained first by Cecily Robinson in Cape Town, now resident in London. Rodrigues is not much interested in abstract dance; he likes themes of a strong dramatic nature or else clearly prescribed stories. *Ile des Sirènes* (1950), *Blood Wedding* (1953), *Café des Sports* (1954) and *The Miraculous Mandarin* (1956), all of which he staged for the Royal Ballet, are full of incident. In Italy, he has mounted three full-length ballets, *Romeo and Juliet* (Prokofiev) in Verona in 1955, *Cinderella* (Prokofiev) at La Scala, 1955, and *Casse-Noisette,* at La Scala in 1957. His sense of the theatre sometimes leads him to stress production at the expense of choreography, but his style is individual and in marked contrast to other young choreographers in England, such as Cranko and MacMillan.

ROERICH Nicolas. Born St. Petersburg 1874, died New York 1947. One of the Russian painters whom Diaghilev introduced to the Western world. Roerich was an authority on Central Asia and on pagan Russia; his designs for *Prince Igor* and for *Le Sacre du Printemps* have an authenticity and a noble simplicity which makes them, in the former case at least, virtually irreplaceable. There is a museum in New York devoted to his work.

ROI NU Le. Ballet in four scenes by Serge Lifar, after Hans Andersen, Music: Jean Françaix. Scenery and costumes: Pedro Pruna. Choreography: Lifar. First performance: Paris Opera, 15 June 1936. Principal dancers: Yvette Chauviré, Serge Lifar, Paul Goubé.

The story of the Emperor's New Clothes.

* New version by Ninette de Valois for the Sadler's Wells Ballet, 7 April 1938. Scenery and costumes: Hedley Briggs. Principal dancers: Pearl Argyle, Robert Helpmann, Harold Turner.

ROMANOV Boris. Dancer and choreographer: born St. Petersburg 1891, died New York 1957. A pupil of Fokine at the St. Petersburg Imperial School, engaged at the Maryinsky Theatre in 1909. Small and well-built, with lively, Mongolian features and a warm and exuberant temperament. He was quickly recognised as an exceptional character dancer. He was engaged by Diaghilev in 1913 to do the choreography for La Tragédie de Salomé (*) and, in the following year, the dances in Stravinsky's opera Le Rossignol (see Chant du Rossignol). He returned to Russia as maître de ballet and choreographer for the operas at the Maryinsky, but left again to found his own company, the Théâtre Romantique Russe, which opened in Berlin in 1921 and subsequently toured Europe. He was the sole choreographer; his ballets included Le Trapèze, Arlequinade and a new version of Giselle which had a great success in Paris in 1924. He worked subsequently at La Scala, Milan (1925), Buenos Aires, Rome, Monte Carlo and Turin. In 1938 he went to America and settled in New York, where he taught and for some years was maître de ballet at the Metropolitan Opera.

ROMEO AND JULIET. Shakespeare's star-cross'd lovers have inspired innumerable ballets, of which only a few can be mentioned here.

In the spring of 1924, for the Soirées de Paris at the Théâtre de la Cigale, Jean Cocteau mounted an astonishing version which blended theatrical dancing with the ideas of such Russian producers as Tairov, Meyerhold and Vakhtangov. Although a financial failure, and not strictly speaking a ballet, the production was a landmark in theatrical history.

Among purely choreographic versions the most complete and most convincing is that by Leonid Lavrovsky, planned in collaboration with the composer, Prokofiev, which was first produced at the Kirov Theatre in Leningrad on 11 January 1940 with Ulanova as Juliet, Sergeyev as Romeo, Koren as Tybalt and Andrei Lopoukhov (brother of Lydia Lopokova) as Mercutio. Later, in 1946, Lavrovsky restaged and revised this production for the Bolshoi Ballet in Moscow. The whole work is conceived in terms of "acting dance" so that it is not possible to say where acting stops and dancing begins. The action follows Shakespeare almost scene by scene and yet the ballet does not become tedious, for ensemble and solo passages are wonderfully contrasted; magnificent spectacle gives way to tiny, intimate scenes; occasionally a huge, soft curtain comes swirling down to isolate just one or two characters, then the whole stage will be opened up on a realistic representation of a street in Verona or the palace of the Capulets. Perhaps no other company than that of the Bolshoi could sustain such a work. Ulanova's Juliet, a complete fusion of movement with music, is justly celebrated, but the ballet retains its tragic beauty when other dancers appear in this role.

* The same music by Prokofiev was used by Frederick Ashton for a three act ballet (shorter than the Soviet one) which he produced for the Royal Danish Ballet in Copenhagen on 19 May 1955. Scenery and costumes were by Peter Rice. Mona Vangsaa and Henning Kronstam danced the principal roles. While the Soviet version was conceived as a whole —it has been described as a rich renaissance fabric with Ulanova's Juliet flowing through it like a golden thread—Ashton's version concentrates on the lovers and therefore on the more intimate episodes. The balcony scene, and the farewell pas de deux for Romeo and Juliet in the latter's bedroom, are among Ashton's most beautiful compositions. The ballet is popular in Copenhagen and was acclaimed in New York when danced there in 1956.

* Shorter versions to the Prokofiev score have been made by Birgit Cullberg in Stockholm (1944), and by Serge Lifar at the Paris Opera, 29 December 1955. The latter was in two acts and ten episodes, with costumes and scenery by Wakhevitch, Liane Daydé and Michel Renault in the principal roles. Despite, or perhaps because of, the cuts, this new version seemed long-winded and verbose. It has since been modified but still contains too much useless and puzzling detail. The choreographer seemed to be interested only in the 'principals and the character of Friar Lawrence, which he himself danced at the opening performance.

* More successful has been Lifar's ballet *Romeo and Juliet* to Tchaikovsky's fantasy-overture of the same name. Made originally for the début of Ludmilla Tcherina, 16 June 1942, at the Salle Pleyel, it was revived at the Paris Opera in 1949, with décor by Moulène, for Chauviré and Kalioujny.

* The Tchaikovsky music was also used by George Skibine for his first ballet, *Tragedy at Verona,* presented by the Grand Ballet du Marquis de Cuevas on 4 May 1950 with Pagava

and Skibine, décor by Delfau. Birger Bartholin used it for his *Romeo and Juliet,* presented at the Royal Theatre, Copenhagen, 8 December 1950, with Vangsaa and Bruhn.

* The *Romeo and Juliet* best known to American audiences (and also seen in Europe) is that by Antony Tudor to music by Delius (arr. Dorati) which was presented by Ballet Theatre at the Metropolitan Opera, New York, on 6 April 1943, with scenery and costumes by Eugene Berman. The choice of music may seem surprising. Tudor selected Over the Hills and Far Away, The Walk to the Paradise Garden (from the opera *A Village Romeo and Juliet*), Eventyr, the prelude to the opera *Irmelin,* and Brigg Fair. These pieces were played straight through, in that order. Yet in the theatre this essentially English music married most happily with the beautiful renaissance designs of Berman. It was an exquisite work, perfectly interpreted by Markova, Hugh Laing, Nicholas Orlov and Tudor himself.

* On 28 June 1955 the de Cuevas company presented a *Romeo and Juliet* in the Cour Carrée of the Louvre. This was an opulent production by Jean-Pierre Grenier, which employed no less

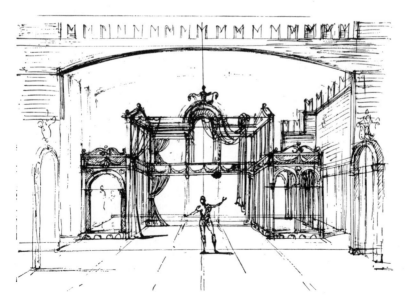

EUGENE BERMAN. SKETCH FOR ROMEO AND JULIET. 1943.

than four choreographers: Taras, Skibine, Golovine and Skouratoff. The music was by Berlioz, décor by François Ganeau, and costumes by Léonor Fini.

* Diaghilev, in the mid-twenties, presented a *Romeo and Juliet* which had nothing to do with Romeo or Juliet. To music by Constant Lambert, with surrealist decorations by Max Ernst and Joan Miró, it was a kind of parody, described as "a rehearsal in two parts without scenery". Karsavina and Lifar appeared as two dancers in love who are rehearsing a ballet about Romeo and Juliet. They arrive late for the rehearsal and escape before the end — by aeroplane. The choreography was by Nijinska and the designs caused enough controversy to give the work a certain notoriety.

ROUAULT Georges (1871-1958). As a boy, Rouault was apprenticed to a painter on stained glass, whom he helped to restore the work of medieval artists. This work left a deep imprint on his own painting, with its richly glowing colours, thick black outlines and mystical intensity. He was an excellent choice as designer for the biblical ballet *Le Fils Prodigue* (Ballets Russes, 1929), his only work for the

JACQUES ROUCHÉ BY ROGER WILD.

theatre, but a distinguished one. Unlike Picasso, Matisse and Léger, Rouault was no scenic innovator. His décors for *Le Fils Prodigue*, bold, simple and glowing with dark colour, were like enlarged paintings or stained glass windows, with moving figures.

ROUCHÉ Jacques (1862-1957). Outside France, Rouché's name is known as director of the Paris Opera during three decades, but he was an important figure in Parisian theatrical life for a whole half-century, a generous and courageous man who placed his personal fortune (he was an industrialist) at the service of his artistic ideals, not a passive patron but an active "animateur" with ideas of his own which he was ready to defend. In 1907 he took over *La Grande Revue* and used its columns to describe the theories of Gordon Craig and Adolphe Appia. In 1910 he published a book on the modern theatre and, in the following year, became director of the Théâtre des Arts in Paris. With the assistance of the producer Durec, he led the French stage into new paths. His choice of designers, who included Drésa, Segonzac and Vuillard, proved that he could be at once eclectic and discriminating. In 1914 he began his thirty years association with the Paris Opera, where he was able to continue his work on a much larger scale. One of the most urgent of the many tasks that awaited him there was the renovation of the old-fashioned and musty décors which had been customary for so long. Some of his collaborators at the Théâtre des Arts — Dethomas, Drésa and Piot, were now attached permanently to the Opéra and in the ensuing years he chose new collaborators from the ranks of modern painters: Maurice Denis, Yves Alix, Valdo Barbey, Paul Larthe, Derain, Pedro Pruna, Chirico, Larionov, Paul Colin, Dignimont, André Hellé, Cassandre, Brianchon, Brayer, among them.

Rouché remained at the Opéra until 1945, mounting a varied repertory, concerning himself with every aspect of the operatic theatre, renovating not only the décors but methods of production. He gave new vitality to the ballet, engaged Serge Lifar to run it, encouraged him to produce new works, attracted young audiences and kept abreast of modern developments. Thus the Opéra, instead of remaining faithful to academic formulas and to established artists, was

ROMEO AND JULIET. DÉCOR FOR JULIET'S BEDROOM BY PETER WILLIAMS. BOLSHOI THEATRE.

able to play a worthy part in the vigorous theatrical life of France in the last fifty years, while remaining decently within the bounds which tradition imposes on a great national theatre.

ROUGE ET NOIR Le. See *L'Étrange Farandole.*

ROUSSEL Albert (1869-1937). His first ballet, *Le Festin de l'Araignée* (1913), was a commission from Jacques Rouché, the perspicacious director of the Théâtre des Arts in Paris. Roussel hesitated, was persuaded by his wife and finally produced a score which is one of the delights of French musical impressionism, in which the small orchestra suggests with Gallic economy the iridescent colours of insect life. The motoric rhythms which are a prominent feature of Roussel's symphonic music are there in suitably attenuated form. In 1914 Rouché moved to the Paris Opera and commissioned another work from Roussel, but the production of *Padmâvati,* delayed by the war and other difficulties, did not take place until 1923. *Padmâvati* was an opera-ballet in two acts (text

by Louis Laloy) based on a 13th century Indian legend about the ruins of Chitor, which Roussel had visited some years previously in the fortuitous company of Ramsay Macdonald. In 1925 the Opéra produced *La Naissance de la Lyre,* a "conte lyrique" after Sophocles, for which Nijinska arranged the dances. Both of his subsequent ballets were based on classical mythology. *Bacchus et Ariane* (Lifar, Paris Opera, 1931) is familiar to concert-goers from the vigorous and colourful orchestral suites drawn from it. *Ænéas* (1935) a choral ballet or dramatic oratorio on a text by the Flemish writer, Joseph Weterings, was written for the German conductor, Hermann Scherchen, who directed the first performance in Brussels (Palais des Beaux-Arts, choreographer Léonide Katchourowsky). It was revived at the San Carlo, Naples in 1937 and (by Lifar) at the Paris Opera in 1938.

ROYAL BALLET (of Great Britain). The organisation which was granted this title by Royal Charter in 1957 comprised two ballet companies, of about 75 and 40 dancers respectively (which now perform in London at the Royal Opera House, Covent Garden) and the former

CRAXTON. COSTUME FOR DAPHNIS AND CHLOÉ.

Sadler's Wells School. The charter represents the culmination of just over twenty-five years' work by Ninette de Valois and her colleagues to create a national ballet in England; it set the whole organisation on a sound and permanent administrative basis, and it also represented an attempt (not wholly successful) to remove the confusion caused by the various names under which the companies had previously been known: Vic-Wells Ballet, Sadler's Wells Ballet and Sadler's Wells Theatre Ballet.

Lilian Baylis, the moving spirit of the Old Vic Theatre in South London, which provided Shakespeare and opera at popular prices, had wanted to add ballet to her repertory for some time before the former Diaghilev dancer Ninette de Valois offered her services and those of the pupils of her recently opened school. The dancers included Ursula Moreton, Joy Newton, Stanley Judson, Hedley Briggs. De Valois began by arranging modest dances for the plays and operas; her first ballet at the Old Vic, *Les Petits Riens,* was given in 1928. In order to extend the Old Vic's work, the Governors had decided to buy and rebuild the derelict Sadler's Wells Theatre in North London. But before

that came about, Diaghilev died, and his company, which included some notable English dancers, was disbanded. In 1930, the Camargo Society was formed in London to give occasional performances of ballet with a few ex-Diaghilev dancers and the most promising pupils of the schools of de Valois and Marie Rambert; its work was of great importance not only for the new ballets produced, but because public attention was drawn to the fund of talent available in England. The new theatre at Sadler's Wells was ready in 1931; de Valois moved her pupils there, and thus the Sadler's Wells School came into being. For the first few years drama, opera and ballet were played in alternation at Sadler's Wells and the Old Vic, hence the name "Vic-Wells Ballet". From now on, complete programmes of ballet were given once or twice a week. De Valois was the company's director; the dancers were led by Markova and Dolin; Lopokova and Idzikowski appeared as guest artists; there were important recruits from Mme Rambert's Ballet Club (Pearl Argyle, June Brae, Frederick Ashton, William Chappell, Leslie Edwards, Harold Turner). The endless journeys between the two theatres soon became a burden, and so the drama remained at the Old Vic, while opera and ballet settled down at Sadler's Wells; in consequence, the ballet company was later renamed "The Sadler's Wells Ballet".

From the creative point of view, the four or five years before the war were perhaps the most exciting of all. De Valois, Ashton (who became resident choreographer in 1935 and embarked on a series of brilliant new ballets) and the excellent musical director, Constant Lambert, won the co-operation of the leading English composers and designers of the younger generation. The formula for one-act ballets in which music, choreography and décor were equal partners, was obviously inherited from Diaghilev. De Valois's ballets (*Job, The Rake's Progress, Checkmate*) inaugurated a deliberate and unmistakable English style; Ashton's work, less literary and relying on dancing rather than on narrative, had an international flavour which no doubt owed something to his cosmopolitan background. Young dancers from the company's school (Margot Fonteyn, Pamela May, Elizabeth Miller, Robert Helpmann) were ready to offset the loss of Markova and Dolin in 1935. The company was firmly anchored to the classical tradition by the presence in the repertory of *Giselle, Coppelia,* the great Petipa-Tchaikovsky ballets (performed in their entirety) and a few works by Fokine. This reliance on tradition was quite deliberate, and in any case the English public has never had the Parisian thirst for novelty.

In the autumn of 1940, when the bombing of London began in earnest, Sadler's Wells Theatre was closed. There followed for the company a long and arduous period of tours in the English provinces relieved by seasons in London, mainly at the New Theatre. The male dancers were called up one by one; when Ashton's turn came, he was temporarily replaced as choreographer by Robert Helpmann, whose dramatic ballets *(Hamlet, Miracle in the Gorbals)* brought a new element into the repertory. The English public's appetite for ballet increased so enormously during the war years that de Valois, who appears to foresee everything, realised that the modest resources of Sadler's Wells Theatre would, in the future, be inadequate for her company. And so, when the war ended, they moved to a larger home in London at the beautiful and historic old theatre at Covent Garden, which for years had been England's semi-official Royal Opera House, run by a series of private syndicates. Now a

TIRESIAS. MARGOT FONTEYN AND JOHN FIELD.

SCENE FROM APPARITIONS.

THE RAKE'S PROGRESS. DROP CURTAIN BY REX WHISTLER. 1935.

COPPÉLIA. DÉCOR BY OSBERT LANCASTER. 1954.

new era began there, with a resident opera company, an annual subsidy from the Arts Council of Great Britain — and the Sadler's Wells Ballet (the old name was, most confusingly, retained), which had the honour of re-opening Covent Garden in 1946 with a new production of *The Sleeping Beauty*.

There was at that time no question of abandoning Sadler's Wells Theatre altogether. A

Rodrigues, MacMillan). In 1957 the link with Sadler's Wells Theatre was finally severed. The two companies are now administered from Covent Garden, one performing there while the other tours at home or abroad. Repertory and dancers are to some extent interchangeable.

The big company soon consolidated its position at Covent Garden, and achieved international fame with several tours of America and

CLOCK SYMPHONY. DÉCOR BY BÉRARD. 1948. *Collection Gilberte Cournand, Paris.*

second and smaller company was formed there, with its own director responsible to de Valois, and was called "The Sadler's Wells Theatre Ballet" in an effort to distinguish it from its older sister. Though there was a fairly constant exchange of dancers between the two companies, the younger one soon developed a lively individuality of its own and became a forcing-house of talent for dancers and choreographers (Cranko,

Europe; in 1954, there was an exchange of companies with the Paris Opera. There have been many new ballets by Ashton (including his masterpiece, *Symphonic Variations*) and the younger English choreographers. Distinguished guest choreographers from abroad (Massine, Balanchine, Roland Petit) have made new works or restaged old ones for the company. A departure from the Diaghilev tradition has

MARGOT FONTEYN IN DAPHNIS AND CHLOÉ.

been the inclusion of new three-act ballets (Ashton's versions of *Cinderella* and *Sylvia*, Cranko's *Prince of the Pagodas*). Apart from Elvin and Beriosova, the majority of the dancers are products of the company's own school, now greatly expanded in new premises; several of the most gifted came there from the British Dominions: Australia, New Zealand, South Africa. The traffic has not been entirely one-way: dancers from the former Sadler's Wells Ballet are now directing companies and teaching on both sides of the Atlantic.

The dancers of the Royal Ballet display an excellent academic training based firmly on the classical school, but allowing great flexibility. Their style has developed certain English characteristics (an emphasis on discipline and teamwork) whose virtues are offset but not outweighed by a certain uniformity and lack of individual personality. A weakness in strong dramatic dancing is compensated by excellent character dancing in comic roles. In the early years, the influx of dancers trained by Marie Rambert to develop their own personality on more positive lines did much to conceal these defects (the choreographers Ashton and Howard, as well as the designers Fedorovitch, Chappell and Stevenson, each of whom made such important contributions to Sadler's Wells, were Rambert's discoveries). But the methods of de Valois have very great merits. Her dancers may not set the audience on fire every night, but their discipline and reliability are, in the long run, invaluable assets to a permanent company.

The credit for the growth and final establishment of what has now become the Royal Ballet lies with its director, Ninette de Valois, whose far-sighted planning has been at once imaginative and practical, with her chief collaborators Constant Lambert and Frederick Ashton, who helped her to shape its artistic policy, and finally with the dancers themselves, many of whom, and most notably the admirable Margot Fonteyn, have been loyal servants throughout their careers.

ROBERT HELPMANN AND PEARL ARGYLE.

ROYAL DANISH BALLET. See *Ballet (Royal Danish)*.

ROYAL SWEDISH BALLET. The company was founded in 1773 by Gustav III, a king much addicted to the theatre, but it has made few bids for international fame. For nearly 150 years the local corps de ballet faithfully supported the work of visiting ballet masters and guest ballerinas but the great talents—Didelot, Marie Taglioni, Christian Johannson, even Borlin—all made their names outside Sweden. A truly native School might have been established by the Swedish ballet master, Anders Selinder (appointed in 1833) but his reign was soon terminated by the directorate. In recent years, however, standards have been rising. An Englishwoman, Mary Skeaping, is now in charge of the ballet and supervises the teaching as well as productions of the classics. In these productions, the young dancers develop their technique while, at the same time, the ballets of the Swedish choreographers Birgit Cullberg, Ivo Cramer and Birgit Akesson, encourage them to develop a distinctive national style. Ellen Rasch, Gunnel Lindgren, Elsa Marianne von Rosen, Mariane Orlando, Gerd Andersson, Bjorn Holmgren, Teddy Rhodin, Willy Sandberg and Caj Selling are among the principal dancers. The company is fortunate in its musical director, Sixten Ehrling.

RUBINSTEIN Ida. When Diaghilev was preparing for his first ballet season in Paris, no suitable dancer could be found for the title-role in *Cléopâtre*. Fokine, supported by Bakst, suggested one of his private pupils, an amateur dancer of great beauty called Ida Rubinstein. Her success in Paris was hardly less than that of her professional colleagues; Fokine designed for her both in *Cléopâtre* (1909) and in *Sheherazade* (1910) roles which made the most of her remarkable appearance and her gift for mime, and concealed her inadequate technical formation. But there was a limit to the amount of roles that could be provided for an artist, however gifted, whose limitations were so marked, and her stay with the Russian Ballet was a short one. She made one reappearance with them, in her old part of Zobeide in *Sheherazade,* at a charity gala

in Paris in 1920. Her ambition to be a great dancer, however, remained. With considerable private means at her disposal, she was able to build up a company of her own, in which she would be the star, and for which she would commission new ballets on the Diaghilev model from the leading choreographers, composers and designers of the day. By the time her company was formed in 1928, when it made its début at the Paris Opera, she had financed a number of spectacular productions such as *Le Martyre de Saint-Sébastien* in which she appeared as dancer or actress, or both. Many of her productions at this time and later were of rare beauty. She employed talents of the highest order. Bakst and Benois did some of their finest designs for her; Honegger, Ibert, Ravel and Stravinsky wrote music for her; choreographers employed by her included Fokine, Massine, Nijinska and Jooss. She was an incurable romantic; to all her enterprises there clung something of the fin-de-siècle aestheticism (typified in its most intense form by d'Annunzio and Debussy's

IDA RUBINSTEIN IN LE MARTYRE DE SAINT-SÉBASTIEN, BY BAKST.

Saint-Sébastien) of the period to which, spiritually, she seemed to belong. Her own performances had the benefit of her languorous and deliberately mysterious beauty, but her technical insufficiency, which the passage of time emphasised rather than eradicated, proved a hindrance to her choreographers and robbed her productions of the chance some of them undoubtedly had of being masterpieces. She was unwilling to make the final sacrifice: to use her taste and wealth and influence to create works of art in which she did not herself figure as the central performer. Ida Rubinstein's earlier productions included *Le Martyre de Saint-Sébastien, Hélène de Sparte* (Bakst-Verhaeren, 1912), *La Pisanelle* (Baskt-d'Annunzio, 1913), *Arthémis troublée* (1922), *La Dame aux camélias* (Benois, 1923). During the 1928 season she presented several ballets by Nijinska with décors by Benois: *Les*

Noces de l'Amour et Psyché (Bach-Honnegger), *Le Baiser de la Fée, La Bien-Aimée* (Schubert-Milhaud), *La Princesse Cygne* (Rimsky-Korsakov) *Boléro* (Ravel). In 1931, *Amphion* (Benois-Honegger-Massine, text by Paul Valéry); in 1934, *Sémiramis* (Benois-Honegger-Fokine), *Perséphone* (Stravinsky-Barsacq-Jooss, text by André Gide), *Diane de Poitiers* (Benois-Ibert-Fokine), *La Valse* (Benois-Ravel-Fokine).

S

IDA RUBINSTEIN IN LE MARTYRE
DE SAINT-SÉBASTIEN, BY BAKST.

SACRE DU PRINTEMPS Le. Ballet in two scenes. Scenario: Igor Stravinsky and Nicolas Roerich. Music: Stravinsky. Scenery and costumes: Roerich. Choreography: Vaslav Nijinsky. First performance: Diaghilev Ballet, Théâtre des Champs-Élysées, Paris, 29 May 1913. New version by Leonide Massine: Théâtre des Champs-Élysées, Paris, 15 December 1920.

Though they are doubtless aware that *Le Sacre du Printemps* was written as a ballet and caused a scandal at its first performance, English-speaking audiences are mainly conscious of it as a concert work which has in recent years become a popular favourite and has been recorded by the world's leading orchestras and conductors. As a ballet, the *Sacre* has acquired an aura of impossibility which is unjustified, as recent revivals in Sweden, Italy and Germany have shown. Its neglect by the permanent companies of England, France and U.S.A. is regrettable. The notorious first performance took place at the newly-opened Théâtre des Champs-Élysées. From the moment the music started there was such an uproar that the dancers could not hear the orchestra, in spite of the valiant efforts of the conductor, Pierre Monteux. Nijinsky stood in the wings, beating out the rhythms with his feet; Stravinsky was holding on to his coat-tails to prevent him jumping on to the stage. There was a determined counter-demonstration led by the composer, Florent

DÉCOR FOR LA PISANELLE BY BAKST. 1912.

Schmitt, shouting "Silence, les p . . . du sei-zième !" One noble lady, who was not from the 16th arrondissement but from the Faubourg Saint-Germain, brandished her lorgnette, ex-claiming "C'est la première fois depuis soixante ans qu'on ose me manquer de respect !" Dia-ghilev rose in his box to implore the audience to be silent. It is easy, today, to laugh at the demonstrators and to forget how incompre-hensible Stravinsky's score, which still has such power to excite, alarm and disturb, must have sounded in 1913.

Nijinsky's version was given six times alto-gether in Paris and London by Diaghilev's company, with Maria Piltz in the exhausting principal role; it had required no less than 120 rehearsals. Whether Nijinsky, who had made a controversial début as choreographer with *L'Après-midi d'un faune* and followed it with the unsuccessful *Jeux,* was the man to undertake the visual realisation of these "pictures of pagan Russia" to the enormously difficult music is a question which those who did not see the result should hardly attempt to decide. The idea of the ballet occurred to Stravinsky in a kind of vision when he was completing *L'Oiseau de feu,* but the composition of *Petrouchka* inter-vened before the vision could be realised. He worked out the scenario with the aid of the designer Roerich, an authority on pagan Russia. The first part, "The Adoration of the Earth" consists of various primitive fertility rites con-cerned with the coming of spring. In the second part, "The Sacrifice" the tribe assembles on a hill-top to watch the girls elect one of their number as the annual sacrifice, the chosen virgin who dances herself to death.

Hardly a subject for entrechats and ara-besques; Nijinsky understandably chose the "terre à terre" school of Jacques Dalcroze to express the scenes of primitive ritual. The inventor of eurhythmics delegated Marie Ram-bert, the future pioneer of English ballet, who found Nijinsky to be a willing pupil, and, though uncommunicative, by no means lacking in intelligence. From their collaboration, clo-sely supervised by Diaghilev, was born this "choreography of stone" with turned-in feet, earth-bound, heavily accentuated movements and groups of massed dancers. After the first shock had worn off, the ballet was treated with more respect, but it was well ahead of its time.

In 1920, when Diaghilev wanted to revive the *Sacre,* Nijinsky's choreography had been completely forgotten, and Massine was entrusted with a new version. The result was favourably received; Lydia Sokolova danced the part of the chosen virgin, and gave the performance of her distinguished career. Massine has revived his version at Philadelphia (1930), Stockholm and Genoa-Nervi (both 1956). It still commands respect, particularly for the ingenious and impressive massed movements of the corps de ballet. Other versions include those by Boris Romanov (1932), Aurel Milloss (1941) and Mary Wigman (Berlin, 1957).

SADLER'S WELLS BALLET. See *Royal Ballet.*

ST. DENIS Ruth. Less well known in Europe than her compatriot and contemporary Isadora Duncan, Ruth Dennis, called St. Denis and, affectionately, "Miss Ruth", is the pioneer of "free dance" in the United States. Unlike Duncan, who was essentially an individualist, Ruth St. Denis was a choreographer, producer and founder of a school. Passionately fond of the theatre from childhood (she was born in 1877), she went on the stage when quite young and appeared in a strange assortment of roles. She says it was in 1904 that she found her vocation. Looking at a picture of the Egyptian goddess Isis she conceived a passion for the

Orient and considered the production of a huge pageant *Egypta.* This was abandoned for financial reasons and she produced instead a Hindu ballet *Radha* (1906). She was always fascinated by the East and many of her ballets had Egyptian, Japanese or Persian subjects. But she also produced lyric, dramatic and historical works which owed nothing to ethnology, and religious works which were performed in churches and were not designed for the stage. From 1906-09 she toured triumphantly in Europe but, again unlike Isadora, she preferred to work in her own country. In 1914 she married her partner Ted Shawn (a former theological student) and together they founded the Denishawn (*) company and school. This was increasingly successful until Shawn and St. Denis separated in 1932, when it came to an end. The ballets that were produced for this company were usually staged with fantastic splendour. One of them, *Ishtar,* required eight tons of scenery. Miss Ruth herself, however, performed many solos with only the simplest properties, although she was meticulous in her choice of costumes. Some of these solos — *White Jade* and *The Nautch* — she occasionally dances today, an exquisite figure with her pale, spiritual face and cloud of white hair. She has retired to Hollywood to devote herself to a cultural and religious foundation bearing her name, but she is still the inspiration of young dancers, the matriarch of the modern dance.

SAINT FRANCIS. See *Nobilissima Visione*.

SAKHAROFF Clotilde and Alexandre. The two names are inseparable, though Alexandre Sakharoff and Clotilde von Deep were known individually as dancers by the time they met in Munich shortly before the First World War. Alexandre, a Russian by birth, was studying painting in Paris when he saw a performance of *L'Aiglon* with Sarah Bernhardt; the beauty of her gestures revealed to him the possibilities of expressive movement. He trained his own body by means of acrobatic exercises and made a successful début as dance recitalist in Munich in 1911. Clotilde, who became his wife and partner, was a German girl of aristocratic family, who had been the leading dancer in productions by Max Reinhardt. The Sakharoffs subsequently toured the world with a repertoire of solos and pas de deux, using both classical and modern music. Alexandre designed the costumes. There was nothing improvisatory about their highly accomplished and carefully worked-out "abstract mime"; musical, expressive, and highly finished. They gave their last recital in Paris in 1953 and retired to Italy to teach.

THE SAKHAROFFS BY GONCHAROVA.

SALADE. Ballet in two scenes. Scenario and texte: Albert Flament. Music: Milhaud. Scenery and costumes: Braque. Choreography: Massine. First performance: Comte Étienne de Beaumont's "Soirées de Paris", Théâtre de la Cigale, Paris, 17 May 1924.

A commedia dell'arte subject which enabled Massine once again to impersonate Pulcinella. The text was sung and spoken (from the orchestra pit).

* Revived at the Paris Opera in 1935 in a new version by Serge Lifar, with admirable scenery and costumes by Derain. Lifar himself danced Pulcinella. The singers doubled the dancers on the stage.

SALOMÉ. See *Tragédie de Salomé*.

SANDERS Dick. A young Dutch dancer, born in Java, of boyish appearance, with an up-tilted nose and unruly hair; a choreographer of distinct promise. He studied with Kurt Jooss (1950-52) before settling in Paris. His work combines modern and academic techniques, thus *Récréation* (Maurice Béjart company), *L'Échelle* (Ballets '56) and the pas de deux *L'Emprise* (Enghien Festival, 1957) which he danced himself with Claire Sombert. He did the choreography for the Visconti-Henze ballet *Maratona di Danza* at the Berlin Festival in 1957.

RUTH ST. DENIS.

CLOTILDE SAKHAROFF IN L'APRÈS-MIDI D'UN FAUNE.

SATIE Erik. Born 1866, died 1925. An eccentric and paradoxical figure, the ultimate value of whose music is still a matter for controversy. His part in the evolution of modern music was both limited and important. Limited, because he was a self-taught musician, ill-equipped to become the leader of a movement; important, because he nevertheless influenced

the reaction against late 19th century romanticism and impressionism towards economy and concision. Satie was a bohemian, who dressed sedately and wore a beard and pince-nez, behind which his eyes twinkled dangerously. His sincere love of music went hand in glove with an irrepressible humour, mordant wit, and a passion for nonsense. When he was over forty, he decided to take his musical education in hand and joined Roussel's counterpoint class at the austere Schola Cantorum, where fooling was not encouraged. Roussel, who was hardly a man to be taken in, described him as "prodigieusement musicien". For a short while, Satie did become the leader of the so-called "École d'Arcueil", which he founded as a mild counterblast to the aggressive tendencies of "Les Six", of which group he had previously, with Cocteau, been a spiritual godfather. He struck a lance for simplicity, austerity and a return to melody. If his place in the musical avant-garde is less considerable than his own pronouncements and the faith of his disciples implied, it was greater than his detractors (whom he so successfully irritated) were willing to admit. He left his mark on Debussy and Ravel and on many younger composers, Stravinsky, Milhaud and Auric included. Much of his music is vacuous, but the best of it has a perky charm which is quite individual and sometimes he achieved a genuinely moving quality of grave simplicity and stillness. The awkward question remains: how far did he take himself seriously? Often the humour which he cultivated so assiduously is more in evidence in the titles

ALEXANDRE SAKHAROFF IN LA BOURRÉE FANTASQUE.

of his little pieces (titles which enchant at first but end by becoming wearisome) than in the music itself: *Trois véritables préludes flasques pour un chien, Pièces froides, Airs à faire fuir,* and so on.

His ballet music is of a piece with the rest of his work. *Mercure* and *Premier amour* (based on the *Morceaux en forme de poire*) for the "Soirées de Paris" (1924) and *Jack in the box,* which Milhaud orchestrated for Diaghilev in 1926, seem to remain voluntarily detached from the action on the stage, a kind of independent musical background. A little jazz, a little "café-concert", some deliberately clumsy progressions—nothing much to shock there. Even in *Relâche* (Ballets Suédois, 1924) Satie caused less scandal by his music than by driving round the stage in a little 5 HP Citroën, raising his bowler hat to the audience. *Parade,* his first ballet (1917), left the deepest impression, and not only for the use Satie made in his orchestra of typewriters, hooters and other strange and unusual noises. The score, scrappy though it is, shows real originality and imagination. Cocteau praised it lyrically, and singled out the dances of the Chinese conjuror, the American girl and the acrobats for their nostalgic quality "never expressed before with such overwhelming fidelity —the poetry of childhood recaptured by a technician".

SAUGUET Henri. Born 1901 at Bordeaux. A pupil of Charles Koechlin. He came as a young man under the influence of Satie and was a member of the École d'Arcueil. His early works showed that he possessed more musical culture than technical assurance, but in the intervening years he has cultivated his small but agreable talent to good purpose, as his numerous ballets show. In 1924 *Les Roses* was given at the "Soirées de Paris" with décor by Marie Laurencin and choreography by Massine. *La Chatte,* for Diaghilev, followed in 1927; *David* for Ida Rubinstein's 1928 season; *La Nuit* for Cochran's 1930 Revue (London). *Fastes,* for the Ballets 1933, was an evocation of orgiastic rites in ancient Italy. It was some years before he wrote another ballet, but when it came, *Les Forains* (1945) proved to be one of his most successful works. The influence of Stravinsky *(Renard)* and of Satie is still discernible, and the ballet is in some respects a throwback to the

'twenties, but the desire to shock has evaporated and the nostalgia for fairground music and café-concert tunes is devoid of any affectation. There is genuine compassion in the score, which makes a more lasting effect than many more imposing works. Sauguet can achieve a simplicity of utterance which Satie would not have disowned, and he has a richer melodic gift than his mentor. Two more ballets followed, both of them distinguished: *Mirages* for the Paris Opera in 1947 and *La Rencontre* for the Ballets des Champs-Élysées in 1948.

ERIK SATIE BY PICASSO. 1920.

SCALA Teatro alla. Ballet made its first appearance in Milan at the Ducal theatre about 1650 in the early melodramas, or *opere in musica.* In 1775 Noverre staged some of his famous ballet-pantomimes there, and from then onwards Milan had a large and well-trained ballet company at its disposal which appeared in all its glory when the newly built Teatro alla Scala opened in August 1778. Salvatore Viganò came as maître de ballet in 1813 and remained until the year of his death, 1821, producing many ballets. In 1812 the Imperial Dance Academy was founded in association with the theatre. Carlo Blasis was appointed director in 1837. The 19th century was the great age of Italian dancing; Grisi, Cerrito, Legnani, Zucchi and other famous dancers from Milan imposed the brilliant Italian style in other European capitals. One son of Milan, Enrico Cecchetti, lived to carry the tradition into the present century. In 1923, an old man, he became Director of the school where he had been a pupil over fifty years earlier.

At the present time the school and the ballet are under the direction of the Anglo-Argentinian Esmée Bulnes, a fine teacher, and Ugo dell'Ara, who is also choreographer and premier danseur. The Scala makes a point of inviting distinguished guest ballerinas (Chauviré, Fonteyn, Markova, Toumanova, etc.). The title of prima ballerina assoluta was last awarded to Nives Poli, in 1936. Nevertheless the home company is a strong one, with Ogla Amati, a fine classical dancer, Luciana Novarro and Giulo Perugini at its head. The younger dancers include Vera Colombo, Gilda Majocchi, Giuliana Barabaschi, Carla Fracci, Fiorella Cova, Dora Ricci, and among the men,

Mario Pistoni, Walter Venditti, Gino Pessina, Roberto Fascilla, Ermanno Savare and Aldo Santambrogio. Guest choreographers are also regularly invited: Charrat, Massine, Lifar, Balanchine, Ashton, Rodrigues, Cranko, etc. Aurel Milloss was engaged for the 1951-52 season. Although the number of completely new works produced at the Scala in recent years has been limited, there have been some of an original type (Noverre might not have disowned them) in which pure dancing played a restricted part. An example was Luchino Visconti's *Mario and the magician,* based on Thomas Mann's story, with choreography by Massine, in which Babilée and dell'Ara spoke as well as danced and there was an important role for a straight actor, Salvo Rondone. The striking décors were by Lila de Nobili. It is conceivable that these works of mixed genre, which employ many of the resources of a great theatre and also show the influence of the cinema (Visconti himself is a distinguished film director) have an interesting future. More conventional tastes have been catered for by sumptuous revivals of classics and modern ballets: Rodrigues put on *Casse-Noisette* (1956), with décor by James Bailey and Fonteyn and Somes as guest artists for the first performances, and John Cranko reproduced his *Prince of the Pagodas* (1957), using the original Piper designs.

SCHANNE Margrethe. A leading Danish dancer, born in Copenhagen and trained at its Royal Ballet school. She was a pupil of Harald Lander, who developed her natural gift for romantic and supernatural roles. She excels especially in the Bournonville version of *La Sylphide.* A light and ethereal dancer of great sensitivity, she has a considerable range, for as well as the romantic roles of the Sylphide and Giselle she can be brilliant and enchanting in the Bournonville character ballets, *Kermesse in Bruges* and *Napoli.* She has appeared as guest artist with several French companies, notably the Ballets des Champs-Élysées and de Cuevas. At the Genoa Festival of 1957 she appeared as her illustrious compatriote Lucile Grahn in the reconstruction of the famous *Pas de Quatre* of 1845, but at home in Copenhagen she dances the role of Taglioni, a dancer whom she must closely resemble.

SALVATORE VIGANO.

LUCIANA NOVARRO AND UGO DELL'ARA.

the work of distinguished artists is in question — are now generally accepted.

SCHAUFUSS Frank. Ballet master (since 1956) of the Royal Danish Ballet. A tall dancer of remarkable strength and fine presence, he trained at the Royal Ballet School in Copenhagen and made guest appearances with the Metropolitan Ballet in England and the Ballets de Paris. Among his best roles are the Hussar in *Beau Danube,* the Drummer in *Graduation Ball* and Mercutio in Ashton's *Romeo and Juliet.* Married to Mona Vangsaa.

SCHERVACHIDZE Prince. An artist and scene painter who has played a self-effacing but valuable role in the history of modern ballet décor. He adapted the 19th century toy-theatre prints used for *The Triumph of Neptune* (Diaghilev, 1926) and designed other décors, including a new version of *Les Sylphides* (de Basil, 1940). But his main contribution lay in the skill and fidelity with which he reproduced the sketches of the artists who designed for Diaghilev and for later companies. Schervachidze contrived to preserve the charm and freshness of the artist's conception, reproducing faithfully the medium (oil or watercolour) in which the sketches had been made and even respecting the accidents of brushwork which give such life to a design. His methods — doubly valuable when

SCHMITT Florent. Born in Lorraine, 1870. A pupil of Massenet and Fauré. His most important ballet, *La Tragédie de Salomé* (1907), is an elaborate score in what one might call the Franco-Russian vein which subsequently produced Ravel's *Daphnis et Chloé,* Dukas's *La Péri* and d'Indy's *Istar. Salomé* was originally written for small orchestra and was produced thus by Loie Fuller, but was later rescored for a large one. Some of its rhythmic features, notably in the "Danse de l'effroi", foreshadow Stravinsky's *Sacre.* There have been numerous revivals in France (see article). In 1924 the Opéra-Comique mounted a ballet, *Le petit Elfe ferme-l'œil,* which was an orchestral version of some children's pieces for piano. Schmitt's third ballet was *Oriane et le Prince d'amour,* designed for production (under a slightly different title) by Ida Rubinstein in 1935, finally presented by Lifar at the Opéra in 1938. This was another sumptuous, highly-coloured and ornamented score: though Schmitt preferred to work on a large scale, he was a meticulous craftsman. He also wrote the incidental music for Ida Rubinstein's production of Shakespeare's *Antony and Cleopatra* in the French version of André Gide (1920). Died 1958.

SCHOLLAR Ludmila. Trained at the school of the Imperial Theatre in St. Petersburg, graduated 1906. She appeared in the early seasons of Diaghilev's Ballets Russes while she was still a member of the Maryinsky company. In 1914 she volunteered as a nurse in the Russian Army, served in the front line, was wounded and decorated, and did not return to the stage until 1917. She left Russia, rejoined Diaghilev in 1921 and then transferred to Ida Rubinstein's company. Her first husband was an officer, Count Vorontzoff; she afterwards married her fellow-dancer Anatole Vilzak. In 1936 she settled in the United States and in 1940, with her husband, opened a school in New York. Schollar was noted for her elevation, which was particularly effective in *Giselle* (Queen of the Wilis), *Carnaval* (Estrella), *Danses du Prince Igor* (Polovtsian Girl) and *Les Sylphides.*

SCOTCH SYMPHONY. ANDRÉ EGLEVSKY.

SCHWARZ Solange. The most celebrated member of a distinguished family of French dancers. Her father, Jean, danced and taught at the Paris Opera; his sister, Jeanne, was a danseuse-étoile there and later taught at the Opéra-Comique and at the Conservatoire National. Her sisters, Nelly, Janine and Christiane are also dancers. Solange joined the Opéra school in 1920, became étoile at the Opéra-Comique in 1933, and returned to the Opéra in 1937 as Swanilda in *Coppelia,* which is her greatest role. In 1940 she became danseuse-étoile at the Opéra and remained there until 1945, dancing leading roles in the new ballets of Lifar, including *Alexandre le Grand* and *Le Chevalier et la Damoiselle.* After the war she danced as guest artist with various companies: Ballets des Champs-Élysées, Maurice Béjart's Ballets de l'Étoile, and de Cuevas. She also reappeared at the Opéra-Comique. Finally, on 16 January 1957, she bade farewell to the Opéra in *Coppelia* and *Suite en blanc.*

She is a small, doll-like dancer, as brilliant and lively on the stage as she is quiet and reserved off it, unsuited to romantic roles but excelling in the rapid, pointed, pizzicato style; at once a reliable technician and a well-defined personality.

SCOTCH SYMPHONY. Ballet by Balanchine. Music: Mendelssohn. Scenery: Horace Armistead. Costumes: Karinska and David Ffolkes. First performance: New York City Ballet, City Center, New York, 11 November 1952. Principal dancers: Maria Tallchief and André Eglevsky.

Balanchine decided to do a ballet on Scottish themes after visiting Edinburgh for the Festival in 1952. He omitted the first movement of Mendelssohn's score, created ensemble dances for the first movement of the ballet, with a pas de trois for a girl and two boys, devised a romantic pas de deux for the second part, and joined soloists and corps de ballet in the finale.

SCUOLA DI BALLO. Ballet in one act, after Goldoni's comedy. Music: Boccherini, arr. and orch. Jean Françaix. Scenery and costumes: Count Étienne de Beaumont. Choreography: Massine. First performance: Soirées de Paris, Théâtre de la Cigale, May-June 1924. An essay in the Italian comedy vein already successfully exploited by Massine in *Les Femmes de bonne humeur* and *Pulcinella.* Revived by the Ballets de Monte-Carlo, 25 April 1933. Principal dancers: Irina Baronova, Tatiana Riabouchinska, André Eglevsky, Leonide Massine and Leon Woizikowski.

SEIGNEURET Michèle. French dancer who won celebrity (and the Prix René Blum) on a summer evening in 1955 when, in the small company run by Jean Laurent and Maurice Béjart in which she had made her début the previous year, she created the female lead in Béjart's *Symphonie pour un homme seul.* Dark, supple and violent as a young animal, an excellent interpreter of Béjart's dramatic style.

SEMENOVA Marina. The first great Russian dancer to emerge after the revolution. A pupil of Vaganova at Leningrad, where she made her début at the Kirov theatre in 1925. She transferred in 1931 to the Bolshoi ballet in

Moscow. Guest appearances in Paris in 1935 (*Giselle* and *Divertissement*). Rather plump, with a pretty head and slender, shapely legs, her ballon and ability to "travel" were remarkable even by Russian standards. Her Odette-Odile and her Aurora were particularly celebrated. She matured at a critical moment for Soviet ballet, and was a stabilising influence. She now teaches in Russia.

SERENADE. Ballet in three movements by George Balanchine. Music: Tchaikovsky (Serenade for Strings). Costumes: Jean Lurçat. First performance: Producing Company of the School of American Ballet, Hartford, Connecticut, 6 December 1934. Given during the American Ballet's first New York season, Adelphi Theatre, 1 March 1935. Principal dancers: Anchutina, Boris, Caccialanza, Mullowney, Dollar, Laskey.

Balanchine's first ballet in America and one of his most felicitous transpositions of music into movement. Since the romantic, elegiac quality of Tchaikovsky is so beautifully captured, "abstract" seems hardly the right term for the

ballet. It is now in the repertory of several companies. The American (and New York City) Ballet versions have no scenery. When Balanchine revived it at the Paris Opera (30 April 1947) Delfau designed the décor.

SERGEYEV Constantin. A product of the Leningrad school attached to the Kirov Theatre, he became one of the principal danseurs nobles in Soviet Russia and is now maître de ballet at Leningrad. Of medium height, strongly built, with firm, virile, features, he is a dancer of unusual authority and strength. He created the role of Romeo in Lavrovsky's *Romeo and Juliet* (1940), partnering Ulanova, and was the first Eugene in *The Bronze Horseman*. Married to Natalie Dudinskaya.

SERGUEEV Nicholas. He was régisseur général at the Maryinsky Theatre from 1914 to 1917 and he wrote down, in the Stepanov method of dance notation, a great number of the ballets in the Maryinsky repertoire, including all the great classics. When he left Russia after

JOSÉ-MARIA SERT, MISIA SERT AND DIAGHILEV
BY COCTEAU.

the revolution, he brought his notes with him and was responsible for nearly all the major classical revivals from Diaghilev's production of *The Sleeping Princess* (1921) onwards. He staged *Coppelia* (1933), *Casse-Noisette, Giselle,* the full-length *Le Lac des Cygnes* (1934) and *The Sleeping Beauty* (1939) for the Sadler's Wells Ballet. For the Ballet Russe de Monte-Carlo he revived *Giselle* and *Casse-Noisette,* and for International Ballet *Le Lac des Cygnes, Giselle, Coppelia* and *The Sleeping Beauty.* He died in Nice in 1951, bequeathing his notes to Mona Inglesby.

SERT José-Maria. Born 1876, died 1947. A Spanish painter and decorator, domiciled in France, the first non-Russian artist to work for Diaghilev (*La Légende de Joseph,* 1914). The choice of Sert represented no new departure, since he had much in common with Bakst, with his love of grandiose architectural conceptions and magnificent costumes. Sert treated the biblical legend as Bakst treated classical ones,

not as opportunity to point a moral but as one for letting his rich and fertile imagination run riot. But while Bakst's imagination ran on oriental lines, Sert remained a Western European in love with the Renaissance and the 18th century. He married, as her third husband, Diaghilev's great friend Misia Godebska. Sert also designed for Diaghilev *Las Meninas* (1916, costumes only) and the Cimarosa opera-ballet *Le Astuzie Femminili* (1920). The dances from this were later produced as a separate ballet, *Cimarosiana* (1924).

SEVENTH SYMPHONY. Choreographic symphony in four parts. Music: Beethoven (Symphony No. 7). Scenery and costumes: Christian Bérard. Choreography: Massine. First performance: Ballets de Monte-Carlo, 5 May 1938. Principal dancers: Alicia Markova, Nini Theilade, Frederic Franklin, Igor Youskevitch.

The fourth of Massine's choreographic symphonies showed increasing freedom in the

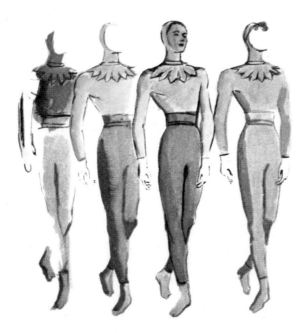

SERENADE. COSTUMES BY DELFAU.
PARIS OPERA. 1947.

JOSÉ-MARIA SERT.
COSTUMES FOR LE ASTUZIE FEMMINILI. 1920.

treatment of the music: Massine no longer felt obliged to produce a plastic equivalent for every phrase. Though the score had, as usual, been carefully analysed, the structure was not laid bare in the dancing. The choice of the music was bold and not entirely justified by the results. "Apotheosis of the dance" the symphony may well be, but the outer movements, at least, are not to be rendered in terms of ballet. Massine used no narrative but chose a general theme for each movement. The first represented the Creation, with the birth of rivers, rocks, plant and animal life and finally man and woman. There was some confusion here, since the idea had no relation to sonata form with its element of recapitulation. The pathetic and impressive second movement was a portrayal of human grief occasioned by the entombment of a dead youth. The processional rhythm suggested the use of stylised, expressionist movement in the manner of Wigman and Jooss: Fokine described it as "Wigman on points". The scherzo was a return to classicism, a celestial interlude on Mount Olympus where the Gods, Markova and Youskevitch, were given the only virtuoso passages in the ballet. The finale showed mankind given over to the lusts of the flesh and the consequent destruction of the world. The bacchanal was all very well, but the catastrophe, for which there is no justification in the exultant music, seemed arbitrary. The designer, Bérard, showed that he was perfectly at home with these cosmic abstractions. Two groups of giant, draped caryatids presided in the wings over the four movements, for which there were different backcloths and costumes, all in keeping with Massine's vision of the music.

SHABELEVSKY Yurek. Polish dancer, born and trained in Warsaw. Later studied under Nijinska. He danced in Ida Rubinstein's company during her 1928 season and was a valuable soloist with de Basil's company from 1932 to 39, where he created roles in *Jeux d'enfants, Scuola di ballo, Choreartium* and *Symphonie fantastique* and danced many of his compatriot Woizikowski's roles with success. A lithe, elegant dancer with enormous charm, great precision and attack, he was ideally cast as the Snob in *Boutique Fantasque* and as the King of the Dandies in *Beau Danube*. Since 1940 he has danced with various companies in America and in Italy.

SHAW Brian. English dancer, born in Yorkshire, 1928. A student of Ruth French and the Sadler's Wells School, Shaw joined the Sadler's Wells Ballet in 1944. Now a leading soloist, he is outstanding in *Les Patineurs* and as the Bluebird in *The Sleeping Beauty,* roles which display his virtuoso technique. Even more famous in America than in his native land, he

MOIRA SHEARER IN CINDERELLA.

has excelled rather in established "show pieces" than in new ballets, although in Cranko's *Bonne-Bouche* he invested the role of the melancholy hero with charm and a nice sense of the ridiculous.

SHEARER Moira. A red-haired ballerina with delicate features and a fragile, porcelain beauty, Moira Shearer's fame, surpassing that of any other English dancers except Fonteyn and Markova, is due less to her performances in ballet than to the popularity of her first film, the technicolour fantasy *The Red Shoes*. Success, in fact, has come easily to Moira Shearer all her life, sometimes causing her distress, because she has a shrewd Scottish awareness of her true abilities. Trained by Flora Fairbairn and Nicholas Legat, she won instant recognition with her first performances in the International Ballet. She joined Sadler's Wells in 1942, and, after four years of hard study and the experience of solo roles, emerged as a ballerina when the company went to Covent Garden. In one year, Shearer danced Aurora, Swanilda, Odette-Odile, and took part in the first performance of *Symphonic Variations*. Later followed Giselle (a notable

performance) and the title-role in Ashton's *Cinderella*. After great success in America, she left the ballet in 1953, to become an actress.

SHEHERAZADE. Choreographic drama in one act. Scenario, scenery and costumes: Léon Bakst. Music: Rimsky-Korsakov. Choreography: Michel Fokine. First presented at the Paris Opera, 4 June 1910. Principal dancers: Ida Rubinstein, Vaslav Nijinsky, Enrico Cecchetti, Alexis Bulgakov.

The above are the official "credit titles": they led to one of they quarrels that beset Diaghilev's inner circle of collaborators from time to time. Benois in his *Reminiscences of the Russian Ballet,* claims that the scenario of *Sheherazade* was his and not Bakst's. There is no reason to disbelieve him. Diaghilev, according to Benois, was rather off-hand about the matter: "You've got *Le Pavillon d'Armide,* let Bakst have *Sheherazade*". It was certainly a painter's conception. Rimsky-Korsakov's symphonic suite has no definite programme, though the composer originally gave the four movements titles taken from the *Arabian Nights*. Diaghilev suppressed the slow movement, and the first movement is played before the curtain rises as an atmospheric (but rather repetitive) prelude. To the two remaining movements, Benois fitted a scenario based on the first tale in the *Nights.* The scene is the gorgeous, tented harem of the Sultan Shahriar. The potentate is uneasy, torn between the desire for distraction and suspicion of his favourite wife, Zobeide. Odalisques dance for him, but he dismisses them and goes off hunting. When the coast is clear, the women bribe the chief Eunuch to release the black slaves. They pour on to the stage from small doors at the back of the stage, and an orgy begins. A further bribe from the imperious Zobeide and the Eunuch opens the last door: a second's hesitation and there leaps towards Zobeide her own favourite, the gold negro. Love-making and feasting are rudely interrupted by the return of the Sultan and his retinue. Scimitars flash and the negroes are swiftly massacred, the gold one last of all. Finally the sultan is confronted with the faithless Zobeide. Preferring death to public dishonour, she snatches a dagger and proudly takes her own life.

Fokine's choreography was based on a study

of Persian miniatures, but the poses were assimilated into the flowing line, economical and dramatic, of which he was such a master. Bakst's vision of the gorgeous east (based on extremely skilful juxtapositions of violent, glowing colour with cunning use of perspective) astonished the first spectators and influenced fashion and interior decoration for years to come. In present-day revivals, *Sheherazade* appears as the worst kind of bogus orientalism, with faded colours, crude or feeble lighting, and a performance more apt to produce titters than sensual thrills. It would be better to bury it once and for all than to betray it by forgetting that the Russian Ballet danced and staged it with all the love, conviction and care for every detail that are nowadays only to be found in the work of the greatest theatre companies, such as the Moscow Arts Theatre. It is true that Diaghilev had the benefit of a wonderful cast: Ida Rubinstein, who might have been born for the role of Zobeide; Cecchetti, waddling and greedy, but never farcical, as the chief Eunuch; lastly, the unsurpassable Nijinsky as the golden negro. His performance had two great moments, the opening leap from a crouching position in the doorway, downstage towards Zobeide, and his death scene, when he fell, slain, to spin on the back of his neck and expire quivering, in his wife's description, like "a fish tossed on to the sand".

SHOSTAKOVITCH Dimitri. Born at St. Petersburg, 1906. The outstanding Soviet composer of his generation, fertile, unequal but very gifted, who has (like so many of his colleagues) more than once fallen foul of official opinion. His ballets have not won the wide recognition of his symphonies and concertos. Both *The Golden Age* (1930) and *The Bolt* (1931) were criticised for their poor scenarios, the former about the adventures of a football team in a big city during a world exhibition, the second a satire on the petty bourgeois. *The Bright Rivulet* (1935), about collective farm life, was also unfavourably criticised. All these are three-act works. To the West, Shostakovitch as a ballet composer is best known by *L'Étrange Farandole* (1939), for which Massine used the remarkable first symphony of 1936.

SKATING RINK. Ballet by Jean Borlin and Fernand Léger. Music: Honegger. Scenery and costumes: Léger. Choreography: Borlin. First performance: Ballets Suédois, Théâtre des Champs-Élysées, 20 January 1922.

SKEAPING Mary. English dancer, ballet mistress and choreographer, now Director of the Royal Swedish Ballet. She has had wide experience — as a dancer, with Pavlova's com-

IDYLLE. GEORGE SKIBINE AND MARJORIE TALLCHIEF.

SHEHERAZADE. DÉCOR BY LÉON BAKST. 1910.

pany and with the Nemchinova-Dolin company, and as ballet mistress with the Sadler's Wells Ballet (1948-52) and companies in Cuba, Finland, and Canada. Her revivals of the classical ballets and her series of period reconstructions for the 18th century theatre at Drottningholm are particularly notable.

SKIBINE George. Strongly built but elegant and distinguished, George Skibine is a remarkable mime and the most convincing of romantic heroes, qualities doubtless inherited from his father, who was an actor and dancer with Diaghilev. Nevertheless the young Skibine was not intended to follow his example; he left school early to earn his living, and it was a chance engagement at the Bal Tabarin that decided his career. He was discovered by Massine, who engaged him for the Ballets de Monte-Carlo, where he made his début in 1938 as a deer in *Seventh Symphony*. He left in 1940 to become premier danseur with Ballet Theatre. He joined the American army in 1942, took part in the Normandy landings, and returned to Paris in the uniform of a Top Sergeant. After demobilisation, he worked as translator and

secretary to a picture dealer in New York. Then he met the celebrated impresario, Sol Hurok, who encouraged him to return to ballet, first with Massine's Ballet Russe Highlights, then the Markova-Dolin Group. Engagements followed with Original Ballet Russe and with the de Cuevas company, where he stayed for eight years until his recent appointment to the Paris Opera with his wife and partner, Marjorie Tallchief, whom he married in 1947 (he has been an American citizen since 1945).

Skibine made a promising début as a choreographer with a version of the Romeo and Juliet story, *Tragédie à Vérone,* for de Cuevas in 1949 (*). Subsequent ballets have included: *Annabel Lee* (*), *Le Prisonnier du Caucase* (*) (1951), *L'Ange Gris* (1953), *Idylle* (*), *Le Retour, La Reine Insolente* (1954), *Achille* and *Le Prince du Désert* (1955), *Concerto,* at the Opéra-Comique (1958). They are the work of an intelligent and cultured artist, who can use the classical dance to express a wide range of feeling.

SKORIK Irène. Born of a Russian mother and a French father, Irène Skorik was a pupil of Preobrajenska and Victor Gsovsky. Her first appearance in 1945 with the Ballets des Champs-Élysées revealed a young dancer of pure line, with a gentle, reserved personality. She was the company's première danseuse throughout its existence, and created roles in *La Fiancée du Diable, La Sylphide, Treize Danses* and *Les Amours de Jupiter* in which she was a chaste and mysterious Leda. In 1950 she became ballerina at the Munich Opera *(Cinderella, Hamlet, Giselle)*, appeared with the "Berliner Ballet" of Tatiana Gsovsky in 1956, and recently with the Ballets 1958 of Miskovitch.

SKOURATOFF Wladimir. The son of emigré Russians, trained by Preobrajenska and Kniaseff in Paris. He started by dancing in cabaret: his chance came in 1946 when he joined the Nouveau Ballet de Monte-Carlo and partnered Renée Jeanmaire in Lifar's *Aubade*. They appeared together with de Basil's company in 1947 and the following year they joined the Ballets de Paris, where Skouratoff created a leading rôle in *La Femme et son Ombre,* a ballet by Paul Claudel with choreography by Charrat. In 1952 he became one of the premiers danseurs of the de Cuevas company, his finest creations being *Piège de Lumière, La Tertulia* and *Boléro*. He has great speed and a strong technique, more suited to dramatic than to romantic roles; he is magnificent in the *Polovtsian Dances*. In 1958 he left de Cuevas to dance the male lead in the Sagan ballet, *Le Rendez-vous manqué*.

SLAVENSKA Mia. A Yugoslav dancer, real name Mia Corak. When she came to France to study with Egorova and Preobrajenska, she astonished Paris not only by her prodigious technique but by the beauty of her red-gold hair and her pale skin. She made her first appearance in 1936 with Lifar in *David triomphant* and in 1938 starred with Chauviré in the film *La Mort du Cygne*. A leading dancer with the Ballets de Monte-Carlo in 1938, she went with the company to the United States

SKATING RINK. DÉCOR BY FERNAND LÉGER. 1922.

where she has remained. She dances *Giselle, Swan Lake* and the great classical pas de deux with brilliance, if not always with subtlety, and excels in dramatic and character parts. One of her most striking roles in recent years was in Valerie Bettis's ballet *A Streetcar Named Desire*, produced for the Slavenska-Franklin Ballet in 1952. She has toured widely, with her own groups and as guest artist with larger companies, and is the choreographer of several ballets, among them *Portrait of a Ballerina* (Dohnanyi) and *Symphonic Variations* (César Franck).

ÉTIENNE DE BEAUMONT BY PICASSO.

SLEEPING BEAUTY. See *La Belle au bois dormant.*

SMIRNOVA Elena. Born in 1888, died in 1935. Trained at the St. Peterburg Imperial School, she prompted the pupil Nijinsky during his final examination. A good technician, excelling in brilliant, dashing roles: *Don Quichotte, Esmeralda.* She danced in Paris with the Diaghilev company in 1909. The last dancer to be nominated "étoile" under the old régime (1916). Later she came to Western Europe

with her husband, Boris Romanov, as the star of his "Théâtre Romantique Russe" and had a triumphant success in 1924 in *Giselle.* She died in Buenos Aires, where she was teaching.

SMITH Oliver. Born 1918 at Waupawn, Wisconsin. One of the leading American stage designers, whose name is associated with some of the most important ballets produced in the United States during the last 20 years. He is a master of precise, economical statement; the economy owes something to French models, but there is no attempt at Parisian elegance and no sign of the desire to charm and amuse which French designers will display in the most unpromising subjects. Oliver Smith makes highly ingenious use of multiple sets, but designs them with such skill that the usual restrictions of space, which would fatally hamper dancers, are avoided. *Fancy Free,* with the sailors' bar and street both visible against a twinkling background, and *Fall River Legend,* with its skeleton house against a lurid sky, are examples. For *Facsimile* he designed an arid, anonymous landscape background appropriate to this ballet of frustration and solitude. There is a calculated coldness in his work which can, for instance in the drop curtain for *Fall River Legend,* become positively disquieting. Since 1947, Oliver Smith has been co-director with Lucia Chase of Ballet Theatre. His décors include: *Saratoga* (1941) and *Rodeo* (1942) for the Ballets de Monte-Carlo; *Fancy Free* (1944), *On Stage!* (1945), *Interplay* (1945), *Facsimile* (1946) and *Fall River Legend* (1948) for Ballet Theatre; *Sebastian* (1944) for Ballet International. Has also designed for straight plays and musicals, including the sets for *My Fair Lady.*

SOIRÉES DE PARIS Les. A series of ballet performances organised in Paris by Count Étienne de Beaumont in the summer of 1924, at the Théâtre de la Cigale. They were a result of the taste for modernity which Diaghilev had so skilfully fostered among a large section of the Parisian upper-class public, and which had increased since the war to such an extent that de Beaumont knew he could count on that public to support the boldest experiments and that they would welcome almost anything except lack of distinction or novelty. These, in fact, were the only qualities common to all the ballets produced. The short season lasted from 17th May to 30th June; the ephemeral nature of the undertaking gave it a particular snob-appeal. Massine was the choreographer, and a number of Diaghilev's most brilliant collaborators were involved. The two productions which caused the greatest sensation were Cocteau's *Roméo et Juliette,* designed by Jean Hugo, and the Picasso-Satie *Mercure.* Other ballets presented were *Le Beau Danube, Salade, Gigue* (décors by Derain) and *Scuola di Ballo.* Four of these were later revived by larger companies.

SOKOLOVA Lydia. The first English dancer to succeed with the Diaghilev Ballet, Hilda Munnings learned to speak Russian, changed her name to Sokolova and was accepted by the company as "one of us". Karsavina said that like the Russians "she possessed that humility of heart, and a fervour almost religious in its intensity that gave her the same attitude towards her work as we had." She received her early training with Pavlova and Mordkin, joined Diaghilev in 1913 and remained until

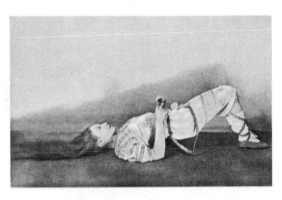

SOKOLOVA IN LE SACRE DU PRINTEMPS.

1929. She was the most loyal and dependable of Diaghilev's dancers, and he regarded her with particular affection. Her knowledge of music was a great asset, particularly in *Le Sacre du Printemps,* in which she danced the chosen virgin. Among her roles were Columbine in *Le Carnaval,* the Rag Mazurka in *Les Biches,* Kikimora in *Contes Russes* and the Miller's Wife in *Le Tricorne.* After Diaghilev's death she danced with Woizikowski's company and arranged ballets for various musicals in London. Now living and teaching in England, she possesses a pungent sense of humour and has an inexhaustible fund of stories about the Diaghilev company.

OLIVER SMITH. SKETCH FOR ON STAGE. 1945.

OLIVER SMITH. DÉCOR FOR FACSIMILE. 1944.

SOLEIL DE NUIT (The Midnight Sun).
Russian scenes and dances. Music: Rimsky-
Korsakov. Scenery and costumes: Larionov.
Choreography: Massine. First performance:
Diaghilev's Ballets Russes, Grand Théâtre,
Geneva, 20 December 1915. Principal dancers:
Massine, Zverev.

Massine's first ballet and the first décor by
Larionov, who worked in close collaboration
with him. The characters (like the choreography) were taken from Russian folklore: the
Midnight Sun, the Snow Maiden, Bobyl the
Innocent, etc. It remained in the repertory for
several years.

SOMBERT Claire. A pupil of Yves Brieux,
launched in 1951 by Janine Charrat, Claire
Sombert was the noteworthy creator of the
rôle of the gypsy girl in *Le Loup* (1953) with the
Ballets de Paris. She appeared in the Gene
Kelly film *Invitation to the Dance* and confirmed
her early promise in Jean Babilée's company,
particularly in *Balance à Trois*. Fair, with
strong slim legs and a beautifully pure line, she
is a distinguished, sensitive dancer.

SOMES Michael. Premier danseur noble of
England's Royal Ballet and partner to Margot
Fonteyn during the years of her greatest
triumphs, Michael Somes has been with the
Sadler's Wells organisation since 1934. He was
the first boy to win a scholarship to the school.
He gradually established a reputation, in the
early ballets of Frederick Ashton *(Horoscope,
Dante Sonata, The Wanderer)* as a sensitive but
virile dancer of noble appearance and fine
elevation. When he rejoined the company
after his war service, he became an admirable
partner as well. He continued to create
important roles in Ashton's ballets — *Symphonic
Variations, Daphnis and Chloe, Sylvia, Tiresias*.
Recently he has assumed increasing responsibilities as teacher and administrator.

SOMNAMBULE La (Night Shadow).
Ballet in one act. Scenario: Vittorio Rieti.
Music: Vincenzo Bellini, arr. Rieti. Choreo-
graphy: Balanchine. Scenery and costumes:
Dorothea Tanning. First performance: Ballet
Russe de Monte-Carlo, New York, 27 Feb-
ruary 1946. Principal dancers: Alexandra

Danilova, Maria Tallchief, Nicholas Magallanes.

The only things the ballet has in common with Bellini's opera are the French title, some of the music (the remainder comes from his *Puritani*) and the sleepwalking heroine. The action is set in the mid-nineteenth century. A Baron is giving an outdoor evening party for his mistress, the Coquette. One of the guests is a Poet, with whom the Coquette is in love; he receives her advances without enthusiasm. Left alone in the garden, the Poet sees a white figure descending the tower staircase of the château. She is the wife of the Baron, walking in her sleep and carrying, at arm's length, a lighted candle. The Poet is enraptured; he dances with her, but she remains asleep, unconscious of his presence. When she goes back towards the house, he follows. The Coquette, however, has seen their departure and warns the Baron. Drawing his dagger, he goes into the house. Shortly afterwards the Poet reappears alone, mortally wounded. The guests draw back in horror; the Somnambulist glides silently into the garden and with supernatural strength lifts the body of the Poet and carries him away to her chamber. The guests watch the light of her candle as it moves along the corridors of the château, slowly mounting the tower.

The choreography, gay and animated for the ball scenes and the colourful divertissements (Pastorale, Negroes, Acrobats, Harlequin), reaches a climax of poetic beauty in the pas de deux for the Sleepwalker and the Poet. Her dance consists almost entirely of pas de bourrées, uninterrupted by his efforts to hold and awaken her. From the beginning, despite the gaiety, the ballet arouses a premonition of impending tragedy.

* Revived for the de Cuevas company on 26 August 1948 at the Cambridge Theatre, London, with Éthéry Pagava, Marjorie Tallchief, George Skibine. Scenery and costumes by Jean Robier, subsequently redesigned by André Delfau.

* Revived for the Royal Danish Ballet 1954 with the Delfau scenery and costumes. Principal dancers: Margrethe Schanne, Mona Vangsaa, Henning Kronstam, and Borge Ralov outstanding as the Baron.

SONGES. Ballet in one act. Book, scenery and costumes: André Derain. Music: Darius Milhaud. Choreography: Balanchine. First performance: Ballets 1933, Théâtre des Champs-Élysées, 7 June 1933, with Tamara Toumanova. Revived 1935 in New York by the American Ballet, with Leda Anchutina.

SOUDEIKINE Serge. Born 1882, died 1946. One of the artists whom Diaghilev took

LA SOMNAMBULE. COSTUMES BY DELFAU. 1948.

to Paris from St. Peterburg to help him organise the Russian Art Exhibition of 1906. Many years later he was to introduce to Diaghilev one of his most faithful collaborators, the young Boris Kochno. He designed *La Tragédie de Salomé* for the Ballets Russes (1913), *Giselle* and *La Fille mal gardée* for the Mordkin Ballet, *Les Noces* and *Petrouchka* (1922) for the Metropolitan Opera, New York, *The Fairy Doll* (1923) for Pavlova and *Paganini* (1939) for de Basil. He was at his happiest working on a intimate scale for the Chauve-Souris company of Nikita Balieff, where he could employ his sense of fantasy and humour, typically Russian even when the subject was Sèvres porcelain, Chinese lacquer or gipsy songs.

SPECTRE DE LA ROSE Le. Choreographic tableau by Michel Fokine. Scenario: Jean-Louis Vaudoyer, after Théophile Gautier. Music: Weber (The Invitation to the Waltz, orch. Berlioz). Scenery and costumes: Léon Bakst. First performance: Diaghilev's Ballets Russes, Monte Carlo, 19 April 1911, with Karsavina and Nijinsky.

A white room, with its windows wide open to the summer night. A young girl returns from a ball, holding a rose to her lips, breathing its scent. Dreamily, she removes her cloak, sinks into a chair and falls asleep. The rose falls from her hand. Suddenly, a spirit, half-youth, half-flower, floats into the room through the open window. He dances, seeming hardly to touch the ground, like a rose petal blown by the wind. Then he bends over the sleeper and draws her into the dance. It becomes more and more delirious, but the dream cannot last. The spectre leads the girl back to her chair, brushes her forehead lightly with his lips, and disappears once more into the night. The girl's eyes open, she awakens drowsily and stoops to retrieve the faded rose at her feet. Its scent recalls her dream and she lingers over the memory, her smile tinged with regret. More than 50 years earlier Théophile Gautier had imagined the episode in his celebrated poem: "Soulève ta paupière close — qu'effleure un songe virginal, — Je suis le spectre de la rose — que tu portais hier au bal". It was Jean-Louis Vaudoyer who had the idea of a short ballet on the theme to Weber's music. Bakst and Fokine realised it to perfec-

tion: a cool, virginal décor in pale colours, many leagues removed from the opulence of *Sheherazade ;* exquisitely tender choreography full of feeling and character, the very opposite of a virtuoso pas de deux. The first interpreters, Karsavina and Nijinsky, remain unsurpassed. Since their time the *Spectre,* constantly performed, has undergone many vicissitudes. Its choreography of the utmost simplicity — jumps and leaps for the man, hardly anything but mime for his partner — requires a male dancer with soft elevation and a girl with exceptional acting ability. The creation of an appropriate atmosphere is all-important. Too many modern versions dispense with a proper setting, ignore the importance of the girl's part, and turn this delicate masterpiece into a mere vehicle for the male dancer. The last leap of the spectre, as he soars through the window into the night, tends to receive so much applause that the final 'cello solo and the pathos of the girl's awakening are obliterated. When this happens, it is a sure sign that the spell has not been cast.

SPESSIVTSEVA Olga (also known as Spessiva). "Spessiva and Pavlova are like two halves of an apple, but the Spessiva half has been in the sun." Diaghilev's judgement must be treated with some reserve, because he could never forgive Pavlova for leaving the Russian Ballet. When we attempt to define Spessivtseva's quality, the vagueness of English terminology becomes cruelly apparent. Everyone agrees that she was one of the greatest classical dancers of the present century. The French, using the term in its precise, period sense, describe her as a "romantic dancer" but we, who are accustomed to use "romantic" in a looser way, remember that her withdrawn, dedicated distinction had little of the warmth, range and power of characterisation of Karsavina, and feel safer with our equally imprecise "classical".

Spessivtseva was a St. Petersburg dancer who graduated from the Imperial school to the Maryinsky in 1913. Her exceptional ability was soon remarked. She joined the Russian Ballet in 1916 (having previously refused) to dance *Spectre de la Rose* with Nijinsky during the American tour. She returned to the Maryinsky in mid-revolution to gain fresh laurels in the great classical roles *Esmeralda* and *Giselle*. With the latter role she felt a particular affinity and worked on it with the passion and relentless tenacity of one possessed, making several visits to a madhouse to observe the patients. The result was a deeply moving portrayal, exquisitely tender and melancholy, with a mad scene of symbolic, almost abstract, quality. In the second act she was an impalpable, transparent wraith, who did not appear to touch the ground; her black hair framed and enhanced the pallor of her face; her eyes were like those of a frightened animal.

In the spring of 1920 Spessivtseva was officially promoted to the rank of ballerina, but fell gravely ill and had to leave the stage for a year. In 1921 she managed to obtain permission to go abroad, as Diaghilev had invited her to appear in his London season as the first of the Auroras in

OLGA SPESSIVTSEVA.

the great revival of *The Sleeping Princess*. She returned to Russia at the end of the season, but left again in 1924 for the last time. There then began an association with the Paris Opera which lasted, with intervals, until 1932. When she appeared for the first rehearsal of *Giselle,* shy and quietly dressed, there was a thrill of disap-

pointment, but it changed to a thrill of a different kind when she began to dance. In 1927 she rejoined Diaghilev for a few months, dancing not only the classics but *Zéphire et Flore* and *Roméo et Juliette,* and creating the title-role in *La Chatte*. She even — she, who many years previously had refused to dance in a Fokine ballet because she "did not understand the style" — prepared *L'Oiseau de feu* for the Paris season, but an injury prevented her dancing it or repeating *La Chatte*. She appeared again in the final London season of 1929, and returned after Diaghilev's death to dance *Giselle* with Dolin for the Camargo Society in 1932. She left the Paris Opera in that year and appeared for six months in Buenos Aires with Fokine. In the autumn of 1934 she sailed for Australia with the Classical Russian Ballet, Pavlova's old company. It was during this tour that the first signs of mental instability declared themselves. After a dance recital at the Opéra-Comique in June 1935 she decided to retire and, except for a short season at Buenos Aires in 1937 with Ekaterina Galantha, she never appeared again. At the beginning of the war she took refuge in the United States. Her mental condition grew worse and she had to be taken to a lunatic asylum on the outskirts of New York, where she is still confined. Like Pavlova, Spessivtseva has become a legend, a legend transmitted less by her actual appearances which, compared to Pavlova's, were few in number, than by fame and hearsay and by the eloquent photographs of her such as adorn the schools of dancing in far-off Japan — a country she never visited, but which honours her name.

STAATS Léo (1877-1952). French dancer, choreographer and teacher, who devoted the sixty-odd years of his busy working life to the preservation and maintenance of the French tradition. He studied at the Paris Opera under Louis Mérante and made his first appearance as a dancer at the age of ten. His first ballet, *Ici l'on danse,* was produced at the Opéra in 1893. As a dancer, his most celebrated role was Jean in Saint-Saëns's *Javotte*. His activities, at the Opéra (where he was maître de ballet from 1909 to 1936) and elsewhere, were manifold. He revived and adapted old ballets, composed new ones. From 1910-1914 he was artistic director of Jacques Rouché's productions at the Théâtre des Arts. After 1915, he produced another thirty or so ballets for the Opéra, including *La Péri* (*) in 1921 and *Cydalise et le Chèvre-pied* (*) in 1923. He taught at his famous school in the rue Saulnier till the time of his death. The Paris Opera is still full of his pupils, who revere the memory of the old man whose heart was as kind as his temper was hasty.

STANISLAVSKY, NEMIROVITCH-DANCHENKO COMPANY. A Moscow ballet company which has been strongly influenced by the teaching of Stanislavsky and which pays particular attention to interpretation and dramatic truth in its productions. A good example is the version of *Le Lac des Cygnes* by its ballet master and chief choreographer, Vladimir Bourmeister. This excels even that of the Bolshoi in creating a fairy-tale world, romantic and beautiful, and in telling the story lucidly and movingly. The company was founded in 1930 by the dancer Victorina Kriger, but Bourmeister from the beginning was the moving spirit. For a time the troupe danced in Moscow and toured widely throughout Russia. Then, in 1939, Nemirovitch-Danchenko recognised the importance of the work which was being done and decided to incorporate the ballet company into his lyric theatre. The dancers are drawn from the state ballet schools and many of them have appeared also at the Bolshoi and in Leningrad. Nevertheless the Stanislavsky Ballet retains a strong personality of its own and has its own devoted public in Moscow. The repertoire includes revivals of the classics, important Soviet ballets *(Fountain of Bakhchisarai, Les Rives du Bonheur)*, and new creations. Among the latter must be mentioned a remarkable production of *The Merry Wives of Windsor* (choreography by Bourmeister and Kourilov, music by Oranski), which brilliantly captures the spirit of Shakespeare's comedy. The Stanislavsky Ballet was the first Soviet company of appear in Paris, in 1956 at the Théâtre du Châtelet. The principal dancers then were Violetta Bovt, Sophie Vinogradova, Alla Ossopienko, Eleanora Vlassova, Mira Redina, Nina Timofeyeva, Alexis Tchitchinadze, Mikhail Salop, Yuri Kondratov, Svatoslav Kouznetsov, and Alexander Klein,

STEVENSON Hugh. English designer, born 1910, died 1956. Hugh Stevenson worked with the Ballet Club and Sadler's Wells from the earliest days. His designs had no great distinction in themselves, but at their best they possessed a sympathetic gift for establishing atmosphere. The Watteau-esque *Gods go a'Begging* and the discreetly Edwardian *Jardin aux Lilas* (one of many ballets he decorated for Tudor) were very pleasing. He designed the first full-length *Le Lac des Cygnes* for Sadler's Wells (1934) and two post-war revivals of *Giselle,* for Rambert and London's Festival Ballet.

STRAUSS Richard (1864-1949). Though neither of his two ballets, *Josephslegende (La Légende de Joseph,* Diaghilev, 1914) and *Schlagobers* (Vienna, 1924) added much lustre to his fame, Strauss's operas show that he was keenly aware of the possibilities of the dance as a theatrical medium. The obvious examples are the final scenes of *Salomé* and *Elektra,* which require to be danced as well as sung by dramatic sopranos, and exhausted sopranos at that. He wrote dance scenes for Molière's *Bourgeois Gentilhomme* and Commedia dell'arte episodes for the originally inset opera *Ariadne auf Naxos.* His last librettist, Joseph Gregor, incorporated dance episodes into *Daphne* and *Danaë,* and they had together planned a work for dancing on the subject of the rivalry between Camargo and Sallé as well as an opera-ballet, *The Revenge of Aphrodite.* Neither of these projects, alas ! was realised.

The *Tanzsuite* after Couperin was danced in Germany in 1926 and reappeared later in augmented form as *Verklungene Feste.* Balanchine used the *Bourgeois Gentilhomme* music for a ballet of that name (Monte Carlo, 1932; revived New York, 1944). Of the symphonic poems, *Till Eulenspiegel* has attracted various choreographers, including Nijinsky (1916), Babilée (1949) and Balanchine (1951). Ashton set *Don Juan* for the Sadler's Wells Ballet in 1948. Tudor used Strauss's *Burleske* for *Dim Lustre.*

STRAVINSKY Igor. The composer of the finest ballet music of our day was born in 1882, the son of a distinguished bass-baritone at the Imperial Opera, St. Petersburg. Though his musical gifts declared themselves early, his parents insisted that he study law at the University, but music absorbed more and more of his time, and he began to take private lessons in composition and orchestration with Rimsky-Korsakov. Two of his early works, *Scherzo Fantastique* and *Feu d'artifice,* were heard by Diaghilev, who sensed the quality of the young man who is now, fifty years later, the most eminent of living composers. The long and chequered association, so immensely fruitful for both men, began with the invitation to orchestrate a piece by Grieg for *Le Festin* and two by Chopin (the opening Nocturne and closing Valse) for *Les Sylphides.* Then, when it became clear that Liadov would never complete *L'Oiseau de feu* in time for the Paris season of 1910, the commission was transferred to Stravinsky. The idea of *Le Sacre du Printemps* came to him before he had finished his first ballet, but *Petrouchka* (1911), originally intended as a concert piece for piano and orchestra, intervened. The *Sacre* (1913) was a Dionysiac outburst, one of the milestones of modern music. Echoes of it have persisted in his own music (Symphony in three movements, *Orpheus*) but after writing it, he felt the need for order and discipline, for what Eric Walter White has described as a "sacrifice to Apollo". He left Russia in 1914 and settled in Switzerland, where he consoled himself by studying Russian folk-poetry. He started work on *Les Noces,* but *Renard* and *L'Histoire du Soldat,* two small but highly original stage works in which dancing is an important element, were finished first. *Renard* is still Russian; the *Soldat* shows signs of increasing cosmopolitanism. Both are written for small chamber combinations. The *Soldat* was first produced at Lausanne (1918), an act of independence which Diaghilev regarded as treachery. But Diaghilev forgave his "spiritual son" and staged many more of his works: *Le Chant du Rossignol* (1920, a shortened, orchestral version of the earlier opera *Le Rossignol*), *Pulcinella* (1920), *Renard* and the miniature opera *Mavra* (1922), *Les Noces* (1923), the opera-oratorio *Oedipus Rex* (1927) and *Apollon Musagète* (1928). In that year also, Ida Rubinstein (to Diaghilev's intense displeasure) mounted the Tchaikovskian *Baiser de la Fée.*

The enumeration of these works gives no hint of their variety. The subject and material of *Les Noces* are still intensely Russian, but their austerely rigorous treatment looks to the future. *Pulcinella,* which antedates the performance of *Les Noces* but not its conception, and *Le Baiser de la fée,* are examples of Stravinsky's habit of deriving a fresh impulse from an intensive study of the music of other composers and other periods—in these two cases 18th century Naples and Tchaikovsky. His devotion to his great compatriot, further proved by the truly Apollonian *Apollon Musagète,* was strengthened by the orchestrations he made for Diaghilev's 1921 revival of *La Belle au bois dormant.* In performing this task he expressed his admiration for classical ballet, which "in its very essence, by the beauty of its regularity and the aristocratic rigour of its forms, corresponds so perfectly to my conception of art". *Perséphone* (1934), a "melodrama" to a text by André Gide, was another commission from Ida Rubinstein. *Jeu de Cartes* (American Ballet, 1937) marked Stravinsky's renewed association with Balanchine, the choreographer of *Apollon* and the one who has understood him best of all.

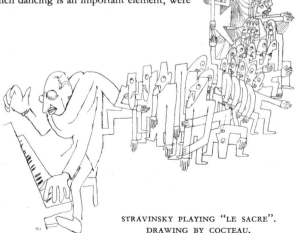

STRAVINSKY PLAYING "LE SACRE".
DRAWING BY COCTEAU.

JEU DE CARTES. BALLET BY CHARRAT AND STRAVINSKY.

In 1939, Stravinsky went to the United States, and became an American citizen seven years later. His remaining ballets were written and first performed there. With the exception of *Scènes de Ballet* (Dolin, Philadelphia, 1944), Balanchine was the choreographer in every case: *Danses Concertantes* (Ballets Russes de Monte-Carlo, 1944), *Orpheus* (Ballet Society, 1948) and *Agon* (New York City Ballet, 1958). Like the earlier ballets, they reflect the main phases of Stravinsky's ceaseless exploration and self-renewal including, in the case of *Agon,* his recent interest in the serial methods of Webern.

All Stravinsky's ballets except the *Sacre,* which has nothing to do with classical ballet, show an instinctive feeling (Tchaikovsky possessed it too) for the classical style, with its turned-out movements, extended lines and use of points. That is not to say that they are easy: the rhythms (or more properly, the metres) are diabolically difficult, the orchestration grows rarer and spikier. Each new score at once excites, bewilders and disconcerts, but is finally seen to be "right". They are quintessential ballet music. They have raised the genre to a new level, and they demand a standard of performance in the orchestra pit which they all too rarely receive.

STRUCHKOVA Raissa. A pupil of the Bolshoi Theatre school and now one of its brightest stars. Her physical beauty is immediately remarkable; her legs are long and slender, her shoulders and neck beautifully modelled, her face, unmistakably Russian, illumined by her bright eyes and radiant smile. She is a superb dancer of effortless elevation, with a great range of style. She has appeared in the majority of Ulanova's roles and has survived the comparison. In some roles, such as Aurora, she allows technique to take precedence over warmth and femininity, but this defect is a minor one in the light of the passionate and exalted interpretation she brings to the roles of Juliet in *Romeo and Juliet* and Maria in *The Fountain of Bakhchisarai.* She moves so naturally that it is a delight to watch her run across the stage, and she throws herself with such joyous abandon into divertissements such as the Moskowski Waltz (which she dances with her husband Lapauri) that she can excite and exhilarate the most blasé or lethargic audience.

SUITE DE DANSES. Ballet by Ivan Clustine. Music: Chopin. First performance:

Paris Opera, 23 June 1913. Principal dancers: Carlotta Zambelli, Albert Aveline.

It was no doubt the popularity of Fokine's *Les Sylphides* (1909) that inspired the Opéra to mount another ballet of pure dancing to music by Chopin. At it is presented today in the version by Aveline made in 1931 for Spessivtseva and Lifar, with décor by Pruna, the formula is even vaguer than the woodland glade "after Corot" which so often serves as background for *Les Sylphides*. *Suite de Danses* marshals a large number of dancers in traditional romantic ballet costumes, including a group of "petits rats", who go through their motions under the full glare of the spotlights in a park where the trees are the colour of burnt bread. Nevertheless, it is one of the hardiest favourites in the Opéra repertoire. There are two star roles, one male, one female.

SUITE EN BLANC. Ballet by Serge Lifar. Music: Édouard Lalo (from the ballet *Namouna*, 1882). Scenario: Dignimont. First performance: Paris Opera, 23 July 1943. Principal dancers: Solange Schwarz, Lycette Darsonval, Yvette Chauviré, Serge Lifar, Roger Ritz, Roger Fenonjois.

Lifar's first non-narrative ballet. The girls wear white tutus, the men black tights and full, white blouses. The stage is arranged in two tiers, connected by flights of steps at either end, which permit a wide range of groupings and a continuous flow of movement. The ballet is a fine opportunity for a large company to display its mastery of technique. It opens with a classical pas de trois by three premières danseuses, followed by the various entrées of the stars (one of them a brilliant pas d'action for a ballerina partnered by four men; another, a male solo based on a Georgian folk dance). After an adage with some curious lifts the general tempo increases till the dancers cross the stage diagonally in a series of coupés jetés and cabrioles en arrière. Finally the dancers are grouped motionless in a circle, while a soloist performs the famous 32 fouettés. The combination of the black and white costumes with Lalo's highly-coloured, pseudo-oriental music is surprisingly effective.

* Revived in slightly modified form as *Noir et Blanc* by the Nouveau Ballet de Monte-Carlo, 1946. A recent revival (1958) of this version by the de Cuevas company was the occasion of the celebrated duel between de Cuevas and Lifar.

ORPHEUS. MARIA TALLCHIEF AND N. MAGALLANES.

SWAN LAKE. See *Lac des Cygnes.*

SYLPHIDE La. Ballet in two acts. Scenario: Adolphe Nourrit, after Charles Nodier's story "Trilby". Music: J. Schneitzhoeffer. Scenery: Ciceri. Choreography: Philippe Taglioni. First performance: Académie Royale de Musique (Paris Opera), 12 March 1832. Principal dancers: Marie Taglioni, Joseph Mazilier.

In the early 1830's the Romantic revival was in full swing; it had spread from literature to the drama and from the drama to the ballet, where it was to find its perfect incarnation in the person of Marie Taglioni. The technique of classical ballet had been enriched by the use of the point. The white tarlatan tutu, diaphanous, chaste and modest, symbol of the preoccupation with sprites and fairies so fashionable at the period of the restoration of the French monarchy, became henceforward the accepted costume for the romantic ballerina. The time was ripe for the flowering of the "ballet blanc", of which *La Sylphide* was the prototype. The curtain rises on a large room in a gloomy Scottish homestead. James, a young Highlander in a kilt, who is to wed the charming Effie on the morrow, is dozing in an armchair by the fire when a Sylphide appears, flutters about him and wakes him with a kiss. Enamoured, he tries to pursue her but she eludes his grasp and disappears. Guests begin to arrive and preparations are being made for the wedding; James, however, is preoccupied, haunted by the vision of the Sylphide. An old witch, Madge, comes in to tell fortunes; she predicts that Effie will not marry James but his rival Gurn. Furiously James sends her from the house and she vows vengeance. General dancing begins, but the Sylphide appears again, visible only to James. She snatches the wedding ring from him and disappears into the forest. James follows her, abandoning the heartbroken Effie. The second act takes place in the forest, home of the sylphs. First we see the witch manufacturing in her giant cauldron a magic scarf. Then James appears, exhausted and forlorn, unable to find the Sylphide. But soon she comes to comfort him, offering him water from a spring and presenting him with birds' nests which she steals from the trees. Other sylphs join in the dance but although James is momentarily happy he is never able to hold the Sylphide. Suddenly all the sylphs disappear and

LA SYLPHIDE. A CONTEMPORARY PRINT.

he is left alone. In despair, he accepts the magic scarf from the witch because she tells him that it will bind his love to him for ever. When the Sylphide returns, he drapes it about her shoulders; her wings drop to the ground and she falls lifeless. She is carried away into the treetops by her mourning companions while the distraught James sees in the distance the wedding procession of Effie and Gurn.

The choreography of the first scene consists of the delicate and charming appearances of the Sylphide, interspersed with mime scenes, pas d'action and general dances which are an Italian ballet master's idea of a highland fling. The second act takes place in a supernatural world and marks the flowering of the "ballet blanc". *La Sylphide* paved the way for *Giselle,* and it was undoubtedly Philippe Taglioni's finest achievement. He took pains to see that his daughter should be the only star in the ballet. The role of the Sylphide, consisting of "held" poses, silent runs on point, arabesques, elevation and grand, majestic developpés, was exquisitely arranged and assured the fame of Marie Taglioni. Ciceri, the master of romantic stage-design, had painted his settings in the "moon-light and ruins" tradition so dear to the times; the first tutu ever to be designed was the work of Eugène Lami. The tinkling music was by Schneitzhoeffer, chorus-master at the Opéra and mediocre composer. Among the heroes of the evening were the Opéra tech-nicians, who devised the flying ballet in act II: in the finale, the Syl-phide's funeral procession ascended to the flies. Accidents did happen, however. One April evening in 1837, the machinery stuck, leaving two of the dancers, to the alarm and dismay of the audience, suspended in space.

Several other great Romantic dan-cers appeared as La Sylphide. When Fanny Cerrito openly challenged Taglioni's supremacy at the Scala, Milan, in 1841, and divided Italy into *Taglionisti* and *Cerrististi,* she was forced to use a reduced version of the ballet by Cortesi. *La Sylphide* was revived by Marius Petipa in 1892 at the Imperial Theatre, St. Petersburg. In our own day, Victor Gsovsky arranged the work for the Ballets des Champs-Élysées in 1946, with scenery by A. Serebriakoff and costumes by Christian Bérard. Nina Vyrou-bova, supported by Roland Petit as James and Nathalie Philipart as Effie, danced the principal role with mysterious and touching poetry. A Bournonville version of *La Sylphide,* mounted in 1836 for Lucile Grahn and with music by Herman Lovenskjold, is still in the repertoire of the Royal Danish Ballet. This retains the French style of the nineteenth century and is the most perfect survival of a ballet from the Romantic period to be seen today. Margrethe Schanne now dances the Sylphide, with Erik Bruhn or Henning Kronstam as James, Gerda Karstens or Niels Bjorn Larsen as the witch. Harald Lander revived this version for the de Cuevas company, with sets and costumes by Bernard Daydé, in 1953 at the Théâtre de l'Empire, Paris. Rosella Hightower was the Sylphide and Serge Golovine James. Two years later, at the Théâtre des Champs-Élysées, the same company presented two guest artists

LA SYLPHIDE. MARGRETHE SCHANNE AND POUL GNATT.

in the ballet, Alicia Markova and Margrethe Schanne.

SYLPHIDES Les. Ballet in one act. Mu-sic: Chopin. Scenery and costumes: Alexandre Benois. Choreography: Michel Fokine. First performance: Diaghilev's Ballets Russes, Théâtre du Châtelet, Paris, 2 June 1909. Principal dancers: Anna Pavlova, Tamara Karsavina, Alexandra Baldina, Vaslav Nijinsky.

One of Fokine's masterpieces: a perfect example of the one-act ballet with no story. The idea of using Chopin for ballet originated with Isadora Duncan, whom Fokine much admired. *Les Sylphides* was evolved in three stages. First of all, Fokine discovered Glazou-nov's *Chopiniana,* an orchestral version of some pianoforte pieces by the Polish composer. A valse was added, and Fokine devised a ballet d'action with various dramatic scenes: Chopin composing in a haunted monastery, a Polish wedding, a Neapolitan Tarantella, etc. This was performed at the Maryinsky in March, 1908. A few weeks later, he produced an entirely different version to a revised selection of Chopin pieces, an evocation of the romantic mood of the music in terms of pure dancing. Diaghilev decided to include it in the repertory for the 1909 Paris season, but insisted on a change of title (the new one was suggested by Benois) and further slight alterations in the music. Stravinsky made some new orchestrations and Benois designed the décor, similar in style to his second act set for *Giselle*. In this moonlit glade, dancers dressed "à la Taglioni" in long, full skirts of white tarlatan are joined by a single male figure in black velvet doublet and white tights. He and the three female soloists each have one solo, subtly contrasted but never destroying the mood. There is a pas de deux of exquisite beauty and ensembles at the opening and close. The corps de ballet also provide links between the solos, when one simple but marvellously effective grouping dissolves into another; in *Les Sylphides* it is they, as much as the soloists, who make or mar the performance.

The Benois décor has frequently been replaced; by a landscape "after" Corot, by new designs by Socrate, Braque, Zack and many others. It remains the most satisfactory, however, and has been reproduced for the Royal Ballet at Covent Garden. There have been several alternative orchestrations. A sensitive performance of *Les Sylphides* (with due attention to such stylistic details as make-up, arm movements, etc.) is still, after fifty years, one of the most rewarding experiences ballet has to offer.

SYLVIA or **The Nymph of Diana.** Ballet in three acts and four scenes. Scenario: Jules Barbier and Baron de Reinach, after Tasso's *Aminta*. Music: Léo Delibes. Scenery: Chéret, Rubé and Chaperon. Costumes: Lacoste. Choreography: Louis Mérante. First performance: Paris Opera, 14 June 1876. Principal dancers: Rita Sangalli, Marguet, Sanlaville, Mérante, Magri.

Sylvia is a nymph of Diana, and as such vowed to chastity. She defies Eros and spurns the love of the shepherd, Amyntas, who is wounded by the arrow intended by Sylvia for the statue of Eros. The statue comes to life and looses a golden arrow at Sylvia. She begins to feel an unwonted tenderness for Amyntas, but further developments are hindered by her abduc-

tion by another admirer, the dark huntsman, Orion. In captivity, Sylvia appeals to Eros, who helps her to escape and return to Amyntas. The goddess Diana is furious at her votary's lapse from grace, but the cunning Eros reminds her of her own adventure with Endymion. She relents, and gives her blessing to the union of the lovers.

The music of Delibes, tuneful, colourful and admirably orchestrated, was far superior to the average ballet score of the period, and had considerable influence on Tchaikovsky. Among the highlights of the choreography are the variations in the first act, with the emphasis on elevation, the dance of seduction in the second act, and the famous "pizzicato" in the last act, a bravura variation which requires impeccable timing and artistry. The ensemble dances, too, are important: the fauns and dryads, the entry of the huntresses, and the procession of Bacchus can only be performed by a large and well trained corps de ballet. The role of Sylvia was one of Carlotta Zambelli's great successes at the Paris Opera at the beginning of the century. Later, Suzanne Lorcia shone by her beauty and style; Solange Schwarz was a Sylvia full of authority, with steel-like points; Lycette Darsonval danced it with spirit and fine technique.

* There have been subsequent versions at the Paris Opera by Staats, Lifar (1941, scenery and costumes by Brianchon) and Aveline (1946).

* Gerdt completed the version on which Ivanov was working at his death (St. Petersburg, 1901, Preobrajenska). The music of *Sylvia* was used for Lavrovsky's first ballet, *Fadetta* (Leningrad, 1934).

* In London, a one-act version was staged at the Empire Theatre in 1911, by C. Wilhelm and Fred Farren. Lydia Kyasht, Phyllis Bedells and Farren himself danced in it. Ashton made a new three-act version for the Sadler's Wells Ballet at Covent Garden in 1952. Scenery and costumes: Robin and Christopher Ironside. Principal dancers: Fonteyn, Farron, Somes, Hart, Grant. This was an opulent production, echoing the conventions of 1870, but rather in the nature of an affectionate *pastiche*. The second act is the weakest, but the dances for Sylvia and her companions in act I, and the third act variation and pas de deux are among Ashton's finest compositions.

SYMPHONIC VARIATIONS. Ballet in one act. Music: César Franck. Choreography: Frederick Ashton. Scenery and costumes: Sophie Fedorovitch. First performance: Sadler's Wells Ballet, Covent Garden, London, 24 April 1946. Dancers: Margot Fonteyn, Pamela May, Moira Shearer, Michael Somes, Brian Shaw, Henry Danton.

Sophie Fedorovitch's setting is like spring sunshine: a great expanse of pale green with flowing black lines; simple, white costumes with touches of black and silver. Christian Bérard compared this décor to a lily of the valley. Ashton's choreography (there is no plot) seems to flow from the finest qualities of Franck's music and yet to shed new light on the familiar score; serene and infinitely peaceful, though demanding the utmost control from the six dancers, who are on the stage throughout the entire ballet. *Symphonic Variations* is the most perfect of Ashton's short ballets and the most distinguished work in the post-war repertory of Sadler's Wells.

SYMPHONIE CONCERTANTE. Ballet in four movements. Music: Mozart. Scenery and costumes: James Stewart Morcom. Choreography: Balanchine. First performance: Ballet Society, New York City Center, 12 November 1947, with Maria Tallchief, Tanaquil LeClercq, Todd Bolender.

One of Balanchine's ballets of pure dancing, set to Mozart's Sinfonia Concertante in E flat (K. 364). The two solo instruments (violin and viola) are each represented by a ballerina. There are six secondary soloists, a corps de ballet of 16 girls and one male dancer, who appears only in the central Andante. The costumes, which have simple, short tutus, harmonise with the golden backcloth.

SYMPHONIE FANTASTIQUE La. Choreographic symphony in five scenes. Scenario and music: Berlioz. Scenery and costumes: Christian Bérard. Choreography: Massine. First performance: de Basil's Ballets Russes, Covent Garden, 24 July 1936. Principal dancers: Tamara Toumanova, Nina Verchinina, Leonide Massine, Yurek Shabelevsky, George Zoritch.

Massine used Berlioz's own scenario for the

RITA SANGALLI IN SYLVIA.

Fantastic Symphony, a typical document of the Romantic period. A Young Musician takes poison in a fit of despair and falls into a state of semi-consciousness between dream and reality. We see five of his hallucinations, in each of which his unattainable beloved appears. The first, Rêveries et Passions, is ghostly and mysterious, vague forms gliding through a landscape with a statue of a sphinx. The second, a Ball Scene, is more precise. He catches sight of his beloved among the waltzing figures and dances with her for an ecstatic moment, but she eludes him. The third movement is a wonderfully serene pastoral. The musician watches a young shepherd dance with a girl; his peace is troubled by a vision of the beloved. In the ensuing March to the Scaffold he dreams that he has murdered her and is being led to execution. As he is about to die, she appears to him once more. The last movement is a Witches' Sabbath. All Hell is let loose, the Dies Irae thunders in the orchestra and — climax of horror — he discovers the beloved dancing in the infernal round among the witches.

La *Symphonie Fantastique* was the finest of a series of ballets on Romantic themes of which Nijinska's *La Bien-aimée* (1928) was a forerunner. Ashton's *Apparitions* (1936) and Fokine's *Paganini* (1939) were other examples. They were, no doubt, a reaction against the anti-romantic movement of the 'twenties. Balanchine can provide a choreographic counterpoint to music. Massine searches for a plastic equivalent; though he weighs every note, his approach is really more intuitive and sympathetic than analytical. When Berlioz becomes vague, Massine becomes confused. But in the main he was wonderfully successful in conveying the atmosphere of fevered hallucination. The three middle movements were the best, the pastoral scene making the strongest impression of all. In the mimed role of the musician Massine once again displayed his remarkable gift for dominating the stage while remaining practically motionless. Bérard's décors, particularly the red arcades of the ballroom and the crumbling Roman aqueduct of the Scène aux Champs, were among his most masterly.

* Revived by Massine at the Paris Opera, with Bérard's décor, 17 April 1957. Principal dancers: Christiane Vaussard and Youly Algaroff.

SYMPHONIE POUR UN HOMME SEUL. Ballet by Maurice Béjart. Musique concrète by Pierre Schaeffer and Pierre Henry. First performance: Ballets de l'Étoile, Paris, 3 August 1955. Principal dancers: Michèle Seigneuret, Maurice Béjart.

A ballet for the times. Man as a prisoner; prisoner of Woman, prisoner of "les autres", prisoner of noise, prisoner of mechanised, modern life. Only the ropes hanging downwards on an otherwise featureless stage seem to offer any hope of escape. It is the world of Kafka, Sartre and Samuel Beckett translated (with force and concision) into terms of ballet. The impression of absolute despair was powerfully reinforced by the use of "musique concrète", a medley of sinister noises which seemed to include a "prepared piano", echoing voices shouting incomprehensible orders, fragments of song, and one intelligible word — "absolument".

SYMPHONY FOR FUN. Ballet in four movements. Music: Don Gillis. Choreography: Michael Charnley. Scenery and costumes: Tom Lingwood. First performance: London's Festival Ballet, Royal Festival Hall, London, 1 September 1952. Principal dancers: Anita Landa, Noel Rossana, John Gilpin.

An invigorating and highly enjoyable mixture

SYMPHONIC VARIATIONS. DÉCOR BY SOPHIE FEDOROVITCH. 1946.

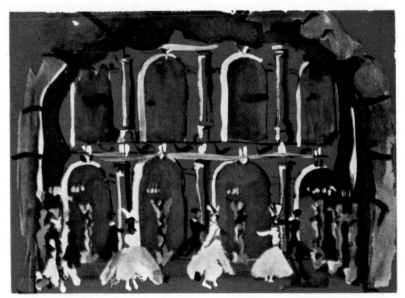

LA SYMPHONIE FANTASTIQUE. DÉCOR FOR THE BALL SCENE BY BÉRARD. 1936.

of jazz dancing and classical ballet, performed by the Festival Ballet with tremendous zest and pace. There is no theme; just simple plays of temperament one against the other, with changes of mood indicated by lighting. *Symphony for Fun* is Festival Ballet's most characteristic work. Dolin commissioned it after seeing experimental works by Charnley at Ballet Workshop. Whether the idiom he has used here is capable of development has yet to be proved, but this ballet is an undoubted winner.

SYMPHONY IN C. See *Palais de Cristal*.

T

TABLE VERTE La (The Green Table). Dance of death in eight scenes. Scenario: Kurt Jooss. Music: Fritz Cohen. Costumes: Hein Heckroth. Choreography: Kurt Jooss. First

performance: Théâtre des Champs-Élysées, 3 July 1932.

Kurt Jooss was almost unknown outside his native Germany when he submitted *The Green Table* at the choreographic competition organised in Paris by Rolf de Maré and his Archives Internationales de la Danse. The Essen Opera, where Jooss was maître de ballet, paid the expenses of the production, which won the first prize. The company from Essen took the ballet to a number of European cities including London, paid a return visit to Paris, and in the following year began an independent existence as the Ballets Jooss.

When the curtain rises ten diplomats, grotesquely baldheaded or bearded, wearing black jackets and striped trousers, are holding a discussion round a green conference table. Their mimed debate grows livelier and livelier and ends with the firing of revolvers — war has been declared. The following scenes take place in the world outside. Under the watchful eye of Death, wearing the attributes of the god Mars (the role was danced by Jooss himself), young soldiers bid farewell to their mothers, wives or sweethearts before marching to the frontier. There follow — all against black curtains — scenes

THE GREEN TABLE. BALLETS JOOSS.

of battle, of refugees in flight, of debauchery; then the survivors return. The diplomats assemble once more round the green table and again fire their revolvers in the air, this time as a sign that negotiations have been resumed. It was a ferociously satirical ballet, a pacifist manifesto. Some of its success was undoubtedly due to the subject, which could leave no one indifferent, but this in no way diminishes its achievement. It was a justification of the theories of Jooss's teacher Rudolf von Laban, and probably the masterpiece of expressionist choreography, but Jooss brought to it positive qualities of his own: passionate sincerity, a mastery of stagecraft and a fine sense of design.

TALLCHIEF Maria. Ballerina of the New York City Ballet and today one of the most brilliant interpreters of the works of Balanchine. The daughter of an American Indian chieftain of the Osage tribe, she was born in Oklahoma and trained in California by Bronislava Nijinska. Her career began with the Ballet Russe de Monte-Carlo, for whom she created the role of the Coquette in Balanchine's *Night Shadow*. In 1947 she joined Ballet Society, the company directed by Balanchine who was then her husband. She is a dancer of remarkable technical strength, not tall but with long, elegant legs. To watch Tall-

chief dancing is to marvel at the perfect execution of neo-classical choreography. Although she performs such roles as The Firebird and Eurydice in *Orpheus* with style and understanding she is not, primarily, a dramatic dancer. *The Nutcracker, Scotch Symphony* and *Caracole* are the ballets which suit her best; she is a skilled pianist and her musicality makes her an ideal exponent of ballets which derive their impetus solely from the music. She was guest artist at the Paris Opera in 1947 and danced again with the Ballet Russe de Monte-Carlo during the season 1954-55.

TALLCHIEF Marjorie. Younger sister of Maria, born in Fairfax, Oklahoma, she studied with Nijinska and Lichine. She danced with Ballet Theatre in *Graduation Ball* and as the Queen of the Willis in *Giselle,* but her greatest successes have been in Europe with the de Cuevas company, which she joined in 1947. She stayed with de Cuevas for ten years, leaving in 1957 to become a star of the Paris Opera—a rare honour for an American. A brilliant, vital dancer, with a very slim and flexible body, Marjorie Tallchief has also a strong stage personality. Her natural, very feminine charm is emphasised by her exotic appearance, inherited from her American Indian forebears. Married to George Skibine (and mother of twins), she is an admirable interpreter of her husband's ballets: *Idylle, Annabel Lee, Le Prisonnier du Caucase, Concerto.* She also dances in Lifar's version of *L'Oiseau de feu* at the Opéra.

TARAS John. Born in New York in 1919 of Ukrainian parents, he made his début at the age of nine in a Ukrainian folk-dance group, directed by Avramenko. At 13 he was arranging dances for plays in a university theatrical company (with which he appeared as a boy actor), but his interest in ballet was really aroused later, by reading a book about Nijinsky. He was 17 when he started to train with Fokine in New York. Subsequently he studied with Vilzak and Schollar and at the Scool of American Ballet. In 1940 he joined the American Ballet Caravan and became a fervent disciple of Balanchine. He was with Ballet Theatre from 1942 to 1946, rising from corps de ballet to soloist level and gaining valuable experience by working as ballet master on the Tudor and Lichine ballets. In 1945 he produced his first ballet *Graziana,* with Nora Kaye, Alicia Alonso, and André Eglevsky. He composed *Camille* for Markova in 1946 (Original Ballet Russe), and *The Minotaur* in 1947 (Ballet Society). 1948 was a busy year: he produced *Persephone* for the San Francisco Ballet, his great success *Designs with Strings* (*) for the Metropolitan Ballet in England, and then became maître de ballet of the de Cuevas company. He stayed with de Cuevas for several years, doing valuable work to build up the company, and producing many ballets, among them *Le Bal des jeunes filles* (1950), *Tarasiana* (1951), and *Piège de lumière* (*). In 1949 he produced two ballets for the Paris season of the Ballets des Champs-Élysées: *Devoirs de vacances,* and *Le Réparateur de radio.* Leaving de Cuevas in 1956, he produced ballets and divertissements at the Aix-en-Provence Festival, and also worked in Copenhagen and Holland. In Monte Carlo he produced, November 1956, *Suite new-yorkaise* and *Entre cour et jardin,* and (1957) the more classical sections of the Sagan ballet *Le Rendez-vous manqué.* He made *Le Rideau Rouge* for Miskovitch's "Ballets 1957" and *Octet* for the Edinburgh Ballet Premières in 1958. Taras is a deeply musical choreographer. His style is varied, but always based on strict classicism. His best works are solidly constructed, dynamic and distinguished by their extreme elegance.

TCHAIKOVSKY Piotr Ilyitch (1840-1893). "I simply cannot understand," wrote Tchaikovsky in a letter, "why the term 'ballet music' should be associated with something *reprehensible.* After all, there is such a thing as good ballet music". The remark suggests that it was rare, and indeed Tchaikovsky, who from his early youth loved dancing and dance music, and made so much use of dance rhythms in his operas and orchestral works, grew to manhood at a time when the ballet in Russia was, artistically speaking, in the doldrums. Music was churned out by such composers as Minkus, Drigo and Pugni (who wrote 300 ballets) beside whom Adam was a Mozart and Delibes a Beethoven. Tchaikovsky himself was commissioned to write a *Cinderella* in 1870, but it came to nothing; according to his nephew Davidov he wrote a one-act ballet, *Le Lac des Cygnes,* in the following year for the children of his sister, who performed it at their house. It contained the "swan" theme which appears in the later ballet. This masterpiece was a commission from the Bolshoi Theatre in Moscow. Tchaikovsky accepted it gladly (and incorporated some material from his

MARJORIE TALLCHIEF AND GEORGE SKIBINE
IN LE PRINCE DU DÉSERT.

first, and unperformed, opera *Undine,* to which the new scenario bore some resemblance) but the first performance in 1877 was a sad failure. It had been produced in the bad old way: the scenery was drab, the dancing dull and much of the music was suppressed on the grounds that it was not sufficiently danceable. No doubt it was Tchaikovsky's fame as a composer of other types of music that led to an invitation in 1888 from the Maryinsky Theatre, St. Petersburg, to compose *The Sleeping Beauty.* The choreographer was Petipa, who gave Tchaikovsky as precise instructions as though he had been one of the official hacks. He was right, of course, to do so. No amount of freedom would have made Minkus or Pugni into great composers; Petipa's precautions ensured that at least they wrote serviceable music. His demands for so many bars in such a rhythm or mood did not impede the flow of Tchaikovsky's melody or his gift for orchestration. He had an innate feeling for classical dancing. What remains miraculous is the way in which he could combine short fragments, of great variety but of the necessary length for virtuoso dancing, with the overall dramatic flow that carries the narrative so surely along. When *The Sleeping Beauty* was produced in 1890, the St. Petersburg balletomanes appreciated the music of the set dances but were shocked by the unaccustomed force and brilliance of the dramatic episodes. Petipa and Tchaikovsky continued their collaboration with *Casse-Noisette* (1892), into which the composer poured a wealth of imagination and craftsmanship, but not even he could bring a consistent dramatic flow to the weak scenario. After Tchaikovsky's untimely death, Petipa sent to Moscow for the score of *Le Lac des Cygnes* and, with Ivanov's assistance, mounted act two in 1894 and the complete ballet in 1895, avenging the initial failure and confirming Tchaikovsky's position as one of the greatest of all composers of ballet music.

It would be impossible here to do more than hint at the number of ballets that have been made out of works by Tchaikovsky that were not intended for dancing: the fifth symphony (Massine's *Les Présages*), the second piano concerto (Balanchine's *Ballet Imperial*), *Romeo and Juliet* (Lifar and others), *Hamlet* (Helpmann), *Francesca da Rimini* (Lichine), the String Serenade (Balanchine's *Serenade*), the A minor trio (Massine's

Aleko and — using the variations only — Taras's *Designs with strings*) are a few examples. Tchaikovsky's style, and some of his melodies, were the inspiration for *Le Baiser de la Fée,* a loving tribute from the greatest of his successors, Igor Stravinsky.

TCHELITCHEV Pavel. Russian painter and stage designer, born in 1898, who spent many years in Paris and finally settled in the United States, where he died in 1957. Tche-

LÉONOR FINI. PAS DE DEUX.

litchev was one of the most gifted stage designers of the century, a creator of mysterious, haunted, insubstantial dream worlds, a romantic poet among the prosaic surrealists. His drawings of dancers give some idea of the powerful atmosphere of his décors, but they cannot indicate the role played in them by his imaginative use of stage lighting. Tchelitchev was a visionary, a designer for the ideal theatre, where time and money are of no importance. The theatre of our day being what it is, his contributions were few in number, but they have left their mark. His ballet décors include *Ode* (Diaghilev, 1928), *Errante* (Ballets 1933), *Orpheus* (the Balanchine production of Gluck's opera for the American

Ballet at the Metropolitan Opera, New York, 1936), *Nobilissima Visione* (Ballets de Monte-Carlo, 1938), *Balustrade* (Original Ballet Russe, 1941), *Concerto* and *Apollon Musagète* (Buenos Aires 1942).

TCHEREPNINE Alexandre. Russian composer, son of Nicholas Tcherepnine, born St. Petersburg, 1899. He was written three ballets: *Déjeuner sur l'herbe* (1945), *Chota Roustaveli* (1946) and *La Femme et son Ombre* (1948).

TCHEREPNINE Nicholas (1873-1945). Russian composer and conductor at the Maryinsky Theatre in his native St. Petersburg and later for the Russian Ballet. He was a member of Diaghilev's advisory committee and conducted his own *Pavillon d'Armide* on the opening night of the first season in Paris (1909), as well as *Cléopâtre,* to which composite score he had contributed. He wrote *Narcisse* for the 1911 season and orchestrated the Schumann music for *Papillons* (1914). He became domiciled in Paris. Other ballets include *The Masque of the Red Death, Dionysius* and *Russian Fairy-Tales.*

TCHERINA Ludmilla. A ballerina whose striking beauty, in addition to her considerable talent, has enabled her to become a star in the widest sense of the word and a figure of Parisian elegance, tall, slender, with jet-black hair and shapely legs. She is half-Russian, half-French. As a dancer she was trained by Alessandri and Preobrajenska. She made her début in 1942 at the Salle Pleyel, in Lifar's *Roméo et Juliette ;* became a leading dancer of the Nouveau Ballet de Monte-Carlo and, in 1945, of the Ballets des Champs-Élysées. She also gave recitals with her dancer husband Edmond Audran, killed in an accident in 1951. Her film career started with *Un Revenant.* Her subsequent films have included: *The Red Shoes, The Tales of Hoffman, Oh, Rosalinda !* In 1957 she made a great impression at the Paris Opera in the title-role of the revival of *Le Martyre de Saint-Sébastien.*

TCHERKAS Constantin. Dancer and choreographer, born St. Petersburg, 1908. A pupil of Cecchetti and Legat. He left Russia and joined the Diaghilev Ballet in 1923, remaining

with it until it was disbanded. He created roles in *The Triumph of Neptune, Ode* and *The Gods go a'begging.* After Diaghilev's death he went to the Paris Opera and then (1933) to the Opéra-Comique, where he remained in charge of the ballet for twenty years, and also danced leading roles. His own ballets produced there include: *La Pantoufle de vair, La Rosière du village, Ma mère l'oye, Un Jour d'été,* etc.

TCHERKASSOVA Ludmilla. A Bolshoi Theatre dancer, conspicuous for her height, her marvellous jump, and her exuberance. The latter quality occasionally jars in her dancing of classical roles, where she is also apt to abuse her exceptional elevation and ballon. But her sheer joy in dancing and her prodigious vitality more than compensate for these lapses from perfect taste. Her best role is probably Zarema in the *Fountain of Bakhchisarai,* but she was a famous Lilac Fairy in *The Sleeping Beauty.*

TCHERNICHEVA Lubov. A St. Petersburg dancer who graduated from the Imperial School in 1908 and remained a member of the Maryinsky company until 1912. She danced in the corps de ballet in Diaghilev's first Paris season of 1909 (she married Serge Grigoriev, the régisseur général, in that same year) and, with her husband, stayed with Diaghilev until the end. She began to make her mark as a soloist during the South American tour of 1913, and became one of the most versatile and reliable dancers in the great company. As a demi-caractère dancer she was invaluable for the modern works such as *Les Femmes de bonne humeur, Pulcinella, Les Noces, Les Biches, Les Fâcheux, Le Pas d'Acier* and *Apollon Musagète,* while her handsome appearance and gift for dramatic mime made her the ideal successor to Karsavina and Ida Rubinstein in such roles as Cleopatra, Thamar and Zobeide *(Sheherazade).* She became ballet mistress to the company in 1926. After disbandment, she and her husband joined in turn the Ballets Russes de Monte-Carlo, the De Basil company and the Original Ballets Russes. The last role she created was in Lichine's *Francesca da Rimini.* Since the war the Grigorievs have done invaluable work for the Royal Ballet, Festival Ballet and other companies in reviving works from the Diaghilev repertory. She recently reappeared in a character part in Cranko's version of *Romeo and Juliet* at the Scala, Milan (1958).

TENTATIONS DE LA BERGÈRE Les. Ballet in one act. Music: Monteclair (1666-1737) arr. and orch. H. Casadesus. Scenery and costumes: Juan Gris. Choreography: Nijinska. First performance: Diaghilev's Ballets Russes, Monte Carlo, 3 January 1924. Principal dancers: Nemchinova, Slavinsky, Woizikowski, Vilzak. An evocation of a 17th century pastoral at the court of Le Roi Soleil. Juan Gris designed a striking but cumbrous set in blue-grey and gold which proved so difficult to handle that the ballet disappeared from the repertory in spite of the high quality of the choreography and the dancing.

TERTULIA La or **Les deux rivales.** Ballet in one act. Scenario: Ana Ricarda and Irène Lidova. Music: Manuel Infante. Scenery and costumes: Capuletti. Choreography: Ana Ricarda. First performance: De Cuevas Ballet, Paris, 11 December 1952. Principal dancers: Ana Ricarda, Jacqueline Moreau, Wladimir Skouratoff.

LES TENTATIONS DE LA BERGÈRE.
COSTUME BY JUAN GRIS. 1924.

The "Tertulia" was a fashionable variety theatre in Madrid in the 1860's. We see the stage from the back, before the performance begins: amid the usual back-stage animation a Spanish dancer finds that her handsome partner's favours are being competed for by a French ballerina. The rise of the curtain cuts short their rivalry, and the performance (clowns, tight-rope dancer, comic turns, solo for the French ballerina, pas de deux for the Spanish couple) takes place. At the end of it the young man goes off with a third admirer.

THÉATRE BOLCHOI (Bolshoi Theatre). In the Soviet Union the Bolshoi or Grand Theatre is considered to be the apotheosis of opera and ballet. The citizens of Moscow are proud of its magnificent auditorium, which is renowned for its splendid acoustics and seats more than 2,000 spectators. The visitor from the West is struck most of all by the vast stage, where it is no unusual thing to see two horsemen galloping among a hundred or more dancers and as many singers. The equipment and machinery are fully worthy of the great stage, and the splendour of the productions show the great importance which the Soviet authorities attach to the capital's leading theatre.

In 1776 Prince Urussov was granted permission to run a theatre in Moscow. With the assistance of an English engineer named Maddox he built a house which opened its doors to the public in 1780 under the name of the Petrovsky Theatre. In 1805, like so many theatres of the time, it was burnt down. It was not until seventeen years later that a second house, the first Bolshoi Theatre, was opened on 6 January 1825 — only to be burnt down in its turn in 1853. All that remained was part of the walls and the eight columns of the façade: these were incorporated in the present structure, which was opened on 20th August 1856, with a performance of Bellini's opera *I Puritani*.

From its predecessor the Bolshoi had inherited a ballet company, which originated in rather curious circumstances. The governing body of the Moscow Orphanage decided to open a dancing class for the children and Filippo Beccari, premier danseur at the Court Theatre of St. Petersburg, offered to run it. There were 82 pupils, out of which he trained 24 as soloists. His successor, Leopold Paradis, presented the first ballet to be seen on the stage of the Petrovsky Theatre, *The Magic School,* in which the majority of the roles were danced by the orphans themselves. At the beginning of the 19th century the Moscow ballet was under the direction of Adam Glushkovsky, a pupil of Didelot. In 1837, when St. Petersburg audiences were lauding Taglioni to the skies, their Moscow counterparts claimed to possess her equal in Catherine Sankovskaya, who was indeed an artist of remarkable quality. When the management of the Imperial Theatres sent E. Adrianova from Petersburg to Moscow and she began to take over roles danced by the "Russian Taglioni", the public became frankly hostile. One evening, a box was handed to her on the stage. She opened it unsuspectingly: instead of flowers it contained a dead cat, with the label "première danseuse". The incident was typical of the antagonism which exists to this day between the two cities. Moscow artists were fond of reproaching their St. Petersburg colleagues with their "coldness", the "solemnity" of their style and their "cult of classical form", themselves preferring temperament, natural spontaneity and freedom of expression. The St. Petersburg style had greater distinction and refinement (it was also more cosmopolitan), the Moscow style was more human, and more Russian. In so far as it was ever justified, the distinction is still valid to-day.

For one reason or another, by the middle of the century the Bolshoi had become little more than a branch of the Maryinsky. In 1848, the great Petipa mounted *Paquita* there, but after the departure of Teodor in 1861, the Moscow theatre no longer had its own maître de ballet and Petipa shared the work with his St. Petersburg colleague, Malavergne. Petipa staged eleven ballets at the Bolshoi, Malavergne eight, Blasis five and Saint-Léon four. It was about this time that the Bolshoi began to gain its reputation for elaborate scenic effects; for example, in one production real water flowed down a sheet of glass the full width of the stage, and fell into a basin illuminated by electricity: dancers seen through the glass appeared to be performing under water. Nevertheless, from 1880 onwards, there was such a shift of public interest from ballet to opera that there was some question of disbanding the company. It was

LA TERTULIA. COSTUME BY CAPULETTI.

saved by Vsevolozhky in 1882 at the price of a reduction in size. He retired 92 dancers and transferred 18 others to St. Petersburg, leaving a mere 70. At the beginning of the next century this number had increased under Ivan Clustine to 208. Volkonsky's brief period on the management committee of the Bolshoi had great consequences, for he was responsible for the transfer of Alexis Gorsky to Moscow. The new maître de ballet arrived at a moment when the theatrical world was in a ferment of reform. He was an enthusiastic supporter of the movement for dramatic realism in the theatre and, warmly seconded by Geltzer, Karalli, Balachova, Fedorova, Mordkin, Zhukov and others, set the ballet on the same path. Nevertheless, he was able to preserve the foundations of the classical school from revolutionary excesses and handed on a first-class company to his successors.

To-day the repertoire of the Bolshoi is substantially the same as that of the Kirov Theatre, that is to say, political ballets like *The Red Poppy* have given way to the classics, both Russian and foreign *(Giselle),* of the pre-Fokine era and new Soviet works, including special ballets for chil-

THE BOLSHOI THEATRE, MOSCOW, IN 1837.
FROM AN OLD PAINTING.

dren, *The Little Stork* and *Dr. Ayi-Bobo*. Fokine is represented only by *Chopiniana,* an early version of *Les Sylphides*. Visitors from the West are invariably surprised by the detailed realism of scenery and costumes, an outworn realism which to our more sophisticated eyes appears inartistic. In fact, from the decorative point of view, Soviet ballet in Moscow and in Leningrad appears to have stuck in the age of Petipa. Innovation is confined to the sphere of choreography, in the supreme importance attached to the scenario. Soviet ballets are mainly narrative and the job of the choreographer is to "tell the story" by all the means at his disposal — dancing, mime and production — in a straightforward manner. The Soviet *Lac des Cygnes,* for instance, is now in its seventh version; the latest of successive attemps at clarification and dramatic truth.

The teaching of Mme. Bocharnikova, Asaf and Shulamit Messerer, Gabovitch and Marina Semenova at the Bolshoi School follows the principles laid down by Vaganova and therefore presents no essential difference from the method taught in Leningrad. First-year study is entirely confined to work on the five positions and elementary exercises at the barre; only later are the girls permitted to start point work, whilst the boys do not attempt batterie (entrechats, etc.) till their fourteenth or fifteenth year. During the first years pupils, whether male or female, only execute simple movements. The school, like the theatre, is richly endowed, and the training

can therefore be very slow and careful. Russian technique is governed by the needs of a choreography where ornament is rare and bravura an exception. On the other hand, it insists on correct placing, suppleness of body, the gracefulness and smooth linking of enchaînements, expressiveness and strength. Particular attention is paid to back and arms while span of elevation and ability to travel are made essential by the dimensions of the Bolshoi stage. Little use is made of small, brilliant steps of batterie but the dancers can perform them if required.

The present company of the Bolshoi Theatre, headed by some of the world's greatest artists, is also remarkable for the amazing quality of the ensemble. The corps de ballet is well disciplined, but every member seems capable of turning soloist at a moment's notice. The dedication of these dancers and their complete absorption in any role they may be playing, no matter how insignificant, can be compared only to the similar qualities of the actors of the Moscow Arts Theatre. In the West, they have not only been acclaimed as executants; they have demonstrated the power, and the value, of the present Soviet methods of ballet-making, typified by the works of Zakharov and, above all, Leonid Lavrovsky.

THÉATRE MARIE (Maryinsky, now Kirov Theatre). Despite the present preeminence of the Moscow Bolshoi Theatre, which the Soviet authorities cherish with particular care, the former Maryinsky Theatre in Leningrad is historically speaking the most illustrious home of opera and ballet in Russia. It witnessed the rise of the classical ballet during the nineteenth century and was the cradle not only of the Diaghilev ballet, but of many contemporary Soviet stars. Although the Imperial Academy of Dancing was founded in St. Petersburg as early as 1738, the Maryinsky tradition only dates from 1783, the year of the erection of a Bolshoi

(Large) Theatre—not to be confused with the one in Moscow. This building was on the site of the present Conservatoire, opposite the Maryinsky Theatre. For more than half a century choreographers and dancers were forging the instrument which was to serve Petipa and Fokine. Among the former, mention must be made of Charles Didelot, who with interruptions of varying length reigned from 1802 to 1829 and mounted some fifty works, and Jules Perrot. Among the latter, were Russian ballerinas like Berilova (1776-1804), Kolossova, Marie Danilova who died when she was 17, Istomina (1799-1848), celebrated by Pushkin, and the galaxy of foreign stars of the Romantic era inaugurated in 1837 by Taglioni and continuing with Lucile Grahn, Fanny Elssler, Carlotta Grisi and Fanny Cerrito. Choreographers and dancers such as Duport, Johansson and Lev Ivanov also made their contribution. The second half of the nineteenth century opened under the guidance of Perrot, but he was gradually ousted by Marius Petipa, who had been dancing in Russia since 1847. From the very start of his appointment as ballet master in 1858, Petipa had a formidable rival in Arthur Saint-

STRUCHKOVA AND LAPAURI
IN CASSE-NOISETTE.

Léon, the dancer-choreographer-violinist, who was also a pioneer in the realm of production (in *Fiametta*, for instance, he represented transparent ghosts by means of convex mirrors). In 1869 Saint-Léon visited Petersburg for the last time; he was to die in 1870. The long dictatorship of Marius Petipa had begun.

By 1869 Petipa was combining the functions of premier danseur, maître de ballet, professor and inspector of dancing at the Imperial School. Thus he was in an excellent position to impose his ideas. Yet he did not make his full contribution until Vsevolozhky had been appointed to the post of director of the Imperial Theatres in 1881. Petipa's career reached its zenith between the years of 1890 and 1898, with the production of the three Tchaikovsky ballets *La Belle au bois dormant, Casse-Noisette* and *Le Lac des Cygnes* (in collaboration with Ivanov), and Glazounov's *Raymonda*. At about the same time, the ballet received fresh impetus from the arrival of the Italian ballerinas Virginia Zucchi, Antonietta Dell'Era and later Carlotta Brianza, Pierina Legnani and others. To their already dazzling technique, Petipa added the poetic lyricism necessary for the great roles in his ballets. The engagement of Enrico Cecchetti as dancer (1887), second maître de ballet (1888) and above all as professor of dancing (1892), decisively enriched the Russian school, up till that time exclusively under French influence. Vsevolozhky was replaced in 1899 by Prince Volkonsky, a man equally cultured and dynamic, but a staunch modernist. Volkonsky wanted to reform the Russian theatres root and branch, and started by appointing some new personnel, among them Diaghilev. But the latter was forced to resign after a quarrel in 1901 which cost him his career in Russia, and Volkonsky himself only outlasted him by three months, having fallen foul of the influential Mathilde Kschessinska. His successor, Colonel Teliakovsky, had several clashes with Petipa, who was retired in 1904, largely at his insistence. Teliakovsky inherited a preponderantly Russian company of whom the stars and future stars were Preobrajenska, Kschessinska, Egorova, Trefilova, Pavlova, Karsavina, Smirnova, Vaganova, Sedova and Spessivtseva; Gerdt, the brothers Legat, Oboukhoff, Kyasht, Nijinsky, Bolm, Vladimirov and the young maître de ballet Fokine. The last-named was the chief reformer of the Maryinsky Ballet: from 1905 onwards he produced 18 new works. His aim was to replace the traditional mime by more realistic and natural dramatic gesture. Under the influence of Isadora Duncan he freed the arms from the tyranny of the classical port de bras and tried to make movement and action more coherent by substituting an appropriate plastique for meaningless technical effects. The period immediately preceding the 1914 war was a brilliant one for the Maryinsky Theatre. It was the age of the painters Golovine, Korovine, Bakst and Benois, of Fokine's early triumphs, and of the bitter controversies started by the articles of Volinsky, Levinson, Svetlov, Volkonsky, etc. Then came the war, followed by the revolution. The theatre experienced its full share of the suffering of civil war. Hungry and cold, the pupils of the former Imperial School wore the same uniforms for over three years and made their own practice costumes from old curtains. But performances went on and attracted a public just as numerous as, but very different from, the brilliant society of former days. Little by little the situation improved. In exchange for its cultural activities, the government gave the company food and increased rations. On the artistic plane the old repertoire was endlessly drawn upon, and there were practically no new productions until circumstances called for ballets with a political bias. These, however, failed to attract the public. A new crisis was caused by the dearth of leading soloists, most of whom had emigrated. Fortunately the skill and perseverance of such teachers as Agrippina Vaganova succeeded in producing new talent. From the Leningrad school have come such dancers and maîtres de ballet as Semenova, Jordan, Ulanova, Vecheslova, Dudinskaya, Shelest, Ossipienko, Lavrovsky, Leontiev, Yermolaev, Chaboukiani, Lopoukhov, Zakharov, etc.

The actual fabric of the Maryinsky, now Kirov, Theatre dates from 1860. It replaced the Circus Theatre, which had been burnt down the previous year. The old Bolshoi Theatre had been burned down long before and meanwhile ballet performances had been given in various buildings. The new theatre has a charming auditorium upholstered in turquoise velvet but a relatively modest seating capacity of 1,760. On the other hand its stage is one of the largest in the world, being 97 feet wide and 72 feet deep (compared with the Bolshoi in Moscow, 85' × 77', and Covent Garden, 40' × 40'), while the lighting and equipment are of the most up to date design. It was here, and not in Moscow, that such famous Soviet ballets as *The Flames of Paris, The Fountain of Bakhchisarai, Laurencia, Romeo and Juliet, Taras Bulba* and *The Bronze Horseman* were first performed. During the last war, when the company was evacuated to Molotov (Perm), *Gayaneh* had its first performance in 1942. The Kirov, which had been damaged by bombs, reopened in 1944.

The Ballet School has not changed its premises, no. 2 Architect Rossi Street, formerly Theatre Street, since 1836. It is an immense building. Severely disciplined and rigorously segregated, boys and girls (mostly boarders) were brought up here in Imperial days in the cult of the theatre. Eminent teachers of French, Italian, Swedish and Russian origin — the Johanssons, father and son, Petipa, Gerdt, Cecchetti, Legat, Sokolova — supervised their studies in the immense studios. Make-up, fencing, mime, music and singing were also taught, but general education was relatively neglected. This is said to have been remedied now, and the ballet classes certainly have not suffered. In 1934 Vaganova published her treatise on the Russian Classical Method (see *Théâtre Bolchoï* and *Vaganova*).

Whatever opinion one may have of present-day Russian aesthetics, the former Maryinsky is unquestionably one of the holy places of contemporary, indeed of all, ballet.

THIRIET Maurice. French composer, born 1906. He has six ballets to his credit. The first of them, *La Nuit Vénitienne,* was written for the Paris Opera in 1939. Ten years later he wrote two works for the Ballets de Paris: *L'Œuf à la Coque* and *Deuil en 24 heures,* light-hearted scores which show a sense of humour and a gift for parody allied to a solid technique. They were followed by *Héraklès* (Charrat, 1953), *La Reine des Iles* (Belgrade Opera, 1955) and *Le Photographe* (Netherlands Opera, Amsterdam, 1956).

THREE-CORNERED HAT The. See *Tricorne, Le.*

THE BRONZE HORSEMAN. DÉCOR BY MIKAIL BOBYCHEV FOR SCENE VI.

TIRESIAS. Ballet in three scenes. Scenario and music: Constant Lambert. Choreography: Frederick Ashton. Scenery and costumes: Isabel Lambert. First produced: Sadler's Wells Ballet, Covent Garden, London, 19 July 1951. Principal dancers: Tiresias as man, Michael Somes; Tiresias as woman, Margot Fonteyn; Pauline Clayden, Brian Shaw, John Field.

Tiresias, who has been both man and woman during his lifetime, is asked by Zeus and Hera which sex derives the greatest enjoyment from love. He pronounces for woman. Hera, in a fury, blinds him. Zeus, in compensation, grants him the gift of prophecy. *Tiresias* was planned by Constant Lambert twenty years before it was produced: he died shortly after the first performance. His dry and incisive music and Isabel Lambert's ominous Minoan settings are more successful than the choreography, which strikes fire only in the lyrical scene where Tiresias as woman dances with her lover. The most controversial of Ashton's later ballets, it has won some passionate admirers. Tiresias-woman was one of Fonteyn's finest modern roles.

TOUMANOVA Tamara. The embodiment of the popular conception of a Russian ballerina.

The dark hair, lustrous eyes and pale skin she has shared with many famous dancers, but few have possessed features of such perfect regularity, at once Slavonic and classical. Accompanied by her devout and attentive "mamoushka", Toumanova moves with imperturbable gravity through a world notorious for its frivolity. On the stage, her smile puts diamonds in the shade. She was born in a railway truck when her parents were fleeing from the civil war in Russia, and was brought up in Paris, where she studied dancing with Preobrajenska. She made a precocious début at the Paris Opera in 1929 in *L'Éventail de Jeanne*. Three years later, Balanchine secured her for the Ballets Russes de Monte-Carlo, with the other "baby ballerinas" Baronova and Riabouchinska. Her dancing in *Concurrence, Cotillon,* and *Jeux d'enfants* had a quality astonishing in a girl of thirteen. She followed Balanchine to become one of the stars of Les Ballets 1933 and then returned to the larger company until 1938, resuming her earlier roles and creating new ones, notably in *Jardin Public* and *La Symphonie Fantastique*. Her later career has been too varied to detail in full. She has danced in Broadway musicals, made films in Hollywood, and appeared as guest artist with several leading ballet companies, including Ballet Theatre, de Cuevas and Festival Ballet. Her most important post-war appearances have been at the Paris Opera, where she created roles in Balanchine's *Le Palais de Cristal* and Lifar's *L'Inconnue* and *Phèdre* as well as appearing in revivals of the classics. But the discipline of regular work with a big company has been lacking; she has not always been able to resist the temptations of facility offered by her virtuosity and her glamorous appearance.

TRAGÉDIE DE SALOMÉ La. In France, the country of its origin, Florent Schmitt's *Tragédie de Salomé* bas rivalled in popularity Ravel's *Daphnis et Chloé* and *La Péri* of Dukas. It was first performed at the Théâtre des Arts, Paris, in 1907 by Loie Fuller, for whom it was written. The scenario by Robert d'Humières follows the nasty story familiar from Wilde's play and Strauss's opera fairly closely,

except that Salomé hurls the Baptist's head into the sea, whereupon it appears, to her horror, in the heavens. Schmitt subsequently rescored the music for a larger orchestra, in which form it was produced in 1912 at the Châtelet by Trouhanova, with décor by Dethomas. Diaghilev mounted a new version in his 1913 season with choreography by Romanov and décor by Soudeikine; Karsavina was the Salomé. It was then Ida Rubinstein's turn: in her production (Paris Opera, 1919) she alternated in the title-role with Yvonne Daunt. The choreography was by Nicola Guerra, the décor by Piot. This version was revived by Spessivtseva. Aveline made a new version for the Opéra in 1944 (Suzanne Lorcia) with décor by Brayer, revived in 1954 for Lycette Darsonval.

* Lifar's *Salomé* (Nouveau Ballet de Monte-Carlo, 1945) used music from Richard Strauss's opera and gave Olga Adabache the role of her life.

TRAILINE Boris. Dancer of Russian extraction, pupil of Julie Sedova and Volinine, with a fine sense of the stage and a sound technique. Leading dancer with the Nouveau Ballet de Monte-Carlo in 1946, when he appeared in *Dramma per musica* and *Chota Rustaveli*. He is an excellent partner and has appeared with several distinguished ballerinas, including Toumanova and Chauviré. He created the male lead in *La Dame à la Licorne* (Munich, 1953).

TRAILINE Hélène. Sister of Boris Trailine —and a great beauty. Made her début in 1947 with the de Cuevas Ballet. Leading dancer in 1950 with the Ballets des Champs-Élysées, later with Janine Charrat's company, and guest artist with Ballet Rambert. Created the female lead in Béjart's *Haut-Voltage* (1956).

TRAIN BLEU Le. "Opérette dansée" in one act. Scenario: Cocteau. Music: Milhaud. Curtain: Picasso. Scenery: Laurens. Costumes: Chanel. Choreography: Nijinska. First performance: Diaghilev's Ballets Russes, Théâtre des Champs-Élysées, Paris, 20 June 1924. Principal dancers: Nijinska, Sokolova, Dolin, Woizikowski.

TOUMANOVA BY TCHELITCHEV.

A topical ballet about the craze for sport, as smart and up to date as Diaghilev and Cocteau could make it. The Blue Train did not appear; it was presumed to have disgorged its passengers on to the fashionable *plage* where, suitably clothed by Chanel, they performed their sporting evolutions: Nijinska as the tennis champion, Woizikowski as the golfer, Sokolova as "Perlouse" and Dolin as "Beau Gosse". It was largely Dolin's ballet; the sight of him performing acrobatics at Monte Carlo in the previous year gave Cocteau the idea for the work.

TREFILOVA Vera (1875-1943). A pupil of the Imperial School of St. Petersburg. She graduated in 1894. Compared with some of her great contemporaries, Trefilova's progress was slow. She became prima ballerina in 1906, on the same day as Pavlova, her junior by six years. She had a reserve, dignity and self-control which coloured her dancing. She was as tiny and as frail-looking as an ivory figurine, but her technique was the equal of the finest Italian dancers and her fouettés dazzled not only by their perfection but by the air of triumph with which she invested them. Levinson called her a "dancing Stradivarius". Curiously enough she never cared passionately for dancing and retired early and willingly at her husband's request. After his death she became an actress and then a dancer once more, soon reaching her former perfection. She appeared with the Russian Ballet in 1921 as the fourth (and in the opinion of many the most perfect) of the Auroras in *La Belle au bois dormant*. She danced in the following year in *Le Mariage d'Aurore* and *Le Spectre de la Rose*. In 1924 she gave dazzling performances of *Le Lac des Cygnes* at Monte Carlo and appeared with the company yet again in London in 1926; age had not impaired the brilliance and purity of her style.

TRICORNE Le (The Three-Cornered Hat). Ballet in one act. Scenario: Martinez Sierra. Music: Manuel de Falla. Scenery and costumes: Picasso. Choreography: Massine. First performance: Diaghilev's Ballets Russes, Alhambra Theatre, London, 22 July 1919. Principal dancers: Tamara Karsavina, Massine, Leon Woizikowski.

Massine's masterpiece was the outcome of the periods spent in Spain by Diaghilev and his dancers during the latter half of the 1914-18 war. On the first of these occasions Diaghilev, who had long wanted to produce a Spanish ballet, sought out Manuel de Falla. The composer played him the music he had written for a pantomime by Martinez Sierra, "El Corregidor y la Molinera" (the Governor and the miller's wife) which had been produced with success in Madrid. It was based on a play by Alarcon, "El Sombrero de Tres Picos", set in Spain at the close of the 18th century. Diaghilev and Massine accompanied Falla to Andalusia, where they discovered a young gipsy dancer of great talent but sullen disposition, Felix Fernandez, whom Diaghilev engaged to teach Massine the traditional Spanish steps. Felix seems to have imagined that he was going to be the star of the ballet; when, in London, he realised the true position, his mind gave way. Meanwhile, Falla had revised and amplified his score, adding the "farucca" as a solo dance for the miller and the joyous final "jota". The tale is a simple one, not very clearly told, about an elderly provincial governor, his badge of office a three-cornered hat, who pursues a pretty young miller's wife and is outwitted by the girl's husband. Massine, though he had soaked himself in the dances of Andalusia, made no attempt to reproduce them with ethnographical fidelity; he achieved the far more difficult and rewarding feat of transposing them into terms of ballet. But it is not only a story told in dancing; it is about people who express themselves most readily in dancing. Picasso' simple, sun-soaked setting is one of the great décors of modern times. Each costume, as it appears, adds something new and yet harmonious to the ensemble. Their effect in motion (aided by the cunning use of an upper level provided by the narrow bridge at the back of the stage) is extraordinary. Massine's own performance as the miller remains unrivalled.

* Massine has revived *Le Tricorne,* in the original setting, more than once: Ballet Theatre (1943), Sadler's Wells Ballet, Covent Garden (1947), Royal Swedish Ballet, Stockholm (1957), etc.

THE TRIUMPH OF NEPTUNE. English pantomime in twelve tableaux. Scenario: Sacheverell Sitwell. Scenery and cos-

LA TRAGÉDIE DE SALOMÉ. PROJECT FOR CURTAIN BY YVES BRAYER.

tumes after 19th century toy theatre prints. Music: Lord Berners. Choreography: George Balanchine. First performance: Diaghilev's Ballets Russes, Lyceum Theatre, London, 3 December 1926. Principal dancers: Danilova, Sokolova, Lifar, Balanchine.

The only "English" work in the repertory of the Russian Ballet: a compliment to Diaghilev's many loyal supporters in London. Scenario and music were entrusted to two of the most talented among them, Sacheverell Sitwell and Lord Berners. It was decided to do a ballet in the style of an old-fashioned pantomime, using toy theatre, "tuppence coloured" prints selected by Diaghilev himself from the shops of Pollock in Hoxton and Webb in Old Street, and adapted by Prince Schervachidze as full-scale settings. The twelve episodes presented the somewhat inconsequential adventures of a British sailor, Tom Tug, between Victorian London and Fairyland. His wife proves unfaithful in his absence, so he marries the Fairy Queen, Neptune's daughter. The most spectacular scenes were Cloudland, the Frozen Forest (complete with flying ballet) and the final Apotheosis in Neptune's palace. There were hornpipes for Sokolova (in a glengarry and a sequin tunic) and,

in the final scene, for Lifar and Danilova as the bridal couple, and a brilliant solo for Balanchine himself as the negro, Snowball. A further solo was added later for Idzikowski, as Cupid.

TROUHANOVA Natasha. A dancer who made adroit use of the new ideas that were in the air at the beginning of the century and showed discrimination in her choice of music and décor. She gave dance recitals with Robert Quinault at the Théâtre des Arts in Paris and later at the Châtelet and Opéra-Comique. In 1912, she presented four ballets at the Châtelet with music by some of the leading French composers of the day: *La Péri* (Dukas), *Istar* (d'Indy), *La Tragédie de Salomé* (Schmitt) and *Adélaïde ou le langage des fleurs* (Ravel's Valses nobles et sentimentales). She died in Moscow in 1956.

TUDOR Antony. A Londoner, born 1909, who has lived for nearly twenty years in America, Antony Tudor's vocation as choreographer was revealed by chance visits to the ballet when, though still a boy, he was already earning his living in unromantic circumstances. He was nineteen before he had the opportunity of taking evening lessons with Marie Rambert. When the Ballet Club was founded, she made him secretary and stage manager, so that he could devote his whole time to the theatre. Her confidence was soon justified by the production of his first ballet *Cross-Gartered*, based on Shakespeare's *Twelfth Night*. Tudor danced for a short time at Sadler's Wells, but his early ballets, including *The Planets, The Descent of Hebe, Jardin aux Lilas* (*) and *Dark Elegies* (*), were done for Mme. Rambert; in them, the unusual nature of his talent became increasingly clear. As a dancer though he often, and most effectively, danced mime roles in his own ballets he was handicapped by his late start. In 1938 he formed his own company, the London Ballet, starting with joint performances with the American Agnes de Mille. Oddly enough, Tudor used the opportunity less for developing his new fields of expression than for producing ballets of a lighter type: *The Judgement of Paris, Soirée Musicale* and *Gala Performance* (*). After the outbreak of war, he was invited to America to work with the newly established Ballet Theatre; there he remained, and with such works as *Pillar of Fire* (*), *Romeo and Juliet* (*), *Dim Lustre* and *Undertow* (*) consolidated his position as one of the outstanding choreographers of our time.

Tudor works for preference with existing music; his choice has been original and revealing. The formal elegance of early composers such as Frescobaldi and Tartini has attracted him, but less frequently than the high emotional content of the late romantics and moderns: Chausson, R. Strauss, Mahler, Schönberg, Bloch, Delius, Holst, Kurt Weill and William Schuman. In the U.S.A. he found, more readily than in England, a public responsive to the social and psychological themes, familiar perhaps to the expressionist dancers but hitherto unexplored by choreographers using the classical vocabulary, which he prefers: bereavement *(Dark Elegies)*, frustration *(Pillar of Fire)*, the marriage of convenience *(Jardin aux Lilas)*, psychopathic murder *(Undertow)*. There is satire in his ballets *(Gala Performance)*, but straightforward entertainment is rare and not always successful. Tudor's ideas mature slowly and need time and patience for their elaboration. America gave him a public but the conditions of work there, with the crippling restrictions of rehearsal time,

have not perhaps proved altogether congenial. He is now in charge of the Ballet School at the Metropolitan Opera House, New York. It is sad that he is no longer working regularly as choreographer with a major company and sad, too, that the repertory of the Royal Ballet contains no work by one of England's foremost choreographers.

TURNER Harold. The most accomplished male virtuoso dancer of the pre-war generation at Sadler's Wells, Harold Turner was born and began his training in Manchester. Massine sent him to Marie Rambert and soon, with her company, he was partnering Karsavina in *Le Spectre de la Rose*. He joined Sadler's Wells, with whom he has spent most of his career, in 1935, dancing leading roles in the classics and in the new ballets. Ashton made for him the principal male role in *Les Patineurs,* which

BAKST. COSTUME FOR TROUHANOVA IN LA PÉRI.

admirably displayed his clean, brilliant technique and his boyish charm, while de Valois cast him as the Red Knight in *Checkmate*. In neither role has he ever been surpassed. Turner now teaches at the Royal Ballet School, and is in charge of the Covent Garden Opera Ballet.

TYL ULENSPIEGEL. Ballet in two scenes. Music: Richard Strauss. Choreography: Balanchine. Scenery and costumes: Esteban Frances. First performance: New York City Ballet, 14 November 1951. Principal dancers: Jerome Robbins, Brooks Jackson, Frank Hobi, Beatrice Tompkins.

Balanchine based his ballet on the epic story by Charles de Coster, in which the legendary rogue is turned into a champion of the liberation of 16th century Flanders; Strauss's symphonic poem *Till Eulenspiegel* has the picaresque roguery without the politics. Hence a fundamental discrepancy between music and choreography which not even Balanchine's rediscovery of the gift for narrative and lusty humour of his first ballets for Diaghilev could disguise. The cho-

reography had much in common with the work of Jerome Robbins, who created the title-role. Scenery and costumes were historically accurate, colourful and humorous.

* On 2 November 1949, the Ballets des Champs-Élysées produced a *Til Eulenspiegel,* also to the music of Strauss, by Jean Babilée, later revived by Ballet Theatre. Scenery and costumes were by Tom Keogh. It was a dynamic work with a vein of poetry even in the burlesque scenes. Babilée himself danced the title-role, with feline grace and acrobatic skill.

* Nijinsky's *Till Eulenspiegel* was produced by the Diaghilev ballet during their American tour (New York, 23 October 1916), with the choreographer in the title-role, and décor by Robert Edmond Jones. It was never performed in Europe, and Diaghilev never saw it.

U

TILL. EULENSPIEGEL. JEAN BABILÉE.

ULANOVA Galina. Before the Bolshoi Theatre Ballet visited Western Europe, Soviet ballet was an unknown quantity except for the already legendary fame of one ballerina—Galina Ulanova, who has now become the idol of the public abroad as well as the pride of the U.S.S.R. She reveals herself at once as a ballerina of the Leningrad school. Both her parents were dancers and her mother taught her the rudiments of dancing before she studied with the great Vaganova. She graduated in 1928 and established herself in the following year as one of the best of the young Soviet dancers.

Ulanova's dancing is a constantly renewed miracle, due to a hyper-sensitive personality, a faultless technique, a magic gift of impersonation and complete identification with the music. A role played by Ulanova is never a mere pretext for brilliant dancing; she creates a character in the round, living the role and expressing every nuance of feeling. She has in the highest degree the rare and precious gift of making the spectator forget the conventions of the theatre. Her

UNDERTOW. Ballet in one act, with prologue and epilogue. Scenario and choreography: Antony Tudor. Music: William Schuman. Scenery and costumes: Raymond Breinin. First performance: Ballet Theatre, Metropolitan Opera, New York, 10 April 1945. Principal dancers: Hugh Laing, Alicia Alonso, Nana Gollner.

A controversial ballet in Tudor's psychological vein; confused, but with scenes of great brilliance. It presented in symbolical form (with classical allusions) the case-history of a psychopathic murderer.

V

interpretations of Maria in *The Fountain of Bakhchisarai* and of Juliet in *Romeo and Juliet* are among her greatest achievements, but it is in the classical repertory, in which so many great dancers have shown their quality, that her wonderful talent is best displayed.

Her Odette-Odile (which she first danced in Leningrad in 1929), her Aurora in *The Sleeping Beauty,* and her Raymonda are famous; equally moving, in its simple romanticism, is her dancing in *Chopiniana (Les Sylphides)*. But greatest of all is her Giselle, now familiar through the film made in London (1956) to thousands who have never seen her on the stage. She is the merriest of peasant girls in the early scenes; in the second act she suggests the power of a love too strong to be conquered by death.

This faultless artist, a slightly-built woman, reserved and quite untheatrical, has attained throughout the Soviet Union a remarkable degree of popularity, affection and respect. She is truly a national heroine and has been showered with official honours. In London (1956) and in Paris (1958) she was acclaimed as a dancer of genius. The Moscow public awaits her retirement with dismay for, in spite of the immense resources of the Bolshoi, Ulanova seems irreplaceable.

VAGANOVA Agrippina (1879-1951). The greatest Russian teacher of her day. She studied (under Ivanov, Gerdt, Legat, Preobrajenska, etc.) at the Imperial School in St. Petersburg, graduated in 1897, became première danseuse in 1906 and ballerina in 1915. Two years later she retired to devote herself to teaching. Her knowledge has been transmitted to a number of famous Soviet dancers, including Semenova, Ulanova, Dudinskaya and Shelest. Another pupil, Vera Volkova, has extended her influence to Europe and America. Vaganova held the chair of choreography in the Leningrad Conservatoire. Her treatise *Fundamentals of the Classic Dance* (1934) has been translated by Anatole Chujoy and has provided instruction and inspiration for teachers and dancers alike.

VALSE La. Few modern ballets have had so complicated a history as *La Valse*. The idea of a "choreographic poem" to be called *Wien* had occupied Ravel for many years before he began it in 1917. In 1920 he offered the completed score to Diaghilev, who turned it down. The music was well known in the concert hall before it was finally produced as a ballet by Ida Rubinstein at the Paris Opera on 23 May 1929. The choreography was by Nijinska, whose first

LE TRICORNE. COSTUMES BY PICASSO. 1919.

version, prepared and rehearsed at Monte Carlo in the previous year, was too abstract for the composer's liking. It was accordingly given new scenery and costumes (by Benois) and revised• choreography by Nijinska more in keeping with Ravel's expressed intentions: "an apotheosis of the Viennese waltz . . . I imagine (it) in the setting of an Imperial Court about 1855." He wanted it to begin as a nebulous vision gradually clearing, as gauze veils are lifted and chandeliers light up, to reveal a huge ballroom full of dancing couples who increase in number as the lights grow brighter and the orchestra louder. The décor was to prolong the architecture of the theatre auditorium, enclosing dancers and public in one space. The difficulty choreographers and designers have experienced in carrying out Ravel's ideas show that it is unwise of composers to work out their ballets in detail before consulting their future collaborators. The principal dancers in the 1929 version were Ida Rubinstein and Anatole Vilzak.

* The work was revived by Ida Rubinstein at the Opéra for her 1931 season with new choreography by Fokine, a stylish evocation of a ball at the Imperial Court of Vienna.

* A very different interpretation was given by Massine at the Opéra-Comique, Paris (17 May 1950). He used a scenario based on a story by Lermontov about a stolen bracelet, jealous lovers and poisoned champagne. In the original version, the lights grew brighter as the climax approached; Massine chose this moment to plunge the stage into darkness. Derain designed a décor in white and green.

* Other versions of La Valse include Balanchine's (New York City Ballet, 1951), which was preceded by the Valses-nobles et sentimentales. This was influenced by a phrase in a letter from Ravel to the Count de Salvaudy: "we are dancing on a volcano". Balanchine introduced Death in the form of a male dancer clothed in black, who presented dark jewels to a woman in white. At certain moments the choreography, like the music, seemed to disintegrate.

* The Valses nobles et sentimentales have had a separate career as a ballet. Trouhanova used them for Adélaïde, ou le langage des fleurs (Théâtre du Châtelet, Paris, 1912. Choreographer: Clustine. Scenery and costumes: Drésa). Ashton has made two versions, both with décor by Sophie Fedorovitch: Valentine's Eve (Ballet Club, 1935) and—under the music's original title—for the Sadler's Wells Theatre Ballet (1947).

* Ashton has also made a new version of La Valse, keeping closely to Ravel's own conception (La Scala, Milan, 1958. Scenery and costumes: André Levasseur).

A dictionary of modern ballet

LE TRICORNE. COSTUMES BY PICASSO. 1919.

VAN DIJK Peter. A German dancer (born at Bremen) who has reached international rank with French companies. He was trained by Tatiana Gsovsky in Berlin, where he made his début at the Municipal Opera in 1950. In 1951-52 he was maître de ballet and leading dancer at the Wiesbaden Opera, when the ballet company was directed by the composer, Hans Werner Henze. He then joined Janine Charrat's company in order to obtain wider experience. With them he appeared in London in 1954, and was singled out for his exceptional promise. He joined the Paris Opera in 1954 and soon became a valued member of the company. Van Dijk is an admirable classical dancer; reserved, meticulous, with an elegant, strong technique and a fine stage presence (*Blue Bird, Black Swan,* etc.) He created important roles in several ballets, including *Les Algues* (Charrat) and *Les Noces Fantastiques* (Lifar), and has danced brilliantly in Lander's *Études.*

VANGSAA Mona. Born in Copenhagen, a pupil of the Royal Danish Ballet School and a leading soloist with the company since 1942. Pretty, charming and lyrical, she has an extensive repertoire and has revealed fresh aspects of her talent under the direction of foreign choreographers. She was a remarkable Street Dancer

in *Le Beau Danube* and a moving Juliet in Ashton's version of the Prokofiev ballet. Of all the Danish dancers she is the one who, in *Serenade,* shows the greatest understanding of Balanchine's style. But she also excels in the ballets of her native country, as Teresina in *Napoli* and in Lander's *Bolero.* She is married to Frank Schaufuss.

VAN PRAAGH Peggy. An English dancer, born in London, who has played an important part in the growth of British ballet both as dancer and teacher. Peggy van Praagh studied with Margaret Craske, Karsavina and Rambert. With the latter's company, and with Tudor's London Ballet, she created important roles in that choreographer's ballets, notably *Jardin aux Lilas, Dark Elegies* and *Gala Performance.* A warm and vivid personality, with an intelligence which enabled her to range from the emotional subtleties of Tudor to the classical brilliance of *Coppelia,* in which she danced Swanilda with great success after joining Sadler's Wells in 1941. When de Valois formed the second company, she invited Peggy van Praagh to be ballet-mistress and subsequently assistant director; for ten fruitful years, she took charge of the young dancers and directed their tours in South Africa, America and Europe. In 1955 she left the company in order, as de Valois's representative, to produce ballets from the Sadler's Wells repertory overseas. She has recently staged *The Rake's Progress* for the Munich State Opera, *Les Rendez-vous* for the Canadian National Ballet and *The Sleeping Princess* for the Royal Danish Ballet. She has also worked with the Royal Swedish Ballet and in Oslo. In 1958 she directed the resident company for the Edinburgh Festival Ballet.

VARIATIONS. "Ballet romantique" by Serge Lifar. Music: Schubert, orch. Tony Aubin. First performance: Paris Opera, 11 March 1953. The work is a Pas de Six in the manner of the famous Pas de Quatre of 1845, and was set to Schubert's Moments Musicaux. It was written for Lycette Darsonval, Madeleine Lafon, Micheline Bardin, Christiane Vaussard, Liane Daydé and Nina Vyroubova, who were étoiles of the Opéra at the time. A seventh variation was added later, after the return of Yvette Chauviré. Lifar designed it to exhibit the special qualities of the six ballerinas, who wore identical white costumes with flowers of different colours.

* Three months later Lifar produced *Grand Pas* (music by Brahms), the masculine counterpart of the above. In white tights and velvet doublets of different colours, Michel Renault, Alexandre Kalioujny, Max Bozzoni, Youly Algaroff and J.-P. Andréani gave displays of virtuosity suited to their individual styles. Both ballets make an effective opening for a programme.

VAUSSARD Christiane. An excellent interpreter of the typically French ballets in the Paris Opera repertory: *Coppelia, Suite de Danses, Soir de fête,* the ballet in *Faust*. A pupil and disciple of Carlotta Zambelli, promoted to the rank of étoile in 1947. Small, lively and precise, brilliant rather than lyrical, and far removed from the classic Russian style, Christiane Vaussard excels in soubrette roles, but she has also portrayed very different characters in *L'Oiseau de feu* (the Princess) and *La Symphonie Fantastique* (the Beloved).

VERCHININA Nina. A valuable interpreter of Massine's first symphonic ballets, to which her supple, sculptural movements, combining the plastic intensity of the modern dance with classical control, were ideally suited. For the de Basil company, she created Action in *Les Présages,* the second movement in *Choreartium* and the young girl in the pastoral scene of *Symphonie Fantastique*.

VERDY Violette. A French dancer of impeccable technique, born in Brittany. She studied with Rousane and V. Gsovsky and made her début under her real name of Nelly Guillerme with the Ballets des Champs-Élysées, as the child acrobat in *Les Forains.* As Violette Verdy, she starred in the film *Ballerina* (1949). Later joined the Ballets de Paris and created the role of the Fiancée in *Le Loup.* She has appeared with Festival Ballet (1954), La Scala, Milan (1955), Ballet Rambert (1958), the American Ballet Theatre and the New York City Ballet.

VERTÈS Marcel. A French painter of Hungarian origin, born in 1895. His style, light, elegant and sketchy, is well suited to ballet, and particularly to works derived from operettas. His décors have the ephemeral charm and freshness of a fashion drawing in a glossy magazine or a Parisian shop window. For Ballet Theatre, Vertès designed *Bluebeard* (1941) and *Helen of Troy* (1943); for Ballet International, *Brahms Variations* (1944); for the Paris Opera, *La Belle Hélène* (1955).

VIE DE POLICHINELLE La. Ballet in six scenes. Scenario: Claude Séran. Music: Nicolas Nabokov. Scenery and costumes: Pedro Pruna. Choreography: Lifar. First performance: Paris Opera, 22 June 1934. Principal dancers: Marie-Louise Didion, Jacqueline Simoni, Serge Lifar, Serge Peretti.

The hero of Lifar's ballet is the Venetian counterpart of Massine's Neapolitan *Pulcinella.* The new ballet was partly based on drawings by the 18th century Venetian painter, G. D. Tiepolo. Polichinelle's adventures, which include a circus scene and a mock execution, are recounted in six scenes with interludes before the curtain. Lifar himself danced the title-role.

VIERGES FOLLES Les. See *Wise Virgins, The.*

VILZAK Anatole. Graduated from the Imperial School, St. Petersburg, in 1915; left Russia in 1921 to join Diaghilev's company for the London revival of *La Belle au bois dormant*. He was a perfect example of a danseur noble of the Russian school and also a fine character dancer *(Les Biches, Les Tentations de la Bergère, Les Fâcheux)*. In 1925 he left the Russian Ballet after a dispute with Diaghilev. He took part in Ida Rubinstein's seasons and later joined the Ballets Russes de Monte-Carlo, for whom he created in 1936 the title-role in Fokine's *Don Juan*, an admirably stylish performance. In that year he went to America, where he now teaches in New York with his wife, Ludmilla Schollar.

VLADIMIROV Pierre. A St. Petersburg dancer who joined the corps de ballet at the Maryinsky Theatre in 1911 and became premier danseur four years later. This rapid promotion was due to his energy and ambition, and also to his exceptional gifts (he was an admirable classical dancer, tall and strongly built; a fine partner). Diaghilev invited him to join the Russian Ballet in 1914, when he replaced Nijinsky as the negro slave in *Cléopâtre*. He joined them again in 1921 to dance Prince Charming in *The Sleeping Princess* and returned once more in 1925. From 1928 to 1931 he was Pavlova's partner. He has lived and taught in New York since 1934. Married to Felia Doubrovska.

VLASSOVA Eleonora. A Moscow dancer who appeared with great success with the Stanislavsky, Nemirovitch-Danchenko company when they danced in Paris at the Châtelet in 1956, particularly in the title-role of *Esmeralda*. Slender, with sparkling eyes and an expressive body, with beautiful port de bras, she showed herself to be a fine actress as well as a magnificent dancer.

VOLININE Alexandre. Born Moscow, 1882, died Paris 1955. A fine dancer and one of the outstanding teachers of his time. He graduated from the Imperial School in 1901 and later became premier danseur at the Bolshoi Theatre

(Coppelia, Le Lac des Cygnes, La Fille de Pharaon). He appeared with Diaghilev's Russian Ballet for their second season (1910), dancing in *Les Orientales* and other ballets with Catherine Geltzer. In 1914 he became Pavlova's partner and remained with her for several years till he retired in 1925 and opened a school in Paris with Mme. Tamara d'Erlanger, which rapidly became famous. His pupils included David Lichine, Anton Dolin, Serge Peretti, André Eglevsky, Jean Babilée, Michael Somes, John Field, as well as Tatiana Riabouchinska, Marie-Louise Didion and Yvette Chauviré. As a dancer, Volinine was memorable for his handsome appearance, his elegant style and his extreme lightness. Stylishness and lightness were qualities found in all his pupils. He was a particularly good teacher of men, imparting strength as well as smoothness, vigour as well as grace. He was a grand seigneur of the dance.

VOLKOVA Vera. Dancer and teacher. Born in Leningrad, she began her training under Maria Romanova (mother of Ulanova) and later worked with Vaganova. She made her début as a dancer in Russia but left soon after the revolution. She spent some years in China (where she met her husband, the English painter Hugh Williams), and danced with her compatriot George Goncharov. The privations of the early 'twenties resulted in a period of ill health, but she fully recovered and began teaching in London in 1943. Her exceptional feeling for the *nuances* of the Leningrad classical style and her gift for vivid explanation enabled her to bring out latent talent even in dancers as experienced as Margot Fonteyn. Violetta Elvin was another pupil, and all visiting dancers found their way to Volkova's famous West Street studio. In 1950 she went to La Scala, Milan, and in 1952 to Copenhagen, at the suggestion of Harald Lander, to instruct the younger generation of Danish dancers in the Russian style.

VYROUBOVA Nina. Born in the Crimea. She trained first with her mother, Trefilova, then with Preobrajenska. She joined the Ballets des Champs-Élysées, appearing in *Les Forains* in 1945 and in the Gsovsky version of *La Sylphide* in the following year. She was engaged by the Paris Opera as étoile in 1949 and remained for seven years, creating leading roles in *Les Mirages, Blanche-Neige* (the wicked stepmother), *The Firebird* (Lifar's revival), *Les Noces Fantastiques,* etc. On leaving the Opera she joined de Cuevas, where her principal creation has been in *The Song of Unending Sorrow* (Ricarda). Vyroubova is one of the most accomplished artists of her generation. Lightly built, with an oval face and slanting eyes, she is ideal in romantic parts *(La Sylphide, Giselle),* but also has the precision and brilliance for classical roles and the temperament for character parts.

W

WAKHEVITCH Georges. One of the most successful stage designers of the post-war years, as prolific as he is skilful. He has worked in Paris and elsewhere for opera, ballet and for straight theatre. He has also designed for the cinema, where he learned to make effective use of perspective. His style is eclectic, sometimes depending for its effect on clear and precise drawing, sometimes on colour and materials. His finest décor for ballet was *Le Jeune Homme et la Mort* (Ballets des Champs-Élysées, 1946) with its striking transformation of a sordid attic interior into an airy terrace lit by stars and twinkling night signs. Other ballet décors include *La Croqueuse de diamants* (Ballets de Paris, 1950), *The Duel* (Ballet Theatre, 1952), *Vilia* (Festival Ballet, 1953), the "Turc généreux" episode in *Les Indes Galantes* (Paris Opera, 1952), *L'Oiseau de feu* (Paris Opera, 1954), *Roméo et Juliette* (Paris Opera, 1955) and *The Miraculous Mandarin* (Sadler's Wells Ballet, Edinburgh Festival, 1956). He has designed several operas for Covent Garden.

WALTON Sir William. Born 1902. The leading English composer of his generation. One of his first works, the overture Portsmouth Point (1925), was played as an interlude during

Diaghilev's London season of 1926. *Façade*, written in 1922 to accompany the recitation of poems by Edith Sitwell, was arranged for orchestra and produced as a ballet by Ashton (Camargo Society, 1931). New numbers have been added for subsequent revivals. It remains one of the most popular ballets in the English repertory.

Ashton was also the choreographer for *Siesta*, a short orchestral piece used as a pas de deux in 1936, for *The Wise Virgins,* an arrangement of music by Bach (1940) and for *The Quest* (1943), Walton's only original ballet, to a scenario adapted from Spenser's "Faery Queen". All these were produced by Sadler's Wells. In 1949, Taras used "Music for children" for *Devoirs de vacances* (Ballets des Champs-Élysées).

WEDDING BOUQUET A. Ballet in one act. Scenario and words: Gertrude Stein. Music, scenery and costumes: Lord Berners. Choreography: Frederick Ashton. First performance: Sadler's Wells Ballet, 27 April 1937.

Lord Berners had the idea of making a ballet out of a play by Gertrude Stein, *They must be*

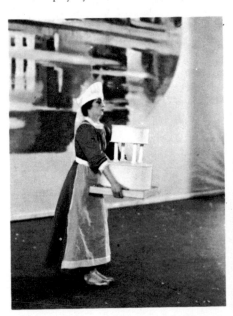

A WEDDING BOUQUET. NINETTE DE VALOIS.

Wedded to Their Wife. He wrote the music and designed the Edwardian costumes and the setting, a plain backcloth with an oval medallion showing a large house behind a river, copied from an American rug in Miss Stein's house in France. The characters involved in the country wedding mostly had Anglo-Saxon names, but their behaviour was provincial French of the wildest burlesque. Certainly no other company could have done such justice to the rich opportunities for character dancing with which Ashton provided them: Mary Honer and Robert Helpmann as the simpering bride and bashful groom; Margot Fonteyn as the forlorn, abandoned Julia (an extraordinary performance, on the boundary of burlesque and realism), Julia Farron as her little Mexican dog Pepe, June Brae as the tipsy Josephine, and many others, not forgetting Ninette de Valois as the maid, Webster, the last role she danced for the company. Gertrude Stein's text, sometimes relevant and sometimes not, was originally sung by the Sadler's Wells chorus, who seemed faintly disapproving. Later the chorus was omitted and the words were declaimed, with inimitable gusto, by Constant Lambert.

WESTERN SYMPHONY.
LECLERCQ AND D'AMBOISE.

WESTERN SYMPHONY. Ballet in four movements. Music: Hershey Kay. Scenery: John Boyt. Costumes: Karinska. Choreography: Balanchine. First performance: New York City Ballet, City Center, 7 September 1954. Principal dancers: Diana Adams and Herbert Bliss, Janet Reed and Nicholas Magallanes, Patricia Wilde and André Eglevsky, Tanaquil LeClercq and Jacques d'Amboise.

Saloon life in the Far West treated by Balanchine in terms of pure dancing. Local colour was assimilated into classical technique, demanding (and obtaining) dancing of prodigious brilliance. The company performed it in such an exhilarating manner that the insufficiency of the music passed almost unnoticed.

WHISTLER Rex. An artist of limited range but exquisite accomplishment, born in 1905. Rex Whistler was one of the most gifted English theatre designers of his generation, also a notable mural painter and book illustrator. He was killed in action in 1944. He made his

name as (a designer for ballet) with *The Rake's Progress* 1935, a loving reconstruction, at once scholarly and imaginative, of 18th century London, displaying to the full his extreme care for detail and his highly professional craftsmanship. No less striking was his magnificent baroque setting for Ashton's *The Wise Virgins* (1940). He also designed a revival of *Le Spectre de la Rose* for Sadler's Wells, two décors for the International Ballet and several plays for theatre companies in London.

WIGMAN Mary. Born Hanover, 1886. This great lady of the German dance has left her mark on a whole generation of dancers in Germany, Switzerland and America. A pupil of Dalcroze and Laban, with whom she worked until 1918, she has danced either alone or with a group of pupils in many of the principal towns of Europe and America. In 1920, she opened a school in Dresden and became ballet mistress at the Dresden Opera. Her pupils included Harald Kreutzberg and Yvonne Georgi. Like her master Laban, Mary Wigman wanted to free dancing from music and to express through movement alone the deepest and most complex of human feelings. According to this theory, the body is an instrument in itself, complete and self-sufficing: it sings and vibrates of its own accord. Having achieved this freedom, she worked back, by means of simple percussion accompaniments, to dancing with music. In spite of the present popularity of classical ballet in Germany, Wigman is still a considerable force there. Her greatest influence has probably been through her teaching and through her generous and warm-hearted personality. As dancer and choreographer she made a greater mark by her solos than by her group arrangements, but her

MARY WIGMAN.

version of *Le Sacre du Printemps* (*) at the Berlin Festival of 1956 showed an imaginative power and a grasp of choral movement which few younger choreographers could bring to this work.

WILDE Patricia. A Canadian dancer, born in Ottawa, now a ballerina of the New York City Ballet. She studied in Canada, then with Dorothie Littlefield and at the School of American

Ballet. She is a dancer of exceptional strength and vitality with remarkable elevation; once rather muscular, she has now fined down and become a brilliant interpreter of the works of Balanchine and Robbins. She is a virtuoso, but she can be tender as well and she has a gift for comedy. A favourite with audiences everywhere, she typifies the American neo-classical style. She created the leading role in Balanchine's *Square Dance* (1957).

WISE VIRGINS The. Ballet-pantomime in one act. Scenario and music: Kurt Atterberg. Scenery and costumes: Einar Nerman. Choreography: Jean Borlin. First performance: Ballets Suédois, Théâtre des Champs-Élysées, Paris, 18 November 1920.

Borlin's *Les Vierges Folles* was a humorous version of the parable, presented in the style of Swedish popular art. The décor recalled the folk paintings of Smaaland and Dalecarlia; the Virgins wore an adaptation of the regional costume, green and black striped dresses with tall hats. The music was based on folk songs.

* Ballet in one act. Music: J. S. Bach, arr. and orch. Walton. Scenery and costumes: Rex Whistler. Choreography: Frederick Ashton. First performance: Sadler's Wells Ballet, 24 April 1940. Principal dancers: Fonteyn, Somes.

Ashton's second wartime ballet, and a complete contrast to the fire and brimstone of its predecessor, *Dante Sonata*. The parable was told simply and majestically with serene, flowing movements for the bride (danced with quiet, rapt intensity by Fonteyn). The music (from the Church and secular cantatas, and including the beautiful "Sheep may safely graze") sounded extraordinarily impressive in Walton's orchestration. Whistler designed a superb baroque décor: golden doors studded with giant nails, surrounded with sculptured angels and set in a rose-pink wall.

WOIZIKOWSKI Leon. The finest character dancer of his day; a Pole, discovered by Diaghilev in 1915. He remained with the Russian Ballet almost continually until 1929. Woizikowski's dancing had extraordinary suppleness, precision and vitality; like most Polish dancers, he had an unerring sense of rhythm.

He shared Massine's interest in folk dancing and his gift for stylisation and characterisation were brilliantly exploited by Massine in his early ballets: *Contes Russes* (the strolling pedlar), *La Boutique Fantasque* (tarantella dancer), *Le Tricorne* (the governor). When Massine left the company in 1921, Woizikowski took over the role of the miller in *Le Tricorne*. He also rivalled the original interpreters in revivals of *Petrouchka* (title-role) and *Prince Igor* (Polovtsian chief), and was incomparable in Nijinska's Three Ivans in *The Sleeping Princess*. He left the company in Massine's wake but returned in 1923 to perform equally valiant services in the new ballets, creating roles in (the list is not exhaustive) *Les Noces, Les Biches, Le Train Bleu* (the golfer), *Les Matelots* (Spanish sailor), *Barabau* (title-role), *Le Pas d'acier* and *The Gods go a'begging* (the shepherd). After the dissolution of the Russian Ballet he joined the Monte Carlo company, and gave them the benefit of his vast experience (master of ceremonies in *Cotillon,* the beggar in *Concurrence,* Fate in *Les Présages,* etc.). Then in 1935-36 he directed his own company with which he toured Europe before settling down in Warsaw as maître de ballet, a post which he still holds, and in which his gift of reproducing ballets from memory has been invaluable.

ALICIA ALONSO AND IGOR YOUSKEVITCH.

WRIGHT Belinda. English dancer, born in Southport. She studied with Marie Rambert and became a leading dancer with the Ballet Rambert, excelling particularly in classical roles. She danced for Rambert in England and in Australia, later with Roland Petit's Ballets de Paris and with the company of the Marquis de Cuevas. She joined Festival Ballet in 1951 and after Marlova's departure became ballerina of the company. A slim, neat dancer she now excels in modern ballets where she can look chic and sophisticated, but she is capable of considerable feeling in classical and romantic ballets. As yet, her true quality has not been fully exploited.

XIMENEZ-VARGAS Spanish Ballet. A small and elegant troupe formed in 1954 by two soloists (both Mexicans) from the Pilar Lopez company. Roberto Ximenez, with his exotic features and wiry frame, excels in flamenco and the dances of South America. Manolo Vargas is a quieter, more lyrical dancer. If the accent is sometimes on pretty girls and low-cut dresses rather than on Spanish dancing, the company nevertheless puts on an admirable show and has been very successful both in Europe and in America.

YERMOLAEV Alexei. A pupil of Vaganova at Leningrad, who transferred from the Maryinsky in that city to the Bolshoi in Moscow in 1930. He is now one of the principal dancers there, renowned for his dramatic gifts and for his phenomenal virtuoso technique, which allow him to perform feats of great brilliance without sacrificing dramatic expression. His "ballon" has been compared to Nijinsky's. He is a notable Albrecht in *Giselle* and Tybalt in *Romeo and Juliet*.

YOUSKEVITCH Igor. Born in Russia, he emigrated to Yugoslavia, where he joined a Sokol group and was trained as an athlete. He is unique in that he made his ballet début at the age of 20, after only two years' study in Paris with Preobrajenska, appearing with the Woizikowski Ballet in 1935. A leading dancer with the Monte-Carlo Ballet from 1938 to 1944 he was one of Massine's favourite interpreters: the Officer in *Gaieté Parisienne,* the Man in *Rouge et Noir,* a God in *Seventh Symphony.* Afterwards he had a brilliant career in the United States with Ballet Theatre and on his return to Europe with this company (in 1951) he was acclaimed in *Black Swan, Helen of Troy, Giselle,* and Tudor's *Romeo and Juliet.* Tall, dark, with high cheekbones and a charming smile, he has excellent elevation and dances effortlessly, with a virile elegance. In spite of his late start, he has become one of the great classical dancers of his day. A favourité partner of Alicia Alonso, he has danced with her in Cuba and also with the Ballet Russe de Monte-Carlo in America.

Z

ZAMBELLI Carlotta. The last Italian star to be engaged at the Paris Opera. The director, Pedro Gailhard, discovered her in the ballet school of La Scala, Milan. She made her début at the Palais Garnier in 1894 as one of the courtesans in *Faust* and soon scored a big success with her dancing of the "mirror" variation. Immediately promoted to the rank of étoile, in succession to the great Rosita Mauri, her first important role was the Snow Fairy in *La Maladetta.* A precise and elegant technician, she was the incarnation of the Milanese style, unrivalled in the famous ballets of the time — *La Korrigane, Namouna, Les Deux Pigeons, Sylvia, Coppelia.*

CARLOTTA ZAMBELLI.

Zambelli was an intelligent and refined dancer with a pure style and strong points. One of the highlights of her distinguished career was her visit to the Maryinsky Theatre, Leningrad, in 1901; the last foreign star to be invited to Tsarist Russia. For many years she directed the school of the Paris Opera and was a decisive influence in the maintenance of the classical tradition there. She trained many outstanding dancers, foremost among them Lycette Darsonval, who has succeeded her as director of the school. Zambelli has been a devoted servant of the dance and nothing describes her better than the device she chose for herself when she was still young: *nel turbine serena* (calm in the midst of the whirlwind).

ZHDANOV Yuri. Trained by the Kirov Theatre in Leningrad, he now dances with the Bolshoi Theatre Ballet in Moscow. An unassuming but stylish dancer, he has exceptional elevation and a sound technique. His dramatic range is limited, but he is excellent in lyrical and tender roles. His Romeo may at times lack fire, but in the later scenes it has anguish and real

sensibility. Perhaps his best part is the romantic Vatslav in *The Fountain of Bakhchisarai*.
A gentle personality, he is a gifted painter and
when not dancing is to be found with his easel
on the banks of the Moskva, the Thames or the
Seine.

ZÉPHIRE ET FLORE. Ballet by Boris
Kochno. Music: Vladimir Dukelsky. Scenery
and costumes: Braque. Choreography: Massine.
First performance: Diaghilev's Ballets Russes,
Monte-Carlo, 28 April 1925. Principal dancers:
Alice Nikitina, Anton Dolin, Serge Lifar.

An attempt to reproduce in modern terms the
type of mythological ballet danced by the private
companies of the Russian nobles in the time of
Alexander I. Didelot used the same subject
in 1795. *Zéphire et Flore* reflected the unsettled
condition of the Russian Ballet at that time.
The choreography had originally been entrusted
to Nijinska, then to Lifar, who was considered
too inexperienced; it was finally undertaken by
Massine. The main attraction was the dancing
of the three young principals, of whom Nikitina
(as Flora) and Lifar (as Boreas, brother and unsuccessful rival to Zephyr) were making their
first appearance in leading roles.

ZORITCH George. Born in Moscow, trained in Paris by Preobrajenska. He made his
début at the age of fourteen in Ida Rubinstein's
Company. He was a soloist with the de Basil
Company (1935-37), with whom he created the
role of the young shepherd in *La Symphonie
Fantastique* (third movement), and from 1938
with the Ballet Russe de Monte-Carlo (Castor in
Labyrinth, 1941). He went to Hollywood
in 1943 but was persuaded to return to ballet by
the Marquis de Cuevas in 1951. He appeared
in *Les Sylphides, Le Spectre de la Rose,* and
L'Après-midi d'un faune. Zoritch is an elegant
dancer something lacking in vigour, but gifted
with a pure style and the appearance of a statue
by Praxiteles.

ZULLIG Hans. A Swiss dancer and choreographer who studied with Jooss at Essen and
Dartington and became a leading dancer of the
Ballets Jooss, unforgettable as the Standard
Bearer in *Green Table,* the poor young man in
Big City and the prince in *A Spring Tale.* His
first ballet was *Le Bosquet* (1945), followed by
Fantasie (1951). Although his dancing was
powerful and dramatic, if elegant, his choreography tended to be rather formless, relying on
charm rather than structure. In 1948 he joined
the Sadler's Wells Theatre Ballet and, notwith-
standing his "modern" training, became a
valuable member of the company. In 1950 he
rejoined Jooss in Essen and danced with the
company until it disbanded in 1953. Now
living and working in Switzerland.

ZVEREV Nicholas. Dancer, and teacher.
His initial, which relegates him to the end of the
alphabet, is a fitting symbol for this modest and
self-effacing Muscovite. He joined Diaghilev
in 1912, became a soloist and remained with the
company until 1926. Short, light and nimble,
with muscular legs, he danced such roles as the
Moor in *Petrouchka,* the male acrobat in *Parade,*
the Innocent in *The Midnight Sun,* the Cossack
Chief in *La Boutique Fantasque,* La Montagne in
Les Fâcheux. He spent the next ten years touring in various companies with Vera Nemchinova
(his first wife), Dolin, and Massine. In 1936 he
took part in the reorganisation of the Ballets de
Monte-Carlo and danced character roles, including Dr. Coppelius in his own version of *Coppelia.*
He remained at Monte Carlo as maître de ballet
until 1945, produced several ballets with Lifar at
La Scala, Milan, and then revived *Petrouchka,
Prince Igor, Sheherazade* and *Le Spectre de la Rose*
for the Paris Opera. He knew the Diaghilev
repertoire, particularly the works of Fokine,
through and through. He has taught in Belgium and Switzerland, and his pupils in France
have included some of the most distinguished
names in French ballet.

LIST OF PHOTOGRAPHERS

GORDON ANTHONY, LONDON : pages 56, 120, 228, 300 B. – BARON, LONDON : pages 10, 53, 145, 164, 204, 173, 300 A, 314, 329. – CECIL BEATON, LONDON : page 349. – BERNAND, PARIS : pages 112, 326. – BERT, PARIS : pages 41, 48 A, 149, 193. – BRASSAI, PARIS : page 306 B. – CHOURA, PARIS : page 196. – J. W. DEBENHAM, LONDON : pages 139, 354. – DETAILLE, MONTE-CARLO : page 69. – D'ORA, PARIS : page 9. – ENKELMANN, BERLIN : pages 108, 356. – ENRIETTI : page 49 C. – ERLANGER DE ROSEN, PARIS : page 24. – FONTEYN, LONDON : page 152. – GERSCHEL, PARIS : page 304. – GJON MILI, NEW YORK : page 349. – GOLDBERG, HOLLYWOOD : page 57. – HOPPÉ, LONDON : pages 109, 192, 240. – IRIS, PARIS : pages 29, 91, 100 B. – ISABEY, PARIS : page 222. – CH. JOURDANET and P. L. GIRAULT, PARIS : page 15. – SERGE LIDO, PARIS : pages 36, 133, 169, 177, 219, 223 A, 223 B, 244, 253, 335, 355. – LIPNITZKI, PARIS : pages 37, 87, 129, 144, 214, 215, 245, 249, 315, 323. – LOWNDS-N. LANGEN : page 33. – MARION-VALENTINE, PARIS : page 248. – MELVIN : page 3. – METRO-GOLDWIN-MAYER : page 11. – JAMES MORTIMER, LONDON : page 296. – MYDTSKOV, COPENHAGEN : pages 117, 232. – NADAR, PARIS : page 359. – WALTER OWEN, NEW YORK : pages 76, 82, 97, 311. – PETIT, PARIS : page 90. – PIC, PARIS : page 233. – PICCAGLIANI, MILAN : pages 200, 309. – PLATT LYNES, NEW YORK : pages 236, 237 B. – HOUSTON ROGERS, LONDON : page 130. – ROY ROUND, LONDON : page 156. – SAEGER : page 48 B. – SASHA, LONDON : page 289. – SEEBERGER : page 184. – MAX SEGAL, PARIS : page 157. – SEVERN MERLYN : page 32. – MAURICE SEYMOUR, CHICAGO : page 94. – STONE, BRUSSELS : page 306 A. – VALENTE, NEW YORK : page 52. – VAN RIEL, AMSTERDAM : page 265. – G. B. L. WILSON, LONDON : pages 26, 128. – PAUL WILSON, LONDON : page 165. – ROGER WOOD, LONDON : pages 297 A, 297 B.

We regret that, since our efforts to trace the identity of some photographers whose work has been reproduced have remained fruitless, the above list is not complete.